The Indigenous Trees of the Hawaiian Islands

THE

INDIGENOUS TREES

OF THE

HAWAIIAN ISLANDS

BY

JOSEPH F. ROCK
Botanist of the College of Hawaii
Consulting Botanist, Board of Commissioners of Agriculture and Forestry,
Territory of Hawaii.

ISSUED JUNE 26, 1913.

With Two Hundred and Fifteen Photo-Engravings

———

PUBLISHED UNDER PATRONAGE.

———

HONOLULU, T. H., 1913.

To the Memory

Of those pioneer Botanists: Gaudichaud, Macrae, Chamisso,

A. Gray, Douglas, Remy, H. Mann and Brigham,

Wawra and Hillebrand,

who first revealed to the world the richness of the Flora

of these Islands, this book is

respectfully dedicated.

Names of Patrons.

Andrew Adams	J. M. Dowsett
Mrs. B. M. Allen	Mrs. J. R. Galt
F. C. Atherton	A. Gartley
C. H. Atherton	Francis Gay
H. A. Baldwin	W. M. Giffard
W. D. Baldwin	J. F. Hackfeld
E. F. Bishop	Mrs. C. S. Holloway
W. A. Bowen	Rev. Hans Isenberg
Geo. H. Brown	Mrs. A. H. B. Judd
Geo. R. Carter	Mrs. Annie S. Knudsen
W. R. Castle	J. D. McInerny
Geo. P. Cooke	W. H. Rice
J. P. Cooke	Aubrey Robinson
S. M. Damon	F. M. Swanzy
R. C. Davies	H. M. von Holt
B. F. Dillingham	Mrs. E. K. Wilder

A. L. Wilcox

PREFACE.

It has long been the writer's desire to give to the public a volume on the native trees of Hawaii, giving popular as well as technical descriptions of the trees peculiar to Hawaiian soil.

At first it was thought that plain popular descriptions would suffice, but it soon became evident that the technical part could not be dispensed with, and in order to make the book valuable for both the layman and the scientist, it was therefore included.

The rather lengthy introduction seemed an advisable feature and necessary, as it gives practically for the first time a more or less detailed description of all the floral regions and their plant associations found in this island group, not being restricted to trees alone but embracing the whole plant covering.

In the sequence of families Engler and Prantl's Natürliche Pflanzenfamilien System has been followed, beginning with the Cryptogams and ending with the Compositae.

Under each species a complete reference and synonomy is given, as far as was possible. Of course, as in all works of this nature, mistakes will undoubtedly be found, which will have to be overlooked on account of the insular position of the writer, as it was not always possible to consult original works, some of them old and out of print and therefore unobtainable. It will not be out of place here to acknowledge the kind assistance of Miss Mary A. Day, the Librarian of the Gray Herbarium, for the loan of books and copies of articles, etc.

Following the reference is a technical description, usually enlarged and based on material in the College of Hawaii Herbarium; only in such instances as when the plant is very common or has not been collected by the writer, are descriptions of old authors quoted. As far as possible native names are given under most of the trees in italics, as well as any legendary or other facts of sufficient interest, together with habitat, plant association, etc. Of a number of trees of which nothing is known of a popular nature, the technical side is enlarged upon, especially in the family Rutaceae (genus Pelea) and Campanulaceae (tribe Lobelioideae).

The writer wishes here to acknowledge above all the kind assistance of Prof. Dr. Ignatz Urban of Berlin, Prof. Le Comte of Paris, Prof. Dr. A. Zahlbruckner of Vienna and Profs. B. L. Robinson and M. L. Fernald of Harvard, in the loan of herbarium material, mainly types, for comparison, without which the authenticity of many determinations would have been doubtful; this refers mainly to the tribe Lobelioideae of the family Campanulaceae, one of the most intricate tribes found in these Islands.

All such plants are included in this book as have been observed by the writer as trees, even if usually occurring as shrubs. To the many species of trees already known the writer has added 1 new genus, 22 new species, 31 new varieties, 3 new forms and 1 new hybrid, which are all described by him. A number of new species were discovered by the writer, but described by various authorities, including 4 new species of Palms by O. Beccari of Florence, Italy, all of which are included in this book. In an addendum the writer describes seven new species, seven new varieties and one new form belonging to the Family Campanulaceae, tribe Lobelioideae. This brings the total number of new plants described by him herein up to seventy-two.

It was also necessary in some instances to make a few new combinations.

Of the 215 photographs nearly all were taken by the writer in the field, with the exception of plates 1, 12, 17, 27, 68, 130, and 131, by Mr. R. S. Hosmer; nos. 29 and 37 by Mr. R. Perkins; no. 2, by Mr. A. Gartley, and nos. 23, 26 and 31, by Mr. R. J. Baker, to all of whom the writer wishes to acknowledge his indebtedness.

The present volume is primarily due to the enthusiasm of Ex-Governor George R. Carter, who headed the list of patrons and secured the necessary funds to insure publication. Credit is due the College of Hawaii for supplying photographic material and part of the writer's time.

It should be stated here that most of the material on which this publication is based was collected by the writer under the auspices of the Board of Commissioners of Agriculture and Forestry of this Territory.

To Dr. H. L. Lyon the writer is indebted for technical advice, and to Dr. E. Hackel and Rev. George Kükenthal for identification of Grasses and Cyperaceae respectively.

To Mr. Francis Gay of Kauai the writer is greatly indebted for knowledge of matters pertaining to Hawaiian names of trees and their uses; he also wishes to express his thanks to all those who extended to him the far-famed Hawaiian hospitality during his many sojourns on the various islands of the group.

Last but not least the writer wishes to acknowledge the kind assistance o' Prof. H. M. Ballou of the College of Hawaii in his painstaking reading of proof-sheets, and expresses his thanks to him and all those who have helped in the preparation of this book.

The volume is herewith presented to the public, who the writer hopes will be lenient towards any mistakes in the construction of sentences, English not being his mother-tongue.

JOSEPH F. ROCK.

College of Hawaii,
Honolulu. T. H., April 23, 1913.

KEY TO THE FAMILIES.

MONOCOTYLEDONOUS OR ENDOGENOUS PLANTS.

Ovary superior, naked flowers unisexual, on spathaceous spadices.
Flowers dioecious, in heads or spikes, leaves elongate, prickly at the edges.

        Pandanaceae   96

Ovary superior, syncarpous, 3-celled, perianth of 6 segments in 2 series.
Perianth regular, wholly corolla-like, cells of ovary 2 to many ovulate.

        Liliaceae   109

Perianth small, calyx-like, fruit drupaceous or baccate, 1-seeded, leaves palmate or pinnate, flowers on a branching spadix...............
Palmae   99

DICOTYLEDONOUS OR EXOGENOUS PLANTS.

I. Perianth simple or none.

Ovary of 3 or rarely 2 or more than 3 united carpels, with 1 or 2 pendulous ovules in each.

Fruit either capsular, separating into as many 2 valved cocci as carpels, or succulent and indehiscent..........
Euphorbiaceae   243

Ovary free with one ovule, styles 2 or rarely 1.

Ovule anatropous or amphitropous.

Fruit indehiscent nut or drupe-like, one seeded....
Ulmaceae   113

Fruit small, drupe-like, milksap present, leaves with 2 axillary stipules.....................................
Moraceae   114

Ovule orthotropous.

Polycarpium or drupe often enclosed by and united with the perianth; usually without milksap..........
Urticaceae   117

Ovary 1-celled with few ovules, seed single.

Perianth partly adnate to maturing ovary, ovules 1-3.

        Santalaceae   126

Ovary 1-celled with a single ovule; embryo curved.

Perianth dry, supported by 3 bractlets, stamens connate at the base, as many as perianth segments...........
Amarantaceae   135

Perianth tube persistent around the fruit, stamens not of the same number as lobes of perianth, hypogynous..
Nyctaginaceae   143

Ovary one-celled, free, with a single ovule, embryo not curved.

Perianth segments 6 in 2 circles, persistent; fruit a one seeded berry or drupe....................
Lauraceae   149

Perianth segments 4, stamens twice as many, sessile in 2 alternate rows, fruit a drupe-like reddish berry......
Thymelaeaceae   315

II. Petals united, at least at the base.

Corolla epigynous, regular.

Ovary 2- or more celled, stamens adnate to the corolla, as many as corolla lobes; leaves opposite....................
Rubiaceae   429

Ovary 1 celled, 1-ovulate; stamens adnate, as many as corolla lobes.

        Compositae   497

Corolla epigynous, irregular.

Stamens 5, filaments and anthers connate, the latter bearded at the top; milk sap present...........................
Campanulaceae   469
        Lobelioideae

Stamens free, stigma surrounded by a hairy indusium...
Goodeniaceae   494

Corolla hypogynous or perigynous, bearing the stamens, regular.

Ovary 3 or more celled; 1 or 2 ovules in each cell.

Stamens 5, alternate with corolla lobes; a single ovule in each cell...
Epacridaceae   365

Stamens indefinite; flowers unisexual............
Ebenaceae   393

Stamens 5-6, opposite the corolla lobes when of some number, often alternating with staminiodia; milky sap present.

        Sapotaceae   380

Ovary 1-celled, with a free central placenta.

Stamens opposite the corolla lobes; drupe with a single basilar seed...
Myrsinaceae   367

Ovary 2 or incompletely 4-celled.
  Corolla contorted in the bud; leaves opposite.
    Capsule 2 or 3-celled, with axile placentas, leaves stipulate.
                                                 Loganiaceae   401
    Carpels 2, more or less distinct, milky sap present.
                                                 Apocynaceae   407
  Corolla not contorted, leaves generally alternate.
    Ovary 2-celled with 1-3 ovules in each cell; corolla colored,
    4-lobed, imbricate......................... **Oleaceae**   397
    Ovary 2-celled, with many ovules in each cell; corolla
    plaited or imbricate, 5-4 lobed............. **Solanaceae**   417
    Ovary 4-celled, with 1 ovule in each cell; corolla 5-lobed,
    imbricate................................. **Borraginaceae**   414
  Corolla perigynous, bearing the stamens, irregular.
    Ovary 2-10 celled, one ovule in each cell; corolla 5-7 lobed, as many
    as stamens.. **Myoporaceae**   425

III. Petals free. Stamens perigynous or epigynous.
  Disc conspicuous, perigynous or hypogynous; flowers small, regular.
    Stamens alternate with petals; ovary 2-5 celled, with 2 or rarely
    1 ovule in each cell.............................. **Celastraceae**   267
    Stamens opposite the small petals; ovary free 2-4-celled with a single
    erect ovule in each cell.......................... **Rhamnaceae**   281
    Stamens alternate with the petals, or twice as many, ovary superior
    1-5 celled, fruit usually a one-celled drupe; leaves pinnate
                                                   Anacardiaceae   262
  Carpels free, or connate only at the base.
    Flowers irregular and imbricate or regular and valvate; fruit a
    2-valved pod..................................... **Leguminosae**   173
  Ovary syncarpous, superior, with axile placentas, ovules 1 or few in each cell.
    Corolla monopetalous, ovary many-celled.............. **Aquifoliaceae**   263
  Ovary syncarpous, with axile placentas and many seeds on each placenta.
    Ovary inferior, stamens indefinite; calyx-lobes imbricate.
                                                 Myrtaceae   319
  Ovary syncarpous with parietal placentas and many ovules on each of
  the latter.
    Ovary partly adnate to calyx, 2-5-celled; leaves opposite.
                                                 Saxifragaceae   151
  Ovary inferior with an epigynous disc, 2- to several celled, with a
  single ovule in each cell.
    Calyx adnate to ovary, the latter 2 to many celled, with one ovule
    in each cell; leaves compound..................... **Araliaceae**   336

IV. Petals free from the calyx and from each other, wanting in *Xylosma*.
  Ovary syncarpous, placentas parietal.
    Petals as many as sepals or none, stamens indefinite... **Flacourtiaceae**   311
    Sepals, petals and stamens isomerous, 5 each; fruit a two to four-
    valved woody capsule............................ **Pittosporaceae**   153
  Ovary syncarpous, placentas axile.
    Disc wanting, sepals imbricate.
      Sepals and petals tetramerous, stamens indefinite; ovary 1-celled;
      leaves opposite............................... **Guttiferae**   309
      Sepals and petals pentamerous, the latter often cohering at the
      base; stamens indefinite, leaves alternate....... **Theaceae**   307
    Disc wanting, sepals valvate.
      Stamens indefinite, monadelphous; fruit capsular; seed usually
      reniform, flowers often showy.................. **Malvaceae**   291
      Stamens indefinite, polyadelphous................. **Elaeocarpaceae**   287
    Disc annular, inside the stamens.
      Leaves entire and opposite or imparipinnate and alternate:
      stamens as many or twice as many as petals; ovary 4-celled
      and in fruit 4 lobed, or of a single carpel....... **Rutaceae**   192
    Disc annular, outside the stamens.
      Leaves entire, impari-pinnate or dissected, alternate; petals
      sometimes wanting; ovary 3-celled............. **Sapindaceae**   269

BOTANICAL REGIONS.

Little attention has hitherto been paid to the various interesting botanical regions of the Hawaiian Islands. The different types of forests, even at the same elevation and often in one district, are so marked that one could draw imaginary lines separating these various types of forests with their peculiar species. There seems hardly to be a transition type present. It is owing to the various lava flows of all ages that such types of forests are at present in existence, but nevertheless climatic conditions, such as wind, rainfall, etc., are also responsible for these peculiarities. This, of course, applies more to the Island of Hawaii, which is the largest and supposed to be the youngest of the group.

If we include the scanty strand vegetation, which consists mainly of a few herbaceous plants and three or four species of trees, which are scattered, single ones here and there on the beaches, we have six botanical regions, each of which has again to be subdivided into sections, owing to topographical changes caused by lava flows and climatic conditions. Many changes on lava flows are caused by rain and exposure to wind, which disintegrates the lava quicker than in other regions more sheltered, and so decides the plants most adaptable to these regions, though this in turn depends again on the nature of the lava itself, whether *aa* (rough) or *pahoehoe* (smooth) lava.

The botanical regions are as follows:

1. Strand vegetation.
2. Lowland region. (This region merges into the lower forest region).
   Section a, dry region.
   Section b, wet region.
3. Lower forest region.
   Section a, windward side.
   Section b, leeward side.
4. Middle forest region.
   Section a, dry region.
   Section b, semi-dry.
   Section c, wet region.
   Section d, *kipukas*, (small areas of lands with no trace of lava, soil black and fertile in dry section, surrounded by newer lava flows; richest in tree species).
5. Bog region.
6. Upper forest region.

PLATE I.

PANDANUS ODORATISSIMUS L. and HIBISCUS TILIACEUS L. on the lowlands on the northern slopes of Mt. Haleakala, Maui.

As already remarked, the strand vegetation of these islands is extremely poor in comparison with the luxurious strand floras of the islands of the South Seas and other countries bordering on the Pacific. Of trees, the most common are the *Hisbiscus tiliaceus (Hau)* and *Pandanus odoratissimus (Puhala).* (See plate I.). While the former may be seen in scattered clumps along the shore, the latter forms dense forests on the windward sides of the islands of Hawaii and Maui, covering the precipitous walls down to the water's edge. They are usually associated with the *Jambosa malaccensis (Ohia ai),* which, however, does not grow on the steep slopes, but at the bottom of narrow ravines, which the mountain streams have cut into the precipitous cliffs. They are also associated with the *Aleurites moluccana (Kukui).*

It is in such places as Pololu, Honokaneiki, Honokanenui, Waimanu, etc.. on the windward side of Hawaii, and Makaiwa, and other valleys on the windward side of Maui, where conditions are still undisturbed, that one can see strand vegetation that would somewhat remind him of the strand floras of the South Seas. But in the true sense of the word it is not a typical beach flora, but belongs to the lowland zone, which in certain localities, as mentioned above, reaches the water's edge. (See plate II.)

On sandy beaches the cosmopolitan *Ipomoea pes caprae (Pohuehue)* is nearly always found, with its long runners reaching almost into the sea. *Cuscuta Sandwichiana* (Dodder or *Pololo*) may often be seen growing on *Ipomoea pes caprae* as well as on *Ipomoea tuberculata.* Among other Convolvulaceae peculiar to the shores is *Ipomoea acetosaefolia (Hunakai),* which is found on the island of Niihau only. *Jacquemontia Sandwicensis* occurs farther inland, as well as on sandy shores, together with the nyctaginaceous *Boerhaavia diffusa (Nena).* Of the Caryophyllaceae, only two endemic species, *Schiedea Remyi* and *Schiedea Lydgatei,* are found on the shores, and those on the island of Molokai only, under the precipitous cliffs on the windward side. Of Leguminosae, the rare *Sesbania tomentosa (Ohai), Vigna lutea* and *Canavalia* sp? are to be found, the two latter especially common near Waialua, Oahu, and also on Molokai, together with the boraginaceous *Heliotropium Curassavicum* and *H. anomalum (Hinahina).* Of Campanulaceae, the very interesting and queer looking *Brighamia insignis* of the tribe Lobelioideae is found on the islands of Niihau, Kauai, Molokai and Lanai, though only on the windward sides, growing on the precipitous cliffs down to a few feet from the waves, where they are within reach of the tremendous spray of the sea. On the latter island it is found at the head of Mauna Lei gorge on the precipitous cliffs.

One of the most common sea-shore plants is the cosmopolitan *Scaevola frutescens,* which is usually in company with *Vitex trifolia.*

Of trees, *Calophyllum Inophyllum (Kamani)* forms usually large groves on the windward sides of most of the islands; but especial mention may be made

3

PLATE II.

PANDANUS ODORATISSIMUS L. (native name: Puhala) on the beach of Hanalei, Kauai.

of the beautiful grove on Molokai in the valley of Halawa, which was spoken of and recorded by the earliest navigators who visited these islands.

Among the plants already mentioned, the following are often met with, though a few are peculiar to certain localities:

Compositae
- A species of Tetramolopium* on the more muddy flats on Molokai.
- (Nehe) Lipochaeta succulenta (Niihau and Kauai)*
- (Nehe) Lipochaeta integrifolia*
- (Nehe) Lipochaeta connata var. littoralis*
- (Kookolau) Campylotheca molokaiensis.

(Koko)	Euphorbia cordata
(Ohelo kai)	Lycium Sandwicense
	Solanum Nelsoni* (Molokai)
	Kadua littoralis (Molokai)*
	Lepidium sp ?*
(Hoawa)	Pittosporum halophilum (Molokai)*
(Heuhiuhi)	Cassia Gaudichaudii (Lanai Manele)
	Scaevola coriacea*
(Hialoa)	Waltheria Americana
	Achyranthus sp.
(Makou)	Peucedanum Sandwicense*
	Lysimachia spathulata
	Ruppia maritima
(Ninika)	Lythrum maritimum (Waikolu, Molokai, only)
(Mao)	Gossypium tomentosum
(Maiapilo)	Capparis Sandwichiana
(Anapanapa)	Colubrina Asiatica
(Kului)	Nototrichium humile*
	Batis maritima
(Iliahi aloe)	Santalum littorale*
(Kaunoa)	Cassytha filiformis (usually on Ipomoea pes caprae)

Of trees the following may be recorded:

(Milo)	Thespesia populnea
(Niu)	Cocos nucifera
(Kou)	Cordia subcordata
(Kamani)	Terminalia catappa
(Noni)	Morinda citrifolia

On the rocks near the sea at Waialua and Cape Kaena, Oahu, the writer observed plants of Myoporum Sandwicense* only one foot high, which at 3000 feet elevation becomes a tree 40 feet in height.

---

* Those which are followed by an asterisk are all peculiar to the Hawaiian Islands and belong to the strand region, with the exception of a few which have descended from the lowlands and are found on the beaches.

PLATE III.

COCOS NUCIFERA L. (Native name: Niu); coconut palm grove near Lahaina, Maui, only short distance from sea. Some of the trees are over 100 feet high.

Of Cyperaceae, the following are to be found:

Cyperus pennatus
Cyperus phleoides
Fimbristylis pycnocephala*
Carex Sandwicensis var. (Makaiwa and Nahiku beach, Maui)
Gramineae
Sporobulus Virginicus, etc.

The *Cordia subcordata (Kou)*, which has followed the Malayan race in its migration, was once much more common than now. Only a few trees can be found along the shores, and those mainly on the less frequently visited islands, in out-of-the-way places. Whether the presence of this tree can be attributed to the ocean currents or to the agency of man can not definitely be determined, though presumably to the latter. The Coconut, of course, needs hardly to be mentioned, though it is not present in such extensive groves as in the South Sea Islands or Central America. (See plate III.)

Of Cryptogams, mention may be made of the *Ophioglossum vulgatum*, which springs up on our shores after heavy rains.

Between the beach formation and lowland zone occur lagoons on some of the islands, which are usually stocked with *Sesuvium Portulacastrum*, very common in company with *Cyperus pennatus, C. laevigatus* and *Mesembrian-themum* of recent introduction. In the ponds themselves, *Lemna minor* and *Wolfia columbiana* are very common, besides *Nelumbium speciosum, Sagittaria sagittifolia* and the cryptogamous *Marsilia villosa, Scirpus maritimus*, and *S. lacustris. Cyperus umbelliferus*, having escaped from cultivation, is found occasionally in patches. The Chenopodiums are numerous, nearly always in company with *Portulaca oleracea* and *Cenchrus echinatus*.

THE LOWLAND ZONE.

Most of the plants mentioned in the strand formation can be found in the lowland zone, though, of course, several species of plants are peculiar to the lowland zone. This formation is usually open grassland on the leeward sides of the islands when spared by lava flows, and has lately been taken up with *Prosopis juliflora (Algaroba)* and *Acacia farnesiana (Klu)*. Of the native vegetation belonging to this zone, *Andropogon contortus (Pili* grass) and *Panicum torridum (Kakonakona)* are the most common. In these fields *Opuntia tuna* occurs frequently with numerous aliens of many countries, of which the most obnoxious is *Lantana camara (Lantana)*, which, however, ascends to an elevation of sometimes 3000 feet and even higher.

Of other native plants, *Sida fallax* and *S. cordifolia (Ilima)* are the most common, with *Waltheria Americana* and a few species of Lipochaeta and perhaps a species of Haplostachys, which is peculiar to the dry, open, grassy districts. *Thephrosia piscatoria* is not uncommon. *Passiflora triloba* and *P. foetida* have become terrible pests in certain parts of the islands, covering large

7

PLATE IV.

LOWER FOREST REGION on Oahu, a typical stand of Aleurites moluccana Willd. (native name: Kukui).

areas to the exclusion of everything else. A striking plant of the lowland zone is the Mexican Poppy, *Argemone Mexicana*, the *Puakala* of the natives. On the lava fields which have reached the shore, especially on the island of Hawaii in South Kona, native trees belonging to the lower forest zone have descended to the lowlands and can be found within a few yards from the sea. The most common is *Reynoldsia sandwicensis*. Even the *Metrosideros polymorpha* (*Ohia lehua*) the writer found growing practically at sea level, together with *Plectronia odorata*, which was covered with the lauraceous leafless parasite, *Cassytha filiformis*. What has just been said of the *Ohia lehua* is also true of *Myoporum sandwicense* (*Naio*), which can be found near the sea on the west end of Oahu near Kaena Point, only a foot in height.

THE LOWER FOREST REGION.

This region is perhaps the most interesting one as far as tree growth is concerned. It ranges from about 1000 feet to 2000 feet elevation, and is exceedingly tropical on the windward side, with a more or less uniform vegetation, though, of course, varying according to locality.

Nothing can be more different in aspect than the lower forest region of the lee sides of some of the islands as compared to that of the windward side. However, there are exceptions, as no two islands are alike in formation, and vary also greatly in age. The vegetation on some of the lava flows of more recent origin differs from that of the lava flows of greater age. On some of the islands, as on Oahu and Kauai, and perhaps Molokai, in certain localities on the leeward side, the vegetation differs very little from that of the windward side; but, nevertheless, each island, with the exception of Kahoolawe, and also Niihau, has its peculiar leeward lower forest flora, which is in all cases richer in species as far as tree growth is concerned than the rain forest.

The island of Hawaii will need a special chapter, as it is the largest of the group and has the most widely ranging regions of all; differing in climatic conditions, rainfall, soil formations, lava flows of all ages, winds, etc., all of which have contributed or are the cause of these marked types of forest or plant coverings belonging to the lower forest region.

The island of Maui, which is the next largest, has also a very striking forest flora that belongs to the region discussed in this chapter. For convenience sake, this lower forest region is here divided into two subsections: (a), the windward, and (b), the leeward forest flora. The island of Hawaii is discussed separately.

The most striking of all trees belonging to this region is the *Aleurites moluccana* or *Kukui*. It can be recognized at once from a distance on account of its pale foliage, which gives this lower forest region a distinguishing character. (See plate IV.) It either forms large groves to the exclusion of everything else or is found in company with *Jambosa malaccensis* (*Ohia ai*) and other trees which will be taken into consideration as a whole. Immediately above the lowland region a few straggling *Kukui* trees may be observed. They grow on the leeward

9

PLATE V.

VEGETATION ALONG A STREAM in the lower forest region on Oahu, Palolo Valley; the trees in the foreground are **Aleurites moluccana** Willd. (Native name: Kukui.)

as well as the windward side, on dry, arid lava flows, in deep ravines, along dry stream beds, in exceedingly dense rain forests, but never going higher than 2200 feet, and sometimes rarely that.

Its associates are, however, not always the same, nor are they confined to the same region. With it in the dry as well as semi-wet districts is to be found the rubiaceous *Plectronia odorata*, usually a shrub or often a small tree. In the valleys back of Honolulu, Oahu, as well as in the valleys of Molokai or other islands (see plate V), it is associated with the *Acacia Koa (Koa)*, which descends on Oahu as low as 600 feet, the *Pandanus odoratissimus (Puhala)*, *Jambosa malaccensis*, and *Elaeocarpus bifidus (Kalia)*, which, however, is not exactly a tree of the lower forest region, as it forms the largest part of the middle forest region on the island of Kauai, from 3000 to perhaps 4000 feet elevation. The rubiaceous trees, *Straussia Kaduana*, *S. Mariniana*, *Gardenia Remyi*, *Bobea elatior*, and on Oahu, especially on the western range, *Santalum ellipticum*, are found in its company at an elevation of perhaps 800 to 1000 feet. The quite numerous *Metrosideros polymorpha*, in its various forms, grows also in this region, but is not confined to it, as it can be found from sea level to an elevation of 9000 feet, and even higher. The nyctaginaceous *Pisonia umbellifera (Papala kepau)* is one of the typical trees of this region, together with the urticaceous genera Pipturus, Boehmeria, and Touchardia, but rarely Urera. The malvaceous *Hibiscus tiliaceus (Hau)*, and also the native white Hibiscus, species Arnottianus, a medium-sized tree, may be found in this region, as well as the anacardiaceous *Rhus semialata* var. *Sandwicensis (Neneleau)*. The latter, however, forms groves by itself.

A form of *Maba Sandwicensis* with narrow leaves may also come into this region. The tree is especially common back of Hilo along the road leading to Olaa. Of shrubs, the pretty white flowered goodeniaceous *Scaevola Chamissoniana (Naupaka kuahiwi)* is very gregarious with Wikstroemia; the latter genus is not confined to this region. Next to the *Kukui*, but not quite so conspicuous from a distance on account of its much smaller size, is the monocotyledonous plant, *Cordyline terminalis*, the common *Ti* or *Ki* of the natives. It clothes, sometimes, the lower slopes of the valleys, on steep sides or precipices, crowding out every other undershrub.

Special mention must be made of the very strong and beautiful climber, *Freycinetia Arnotti*, which covers the trunks of trees (mainly *Ohia lehua*), smothering them beneath its great masses of runners with their peculiar cling roots.

In this very interesting region the first signs of Lobelioideae, a tribe of the family Campanulaceae, occur, to the wonderful development of which the writer wishes to call attention. (See plate VI.) It is the largest of all other families which occur in this Territory, the Hawaiian Islands. The most extreme forms can be found, from two to over forty feet in height. They are represented at from 800 to 2000 feet elevation by the very common *Clermontia macrocarpa*,

11

PLATE VI.

CYANEA TRITHOMANTA Gray, a typical lobelioideous plant of the lower forest region on Hawaii; the vine in the background is Freycinetia Arnotti Gaud. (native name: Ieie).

which can be found on nearly all the islands. Higher up, its place is taken by the most interesting and peculiar as well as handsome forms, such as *C. persicaefolia, C. oblongifolia, C. drepanomorpha*, etc. On Oahu the genus Rollandia, also of the tribe Lobelioideae, is represented in the lower forest region by the species *R. lanceolata* and *R. grandifolia* and another species of Rollandia found to be new and named *R. truncata* by the author.

Clermontia Kohalae, a strictly lower forest zone type, is also new to science. It is found at Kohala on the island of Hawaii, where it is gregarious at 1500 to 2000 feet elevation, after which place it is named. It is a small, handsome tree, flowering in the summer. To this region belongs also *Cyanea angustifolia, C. acuminata, C. grimesiana, C. scabra*, all of which are peculiar to this region.

The gesneriaceous genus Cyrtandra, with its many species, characterized by the often bilabiate corolla, which is invariably white, having a fleshy berry of the same color as the flower, with minute, almost microscopic seeds, belongs to this zone; but not exclusively. These Cyrtandras have very few species in this region, but reach their best development in the middle forest zone.

The euphorbiaceous Claoxylon, a small shrub, may be found occasionally in this zone, though most plentifully on West Maui in the valley of Waikapu. Of vines, several Convolvulaceae, especially the genus Ipomoea, are found trailing over guava, lantana and other introduced shrubbery which have established themselves in the lower forest region. Besides the Convolvulaceae, *Dioscorea sativa* and *D. pentaphylla (Yam)* are common, as well as the liliaceous *Smilax Sandwicensis (Pioi)*, trailing over trees.

The Hawaiian Labiatae are conspicuous by their absence in this region, at least in the region belonging to the windward subsection, though two are found in the dry section.

Of monocotyledonous plants, the following remain to be mentioned: The *Alocasia macrorrhiza (Ape)*, one of the huge species of taro, but not edible, though in times of scarcity the stem was cooked and eaten by the natives. With leaves several feet long, they can occasionally be found in shaded ravines or valleys, besides the useful *Tacca pinnatifida (Pia)*. The last, but not least, is *Musa sapientum*, the Banana, of which the natives recognized some forty odd varieties, which is a typical feature of the lower forest zone, and with it is the ginger, *Zingiber zerumbet (Awapuhi)*.

The cryptogamous flora is also represented in this region, its most conspicuous and typical representative being the *Asplenium nidus* or bird's-nest fern, which usually is plentiful in the forks of the branches of the *Kukui*, with which it is invariably growing when not terrestrial. Of other ferns, mention may be made of the everpresent *Nephrolepis exaltata* and the very troublesome *Gleichenia linearis (Uluhe)*, which covers the ground so thickly with its far-reaching branches that it is next to impossible to penetrate any country taken up by this robust fern. It is usually in layers of four to five or even more feet thick, the lower ones usually dead, forming a canopy over which one crosses only with great diffi-

13

PLATE VII.

SCRUB VEGETATION on aa (rough) lava field on the leeward side of Mt. Haleakala, Maui; elevation 1500 feet; the tree to the right is *Reynoldsia sandwicensis* Gray (native name: Ohe), the one at the left is *Rauwolfia sandwicensis* A. DC. (native name: Hao).

culty. It is often dangerous to cross places where this fern grows, as it completely hides the ground underneath, sometimes concealing the holes, into which one is likely to fall should he entrust himself to this treacherous fern. Several species of Polypodium are present, as *P. spectrum*, etc. Dryopteris and Asplenium have also species in this locality. In the more open places the ground is usually covered with *Commelina nudiflora (Honohonowai)* and several grasses, with a few cyperaceous plants, such as *Rhynchospora thyrsoidea* and *Gahnia Beecheyi*. In the more open glades on the outskirts of the lower forests *Microlepia strigosa* and *Odontosoria chinensis*, the *Palapalae* and *Palaa* ferns, are quite common, while occasionally Cibotium and Sadleria occur in this region also.

The family Flacourtiaceae is represented by two species in these islands, both of the lower forest zone, though one, *Xylosma Hawaiiensis*, is peculiar to the wet, the other, *X. Hillebrandii*, to the dry. This holds good of the euphorbiaceous genus Antidesma, with its two species, *A. platyphyllum* and *A. pulvinatum*, the former occurring in the wet section as well as in the dry, while the latter is found mainly in the dry section of the lower forest zone.

SUBSECTION B—LEEWARD LOWER FOREST FLORA.

No two forest floras could be more different and strikingly peculiar than those in question. The plant covering of the leeward regions, as for example the Waianae mountains, Oahu, the southern slope of Haleakala, Maui, the west end of Molokai, etc., is the richest in species as far as tree growth is concerned. Nearly all trees growing on these more or less arid lava fields have developed extremely hard, close-grained wood. Only four or five species, as Reynoldsia, Erythrina, Nothocestrum, etc., are soft-wooded, and possess exceedingly thin bark, while those of hard wood possess a usually rough, scaly bark of perhaps half an inch or more in thickness. This striking flora gives the region a most peculiar aspect, and more so in such places which were disturbed by more or less recent lava flows, destroying the original vegetation, which is then succeeded by an entirely different plant growth. These districts which harbor such an interesting flora are not very large, being only perhaps two to four miles long at the most and much less wide. It is in these peculiar regions that the botanical collector will find more in one day collecting than in a week or two in a wet region, and may it be said here that it is indeed astonishing that these various places like Puuwaawaa, North Kona, Hawaii, and Kahikinui, Maui, have been entirely neglected by the botanical collectors who have previously visited these islands. It may be of interest to know that not less than 60 per cent of all the species of indigenous trees growing in these islands can be found and are peculiar to the dry regions or lava fields of the lower forest zone, which in certain localities gradually passes into the middle forest region, carrying a few trees up into the latter zone.

Exceptions are certain *kipukas* on Hawaii, at an elevation of between 4000 and 5000 feet, which possess a flora which is otherwise entirely restricted to the

15

PLATE VIII.

XEROPHYTIC VEGETATION, trees in foreground Plectronia odorata, one of them covered with Cassytha filiformis, a leaf-less parasite; on lava flows at Hilea, Kau, Hawaii.

lower forest region. In these restricted areas one may find from 40 to 50 species of trees, some of which are confined to one locality only. It is in these places that the writer has found many new species of trees and rediscovered some which were thought to have become extinct. Of course, most of the Hawaiian plant genera have representatives in both wet and dry districts, which differ so greatly from each other that one cannot help coming to the conclusion that they must have originated in different periods, meaning that their evolution was not carried on simultaneously.

The *Kukui* is sparingly represented in these floral districts and is replaced by the araliaceous *Reynoldsia sandwicensis*, a striking tree of sometimes 50 feet in height. (See plate VII.) It is one of the trees which possesses a soft wood and an exceedingly thin bark. Its most plentiful associate is the leguminous *Erythrina monosperma*, the *Wiliwili* of the natives, whose wood is also very light and soft.

Nearly all Hawaiian Araliaceae come into this region, with the exception of a very few species, such as *Tetraplasandra Waialealae*, the Oahuan varieties of *T. meiandra*, *Cheirodendron platyphyllum*, and *Pterotropia gymnocarpa*, which are characteristic of the rain forest. *Pterotropia dipyrena* is peculiar to the region discussed in this chapter, though sometimes going over into the middle forest zone, to which *Pterotropia Kavaiensis*, a handsome tree found only on the island of Kauai, is peculiar.

The Apocynaceae have three arborescent species represented, *Rauwolfia sandwicensis (Hao)*, either a shrub or more often a tree, and *Ochrosia sandwicensis (Holei)*, not uncommon, and *Pteralyxia macrocarpa (Kaulu)*, only found on Oahu in the valley of Makaleha. The latter is a small tree, with large, bright red, double fruits. The *Gynopogon oliviformis (Maile)*, also belonging to this family, has a variety *myrtillifolia* occuring in the dry forests, usually climbing over trees, and sometimes strangling them to death.

The most common tree is the liliaceous *Dracaena aurea*, or *Halapepe* of the natives. It is entirely restricted to this region and only very rarely is found outside of it.

These dry or mixed forest regions occur, however, in other tropical countries, as in East Java and India, and are peculiar in so far as they are composed of periodically deciduous trees. In Hawaii only three or four species lose their leaves in the dry season, as *Erythrina monosperma*, *Reynoldsia sandwicensis*, *Kokia drynariodes*, and *Sapindus saponaria*. The same may be said of Nothocestrum, which also sheds its leaves, but without ever becoming leafless, as its defoliation immediately precedes its acquisition of new foliage. These dry, forest regions or mixed woodlands have hardly ever been investigated, previous explorers confining their investigations to the wet forests, which appear from a distance much more promising. These rain forests, however, display much less variety than the mixed forest, where not a single tree species can be called dominant. Of course, there are exceptions, as for example in South Kona, on Hawaii,

PLATE IX.

FERN OR RAIN FOREST in the middle forest region near the Volcano Kilauea on Hawaii, elevation 4000 feet; the trees are mainly: Metrosideros polymorpha Gaud, the ferns: Cibotium Menziesii Hook. and C. Chamissoi Kaulf.

where *Metrosideros polymorpha (Ohia lehua)* got the upper hand and now forms nearly pure stands, with perhaps a few other trees, like Straussia and Suttonia, on the more recent lava flows which intersect the mixed forests. This, however, is due to the wonderful adaptability of the *Ohia* to nearly any environment and to its quicker growth, while the trees of the mixed lower forests are extremely slow growing and their seeds usually do not germinate before one or two years, or perhaps much longer, after which the two cotyledons remain for another year before a third leaf appears. Trees of these mixed forests have practically no epiphytes and only one or two lianes are present, *Embelia* sp., whose huge, rope-like stems are entangled in the tops of the trees, having a thickness of several inches near the ground, on which they are twisted like the coil of a rope before ascending the trees. This giant Embelia has only been observed so far by the writer in the *kipuka* Puaulu, near the volcano on Hawaii.

Caesalpinia bonducella is very common on the lava fields, and the writer met with huge plants whose rope-like stems climbed the tallest trees, forming also an impenetrable mass on the ground, very treacherous on account of their recurved sharp thorns and very spiny seed pods. Besides these lianes, two parasites are exceedingly common, one being the Hawaiian mistletoe, *Viscum articulatum*, which at that locality infests mainly the ebenaceous *Maba sandwicensis*, while the leafless parasite, *Cassytha filiformis*, with its thousands of thread-like, yellow stems, covers the tops of trees (usually *Plectronia odorata)*, which in due time succumb to this pest. (See plate VIII.)

Strange to say, these mixed forests have hardly any native undergrowth, with the exception of a few ferns and grasses, though in late years lantana and guava have driven out the few native plants which formed this undergrowth. In dry forests of normal conditions a few composites thrive, such as Lipochaeta, and a menispermaceous vine, *Cocculus Ferrandianus*, and a species of the cucurbitaceous genus Sicyos. Some of the trees belonging to the mixed or dry forests, as the handsome *Pelea multiflora, Alectryon macrococcus* and *Hibiscadelphus*, but mainly the former, are covered with a species of lichen which gives the trees a mournful appearance and is really injurious to them. This particular species *(Usnea australis)* does not infest all trees, but only certain species, mainly *Pelea multiflora*, in the dry forest of Auahi on the southern slope of Haleakala.

Though it is said that the more conspicuous lichens are common on unhealthy trees, rather than on thrifty ones, nevertheless when they do occur in such quantities as on some of the trees of the mixed forests, they must interfere with the functions of the bark. It also may be said that nowhere is the lichen flora richer in species than in the mixed or dry forest of the lower zone.

On Kauai, the dry or mixed forest zone has almost entirely disappeared and only a few trees can still be found. Most of the land has been cleared for sugar cane fields up to an elevation of nearly 2000 feet; above Makaweli only little is left, while above Kekaha only grass land spreads up to an elevation of nearly 3000 feet.

19

PLATE X.

INTERIOR OF FERN FOREST on Hawaii, near Volcano Kilauea, elevation 4000 feet. The tree ferns are **Cibotium**; undergrowth ferns, **Dryopteris, Asplenium, Aspidium,** etc.

That there was once a mixed woodland is told by the very few remaining trees, such as the white Hibiscus *(Hibiscus Waimeae)*, a handsome tree with large, white, showy flowers, which still exists in a small valley in company with *Osmanthus sandwicensis.* At an elevation of 1000 feet, back of Makaweli, the most common tree is *Sapindus oahuensis,* remarkable for its simple leaves. This tree has hitherto not been reported from Kauai, from whence it must have come to Oahu, being much more numerous on Kauai than on the latter island.

The plants which make up the mixed woodlands are usually the same on all the islands, with the exception of certain species which are peculiar to certain localities. Among them are the following: *Hibiscus Waimeae* to Kauai; *Pteralyxia macrocarpa,* an apocynaceous tree with bright red double fruits, to the Waianae mountains on Oahu; *Pelea multiflora,* a newly described species, together with *P. cinerea* var. *racemosa, Hibiscadelphus Wilderianus, Sideroxylon auahiense,* all new to science, peculiar to the lava fields of Auahi, southern slopes of Haleakala; and *Pittosporum Hosmeri, Xanthoxylum dipetalum* var. nov., *Kokia Rockii,* and others, to Puuwaawaa, Kona, Hawaii; while *Tetraplasandra Lanaiensis* and a few other species are found on Lanai only.

Not all dry forests of the lower zone are, however, alike, some differing very materially in possessing fewer species of trees than others, and thus form, so to say, a transition type. On Maui the forest above Makawao, which gradually passes into the middle forest zone, has a similar aspect to the dry forest on the southern slope, but, being more to the windward side, and therefore receiving more rain, is unsuitable for certain tree species, and thus less rich in species. Between this forest, which is somewhat a mixture of rain and dry forest, since it has suitable conditions for plants of both regions, and Kula, is now a large treeless plain, with the exception of the intervening valleys, or rather old lava gulches, with their precipitous walls, which show still a very interesting tree growth, mainly composed of Sideroxylon, Xanthoxylum, Pseudomorus and Dracaena. The slopes of Kula, where once a beautiful dry forest existed, are now bare owing to cattle, and the only trees still to be found are *Dracaena aurea.*

At Ulupalakua native vegetation has disappeared entirely and only planted Eucalypti are to be seen. The land of Ulupalakua must be extremly old, as not much lava is visible, while the immediate vicinity shows lava flows of little age. Several lava flows of various ages must have flowed down the mountain at intervals of a century or perhaps more, which can be judged by the presence of the various floral aspects on these different lava flows. The older lava flow has been taken possession of by tree growth of such species belonging to the typical dry forest as are more easily transported by either winds or birds and have the advantage of becoming more easily established than others, while the newer and also somewhat blacker flow is covered by a somewhat different vegetation, mainly of introduced weeds, with here and there a native shrub. Beyond these flows is the typical mixed or dry forest, undoubtedly of great age; its area is about 500 acres, and is mainly *aa* (rough) lava, very much disintegrated in some places,

21

though where it is not covered with vegetation other than lichens it shows still all its characteristics.

Beyond Auahi, with its fifty species of trees, is open, flat, rough country with a few scattered trees of Xanthoxylum, the last stragglers from the dry forest which have ventured out into the open, or perhaps are the survivors of an old forest previously existing in this locality. Close to it lies the Kaupo Gap, or southern outlet of Haleakala crater, beyond which seems to be a semi-wet district, followed immediately by the rain forest.

THE VARIOUS FOREST REGIONS ON THE ISLAND
OF HAWAII

The Island of Hawaii is composed mainly of the three mountains, Mauna Kea (13,823 feet), Mauna Loa (13,675 feet), and Hualalai (8273 feet), while the western end, the mountains of Kohala, are said to have formed once a separate island, being about of the same age as West Maui. The now extinct volcano, Mauna Kea, the highest mountain of the Pacific, is the oldest volcano on Hawaii, while Mauna Loa, whose summit crater, Mokuaweoweo, still becomes periodically active, is the youngest. Mt. Hualalai, the lowest of the volcanoes on Hawaii, now supposed to be extinct, was last active a little over a century ago, its last eruption, in 1801, being thought to have been witnessed by an Englishman.

Naturally an island like Hawaii, still in process of formation, represents widely ranging districts: ancient lava flows, deserts, dense tropical rain forests, dry or mixed forests, new lava flows bare of any vegetation, alpine zones, and almost any climate from dry desert heat to the most humid air of the rain forest, from tropical heat to ice and almost perpetual snow at the summits of the mountains, where a temperature of 13 degrees Fahrenheit in midsummer is nothing uncommon. From a phytogeographic standpoint the island of Hawaii offers the most interesting field in the Pacific.

All these various districts, with their peculiar climates, support many interesting types of plant coverings.

The windward side of Hawaii, as of nearly all the other islands, is very precipitous, especially along the western end, the Kohala mountains, where vertical cliffs nearly 3000 feet in height are covered with verdure almost to the the water's edge. The rainfall is exceedingly heavy in this district, and the waters have cut huge gorges into these rocky walls, such as the valleys of Waipio, Waimanu, Pololu, Honokaneiki, etc. The vegetation of these valleys is rather uniform, and has been described under the lower windward forest region.

Between Kohala and Mauna Kea is a large plain of many thousands of acres, now mainly grassland, at an elevation of 2000 to 3700 feet, after which the slopes of Mauna Kea rise more steeply. At from 3700 feet up to 7000 feet, on this big plain, is a belt of forest composed mainly of *Sophora chrysophylla*, while lower down are scattered trees, usually *Osmanthus sandwicensis*, the Hawaiian olive, with *Myoporum sandwicense*, the *Naio*, etc. To windward, the mountain slopes rather gently, forming the Hamakua coast, which at the lowlands has been planted with sugar cane exclusively up to an elevation of 2000 feet. From thence

PLATE XI.

SUBXEROPHYTIC VEGETATION near Volcano Kilauea on Hawaii: ferns in foreground: **Sadleria cyatheoides**; Volcano Mauna Loa (13675 ft.) in the distance.

up is a stretch of forest which receives a heavy rainfall, and is composed mainly of *Metrosideros polymorpha*, with Perottetia, Straussia, Suttonia, Pipturus and other trees peculiar to such a forest type. Epiphytic plants occur in great numbers, especially Pteridophytes and vines like the *Freycinetia Arnotti (Ie-ie)*, while the lobeliaceous *Clermontia parviflora* is found on trunks of trees and on tree ferns. The whole forest, however, has suffered greatly, not only from the invasion by cattle, but also by forest fires, which have destroyed large areas. *Ilex sandwicensis* is found in great numbers, besides huge tree ferns, *Cibotium Menziesii*, some of which measure 25 to 30 feet in height, with a diameter of 3 feet. The fibrous trunks are usually covered with multitudes of species. Vaccinium is plentiful, also Clermontiae and *Rubus Macraei*. The *Ohia*, which becomes a tall tree, is festooned with the liliaceous *Astelia veratroides*, besides Smilax and other plants.

Between 2000 and 3000 feet elevation the forest has disappeared and only stragglers of tree ferns can be found standing, though ten times as many are lying dead on the ground and overgrown with all possible weeds, which the ranchmen have imported with their grass seeds. Among them is the composite climber, *Senecio mikanioides*, an awful pest, which has become well established on Hawaii. At 3000 feet a few *Koa* trees can be found, together with *Naio*, and here also was found a single native palm, *Pritchardia* sp., windswept and half dead. If one considers the natural condition in which this palm flourishes, as for example in the dense tropical rain forests in Kohala, and then looks at the single plant all alone in a field of *Paspalum conjugatum*, as the accuser of man the destroyer, it stands a witness to the fact that there, surrounding it, was once a beautiful tropical jungle. Above this dead forest belt is grass land only, while a little higher up *Sophora chrysophylla* forms a belt of forest together with *Acacia Koa*, on whose trunks grows *Asplenium adiantum nigrum*. Farther up the *Koa* gives place to the *Mamani*, which forms the sole vegetation besides a few straggling shrubs of the rosaceous *Osteomeles anthyllidifolia* at 6000 feet.

In this locality are three cinder cones or craters on the mountain slope, Kaluamakani, a little over 7000 feet, Moano, and Nau. The vegetation on these cones is scanty. The crater holes are very shallow and sandy and harbor only few plants. On the rim of the cones grows the monocotyledonous *Sisyrynchium acre*, a glabrous plant 6 to 10 inches in height, with small yellow flowers. In the shade of the *Mamani*, as well as on the slopes, grows *Ranunculus Hawaiiensis*, while in the cracks of the crater wall several grasses, *Cynodon dactylon*, *Koehleria glomerata*, and *Deschampsia australis* var. were found in company with *Gnaphalium luteo-album*. At an elevation of 7000 feet on the windward slope, *Raillardia arborea*, one of the Hawaiian tree composites, grows in company with the epacridaceous Cyathodes. On the crater Nau several Compositae were found, mainly Raillardia, but also Campylotheca and Lipochaeta, besides a tree, *Euphorbia lorifolia*, and several herbaceous Labiatae of the genus Ste-

25

PLATE XII.

EXTERIOR VIEW OF FERN FOREST near Volcano Kilauea, elevation 4000 feet; the trees are **Acacia Koa** Gray and **Metrosideros polymorpha** Gaud.

nogyne. Encircling the base of the cone Nau is a deep lava gulch with precipitous walls, inaccessible to cattle. Here a composite vegetation with Labiatae flourishes; while outside only the hardy *Mamani* trees have survived the ravages of cattle.

The forests of Puna near Hilo are extremely rich and are situated almost between the slopes of Mauna Kea and Mauna Loa. Immediately back of Hilo is a somewhat mixed forest composed of species of trees peculiar to the dry and wet regions. The nearly impenetrable forests of the Hilo district are composed mainly of *Metrosideros polymorpha*, which forms almost pure stands.

FLORAL ASPECTS IN THE NEIGHBORHOOD OF THE VOLCANO KILAUEA ON HAWAII.

The floral aspects of the country surrounding Kilauea are exceedingly interesting, as there are many peculiar types of vegetation which are limited to certain small areas. Immediately back of the Volcano House is the fern or rain forest (see plate IX), composed of the tree ferns *Cibotium Menziesii* and *Cibotium Chamissoi*, which reach here a wonderful development as far as fronds are concerned, though the trunks are not so high as in the mountains of Kohala. The main trees are *Cheirodendron Gaudichaudii, Ilex sandwicensis, Suttonia Lessertiana*, while lobeliaceous species such as *Clermontia parviflora* var. *pleiantha* and others grow in the forks of trees. *Metrosideros polymorpha* is also extremely common. The trunks of these trees are usually covered with moss a foot or so thick, holding a tremendous amount of water. In the moss on these trees epiphytes are numerous; 10 to 15 species of ferns can sometimes be found on one trunk, mainly *Polypodium tamariscinum, P. lineare, P. pseudogrammitis, P. sarmentosum, Asplenium horridum, A. pseudofalcatum, Elaphoglossum gorgoneum, E. reticulatum, E. Wawrae*, etc., while an occasional Lycopod may be found also. Besides these numerous ferns, the liliaceous plant *Astelia veratroides* forms dense beds, especially on horizontal tree trunks, while *Vaccinium penduliflorum* and another variety occur quite frequently on the same trees. The undergrowth is mainly of ferns of the genera *Asplenium* and *Aspidium*. (See plate X.) From the trunks of tree ferns a beautiful Labiate, with large pink flowers, *Stenogyne calaminthoides*, hangs gracefully and sometimes interlaces several tree ferns with a number of its runners. Of shrubs, *Broussaisia arguta* and several species of Cyrtandra are not uncommon, while in certain localities the cyperaceous *Uncinia* sp. covers the ground. However, the native undergrowth is now being driven out by the tenacious *Rubus jamaicensis*, or thimble berry, an introduced pest, which makes walking very difficult on account of its nasty recurved thorns. The plant grows luxuriously in the shade of the tree ferns. Besides this obnoxious plant, another one has been introduced of late, the ordinary blackberry, which already shows signs of having taken a strong foothold.

Before one reaches the true rain or fern forest, where rich, black, muddy soil abounds, a sort of semi-wet forest, or rather shrubby vegetation, is passed

27

PLATE XIII.

ACACIA KOA FOREST in open flat country joining dry or mixed forest, near Volcano Kilauea, Hawaii; elevation 4000 feet.

through. Sadleria ferns, which like the open country, are numerous, with an occasional Cibotium (see plate XI); the trees are the same as in the rain forest, but are more stunted, while the shrubs are composed of different species. *Vaccinium reticulatum* ranks first, then *Cyathodes tameiameia*, an epacridaceous plant with pretty white and red berries, and also the poisonous thymelaeaceous plant *Wikstroemia* sp. On the open lava fields *Ohia lehua* abounds, and especially along the hot sulphur cracks, where the small trees are covered with the yellow crystals. Many cyperaceous plants can be found; among them are the following indigenous species: *Cyperus mauiensis, Carex sandwicensis, Gahnia Gaudichaudii, Cladium angustifolium, Cladium Meyenii,* etc. In the old cracks, *Santalum Freycinetianum* var. *latifolium* is common, besides several species of Coprosma and the composite shrub *Raillardia laxiflora*, the sapindaceous cosmopolitan *Dodonaea viscosa*, besides the common fern, *Polypodium pellucidum, Lycopodium cernuum,* etc. Adjoining this open scrub vegetation is the Koa forest (see plate XII), where giant trees can be seen, some reaching a height of 80 feet with a trunk 6 feet or so in diameter. It is mixed with *Ohia lehua,* Straussia, Suttonia, Perrottetia, and tree ferns, while in the forks of its branches small trees of a new lobeliaceous plant, *Clermontia* sp.,* have established themselves. Miles of this forest exist in which one can easily lose his way if he tries to penetrate into the interior, which in certain localities is inaccessible. The *Ie-ie* vine is occasionally met with, but 4000 feet elevation is its limit. Bordering this forest to the south are extensive lava flows of *aa*, which have now been taken possession of by *Acacia Koa* solely. (See plate XIII.) Here the trees do not grow straight, but have short trunks with very crooked branches, of which the lower invariably trail on the ground. In contrast to the lowland *aa* flows, which are taken possession of by *Ohia*, at this elevation *Koa* is the predominant or sole tree.

Three or four miles from the Volcano House, in the midst of *aa* lava just described, is a bit of land composed of 56 acres, which is called Kipuka Puaulu by the natives. This little oasis, as it should properly be termed, shows no sign of lava rock, but has rich, deep, black soil which supports a marvelous mixture of vegetation. As many as forty species of trees are present in this beautiful park-like spot. (See plate XIV.) It is of a similar nature to the mixed or dry forest of the lower forest zone. This *kipuka* or oasis is situated at an elevation of 4000 to 4500 feet, and is surrounded on three sides by old *aa* flows, 20 to 30 feet thick, while on the southeast side it is cut off by an old *pahoehoe* flow, which supports a scanty *Ohia lehua* growth. Many unique species of trees occur in this beautiful spot, and have not been found on the other islands and not even in other localities on the same island.

It is the writer's opinion that this forest is the sort of type which covered the slopes of Mauna Loa at this elevation for quite a large area but was destroyed by the many lava flows which broke out on the flanks of the mountain. Fortunately this little oasis, which will soon be reserved as a National park,

---

* Clermontia Hawaiiensis (Hbd.) Rock.

29

PLATE XIV.

DRY AND MIXED FOREST at an elevation of 4000 feet (Kipuku Puaulu) not far from the Volcano Kilauea on Hawaii; the main trees are: Straussia, Pelea, Xanthoxylum, Suttonia, Sophora, etc.

escaped the fiery streams by its elevation. It is now used as a fattening paddock for cattle, and it is indeed high time that something is done, or else these wonderful trees, many of them new and unique, will be a thing of the past, in even the nearest future. No undergrowth exists, with the exception of a few ferns, mainly Aspidium and Asplenium, the most common being *Polystichum falcatum* var.

One of the most interesting trees is a Malvaceae nearest to Hibiscus. Only one tree is in existence, and was described by the writer as a new genus under the name "Hibiscadelphus." Two other species have since been discovered by the writer belonging to the same new genus, which will be mentioned in their respective places. Among the biggest trees is a new variety of Xanthoxylum, with a straight trunk of over a foot in diameter. (See plate 83.) Several species of Pelea, besides other Xanthoxyla, *Sapindus saponaria,* and Suttonia, etc., make up this beautiful park.

Beyond this oasis is another *aa* lava flow of more recent age, as it is still covered with a sort of scrub vegetation. Dodonaea, *Rumex giganteus, Coprosma ernodeoides*—the *Kukainene* of the natives, *Cyperus mauiensis, Carex, Koehleria glomerata, Styphelia,* and a few others form the main vegetation, while a little lower is a triangular spot which was saved from the lava flows and supports a number of trees of *Pittosporum Hosmeri* var.,* the only Pittosporum representative in the whole district. It is most remarkable that not a single species of Pittosporum or Sideroxylon can be found in the Kipuka Puaulu, which has most of their associates represented, while these two genera are conspicuous by their absence. With these Pittosporum are *Pelea volcanica, Pelea* sp? and *Cheirodendron Gaudichaudii.* This strip of lava beyond the little oasis is about half a mile wide. On its other side is an *aa* flow of much greater age. *Ohia lehua* has covered it densely, together with other species, the former, however, being the dominant tree.

Adjoining this flow is another *kipuka* called Ki, similar to Puaulu, though much younger, as the vegetation is not half as rich in species as that of the latter. *Sapindus saponaria* is the predominant species, forming 50 per cent of the tree growth, while *Acacia Koa, Sophora chrysophylla,* Straussia, *Pelea volcanica,* and others make up the rest of the forest. *Sapindus saponaria* is the largest tree present, reaching a height of about 80 feet, with trunks of 2 to 3 feet in diameter. There is no undergrowth now with the exception of a few Aspidium and Polystichum ferns. Lichen growth is extremely rich in species, especially on the bark of *Sapindus saponaria.* This last *kipuka* is at an elevation of about 4600 to 5000 feet. Above it is still another *aa* flow occupied by *Acacia Koa,* while below it is a forest of *Sophora chrysophylla,* which at this elevation, 4000 to 5000 feet, reaches its best development.

Another *aa* flow joins this *kipuka* on the southwest side, supporting a vegetation similar to the one adjoining it on the other, but is still younger. This flow is perhaps two miles wide, and must have come from the west flank of

---

* Pittosporum Hosmeri var. longifolia Rock v. n.

31

PLATE XV.

TYPICAL JUNGLE OF THE LOWER FOREST REGION, at Hilea, Kau, Hawaii, elevation 1800 feet. Ferns to left, **Sadleria**; to right, **Cibotium**; vine in background, **Freycinetia Arnotti** Gaud.

Mauna Loa. The vegetation is extremely uniform, *Ohia lehua* being the only tree, while in certain localities it is entirely bare of vegetation.

At 5000 feet elevation is a large area of land with rich soil supporting a number of species of native grasses, mainly *Koehleria glomerata*, with *Carex sandwicensis* var. *lavarum*. Most beautiful *Koa* trees of great size form clumps of forests, together with *Mamani*. This land, which has been reserved as a paddock, must be extremely old, as no lava is visible, and is sharply contrasted by the rugged, sharp, black *aa* lava flows bordering it. Above this paddock, which is of considerable extent, is the again everpresent lava. It is only on this side, but mainly above Kapapala, that the silversword, *Argyroxiphium sandwicense*, is found as low down as 7000 feet elevation on Mauna Loa. The vegetation from the volcano until one reaches Hilea, in Kau, is extremely uniform and quite uninteresting. At Hilea, the slopes of Mauna Loa are cut into many divisions, mainly valleys and ridges with very precipitous slopes. From Naalehu the country slopes very gradually.

FLORAL ASPECTS OF KAU.

LAVA FORMATION.

Immediately below Hilea proper the land is all under cultivation, sugar cane being the only crop. At an elevation of about 2000 feet is a small plateau, mainly composed of *pahoehoe* lava of apparently great age, on both sides the mountain of Kaiholena rising to about 1000 feet, with very precipitous walls. The *pahoehoe* plain, which is called Kanalohu, is all hollow underneath. Great subterranean channels undermine the whole plain, and are now used for reservoirs. The lava walls are perfectly smooth and black and form complete arched tunnels for a long distance. These were undoubtedly subterranean outlets of rushing lava streams. In fact, some of the channels can be traced right down to the water's edge. The main vegetation of this plateau is *Paspalum conjugatum* (Hilo grass), besides a number of ferns.

Emerging into this flat plateau are several valleys, one of which, Kumauna, is of interest. The forest from Hilea to Waiohinu, though being on the lee side of Hawaii, belongs to the rain or wet forest type. At Hilea proper it is somewhat mixed, being composed of trees belonging to both wet and dry forest types. The forest as a whole is more uniform than similar forest types in other localities, due mainly to the land being geologically much younger than in similar localities on the other islands where volcanic activities ceased thousands of years ago, as it is situated on the southern slopes of the still active volcano Mauna Loa. The land, nevertheless, has extremely rich soil, which is black and somewhat muddy. The principal tree of which the Hilea forest is composed is *Metrosideros polymorpha*, which is the most numerous. Its associates are *Antidesma platyphyllum (Hame)*, Straussia, *Perrottetia sandwicensis (Olomea)*, Pipturus, Suttonia *(Kolea)*, *Pelea volcanica*, *Pelea clusiaefolia*, *Bobea* sp., *Tetraplasandra*

33

meiandra var., *Eurya sandwicensis (Wanini)*, and several species of Gouldia, Coprosma being very common at lower levels.

On the slopes of Kumauna and Kaiholena valley is found *Pterotropia dipy-rena* var., which reaches here a beautiful development. Trees 60 feet tall and more, with trunks of nearly two feet in diameter, are not uncommon in the valley, while at higher elevation it is a tree 30 feet in height with rather rambling branches. The *ie-ie* is gregarious, besides Smilax and Embelia, which are all lianes, climbing over trees. Of Leguminosae, a beautiful climber, *Strongylodon lucidum*, called *Nukuiwi* by the natives, covers the tops of the numerous *Kukui* trees in Kumauna valley. In few places has the writer seen such a beautiful forest as the one in question, reaching from Hilea to Waiohinu. Its natural condition is undisturbed, and therefore presents a marvelous display of growth up to an elevation of nearly 6000 feet. (See plate XV.) Several Lobeliaceae occur, such as *Cyanea tritomantha*, which is exceedingly common in this locality, favored by the very shaded situation under the rank growth of trees, ferns and lianes. It belongs to the section Palmaeformes, which is peculiar to the middle forest region, but occasionally going a little lower. *Clermontia coerulea, Cl. parviflora*, are also common, both being trees sometimes growing in the forks of other trees. The solanaceous genus Nothocestrum is represented by the species breviflorum, which is here a little tree 20 feet in height.

The only plant cultivated near the Hilea plain is *Piper methysticum*, the *awa* of the natives. Pittosporums are absent as well as Sideroxylon and its associates. In Kumauna valley proper, *Pisonia inermis* var. *leiocarpa (Papala kepau)* is very common.

The country just below Hilea is called Kalaiki, and is mainly *aa* lava, which supports a strictly speaking dry or mixed forest flora, though not as rich in species, as the area is limited. It consists mainly of large groves of *Kukui*, besides stunted forms of Straussia and a few trees of *Antidesma pulvinatum; Osmanthus sandwicensis* is very common besides *Plectronia odorata (Walahee)*, a pretty little tree or shrub with horizontal branches and a dark green, glossy foliage, which is pleasingly contrasted by the white, birch-like bark. A white flowered and white fruiting variety of the *Ohia ai* or mountain apple is also to be found among shrubs of the *tapa* plants Pipturus *(Mamake)* and *Broussonetia papyrifera (Wauke)*, the latter having of late become exceedingly scarce, as its cultivation has been discontinued since about fifty years or more ago.

A few hundred feet below this small grove of mixed forest we find the typical lowland formation on *aa* lava fields, which is characterized by the leguminous trees, *Erythrina monosperma, Reynoldsia sandwicensis, Myoporum sandwicense*, Nototrichium, Dodonaea, several Cyperaceae, besides the following climbers, of which the leguminous thorny *Caesalpinia bonducella (Kakalaioa)* is the most common, in company with the convolvulaceous *Ipomoea insularis (Koaliawahia)* and *Argyreia tiliaefolia (Pilikai)*. Large yellow patches are discernable on the tops of trees from the distance, and on examination are found

34

to be the very troublesome leafless parasite, *Cassytha filiformis* or *Kaunoa* of the natives, which is here more plentiful than in any other district of the islands of the group visited by the writer.

THE FOREST BACK OF NAALEHU UP TO AN ELEVATION OF 6000 FEET.

Above the cane fields, which are situated on the rather steep slopes back of Naalehu, is a more or less flat stretch of land clothed in a rather scanty vegetation, mainly Sadleria ferns; the soil is muddy and numerous species of weeds abound, besides the everpresent Hilo grass, forming a dense carpet. Joining this open stretch of land at an elevation of about 2300 feet commences an almost impenetrable jungle which ascends uninterruptedly to an elevation of 6000 feet. The main vegetative feature is fern growth, intermixed with Scaevola shrubs, Straussia, Broussaisia, *Clermontia parviflora, Cl. coerulea,* the latter one of the most common trees. The larger trees are mainly Suttonia, Pelea, Perrottetia, Metrosideros, and as we ascend a species of Pittosporum is not uncommon. The forest is strictly of the rain forest type, and becomes more uniform with increased elevation. For example, at from 3000 feet to 5000 feet elevation three species of trees, *Suttonia Lessertiana, Cheirodendron Gaudichaudii* and *Metrosideros polymorpha,* are the principal ones, while an occasional straggler of Pittosporum, Gouldia, and Straussia can be observed. *Tetraplasandra meiandra* var. belongs to the 3000 foot level. The undershrubs are mainly *Broussaisia pellucida* and several species of Cyrtandra, with many species of ferns and a few Labiatae, such as Phyllostegia and Stenogyne.

Pipturus albidus is the most common plant of all, reaching the size of a handsome tree with a trunk of sometimes a foot or more in diameter. It ascends to an elevation of 5000 feet. Along the fern trail toward the mountain springs, from which the sugar plantation obtains its main water supply, the vegetation becomes richer; the ground is covered with thick moss. Here the writer was fortunate enough to discover three species of Lobelioideae new to science, two belonging to the genus Cyanea, one very remarkable for its creeping root stock; the third is a handsome shrub of the genus Clermontia with pinkish flowers. *Lobelia hypoleuca* and the exceedingly handsome *Lobelia macrostachys* occur here also, as well as at the higher levels.

Of a species of Pritchardia 18 to 20 feet high (a native palm) with a smooth trunk about 8 inches in diameter, the writer found a few individual trees.* It differs from all the other native palms in its flowering spathes, which are thickly covered with a salmon-colored wool or tomentum. Its fruits are oval and little more than an inch long. It may be the same species that is found near Glenwood on the road to the Volcano Kilauea from Hilo, which the writer had no opportunity of examining. This conclusion is drawn from the fact that the forest flora at this latter locality has many species in common with the one just described.

---

* Since described by Beccari as *Pritchardia eriostachia* sp. n.

The writer crossed the Naalehu forest diagonally toward Kahuku up to the source of the 1868 lava flow, at an elevation of about 6600 feet. The main trees above 5000 feet elevation are *Metrosideros polymorpha*, the *Ohia lehua*, usually tall trees with rather straight trunks, which are enwrapped with moss and epiphytic ferns; the *Cheirodendron Gaudichaudii (Olapa)* is the next most common, with *Suttonia Lessertiana*.

The undergrowth is exceedingly dense and is composed mainly of *Rubus Hawaiiensis*, which is covered with fine aculeate spines which adhere to and penetrate into the flesh very easily when touched. It grows here erect, 5 to 8 feet high, and was almost void of foliage (January). It has one main stem tapering toward the end without even small branchlets, having the shape of a whip. Ferns are also common, mainly *Dryopteris globulifera*, Sadleria, and here and there a Cibotium. At an elevation of 5600 feet *Ohia lehua* is the principal tree. Associated with it, curiously enough, is the small-leaved *Suttonia sandwicensis (Kolea)*, which is here a tree 18 to 25 feet in height with a straight trunk of 5 to 6 inches in diameter. The undershrubs are mainly Coprosma with rambling branches, *Broussaisia pellucida,* and Pipturus. The soil is still rich and muddy, and is often covered with tussocks of *Astelia veratroides,* the large-leaved form usually found to be terrestrial. At about 5000 feet, where in other localities a forest of this type would gradually change into an open, flat swamp like Puukukui on West Maui, or Waialeale on Kauai, the land here becomes drier, and the first *pahoehoe* lava becomes visible. The transition vegetation is stunted, though some straight, tall *Ohia* trees are not uncommon, while a peculiar low-growing Sadleria forms the undershrub. The most interesting fact is the absence of *Acacia Koa* in the entire stretch of forest between Hilea and Waiohinu, as well as of *Sophora chrysophylla,* which is not found even on the open *pahoehoe* lava field which supports the following vegetation belonging to the upper forest zone: *Raillardia* sp., a small shrub 4 to 5 feet high, grows together with *Vaccinium reticulatum,* and an undescribed variety of the same which is much taller and has a bluish-purple glaucous berry, with orbicular glaucous leaves. *Geranium cuneatum var. β.* forms small shrubs with stout, stiff branchlets; the leaves are silvery underneath. It is usually plentiful on elevated crusts of *pahoehoe* lava which have become fissured, and covers them completely together with *Styphelia tameiameia* and *St. imbricata* and Raillardia, forming densely-wooded mounds. *Coprosma ernodeoides,* a rubiaceous creeper with black, round berries, abounds, besides the Chilean strawberry, *Fragaria Chilensis,* the cyperaceous *Gahnia Gaudichaudii, Carex sandwicensis,* while the juncaceous *Luzula Hawaiiensis* Buch., which has all the aspects of a Cyperaceae, and *Sisyrynchium acre* of the order Iridaceae are growing scattered between the lava cracks. *Lycopodium venustulum* and the Gramineae *Koehleria glomerata* and *Deschampsia australis* can also be met with.

This is the limit of tree growth. Above this, old and more recent lava flows cover the ground, which is either bare or covered with a scrubby vegetation such as just described.

VEGETATION OF THE LAVA FLOWS OF KAU AND SOUTH KONA FROM SEA LEVEL TO AN ELEVATION OF 4200 FEET.

Between Waiohinu and Kahuku the vegetation is mainly composed of *Ohia*, with an occasional sandalwood tree, *Santalum Freycinetianum* var. *latifolium*. Lava flows of various ages have descended from the upper as well as the lower slopes of Mauna Loa, some having reached the sea, others having just crossed the government road (1200 feet), while minor flows have descended for only about a mile from their source, after which they cooled and stopped. The neighborhood of Kahuku is the seat of many eruptions, some within the memory of man, as two flows came forth from the southern slopes of Mauna Loa, one in 1867, and another in 1887, while as recently as January 9, 1907, after a few slight earthquakes, another flow proceeded in the same direction from an elevation higher than that of the two previous flows. This last eruption emerged considerably below the summit of Mauna Loa, pouring forth a stream of *aa* (rough lava) which divided into two nearly equal streams, with a smaller one between This is, however, not the place to give a description of the behavior of lava flows, and the writer wishes to refer the reader to Dr. Wm. T. Brigham's valuable publication on the Volcanoes of Kilauea and Mauna Loa. All three flows mentioned above are entirely bare of vegetation, and the half century intervening has not changed the appearance of these various flows in the slightest. The older ones look exactly as does the one of 1907, the only difference being in the color, which is a trifle lighter shade of brown. It is most interesting to note little areas of more ancient flows, perhaps only an acre or smaller in extent, which have not been covered by these flows, and bear an occasional shrub of Nototrichium, with Sadleria ferns, or a small, stunted *Ohia*. These more recent flows are very irregular in outline, and in the actual flow little islands of many shapes have remained—that is, islands of old lava beds, bearing a typical dry scrub vegetation which was spared by the fiery streams. The last flow at first came forth as *pahoehoe* (smooth lava), while lower down it assumed *aa* form, as can be seen along the government road.

The first plant to settle along the margins of these various flows is *Nephrolepis exaltata*, a cosmopolitan fern. Sadleria ferns follow after it or perhaps at the same time, but the former was always to be observed when hardly a grass or weed of any kind was visible. Two branches of the recent 1907 flow are about four miles apart, and this stretch of land is covered by a dry scrub vegetation and occasional trees, such as *Xylosma Hillebrandii (Maua)*, which is by far the most common tree next to *Ohia*, *Antidesma pulvinatum (Hame* or *Haa)*, Pipturus *(Mamake)* and Sadleria ferns. The land of Kahua, which is apparently older than Manuka, is of a rough lava nature, with occasional *kipukas*, and

37

supports a vegetation mostly composed of *Nototrichium sandwicense* and *Dracaena aurea*, which are the predominant trees in this district. An occasional Pittosporum, Straussia, and Santalum can be observed, but the two first mentioned form the main plant growth. On the *kipukas*, which were originally covered with *Cynodon dactylon (Manienie* grass), the guava has established itself to such an extent that it is difficult to penetrate far into these *kipukas* without a cane knife or an axe.

From Manuka toward Honomalino are several stretches of *aa* lava flows geologically younger than the rest of the country. These flows have originated at an elevation of about 4000 feet and can be distinguished from afar by the entirely different vegetation which they support. These flows, of which Kaulanamauna is an example, are sharply outlined against the sky from the country which they intersect, by the tall, straight trees of *Metrosideros polymorpha (Ohia)* which form the main plant covering. It is only on the margins of these flows that intruders from the surrounding country, such as Reynoldsia, Pittosporum, and others have taken a foothold, while *Alphitonia excelsa (Kauila)* has become a part of these *Ohia* forests. The scrub vegetation is mainly composed of the following plants: *Styphelia tameiameia (Pukeawe), Santalum Freycinetianum (Iliahi),* the above mentioned Alphitonia, *Gouldia* sp., with very large, black berries, *Vaccinium reticulatum, Coprosma montana, C. ernodeoides, Gahnia gaudichaudii,* and *Rumex giganteus (Pawale),* besides the two species of Cladium, *Pellaea ternifolia* and the everpresent *Nephrolepis exaltata,* which seems to thrive as well on *aa* lava as in the dampest lower forests. The vegetation of Manuka is more or less uniform and not as interesting as that of Kapua, only a few miles distant.

Besides the Kipuka Puaulu near the Volcano House, there are only two districts on Hawaii which possess an extremely rich and xerophilous flora, namely, Puuwaawaa in North Kona, and its rival Kapua in South Kona. There is no doubt in the writer's mind that a vegetation such as is represented in both these districts encircled the southern slopes of Mauna Loa, but was consumed by the various lava flows, leaving these two districts unmolested. Kapua is small in area, and so is Puuwaawaa; their vegetative growth is very similar, though the latter is richer in species. They are about 50 miles apart, and the intervening country is taken up by more or less uniform vegetation which has little in common with either Kapua or Puuwaawaa. Beginning with the lowlands at Kapua to an elevation of about 2000 feet, the vegetation covering this area, which is on a gradual slope, belongs strictly to the dry or mixed forest type, while above it, between 2000 and 4200 feet, the vegetation is of the rain forest type, but by far not as wet as the rain forest above Naalehu, Kau. Species of the lower levels have ascended into the wet forest, or vice versa.

Immediately above the lowland zone, which is composed of the ordinary types of plants common to that region, commences an exceedingly interesting and very varied xerophilous vegetation. The most common tree, forming 60

38

per cent of the vegetation, is *Maba sandwicensis (Lama)*, which fruits prolifically during the winter months, and is associated with *Erythrina monosperma (Wiliwili), Reynoldsia sandwicensis (Ohe), Plectronia odorata (Walahee)*, here a little shrub, *Pandanus odoratissimus (Puhala), Aleurites moluccana (Kukui)*, and here and there in open places by itself *Capparis Sandwichiana (Maiapilo)*, which becomes here a shrub 8 to 10 feet high with a thick stem and rambling branches. *Opuntia tuna* has ascended from the lowlands. The country is extremely rocky, loose *aa* of ancient origin covering the ground for many feet in thickness.

The undershrub is solely composed of the troublesome *Lantana camara*, now dead, killed by the insects introduced by Koebele, but still the country is almost inaccessible, as the dead, thorny shrubs stand more than 15 feet high in certain localities. It ascends to an elevation of 2000 feet, above which its place is taken by the guava, *Psidium guayava*, which forms thick stands on forsaken *kuleanas* or old native homesteads.

As we ascend above 1000 feet elevation the vegetation becomes more interesting. (See plate XVI.) *Osmanthus sandwicensis* and *Maba sandwicensis* remain still abundant, but are associated with *Nototrichium sandwicense (Kului), Charpentiera ovata (Papala)*, and *Pisonia sandwicensis (Papala kepau* or *Aulu)*. The euphorbiaceous trees *Antidesma pulvinatum* and *A. platyphyllum* are here the most numerous, and are indeed very characteristic. They can be recognized by their deeply, longitudinally furrowed, fibrous gray bark and broad, heart-shaped, dark leaves. *Pittosporum Hosmeri* var. is also exceedingly common, together with *Dracaena aurea (Halapepe), Straussia* sp?, *Xylosma Hillebrandii*, an occasional *Colubrina oppositifolia (Kauila)*, while the other native *Kauila (Alphitonia excelsa)* is here absent and only found on lava flows of more recent origin, where *Ohia lehua* forms almost pure stands. Rutaceous genera are entirely absent, such as Pelea and Xanthoxylum, which reach such a wonderful development on the lava fields of Puuwaawaa, so similar in floral aspects to that of Kapua. *Reynoldsia sandwicensis*, while stunted at the lower elevation, together with the *Lama*, is here a tall tree reaching a height of 40 to 50 feet, with trunks of two feet in diameter.

Of shrubs, the very strong, tenacious *Osteomeles anthyllidifolia* forms almost 80 per cent. Its white rosaceous flowers are very fragrant. The wood is exceedingly tough and can be bent into almost any position without breaking it. When growing on the slopes of the lowlands on the windward sides of the islands it is a small vine, while on the dry lava fields it develops many erect stems from a common root-stock, which are several inches thick and sparingly branched, reaching a height of 15 to 20 feet. *Plectronia odorata* is again very common, while the araliaceous *Tetraplasandra Hawaiiensis* is only sparingly represented. It reaches here a height of only about 25 feet. Of Sapotaceae, *Sideroxylon auahiense* var. is found, but is not numerous, being restricted to a single locality along a little gulch at 1600 feet elevation. *Santalum Freycine-*

39

PLATE XVI.

DRY OR MIXED FOREST on aa (rough) lava flows in South Kona, Hawaii; elevation 1500 feet. The trees from left to right are: **Tetraplasandra hawaiiensis** Gray, **Antidesma pulvinatum** Hbd., besides **Maba, Sophora, Colubrina,** etc., in the background. Shrub in front: **Osteomeles anthyllidifolia** Lindl.

tianum var. occurs also, but only small trees can be found. Malvaceous trees are entirely absent, though we might expect to find the newly discovered genus Hibiscadelphus, which is peculiar to such localities, one species, *H. Hualalaiensis*, occuring on Puuwaawaa. Besides *Tetraplasandra Hawaiiensis*, no other species of that genus, nor of Pterotropia, are present, though several can be found in similar localities. Neither can any urticaceous trees be observed. The Pipturus, so common in Kau, is not found in the district here described, and is only sparingly represented in the forest above it, where one would naturally expect it in abundance, as in forests of Kau. *Suttonia Lessertiana (Kolea)* is scattered here and there.

Nearly all the species of trees were in full fruit when visited by the writer during the month of February, 1912, with the exception of one tree, which is undoubtedly new and of which only three individuals were seen. As the tree had neither flowers nor fruits, and as a careful search on the ground below the tree did not reveal any sign of fruits or seeds of a previous season, the writer was unable to classify it. The writer, however, had occasion to visit that district again in the month of July when in company with Mr. W. M. Giffard; the trees, which were then in flower and fruit, proved to be new, and are described in this volume; two male and one female trees were observed.

Several Convolvulaceae flourish, such as *Ipomoea insularis*, and others of the same genus. Of Crassulaceae, the common *Bryophyllum calycinum* (air plant) grows very gregariously along the roadside together with *Cassia gaudichaudii*, *Pteridium aquilinum*, *Nephrolepis exaltata*, *Stachytarpheta dichotoma*, and many other weeds. On old native homesteads or *kuleanas* which have been forsaken for many years, orange trees are bearing very prolifically, while the Cherimolia, or *Momona*, as it is called by the natives, fruits seldom. One other remarkable fact is the absence of any leguminous tree, such as *Mezoneurum Kauaiense*, or the *Sophora chrysophylla*, or *Mamani*, so common on lava fields, and invariably associated with *Myoporum sandwicense*, the *Naio*, another tree which is absent on the lower half of the district of Kapua. It may be remarked that the inflorescences of *Maba sandwicensis* are attacked by a species of Acari, causing them to have the same appearance as the deformed inflorescences of *Elaeocarpus bifidus* on Oahu.

Of interest is also the fact that it is difficult to find a sound capsule of *Pittosporum Hosmeri* var., as they are almost invariably pecked open by the native bird *Alala (Corvus hawaiiensis)*, which feeds on the very oily black seeds. The bird is very abundant in this district.

About a mile above the government road at an elevation of about 2000 feet we find an entirely different type of forest. It is neither exactly a wet nor is it a dry forest, but has all the characteristics of the former. Of the first, tall *Ohia lehua* trees form almost pure stands, with trunks, as elevation increases, covered by the climber *Freycinetia Arnotti*, the *ie-ie*. *Straussia Hawaiiensis*, a very handsome tree peculiar to Kona and Puna, reaches a height of about 40

41

feet, with a straight trunk and black bark of half an inch thickness. *Xylosma Hillebrandii* becomes here a beautiful big tree with a trunk of one and a half feet in diameter, straight ascending and clothed in a gray bark. *Tetraplasandra Hawaiiensis* is here a large tree 60 feet in height, with a fine trunk ascending for 30 feet or so before branching. It is about two and a half feet thick and vested in a whitish bark three-quarters of an inch thick. It is the only representative of the family Araliaceae in this forest. *Myoporum sandwicense* is here a slender shrub, and only a few individual specimens can be observed. Coprosma, Perrottetia, Pipturus, *Pelea volcanica* only, *Cheirodendron gaudichaudii*, *Antidesma platyphyllum* and a species of Suttonia form the tree growth, together with Pittosporum and Ilex, up to the *Koa* belt at an elevation of 4200 feet. *Sadleria cyatheoides, Cibotium Menziesii,* and the lobeliaceous *Clermontia coerulea,* which ranges from the extreme eastern end of Kau to North Kona, form the undergrowth. The latter ascends, however, up into the *Koa* belt, where it can be found on *Koa* trees, growing in the forks of their branches.

Several *aa* flows of more recent origin intersect this forest. The flows are covered with a scanty vegetation, such as Vaccinium, Styphelia, *Coprosma ernodeoides, Raillardia scabra* (very common), and stunted *Ohia;* while the lava itself is entirely hidden by a species of lichen. At 4200 feet elevation the trees described above are replaced by *Acacia Koa,* which grows here under similar conditions as near the Volcano House, together with *Urera* sp. and the tree ferns. Cattle, however, have played serious havoc with this beautiful forest. The undergrowth is mainly composed of *Polystichum falcatum* var., Dryopteris, Asplenium, and Cibotium.

The most interesting vegetation, however, occupies the area between 1500 to 2000 feet, above which the forest is very uniform. Nowhere has the writer found such beautiful stands of the ebenaceous *Maba sandwicensis (Lama)* as in this district, where it associates mainly with tall-growing *Kukui* trees. Trees 30 to 40 feet in height with trunks of a foot or more in diameter are not uncommon. Beyond Kapua the country is covered mainly with *Ohia lehua,* and is as a whole very uniform, until we reach the boundary of South Kona, where a forest similar to that back of Naalehu, Kau, forms the lower and middle forest zones. Most of the land about 600 to 2500 feet elevation is under cultivation, *Coffea arabica* being the crop.

THE MIDDLE FOREST ZONE IN KONA AND FLORAL ASPECTS OF THE GREAT CENTRAL
PLAIN BETWEEN MAUNA LOA, HUALALAI AND MAUNA KEA.

If we ascend from Kealakekua up the slopes of Mauna Loa, we at first pass through large areas of *Psidium guayava,* which has taken possession of the land and is the only shrub up to an elevation of about 1200 feet. The country then becomes more open and old *pahoehoe* flows are visible, which are covered with a

42

scanty grass vegetation. The trees on this lower plain are mainly Straussia and its associates, such as *Charpentiera obovata, Pisonia inermis,* var. *leiocarpa,* with occasionally a Pelea. The trees are so scattered that one can count them easily. This somewhat mixed forest passes gradually into an *Ohia lehua (Metrosideros polymorpha)* forest, with *Suttonia Lessertiana (Kolea).* Here also the lobeliaceous shrub *Clermontia coerulca,* somewhat different from that of Kau, is present. It descends, however, as low as 1500 feet, but then only on the *aa* flows, as will afterwards be described. The forest in this section is as a whole very uniform.

The *Ohia lehua* gradually passes into the *Koa* forest, if such it can still be called; for nowhere has the writer found such a pitiable sight as the *Koa* forest presents in this district at about 3000 feet up to 5000 feet elevation. Here 90 per cent of these giant *Koa* trees are dead; their huge limbs dangle in the air on pieces of fibrous strings of bark, ready to drop, if stirred by the slightest breeze. The remaining 10 per cent of trees are in a dying condition, and in a very few years the country will be entirely denuded. Huge masses of trunks and limbs are scattered over the ground, and it is really difficult to ride through this remnant of forest. It is also dangerous, as any minute a few huge limbs may drop from the heights above. Trees reach here a height of 80 feet or more. This condition is mainly due to the cattle, which have destroyed all the undershrubs and also injured the trees, which are then readily attacked by insects. It may be remarked that native insects, especially beetles, do not attack healthy trees, but only such as have been injured.

As we ascend farther the dead *Koa* trees are associated with *Myoporum sandwicense (Naio), Sophora chrysophylla, Suttonia Lessertiana,* and *Santalum Freycinetianum,* the *Iliahi,* or true Sandalwood of commerce, of which trees 50 feet in height and trunks a foot and a half in diameter, are not uncommon. Next to *Koa,* Sandalwood is most numerous; but, like the former, most of it is destroyed. It differs from the Sandalwood found in other parts of Hawaii in its smooth, black bark and very dark green, glossy leaves. The wood is also exceedingly fragrant.

That the undergrowth must have been intensely interesting is evidenced by the fact of the abundance of vines on *aa* flows which intersect this forest area, and are very seldom frequented or even crossed by cattle. Lower down at an elevation of 1500 feet these *aa* flows present a dense jungle of *ie-ie* vines, many species of trees, mainly the rubiaceous Straussia and urticaceous Urera and Pipturus. Ferns are abundant as well as one or two lobeliaceous Clermontia. Higher up the main tree is *Ohia lehua* together with Sandalwood, which on these flows is in splendid condition. At an elevation of 4600 feet *Sophora chrysophylla* has encroached on the *aa,* but not the *Koa.* On the margins of the flows and in cracks and fissures many species of Labiatae thrive, the most numerous representative of which is the genus Stenogyne. Trailing over *aa* lava we find *Stenogyne rugosa* var. *β., St. cordata, St. sessilis,* while climbing over

43

PLATE XVII.

DELISSEA UNDULATA Gaud., in the upper forest regions on the slopes of Mauna Loa, elev. 5200 feet. The tall specimen to the left is 35 feet high. The trees are mainly **Acacia Koa** Gray, **Sophora chrysophylla** Seem., and **Myoporum sandwicense** Gray.

Naio shrubs are *St. calaminthoides* and *St. scrophularioides,* the latter with small pale yellow flowers covered with silky hair. The genus Phyllostegia, also of the Labiate family, has several species. *Raillardia scabra* is also common on the *aa* as well as *Smilax sandwicensis,* and several ferns, of which *Pellaea ternifolia* and *Sadleria cyatheoides* are the most common. And all of these in a comparatively small area. *Clermontia coerulea* is here a fine tree, growing to a height of 20 feet or so, on the *aa* lava, shaded by *Ohia* and Sandalwood.

This forest merges gradually into the great central plain at an elevation of 5000 feet. Of course, clumps of tall trees can be found in certain localities and on the plateau also, as well as higher up on the slopes of Mauna Loa. The trees become smaller and only a few stunted *Naio* and Sophora trees *(Mamani),* together with Santalum, are here to be found.

At Pulehua and beyond toward Mauna Loa a nice *Koa* forest, mixed with trees peculiar to this elevation, such as mentioned above, extends up to an elevation of 6000 feet. *Koa* is the principal tree. The country is composed of rich, black soil, now supporting a rank growth of undesirable weeds. A most interesting feature in this forest is the lobeliaceous *Delissea undulata.* Previously this plant has only been recorded from Niihau, Kauai and Maui, and that at a low elevation on exposed open cliffs, only reaching a height of 10 feet. Here at 6000 feet it grows under the shade of giant *Koa* trees on the slopes of the numerous crater hills with which the country is covered. The plant grows here 35 feet tall, perfectly straight, with a bole only two inches in diameter, not branching, and bearing at its apex a crown of leaves only one and a half feet in diameter. (See plate XVII.) These beautiful little round crowns are often hidden in the foliage of the *Koa,* so that only the gray, straight stems covered with leaf-scars can be seen. The plants are exceedingly numerous, but especially on the crater bottoms of the numerous volcanic cones, where they form the main vegetation. Looking down into one of these cones, one sees the tops of this curious plant like cabbage heads protruding up to the rim of the cone. This is the only lobeliaceous plant at this elevation.

THE GREAT CENTRAL PLAIN.

When we step out on this great plateau from the South Kona side, we have Hualalai to the left, Mauna Loa to the right, and Mauna Kea in front of us. This great plain is composed mainly of *pahoehoe* lava and black cinder. The *pahoehoe* lava has often broken through, and huge caverns or caves are visible, which expose again old *pahoehoe* lava or black cinder. The clouds gather at about eight o'clock in the morning around the slopes of Mauna Loa up to an elevation of 4000 feet, where they remain under normal weather conditions up to noon. At about two o'clock they encroach on to the central plateau, which by three o'clock is completely covered by the clouds. When caught out on this plain without a compass in the fogs it is indeed exceedingly difficult to find one's way. The plain is about fifty miles across and almost level, full of holes and cracks into which one is likely to fall, and by going round about them one gets lost in no time. The slopes of Mauna Loa are very gradual on this side, while those of Mauna Kea and Hualalai are steep. On this plain are scattered many volcanic cones, mainly composed of black cinder and covered with dense vegetation. But especially on the crater bottoms one is likely to find interesting plants which have disappeared from the open plain, where they are eagerly devoured by cattle and goats, while at the bottom of these craters they are safe from their ravages. Anyone collecting on this plain should direct his steps to all these cones, as it is here only that he can obtain things of interest.

Curiously enough, the plants found on these various cones are not always the same. On the plain itself, *Geranium cuneatum* is plentiful, besides *Raillardia* sp.?, *Coprosma ernodeoides*, a rubiaceous creeper with black, round berries, the main food of the native geese, besides *Ohelo, Rumex giganteus, Styphelia tameiameia*, an epacridaceous plant, *Myoporum sandwicense (Naio), Sophora chrysophylla*, the iridaceous *Sisyrynchium acre*, while in the black cinder the caryophyllaceous *Silene struthioloides* and *S. lanceolata* thrive best. Both species develop a large root system having a main tap root, sometimes tuber-like, and often 5 inches in diameter and over a foot and a half long. The root is sweet to the taste, and is eaten by the natives.

Here and there are shrubs or small trees of *Mamani* and *Naio*, among which one sometimes finds Suttonia and a stunted variety of *Pittosporum Hosmeri. Dodonaea eriocarpa* forms straight trees some 25 feet in height with trunks of 8 inches in diameter. At Naahuaumi, a historic place where King Umi took the first Hawaiian census, near the old Judd road which leads to the 1859 flow, the santalaceous *Exocarpus gaudichaudii*, a shrub, is not uncommon, and extends up the slopes of Hualalai. *Stenogyne rugosa* var. must once have been exceedingly common, but can now only be found growing in deep fissures, which cover them completely, where they are safe from cattle. *Osteomeles anthyllidifolia*, a rosaceous vine of great toughness, forms dense tangles over thrown-up fissures in *pahoehoe* lava. During the morning sunshine thousands of Odynerus (Hawaiian wasps) and bees can be found flying over the sweet-scented flowers of the above-mentioned vine, which is called *Ulei* by the natives.

The only poisonous plant in this district is a shrub, a species of Wikstroemia, with long, drooping, slender branchlets. The bark, like that of all other Hawaiian Wikstroemia, or *Akia*, as they are termed by the natives, is extremely tough and very suitable for cordage.

The crater cones in the neighborhood of Puulehua are Puuokeanue, Puuoikaaka, Pohakuloa and others. These cones support a very interesting vegetation. Besides the plants found on the plain proper, *Lipochaeta subcordata*, described by Gray, is very numerous at an elevation of 5300 feet, and forms dense masses on Pohakuloa crater to the exclusion of everything else. It has previously only been reported from the sea shore, where it is one or two feet high, while at this elevation it branches diffusely, covering the whole crater, being almost similar in habit to *Gleichenia linearis,* the well-known *Uluhe* or staghorn fern. The writer has found it also on one of the other craters, but sparingly, and again on the lava fields of Puuwaawaa, in North Kona.

An arborescent Raillardia about 15 feet high grows on Puuokeanue in company with *Solanum incompletum,* also found in North Kona, where it is a shrub 5 to 8 feet tall. *Campylotheca micrantha,* another shrubby composite, was associated with it. *Campylotheca Menziesii* var. γ, was only found on one crater on the slopes of Hualalai on Puuoikaaka. It, however, is not uncommon on the Waimea side on the slopes of Mauna Kea, especially on Nohonaohae and Kemole crater. A species of Sida not found on the central plain proper is confined to Pohakuloa, where it forms dense thickets. Of trees, *Santalum Freycinetianum,* Suttonia, Wikstroemia, etc., form the main vegetation, besides *Sophora chrysophylla,* the everpresent *Naio,* and *Acacia Koa.* The slopes of Mauna Loa are covered with a dense growth up to an elevation of 8000 feet, after which the plants become very stunted and few until we find nothing but a species of grass, *Koehleria glomerata.*

The main trees are Sophora and Myoporum, but *Koa* is wanting. Of shrubs, the epacridaceous Styphelia is common, together with a species of Raillardia; of Rubiaceae, two species of Coprosma are present, one being a creeper, the other a small shrub. *Gahnia Gaudichaudii,* Carex, and Cyperus are scattered here and there. The main plant covering at an elevation of 6000 feet is the grass *Keohleria glomerata,* which grows exceedingly rank and stands sometimes three feet high. As already mentioned, it is the last plant one sees at an elevation of 11,000 feet. Of course, the *Ohelo* is also common. Noteworthy is the fact that *Argyroxiphium sandwicense* is not to be found on this side of Mauna Loa, but only above Kapapala at an elevation of from 7000 to 9000 feet. Besides, one looks in vain for the tree composites which can be met with so frequently on Mauna Kea up to 11,500 feet. Here on Mauna Loa only one species is present. The slopes of the mountain on the Kona side are mainly composed of *pahoehoe* which is of great age, and very much disintegrated; the country is covered with holes, which are usually overgrown with *Stenogyne rugosa* at the lower levels, 5000 to 6000 feet, and harbor Vaccinium shrubs or *Mamani* at the higher levels. The lava crust is very thin and cracks like ice, which makes traveling very uncomfortable. At about 9000 feet we meet the first *aa* flow, which covers the *pahoehoe* for miles. It was ejected from a crater situated at that elevation. It is a triangular steep cone with sharp rims, and is called Puuouo. The *aa* flows are barren and of great thickness. Many *aa* flows intersect the ancient *pahoehoe* at the higher levels. In traveling it is a continuous going round these flows, which one is occasionally forced to cross. Above 11,000 feet perfectly black, shining *pahoehoe* covers the mountain. It is extremely thin and glassy in appearance, breaking in at nearly every step. When the writer ascended Mauna Loa on February 17, 1912, snow was to be found only in patches several feet thick. The steep crater walls were more or less covered with snow, which was

PLATE XVIII.

AT THE SUMMIT OF MAUNA LOA elevation 13,675 feet; vegetation ceases at 11,000 feet; aa (rough) lava and snow in the foreground, Mt. Hualalai in the distance.

beautifully contrasted from the red, yellow and black colored walls of cinder. (See plate XVIII.)

The crater itself showed no activity. Two small cones of reddish-yellow cinder mark the outbreak of 1907. The temperature at nine o'clock in the morning on the upper lava flows was 92° Fahr. at an elevation of about 8500 feet. At the summit the temperature was at 60° Fahr. about noon, and sank during the night to 35° at an elevation of 7000 feet. A most peculiar fact is the presence of millions of flies at the summit of the mountain, which make a stay of even a few minutes most disagreeable. Besides these flies, only another small insect, similar to an Ichneumon, was found, covering the patches of snow thickly. Only a few hundred feet lower, remarkable to say, not a single fly could be detected. They evidently had been blown up by the wind.

HUALALAI AND PUUWAAWAA, NORTH KONA.

From Kealakekua toward North Kona the forest is very uniform and of a similar nature to that between Kapua, South Kona, and Napoopoo. At the lower levels *Kukui* forms the main tree growth, together with introduced shrubs, such as lantana and guava. Coffee is extensively cultivated, also sisal, and in certain localities sugar cane. The vegetation begins to become interesting at Huehue, near the lava flows on the northern flanks of Hualalai, and reaches its culminating point at Puuwaawaa, the richest floral section of any in the whole Territory.

It is only as recently as 1909 that this region was botanically explored. The whole country was until ten years ago a wilderness of lava fields, and only since the opening of the country through the government road, ten years ago, was this beautiful floral region made accessible.

MT. HUALALAI AND ITS FLORAL ASPECTS.

Mt. Hualalai, which is the smallest volcano on Hawaii, has an elevation of 8273 feet. Its last eruption was in the year 1801, not from the summit, however, but at an elevation of about 1800 feet, where huge lava masses poured forth which changed the coast line of the region about Huehue for twenty-five miles from a bay to a headland. This lava flow is still bare of vegetation, with the exception of a few ferns and weeds.

The lowland belt is extremely arid, rainfall being exceedingly scarce. *Opuntia tuna* grows gregariously and is associated with many other introduced plants, such as *Leucaena glauca, Datura stramonium, Waltheria americana, Nicotiana tabacum, Acacia farnesiana,* and many others.

The interesting native vegetation, which is of a similar nature to that of Kapua in South Kona, begins at Huehue proper. *Aleurites moluccana* is still the principal tree, though as one advances toward Puuwaawaa it becomes more scarce. *Antidesma platyphyllum* and *Antidesma pulvinatum,* besides *Dracaena aurea (Halapepe), Maba,* and their usual associates are predominant. In this

49

district, however, occur many species of trees which are not found in other places, not even on the same island. The most prevailing tree is the rubiaceous *Plectronia odorata (Walahee)*. *Gardenia Brighami (Nau)* of this same family, only common on Molokai and Lanai, is here also to be found, but will have to be termed for here a rather rare plant; it has not been recorded previously from the Island of Hawaii. Nearly all the trees occurring at Kapua, South Kona, can be found also in North Kona, with possibly one or two exceptions, though numerous trees occur here and not in the former locality.

Of Leguminosae, the elsewhere very rare *Mezoneurum Kauaiense (Uhiuhi)* is here plentiful. It forms small groves by itself, while only here and there can a single tree be found, usually in company with the rhamnaceous *Colubrina oppositifolia*. Hillebrand records this species as a small tree. Here in this locality it grows to quite a good sized tree with trunks of over a foot in diameter. It is much more numerous in North Kona than in South Kona, outside of which the tree is not found. Of Rutaceae, which are absent in Kapua, two genera are represented, Pelea and Xanthoxylum. *Pelea cinerea*, not uncommon at an elevation of 4000 feet near the Volcano Kilauea, grows gregariously at 500 feet elevation and even lower, on rough aa lava fields.

Of great interest is the genus Xanthoxylum, which has here four species; two belong to the *X. dipetalum* type, the other two are variations of *X. Kauaiense* and *X. Mauiense*.

Pittosporum Hosmeri is also met with quite frequently, the trees found at Kapua being a variety. At Puuwaawaa the fruits are nearly twice the size of those from South Kona, while the tree itself is also larger.

Euphorbia lorifolia (Akoko) is a shrub at 2000 feet elevation, while 700 feet higher it is a tree about 25 feet high, with a diameter of 10 inches. The tree yields a large amount of latex, which owing to its predominance in an area of 5000 acres will undoubtedly prove a valuable commercial product. Of Araliaceae, *Reynoldsia sandwicensis* is quite plentiful, besides *Tetraplasandra* sp., and *Tetraplasandra Hawaiiensis* growing at 3500 feet. Of Sapindaceae, *Sapindus saponaria* is quite common, especially at Puuwaawaa proper, a rugged hill of 3000 feet elevation. Associated with it are *Acacia Koa, Claoxylon* sp., *Delissea undulata*, a lobeliaceous plant also found on Mauna Loa, but in this locality much smaller in size, *Xanthoxylum* sp. and *Charpentiera obovata (Papala)*. *Nothocestrum breviflorum* occurs on the lava fields surrounding the crater. A very interesting tree is *Hibiscadelphus Hualalaiensis*, of which species several trees are in existence, while of the two other species, also peculiar to the dry districts, only one specimen of each species has been discovered.

Sandalwood is frequently met with, as well as *Pisonia inermis* var. *leiocarpa*, and *Ochrosia sandwicensis*, the latter, however, being scarcer. *Chenopodium sandwicheum (Alaweo* or *Aweoweo)*, which in other localities is herbaceous, is here a small tree and very plentiful. Of vines, *Canavalia galeata, Mucuna gigantea, Cocculus Ferrandianus*, two species of Ipomoea and one of Breweria can be observed. *Asplenium adiantum nigrum, Asplenium trichomanes, Polypodium pellucidum* and *Pellaea ternifolia*, besides *Psilotum triquetrum*, represent the cryptogams.

About a mile above the government road *Sophora chrysophylla (Mamani)*, together with *Myoporum sandwicense*, are the predominant species, with undershrubs of *Solanum incompletum, Campylotheca* sp., and a Labiate vine of the genus Phyllostegia. Still higher up the lava fields are bare for a certain distance, especially lava fields of more recent origin. The only plants observed on these flows are *Rumex giganteus (Pawale), Gnaphalium sandwicense, Raillardia scabra*, and xerophytic ferns, as just mentioned above.

The region called Waihou is composed of a semi-wet forest and is situated at an elevation of 3500 feet. The predominant tree is first *Metrosideros polymorpha (Ohia lehua)*, which inhabits an old *pahoehoe* lava flow adjoining the rough *aa* lava fields; here the trees are about 40 feet high. This grove of *Ohia lehua* passes gradually into a more mixed forest, mainly *Acacia Koa*, Sophora, Myoporum, and *Euphorbia lorifolia (Akoko)*, which in places is so thick that it is almost impossible to pass through it. A species of Urera grows quite tall, besides *Cheirodendron Gaudichaudii, Suttonia Lessertiana (Kolea)*, Ilex, and others. Higher up occur *Pelea volcanica, Pipturus albidus*, tree ferns, Cibotium, *Broussaisia pellucida*, and on the trunks of tree ferns, *Clermontia coerulea*.

At 4500 feet, *Metrosideros polymorpha (Ohia lehua)* is stunted, as it grows on *aa* lava flows, which intersect the old forest with its trees of 80 feet in height at this elevation. It is the predominant tree on these flows; only occasionally one observes *Suttonia sandwicensis* and *S. Lessertiana*.

Vaccinium penduliflorum β var. *gemmaceum* assumes here the size of a tall shrub; here and there *Stenogyne sessilis* can be observed clinging to *Ohia lehua*.

At 5000 feet, this vegetation gives place to a gravelly plain which is bordered on its northern and southern limits by heavily-forested hills or ancient craters. The principal trees on these hills are *Acacia Koa, Ohia lehua, Styphelia tameiameia*, and *Coprosma rhynchocarpa*. This latter tree reaches quite a size in height and diameter of trunk, though nearly all trees are diseased, their trunks being all hollow and the abode of a species of sow bug *(Philoscia angusticauda)*, which can be found by millions.

It is here that the wild native raspberry, *Rubus Macraei (Akala)*, attains its most wonderful development; its runners vary from 10 to 15 feet in length and are two inches in diameter, climbing over *Koa* trees and trailing over the ground, thus forming almost impenetrable thickets.

Here and there in the extensive barren lava fields and cinder plains are beautiful green hills covered with old giants of *Acacia Koa*, which from their elevation escaped destruction by the fiery streams, and now appear like oases in a desert.

On the northern border of this dismal plain, on the slopes of a crater, grows

PLATE XIX.

VEGETATION ON THE SUMMIT OF HUALALAI elev. 8273 mainly composed of **Pteridium aquilinum** (L.) Kuhn, **Dodonaea viscosa** var. **spathulata** Hbd., and **Coprosma montana** Hbd.

Dubautia plantaginea, here a small tree, in company with *Pelea volcanica* *(Alani)*.

Finally tree growth ceases, with the exception of a few straggling shrubs of *Sophora chrysophylla (Mamani)*; the ground is covered with a scrub vegetation of which *Raillardia scabra* is predominant, besides Geranium, *Coprosma ernodeoides, Fragaria chilensis,* and also *Plantago pachyphylla.* The cryptogamous flora is composed of *Asplenium trichomanes, Asplenium adiantum nigrum* and *Polystichum falcatum* var.

At 7000 feet, *Sophora chrysophylla* and *Myoporum sandwicense*, both trees of about 20 feet in height at this elevation, have gnarled trunks and form the main tree growth. *Keoleria glomerata* and *Panicum nephelophilum* represent the Gramineae.

At the summit of Hualalai the vegetation is scrubby, with the exception of a few *Ohia lehua* trees *(Metrosideros polymorpha* var. *ȝ)*, with thick, woolly orbicular leaves, which grow on the rim of Honuaulu crater. The crater floors and slopes are covered with the ordinary eagle fern, *Pteridium aquilinum,* which on the northern side of the mountain summit forms the sole vegetation.

The slopes of Honuaulu are covered with *Styphelia tameiameia (Pukeawe)*, *Dodonaea viscosa* var. *spathulata,* and *Coprosma Menziesii.* (See plate XIX.)

The summit of Hualalai is composed of a series of large craters, 200 to 500 feet deep and several thousand feet in circumference. The highest point is Honaulu, 8273 feet above sea level. Some of the walls of the craters are solid or composed of cinder, and almost vertical. In the rock crevasses of the crater walls one frequently meets with the composite *Tetramolopium humile,* the Hawaiian daisy.

Northwest from Honuaulu, a half mile distant, is a series of craters and cones, one being especially remarkable for its unfathomable depth. Of these cones there are many. They are usually built up of *aa,* and have the shape of the well-known tufa cones. The one in question is a veritable chimney, about 100 feet high, with a blow-hole of ten feet in diameter, the inner walls of which are perfectly smooth. A stone dropped by the writer in this chimney fell for sixteen seconds before the first reverberation could be heard. Between this cone and Honuaulu is a plain of *pahoehoe* lava, with a very thin crust which breaks at nearly every step, making it dangerous for man and animal to cross it.

The slopes of Hualalai, from the Puuwaawaa side, are very steep and bear only one crater of considerable size, at an elevation of 5000 feet.

This mountain is usually wrapped in clouds and only occasionally the very summit can be seen appearing like a little island above a sea of clouds, while Mauna Loa and Mauna Kea are hardly ever completely hidden from view. (See plate XVIII.)

Back of Puuwaawaa its wonderful vegetation ceases and its place is taken by the leguminous *Sophora chrysophylla* and *Myoporum sandwicense.* Here and there a few composites can still be found and an occasional *Euphorbia lorifolia*, together with *Pseudomorus Brunoniana*, form the last stragglers. From here the country merges into the great central plateau whose vegetative characteristics have already been described.

Adjoining Puuwaawaa on the north is another interesting strip of land called Puuanahulu. The plant formation on this land is very similar to that of Puuwaawaa, but harbors species of trees which can not be found in the latter locality. In this respect the vegetation approaches very much that of Kapua or Manuka in South Kona.

On the way to Puuanahulu the road leads over a bluff of about 100 feet in height, over which the lava flowed cascade-like. The trees growing on this bluff are mainly *Reynoldsia sandwicensis (Ohe)* and *Dracaena aurea (Halapepe)*. The land forms a promontory and is in reality an ancient crater; the soil is a yellow loam, and no trace of lava is visible. *Opuntia tuna* is exceedingly numerous, together with *Brousonettia papyrifera*, which has been cultivated by the natives living there. It is one of the driest districts and very few trees can be found, such as the above mentioned and *Erythrina monosperma (Wiliwili)*, all of them trees adapted for districts with very little rainfall.

Immediately beyond the bluff, the 1859 flow, which found its source on the flanks of Mauna Loa, crossed the government road. The lava is *pahoehoe* (smooth), and is bare of any vegetation with the exception of some weeds, such as *Solanum pseudocapsicum*, which is very numerous in that neighborhood. Beyond this comparatively recent flow is an old *aa* (rough) lava flow which supports a very interesting xerophytic vegetation. Here we find *Xanthoxylum Hawaiiense*, a small tree, also *Kokia Rockii*, and *Alphitonia excelsa*.

Adjoining Puuanahulu is Keaumoku, a large plain with a scrub vegetation which merges into the Parker ranch, and is really a continuation of the slopes of Mauna Kea. The shrubs found here are mainly *Dodonaea viscosa (Aalii)*, *Wikstroemia phyllyreaefolia (Akia)*, a low shrub with brick-red globose berries; and a few others also common to the central plateau. From Keaumoku on, the country is flat and mainly grassland; the grasses growing there are of recent introduction, such as *Cynodon dactylon, Melinis rosea, Bromus villosus*, and others; mixed with them are *Sida falax, Argemone mexicana, Waltheria americana, Silene gallica*, etc. The country is extremely dry, and when very windy the dirt is carried for miles and so thickly that everything appears to be hazy as in a dense mist or fog.

Of interest in this locality is the large crater Nohonaohae, as it harbors still some of the original vegetation which covered these lands before they were stocked with cattle and sheep.

Of great interest is the Labiate *Haplostachys Grayana*, an exceedingly scarce plant which, like its congeners *Haplostachys rosmarinifolia* and *H. truncata*, belongs to the dry, open grasslands. As these lands are usually used for ranching, these beautiful plants were of the first to be devoured by sheep and cattle alike. It is also only in such places as Nohonaohae, owing to the partial inaccessibility to cattle, that one can still find *H. Grayana;* with it grows Wikstroemia, Campylotheca, several species of Lipochaeta, *Dodonaea viscosa, Raillardia ciliolata* and *Xanthoxylum Hawaiiense,* the latter a small tree or shrub with strongly lemon-scented leaves.

The treeless plain extends over to the Waimea village, situated at the foot of the South Kohala mountains, at an elevation of 2700 feet. The country north of Waimea is extremely wet, while south of it the land is comparatively dry, especially so at Kawaihae. From Puukawai, a crater situated about three miles south of Waimea, the land is known as Kawaihaeiuka, and must have been once upon a time covered with a plant growth similar to Puuwaawaa now. Nearly all the common trees found in North Kona occur here; the only species not found in Kona and growing on the slopes of South Kohala that is in Kawaihaeiuka is *Acacia Koaia (Koaia),* a tree resembling very much the *Koa,* but differing from it in size, in its rather gnarled trunk, harder wood and very narrow seed pods. It can be found, however, on the slopes of Puuanahulu, the boundary of North Kona. The tree is peculiar to the very dry districts and never occurs in wet forests, as is the case with the *Acacia Koa.* Hillebrand in his Flora reports the araliaceous *Pterotropia dipyrena* as growing at Kawaihaeiuka, but the writer was unable to find it. In fact, the land is now very open and only few trees can still be found, cattle having destroyed them very rapidly. At 3000 feet elevation the land is swampy and the main plant covering is *Paspalum conjugatum,* with a few Sadleria ferns, instead of the dense forest which once here existed.

In conclusion, the writer wishes to state that owing to the similar age of the Kohala Mountains to that of the West Maui Mountains, he finds it advisable to treat that district either separately or in conjunction with the West Maui forests and those of Waialeale, Kauai.

THE MIDDLE FOREST ZONE.

Next to the xerophytic forest on the leeward sides of the various islands, the middle forest region is one of the most interesting, as it is here that certain plant families, such as the Campanulaceae, tribe Lobelioideae, and Labiatae, as well as Rutaceae, reach their best development and become highly specialized.

As is the case with the lower forest regions on the various islands, in regard to non-uniformity, so it is with the middle forest region, but still more pronounced as the various islands are of different ages, Kauai being the oldest.

Owing to the fact that there is no typical forest for all the islands as far as the middle forest zone is concerned, it will therefore be of greater interest and value to describe the vegetative formations of this particular region on each island separately.

The Island of Kauai is almost orbicular in outline and is intersected on the leeward side by a large canyon and several valleys, of which Kalalau, Miloli and Olokele are the most noteworthy.

At 3800 feet elevation *Metrosideros polymorpha (Ohia lehua)* is a very common tree and inhabits the outskirts of the middle forest zone. It is, however, associated with *Sideroxylon sandwicense (Alaa)*, *Tetraplasandra Waimeae*, the lauraceous *Cryptocarya Mannii*, previously thought to be peculiar to Kauai, but since found by C. N. Forbes on the Kaala Mountains on Oahu, *Xanthoxylum dipetalum* var. *γ*, *Broussaisia arguta*, usually found along streams with the lobeliaceous *Cyanea leptostegia (Hahalua)*, a truly superb plant of palm-like habit which reaches sometimes a height of 40 feet. It is associated with *Cyanea hirtella*, and *Cyanea spathulata*, both of which are shrubs with small flowers. *Santalum pyrularium*, the Kauai Sandalwood, forms an important tree of this region, while *Elaeocarpus bifidus (Kalia)* forms about 30 per cent. of the forest, following immediately after the *Ohia lehua*. This particular elevation has still some species of the lower forest zone present, as can be seen by the occurrence of *Pterotropia Kauaiensis*, *Osmanthus sandwicensis*, Antidesma, and others; while, as we enter the interior of the island, a wealth of foliage is displayed which can hardly be equaled anywhere in the group.

Members of the Rutaceae are the most prominent, besides Pittosporum, of which *P. Kauaiensis*, *P. acuminatum*, and *P. Gayanum*, a species new to science, are of interest. The latter species occurs only on the high plateau at the foot of Mt. Waialeale, where the rainfall is immense. As already mentioned, the family Rutaceae is well represented in this floral zone. The genus Pelea, which has a few species in the drier regions, has not less than 14 or 15 species here, 10 of which are peculiar to Kauai, in the middle forest zone. They like heavy, gray, loamy soil, where water is often stagnant, forming small pools all the year round. *Pelea cruciata (Piloula)*, and *P. microcarpa (Kolokolo Mokihana)*, both recently described species, are quite common in company with *Wikstroemia sandwicensis* var. *furcata (Akia)*, *Pelea Kauaiensis*, *P. Knudsenii*, *P.*

sapotaefolia and var. *procumbens, P. macropus, P. oblongifolia* (not peculiar to Kauai), *P. barbigera (Uaheapele),* and the well-known *P. anisata (Mokihana),* all are old denizens of Kauai and particularly of the middle forest zone. On the other islands several species of Pelea are found, but by far the most numerous species are found on Kauai. On Oahu we find *P. Lydgatei* and *P. clusiaefolia,* but the most common species is *P. sandwicensis,* whose place is taken on Hawaii by *P. volcanica,* which ascends, however, up to 6000 feet. *Platydesma rostrata* and *Pl. campanulata* var. *macrophylla,* both species belonging to a strictly Hawaiian genus with almost no affinities, are to be found. Of these two species, the former inhabits the more dry districts, as in the forest of Kopiwai in company with *Alphitonia excelsa,* while the latter is usually found in the interior of the island, but in the Elaeocarpus forest belt. *Solanum Kauaiense (Popoloaiakeakua)* forms the undershrub, with several species of Cyrtandra and the very handsome composite *Campylotheca cosmoides (Poolanui),* a shrub with long, rambling branches and very large yellow, drooping flowers. The genus Raillardia, with its many species on Maui and Hawaii, has only one species represented in the middle forest zone of Kauai, but this species, *Raillardia latifolia,* is so different from those found on the other islands that one would not recognize its relationship at the first glance. While all Raillardiae are either shrubs or small trees, the species in question is really a vine or climber. The writer observed it on *Bobea Mannii* and also on Xanthoxylum, both trees of about 30 feet in height. The genus Dubautia, also of the composite family, consists of seven species, all of which can be found on Kauai, five of them being peculiar to the island. *Dubautia plantaginea* is found on all the islands of the group, but has many variations on Kauai, where it is very common along Waialae stream. *Dubautia Knudsenii* usually grows on more open slopes and ridges and is a small shrub, while *D. raillardioides* is a small tree still belonging to the Elaeocarpus belt. Of other Compositae especial mention must be made of the highly interesting *Wilkesia gymnoxiphium,* a very beautiful plant usually found on the edge of canyons and bluffs, nearly always in company with the tall and handsome blue-flowered *Lobelia yuccoides,* which becomes 15 to 20 feet in height; they are usually found in company with *Styphelia tameiameia, Bobea Mannii, Dodonaea viscosa,* and *Acacia Koa,* and belong to the outskirts of the middle forest zone.

If we follow the Waialae stream at an elevation of 4000 feet we find many interesting plants, among them the new lobeliaceous *Cyanea rivularis* with its large, bright-blue flowers. It covers the steep banks or walls of this wonderful valley, almost to the exclusion of everything else. At the head of this stream these beautiful plants stand erect like palms, with their large crown of leaves at the top of a single 15 to 20 feet tall stem, waving gracefully in the wind. With it is usually found *Lobelia hypoleuca, Cyrtandra begoniaefolia,* and *C. Wawrae,* as well as the new *Cyanea Gayana,* another of the numerous Lobelioideae inhabiting this wonderful island.

As we advance into the interior of the island, *Elaeocarpus bifidus* and its associates give place to the araliaceous *Cheirodendron platyphyllum (Lapalapa)*, which is the predominant tree with *Metrosideros polymorpha;* here dwell *Scaevola glabra,* also known from Oahu, *Labordea tinifolia, L. Waialealae,* and several other species of this genus, some of which are new to science. The forest becomes wetter and wetter, thick, light-green moss covers the trees and ground alike, fern growth is abundant, and Hepaticae together with Hymenophyllums and Trichomanes ferns hang gracefully from every tree. The narrow leaved *Astelia Menziesiana* covers fallen trees; with it can be found the very peculiar caryophyllaceous *Schiedea lychnoides,* with large white flowers, while *Schiedea stellarioides* inhabits the drier districts. In these swampy forests the newly-described *Lysimachia glutinosa,* with large, beautiful cream-colored flowers, forms part of the undershrubs, but only in one locality, and that at the summit of the ridge leading to Kalalau. It is here that the writer discovered a species of Palm new to science, which has since been described by Dr. O. Beccari of Florence, Italy, as *Pritchardia minor.* It is a very distinct species and differs from all the rest of Hawaiian palms in the oval black fruits, which are of the size of a black olive, while the other species have fruits of the size of a small hen's egg; besides the whole aspect of the palm is different. Of Rubiaceae, *Straussia Mariniana* and *S. oncocarpa* var. β. grow side by side with *Psychotria hexandra,* since also found on Oahu in the Punaluu Mountains. *Psychotria grandiflora,* a small tree or shrub with beautiful cymosely-arranged white flowers, inhabits the dense, swampy jungle, with *Cyrtandra Gayana* and several vines, such as *Stenogyne purpurea* var. *brevipedunculata,* and one or two species of Phyllostegia with fragrant flowers.

The genera Kadua and Gouldia, both endemic genera of the Family Rubiaceae, are represented in this zone by many species, of which *Kadua Knudsenii, K. Waimeae,* and *K. glaucifolia* are the most common. These with Gouldia species inhabit rather the more open places where *Cyanea leptostegia* abounds.

In the smaller streambeds occur several species of Pipturus, as *P. ruber, P. Kauaiensis,* and others, besides Urera, *Neraudia* sp. nov., *Perrottetia sandwicensis, Dubautia laxa, Rubus hawaiiensis* var. *inermis,* several species of Phyllostegia, *Cyanea spathulata, Artemisia australis,* and others.

What is true of other genera is also true of the genus Suttonia (Myrsine). This genus, with its species Lessertiana, common on all the islands of the group, has four species peculiar to Kauai, which inhabit the swampy forests. Most peculiar is the fact that of the lobeliaceous genus Clermontia, which has reached such a wonderful development on Oahu, Maui and Hawaii, only one species *(C. Gaudichaudii)* occurs. It is a small tree, usually growing along water courses, either terrestrial or epiphytic on other trees.

Mention may also be made of the herbaceous *Dianella ensifolia (Uki)* with its lilac berries, which covers the ground thickly in the Elaeocarpus forest belt. *Syzygium sandwicense (Ohia ha)* attains quite a height and is associated

58

with *Ohia lehua, Kalia,* and the rubiaceous genus Coprosma, of which *C. pubens, C. Kauaiensis* and *C. Waimeae (Olena)* belong here.

The third species, *C. montana* var. ₎., is only found on the high, swampy plateau itself in company with *Lobelia Kauaiensis* and *L. macrostachys* var. *Kauaiensis* var. nov., several species of Dubautia, and others.

The further we penetrate into the interior the denser becomes the growth. Soil is no longer visible, as the ground is covered with a beautiful green carpet of moss, often two feet thick and saturated with water. The same can be said of the trees; their trunks appear to be two feet in diameter, but on investigation we find the true diameter to be only 4 to 5 inches, the rest being mosses and hepaticae of all description. It is on such trees that *Polypodium hymenophylloides, P. serrulatum, P. adenophorus,* and *Lycopodium Mannii* occur.

The genus Diellia has several species peculiar to Kauai, as *D. centifolia, D. laciniata,* and *D. Knudsenii,* which belong to the swampy region. The same holds good of many Asplenium, Polystichum and Dryopteris species.

In these dense forests, which harbor many species undoubtedly new to science, which will be described as soon as the bulky material can be worked up, we find large open places of several acres in area which resemble the peat bogs of Northern Europe. The vegetation is naturally stunted and only few shrubs occur. The soil in these bogs is of a gray color, loamy and heavy, and decayed vegetation is often found to be 10 to 15 feet deep. A bunch grass, *Panicum monticola,* forms large round mounds or tussocks, together with *Panicum isachnoides* of similar habit. In these tussocks we find *Selaginella deflexa* and *Lycopodium erubescens,* the latter, however, often submerged on the rocks in the middle of streambeds. The most interesting plant is *Drosera longifolia (Mikinalo),* one of the so-called insect-eating plants, which also occurs in the northern parts of Europe. Outside of Kauai the plant has not been found on the other islands of the group.

Back of Kaholuamano, in the midst of a dense forest, is such a bog, which bears the name *Lehua makanoe* or ''Lehua in the fog.'' The only shrub in this bog is *Metrosideros pumila,* probably a stunted sport of *Metrosideros polymorpha,* in whose shade the beautiful herbaceous violet, *Viola Kauaiensis (Pohe hiwa)* thrives. It is, however, not confined to this locality, but can also be found throughout the swampy forest, mainly on moss-covered tree trunks, as well as in Kauluwehi swamp (4210 feet), and on the summit of Waialeale, whose vegeta tion will be described under ''bog formations.''

Denser and wetter becomes the forest as we ascend the gradual slope which leads to Waialeale. We cross the first stream, Wailenalena, on whose banks the writer discovered a new violet, a variety of *Viola robusta,* which was named after the stream, var. *Wailenalenae,* outside of whose banks it has not been observed. It reaches a height of 3 to 6 feet, and has a woody stem, such as many of our violets possess. Two new shrubby species of Pelea grow in its company. As we approach the streams of Kailiili, Kaluiti, and Kanaholo, we find for the first

59

PLATE XX.

A DENSELY FORESTED WATERSHED on the Island of Oahu, Koolau range.

time the very interesting haloragaceous *Gunnera petaloidea (Ape ape)*, with its huge, thick, rugose, reniform leaves of sometimes five feet in diameter. Both banks of the streams are lined with these handsome plants, under whose leaves the traveler finds as perfect a protection from rain as under an umbrella. The stems of the plants are 4 to 5 feet tall, and can be cut with one stroke of the knife, though almost six inches in diameter. Associated with it is the newly-described araliaceous *Tetraplasandra Waialealae*, which ascends, however, up to the summit of Waialeale, where it is most common.

One would expect that in such a locality the tribe Lobelioideae would have many forms, which, however, is not the case. Only one species is found, which occurs also in the Elaeocarpus belt, and is new to science. The two species of Lobelia, *L. Kauaiensis* and *L. macrostachys* var. *Kauaiensis* var. nov., are found in great numbers, especially the former, which forms often pure stands of several hundreds of plants in open spots.

In the neighborhood of Kauluwehi swamp, *Suttonia Kauaiensis* and its tomentose variety form more or less tall shrubs. Cyperaceae are plentiful in the open swamps and forest as well, and will be mentioned under "bog formations."

A very peculiar cyperaceous plant was found on a dry ridge leading to Waiakealoha. It was unfortunately neither in flower nor fruit, but was sent to Dr. Kükenthal, the authority on this family.

The common species of Gahnia and Cladium can be found at Kaholuamano as well as in the neighboring districts.

THE MIDDLE FOREST REGION OF OAHU AND MOLOKAI.

The Islands of Oahu and Molokai have many species of plants in common. As we have seen, *Elaeocarpus bifidus (Kalia)* is almost the predominant tree of the first belt of the middle forest zone on Kauai; on Oahu the tree belongs to the lower forest zone and is only sparingly found above 2400 feet. On Molokai the tree is entirely absent, as well as on the rest of the islands of the group. The reason for this is probably to be found in the awkward size of the seed, which is about as large as a small pigeon's egg, and dispersed by nature's agents only with great difficulty or now not at all.

Of Lobelioideae, the genus Clermontia, only represented by one species on Kauai, achieved a wonderful development on Molokai and Oahu. The most common species is *Cl. macrocarpa*, found also in the lower forest zone at 1200 feet elevation. Since the dying out of the once beautiful forest on the northern slope of Haleakala, especially between Kailua and Honomanu, this shrub has taken possession of the land and seems to thrive where *Ohia lehua* trees could not exist. On Oahu we find the sharp ridges of the main range covered with dense vegetation (see Plate XX), especially so in the valleys of Punaluu and Kahana, until we reach the drier districts of Kahuku. Compositae are scarce on Oahu, and the genus Raillardia is practically absent. On Konahuanui several

61

species of Clermontiae abound, such as *Cl. oblongifolia*, which has a variety on Maui and is also not uncommon on Lanai; *Cl. persicaefolia* is, however, peculiar to Oahu. It is a small, handsome tree with white flowers, and is not uncommon in Palolo Valley along the ridge leading to Mt. Olympus. On Molokai, *Cl. arborescens* and *Cl. grandiflora* take the place of *Cl. macrocarpa* on Oahu, the former being especially common not only on Molokai, but also on Maui, where trees of 20 to 25 feet in height can be found. At the Pali of Wailau, Molokai, we find *Cl. pallida* as the third and last species of that genus on Molokai.

The genus Cyanea, however, finds a larger development. On Oahu, the most common species are *Cyanea angustifolia* and *Cyanea acuminata*, the latter not unlike a Delissea at first appearance, to which supposition its white flowers would lead one. *Cyanea Grimesiana*, one of the few Lobelioideae with pinnate leaves, is often found hidden among ferns, and when not in flower could easily be overlooked as such. On Molokai we find *Cyanea Mannii, C. solenocalyx,* and *C. ferox*, which, however, has a close relative on East Maui. *C. procera* belongs to the 2000-foot level above Kamolo, in which district, however, the forest has suffered tremendously from cattle, and no doubt the introduced Japanese deer have contributed their share of uselessness. The trees in this section are again *Ohia lehua,* mainly with *Cheirodendron Gaudichaudii (Olapa), Suttonia Lessertiana,* and several species of Pelea, such as *Pelea Molokaiensis, P. oblongifolia, P. sandwicensis,* etc. Of Rubiaceae, *Straussia kaduana* is the most common tree, and is distinguished from its ally *S. mariniana* in its drooping peduncle, which is usually of various lengths. *Psychotria hexandra* has also been found outside of Kauai, to which island it was once thought to be peculiar. It grows in the mountains of Punaluu in company with *Pittosporum glomeratum, P. glabrum (Hoawa), Perrottetia sandwicensis,* numerous species of Rollandia, and in its shade grows an exceedingly interesting species of Lysimachia, which was discovered by the writer in the year 1908, and has later been named by C. N. Forbes as *L. longisepala.* In the same locality grows a tree of the family Euphorbiaceae; it is a true Euphorbia, and has been named after its discoverer as *Euphorbia Rockii* by C. N. Forbes, who also named a species of violet found by the author as *Viola Oahuensis.* The genus Cyrtandra of the family Gesneriaceae reaches here a wonderful development, and it can safely be said that Oahu harbors more species of that genus than any other island of the group.

Of Palms, we find *Pritchardia Martii* on Oahu, while on Molokai in the swamps of Kawela grows *Pritchardia Hillebrandii.* Of Araliaceae, Tetraplasandra grows in the dense forests as well as on open, exposed ridges, in company with *Scaevola glabra,* Pelea, Campylotheca, and *Xanthoxylum oahuense,* a small handsome tree. On Oahu we find *Tetraplasandra meiandra* in many varieties on the exposed ridges, while the variety β of the same species occurs along a large gulch near Kawela swamp in company with *Pittosporum glabrum, Lobelia gaudichaudii,* and *Raillardia Molokaiensis. Tetraplasandra hawaiiensis* is not uncommon on Molokai, especially above Kaluaaha and in Wailau valley, as well as on the Island of Lanai on the main ridge of Haalelepakai, from which place it had not been reported previously. Hillebrand in his Flora reports *Pterotropia dipyrena* from Lanai, especially from the main ridge; the writer, however, failed to find a single tree of this species, but *Tetraplasandra hawaiiensis* being very common he comes to the conclusion that there is a possibility of Hillebrand having mistaken the identity of the trees in question, which resemble each other very much and perhaps could be mistaken one for the other when not in flower.

The middle forest zone is also the home of the loganiaceous genus Labordea, of which many species exist, as new ones have come to light since the exploration of this group has been commenced systematically. Mention must also be made of the extraordinary species of Compositae belonging to the genus Hesperomannia. Mr. Forbes has described an interesting species which he found on the Island of Kauai, and the writer has found trees 30 feet in height of *H. arborescens* on Mt. Konahuanui, Oahu. The trees were originally found on the Island of Lanai on the highest ridge, where Hillebrand says he found about eight specimens of this tree. Dr. R. C. L. Perkins told the writer that he found two trees about ten years ago. A careful search during a six-weeks' stay on that island did not reveal even a sign of such a tree once having existed. Our three species of Hesperomannia are very closely related to the Tahitian Fitchia, a genus of two arborescent mountain species.

Of Goodeniaceae, several species belong to this region, *Scaevola mollis* being peculiar to Oahu, as well as *S. chamissoniana*, the latter, however, descending into the lower forest zone, while *S. procera* inhabits the mountains of Molokai, Maui, and Kauai; *S. cylindrocarpa* being only found on Lanai on the highest ridge. The epacridaceous shrub, *Styphelia tameiameia*, is also an inhabitant of this zone, together with *Vaccinium penduliflorum*.

Of herbaceous plants, several species of Campylotheca belong here, as well as several vines, as *Gynopogon oliviformis (Maile)*, the liliaceous *Smilax sandwicensis (Pioi)*, and the myrsinaceous *Embelia pacifica*. Besides *Euphorbia Rockii*, a number of other species belong to this zone, such as *E. clusiaefolia* and *E. multiformis*, the former on more exposed ridges, especially back of Honolulu on one of the ridges leading to Konahuanui, where it is associated with a stunted form of *Syzygium sandwicense (Ohia ha)*.

Of Violaceae, *Viola robusta*, a very stout species 3 to 5 feet tall, is very common in the dense, mossy forest, while *V. Chamissoniana*, a shrubby species with pink flowers, is found mainly along stream beds (see Plate XXI) in company with shrubby species of Plantago, such as *Plantago princeps*, not uncommon back of Kamoku camp, Molokai, where it grows over 6 feet tall. The Labiatae take here also an important place, Phyllostegia being represented by numerous species. Especial mention must be made of the truly superb specimens of *Stenogyne Kamehamehae*, which trail over the swampy ground with large clusters of

63

PLATE XXI.

VEGETATION ALONG A STREAM BED on Molokai, ferns **Sadleria cyatheoides.**

deep magenta flowers which are over 3 inches long. On Hawaii its place is taken by the also handsome species *S. calaminthoides*, while on Oahu only two are recorded, of which one is doubtful.

The amarantaceous *Charpentiera ovata*, as well as *Ch. obovata*, ascend occasionally into the middle forest zone, but are really typical of the lower forest region. The biggest trees of the species *Ch. obovata* were found at Puuwaawaa, Hawaii, where the writer measured trunks two feet in diameter.

A handsome plant growing along streambeds and waterfalls is the begoniaceous *Hillebrandia sandwicensis*, the native Begonia or *Akaakaawa*, or as it is often called, *Puamakanui*, the big-eyed flower. It is common on Kauai as well as Molokai, and may still be found on Oahu. On Maui the writer found it at about 6000 feet elevation, in the crater of Haleakala in the Koolau gap, where it grew over six feet high under the shade of *Perrottetia sandwicensis (Olomea)*.

The queen of all is the lobeliaceous *Cyanea superba* var. *regina*, an exceedingly beautiful plant found only on Oahu, in the gulches of Wailupe and Niu, and in Makaleha of the Kaala range.

Cryptogams reach also a wonderful development, especially the tree ferns, which have been referred to under the chapter on the Island of Hawaii proper. *Marattia Douglasii* may be called a typical fern of the middle forest zone; it is known to the natives as *Pala* or mule-hoof fern on account of its large, fleshy auricles, which cover the caudex and are a source of food, as they abound in starch and mucilage.

THE MIDDLE FOREST ZONE ON THE ISLAND OF MAUI AND KOHALA, HAWAII.

Many of the trees found on Oahu and Molokai are common on Maui and also in the Kohala mountains on Hawaii, and need not be reenumerated; only mention will be made of such plants as are peculiar to the localities treated in this chapter.

WEST AND EAST MAUI.

Undoubtedly West Maui once upon a time formed a separate island and was in no wise connected with the extinct volcano Haleakala, which forms the bulk of East Maui, ascending to a height of 10,030 feet. West Maui is very much older than Haleakala, as no trace of a crater is visible at its summit, with the exception of the flat swamp called Mauna Eeke, which has the resemblance of a crater floor. West Maui is connected with East Maui by a narrow strip of land or isthmus with a mean elevation of 160 feet. The mountain mass of West Maui is intersected by many deep valleys or gorges, which find their source in the very heart of the mountain. Of these valleys, Iao is the biggest, on the eastern side, while it is separated on the western side by a low ridge from another valley, called Oloalu, which has a rather narrow entrance but widens out amphitheatrically.

65

The extreme western side is intersected by the valley Honokawai, which reaches almost to the head of Puukukui, the summit of West Maui, with an elevation of 5788 feet. This valley is much narrower than either Iao or Oloalu, but resembles very much the northern valley called Honokahau, which finds its source at the head of Mauna Eeke at a height of approximately 4500 feet. On the northeastern side are still other valleys, the most interesting one being Waihee, which has a very interesting vegetation; but owing to the enormous amount of rainfall is not often accessible. The streambed is narrow and enclosed between steep walls, which makes it very dangerous should one be caught in even a slight rain storm. The same is practically true of Waikapu, which is south of Iao valley.

The vegetation in most of these valleys is rather uniform and belongs to the lower forest zone. As the walls are very steep. in reality vertical, it is impossible to investigate these, but one has to satisfy himself by exploring the gradual slopes on each side of the valleys, which culminate into a more or less flat plateau with a stunted swamp vegetation. In the Kohala Mountains on Hawaii, however, the plateau is much more extensive and is covered by a typical middle forest zone formation. *Metrosideros polymorpha* is again a predominant tree, with *Cheirodendron Gaudichaudii*, several species of Suttonia, *Pelea clusiaefolia*, *Cyrtandra pilosa*, the rubiaceous *Kadua formosa*, together with *Schiedea diffusa* and again *Gunnera petaloidea*, which covers the walls of the valleys to the exclusion of nearly everything else.

The ground on the slopes at 4000 feet elevation is covered with moss, holding a tremendous amount of moisture. In such places, under the dense shade, grow many species of Cyrtandra, which are nearly all dense shade-loving plants. With it we find the terrestrial *Lycopodium serratum*, while *Lycopodium errubescens* is found on rocks in streambeds. Here also is the home of the genus Labordea of the family Loganiaceae, herbaceous species with orange-colored flowers, growing in the thick moss, while shrubby or even arborescent species are found mostly along streambeds together with *Urera* sp., *Gouldia axillaris*, and *Pittosporum insigne*, the latter a common but handsome tree in this locality.

Of Compositae, we find *Dubautia laxa* along the edge of Honokawai gulch, with species of Pelea and the rubiaceous genus Coprosma. Campylotheca has several species at an elevation of 4500 feet, while it is also represented in the lowlands by one or two species. *Cladium angustifolium* and *Cladium Meyenii* occur on the rather windswept edges of the gulches, together with *Scaevola chamissoniana*, Styphelia and other plants.

Of interest is the tribe Lobelioideae, which is represented here by the genera Lobelia, Clermontia and Cyanea. The genus Lobelia is found only near the swampy plateau in the more open forest which leads into the great bog, the only species being *L. Gaudichaudii*.

Immediately below the swampy plateau are one or two miniature bogs which harbor *Plantago pachyphylla*, with its many varieties peculiar to high elevations.

Here also occurs a creeping species of Lysimachia, together with Lycopods, and other cryptogams, besides *Lagenophora mauiensis*, which has descended from the bogs above.

One of the interesting lobelioideous plants is *Cyanea atra*, a plant of the aspect of *Cyanea tritomantha* (see Plate VI), to which it is related. The flowers, as the name *atra* implies, are almost black. The plants are 10 to 15 feet tall, and grow either along streambeds shaded by *Gunnera petaloidea*, or also in dense jungles in mossy forests. In the more open forests grow *Clermontia arborescens*, *Clermontia grandiflora*, and, at an elevation of nearly 5000 feet, *Clermontia multiflora* var. *micrantha* forma *montana* f. n. This latter plant is an exceedingly handsome lobelioideous shrub, with most beautiful foliage and bright pink flowers. It grows neither lower nor higher, but is peculiar to about 4800 to 5000 feet elevation.

The variety *micrantha* is found, according to Hillebrand, in Waihee Valley in the bare gravel along the stream, while the species is found in the same valley and also on Oahu, in Wailupe. Another lobelioideous plant, *Cyanea macrostegia*, resembles *C. atra* closely, and is found often in its company. Other species of the same genus are found in Waikapu, Iao Valley, and above Kaanapali, but more in the lower forest zone. Of trees, the araliaceous *Tetraplasandra meiandra* var. may be mentioned, which is found at an elevation of 4300 feet. Here also belong the Labiate vines, such as Phyllostegia and Stenogyne, though sparingly represented.

EAST MAUI—HALEAKALA.

Haleakala, an extinct crater over 10,000 feet high, makes up the whole of East Maui. Its vegetative covering is indeed of great interest, but has suffered severely the last fifty years, and represents probably an entirely different aspect from what it was before the slopes of Haleakala were given over to the ranchman and his cattle. The lower forest zone has already been described, and we have to consider now mainly the vegetation between 3000 to 5000 feet on the northern slopes of the mountain, as on the western and partly southern slopes nothing remains to be considered, as the grassy plains have not even a remnant of the once existing forest, except in deep gulches inaccessible to cattle, from which we can judge of what the forest was once composed.

The western slope of the mountain is not much intersected by gulches, the only one of interest being Waihou gulch. The northern slope, however, is cut into many gorges, such as Waikamoi, Puohaokamoa, and Honomanu. The biggest, however, in the northern outlet of Haleakala at Keanae, called Koolau gap, while the western outlet is known as Kaupo gap.

The interesting forest commences at Olinda in the district of Hamakuapoko and up to Ukulele, from which latter place the upper forest zone begins. We find practically the same trees in this district as on West Maui, the most common and predominating trees being *Cheirodendron gaudichaudii (Olapa)*, Co-

PLATE XXII.

A TYPICAL JUNGLE of the middle forest zone, Waikamoi trail, East Maui; elevation
4000 feet.

prosma, *Metrosideros polymorpha (Ohia lehua)*, and *Acacia Koa*, which has ascended from the upper edge of the lower forest zone. It is, however, still a common tree in this zone, and rivals with *Olapa* and *Ohia lehua* in predominance. *Straussia oncocarpa* and *Straussia leptocarpa*, of the family Rubiaceae, belong to the 3500 foot level.

On the open grassland between 3000 feet to almost 5000 feet, but especially a little over 3000 feet, is a belt of an endemic Labiate, *Sphacele hastata*, peculiar to Haleakala. It is really marvelous that this plant is still to be found in large numbers, as it is in the midst of a cattle ranch. On investigating, we find it owes its survival to its peculiar mint odor, apparently offensive to the taste of the cattle. All other vegetation has disappeared, though, as mentioned before, traces can still be found in inaccessible gulches.

The semi-dry forest above Makawao gradually merges into the middle forest zone. Southeast of Olinda only grasslands prevail, though here and there many species of Eucalypti have been planted into symmetrical squares.

The forest beginning at Olinda and extending all along the windward side of Haleakala is, however, the object of our investigation. Besides the trees already mentioned, we find other araliaceous genera, such as *Tetraplasandra meiandra* var. and the tall *Pterotropia dipyrena (Oheohe)*, most common on Puukakai, an extinct crater between Ukulele and Olinda. *Pittosporum insigne* var. β, *Nothocestrum longifolium*, *Gouldia axillaris*, *Perrottetia sandwicensis*, and *Raillardia Menziesii*, an arborescent composite which reaches its best development at the lower edge of the upper forest zone, are the more common trees.

Of Lobelioideae, *Clermontia arborescens* is the most common, while *Cl. tuberculata* is the rarest. Of shrubs, we find *Platydesma campanulatum* var.? with a small Gouldia, and one or two species of Kadua, numerous Cyrtandra, a species of Scaevola, a few species of the rutaceous genus Pelea, and also the leguminous *Sophora chrysophylla*, which inhabits here the wet forest with *Suttonia Lessertiana*. *Dubautia plantaginea* is occasionally met with, as well as an introduced Cassia.

Of herbaceous plants, we find *Ranunculus Mauiensis* quite common in company with numerous species of Labordea. Surprising is the dense undergrowth of *Rubus hawaiiensis* on the outskirts of the middle forest zone. As we penetrate into the interior the forest becomes dense, moss covers the ground and trees (see Plate XXII), and many epiphytes, such as *Astelia veratroides*, with numerous species of ferns, especially of the genus Polypodium, abound. Peperomiae form a dominant feature of the herbaceous growth; and it is here also that we find two species of our Orchids, poor, measly representatives of a family which reaches such wonderful development and floral beauty in other tropical countries. Labiatae are at home in this floral zone and display a beautiful variety of forms, many of which possess beautiful flowers worthy of cultivation. The genus Phyllostegia displays not less than nine species, of which *P. grandiflora*, *P. glabra*, and *P. racemosa* are the most common and beautiful. They are only surpassed in beauty by the species of Stenogyne, which flower in the late winter months. Their large curved corollas, which are borne in large whorls, vary in shades from deep magenta to crimson, pink, yellow and pure white, interlacing trees or gracefully festooning branches, or, as is often the case, forming dense carpets covering the ground in small spots to the exclusion of other plants. The handsomest species are *St. Kamehamehae* and *St. longiflora*.

Another very important feature of the vegetation is the tribe Lobelioideae, of which most of the species found here are new to science; they belong nearly all to the Sect. III., Palmaeformes, and are more or less closely related. The most interesting is *Cyanea aculeatiflora*, which, as the name implies, is covered with spines even to the lobes of the corolla; another peculiar new species is *Cyanea hamatiflora* with broad sessile leaves, dark-red flowers, and large purple fruits; the latter plant is most common on Puukakai, where it reaches a height of 15 to 20 feet, similar to *C. aculeatiflora*. *C. macrostegia* with lobed leaves is not uncommon, and so is *C. atra*, but differing from the specimens found on West Maui. *Cyanea ferox* is here a shrub 15 feet in height with straight ascending branches, which together with the stem are covered with thorns; the leaves of this latter species are sinuate and remind one somewhat of *Cyanea Grimesiana*.

Besides these tall species, two subherbaceous ones are found in the dense shady moss forest, the taller one of the two, *Cyanea Bishopii* (a new species, but first collected by the late E. Bishop, and referred by Hillebrand doubtfully to *Cyanea Kunthiana?*), with purple flowers, is the most common, but flowers, unlike the other species, in the winter months. As we cross Waikamoi, where we meet again with *Gunnera petaloidea* and *Hillebrandia sandwicensis*, the Hawaiian begonia, the forest becomes more uniform. At the edge of Waikamoi proper, we find *Lobelia macrostachys* and a species of Wikstroemia, probably a new species. The writer crossed this forest belt from Olinda to Honomanu and followed along the ditch trail to Kailua. A forest as described in the above pages covers this stretch of land, and it may be remarked that at about 3000 feet elevation, above Honomanu, there are two clumps of Palms, *Pritchardia arecina* Becc. This palm, discovered by the writer, is new to science, and is described by Beccari in Webbia Vol. IV. Lower down along the ditch trail proper the forest has died for miles, the cause being still unascertained. All the *Ohia* trees are dead, and only here and there a species of Tetraplasandra is struggling for existence. Since the death of the tree growth the lobeliaceous *Clermontia macrocarpa*, so common on Oahu, has become almost the sole underbrush, with here and there a species of *Cl. arborescens*.

What has been said of this forest belt up to Honomanu holds good for Keanae and Nahiku, the only exception being the presence of *Sideroxylon rhynchospermum* at Nahiku, besides several species of Cyanea.

The forests spoken of by Hillebrand at Ulupalakua have entirely disappeared and only remnants of them can be found. *Cheirodendron Gaudichaudii* is still common, besides Suttonia, and *Ohia lehua;* numerous still is the araliaceous

Pterotropia dipyrena. The undershrub is again mainly *Rubus hawaiiensis.* The species of Cyanea found by Hillebrand are gone forever; and where they once reared their proud palm-like crowns toward the sky there is now only grassland, with herds of cattle and ugly Eucalypti. The writer was fortunate enough to find a specimen of the long-sought-for, gorgeous *Cyanea arborea* in that locality in a small gulch inaccessible to cattle. It was the last of its race. He scoured the country for miles searching for the handsome *Cyanea comata,* but his searches were in vain: it had vanished forever.

THE MOUNTAINS OF KOHALA, HAWAII.

Above 3000 feet in the mountains of Kohala we find the vegetation similar to that of East and West Maui. *Metrosideros polymorpha, Cheirodendron Gaudichaudii,* and a host of species of Pelea are the most common trees. Like West Maui, the Kohala mountains are intersected by many deep gorges, of which the biggest are Waipio and Waimanu valleys, which are followed toward the west by Honokanenui, Honokaneiki and Pololu valleys; beyond them the country becomes flatter and only little gulches descend to the sea. (See Plate XXIII.) All the sugar plantations of this part of the Island of Hawaii are situated here. As we advance farther west the land becomes very dry and is bare of vegetation.

Back of Waimea village, which is situated at an elevation of 2700 feet, the mountains are intersected by only a few small gulches. The summit is called Kaala, and has an elevation of 5500 feet. The most prominent gulch on this side is Holokaiea. The valley of Waipio is very large and is divided into many other gorges of great interest. Hiilawe and Waima are minor valleys, while Alakahi and Kawainui, the latter a continuation of the former, reaches almost to the center of the mountain. The walls of these valleys are vertical and nearly 3000 feet in height, with hundreds of waterfalls. Clouds hover nearly constantly over the ridges, and the traveler is lucky if he gets a glimpse of the depths below him. It is on these flats on each side of the valleys that the botanist finds a most interesting collecting ground.

It is only recently that this part of the land was made accessible through the so-called upper Hamakua ditch trail, which leads to the headwaters of Kawainui gorge, opening to the botanist a most interesting field. Not less interesting is the land back of Awini in Kohala proper. On these flat forest lands the trees do not grow to any size, but are more or less stunted and covered with numerous mosses and hepatics, and are also festooned with *Astelia veratroides,* Vaccinium, and many ferns. Of great interest is the rutaceous genus Pelea, which has many forms here. One species new to science has extremely large capsules, and when bruised emits an even stronger odor than *Pelea anisata* of Kauai. Xanthoxylum is represented only by one species, which is new, and shall be known as *Xanthoxylum Bluettianum* sp. n., in honor of Mr. P. W. P. Bluett of Kohala, through whose courtesies the writer was enabled to explore this won-

71

PLATE XXIII.

VEGETATION ALONG ONE OF THE MANY STREAMLETS which descends to the sea;
Kohala Mts., Hawaii.

derful country. Labiatae are represented numerously, the most common being *Stenogyne calaminthoides* and several species of Phyllostegia.

The tribe Lobelioideae reaches a most remarkable development, but especially the genus Clermontia, the species *parviflora* being the most common, not only in this district but in all the wet forests on Hawaii. *Clermontia Kohalae*, a new species with dark-purple flowers, is found on the lower Kohala ditch trail as well as Awini. The largest flowered species, however, occurs at an elevation of 4200 feet, and is very variable in leaf as well as flower. It is also new, and was named by the writer *Cl. drepanomorpha*. It is associated with another new species of the same genus named *Cl. leptoclada*. At least five more species of this genus can be found, nearly all of which are new and were discovered by the writer. The genus Clermontia forms a large percentage of plant growth in the upper Kohala mountains, which is not the case either on Waialeale, Kauai, or Puukukui, West Maui. As on the other mountains so also here we find Coprosma, Cyrtandra, Tetraplasandra, and at an elevation of 3000 feet the interesting palm *Pritchardia lanigera*, differing from the other Hawaiian palms in its woolliness of leaf and spadix. *Schiedea diffusa* makes here also its appearance with several Labordea, and the lobeliaceous *Cyanea pilosa*.

In more open boggy places we find *Raillardia scabra, Raillardia* sp., a new species of Plantago covered densely with long gray hair, Lycopods, *Selaginella deflexa, Schizaea robusta,* and other species. *Suttonia sandwicensis* is also not uncommon. At 4500 to 5000 feet elevation the forest is exceedingly wet and the ground covered with mosses two feet or more thick. On this high plateau are numerous volcanic blow-holes which are a constant danger to the traveler, as they are hidden from view by shrubs which grow on their sides and also by vines and moss. These blow-holes are often several hundred feet deep, and sometimes only 10 feet or so in diameter. As already said, they can seldom be perceived, but can always be heard, as water from the swamps drains into them, making the sound of a miniature waterfall. In this extremely wet, mossy forest the writer collected a great quantity of material which, owing to continuous field trips, has not yet all been worked up, but undoubtedly will result in the determination of many new forms.

Here also the writer found growing in the beautiful light-green moss a variety of *Viola mauiensis* which he named var. *Kohalana*. This is the first violet recorded from the Island of Hawaii. The flowers are blue, while the plant stands about five feet high. At the summit of the mountain a white-flowering form was found.

Until the material of this region has been thoroughly worked out the description now given will have to suffice. In general, the vegetative characteristics are the same as on West Maui. On the steep slopes of the valleys, especially along the sides of the enormous waterfalls, we find *Gunnera petaloidea*, the *Ape ape* of the natives, besides many ferns usually common to all wet districts of the higher levels.

PLATE XXIV.

LOBELIA MACROSTACHYS growing in the open swamps of Molokai.

Of Gramineae, the following may be recorded: *Polypogon monspeliensis*, found in open places, often in pools; *Isachne distichophylla*, and *Eragrostis grandis*, the latter usually at lower elevation along streams. Cyperaceae are also more or less common, especially on the edges of the cliffs of Kawainui and Alakahi. Mention may be made of *Cladium Meyenii, Uncinia uncinata*, usually along streambeds and waterfalls, *Cladium angustifolium*, and *Cyperus strigosus* var. *insularis* Kükenth. The juncaceous *Luzula hawaiiensis*, resembling very much a Cyperaceae, is also very common.

THE BOG REGION.

The bog region is usually confined to the summits of the mountains of the older islands or portions of islands, with an altitude of little over 5000 feet.

Waialeale, the summit of Kauai, at an elevation of 5280 feet, represents such a bog, as well as Puu Kukui, the summit of West Maui (5788 feet) and Kaala, the summit of the Kohala mountains on Hawaii (5505 feet). All these three localities have many species of plants in common, but also each locality has again its peculiar species.

The summits of these mountains are nearly always throughout the year enwrapped by clouds, with the exception of a short period during which the south wind prevails. The best season for visiting these wonderful places is in October and the first part of November. The rainfall in these localities is enormous, but no definite record has been kept in these places, with the exception of Waialeale, where the U. S. Geological Survey placed a rain gauge with the capacity of holding 120 inches. The writer ascended Waialeale for the second time on October 20, 1911. One month before the rain gauge had been emptied. On arrival at the summit on the above date the rain gauge was found overflowing.

It may, however, be remarked that these bogs, with their peculiar flora, are not always confined to the summits of the mountains of an altitude of 5000 feet, but can also be found in the midst of the middle forest zone at an elevation of usually 4000 feet. Thus we have four bogs on Kauai besides Waialeale. The biggest one is situated a few miles back of Halemanu and extends almost to the edge of Wainiha gorge; this bog is known as Alakai swamp, and is about one and one-half miles across. Another much smaller bog is Kauluwehi swamp, situated at an elevation of 4200 feet, back of Kaholuamano on the trail to Waiakealoha waterfall; the smallest one is Lehua makanoe, "Lehua in the fog"— only about a mile back of Mr. F. Gay's mountain house. The next, though larger than either Kauluwehi or Lehua makanoe, is the bog of Wahiawa, at a much lower elevation than those previously mentioned.

On Molokai there is only one bog worth mentioning, and that is Kawela swamp, back of Kamoku, not far from Pelekunu gorge. (See Plate XXIV.)

On Maui we have besides Puu Kukui, the bog Mauna Eeke, situated above Honokahau gulch at an elevation of about 4100 feet. It is indeed of interest to note that most of the species of plants found on Puu Kukui are not peculiar to the bog region, but have been found by the writer on the steep walls in Kaupo gap in the crater of Haleakala.

In the Kohala Mountains there are several bogs besides the main one at the summit, the names of which are not known to the writer.

THE BOGS OF KAUAI.

In the bogs situated on the central plateau we find the vegetation the same, while the great bog of Waialeale has its peculiar species besides most of those found in lower situated bogs.

The turfy soil is covered with tussocks of Gramineae and Cyperaceae, mainly *Panicum monticola, Panicum imbricatum* and *P. isachnoides*, together with the cyperaceous *Oreobulus furcatus*.

On these tussocks of grasses and Cyperaceae we find the European *Drosera longifolia (Mikinalo)*, the so-called insect-eating plant, embedded. It has been said that *D. longifolia* is hardly ever found without its associate *D. rotundifolia*, but here on Kauai it is the only representative of the family Droseraceae. *Drosera longifolia* is more common in the lower swamps than on the summit, where only few specimens of it have been found. Between these tussocks grow small bushes of *Ohia lehua*, or really called *Lehua makanoe*, from which one locality derives its name. The plant has been named by Heller *Metrosideros pumila*. In its shade grows the handsome blue-flowered violet, *Viola Kauaiensis. Habenaria holochila* was found by the writer in Alakai swamp in the turf, growing erect about three feet in height. It is the third species of our poor orchids.

The swamps are bordered by many tall-growing Cyperaceae, as *Carex sandwicensis*, which forms stands 4 to 5 feet high, together with *Cladium* sp., probably new, a tall plant with long, scaly, creeping rhizomes, with stems often 10 feet high. In the swamp proper we find *Carex montis Eeka, Rhynchospora glauca* var. *chinensis, Deschampsia australis, Selaginella deflexa, Schizaea robusta, Styphelia imbricata* var. *struthioloides*, a creeper, a species of Wikstroemia, *Suttonia sandwicensis* β var. *denticulata, Vaccinium penduliflorum*, etc.

The summit of Kauai, Mt. Waialeale, was visited first by Wawra, the botanist of the Austrian exploring expedition, in the year 1871; and it is peculiar that no other botanist or botanical collector had cared to visit the mountain again.

The writer ascended Waialeale in the year 1910 and again in 1911. The second time the ascent was very much facilitated through the trails which had been cut by the men of the U. S. Geological Survey. The vegetation of Waialeale is extremely interesting, and several new species were found and described by the writer. The ridges leading to the summit have an entirely different plant formation, composed of peculiar species. One of the striking plants is *Pelea Waialealae (Anonia* or *Alaniwai)*, which grows together with *Suttonia lanceolata*, a very distinct species, both being shrubs but occasionally becoming small trees. Of Compositae we find *Dubautia laxa* var. *pedicellata* Rock v. n., which is here a shrub 10 to 15 feet high, in company with the rutaceous *Pelea orbicularis* var. ? and *Pelea* sp. ? and *Dubautia paleata*. A few small species of La-

76

bordea are not uncommon on the mossy tree trunks. Here we also meet with *Lobelia Kauaiensis* and *Lobelia macrostachys* var. *Kauaiensis* with deep crimson flowers. As we ascend, we enter the open plateau or bog with still a few shrubs, and even higher up in little depressions we find trees such as the newly-described *Tetraplasandra Waialealae*, the second species of Tetraplasandra that is to be found on this island. *Cheirodendron platyphyllum* is also found here as a small tree with sinuate-serrate leaves, while at lower elevation the leaves are entire. Among such shrubbery grows *Lobelia macrostachys* var. *Kauaiensis*, while *L. Kauaiensis* with either a simple or compound candelabra-like spike, with cream-colored purplish-streaked flowers, prefers the open, flat swamp where the vegetation is stunted. *Labordea Waialealae*, a shrub, is peculiar to this locality, as well as *Labordea fagraeoidea* var. *pumila*, which is subherbaceous. *Pittosporum Gayanum* var. is here a shrub, differing from the species in its being glabrous throughout; with it occurs a stunted form of *Eurya sandwicensis* var. with rather large fruits; and also a species of Wikstroemia.

In the open bog proper, we meet with the already-described Cyperaceae and Gramineae, besides a species of Cyperus and *Deschampsia australis* var. *pumila. Astelia Waialealae* is scattered over the ground plentifully, but is, however, not peculiar to Kauai, as it has been met with by the writer in Kawela swamp on Molokai.

A curious species of Dubautia, named *D. Waialealae*, grows at the summit proper. On the outskirts together with the other shrubs grows *Lysimachia Hillebrandii* var. *venosa*, with rather long herbaceous branches.

In the grassy tussocks we find again *Viola Kauaiensis*, but only very small plants; in Sphagnum moss the pretty *Geranium humile* var. *Kauaiensis (Nohuanu)* occurs together with *Plantago pachyphylla* var. *Kauaiensis*, and *Acaena exigua*, as well as *Sanicula sandwicensis* var. *β.*, with leaves much less incised; this latter plant had not been recorded previously from Kauai. Wawra's *Plantago pachyphylla* var. *pusilla* occurs only in one locality, called Kawakoo. *Metrosideros pumila* is here a small glabrous creeper only a few inches in length. Another variety of *Plantago pachyphylla*, which is wholly glabrous, occurs at the summit, and is here named var. *glabrifolia* Rock v. n. *Lycopodium venustulum* var. *herpeticum* is found trailing at the summit in company with *Stenogyne purpurea* var. *Lobelia Kauaiensis* is an exceedingly handsome plant and is quite common at the summit. It differs very materially from *L. Gaudichaudii*, so common on Puu Kukui, West Maui, and when seen in the field no botanist can help but see the specific distinction.

Of interest may be the names of the various localities on the summit of Waialeale. Immediately after leaving the ridge leading into the open plateau a large patch of bright-red dirt is discernable; the natives used to go to this place, which they called Kaluaalaea, for this dirt, which they used for paint. The first point or hill on the plateau is called Honunamanu; where the rain gauge is situated the place is known as Manakauaalakai; the highest point, on which the copper plate of the U. S. Geological Survey is enclosed in cement, is Kapailoahiki. Where the *Heiau* is situated is Kawakoo, then comes a pool called Waialeale, and beyond it a hill overlooking Wailua, which is known as Waikini.

THE SUMMIT BOG OF WEST MAUI, PUU KUKUI, ELEVATION 5788 FEET.

Puu Kukui is a large, open, more or less flat plateau, composed of light-gray, heavy, loamy soil. The vegetation is stunted, with the exception of such as occurs in depressions or small gulches, and at the head of Iao Valley, where trees belonging to the middle forest region abound.

The whole of Puu Kukui is a second Waialeale of Kauai, though a number of plants are peculiar to the former. We find the same globose tussocks of *Oreobulus furcatus* and the very interesting *Carex montis Eeka*, besides Gramineae, such as *Deschampsia australis* forma *longius aristata, Calamagrostis Hillebrandii* Hack. (nov. nom.), and others, while the juncaceous *Luzula hawaiiensis* var. *glabrata* grows in their company. One of the most striking vegetative features is the great abundance of the very beautiful *Lobelia Gaudichaudii.* In certain parts this plant covers the ground, and in the month of August it is indeed a beautiful sight. At about 5000 feet elevation these Lobelias are only about 3 to 4 feet high, while at the extreme eastern end of this interesting bog the plant is from 8 to 15 feet high and branches candelabra-like into usually five erect racemes, bearing from 40 to 80 flowers each, while the plants in the open bog have only one pyramidal raceme about 2 to 3 feet long. The flowers are much larger than those of *L. Kauaiensis*, found on Waialeale, and also handsomer; they are cream colored with a slight pinkish tinge, and are three inches long and an inch wide. *Lobelia macrostachys* is here absent, while represented on Waialeale, Kauai, by a new variety. The beautifully branching *Lobelia Gaudichaudii* found on the brink of Iao Valley is certainly distinct from the one described by DeCandolle in many particulars, especially in the very long lanceolate acuminate bracts, and shall from now on be known as var. *longibracteata* Rock, var. nov.

Next to the Lobelioideae found at the summit, the Compositae have three representatives. Of greatest interest is the very handsome *Wilkesia Grayana,* with its 5 to 8 feet tall stem, bearing a dense crown of verticillate leaves, out of whose center the inflorescence comes forth as a large foliaceous raceme of one and one-half to two feet in length, bearing yellow globose flower heads of about 10 lines in diameter. There is only one other species known of this interesting genus, *W. gymnoxiphium.* It occurs in the dry districts of Kauai, especially on open wind-swept cliffs in company with *Lobelia yuccoides;* while *W. Grayana* grows in the open bog, which receives an enormous amount of rainfall.

The second interesting genus is Argyroxiphium, which also belongs to the most ancient of Hawaiian Compositae, though of American affinity. These two genera are undoubtedly the oldest denizens of the Hawaiian Islands. The genus

78

Argyroxiphium with its two species, *sandwicense* and *virescens*, has hitherto been found only in the drier upper forest region in black volcanic ash at an altitude of from 8000 to 10,000 feet. At the summit of Puu Kukui is a small species of this genus growing in a veritable pool, but only in one locality. The plant was not in flower at the time of the writer's visit, but it can be said that when the plant is fully known it will undoubtedly represent a new variety or intermediate form between *A. sandwicense* and *A. virescens*. The leaves of the plants in question are neither silvery nor green, but are covered with a bluish, somewhat silvery or glauceous pubescence.

Lagenophora mauiensis is very common in the turfy soil in company with the creeping *Geranium humile* with pink flowers. *Acaena exigua*, which is very scarce on Waialeale, is here exceedingly common, together with *Viola mauiensis*. Remarkable to say, *Drosera longifolia*, so common on Kauai, is here absent. A small creeping Metrosideros is also present with *Lycopodium venustulum* var. and *Styphelia imbricata* var. *struthioloides*.

The writer met with a single plant of *Lycopodium Haleakalae* resembling very much *L. erubescens*, but stouter and not reddish. Several species of lichens grow on the exposed gray loam, such as Cladonia, Stereocaulon and others.

At the extreme eastern end of the bog on the brink of Iao Valley the tree growth is mainly *Cheirodendron Gaudichaudii, Suttonia* sp. ?, *Pelea* sp., *Metrosideros polymorpha*, and the lobelioideous *Clermontia grandiflora*. All the trees are covered thickly with moss and hepaticae or Liverworts. The swamp of Mauna Eeke harbors the same vegetation as that of Puu Kukui with possibly one or two exceptions.

THE UPPER FOREST REGION.

The upper forest region extends from about 5500 feet elevation up to 11,500. Of tree growth we can practically say that four species form the main trees. The most predominant of these is the leguminous *Sophora chrysophylla (Mamani)*, and, secondly, *Myoporum sandwicense (Naio)*, and on the lower edge of the upper forest zone, or as on Mt. Haleakala at 7000 feet elevation, *Acacia Koa (Koa)*, with *Metrosideros polymorpha (Ohia lehua)*. These four species form the main tree-growth, while here and there we find the rubiaceous *Coprosma montana* at 9000 feet elevation and with it the arborescent Compositae *Raillardia arborea* up to 10,000 feet, while *R. struthioloides* can be found up to an elevation of 11,500 feet; the two latter, however, only on Mauna Kea (13,823 feet), Hawaii. *Raillardia Menziesii* is found at an elevation of 6000 to 8000 feet, and on Mt. Haleakala is the largest species in the genus Raillardia, but is a shrub at the higher levels up to the summit.

On Mauna Loa tree-growth ceases at a little above 8000 feet; the tree compositae found on Mauna Kea and Haleakala are, however, absent on Mauna Loa. *Santalum Haleakalae*, a species of *Iliahi* or Sandalwood, is peculiar to Haleakala, Maui, and can be found at from 7000 to 8500 feet elevation. This same species

79

PLATE XXV.

ARGYROXIPHIUM SANDWICENSE var. **MACROCEPHALUM** (Ahinahina, Silversword)
growing in the crater of Haleakala, Maui, elevation 7500 feet.

was, however, observed by the writer on the lava fields of Auahi, southern slopes of Mt. Haleakala, at an elevation of 2000 feet. Naturally the species was not stunted but developed to a fine looking tree; only a single tree was found at the lower level, while at 8000 feet it is not uncommon, especially at the very head of Waikamoi or Honomanu gulch.

The Compositae form quite a large part of the vegetation of the upper forest zone and are most numerously represented on Haleakala.

The mountains which possess an upper forest flora are, according to age, Haleakala (10,030 feet), Maui; Mauna Kea (13,873 feet), Hualalai (8273 feet), and Mauna Loa, the youngest, (13,675 feet), Hawaii. All four mountains are volcanoes, three of them extinct, while Mauna Loa becomes still periodically active.

Haleakala is entirely different in formation from the other mountains; it has a summit crater of huge dimensions having a circumference of nearly 23 miles, is 2000 feet deep, and is covered at the bottom with numerous cinder cones, of which the highest is 1030 feet.

The crater has two outlets, one on the north side called Koolau gap, and another on the southern side called Kaupo gap. The former gap is, up to an elevation of 6000 feet, an impenetrable tropical jungle, while the latter is comparatively dry and covered with more or less scrub vegetation. The largest portion of the crater is bare of vegetation, being composed mainly of extensive *aa* (rough) lava flows and huge fields of black volcanic ash; it is in the latter that the most beautiful *Argyroxiphium sandwicense* var. *macrocephalum (Ahinahina* or Silversword) thrives best. They still occur in thousands in Haleakala crater, but are indeed very scarce on Mauna Kea, and more so on Mauna Loa and Hualalai. The steep slopes in the upper part of Kaupo gap are covered with this most beautiful plant (see Plate XXV), which flowers from July to October. Wild goats are doing great damage to it, as they devour it eagerly, and so also do cattle, the arch-enemy of the Hawaiian forests. In earlier days this interesting plant was also found plentifully on the slopes of the mountain, but it has now vanished since tourists began to ascend to the mountain summit.

Raillardia platyphylla, a shrubby composite, is quite gregarious along dry streambeds, especially along the upper part of Waikamoi near Puunianiau crater, while *R. Menziesii* grows as a tree at 6000 feet elevation and becomes a common shrub at 9000 feet near the summit. Of great interest is the green sword-plant, *Argyroxiphium virescens*, which is peculiar to Haleakala and found together with the plants just mentioned. It usually grows on the edges of cliffs in company with the silversword, and is especially common near the base of Puunianiau crater. It has been observed in the crater of Haleakala itself, but not on the ash fields, as its congener, but in Kaupo gap along dry streambeds between rocks, together with *Lobelia hypoleuca* var., *Dubautia plantaginea* var., *Raillardia* sp., etc.

Vaccinium reticulatum (Ohelo), with its delicious berries, covers the mountain slope, with another species which has lately been described as *Vaccinium Fauriei*, a very distinct plant, with large, glaucous berries and small leaves; it grows much taller than *V. reticulatum*, and its berries are better tasting than those of the latter.

Rubiaceae are also not uncommon. We find again *Coprosma ernodeoides (Kukainene)*, *Coprosma montana*, and *C. menziesii*, with *Sanicula sandwicensis*, *Plantago pachyphylla*, *Fragaria chilensis* (the Chilean strawberry), and the iridaceous *Sisyrynchium acre*, once employed in tattooing by the Hawaiians.

Ranunculus Hawaiiensis (Makou), the Hawaiian buttercup, is not uncommon on Puunianiau crater, and exceedingly plentiful on Mauna Kea, especially above Waiki and the craters Kaluamakani, Moano, etc. *Silene struthioloides* is found in black cinder in the crater, as well as on the slopes. *Metrosideros polymorpha* var. *β.* and *δ* are usually found in gulches, together with *Suttonia* sp., *Dodonaea eriocarpa*, *Sophora chrysophylla*, and others.

Special mention must be made of the wonderful development which the temperate genus Geranium has reached in these islands. Like the Violaceae, it has become arborescent and evolved into many species. The Hawaiian species of Geranium form a distinct section in the family, called *Neurophyllodes*. All species have a peculiar type of leaf which varies in size, shape, and pubescence.

Geranium tridens is the common shrubby form which can be seen mixed with *Sophora chrysophylla*; its leaves are covered with a bright-silvery pubescence, and are tridentate at the apex, whence the name. It is the most common species on Haleakala, while *G. arboreum* is scarcer. It is usually found in sheltered places near Puunianiau crater. The leaves are the largest of any of the Hawaiian Geraniums, and are not silvery; the flowers are a purplish-red; the petals are unequal, giving it the appearance of a violet. The name arboreum would have fitted better to *G. multiflorum* var. *canum*, which is, indeed, a small tree, 15 feet in height, with a trunk of about 10 inches in diameter, while the former is a large shrub with drooping, rambling branches. *G. multiflorum* var. *canum* is not uncommon in the crater, but is found especially in Kaupo Gap, where it grows on upheaved *aa* lava, or fissures, together with *Artemisia australis*. *Geranium ovatifolium*, also a shrub, is found on the north bank of Haleakala crater.

Labiatae are not very conspicuous in this region, though a few species of Phyllostegia and Stenogyne are not uncommon. One *St. microphylla* the writer found entangling *Santalum Haleakalae;* the leaves are very small, measuring only about three lines in length; the flowers are very inconspicuous and green. The epacridaceous shrub *Styphelia tameiameia (Pukeawe)* is the most common, while *St. imbricata*, very common on Mauna Kea, is only found near the summit of Haleakala. *Tetramolopium humile* and *T. Chamissonis* var. *arbuscula*, the Hawaiian daisies, occupy cracks between rocks and can also be found in black cinder.

The most interesting discovery, however, made by the writer is a new species

82

of the large tribe Lobelioideae. It is a rather handsome tree, undoubtedly one of the oldest types of Lobelias, and has an almost antediluvian appearance. This striking plant, of which only three trees are now in existence, is a species of Clermontia, and is described in this volume under the name *Clermontia Haleakalensis.* It was found on the inner slopes of Puunianiau crater at the head of one of the numerous small gulches which find their origin in this crater basin. The trees were thickly surrounded by *Rubus hawaiiensis* and *Sophora chrysophylla.* It flowered during the month of October. If not protected from the cattle, which are very fond of the thick, fleshy leaves of this wonderful plant, it also will join the others of its race, as *Cyanea arborea* and *Cyanea comata,* which have vanished forever.

Of Gramineae, or grasses, mention may be made of the following: *Koeleria glomerata,* and var. nov. *rigida* Hack., and the newly-described *Argrostis Rockii* Hack., which was discovered by the writer at an elevation of 9700 feet between rocks near the summit of the mountain. Hackel, who described the plant, says that it is an excellent species and is nearest related to *A. varians,* which, however, is no xerophyte, as is *A. Rockii.*

The vegetative formation of the upper forest zone on Mauna Kea and Mauna Loa has already been described in the chapter on Hawaii. Mention may be made, however, of the introduced, or rather naturalized, flora of this region. *Veronica arvensis* grows as a weed among rocks and on the pasture lands above 6000 feet elevation with *Sonchus oleraceus,* which, by the way, was the last plant observed on Mauna Kea at an elevation of 12,000 feet, where it was prostrate with leaves and flowers closely pressed to the ground, with a long root-stock. *Gnaphalium sandwicensium* and *G. luteo-album* grow side by side in the black cinder and between rocks. One of the most common plants is *Senecio vulgaris,* which can be observed up to an elevation of 10,000 feet and even higher; *Chenopodium album* is often found in its company.

Since the introduction of grass seeds by the ranchmen to improve their pasture lands, many undesirable grasses and weeds have come with them. We find *Poa annua* on the slopes of Mauna Kea together with *Cynodon dactylon, Bromus unioloides,* and *Eragrostis atropioides,* which, however, is a native grass originally found on Haleakala, Maui. Also *Hordeum murinum* var. *leporinum, Lolium multiflorum,* a very tall grass, usually found in company with *Malvastrum tricuspidatum,* which for that part of the district forms a valuable fodder plant, owing to the absence of anything better. *Bromus villosus* occurs here and there in patches, while *Poa pratensis* is found scattered.

The following Cyperaceae occur in this region: *Carex macloviana* on Moano hill, *Carex sandwicensis* scattered over the whole of Mauna Kea, and a new variety of the same about to be published by Rev. G. Kükenthal.

In conclusion, a few words may here not be out of place, describing briefly the floral aspects of Lanai, Niihau and Kahoolawe.

The Island of Lanai is the best forest-covered island of the three last men-

PLATE XXVI.

STAND OF ALEURITES MOLUCCANA (Kukui) at the head of Mauna Lei gorge, Lanai.

tioned. It has an altitude of about 3400 feet. Two main ridges run parallel the length of the island, and are called Lanai hale and Haalelepakai, the former being the highest. On the leeward side of these mountain ranges is a flat plateau consisting of about 24,000 acres, having an elevation of approximately 2000 feet; the southeastern end toward Manele is covered with the cactus *Opuntia tuna (Panini)* exclusively. This plateau must have been once upon a time covered with a xerophytic vegetation similar to that of the Kipuka Puaulu on Hawaii near the Volcano Kilauea.

The main ridges of Lanai are covered with a similar vegetation to that of Molokai above Kamolo, but are not as wet as the latter, though here and there swampy spots can be found in which the newly-described var. *lanaiensis* of *Viola Helena* occurs. Peculiar to these ridges are the thymelaeaceous *Wikstroemia bicornuta*, the lobelioideous *Cyanea Gibsonii*, and the goodeniaceous *Scaevola cylindrocarpa*. The most common composite at the summit ridge is *Dubautia laxa* var. *hirsuta*. One of the rare and interesting compositae, *Hesperomannia arborescens*, of which a few trees were seen about ten years ago, has vanished forever. Xanthoxylum has several species present, and so has also the genus Pittosporum, which on Lanai has the most varying species. That this particular genus is in these islands dependent on insects for fertilization is brought out by these numerous variations. It is difficult to arrange the classification of the various species according to their capsules, as the writer had observed on Lanai not less than three capsules of different species on a single flower cluster.

Araliaceae has several species here, especially the genus *Tetraplasandra*, of which the newly-described *T. Lanaiensis* is peculiar to Lanai; with it occurs *Suttonia Lanaiensis* and *Sideroxylon spathulatum*, the latter a small tree with cone-shaped yellow fruits.

Very interesting is the vegetation in the valleys of Mahana, Koele, and Kaiholena, which is of a xerophytic character. Lobelioideae are here rather scarce, and, as already mentioned, the tribe has only one species peculiar to Lanai.

The extreme western district of Lanai is covered with an interesting mixed or dry forest, mainly composed of *Osmanthus sandwicensis*, *Sideroxylon spathulatum*, *Nothocestrum* sp., *Chrysophyllum polynesicum*, *Suttonia* sp., *Plectronia odorata*, *Gardenia Brighami*, *Bobea Hookeri*, and others.

The land has been very much eroded and portions of this interesting woodland are now buried beneath earth and sand dunes, only the tips of trees protruding through the earth.

The windward side is exceedingly barren and only the xerophytic *Pili* grass, *Andropogon contortus*, grows between the rocks, together with *Waltheria americana*, *Sida fallax*, and, lower down, *Gossypium tomentosum*. The gulches of Mauna Lei and Nahoku are almost barren, the latter very much so. Mauna Lei is exceedingly interesting from a geological standpoint. Vegetation is very scarce and only few trees can be found, as *Erythrina monosperma (Wiliwili)* and some of those already mentioned above. At the very head of this gorge, which near

85

PLATE XXVII.

ERYTHRINA MONOSPERMA (Wiliwili), the only native tree species left on the barren island of Kahoolawe.

the entrance divides into two main valleys, the vegetation becomes more interesting, a few Compositae cling to the rocks, such as Artemisia, and to the writer's surprise, he found the interesting lobelioideous *Brighamia insignis* growing on the vertical cliffs, even inaccessible to the multitude of goats inhabiting this region.

On the bottom, at the very head of the gulch, are huge trees of *Aleurites moluccana (Kukui)* (see Plate XXVI), the trunks of some of which are torn into shreds by huge boulders which are constantly coming down from the heights above, which, when loosened by the goats, bring with them avalanches of rocks to the depths below. Nahoku gulch is the narrowest and steepest, and is void of vegetation, but in the early days enough water came down in the now dried-up streambed for the natives to carry on the cultivation of taro.

The Island of Kahoolawe is the most eroded of the whole group and the only native tree growth which remains is composed of perhaps a dozen *Erythrina monosperma (Wiliwili)*. (See Plate XXVII.) The urticaceous *Neraudia Kahoolawensis*, the only plant thought to be peculiar to Kahoolawe, was found by the writer on the lava fields of Auahi on the southern slopes of Mt. Haleakala, Maui. Most of the land on this island has no soil, all having been blown into the sea by the wind, after it had been robbed of its vegetation by cattle, sheep, and goats, with which the island was overstocked. The result is that there is nothing left but pure hard-pan, several feet thickness of soil having been blown away. Even now on a windy day the island is not visible, as it is enshrouded in a cloud of red dirt which, when the south wind prevails is carried across the isthmus of the Island of Maui, to be deposited on the already fertile sugar cane fields.

The Island of Niihau is in a similar state, though is not as eroded as Kahoolawe. The native vegetation of this small island has, however, disappeared. *Acacia farnesiana* and *Prosopis juliflora (Kiawe* or Algaroba) have been planted on the lowlands.

In this rather lengthy introduction, the writer has tried to give a more or less detailed description of the various interesting botanical regions of this island group. The present paper by no means claims to be the result of an ecological study, but a mere foundation for such work, which undoubtedly will have to follow. The whole of the introduction is devoted to the floral aspects of this interesting island group, and is merely floristic work with here and there an attempt to explain some of the ecological features.

The writer has had occasion, as Botanist of the Board of Agriculture and Forestry and of the College of Hawaii, to visit all the islands of the group, each several times at the various seasons during five years, making a thorough botanical survey of each island, some of the results of which are herewith published.

Note:—All plants mentioned in this introduction as new to science (trees excluded) are briefly described in the appendix. All new trees mentioned are described in their respective places according to the natural system of classification.

EMBRYOPHYTA ASIPHONO-GAMA

CRYPTOGAMIA

Plants not bearing true flowers—that is, having no stamens nor ovules and never producing seeds containing an embryo.

Pteridophyta

FILICES (Ferns)

Sporangia minute, placed on the margin or under-surface of the leaf or frond, rarely somewhat larger and arranged in spikes or panicles. Spores all of one kind.

CYATHEACEAE

The Cyatheaceae are mainly tropical, and are distributed over the old and new world more or less evenly. The family is restricted to localities with a very moist and uniform climate. They are found rarely in areas with a precipitation of less than 100 cm. annually. Against temperature they are more or less independent, as they still thrive prolifically in regions where mild frosts occur, as, for example, in Tasmania. With the appearance of this family in the Stewart Island of New Zealand, it has reached the border land of the Polar region.

CIBOTIUM Kaulf.

Pinonia Gaud., *Dicksoniae* sp. autt., Hk., Bk.

Sori globose at the apex of a vein, marginal, enclosed in a prominent coriaceous, deeply 2-valved involucre, the outer box-shaped valve proceeding from the margin of the segment, but being of different texture. Sporangia stipitate. Annulus with a stomium consisting of thin walled cells, which can easily be distinguished from those of the walls of the sporangium.—Tree ferns with very large leaves, which are usually tripinnate, the last pinnae with linear oblong segments.

The distribution of the six or eight existing species, which seem to be very closely related, is very remarkable. *C. guatemalense* and *C. Wendlandi* occur in Guatemala, as well as *C. Schiedei* in South Mexico and Guatemala, in cultivation for a long time. *C. Barometz* occurs in the monsoon districts of East Asia; another subspecies *(C. Cumingi)* is endemic in the Philippine Islands, while three are peculiar to the Hawaiian Islands.

PLATE 28

CIBOTIUM MENZIESII Hook.
Hapu Iii or Heii.
Showing part of frond with sporecases, and part of the stipe to left; reduced.

Stipes tuberculate, and clothed with long blackish-brown hairs............ **C. Menziesii**
Stipes smooth and glabrous in the upper portion...................... **C. Chamissoi**

Cibotium Menziesii Hook.
Hapu Iii or *Heii.*
(Plates 28, 29.)

CIBOTIUM MENZIESII Hook. Spec. Fil. I. (1846) 84, t. 29 c;—Brack. Fil. U. S. E. E. (1854) 280;—H. Mann. Proc. Am. Acad. VII. (1867) 212;—Hbd. Fl. Haw. Isl. (1888) 546;—Heller in Minnes. Bot. Stud. IX. (1897) 776;—Diels in Engl. et Prantl Pflzfam. I. 4, (1902) 121;—Christens. Index Fil. (1906) 183;—Robinson in Bul. Torr. Bot. Cl. 39, (1912) 243.—**C. pruinatum** Metten et Kuhn in Linnaea, 36, (1869) 150.—**Diksonia Menziesii** Hook. et Bak. Syn. (1866) 49 et II ed. (1874) 49;—Del Cast. Ill. Fl. Ins. Mar. Pac. VII (1892) 356.

Stipes green, stout, with a ventral and two lateral furrows, tuberculate and shaggy at the base with a straightish and long brownish yellow glossy *pulu* which changes higher up into stiff long blackish hair, and as such often covers the entire stipes; frond with stipes 18 to 36 dm or more long and 9 to 15 dm or more broad, pyramidal-oblong, coriaceous, naked underneath or sometimes with minute furfuraceous dots; the rhachis asperous with scattering tubercles; pinnae with a stipe of 25 to 50 mm, oblong, 4.5 to 7.5 dm long, bearing 18 to 24 pairs of free pinnules besides the pinnatifid apex; most pinnules shortly stipitate, linear lanceolate, acute, cut halfway or more, often to the rhachis at the base, into oblong rounded or entire segments, which are separated by broad sinuses; veinlets very prominent, simple or forked; sori 8 to 14 on a lobe, also fringing the sinus. Invol. corneous, large, a little more than 1 mm to nearly 3 mm in width, the outer valve fornicate and large, the inner flat and narrower.

Cibotium Menziesii or *Hapu Iii* of the natives is the most stately tree fern of the Hawaiian forests. Nowhere in the islands does this handsome fern reach such a wonderful development as on Hawaii in the forests of Puna, Hilo, and especially in the Kohala mountains. In the district of Paauhau, on the windward slopes of Mauna Kea (13823 feet) the writer saw the biggest specimens. The fibrous trunks of these immense ferns have often a diameter of three feet and reach a height of about 24 feet or so, not including the almost erect fronds, which measure occasionally more than 12 feet, giving it a total height of sometimes 36 feet. Thanks to the hardiness of these ferns, they were and are able to withstand attacks from cattle, and even when uprooted by wild pigs, and laid prostrate, they continue to grow.

Nothing is more beautiful than a stand of pure *Ohia* forest with trees of about 80 feet in height, when growing together with this beautiful fern, which forms the dense undergrowth. Their bright-green fronds produce a pleasing contrast to the rather grayish *Ohia lehua* trees, which contrast is enhanced when the latter are displaying their beautiful red blossoms. Such a forest, when not in the vicinity of human dwellings, is inhabited by native birds of all colors, red (the *Iiwi*), however, predominating. These birds feed on the pollen of the *Ohia* flowers, and can be seen in great numbers, often sitting on the bright-green fronds of the majestic tree ferns.

The *Hapu Iii* occurs, however, on all the islands at an elevation of from 2000 to 6000 feet and perhaps higher. Ordinarily the trunks are not taller than 8 feet or so, but, as already mentioned, the fern reaches its best development on

PLATE 29.

CIBOTIUM MENZIESII Hook.
Hapu Iii Fern.
Growing in the forests of Kohala, Hawaii; elevation 4000 feet.

Cyatheaceae.

the Island of Hawaii. The wool or *pulu* of this fern, as well as of the two other species, was used in stuffing pillows, etc., and the trees were ruthlessly cut down by the *pulu* gatherers in order to get easily at the wool. Since the *pulu* is no longer in demand and as hardly any is being gathered at present, the ferns have begun to thrive again, and fine specimens can be met with in all the Hawaiian rain forests.

It might be of interest to remark that the *Ohia lehua (Metrosideros polymorpha)* is a close associate of the *Hapu Iii.* Both the fern and the tree are often found growing together to such an extent that it is difficult to distinguish the tree trunk from the trunk of the fern.

The natives have an idea that the *Hapu Iii* fern is the mother of the *Ohia lehua.*

The seeds of the *Ohia lehua* often germinate in the crowns of the tree ferns, sending down their roots along the very fibrous, often water-soaked trunk. In time the fern begins to die and the *Ohia lehua* is left standing with stilt roots of often 15 feet or more in height, after which the real trunk of the tree commences. Such examples are very numerous in the Hawaiian forests, and undoubtedly led the Hawaiians to the belief that the tree fern is the parent of the *Ohia lehua.*

Cibotium Chamissoi Kaulf.
Hapu.
(Plate 30.)

CIBOTIUM CHAMISSOI Kaulf. Enum. Fil. (1824) 230, t. 1, f. 14;—Spreng. syst. IV. (1827) 127;—Presl Tentam. Pterid. (1836) 69, t. 11, f. 8;— Endl. Fl. Suds. (1836) no. 512;—Hook. Spec. Fil. I. (1846) 83;—Brack. Fil. U. S. E. E. (1854) 279;—Moore Ind. Fil. (1857-62) 259;—H. Mann. Proc. Am. Acad. VII (1867) 212;—Hbd. Fl. Haw. Isl. (1888) 547;—Christ Farnkr. (1897) 316;—Heller in Minnes. Bot. Stud. I. (1897) 776;—Diels in Engl. et Prantl. Pflzfam. I. 4 (1902) 121;—Christens. Ind. Fil. (1906) 183;—Robinson in Bull. Torr. Bot. Cl. 39 (1912) 243.—**C. pruinatum** Mett. et Kuhn in Linnaea 36 (1869) 150.—**Dicksonia Chamissoi** Hook. et Bak. Synops. Fil. (1866) 50, et II. ed. (1874) 50;—Hook. Icon. Plant. XVII (1886) pl. 1603.—**C. Chamissoni** Del Cast. Ill. Fl. Ins. Mar. Pacif. VII (1892) 356.—**Pinonia splendens** Gaud. Ann. Sci. Nat. III (1824) 507, idem Gen. p. 96, et Bot. Voy. Uranie (1826 title page, appeared 1830) 370, t. 21.—**Dicksonia splendens** Desv. Prodr. (1827) 318.—**Dicksonia**, Smith ex R. Brown.

Stipes 12 to 24 dm, brownish, smooth, clothed at the base with a pale fawn-colored lustreless matted or cobwebby pulu, furfuraceous or naked above; frond 12 to 24 dm long, chartaceous, the under face green or dull glaucous and generally covered with a pale cobwebby pubescence; lowest pinnae 4.5 to 7.5 dm long, with 24 to 28 pairs of pinnules, these shortly stipitate, linear lanceolate 12.5 to 15 cm by 16 to 20 mm, acute, the lower ones cut to near the rhachis into oblong, straightish, rather obtuse segments with narrow sinuses, the basal segments entire and not deflected; veinlets little prominent; sori 8 to 14 to a segment, the involucre small about 1 mm wide, chartaceous.

The *Hapu*, which is of much smaller stature than its congener, the *Hapu Iii* or *Heii.* is one of the most common tree ferns of the group. It occasionally has a trunk of 16 or more feet in height, but never reaches the size of *Cibotium Menziesii.* Both are, however, found growing together and are most numerous on Hawaii, especially in the forests of Puna and back of Hilo. Near the Volcano House pure stands of these two species can be found, usually associated with

93

PLATE 30.

QIBOTIUM CHAMISSOI Kaulf.
Hapu.
Showing fruiting pinnae of frond and pulu to right

Cyatheaceae.

Metrosideros polymorpha or *Ohia lehua* of the natives. Where these ferns grow with a typical *Ohia lehua* forest, the soil is usually not deeper than 2 or 3 feet at the most, below which we find the arched *pahoehoe* lava.

The *Ohia lehua* is, however, not their only associate. In the older forests we find them growing together with *Cheirodendron Gaudichaudii* (*Olapa*), *Ilex sandwicensis*, *Perrottetia sandwicensis* (*Olomea*), and especially with *Suttonia Lessertiana* (*Kolea*). In the drier or semi-wet forest we find it again with *Acacia Koa* (*Koa*), while it can also be met with in a typical xerophytic forest, but then only at an elevation of 4000 feet or so, and not at all common. Only a few stragglers can be found scattered in these interesting dry regions. On Oahu the *Hapu* is much smaller than on Hawaii and not quite as common, as it never forms pure stands or covers large tracts of land as is the case on Hawaii.

On the Island of Kauai occurs a variety of this species named var. *β.* by Hillebrand, which differs from the species in its smaller frond, which is dull glaucous underneath.

The young stems of this species are farinaceous, and used to be eaten by the natives in times of scarcity. They are baked in hot ashes and are then quite palatable.

The trunks of the *Hapu*, as well as of the *Hapu Iii*, are used for forest trails, where they make an excellent pathway through the otherwise hardly-penetrable swampy jungles. Portions of trunks, when used for fern trails, sprout usually at one end, forming quite a handsome hedge of young fronds. The *pulu* wool, which densely covers the base of the leafstalks, is glossy and of a fine, silky texture, and was used together with that of the *Hapu Iii* for stuffing pillows and mattresses, and formed a regular article of export to California. According to Hillebrand, the hairs consist of a single series of flat, thin-walled cells which break readily at the joints. The cells are shorter in *Cibotium Chamissoi*.

Cibotium glaucum is occasionally found with the other two species, but is rather rare. All three species are peculiar to the Hawaiian Islands, outside of which they have not been recorded.

EMBRYOPHYTA SIPHONOGAMA

Angiospermae

MONOCOTYLEDONEAE

Embryo with only one cotyledon.   Stem consisting of bundles of vascular fibres.

PANDANACEAE

The family Pandanaceae is peculiar to the tropical regions of the old world, and is represented in America by the Cyclanthaceae.   The Pandanaceae are especially rich in the Malayan region, in Micronesia, in Madagascar, Bourbon (Reunion) and Mauritius.   Little is known about the distribution of this family in West Africa.   The Pandanaceae are related to the Palms and Araceae.

Here in Hawaii we have two species of two different genera which belong to this family.   One is the well-known *Hala* or *Puhala (Pandanus odoratissimus)* and the other, the climber *Freycinetia Arnotti* or *Ie ie.*   Only the former is here considered, being the only arborescent representative of this family.

PANDANUS L.

Erect trees or shrubs with simple or variously branched stems, mostly with aerial roots.   Never climbers.   Inflorescence often of immense size.

The genus Pandanus, with its many species, is so far little known, owing to its dioecious character.   In Hawaii there is only one species represented, which is however not peculiar to the islands, as it extends from Hawaii to the Seychelle Islands and Arabia.

In German New Guinea eleven species have been found so far, six of which are endemic.

Pandanus odoratissimus L. has been sunk by Warburg and made a synonym of *P. tectorius;* which he records as occurring in "Hawai."   On the same page he creates a variety γ. *sandvicensis* from the Sandwich Islands.   Prof. Warburg evidently regards Hawai and the Sandwich Islands as two different groups, and it is possible that his variety came from the higher levels, whence, of course, it would differ somewhat from the tree found on the shores, where they are exposed to the salt air; while the higher altitude (1800 feet), larger precipitation, wind, etc., would undoubtedly cause some differentiation, which would not, however, warrant the creation of a new variety.   On the strength of this, the name *Pandanus odoratissimus* is here retained.   The genus consists of about 156 species.

Pandanaceae.

Pandanus odoratissimus L.

Hala, Puhala, Lauhala, or Screw-pine.

(Plate 31.)

PANDANUS ODORATISSIMUS L. f. Suppl. (1781) 424;—Forst. Pl. escul. (1786) 38, et Prodr. (1786) no. 368;—Endl. Fl. Suds. (1836) no. 738;—Guillem., Zeph. Tait. (1837) No. 136;—Jardin, Hist. Nat. Iles Marqu., (1858) 27;—Pancher in Cuzent, Tahiti (1860) 241;— Nadeaud, Enum. (1873) 286;—Hbd. Fl. Haw. Isl. (1888) 453;—Del Cast. Ill. Fl. Ins. Mar. Pacif. VII. (1892) 324, et Fl. Polyn. Franc. (1893) 232.—**Pandanus verus** Rumph. Herb. amb. IV. (1744) 140 t. 74;—H. Mann Proc. Am. Acad. VII (1867) 204;—Seem. Fl. Vit. (1873) 281;—Wawra in Flora (1875) 245.—**Pandanus tectorius** Sol. Prin. Fl. Ins. Pacif. Ined. 350;—Parkins Draw. Tahiti Pl. 113 (ined.);—Warburg, Pflzreich. IV. 9 (1900) 46, fig. 13 F. et var. **sandvicensis** Warburg l. c. p. 48.

Leaves crowded at the ends of the branches, abruptly narrowing toward the apex into a long acumen (point); prickly at the margins and keeled midrib, coriaceous; spadix of male flowers compound pendulous, spikes sessile, supported by very odoriferous spathes; stamens racemosely fasciculated, the filaments shorter than the column, anthers linear, long mucronate; syncarpium surrounded by 3 sets of white imbricate leaf-like bracts, erect, globose, of the size of a child's head when mature, about 50 to 80 drupes in a syncarpium, reddish when mature, each about 4 to 10 cm long, 2 to 6 cm broad, angular, composed of 5 to 12 carpels, the flat top divided by shallow grooves into as many spaces as there are carpels; the sessile stigmas at first oblique but finally apical, uniform.

The *Puhala* or *Hala* is a small tree reaching the height of 15 to 20 feet. The trunk is short and branches in a dichotomous manner, having many aerial roots above the base and also from the branches. The bark is whitish and covered with prickly lenticels. In the female tree the outer cortex is exceedingly hard, while the inner pith is very fibrous and soft. In the male mature tree, however, the trunk is more or less solid throughout. The male flowers, which are called by the natives *Hinano Hala,* are very fragrant, and are pendulous from the center of the leaf-whorls; the spadix of the female flowers is solitary, globose, and reaches the size of a child's head when mature, and is orange-colored to red. The leaves, which are prickly at the margins, are arranged like a corkscrew, from which the tree derives its name.

The *Puhala* is most common on the windward sides of all the islands, inhabiting the lowlands from sea-level up to 2000 feet. It is most common on the coast of Puna, Hawaii, and also on the northern slope of Haleakala, Maui, where, on the flat plateau above the cliffs between Keanae, Nahiku and Hana, it forms a thick forest exclusive of everything else. It is the landmark of the lower levels, and is often found with the *Kukui* and the *Koa* on Oahu.

Many, indeed, are the uses of the *Puhala.* From the leaves handsome mats are made, while the wood of male trees, which is of exquisite beauty and exceedingly hard, was employed for many purposes.

The orange-colored seeds are strung into leis together with the fragrant leaves of the *Maile (Gynopogon oliviformis* Gaud.) and worn by men and women alike. The seeds, after having become dry, were used as brushes, and with the fibrous end the various dyes were applied onto their *tapa* or cloth. In

PLATE 31.

PANDANUS ODORATISSIMUS L.
Puhala.
A Pandanus forest at the lower zone on East Maui.

Pandanaceae.

Mauritius, where the tree is plentiful, the fiber derived from the leaves is used for making sacks for coffee, sugar and grain; the roots are also fibrous and are used by basket makers as binding material. An oil is obtained by distilling the fragrant bracts of the male flowers and is called *Keora* in India.

The natives of Burma make matting sails, by sewing together the leaves of the *Hala*; the very fragrant male flowers are used as hair decorations. The etheric oil expressed from the flowers is used as a stimulant, and is also applied as a remedy for headaches and rheumatism. The seeds are used in India as spools for twine.

The wood of the female trees is often used, after the removal of the fibrous pith, as water pipes on the richly-wooded volcanic islands of South Polynesia. The native name in Tahiti is *Fara*, in Viti or Fiji *Balawa* and *Vadra*.

The *Puhala* or *Lauhala* is distributed from the Seychelle Islands to Arabia, all over the South Sea Islands, to Guam and India. It is called *Aggag* in Guam, *Pandan* or *Sabotan* in the Philippines, and *Fala* or *Laufala* in Samoa.

In India, where the tree is cultivated, female trees are a rare occurrence, while male trees are common; this is just the reverse in the Hawaiian Islands.

PALMAE

The family Palmae is characteristic of the tropics. It is distributed over the old as well as the new world, and finds its northern boundary in the south of Spain, South Italy and Greece to the southern part of Asia Minor, and from there to the Himalayas, South China and to the most southern part of Japan. In the new world it is distributed from Southern California to Arizona and Mexico. The southern boundary of the Palms of the old world describes a circle through the arid interior of Africa to Madagascar, Australia, the South Island of New Zealand and through the Pacific Islands, including Hawaii. In equatorial Africa the family is poorer in species, but becomes richer in the West Indies, Central and South Brazil.

This order consists of about 1000 species. Of interest, so far as Hawaii is concerned, is the Pacific genus Pritchardia, which is represented in the Hawaiian Islands by ten species. *Cocos nucifera*, the *Niu* of the natives or coconut of the foreigner, is, of course, also present, but is too common to be described or otherwise mentioned.

The most interesting species are the native Pritchardias or *Loulu* Palms, all of which are endemic and found only at an elevation of about 2000–3000 feet, in the wet or rain forest zone, though occasionally *Pr. Gaudichaudii* occurs near the beach and often at 1000 feet elevation.

PRITCHARDIA Seem. et H. Wendl.

Flowers hermaphrodite, singly on the branches of the panicle; stamens 6, connate at the base into a cup; ovary three-lobed with a single style, the latter tri-sulcate with 3 minute stigmas. Drupe dryish, with a single nut or coccus, the pericarp thin fibrous, the endocarp crustaceous. Seeds with uniform albumen, and embryo at the base.—Tall trees with terminal, fan-shaped palmatisect leaves, and unarmed petioles.

99

Palmae.

Here in Hawaii only 2 species of Pritchardia were formerly known to exist, namely: *Pr. Gaudichaudii* and *Pr. Martii*. O. Beccari, the world's authority on Palms, described three species since the publication of Hillebrand's Flora, based on the latter's herbarium material.

In the month of February, 1909, the writer discovered an interesting species, with very small olive-shaped, black, shining fruits, which was named by Beccari and published in Webbia Vol. III. 137 as *Pr. minor*. Since then the writer has carried on extensive explorations on all the Islands of the group under the auspices of the Board of Agriculture and Forestry, as well as under the College of Hawaii, with the result of bringing to light new plants of many families, among which the Palmae were represented by four new species, as follows, the first discovered by G. P. Wilder: *Pr. eriophora* Becc., from Halemanu, Kauai; *Pr. arecina* Becc., from Honomanu, Maui; *Pr. Rockiana* Becc., from the Punaluu Mts., Oahu; and *Pr. eriostachia*, from the slopes of Mauna Loa, Hawaii. This brings the species of Hawaiian Pritchardia up to ten. As O. Beccari remarks in a letter to the writer, he believes that other species of Pritchardia yet remain to be discovered in these Islands, to which the writer cannot but agree.

The writer has held back the manuscript on the Palms, as he had hoped to receive Beccari's publication of the above-mentioned new species in Webbia Vol. IV, as was promised by him. In fact, the writer cabled to Beccari in Florence, Italy, for prompt despatch of the publication, but no answer has been received. It is, however, hoped that the publication has been issued before this book appears off the press.

In order to have this book on the native trees as complete as possible, it was thought advisable to include all the species of palms so far known to be natives of Hawaii, and brief descriptions are given of the new ones by the writer, giving O. Beccari credit as the author of the new species.

In regard to the usefulness of the *Loulu* palms, it may be stated that excellent hats are made from the young fronds by the natives. This, however, has caused much havoc; the present generation, being more or less afflicted with the hookworm, finds it easier to cut the palms down rather than climb them for the single young frond necessary for a hat. The Japanese have imitated the natives, and consequently many beautiful trees are being destroyed.

The genus Pritchardia, which consists of about 14 species, is represented in Hawaii by 10 species. Of the remaining four, two belong to Fiji (*Pr. pacifica*, also cultivated in Honolulu, and *Pr. Thurstonii*) and two to the Dangerous Archipelago, on the Island of Pomotu.

Pritchardia Gaudichaudii H. Wendl.

Loulu.

PRITCHARDIA GAUDICHAUDII H. Wendl. in Bonpl. X (1862) 199;—Seem. Fl. Vit. (1868) 274;—H. Mann in Journ. of Bot. VII. (1869) 177;—O. Beccari in Malesia III. (1889) 295. tab. XXXVIII. fig. 11-13.—**P. Martii** (non H. Wendl.) Hillebr. Fl. Haw. Isl. (1888) 450 (pro max. parte).—**Livistona** (?) **Gaudichaudii** Martius

Hist. Nat. Palm. III. (1836-50) 242 et 319.—**Washingtonia Gaudichaudii** O.
Ktze. Rev. Gen. Pl. II. (1891) 737.—**Eupritchardia Gaudichaudii** O. Ktze. Rev.
Gen. Pl. III. 2. (1898) 323.

Candex of medium height 1.5 to 2 m; 30 cm in diameter; young fronds squamose underneath, small, narrow lanceolate, attenuate on both ends, with scattered silvery pubescence,
with about 20 or more segments connate to the middle; spadices about 1 m, spathes with
a scattered glaucous scaliness, sheathed, panicles rather short, erect; branchlets sinuous,
glabrous; flowers alternately distichous, calyx tubular-campanulate, sharply 3-dentate, outside conspicuously striate-nervate; fruits large spherical, 4 cm and more in diameter, the
very minute subsymmetrically apiculate style deciduous from the carpels, pericarp fibrous-
grumose, 3 to 4 mm thick, endocarp osseous, 1 mm; seeds globose, embryo subbasal.

This species was discovered by Gaudichaud, probably on Oahu. The above
description is a translation of Beccari's Latin description as published in Malesia, and is based on the original material. He says, ''For the description of
the floriferous spadix Hillebrand's specimens served me, and as I have said, referred *Pr. Martii* of Hillebrand to *Pr. Gaudichaudii*. The fruits which I at-
tribute to *Pr. Gaudichaudii* and are here described were communicated to me
from Kew, and were collected by Stephen Spencer in the year 1884 on the small
island off Molokai (a small rock supposedly cast off from the face of Waikolu
cliff, Molokai, where also trees of Hillebrand's second species grow, by him referred to *Pr. Martii*).''

He then describes in detail specimens in the various Herbaria, as fronds to
be found in the Herbarium Webb at Florence, etc. Suffice it to say, the writer,
according to Beccari, to whom all the palm material was submitted, has not as
yet collected *Pr. Gaudichaudii* in a wild state, though specimens are cultivated
in Honolulu.

Pritchardia Martii H. Wendl.

Loulu.

PRITCHARDIA MARTII H. Wendl. in Bonplandia X. (1862) 199;—Seem. Fl. Vit. (1868)
274; H. Mann in Journ. of Bot. VII. (1869) 177;—Hlbd. Fl. Haw. Isl. (1888) 451
(tantum quoad Spec. Lydg. e Niu?).—O. Beccari in Malesia III. (1889) 297 tab.
XXXVIII. fig. 14, 15.—**Livistona** (?) **Martii** Gaud. Bot. Voy. Bon. (1844-52) t.
58-59;—Mart. Nat. Palm. III. (1836-50) 242 et 319.—**Washingtonia Martii** O. Ktze.
Rev. Gen. Pl. III. 2. (1898) 323.

Trunk of medium height. Petioles unarmed, ligule rotundate, leaf pluri-radiate, suborbicular, with 40 segments connate not quite to the middle, coriaceous, intermediate
threads to 1/3 bifid, densely covered underneath with a griseous-furfuraceous tomentum;
fruit elliptical, the albumen in the ventral part not ruminate, testa only thickened; fruit
of the size of an ordinary plum with the residuous stigmas at the acute vertex, glabrous;
fruit-flesh about 4 mm thick; seeds globose-elliptical, testa dusky, shining, thicker in the
part in which the embryo is imbedded; embryo subbasal, the small wart produced, conical,
2 mm long.

Gaudichaud has not indicated the precise location where he collected this
species, but it is believed to have come from Oahu. Beccari says that he himself has correctly referred to *Pr. Martii* the specimens often cited by Lydgate;
this species can be found growing at Cape Niu. He continues, ''*Pritchardia
Martii* is in all probability very close to *Pr. Gaudichaudii*, but can be distinguished from the latter above all in the elliptical fruits and not globose ones,

PLATE 32.

PRITCHARDIA LANIGERA Becc.
Loulu Palm.
Growing in the mountains of Kohala, Hawaii; elevation 3000 feet.

Palmae.

in the larger dimension of all parts, in the calyx which is more distinctly campanulate, and in the style which surpasses the urceolate androphore. The flowers are a little larger, very attenuate at the base and broader at the mouth, striate-nervose."

The writer has never collected the typical *Pr. Martii*, which undoubtedly occurs on Oahu. In the Punaluu Mts., Oahu, quite a number of native palms occur, some of which may have to be referred to this species.

Pritchardia lanigera Becc.
Loulu.
(Plate 32.)

PRITCHARDIA LANIGERA Becc. in Malesia III. (1889) 298. tab. XXXVIII. fig. 1-3.—
Pr. Gaudichaudii (non H. Wendl.) Hbd. Fl. Haw. Isl. (1888) 450 ex parte.—**Washingtonia lanigera** O. Ktze. Rev. Gen. Pl. II. (1891) 737.—**Eupritchardia lanigera** O. Ktze. Rev. Pl. III. 2. (1898) 323.

Spadix long pedunculate, spathes 7 to 8, broadly lanceolate-oblong with auriculate, densely silvery-woolly clasping sheath, rhachys lanate, panicles short compact, ovate-thyrsoideous (12 to 15 cm long) branchlets densely woolly to pilose, erect-spreading, short; flowers somewhat large, calyx ovate, urceolate, rounded at the base, not striate outside, apex crowned by 3 rather short ciliate teeth; corolla-lobes not striate, coriaceous; the urceolate androphore as long as the calyx, filaments subulate, erect after the expansion of the flower; fruits oblong (rather large?).

This species occurs on the Island of Hawaii and was collected first by Mr. J. Lydgate. It was again collected in the type locality by the writer in the Kohala Mountains above Awini at an elevation of 3000 feet in the dense tropical rain forest. It was in flower only, so that the mature fruits remain still undescribed.

Beccari says: "A very distinct species, and uncomprehensible how Hillebrand could confuse it with *Pr. Gaudichaudii*." He states that fruits (as described above) were attached to the sheet in a separate envelope; he, however, believes for some reason that they do not belong to *Pr. lanigera*, and it is therefore wise to restrict the specific distinction to the floriferous spadix. Specimens of this species, together with other palm material, were forward to O. Beccari, who pronounced No. 8820 in the College of Hawaii Herbarium the typical *Pritchardia lanigera*.

Pritchardia Hillebrandi Becc.
Loulu.

PRITCHARDIA HILLEBRANDI Becc. in Malesia III. (1889) 292 tab. XXXVIII fig. 4-10.—**Pr. Gaudichaudii** (non H. Wendl.) Hbd. Fl. Haw. Isl. (1888) 450 (excl. specim. e Kohala ridge et e Bird Island).—**Washingtonia Hillebrandi** O. Ktze. Rev. Gen. Pl. II. (1891) 737.—**Eupritchardia Hillebrandi** O. Ktze. Rev. Gen. P. III. 2. (1898) 323.

Caudex 6 to 7 m high, 30 cm in diameter; petiole 60 to 90 cm long, limb suborbicular 1 m to 1.3 m in diameter, woolly-furfuraceous underneath to one-third divided into 60 acute bifid segments; spadices 50 to 60 cm long; panicle glabrous, diffuse, thyrsoid-ovate, inferior branches simple or divided into 7 to 8 furcate branchlets, superior ones simple; flowers oblong, apiculate; calyx cylindrical tubular or subcampanulately-dilated at the apex, truncate at the base, not striate-nervose outside, the urceolate androphore shortly exserted, filaments erect or spreading; fruits globose-ovate, symmetrical, 20 to 22 mm long, 17 to 18 mm wide, seeds globose, 11 to 12 mm in diameter. (Descript. ex Becc.)

Palmae.

Beccari in his notes following the description says*: "According to Hille-brand this palm seems to appear to grow spontaneously in the Hawaiian Islands upon cliffs of the northern coast of Molokai, but is also frequently cultivated on the other islands. (Native name *Loulu lelo.*)"

He continues as follows: "I have not seen fronds which could be referred with certainty to this species. Therefore their characters, as well as relative indications of the trunk, I have taken from Hillebrand's description.

"The spadices examined by me measure all together 55 cm, of which 23 cm fall to the peduncle, but of this, probably there is a small portion missing; the one at hand is slightly compressed and fugaciously pubescent. The panicle is rather diffuse, as a whole ovate—thyrsoid, a little unilaterally incurved. Of the spathes there ought to be five (Hillebr.), but of the mentioned specimen the first portion of the peduncular part is missing."

This species was not collected by the writer, but numerous palms were ob-served growing on the cliffs of Wailau, Molokai, near the sea, which probably belong to this species.

Pritchardia remota Becc.

Loulu.

PRITCHARDIA REMOTA Becc. in Malesia III. (1889) 294.—**Pr. Gaudichaudii** (non H. Wendl). Hillebr. Fl. Haw. Isl. (1888) 450 (partim).—**Washingtonia remota** O. Ktze. Rev. Gen. Pl. II. (1891) 737.—**Eupritchardia remota** O. Ktze. Rev. Gen. Pl. III. 2. (1898) 323.

Spadix more ample than in Pr. Gaudichaudii, inferior branches divided into numerous simple subspirally disposed sinuous branchlets, calyx sharply 3-dentate.

Hillebrand writes (p. 451) that this palm covers a part of Bird Island, a small volcanic rock 400 miles N. E. of Kauai, and also writes that seeds were brought to Honolulu in the year 1858 by the late Dr. Rooke, and that the palm is supposed to grow in the Palace court.

Beccari says that the above description was drawn from a floriferous spadix sent to Kew by Hillebrand.

This palm is not known to the writer, but on Laysan Island Prof. Bryan saw a single palm with a short trunk which is probably Beccari's *Pr. remota.*

Pritchardia minor Becc.

Loulu.

PRITCHARDIA MINOR Beccari Webbia III. (1910) 137.

Under the above name, O. Beccari published a species of Pritchardia which was collected by the writer back of Halemanu in the swampy forest near Alakai swamp. Only mature fruits were collected by the writer, as the palm was then not in flower and only a single panicle with old fruits had remained on the tree. The seeds were taken to Honolulu and were sent to Dr. Francesci of

---

* Translated from the original.

Palmae.

Santa Barbara, California, by the Government Nurseryman of the Board of Agriculture and Forestry, without the knowledge of the writer. Dr. Francesci forwarded the seeds to O. Beccari, on which the above species was based; from where and whom Beccari received the description of flowers, leaves, etc., is a mystery, as no one but the writer had ever collected that species and only the seeds at that. The description as given in Webbia III, pl. 137, is therefore apocryphal and entirely unreliable.

Mr. Gerrit P. Wilder, while on an excursion to Halemanu, Kauai, was requested by the writer again to collect *Pr. minor*, as flowers, leaves, etc., were wanted. On May 11th Mr. Wilder sent a box of specimens of a palm, which was, however, not the desired *Pr. minor*, but a new species named since by Beccari *Pr. eriophora* sp. nov. The *Pr. minor* was again collected by the writer on Kauai in the forests of Kaholuamano in October, 1911, differing, however, somewhat from the one found at Halemanu. The palm from the latter place has a slender stem and is quite tall, 20-30 feet in height, with a trunk of about 10 cm in diameter; the leaves are small and pubescent or woolly underneath; the fruits are of the size of a small, black, ripe olive, and are covered with a black glossy pericarp. The specimens from Kaholuamano agree well with the writer's notes of the palm from Halemanu, with the exception of its general appearance; the trunk is shorter and thicker and the whole palm has not the slender aspect of that from Halemanu. No type exists of *Pr. minor*, except the seeds now in Beccari's possession.

Pritchardia eriophora Becc.
Loulu.

PRITCHARDIA ERIOPHORA Becc. in Webbia IV. p. †

A tall slender palm 12 m or more high with a slender trunk; leaves small on short petioles which are densely covered with a matted light brown wool; spadices short; panicles short, the branches almost hidden by the thick matted wool which unites the branchlets almost into a compact mass as if covered with cotton; fruits very small, 12 to 15 mm long, 8 to 10 mm wide, black, shining.

This species was discovered by Mr. Gerrit P. Wilder in the forest-swamps of Halemanu, Kauai, and specimens were sent to the writer by him in May, 1911. It is an exceedingly interesting species and quite unique among Hawaiian Pritchardias. It is, however, close to *Pr. minor*, from the same island. None of the palms so far found on Kauai have as large fruits as those found on the other islands of the Hawaiian group, another incident showing the great difference of species on Kauai from those of the geologically younger islands. The co-type is no. 8846 in the College of Hawaii Herbarium.

Pritchardia Rockiana Becc.
Loulu.

PRITCHARDIA ROCKIANA Becc. in Webbia IV. p. †

A small tree 5 m high, trunk 3 dm in diameter, and of a gray color; leaves large, glabrous above but furfuraceous and lighter colored underneath; panicle open and spreading, freely branching, subglabrous; fruits large, obovate.

105

PLATE 33.

PRITCHARDIA ERIOSTACHIA Becc.
Loulu Palm.
Showing flowering and fruiting spadices, and parts of leaf; reduced.

Palmae.

Specimens of this species were collected by the writer in the Punaluu Mts., Oahu, in August, 1911, and were sent to O. Beccari, together with other specimens of Pritchardia from various islands of the Hawaiian group, all of which proved to be new, including the species in question. The co-type is no. 8822 in the College of Hawaii Herbarium. It grows in the rain forests of the Koolau range, Punaluu, at an elevation of 2500 feet. All four species are here only very briefly described: for complete descriptions see Webbia Vol. IV.

Pritchardia eriostachia Becc.

Loulu.

(Plate 33.)

PRITCHARDIA ERIOSTACHIA Becc. in Webbia IV. p. 1

A small tree 6 to 7 m high, with a gray smooth trunk of 15 to 20 cm in diameter, petioles of leaves 6.5 to 10 dm long, spadices over 1 m long, covered, as are the panicles and spathes, with a dense salmon-colored wool; panicles very small, few branched; fruits elliptical-obovate, about 4 cm long.

This exceedingly interesting species was also discovered by the writer. It occurs on the southern slopes of the active volcano Mauna Loa on Hawaii, in the dense rain forests of Naalehu, district of Kau, at an elevation of 3000 feet.

Pritchardia arecina Becc.

Loulu.

PRITCHARDIA ARECINA Becc. in Webbia IV. p. 1

A tall palm 10 m or more high, with a trunk of about 25 cm in diameter, bark somewhat longitudinally furrowed; leaves very large on long stout broad woolly petioles; spadices over 1 m long, woolly, panicle short, few-branched, furfuraceous; fruits large, ovate or obovate, 5 cm or more long.

Only two clumps of this species, which was discovered by the writer, were found on the northern slopes of Mt. Haleakala in the dense swampy forest above Honomanu gorge, at an elevation of 3000 feet. One single tall specimen was also observed above Nahiku on the same mountain at 4000 feet elevation along a stream bed. It is one of the largest species next to *Pr. lanigera*, of the Kohala Mts., Hawaii. Co-type in the College of Hawaii Herbarium no. 8821.

PLATE 34.

DRACAENA AUREA Mann.
Halapepe.
A flowering branch, much reduced.

LILIACEAE.

The family Liliaceae consists of about 2450 species, and is distributed all over the tropics of both the old and new world and also in the temperate zone. Hawaii is extremely poor in Liliaceae, as only 5 genera with 8 species can be found. Of interest here is the arborescent genus *Dracaena*, which is represented in these islands by a single species.

DRACAENA Vandelli.

Perianth whitish or golden. Ovules ascending, single in each cell of the ovary. Stigma entire, or scarcely divided, style filiform. Berry 3 to 1 seeded, with large globose seeds which are entire, whitish or black to brown. Trees or shrubs without stolons. Leaves linear lanceolate. Inflorescence a terminal foliaceous panicle.

The genus Dracaena consists of about 50 species, distributed over the warmer regions of the old world. Only one species, *Dracaena aurea* (*Halapepe*) is found in these islands, outside of which it has not been recorded. In fact, *Dracaena aurea* is the only representative of this genus in Polynesia.

Dracaena aurea H. Mann.
(Plates 34, 35, 36.)
Halapepe.

DRACAENA AUREA H. Mann Proc. Am. Acad. VII (1867) 207;—Wawra in Flora (1875) 244;—Hbd. Fl. Haw. Isl. (1888) 443;—Del. Cast. Ill. Fl. Ins. Mar. Pac. VII (1892) 318;—Heller Pl. Haw. Isl. (1897) 806. Draco aurea O. Ktze. Rev. Gen. Pl. II (1891) 710.

Leaves sessile, linear ensiform, with entire margins, acuminate at the apex, broad at the base, without midrib; panicles terminal, recurved, pendulous, about 6 dm long, foliose bracteate, flowers single or 2 or 3 together on slender pedicels; perianth tubular, golden yellow, divided to one-third into linear-lanceolate erect lobes; stamens inserted at the base of the lobes and of the same length as the latter; style shortly exserted; berry bright red globose, brownish when dry, 8 to 16 mm in diameter; seed generally single, globose.

The *Halapepe* reaches a height of 25 to 35 feet or even more in certain localities, and has a straight trunk of 1 to 3 feet in diameter,and is freely branching. The branches, which are densely ridged with leaf-scars, are erect and stiff, bearing at their ends a whorl of long linear sword-shaped leaves.

The *Halapepe* is a xerophyte; that is, a dry district loving tree or plant. It is especially common on the *aa* (rough) lava fields on all the islands of the group, and is usually to be found at an elevation of from 1000 to 2000 feet. The golden yellow flowers, which are arranged in long drooping terminal panicles, appear in the early spring in the drier localities, while it often flowers during the summer months in districts with more rainfall.

The *Halapepe* is very common in North and South Kona, Hawaii, as well as in Kau, in the district Hilea. On the Kula slopes of Maui there once existed a forest of this tree, the remnants of which can still be seen. While the tree is very common on the other islands, it is rather scarce on Oahu, and not quite as plentiful on Molokai as on Kauai, where it forms almost pure stands at the bottom of the cliffs below Kaholuamano, near Waimea.

PLATE 35.

DRACAENA AUREA Mann.
Halapepe.
A fruiting branch; reduced.

PLATE 36.

DRACAENA AUREA Mann.
Halapepe Tree.
Growing on the lava fields of Kapua, South Kona, Hawaii; elevation 2000 feet.

Liliaceae.

On the lava fields of Auahi, on the southern slope of Haleakala, the tree is most numerous, but differs in many regards from the specimens found in the forest of Makawao on the same mountain. The leaves of the Auahi specimens are much smaller and more graceful.

The wood of the *Halapepe* is white, with reddish streaks, and is extremely soft. On account of its softness it was used by the natives for carving their idols. Certain gods, however, were carved, each from a particular wood, like the goddess Laka, who was represented on the altar by a large block of wood of the *Lama (Maba sandwicensis)* tree.

The branches of the *Halapepe* were used by the natives in decorating the *kuahu* or altar of the goddess Laka, which was erected in the *halau* or hall in which the *hula* dances were performed, Laka having been the patron of the sacred *Hula.*

Much of interest in regard to the decoration of the *Halau* and *Kuahu* can be found in Dr. N. B. Emerson's book, "Unwritten Literature of Hawaii."

DICOTYLEDONEAE.
ULMACEAE.

The family Ulmaceae is at present to be found nearly everywhere in the tropical and extra tropical regions, though they are only sparingly represented in the western part of North America, and are entirely absent in the prairie regions as well as in the Asiatic and African deserts, and also in South and West Australia. As far as Hawaii is concerned, the genus Trema is alone of interest. The family consists of 13 genera, with about 117 species.

TREMA Lour.
(Sponia Comm.)

Perigone of the male flowers 5-, rarely 4-parted, as many stamens as segments. Ovary sessile, with permanent styles. Drupe small ovoid or subglobose, crowned by the styles, and enclosed in the perigone. Seeds with a fleshy albumen. Embryo curved or spiral with narrow cotyledons. Trees or shrubs with short petioled, triply or pinnately nerved leaves, and subsessile cymes; monoecious or dioecious. Flowers very small.

This genus consists of about 30 species, which are all closely related, and occur in the tropics of the old and new world. The most common is *T. amboinensis* Blume, which occurs in subtropical and tropical Asia and Australia and the Hawaiian Islands.

Trema amboinensis Blume.

TREMA AMBOINENSIS Blume Mus. Lugd. Bot. II (1852) 63;—Del Cast. Ill. Fl. Ins. Mar. Pac. VII (1892) 294, ,et Fl. Polyn. Fr. (1893) 190;—Engler in Engl. et Prantl Pflzfam. III, 1 (1893) 65.—Celtis amboinensis Willd. Spec. Pl. IV. (1806) 997;—Decaisne, in Brongn., Voy. Coqu. (1828-29) 212, t. 47.—Sponia velutina Planch. in Ann. Sc. Nat. 3, ser. X. (1848) 327;—Seem. Fl. Vit. (1873) 235.—Sponia amboinensis Planch. in A. DC. Prodr. XVII. (1873) 199;—Hbd. Fl. Haw. Isl. (1888) 405.

Leaves ovate oblong, cuspidate, cordate or rounded and often oblique at the base, margins serrate, very rough above, silky tomentose underneath when young; cymes with male, female and hermaphrodite flowers, shortly pedunculate or subsessile; male flowers sparingly pilose, perigone 5-parted to the base; stamens as long as the lobes; ovary obovate without style; female flower 5-fid to the middle; ovary 2-celled; drupe ovoid, puberulous, little fleshy.

Trema amboinensis, which has no Hawaiian name as far as can be ascertained, is a small tree, 20 to 30 feet in height, whose young branches are covered with a soft gray pubescence. As has already been remarked, the tree is not peculiar to Hawaii, but is found on nearly all the other islands of the Pacific, as, for example, in Samoa, Viti (Fiji), Tahiti, etc., where the tree is much more common than in Hawaii, and where it is also known by several native names. In Hawaii the tree has so far only been found in Manoa Valley and on the northern slope of Kaala, on Oahu, and also at Mapolehu, on the island of Molokai.

Parts of the tree are used medicinally, mainly for their purgative properties, which are expressed in the Samoan names *tio* and *ui*; the most common name by which the tree is known in Samoa is *fauui*, and on Tutuila the name *ti'ovale* is in use. The name *fausoga* occurs also in Samoa for this particular tree. From the bark of the *fauui* or *fausoga* the natives manufacture a strong fiber which they use for their fish nets.

113

MORACEAE.

The family Moraceae consists of 55 genera which have a distribution similar to the Urticaceae; though the number of species of the former is larger in tropical America. The family is closest related to Ulmaceae, but can be distinguished from them very easily by their inflorescence. It is less allied to the Urticaceae. The family Moraceae is an exceedingly useful one, primarily in their latex, which contains rubber in many species; second, in their fruits, which have a very pleasant taste, as figs, breadfruit, etc.; and, third, in the fiber, which is used for various purposes.

The family is represented in the Hawaiian Islands by two genera, with two widely-spread species.

KEY TO THE GENERA.

Flowers dioecious or monoecious.
    Female flowers in spikes...................................... 1. **Pseudomorus**
Flowers monoecious.
    Female flowers on a globose receptacle......................... 2. **Artocarpus**

PSEUDOMORUS Bureau.

Embryo subglobose, with a large, curved cotyledon, which encloses the other smaller ones. A tree or shrub with entire or dentate leaves. Flowers monoecious or dioecious; female inflorescence short cylindrical, few flowered.

The genus Pseudomorus consists of a single species only, which is of wide distribution. Originally found on Norfolk Island.

Pseudomorus Brunoniana (Endl.) Bureau.

Ai ai.

PSEUDOMORUS BRUNONIANA (Endl.) Bureau, in Ann. Sc. Nat. 5 ser. XI. (1869) 371 et in DeCand. Prodr. XVII. (1873) 249;—Hbd. Fl. Haw. Isl. (1888) 405;—Del Cast. Ill. Fl. Ins. Mar. Pacif. VII. (1892) 296;—Engler in Engl. et Prantl Pflzfam. III, 1 (1893) 72.—**Morus Brunoniana** Endl. Atakta Bot. (....) t. 32.—**Morus pendulina** Bauer Ill. Pl. Norfolk. tab. 186, ined., et in Endl. Prodr. Fl. Norfolk (1833) no. 84;—H. Mann Proc. Am. Acad. (1867) 201.

Leaves distichous, ovate-oblong or lanceolate, acute, sinuate dentate, rounded or truncate at the base, thin pale shining, glabrous on both faces, chartaceous, flowers monoecious; male spikes in the upper axil, slender 7.5 to 10 cm long on peduncles of about 2 to 4 mm; perigone 2 mm, 4- rarely 3-parted; stamens 4, twice as long as the perigone; pistil obcordate, naked; female spikes shorter, often ovoid, at most 12 mm long by 8 mm broad, with few drupes when mature, ovary ovoid, peaked; fruit a fleshy drupe; subglobose, 6 to 8 mm, 2 horned with the conical style-bases.

The *Aiai* is a milky tree or shrub, reaching a height of sometimes 40 feet. It is clothed in a whitish gray bark and has a trunk of up to 2 feet in diameter. The leaf resembles somewhat the mulberry at first appearance.

The *Aiai* is not endemic to Hawaii, but is also found on Norfolk Island and in Australia. In the Hawaiian Islands it may be found on Lanai in the gulches of the main range of Haalelepakai, at an elevation of 2300 feet. It is common on the island of Maui, especially in the dry gulches above Makawao, where the

Moraceae.

writer met with very large trees, about 40 feet high. The flowering and fruiting season falls during the summer months, and trees can be seen loaded with the small fruits in October. At Auahi, southern slopes of Haleakala, in the dry forest, it is again not uncommon in company with *Ochrosia sandwicensis, Sideroxylon auahiense, Pelea multiflora,* etc., as well as at Ulupalakua at an elevation of 3000 feet, and at Puuwaawaa, Kona, Hawaii. It also inhabits the dry regions of Kauai, Hawaii and Oahu, on the latter island in Wailupe Valley and in the Waianae range.

The wood of the *Aiai* is light brown, close-grained, hard, and tough. The aboriginals of New South Wales employed the wood for their boomerangs. When properly dressed and polished it has a remarkable resemblance to Oak. A well-seasoned specimen has an approximate weight of 56 pounds per cubic foot. It is known by the aboriginals of the Richmond and Clarence rivers of New South Wales as "*Mail*" or "*Legaulbie.*" By the whites it is called "Whalebone tree."

ARTOCARPUS Forst.

Perigone of the male flowers 2 to 4 lobed, with only one stamen; perigone of the female flowers tubular, obovate, or linear; style with spathulate stigma, rarely 2-3 fid. Seeds without albumen. Embryo straight or curved, with thick fleshy equal or unequal cotyledons. Trees with large coriaceous leaves which are either entire or incised, with deciduous axillary stipules, and single, short or long peduncled inflorescences. Flowers monoecious, on globose or club-shaped often elongate receptacles.

The genus Artocarpus consists of about 40 species distributed from Ceylon through the Indian Archipelago to China. Of interest is *Artocarpus incisa*, the *Ulu* of the natives or Breadfruit tree, which is indigenous in the Sunda Islands and has been cultivated for ages everywhere in the tropics, but especially on the islands of the Pacific.

Artocarpus incisa Forst.
Ulu, Breadfruit.
(Plate 37.)

ARTOCARPUS INCISA Forst. Pl. escul. (1786) 23, et Icon. (ined. cf. Seem.) t. 250-252;— Endl. Fl. Suds. (1836) no. 882;—Guill. Zeph. Tait. (1836-37) 172;—Trecul, in Ann. Sc. Nat, 3 ser. VIII. (1847) 110;—Pancher in Cuz. Tahit. (1860);—H. Mann Proc. Am. Acad. VII. (1867) 201;—Seem. Fl. Vit. (1873) 255;—Nadeaud, Enum. Pl. Tah. (1873) n. 305;—Hbd. Fl. Haw.Isl.(1888) 407;—Engl. in Engl. et Prantl Pflzfam. III. 1 (1888) 82 fig. 61;—Del Cast. Ill. Fl. Ins. Mar. Pacif. VII. (1892) 298, et Fl. Polyn. Franc. (1893) 196;—Wilder Fr. Haw. Isl. (1911) pp. 101-106, pl. 48-51.—**Rademachia incisa** Thunb. in Vet. Akad. Handl. Stockh. 38 (1776) 253.

Leaves coriaceous, pubescent, 3 dm or more in length, oblong in outline, pinnatifid, with acute or obtuse lobes; stipules 2, free, very large, rolled round the bud, soon caducous; male flowers on thick oblong, female flowers on large globose receptacles, both at first covered by 2 large bracts; male perigone of 2 divisions; style simple or 2-3 fid.

The *Ulu* or Breadfruit has only one variety in the Hawaiian Islands, but has many in the South Seas which are well known to the islanders of the Pacific, as, for instance, in Samoa, Fiji and Tahiti, where they distinguish more than 24 sub-species or varieties, each one having its native name. The milky sap of the tree is used by the Hawaiians for bird lime, and is chewed by the boys and girls in Samoa.

PLATE 37.

ARTOCARPUS INCISA Forst.
Ulu, Breadfruit.
Showing a fruiting branch, much reduced.

The *Ulu* has accompanied the Polynesians in all their migrations and was planted by them wherever it could possibly live. Here in the Hawaiian Islands we can find the *Ulu* always near native dwellings or in the valleys and ravines of the low lands, near by forsaken grass huts or native houses. In Hawaii the Breadfruit has not played a very important part in the household of the aborigines, as it did with their relatives in the South Seas. The fruiting season in Hawaii is very short, being from June to August, and the art of preserving the fruit as is done in the South Seas (as will be explained in a special paragraph) was not understood.

The Hawaiian *Ulu* never bears seeds, and is therefore cultivated by suckers. The fact that the tree does not bear seed is sufficient to show that it could not have been found here originally, but must have been brought here with the arrivals of that race which we now call Hawaiians. The seed-bearing species found in the islands is of comparatively recent introduction and came from the Carolines. Since then the Jack fruit (*A. integrifolia*) has been added to the stock of cultivated fruits.

The *Ulu* often reaches a very large size, ranging from 40 to 60 feet or more in height; the bark of the trunk is smooth, the latter often 2 feet in diameter. It is usually found together with the *Ohia ai* or mountain apple (*Jambosa malaccensis*) and the *Kukui*. The wood of the *Ulu* was used in the construction of doors and houses and for the bodies of canoes. The fruit was often made into a delicious poi, and the root was used medicinally as a purgative.

The name *Ulu* occurs again in Samoa, though also known by 24 other names designating the various sub-species; the most common in use are *uluea, ului, ulufauluma'a* (meaning many seeded), *ulumanua*, etc.

In times of superabundance of breadfruit, which is usually from January to March in Samoa, the fruits are preserved. They are thrown into a hole in the ground which has been laid out with banana leaves. Most of the fruit is placed in whole, while a few are cut up, and then covered with leaves and buried. These preserves are very useful in times of scarcity, as they do not spoil as long as they are buried. The *Ulu* preserve is known as *Masi*. The Tahitian name of the Breadfruit is *Uru*, and in Fiji *Uto* and *Uto sore*. For references of similar nature consult Safford's "Useful Plants of Guam," p. 189, and Seem. Flora of Fiji, p. 255.

URTICACEAE.

The Urticaceae are differentiated from the Ulmaceae by the inflorescence and inflexed anthers, and from the Moraceae by the absence of laticiferous vessels; the only exception being Neraudia and Urera.

The family Urticaceae is only sparingly represented outside the tropics, especially so in Europe. The family consists of 41 genera with about 500 species, of which 33 per cent. are to be found in the new world, and perhaps as many

PLATE 38.

URERA SANDVICENSIS Wedd.
Opuhe.
Showing branch with male inflorescence; reduced.

Urticaceae.

in Asia and the Indian archipelago; about 14 per cent. in Africa, 14 per cent. in Oceanic Islands and only 3 to 4 per cent. in Europe. In the Hawaiian Islands the family is represented by 9 genera, of which two only are endemic (Neraudia and Touchardia). Two genera, Pipturus and Urera, however, have arborescent species only. The usefulness of the Urticaceae is mainly in the long and very strong fiber which is obtained from the bark of some species. The fibre of the Hawaiian *Olona* (*Touchardia latifolia*) is one of the strongest in the world.

KEY TO THE GENERA.

Urereae.   Perigone of the female flowers four parted or four lobed.
    Flowers in cymes.
        Cymes divaricately dichotomous, corymbose, achene covered by the fleshy
           perigone.. 1.   **Urera**
Boehmerieae.   Perigone of the female flowers tubular, free.
    Flowers in axillary clusters.
        Female flowers on a globose receptacle, the perigone dry with fruit. 2.   **Pipturus**

URERA Gaud.

Perigone of the male flower 4-5 parted, stamens 4-5, and a globose or cupshaped rudimentary ovary. Female flower with equally large, or smaller outer segments. Stigma globose-penicillate or cylindrical, subsessile. Achenes enclosed in the fleshy perigone. Seeds with scanty albumen.—Trees or shrubs with alternate leaves, and punctiformous to elongate, in the Hawaiian species ovate-elongate cystolithes, flowers in dichotomous or irregularly branching, loose cymes or corymbs.

The genus Urera consists of about 22 species distributed over the tropics of America and Africa and the islands of the Pacific. In the Hawaiian Islands we have only two species with several varieties, both species being peculiar to the islands, outside of which they have not been found. The native name for both species is *Opuhe.*

Urera Sandvicensis Wedd.

Opuhe.

(Plates 38, 39, 40.)

URERA SANDVICENSIS Wedd. in Ann. Sci. Nat. ser. 3. XVIII (1852) 177,—et in DC. Prodr. XVI (1869) Sect. I. 92;—H. Mann Proc. Am. Acad. VII (1867) 200;— Hbd. Fl. Haw. Isl. (1888) 410 inclus. var. β.;—Del Cast. Ill. Fl. Ins. Mar. Pac. VII (1892) 299.—**Villebrunea crenulata** Gaud. Bot. Voy. Bonite (1844-52) t. 92.

Leaves oblong, 15 to 20 cm x 7 to 9 cm, on petioles of 3 to 5 cm, acuminate, moderately elliptico-contracting but more or less obtuse at the base, wavy crenulate in the upper, entire in the lower portion, chartaceous, or thick somewhat fleshy, pale underneath, either glabrous or pubescent along the veins and midrib, veins impressed in fresh specimens, penninerved, with 12 to 15 strong nerves on either side, all parallel, straight, the lowest equally long or often longer (not shortest as given in Hillebrand's Flora); stipules lanceolate about 4 cm; flowers dioecious; cymes in the lower axils, often rising from the naked branch, regularly and repeatedly dichotomous, corymbiform, 5 to 8 cm in diam. with a peduncle of about 15 mm in the female and 30 to 35 mm in the male flowers; male perigones 8 to 20 in a glomerule, subsessile, each about 3 mm in diam., pale reddish or yellow, with 4 to 5 segments; anthers pale usually 5 in number; female perigone surrounded by a deciduous cup of bractlets, shortly pedicellate, 3 to 4 toothed, at length fleshy and orange yellow, about 2 mm or less; achene suboblique, with yellow stigma, ovate, tuberculate on both faces, entirely enclosed by the perigone.

119

PLATE 39.

URERA SANDVICENSIS Wedd.
Opuhe.
Showing (female) fruiting branch; reduced.

Urticaceae.

The cystolites in the specimens from near the volcano Kilauea, Hawaii, are ovate elongate, while those from the Kohala mountains of the same island are punctiform; besides, the male inflorescence of specimens from the latter locality is only about 3 cm. in diameter, and the leaves are shortly petioled. The specimens found at the slopes of Mauna Loa, Hawaii, seem to be the typical *U. Sandvicensis* and coincide exactly with Gaudichaud's most excellent plate. Hillebrand's var. *β*. is here united with the species, as the pubescence, which seems to be his only distinctive character, occurs in nearly all the specimens from various localities. Hillebrand's var. *γ*. from Molokai, Oahu and Lanai differs from the species mainly in the leaves, which are shorter petioled and are rounder or rather broadly truncate to cuneate at the base, making the leaf almost deltoid. The leaves are nearly all pubescent underneath in the writer's specimens, especially along the veins and midrib. Heller suggests to uphold Weddel's *Urera glabra*, which is a synonym of Hillebrand's var. γ, merely on account of geographical range: the difference is in reality slight, and Hillebrand's variety is here retained. The latter author's var. δ or Wawra's *Urera glabra* var. *mollis*, which is cited as a synonym by Hillebrand, does not warrant being separated from var. γ, with which it is here united. In Olokele Valley, on Kauai, the writer collected specimens of *Urera Sandvicensis*, which he refers to var. γ. They differ somewhat from the plants found on Molokai in the longer petioled leaves which are slightly cuneate at the base, and the very large loose male inflorescence; the leaves are more or less deeply serrate even to the subtruncate-cuneate base, and wholly glabrous.

The *Opuhe* is a medium-sized tree with a straight trunk which is clothed in a smooth, very fibrous bark. It is distributed all over Hawaii, where it is nearly always a tree, while on the other islands it is merely a shrub. Near the Kilauea volcano, on Hawaii, slopes of Mauna Loa, especially at the Kipuka Puaulu (4000 feet), it is a very common tree, 25 feet or so in height, with rather long, thick, drooping branches. The tree is dioecious; that is, male and female flowers are borne on separate trees. It is associated with *Koa*, and *Naio* trees near Shipman's ranch, and with many other trees at Puaulu, such as Straussia, Pelea, Xanthoxylum, etc. At Puuwaawaa, North Kona, Hawaii, it is not uncommon in Waihou forest (elevation 3000 feet), where trees 35 feet in height can be found. It is here that the writer met with the biggest trees; some had trunks of one foot in diameter. In the Kohala mountains on the same island it is a shrub. Varieties of this tree occur on all the islands of the group, but not with well-defined characteristics. Like Neraudia, it also exudes a milky, watery fluid which is otherwise lacking in the family Urticaceae. It is not a very dry district plant, but favors regions with more frequent and heavier precipitation.

The bark was used by the natives in a similar manner to that of the *Olona*—for fish-nets, and even at times for their tapa cloth. It is, however, not as strong as *Olona*. The trees are free from insects. The wood is soft and light.

121

PLATE 40.

UREBA SANDVICENSIS Wedd.
Opuhe.
Female tree growing in the Kipuka Puaulu, near the Volcano Kilauea, on Hawaii;
elevation 4000 feet.

Urticaceae.

On the island of Kauai, on the leeward side in the forest of Kaholuamano, grows a small tree about 18 feet high, which differs very materially from *Urera sandvicensis*, found on Hawaii. It is here described as a new variety under the name *Urera sandvicensis* var. *Kauaiensis*. The native name of this tree is *Hona*.

Var. **Kauaiensis** var. nov.
Hona.

Leaves broadly ovate, bluntly accuminate at the apex, truncate to cuneate at the base, evenly crenate to serrate, thick coriaceous, dark green, with bright red midrib and veins, pinnately nerved, glabrous on both sides, 6 to 9 cm wide and 10 to 14 cm long, on petioles of 4 to 12 cm; male flowers bright red, perigone tuberculate, stamens purple to pink, 5 in number, inflorescence in the axils of the upper leaves and all along the naked branch, very shortly peduncled, branching cymosely or paniculate, flowers larger than in the species.

The tree, which is called *Hona* by the natives, was the only one observed in the forests of Kaholuamano, Kauai, along a streambed. It was collected by the writer in August, 1909, and October, 1911. The number of the type is 9006 in the College of Hawaii Herbarium. It differs from the species in its very long petioled coriaceous leaves, shortly peduncled male inflorescence, which is of a bright red color, purple anthers and large perigones.

Mention may be made here of *Urera Kaalae* Wawra, a small tree found in the Waianae range of Oahu. It differs from *U. Sandvicensis* in the palmately nerved, cordate leaves, small triangular stipules and bracteolate inflorescence. The plant was discovered by Wawra and described in Flora (1874), p. 542. His specimens came from Mt. Puakea of the Kaala range. Not collected by the writer.

PIPTURUS Wedd.
(*Nothocnide* Blume.)

Perigone of the male flower with 4 to 5 ovate lobes. Perigone of the female flower thin and fleshy with the mature fruits. Embryo with scanty albumen and broad cotyledons. Trees and shrubs with alternate 3 to 5 nerved leaves, which are usually covered with a gray pubescence underneath, entire to serrate leaves; stipules bifid, easily caducous. Flower clusters globose, single in the leaf axils, or in some plants, not from the Hawaiian Islands, arranged in catkins.

The genus Pipturus consists of about 12 species, which are distributed over the Oceanic Islands, Hawaiian Islands, and Mascarene Islands to Australia. The Hawaiian species are all called *Mamaki* or *Mamake;* they furnished, next to *Wauke* (*Brousonetia papyrifera*), the fiber for their *tapa* or paper cloth.

Pipturus albidus A. Gray.
Mamaki or *Mamake.*
(Plate 41.)

PIPTURUS ALBIDUS A. Gray (ined.) in H. Mann, Proc. Am. Acad. VII (1867) 201;—Weddl. in DC. Prodr. XVI (1869) Sect. I. 235¹⁷;—Nadeaud, Enum. (1873) n. 313;—Wawra in Flora (1874) 547;—Hbd. Fl. Haw. Isl. (1888) 413;—Del Cast. Ill. Fl. Ins. Mar. Pac. VII (1892) 303, et Fl. Polyn. Franc. (1893) 203;—Heller Pl. Haw. Isl. (1897) 814.—**Boehmeria albida** Hook. et Arn. Bot. Beech. (1832) 96;—Endl. Fl. Suds. (1836) no. 866.—**Pipturus tahitensis** Wedd. in Ann. Sc. Nat. ser. 4. I (1854) 197, et **Pipturus Gaudichaudianus** Wedd. 1. c. p. 196.—**Perlarius albidus** O. Ktze. Rev. Gen. Pl. II (1891) 630.

PLATE 41.

PIPTURUS ALBIDUS A. Gray.
Mamaki or Mamake.
Branch with female inflorescence.

Urticaceae.

Leaves ovate to oblong acute or accuminate at the apex, cordate, truncate or rounded at the base, crenate to serrate, 10 to 14 cm long, 4.5 to 10.5 cm wide, chartaceous to coriaceous, shortly white-tomentose underneath (Oahu) often light green, to dark brown especially in specimens from the other Islands; tripli-nerved, the nerves often red in the living plant; stipules triangular bifid to the middle into subulate lobes; flowers all sessile in axillary clusters of 6 to 12 mm either all male or all female or male and female flowers in one glomerule (in Lanai specimens), white tomentose or very hispid; male perigone reddish acutely 4-fid to the middle or less; stamens little or much exserted (in plants from Paauhau, Hawaii); female perigones on a thick, finally fleshy receptacle, the uncinate stigma much longer than the perigone; fruit about 1 mm.

This is a most variable species, and if one should undertake to separate the various forms, one would have to name individual trees. The leaves vary greatly in shape and size as well as in pubescence, some being densely gray tomentose underneath, others light green to brown; the same holds good of the nervature, which is often bright red.

On Oahu the plant is only a small shrub about 8 feet in height, while in the forests of Naalehu in Kau, Hawaii, the writer observed the biggest trees, which occasionally attain a height of 30 feet with a trunk of often one foot in diameter. When a tree grows in the open it has long drooping branches, which are arranged pyramid-like. The trunk is clothed in an exceedingly strong fibrous smooth bark of a light brown color. As already stated, it is a very variable species and occurs on all the islands of the group, avoiding dry districts; it inhabits the mesophytic forests at an elevation of 1500 to 4000 feet, but does not go higher. Occasionally it can be found in a sub-xerophytic district, but never on the lava fields as is the case with the Hawaiian genus Neraudia, which can be found in the hottest and driest districts, as well as in the rain forests. Two species of Pipturus were described by Heller from Kauai, as *P. Kauaiensis* and *P. ruber*. The latter is a good species and was even distinguished by the natives from their *Mamaki;* it is known to them as *Waimea* on Kauai.

The *Mamake* furnished the natives of old with the fiber for their *tapa* (*kapa*) or paper cloth, which they obtained from the bark of the tree. It is said that *Mamaki* fiber made the finest *tapa* and was preferred to that made of the *Wauke* bark. For further information on the *tapa* making and the fibers used, the writer wishes to refer the reader to Dr. Wm. T. Brigham's valuable book ''Ka Hana Kapa,'' which is an exhaustive treatise on the subject. The wood of the *Mamaki* is exceedingly hard and durable. It is of pinkish color when newly cut, and turns brownish with age. The bark and fruits of the Mamaki are supposed to have been employed by the natives medicinally for consumption.

In Samoa several species of Pipturus occur under the name *fausoga* or *soga*. The bark of these trees is used by the natives in a similar manner as was that of the Hawaiian species—for their *tapa* or paper cloth. The Hawaiian species is supposed to occur also in Tahiti.

125

SANTALACEAE.

The family Santalaceae, which consists of 26 genera and about 250 species, is divided into two groups: Holoparasites or genuine, and Hemiparasites or half parasites. To the latter group, among others, belongs the genus Santalum, which is represented here in the Islands by several species. The Hemiparasitic Santala root in the ground and partly extract nutriment from the roots or stems of other plants by means of haustoria or suck-organs. It has been proved in *Santalum album*, the Indian Sandalwood, that it can exist and grow in soil perfectly devoid of foreign roots. Botanists are of the opinion that parasitism in this group must have played an important part in the existence of these plants in previous periods, on account of the large number of haustoria on their rootlets, and the small number of which succeed in bringing about adhesion to roots of other plants; while in genuine parasites, as the Loranthaceae, no such extravagant endowment is to be found. The opinion has been expressed that these Hemiparasites, which root in the ground, form an intermediate step to those parasites which live on tree branches, rather than being reduced forms of the latter or genuine root parasites.

The Santalaceae are distributed over the tropics and the temperate zone. A majority of the genera occurs only in dry regions and comparatively few belong to regions with heavy precipitation.

In Hawaii the family is represented by two genera, Exocarpus and Santalum; of the former two species are to be found, while of the latter four or five species occur in the mountains of all of the Hawaiian islands.

It may be of interest here to remark that in the days of Vancouver, Sandalwood was the main export from these Islands, which was shipped to China. An interesting account is given in regard to Sandalwood export from the South Pacific islands to various parts of the world, in Seeman's Flora of the Fiji Islands.

The Chinese term the Sandalwood *Tanheong*. i. e., scented tree. The Hawaiian Islands are called *Tan-shan* or Sandalwood mountains by the Chinese, on account of the Sandalwood trade which was carried on with China.

SANTALUM Linn.

Flowers hermaphrodite, perigone 4 to 5 lobed. Tube of perigone campanulate or ovate. Lobes of perigone free to the discus, each lobe with a tuft of hair at its base. Stamens inserted at the base of the perigone, and shorter than the latter; filaments short. Discus drawn out into fleshy, spathulate triangular lobes, between the stamens. Ovary at first superior, later on partly inferior. Style simple, stigma short, 2 to 4 lobed. Ovules 2 to 4, pendulous. Drupe. ovoid to globose crowned with the scars of the fallen lobes; exocarp thin, somewhat fleshy and hard rugose endocarp. Seeds ovoid to globose. Embryo in the center of the albumen, obliquely embedded; radical longer than the cotyledons. Glabrous hemiparasitic trees or shrubs with opposite rarely alternate, entire leaves, and relatively large panicles or racemes which are either terminal or axillary Bracts not present.

The genus Santalum consists of about 10 species which are all closely related and occur in East India, on the islands of the Malayan Archipelago, on the islands of the Pacific and in Australia.

Santalaceae.

In the Hawaiian Islands four species are to be found, which are perhaps only variations of a single species. Since the large export of Sandalwood from these Islands to China, the trees have became rather scarce and only individual ones can be found scattered through the drier forests. On Oahu, Sandalwood trees or *Iliahi* are still plentiful in certain districts, such as Kahuku, and in Palolo Valley, where they are very numerous at the lower elevation in company with *Acacia Koa* (*Koa*).

KEY TO THE SPECIES.

Inflorescence axillary and terminal.
  Perigone reddish, 8 to 10 mm.
    Drupe ovoid, smooth.................................... **S. ellipticum**
  Perigone reddish, large, 12 to 14 mm. cylindrical.
    Drupe obovoid, rough................................... **S. pyrularium**
  Perigone yellowish, 6 mm campanulate.
    Drupe ovoid, smooth, mucronate........................ **S. Freycinetianum**
Inflorescence a terminal cymose densely flowered panicle.
  Perigone bright red...................................... **S. Haleakalae**

Santalum Freycinetianum Gaud.
Iliahi.
(Plates 42, 43.)

SANTALUM FREYCINETIANUM Gaud. Bot. Voy. Uranie (1826) (1830) 442, t. 45;—Hook. et Arn. Bot. Beech. (1832) 90;—Endl. Fl. Suds. (1836) no. 939;—Guill. Zeph. Tait. (1836-37) no. 184;—DC. Prodr. XIV. (1857) 682;—Jardin, Hist. Iles. Marqu. (1858) 184;—A. Gray in Proc. Amer. Acad. IV. (1860) 326;—et in Bot. U. S. E. E. ined;—Panch. in Cuzent, Tahiti (1860) 233;—H. Mann Proc. Amer. Acad. VII (1867) 198;—Wawra in Flora (1875) 171;—Hbd. Fl. Haw. Isl. (1888) 389;—Hieronym. in Engl. et Prantl. Pflzfam. III, 1 (1889) 221;—Del Cast. Ill. Fl. Ins. Mar. Pacif. VII (1892) 282 et Fl. Polyn. Franc. (1893) 173.—**Santalum insulare** Bertero, in Guill. l. c.;—Nadeaud Enum. (1873) no. 328.

Leaves opposite, ovate to obovate or elliptico oblong, 4 to 8 cm long, 2.5 to 4 cm wide, on petioles of 2 to 15 mm; either obtuse or acute at both ends, chartaceous, glabrous, glossy and darker green above, lighter underneath or in specimens from North Kona golden yellow; cymes paniculate terminal or in the axils of the upper leaves 2.5 to 5 cm long, few flowered in axillary inflorescences, densely flowered in terminal ones; the flowers in almost sessile clusters or 3 to 9 or more; perigone yellowish green, with slight reddish tint, campanulate about 6 mm, the somewhat acute lobes as long or longer than the tube; disc lobes short and broad, tufts of hair very scanty and short; anthers longer than the filaments; style little shorter than the perigone, shortly 3 to 4 cleft; drupe ovoid, about 15 mm long when mature, the apex somewhat truncate, very shortly mucronate, and crowned with depressed annulus; putamen smooth.

Santalum Freycinetianum, the Hawaiian Sandalwood of the commerce of bygone days, is a most variable species. It is often a small shrub, but usually a medium-sized tree, and is peculiar to the dry regions of these Islands. It loves the lava fields of the Island of Hawaii, where it is especially common, comparatively speaking. It occurs as a small tree in South Kona on the lava fields of Kapua, and Manuka, while in North Kona on the old lava flows of Mt. Hualalai it reaches a handsome size. Here the tree grows 35 feet or so tall, with a trunk of 10 to 12 inches in diameter, which is clothed in a rather rough scaly bark.

On the slopes of Mauna Loa above Kealakekua, at an elevation of about 5000 feet, the writer met with the biggest Sandalwood trees to be found in the whole group. They differ very much in their outward appearance from the other varieties known to the writer. The trees reach a height of over 50 feet and have a

127

PLATE 42.

SANTALUM FREYCINETIANUM Gaud.
Iliahi, Sandalwood.
Growing on the lava fields of Puuwaawaa, North Kona, Hawaii; elevation 2800 ft. Showing flowering and fruiting branch pinned against trunk of tree. Note the rough bark.

trunk of over one and a half, and occasionally two, feet in diameter. The bark is black and smooth, the leaves very dark green and glossy, and drupes olive shaped and black, with somewhat fleshy exocarp. It occurs mainly on the rough *aa* flows intersecting this beautiful country, but can also be found in the Koa forest, where it is very numerous; many large trees were found dead, undoubtedly due to the dying off of their hosts. Nearly 90% of the trees which formed this once beautiful forest are now dead.

Santalum Freycinetianum occurs on all the islands. On Lanai it can be found on the extreme eastern end, scattered about on the exposed open grasslands. At Puuwaawaa, North Kona, Hawaii, it grows on the lava fields at 2000 feet and higher up on the slopes of Hualalai large trees can be observed. This species of Santalum has several varieties, found on the various islands. On Lanai and East Maui on the southern slopes of Haleakala occurs Hillebrand's var. γ. *cuneatum*, which differs from the species in its small thick, fleshy, suborbicular leaves, which are slightly cuneate at the base. It is usually a shrub, but to the writer's astonishment it grew as a veritable vine, completely covering a species of Sideroxylon.

At the volcano of Kilauea, Hawaii, elevation 4000 feet, occurs another variety called β. var. *latifolium* Gray. Its leaves are coriaceous pale glaucous underneath and quite broad; the flowers are arranged in numerous panicles which are axillary and terminal. It grows plentifully on the cliffs surrounding the main crater, but always as a shrub.

On Diamond Head crater, the landmark of the Island of Oahu, and in Kailua, Hawaii, as well as at Cape Kaena, Oahu, grows a small much branching shrub, which is another variety called var. ε. *littorale* Hbd., as it grows in the vicinity of the seashore.

On Lanai on a spur of the main ridge, Lanaihale, the writer found a tree quite distinct from any of the other varieties known. It has the largest leaf of any Santalum known, and also flowers which almost exceed in size those of *Santalum pyrularium* of Kauai. It is here described as follows:

Var. **Lanaiense** var. nov.

Branches robust, stiff; leaves orbicular in outline, mucronate at the apex, slightly contracting at the base into a petiole of 5 mm, 7 to 10 cm each way, dark green above, bright glaucous underneath with red veins, chartaceous; panicles very small, axillary, 25 mm long, flowers two or single on minute pedicels, flowers large, bright red with glaucous hue; perigone 12 mm long, campanulate to cylindrical, the acute lobes a third the length of the tube; anthers as long as the perigone; drupe unknown.

A medium-sized tree with stiff gnarled branches, growing at an elevation of about 3000 feet in company with Straussia, Bobea, Dubautia, etc. It has the largest leaf in the genus and is almost worthy of specific distinction. Collected in July, 1910. Type in the College of Hawaii Herbarium; co-type in the author's Herbarium no. 10061.

It may be of interest here to relate the rise and fall of the Sandalwood trade in the Hawaiian Islands. In the year 1778 the attention of the commercial world was first drawn to the existence of Sandalwood in these islands; a Captain Ken-

PLATE 43.

SANTALUM FREYCINETIANUM Gaud.
Iliahi, Sandalwood.
Growing on the lava fields of Puuwaawaa, North Kona, Hawaii.   One of the biggest
Sandalwood trees in the Hawaiian Islands.

Santalaceae.

drick, of a Boston brig, is known to have been the first who left two men on Kauai to contract for several cargoes. Under the able government of Kamehameha, vast quantities of the wood were exported. The Sandalwood was to these islanders the start in life. From 1790 to 1820 numerous vessels called for this wood, bringing many and various things in exchange, and about 1810 Kamehameha I. and his people began to accumulate considerable wealth. In one year nearly 400,000 dollars were realized. Under the reign of Liholiho the Sandalwood began to be exhausted, though in the year 1820 we still hear of 80,000 dollars' worth of the wood being paid for the yacht "Cleopatra's Barge," and in 1822 of a voyage to Kauai to collect the annual tribute of the wood in that island; though the produce became every day more difficult to procure, and could no longer be demanded in payment of taxes. Finally a substitute was discovered, the *Naio* (*Myoporum sandwicense* A. Gray) or Bastard Sandalwood, though no relation to true Sandalwood; it, however, could not revive the trade.

Thus came to an end the export of the *Iliahi* or *Laau ala* (fragrant wood) as the natives termed the wood.

For further particulars in regard to Sandalwood trade in Hawaii, consult J. J. Jarves' History of the Hawaiian Islands.

Santalum ellipticum Gaud.
Iliahi.

(Plate 44.)

SANTALUM ELLIPTICUM Gaud. Bot. Voy. Uranie (1826, 1830) 442;—Endl. Fl. Suds. (1836) 940;—DC. Prodr. XIV (1857) 682;—A. Gray Proc. Am. Acad. IV (1860) 327;—Mrs. Sinclair Indig. Fl. Haw. Isl. (1885) pl. 34;—Heller, Pl. Haw. Isl. (1897) 818.—Santalum Freycinetianum var. *e.* ellipticum Gray Bot. U. S. E. E. ined;—H. Mann, Proc. Am. Acad. VII (1867) 198;—Hbd. Fl. Haw. Isl. (1888) 390;—Del Cast. Ill. Fl. Ins. Mar. Pacif. VII (1892) 283.

Branches slender, more or less drooping; leaves thin chartaceous, elliptical-oblong, reddish, about 17 cm long and 3 cm wide, on slender petioles of 18 mm, acuminate glabrous; panicles in the axils of the upper leaves, rather loose, the flowers on distinct pedicels of 2 mm; perigone 8 to 10 mm reddish, the lobes as long as the tube or longer, with long tufts of hair; drupe as in *S. Freycinetianum.*

Santalum ellipticum or *Iliahi* is not uncommon on the islands of Kauai and Oahu; on the latter island trees of this species are very numerous on the eastern end, especially in the valley of Palolo, where they are associated with *Acacia Koa* (*Koa*) mainly, which is probably its host. It extends from an elevation of 600 feet up to about 1500 feet, at which latter elevation it grows together with *Straussia Kaduana* (*Kopiko*). *Elaeocarpus bifidus* (*Kalia*) and others. It has a short, straight trunk and a rather round crown, formed of slender branches. It is very conspicuous from a distance on account of its reddish tinted foliage.

The Hawaiian Sandalwood, according to old natives, grows to a height of often 80 feet, with trunks of often three feet in diameter. The older and bigger the tree the more valuable it becomes, as its fragrance increases with age. It is only the very heart wood that is scented, and in small or young trees the roots only are fragrant.

131

PLATE 44.

SANTALUM ELLIPTICUM Gaud.
Iliahi, Sandalwood.

Santalaceae.

Santalum pyrularium A. Gray.

Iliahi.

SANTALUM PYRULARIUM A. Gray Proc. Am. Acad. IV (1860) 327, et in Bot. U. S. E. E. ined;—H. Mann, Proc. Am. Acad. VII (1867) 198;—Wawra in Flora (1875) 172;— Hbd. Fl. Haw. Isl. (1888) 390;—Del Cast. Ill. Fl. Ins. Mar. Pacif. VII (1892) 283.

A medium sized tree, leaves as in *Santalum ellipticum* of Oahu, but glaucous under-neath; panicles axillary, loose, few flowered; flowers on pedicels of 3 mm, perigone dull red, cylindrical 12 to 14 mm, the lobes as long as the tube or shorter; anthers as long as the filaments; style nearly as long as the perigone, 3-cleft; drupe large 14 to 24 mm long, the putamen rough, runcinate, crowned with membraneous annulus below the apex.

This species is peculiar to the Island of Kauai and occurs in the forests of Hale-manu at an elevation of 3000 to 4000 feet, where it is a tree 35 to 40 feet high, occasionally. It can also be found in the woods of Kaholuamano, on the same leeward side, above Waimea in the more dry regions in company with *Elaeocarpus bifidus* (*Kalia*), *Tetraplasandra Waimeae* (*Ohe kikoola*), *Pterotropia Kauaiensis* (*Ohe ohe*), Straussia (*Kopiko*), *Bobea Mannii* (*Ahakea*) and others. It also en-croaches on the border of the rain forest where it is a straighter and taller tree than when growing on the drier forehills.

On the road to Halemanu, near Puu ka pele of the Waimea canyon, the writer saw a fine specimen which was loaded with fruit, and the ground beneath was covered with thousands of seeds, but none had sprouted.

It may be remarked, that any attempt to germinate seeds of the Hawaiian Sandalwoods resulted in failure. Hillebrand records a similar fate in his Flora of the Hawaiian Islands.

Santalum Haleakalae Hbd.

Iliahi.

(Plate 45.)

SANTALUM HALEAKALAE Hbd. Flora Haw. Isl. (1888) 390;—Del Cast. l. c. p. 283.— Santalum pyrularium var. β. A. Gray, mss. Bot. U. S. E. E. ined;—H. Mann, Proc. Am. Acad. VII (1867) 198.

A small tree with stiff erect branches; leaves thick, coriaceous to chartaceous (at lower elevations) dull light green, ovate-obovate oblong 3 to 5 cm long, 25 to 30 mm broad, on petioles of 4 to 6 mm, bluntly acuminate or rounded; panicles crowded near the end of each branch, constituting a terminal corymb of 3 to 8 cm in length and also in width; flowers subsessile, of a deep scarlet red, the perigone 8 to 10 mm, with the lobes as long as the tube or longer; disc-lobes lanceolate, longer than the filaments; anthers on short filaments, their cells diverging at base and apex; style subexserted, 3-cleft; drupe ovoid 12 to 16 mm long, truncate at the base, and with a conical vertex at the apex and a short annulus below the same, putamen minutely runcinate.

This species, which is easily distinguished from the other Hawaiian Sandal-woods by its dense corymbose inflorescence, which is bright scarlet, is peculiar to the Island of Maui, and at that confined to the eastern part Mt. Haleakala, after which mountain it was named by Hillebrand, who records it as a shrub.

It is, however, also a tree, though not of any size; the highest trees observed by the writer were about 25 feet. · It grows around the crater of Puunianiau, on the northeastern slope of Mt. Haleakala, at an elevation of 7000 to 9000 feet. It was

133

PLATE 45.

SANTALUM HALEAKALAE (Gray) Hbd.
Iliahi, Sandalwood.

also found as a small tree 15 to 18 feet in height on the floor of Haleakala crater in Koolau gap and Kaupo gap, in company with *Sophora chrysophylla* (*Mamani*), *Geranium tridens* (*Hinahina*), and the well-known Silversword (*Argyroxiphium sandwicense* var. *macrocephalum*).

It has been reported by Hillebrand to grow only at very high elevations near the summit of the mountain, together with Raillardia and Geranium. It may, however, be of interest to state that it was observed by the writer on the southern slopes of Haleakala on the lava flows of Auahi, Kahikinui, at an elevation of 2600 feet. At this latter locality, which is one of the richest botanical districts in the Territory, it is a fine-looking tree and does not show any signs of stiff branches and short, gnarled trunks, as, of course, must be expected at high altitudes. Were it not for the dense inflorescence and bright scarlet perigones, one could easily mistake it for *Santalum ellipticum* of Oahu, which it, in reality, resembles greatly.

The wood of trees from the high levels is exceedingly fragrant, and of a dark yellowish brown color.

AMARANTACEAE.

The family Amarantaceae occurs in all floral regions of the world, with the exception of the frigid zones. It consists of about 40 genera, with about 655 species.

In the Hawaiian Islands only five genera are represented, two of which are endemic (Charpentiera and Nototrichium) and have arborescent species.

KEY TO THE GENERA.

Style simple with a capitate stigma.
    Flowers villous or hispid; in terminal or axillary spikes.......... 2. **Nototrichium**
Style deeply divided into 2 stigmatic branches.
    Flowers glabrous, in long paniculate spikes..................... 1. **Charpentiera**

CHARPENTIERA Gaud.

Flowers inconspicuous, arranged on long slender branched paniculate spikes. Ovary ovoid, with two stigmas. Androeceum consisting of a shortly 5 lobed discus-cup, with 5 stamina, alternating with the discus lobes. Pericarp dry. Trees or shrubs with always long petioled, ovate to obovate or elliptico-lanceolate leaves.

The genus Charpentiera is peculiar to the Hawaiian Islands and consists of two species, *Ch. elliptica* (Hbd.) Heller, and *Ch. obovata* Gaud. The former is a shrub peculiar to Kauai, the latter a tree found on all the islands. The native name of the species is *Papala*.

Charpentiera obovata Gaud.

Papala.

(Plates 46, 47, 48.)

CHARPENTIERA OBOVATA Gaud. Bot. Voy. Uranie (1826, 1830) 444, pl. 48;—Hook. et Arnott. Bot. Beech. (1832) 94;—Endl. Fl. Suds. (1836) no. 718;—Moquin-Tandon in DC. Prodr. XIII (1849) 2. p. 232;—Wawra (1875) 188;—Sinclair Indig. Fl. Haw. Isl. (1885) pl. 44;—Hbd. Fl. Haw. Isl. (1888) 375;—Del Cast. Ill. Fl. Ins. Mar. Pac. VII (1892) 269;—Schinz in Engl. et Prantl. Pflzfam. III. l. a. (1893) 101, fig. 52;— Heller Pl. Haw. Isl. (1897) 820.—**Ch. ovata** Gaud. l. c. pl. 47;—H. et A. l. c.;— Endl. l. c. no. 919;—Moqu. l. c.;—Mann Enum. (1867) no. 423 (ex parte);—Hbd. l. c. etc.

135

PLATE 46.

ÇHARPENTIERA OBOVATA Gaud.
Papala.
Flowering and fruiting branch, reduced one-half.

PLATE 47.

CHARPENTIERA OBOVATA Gaud.
Papala.
Growing on the lava fields of Kapua, South Kona, Hawaii; elevation 2000 feet. Fruiting
branch pinned against trunk of tree.

PLATE 48.

CHARPENTIERA OBOVATA Gaud.
Papala.
Growing on the lava fields of Kapua, South Kona, Hawaii.   Tree about 25 feet tall.

Amarantaceae.

Leaves ovate or obovate-oblong 6 to 30 cm long, 4 to 12 cm wide, on petioles of 2 to 8 cm rounded at both ends, slightly decurrent into the petiole, fleshy, thick or chartaceous when fresh, glabrous, dark green, with impressed straight parallel veins; panicles compound, red, often 40 to 50 cm long, but smaller in the specimens from dry districts, on peduncles of sometimes more than 12 cm; flowers 2 mm, thin rather pale; bracts about 1 mm, ovate; sepals ovate, stamens about as long as the sepals; utriculus 2 to 3 mm, enclosed or partly exserted; stigmas deeply bifid exserted.

This is a tree of 15 to 35 feet in height, and reaches its best development in the dry regions. It is a very variable species, and was, as a matter of fact, described by Gaudichaud as two different species, mainly on the shape of the leaf.

The *Papala* occurs on all the islands of the group in the rain as well as the dry forests. It is not uncommon in Manoa and Pauoa valleys, Oahu, as well as in the whole Koolau range, where it grows in densely shaded ravines and on mountain slopes. On Kauai it is plentiful at Hanalei and neighborhood. We find it again in all the valleys of the Kohala mountains, but not higher than about 4000 feet. The biggest and finest specimens of this tree the writer observed in North Kona, Hawaii, at Puuwaawaa, where the trunks reached a diameter of two and a half feet, being perfectly straight and clothed in a very smooth, light brown, thin bark. The trunk, in its lower portion, usually divides into several column-like parts, in the form of buttresses. When in full bloom it is a rather attractive looking tree. The wood is very soft and fibrous, and when dry exceedingly light, and will burn like paper. It is the very tree which was used by the natives for a most original and grand display of fireworks, owing to the easiness with which the wood can be ignited. Mrs. Sinclair in her beautiful book on the "Indigenous Flowers of the Hawaiian Islands," says the following in regard to this sport: "On the northwest side of Kauai the coast is extremely precipitous, the cliffs rising abruptly from the sea to a height of from one to two thousand feet, and from these giddy heights the ingenious and beautiful pyrotechnic displays take place.

"On dark moonless nights upon certain points of these awful precipices, where a stone would drop sheer into the sea, the operator takes his stand with a supply of *papala* sticks, and, lighting one, launches it into space. The buoyancy of the wood causes it to float in mid-air, rising or falling according to the force of the wind, sometimes darting far seaward, and again drifting towards the land. Firebrand follows firebrand, until, to the spectators (who enjoy the scene in canoes upon the ocean hundreds of feet below), the heavens appear ablaze with great shooting stars, rising and falling, crossing and recrossing each other, in the most weird manner. So the display continues until the firebrands are consumed, or a lull in the wind permits them to descend slowly and gracefully to the sea."

On the Island of Kauai in the forest of Kaholuamano occurs another species of this genus—*Ch. elliptica* (Hbd.) Heller. It is certainly quite distinct from *Ch. obovata* in the long elliptical-lanceolate leaves, and very short inflorescence which is almost erect and not drooping. Hillebrand mentions it as a variety *elliptica*.

NOTOTRICHIUM Hbd.

Flowers hermaphrodite, small conical, hispid villous or pubescent. Perianth deeply 4 parted, the lobes equal, an outer pair enclosing the inner one. Stamens slightly con-

139

PLATE 49.

NOTOTRICHIUM SANDWICENSE Hbd.
Kului.
Showing flowering branch.
Photographed from Herbarium specimen; nearly one-half natural size.

nected at the base. Ovary one-celled, one-ovulate. Style slender; stigma capitate. Fruit an oblong or obovoid thin utricle, enclosed in the perianth. Seed lenticular, with thin testa.—Shrubs or trees with dichotomous branches and opposite penninerved leaves. Flowers in terminal and axillary spikes with a woolly or pubescent rhachis.

The endemic genus consists of three closely-related species. In Engler and Prantl's Natürl. Pflzfam. the genus Nototrichium is merged with Psilotrichium, from which it differs, however, in the equal perianth lobes and tetramerous flowers.

Only one species, *N. sandwicense*, becomes arborescent; the other two species are shrubs. One of them occurs on Kauai, the other on Oahu, while *N. sandwicense* or *Kului* occurs on nearly all the islands of the group.

Nototrichium sandwicense Hbd.
Kului.
(Plates 49, 50.)

NOTOTRICHIUM SANDWICENSE Hbd. Flora Haw. Isl. (1888) 373;—Heller Pl. Haw. Isl. (1897) 821.—**Ptilotus sandwicensis** A. Gray in Bot. U. S. E. E. ined;—H. Mann Proc. Am. Acad. VII (1867) 200.—**Psilotrichium sandwicense** Seem. Fl. Vit. (1867) 198, adnot;—Wawra in Flora (1875) 186;—Del Cast. Ill. Fl. Ins. Mar. Pac. VII (1892) 270;—Schinz in Engl. et Prantl. Pflzfam. III. 1. a. (1893) 111.

Branches slender, articulated, covered with an ochraceous tomentum; leaves opposite, ovate, acuminate, covered with a silky adpressed tomentum especially the underside of the leaf, which is silvery tomentose, contracting into a petiole of 12 to 18 mm, 2 to 8 cm long, 1.5 to 4 cm wide; spikes generally 3 or 5 at the end of a branch; thick ovoid to cylindrical, 1.5 to 3 cm long on peduncles of 6 to 30 mm, the rhachis densely villous; flowers crowded, ovoid 2 to 3 mm long, villous with spreading hairs at the base; perianth lobes ovate lanceolate 3 to 5 nerved, hispid at the back; stamens nearly as long; ovary oblong, truncate; style as long as the perianth, with punctiform stigma.

The *Kului*, which is usually only a shrub several feet high in the lowlands, becomes a small tree of about 15 to 20 feet in height in the lower forest zone at 2000 to 3000 feet altitude.

It is a handsome little tree and quite conspicuous by its silvery gray foliage and its pretty catkins which droop from the end of every branchlet. It is peculiar to the very dry regions and may be found as a straggling shrub where nothing else can live.

In Kona, Hawaii, especially near Puuwaawaa, it forms a regular hedge along the government road on the rough aa lava fields. On Molokai it grows on the western end in gulches, on the slopes of Mauna Loa, where it forms, together with the *Nau* (*Gardenia Brighamii*), the *Ohe* (*Reynoldsia sandwicensis*) and the *Wiliwili* (*Erythrina monosperma*), the last remnants of what was once a xerophytic forest. At Puuwaawaa, Hawaii, proper, it grows to a small tree about 15 to 20 feet in height at an elevation of 3000 feet, besides also at Kawaihaeiuka (2500 feet), together with *Maua* (*Xylosma Hillebrandii*) and the *Mamani* (*Sophora chrysophylla*). It also is not uncommon on Maui and Oahu. On the latter island it inhabits the arid regions of the Waianae Mountains. It occurs as a tree on the lava fields of Kau, and South Kona, on the slopes of Mauna Loa, Hawaii, and forms, in certain districts as Manuka, about 80% of the growth.

PLATE 50.

NOTOTRICHIUM SANDWICENSE Hbd.
Kului.
Growing on the slopes of Mauna Loa, Molokai; elevation 2000 feet. Tree in background, Erythrina monosperma (Wiliwili).

Nyctaginaceae.

Two varieties have been described, one from Kauai by Asa Gray, and another from the Pali of Kalaupapa, Molokai.

The wood is coarsely grained and very light. resembling the wood of the *Papala*.

NYCTAGINACEAE.

This family is one of the most interesting in the vegetable kingdom, on account of its many peculiarities. All Nyctaginaceae are void of corollas, but possess, however, a perigone of often remarkable beauty. The family consists of 18 genera, with about 155 species; it is represented in the Hawaiian Islands by three genera, only one of which, Pisonia, has arborescent species.

The Nyctaginaceae are either herbs, shrubs or trees, and are distributed over the warmer regions of the whole world, especially in tropical America.

PISONIA Plum.

Flowers rarely hermaphrodite, usually unisexual, with 2 to 3 small triangular to linear bracts at their base. Male flower campanulate, with a 5-lobed perigone and 5 to 30 (usually 6 to 8) stamens, which are very shortly united at their base, and exserted, surrounding a rudimentary ovary. Female flowers tubular, 5 lobed, with staminodia and an often plainly stipitate, elongate ovary, with a filiform style and fringed capitate stigma. Anthocarp of variable form, elliptical to long prismatic, etc., smooth or angular with viscous glands. Shrubs or trees with small often fragrant flowers and usually opposite, elliptical, lanceolate or obovate leaves.

The genus consists of about 40 described species which occur in the tropics and their neighboring regions. Only one species is found on the African coasts.

The fruiting perigone of the Hawaiian species exudes a very viscous substance, which was used by the natives as a bird lime.

The nomenclature of the species of Pisonia is very much confused, different authors having referred our species to plants from other parts of the world. A. Heimerl expresses the possibility of our endemic species (*P. sandwicensis*) being identical with *P. artensis* from New Caledonia.

The writer has adhered to Hillebrand's nomenclature as regards this latter species, rather than Heimerl's, who says that our Hawaiian Pisonia is not well known to him.

KEY TO THE SPECIES.

Limb of perigone lobed.
    Leaves cuneate, inflorescence a terminal loose umbel or contracted panicle
                                                            P. umbellifera
    Leaves broad at the base, inflorescence a globose head.............   **P. sandwicensis**
Limb of perigone entire.
    Leaves elliptical oblong, inflorescence a loose open panicle.........   **P. inermis**

143

PLATE 51.

PISONIA SANDWICENSIS Hbd.
Aulu.
Female flowering branch and fruits, reduced one-half.

Nyctaginaceae.

Pisonia umbellifera (Forst.) Seem.
Papala kepau.

PISONIA UMBELLIFERA (Forst.) Seem. in Bonpl. X. (1862) 154;—et Fl. Vit. (1866) 195;—Nadeaud, Enum. Tahit. Pl. (1873) no. 326;—Hbd. Fl. Haw. Isl. (1888) 368;— Del Cast. Ill. Fl. Ins. Mar. Pac. VII (1892)268, et Fl. Polyn. Franc. (1893) 157;—Heller Pl. Haw. Isl. (1897) 823.—**Ceodes umbellifera** Forst. Charact. Gen. (1776) 141, t. 71.—**C. umbellata** Forst. Prodr. (1786) no. 569.—**Pisonia excelsa** Blume, Bijdr. (1825) 735;—Choisy in DC. Prodr. XIII. 2. (1849) 441;—H. Mann Proc. Am. Acad. VII (1867) 198.—**P. macrocarpa** Presl. Symb. (1833) t. 56.—**P. Forsteriana** Endl. In Herb. Meyen ex Schauer et Walp. Nov. Act. Nat. Cur. XIX., Suppl. (1843) 403 t. 51.—**P. Sinclairi** Hook. f. Fl. New Zeal. I. (1853) 209 t. 50.— **P. Mooreana** F. Muller Fragm. I. (1858-59) 20.

Branches large and stiff with long internodes; leaves broadly obovate, cuneate at the base, obtuse or shortly acuminate but sometimes broad at the base and suborbicular, 12 to 26 cm long, 8 to 12 cm wide, on petioles of about 12 mm, fleshy, the upper ones crowded in a whorl at the internodes of the branches, the lower sub-opposite; inflorescence terminal, subumbellate, one or several peduncles rising from the apex of a branch, dividing at or near the apex into loose umbel or contracted panicle; perigone greenish to yellowish, smooth, with the limb 5-fid; fruiting pedicels of 6 to 18 mm, obtusely 5-ribbed, viscid, but smooth; utricle 1/2 to 2/3 the length of the perigone.

A low tree 15 to 30 feet high, common on most of the islands, inhabiting the forests of the lower regions. On Oahu it is a common feature of the vegetation back of Tantalus and adjoining valleys. Unlike the other species, it is moisture loving, and forms large clumps in the valleys on the windward side, where the rainfall is very large. Logs of this tree, which the writer collected for wood specimens, shriveled to such an extent that it was impossible to recognize them afterward, resembling the stems of shriveled banana plants. Trunks of a foot in diameter can be felled with one stroke of the axe. It is of a very wide geographical distribution, ranging from Polynesia to Australia and the Philippines. On Oahu it is found at an elevation of 200 to 1600 feet, and possibly higher. It is very difficult to find good specimens on account of an insect which feeds on the leaves, and thus most of the trees have a very ungainly appearance.

Pisonia sandwicensis Hbd.
Aulu on Kauai.
(Plate 51.)

PISONIA SANDWICENSIS Hbd. Fl. Haw. Isl. (1888) 369;—Heimerl in Engl. et Prantl Pflzfam. III. 1. b. (1889) 29;—Heller Pl. Haw. Isl. (1897) 823.—**Pisonia umbellifera** Del Cast. Ill. Fl. Ins. Mar. Pac. VII (1892) 268 (ex parte) et Fl. Polyn. Franc. (1893) 157.

Leaves thick coriaceous 10 to 30 cm long, 6 to 15 cm wide, on petioles of 3 to 5 cm, ovate oblong, obtuse or rounded or bluntly acute at the apex, often even emarginate, the base rounded, the ribs and veins prominent; peduncles in the axils of the uppermost leaves, 3 to 6 cm long, dividing in few short rays, forming a globose head of about 5 cm in diam., flowers sessile; male perigone 5 to 6 mm, deeply parted into 5 to 6 obtuse lobes; stamens 18 to 20, long exserted, twice the length of the perigone; female perigone tubular, style exserted, fringed along its upper clavate portion; fruiting perigone (mature) 4 cm long, ovoid-cylindrical, crowned with the lobes of the limb and style; not muricate, but faintly many ribbed.

The *Aulu*, as the tree is called on Kauai, is a tall tree, reaching a height of 50 to 60 feet, with usually 2 to 3 trunks of 1 to 2 feet in diameter, rising from

145

PLATE 52.

PISONIA INERMIS Forst.
Papala kepau.
Fruiting branch.   Note insects caught on viscous fruits.   One-half natural size.

Nyctaginaceae.

a common base. The writer has observed splendid specimens on the Island of Kauai, in the dry districts and gulches below Kaholuamano about 2500 feet above sea level, where it is to be found in company with *Cryptocarya Mannii, Hibiscus Waimeae, Urera* sp., *Xylosma Hawaiiense (Maua), Osmanthus sandwicensis,* the native olive, *Olopua* or *Pua,* and others. The tree is conspicuous from the distance on account of its large and very dark-green leaves; the wood, like that of the other species, is soft, and trees are never cut for the sake of the wood. The flowers, which are arranged in globose heads, are very fragrant and not altogether unattractive. On Lanai, where it does not grow to such a height as on Kauai, it associates with *Rauwolfia sandwicensis, Sideroxylon* sp., *Suttonia Lanaiensis,* etc., and thrives best at an altitude of about 2000 feet, on the dry ridges of Kaiholena and Mahana valleys. It has also been recorded from Molokai and Maui. The *Aulu* flowers usually during the summer months, from June to August, though fruits, which have the same properties as the *Papala kepau,* may be seen together with flowers on one and the same tree. It is peculiar to the Hawaiian Islands. The largest leafed specimens the writer observed on the lava fields of Kapua, S. Kona, Hawaii, where it is a small tree.

The wood is very light when dry and very porous; the branches are very brittle and break easily.

Pisonia inermis Forst.

Papala kepau.

(Plates 52, 53.)

PISONIA INERMIS Forst. Prodr. (1776) 75. no. 397;—Seem. Fl. Vit. (1866) 195.—
P. inermis var. leiocarpa Hbd. Fl. Haw. Isl. (1888) 369.—P. grandis R. Brown Prodr. Nov. Holl. (1810) 422;—H. Mann Proc. Am. Acad. VII (1867) 197;—Heimerl in Engl. et Prantl Pflzfam. III. 1. b. (1889) 29.—P. procera, Bertero, mss. in Guill. Zeph. Tait. (1837) 39;—Delles. Icon. Select. III. t. 87.—P. Brunoniana Endl. Fl. Norf. (1833) 43. n. 88;—F. Bauer, Illust. Pl. Norf. t. 145.—P. umbellifera Del Cast. Ill. Fl. Ins. Mar. Pac. VII. (1892) 268 et Fl. Polyn. Franc. (1893) 157, ex parte.

Leaves opposite, elliptico or obovate oblong 8 to 14 cm long,, 3 to 8 cm wide, on petioles of 15 to 20 mm, bluntly acuminate, contracted at the base, thin; flowers mostly hermaphrodite in a loose open panicle of 15 to 35 cm in length; perigone pale, 4 to 6 mm, tubular funnel shaped, the spreading limb entire, plaited with 5 to 10 crenatures; stamens 8 to 12 exserted; style as long as the stamens, stigma oblique, not fringed; fruiting perigone fusiform 35 mm long, 5-ribbed.

This tree, as well as *Pisonia umbellifera,* is known to the natives as *Papala Kepau* (*kepau* being the general name for substances such as tar, pitch, etc.), on account of the viscid glue which exudes from the fruits. It is a small tree 15 to 18 feet high, with elliptical-oblong thin leaves; it differs from the other two species in its large, loose panicle and in the flowers, which have the perigone not parted but entire. It inhabits the dry or semi-dry districts. It may be found in gulches back of Makawao, Island of Maui, in company with *Pelea cinerea, Xanthorylum* sp., *Pseudomorus Brunnoniana,* etc., as well as on the lava fields of Auahi, crater of Haleakala. On Hawaii it grows on the outskirts of the lava fields

PLATE 53.

PISONIA INERMIS Forst.
Papala kepau.
Growing in the Kipuka Puaulu, near Volcano Kilauea, Hawaii; elevation 4000 feet.

in Kona, slope of Mt. Hualalai, elevation 2000 feet, and on the slopes of Mauna Loa, land of Keauhou, at an elevation of 4000 feet, near Kilauea volcano; on the Parker Ranch near Waimea, and also on Molokai.

The fruits of this, as well as other species, were used by the natives for catching birds, and was spoken of as the *"he kepau kapili manu,"* or bird lime. The wood is very soft and of no value. *Pisonia inermis* extends over the Society, Gambier, Fiji, and Tonga groups, as well as Australia and Ceylon. It forms part of the beach forests of the Andaman Islands. The fresh leaves are used in India medicinally to subdue elephantiac inflammation in the legs or other parts. It is not uncommon in New Zealand, where it is called *"Para-para"* by the northern Maoris.

LAURACEAE.

The family Lauraceae is distributed over the tropical and subtropical regions of both hemispheres. It consists of 39 genera, with about 950 species. The genus Cassitha, also occurring in the Hawaiian Islands, is the only genus with parasitic species, which reminds one very much of the Dodder or Cuscuta species.

In these islands only one genus (Cryptocarya) has a single arborescent representative, which is peculiar to Kauai and the Waianae range of Oahu.

CRYPTOCARYA R. Br.

Flowers hermaphrodite. Tube of perianth, after flowering, constricted. Staminodia of the 4 circles ovate, shortly stipitate. Fruit dry, but entirely enclosed within the fleshy periantheal tubes. Testa of the seed hardly separable from pericarp. Flowers small in short axillary panicles. Trees with alternate penninerved leaves.

The genus Cryptocarya, which consists of about 40 species, reaches its best development in South-east Asia, especially Java and the Sunda Islands. A few occur in South Africa, nine in tropical Australia and a single one in the Hawaiian Islands. Ten species are American, especially Brazilian. To this genus belongs *Cr. moschata* Mart., the American nutmeg.

Cryptocarya Mannii Hbd.
Holio.

CRYPTOCARYA MANNII Hbd. Fl. Haw. Isl. (1888) 382;—Del Cast. Ill. Fl. Mar. Pac. VII. (1892) 278;—Heller Pl. Haw. Isl. (1897) 826.—Oreodaphne? Mann in Proc. Am. Ac. VII. (1867) 199.

Branches angular, the young leaves and inflorescence silky with a brownish tomentum; leaves thick coriaceous, glabrate, oblong 7 to 10 cm long, 30 to 40 mm wide, obtuse, narrowing at the base, the flat midrib prolonged into a flat margined petiole of 8 to 16 mm; panicles or racemes axillary, 12 to 18 mm long, few flowered; flowers hermaphrodite; perianth silky outside and within, funnel shaped 4 to 5 mm; lobes 6 in two series, the inner ones larger, rounded; stamens 9 of nearly equal length, the 6 outer ones inserted at the base of the lobes and shorter, anthers longer than the broad hairy filaments; the 3 inner anthers extrorse, ovoid, alternating with broad triangular staminodia. Ovary free, ovoid; style short obtuse; drupe ovoid globose, bluish-black, about 16 mm long, 12-ribbed, the thin putamen closely adherent to the perianth; seed with thin testa; the drupe is crowned by the remains of the perianth.

149

PLATE 54.

BROUSSAISIA PELLUCIDA Gaud.
Kanawau and Puahanui.
Male and female branch, the latter with mature fruits; reduced.

The *Holio* is a very common tree in the forests of the leeward side of Kauai, where it associates with *Bobea Mannii* (*Ahakea*), *Elaeocarpus bifidus* (*Kalia*), *Alphitonia excelsa* (*Kauila*), and others. It is a medium-sized tree, reaching a height of 20 to 30 feet, but rarely more. The trunk is somewhat rough and not exceeding 10 to 12 inches in diameter. It inhabits the drier districts of Kauai at an elevation of 3000 to 4000 feet, is light-loving and therefore mostly found on the outskirts of the forests. Mr. Forbes has found this tree, which was thought to be peculiar to Kauai, on the Waianae range of Oahu, whose vegetation is very similar to that of Kauai. Nothing could be ascertained from the natives as to the uses of this tree. Even the name *Holio* was not known to many of them.

SAXIFRAGACEAE

The family Saxifragaceae, which consists of 69 genera and about 581 species, is very widely distributed from tropical Asia to Africa and Australia, also in America and insular regions. In the Hawaiian Islands the family is represented by a single endemic genus with two species, which belongs to the section Hydrangeoideae, as it is a relative and representative of the well-known Hydrangea.

BROUSSAISIA Gaud.

Flowers through abortion unisexual. Male flowers with flat receptacle, 5 lanceolate sepals, and 5 valvate petals. Stamens 10, with thick subulate filaments, ovate anthers, and sterile gynoeceum. Female flowers with cup-shaped to ovoid receptacle, triangular sepals, and small scale-like petals, without stamens. Ovary inferior, five-celled; ovules numerous on thick bipartite placentas, with thick style and thick 5-lobed stigma. Berry globose, fleshy, many seeded. Trees with thick densely tomentose terete branches, opposite or whorled serrate leaves, and small flowers arranged in terminal corymbs.

KEY TO THE SPECIES.

Leaves opposite; petals bluish green.................................... **B. arguta**
Leaves ternate; petals reddish... **B. pellucida**

Broussaisia arguta Gaud.
Kanawau and *Puahanui*.

BROUSSAISIA ARGUTA Gaud. Bot. Voy. Uranie (1826, 1830) 479-80 t. 69;—DC. Prodr. IV. (1830) 17;—Hook. et Arn. Bot. Beech. (1832) 84;—Endl. Fl. Suds. (1836) no. 1417;—A. Gray Bot. U. S. E. E. (1854) 683. t. 87;—H. Mann, Proc. Am. Acad. VII. (1867) 165, et Fl. Haw. Isl. (1867) 240;—Mrs. Sinclair Indig. Fl. Haw. Isl. (1885) pl. 36 (is not *B. pellucida*);—Hbd. Fl. Haw. Isl. (1888) 120;—Del Cast. Ill. Fl. Ins. Mar. Pac. VI. (1890) 163;—Engler in Engl. et Prantl. Pflzfam. III. 2. a, (1891) 77;—Heller Pl. Haw. Isl. (1897) 828.

Leaves opposite (never ternate) obovate oblong, slightly acuminate, closely serrate, gradually tapering into a thick fleshy petiole which is dilated at the base, coriaceous glabrous, quite opaque, dark green above with impressed veins which are shortly hirsute; corymb 5 to 7 cm in height and about 10 cm in width, hirsute, the branches subtended by foliaceous sessile bracts of 12 to 25 mm, the bractlets smaller, caducous; male flowers: petals greenish-blue, spreading triangular, coriaceous, much longer than the acute sepals; stamens exserted; female flowers calyx ovoid, the narrow acute teeth 2 mm, petals scale-like, 1 mm, ovary adnate to about ¾ of its length; berry dark red, globose with a free conical apex, with distinct persistent style and crowned by the calycine teeth and petals; seed ½ mm.

Saxifragaceae.

This is one of the most common trees or shrubs which the traveler will meet in the Hawaiian rain forests. It occurs in all the islands of the group at elevations of 1000 to 3000 feet. It is conspicuous by its dark green shiny leaves, and when in fruit it is not at all unattractive. The native name of this, as well as of the other species, is *Puahanui* and *Kanawau*. It is never found in the dry districts, but is confined to the rain forests, where precipitation is heavy. It is easily distinguished from the other species by its small corymb and opposite leaves, which are not transparent.

Broussaisia pellucida Gaud.

Puahanui.

(Plate 54.)

BROUSSAISIA PELLUCIDA Gaud. Bot. Voy. Bon. (1844-52) pl. 9. (exclus. fig. 11 & 12);— Hbd. Fl. Haw. Isl. (1888) 121;—Del Cast. Ill. Fl. Ins. VI (1890) 163;—Engl. in Engl. et Prantl Pflzfam. III. 2. a. (1891) 77.

Leaves whorled, ternate, narrower, 4 to 6 cm in width; corymb larger and more open; male flowers: calyx about 2 mm; petals 4 mm, reddish; female flowers: calycine lobes short dentiform, not longer than the petaloid scales; ovary adnate only in the lower half; berry smaller, the stigma sessile on the free conical apex.

This species is certainly quite distinct from *B. arguta*, but is not confined to Puna, Hawaii, as it occurs on all the islands of the group, but at higher elevations than *B. arguta*. This latter species practically goes not higher than 3000 to 3500 feet, while the other species takes its place up to 5000 and nearly 6000 feet elevation. It differs from *B. arguta* in the larger female corymb, which is more open and almost as long as broad, while the male corymb is smaller and denser. A characteristic is the ternate leaves, which are not as broad as in *B. arguta*, and are perfectly pellucid, a characteristic not found in *B. arguta*, whose leaves are opaque. All these characteristics are constant; Gaudichaud's plate in Bot. Voy. Bonite is most excellent and shows at a glance the specific distinction from *B. arguta*. (Excluding figures 11 and 12.)

The figs. 11 and 12 in Gaudichaud's plate certainly do not represent *B. pellucida* as the stigmas in all specimens examined are sessile and not raised on a columnar style as is the case in *B. arguta*. As no text was published with the plate, they perhaps were introduced for comparison.

The native names for this and the previous species are *Puahanui* and *Kanawau*. It occurs on all the islands of the group, and is not confined to Puna, Hawaii, as given by Hillebrand. The writer collected it on the high plateau of Kauai and at the summit of Waialeale, on the same island: on Haleakala, Maui, it is not uncommon in the rain forests at an elevation of 4000 to 6000 feet. It is found on all the mountains of Hawaii, Mauna Loa, Kau, Hualalai, South and North Kona, Hamakua, and on the summit of the Kohala Mountains. The red berries are much sought for by the native birds.

It is a small tree, but often a shrub with stout and soft branches which are hirsute at their ends.

PITTOSPORACEAE.

With the exception of the genus Pittosporum, this family is exclusively Australian. It consists of 9 genera, 8 of which are peculiar to Australia. The genus Pittosporum is distributed over the tropics of the old world, from tropical and extra-tropical South Africa to the Hawaiian Islands, and reaches its northern boundary in Japan and from there to the Canary Islands. Its position in the natural system has been a varied one, as the relationship of this family to other plant families has been rather a mystery. Pax, in his treatise in Engler & Prantl, places it near the Hamamelidaceae, in common with which it has the resin ducts.

PITTOSPORUM Banks.

Calyx lobes free or united at the base, petals sometimes united; stamina subulate; anthers erect. Ovary sessile or shortly stipitate, incompletely 2, rarely 3-5celled. Style short. Capsule often laterally compressed, with coriaceous or woody valves. Seeds smooth or rugose, covered with a viscous resinous milky white pulp. Evergreen shrubs or trees, glabrous or tomentose. Leaves entire or dentate, often crowded in spurious whorls. Flowers in terminal or axillary racemes, panicles or clusters.

The genus consists of more than 70 species, and is distributed from Africa to the islands of the Pacific, as in Fiji, Timor, New Guinea and in the Hawaiian Islands, where they have reached a wonderful development. The species are dependent on the insects for pollination. The flowers of the Hawaiian species are dimorphous; that is, they are of two kinds—fertile and sterile. It is very difficult to render the exact limitation of each species, which is shown by the fact that the writer has found capsules belonging to three different species on a single inflorescence, on a tree found on the island of Lanai. Hillebrand, who had no mature capsules of each species, but of only a few, based his key to the species on the flowers. Ten species were originally described, to which number the writer has added three new ones.

KEY TO THE SPECIES.

Inflorescence axillary or cauline.
  Leaves glabrous; flowers white or cream-colored, the raceme pedunculate, seeds smooth.
    Flowers pedicellate.
      Sepals ovate, capsule smooth or occasionally roughened, leaves spathulate to oblong lanceolate........................... **P. glabrum**
      Sepals lanceolate acute or subulate, capsule rough.
        Pedicels and peduncle very long, leaves acuminate... **P. acuminatum**
        Pedicels short, leaves thick dark green rounded...... **P. spathulatum**
    Flowers sessile or glomerate at the end of a long peduncle.... **P. glomeratum**
  Leaves tomentose, obtuse or acuminate, flowers subsessile or pedicellate; seeds often rough at the back.
    Flowers small in a sessile cluster; capsule smooth........... **P. terminalioides**
    Flowers larger on a distinct peduncle, capsule smooth........ **P. cauliflorum**
    Flowers glomerate pedicellate, capsule very large 5 to 7 cm long, smooth
                                         P. Hosmeri
    Flowers pedicellate, capsule small, rough, densely tomentose, leaves strongly curved... **P. Gayanum**

153

PLATE 55.

PITTOSPORUM GLABRUM Hook. et Arn.
Hoawa.
Fruiting branch about one-half natural size.

Pittosporaceae.

Inflorescence terminal, axillary and cauline.
  Leaves glabrous, seeds smooth.
    Flowers large pedicellate, capsule rough, glabrous............ **P. insigne**
  Leaves tomentose, seeds smooth.
    Flowers large, capsule bluish glaucous, deeply wrinkled...... **P. Hawaiiense**
    Flowers subsessile, capsule small, quadrangular smooth....... **P. Kauaiense**
  Leaves tomentose, seeds rough.
    Flowers nearly always terminal, capsule rough, tomentose..... **P. confertiflorum**

Pittosporum glabrum Hook. et Arn.

Hoawa.

(Plate 55.)

PITTOSPORUM GLABRUM Hook. et Arn. Bot. Beech. (1832) 110;—End. Fl. Suds. (1836) no. 1585;—Gray, Bot. U. S. E. E. (1854) 229;—H. Mann, Proc. Am. Ac. VII. (1867) 151 et Fl. Haw. Isl. (1867) 125;—Hbd. Fl. Haw. Isl. (1888) 23;—Del Cast. Ill. Fl. Ins. Mar. Pac. VI (1890) 110;—Heller Pl. Haw. Isl. (1897) 829.

A small tree glabrous throughout; only the young shoots pubescent; leaves thin coriaceous, on slender branches, in loose whorls; spathulate to ovate oblong or oblanceolate, tapering at the base into a short petiole, the apex obtuse, rounded or acuminate; peduncles terminal, axillary or below the leaves, corymbose racemose, 6 to 12 flowered; sepals ovate acute 3 mm, glabrous; corolla 12 mm, white or cream-colored, the spreading tips 4 mm long; stamens nearly as long as the tube; style twice the length of the glabrous ovary; stigma truncate; capsule subglobose smooth, or rough, (wrinkled) two to three valved, the valves coriaceous, 25 mm in diam.; seeds smooth, angular.

This is a variable species and presumably occurs on the whole Koolau range. It was collected by the writer in Manoa and Pauoa valleys, also in Nuuanu Valley, on Konahuanui, Mt. Olympus, and especially Palolo Valley, where it is exceedingly common. In Niu Valley occurs a plant which agrees fairly well with those from the mountains back of Honolulu; the leaves are little shorter and not acuminate, neither are the capsules rough, but smooth and more or less oblong rather than subglobose. It must, however, be referred to this species.

It is a small tree 15 to 20 feet high and is peculiar to the rain, as well as the drier forests of the main mountain range of the island of Oahu at an elevation of 2000 feet.

Pittosporum acuminatum Mann.

Hoawa or *Papahekili.*

PITTOSPORUM ACUMINATUM Mann Proc. Am. Acad. VII (1867) 152, et Fl. Haw. Isl. (1867) 125;—Hbd. Fl. Haw. Isl. (1888) 22;—Del Cast. Ill. Fl. Ins. Mar. Pacif. VI. (1890) 110;—Pax in Engl. et Prantl Pflzfam. III. 2 a (1891) 111;—Heller Pl. Haw. Isl. (1897) 828.

Leaves chartaceous, oblanceolate-acuminate, perfectly glabrous, 8 to 20 cm long, 2 to 4 cm wide, gradually merging into a short petiole of about 1 cm; axillary peduncles very slender 2.5 to 6 cm with flower, with fruit 8 cm, corymbose-racemose, the peduncle and pedicels hirsute, bracts subulate; flowers very fragrant, 5 to 12 or even more, on pedicels of 7 to 20 mm, sepals very narrow subulate, pubescent, petals cream colored, stamens as long as the tube, anthers sagittate; style slender, as long as the corolla, often exserted, stigma capitate; capsule subglobose, tomentose, rugose (wrinkled), seeds black, minutely tuberculate.

A very handsome, graceful tree with beautiful cream-colored, fragrant flowers. Tree about 18 to 20 feet high. It is a very distinct species and differs from all the rest of the Hawaiian Pittosporums in the slender long peduncles and pedicels.

155

PLATE 56.

PITTOSPORUM SPATHULATUM Mann.
Hoawa.
Fruiting branch, about one-half natural size.

Pittosporaceae.

Wawra in Flora writes that *P. acuminatum*, described by Mann, may belong to the group of *P. terminalioides*. This view the writer does not share with Wawra, but he thinks it to be closer to *P. insigne* var. β Hbd. However, it is quite a distinct species. Specimens were collected by the writer on Kauai, to which island the tree is peculiar. It is plentiful at Halemanu, and Kaholuamano at an elevation of 4000 feet, where it grows in the drier forests or on exposed ridges. It was also observed above Makaweli at an elevation of 2000 feet. Specimens from this locality differ somewhat from those of the higher elevations in being much stouter, and in having coriaceous instead of chartaceous leaves.

Pittosporum spathulatum Mann.
Hoawa.
(Plate 56.)

PITTOSPORUM SPATHULATUM Mann. Proc. Am. Ac. VII. (1867) 151, et Fl. Haw. Isl. (1867) 125;—Hbd. Fl. Haw. Isl. (1888) 24;—Del Cast. Ill. Fl. Ins. Mar. Pac. VI. (1890) 111;—Pax in Engl. et Prantl. Pflzfam. III. 2. a. (1891) 111.—**P. terminalioides** Planch. var. **spathulatum** Gray, Bot. U. S. E. E. (1854) 231;—Wawra in Flora (1873) 169.

Branches stiff, densely foliose, the leaves dark green, sub-coriaceous glabrous, cuneate or obovate-spathulate, gradually narrowing from an obtuse and rounded apex into a short petiole of 1 to 1.5 cm; 6 to 12 cm long, 2 to 4 cm wide; inflorescence axillary with a yellowish pubescence; peduncle very short, about 6 mm or more, pedicels of the same length; sepals ovate-elongate, obtuse or acute, sparingly pubescent; stamens shorter than the tube, anthers sagittate; ovary densely tomentose, style the length of the ovary, stigma capitate; capsule glabrous when old, subquadrangular, deeply furrowed or runcinate, seeds smooth.

A tree of 15 to 18 feet in height, occurring in the rain forests of Oahu, especially in the Koolau range. It is a very distinct and not variable species, as its characteristics are quite constant. It is a rather handsome, though somber, plant, and is conspicuous from a distance on account of its dark green foliage. It is quite common on the upper slopes of Konahuanui, elevation 3000 feet, and in the mountains of Punaluu, Waiahole, and Waikane. In the upper forests of Oahu it takes the place of *P. glabrum*, which grows up to 2000 feet elevation. Horace Mann's specimens came from Kaala Mt., Waianae range.

Pittosporum glomeratum Hbd.
Hoawa.

PITTOSPORUM GLOMERATUM Hbd. Fl. Haw. Isl. (1888) 23;—Del Cast. l. c. p. 110;—Pax l. c. p. 111.

Leaf whorls at intervals of 5 to 10 cm, the young shoots cinereous-pubescent; leaves spathulate elongate, 15 to 25 cm x 2.5 to 5.5 cm, acuminate or obtuse, gradually narrowing into a petiole of 25 mm or less, chartaceous glabrous; peduncle axillary 25 to 32 mm, bracteate, with a dense cluster of almost sessile flowers at the apex, pubescent, the lanceolate bracts 3 to 6 mm; sepals ovate, obtuse 2 to 3 mm, tomentose; corolla white; with a tube of 10 mm; ovary tomentose; capsule and seeds as in *P. glabrum*.

A small tree occurring at the eastern end of Oahu in Wailupe Valley. Hillebrand also describes a variety β. *acutisepala* from the same region, evidently a slight variation.

The species comes very close to *P. glabrum* and is perhaps only a form of it.

PLATE 57.

PITTOSPORUM TERMINALIOIDES Planch.
Flowering and fruiting branch, less than one-half natural size.

Pittosporaceae.

Pittosporum terminalioides Planch.

Hoawa.

(Plate 57.)

PITTOSPORUM TERMINALIOIDES Planch. in Herb. Hook;—A. Gray Bot. U. S. E. E. (1854) 231;—H. Mann Proc. Acad. VII. (1867) 151;—et Fl. Haw. Isl. (1867) 123;—Hbd. Fl. Haw. Isl. (1888) 24;—Del Cast. Ill. Fl. Ins. Mar. Pac. VI (1890) 111.—**P. glabratum** Putterl. Syn. Pittosp. 11. (pro parte non Hook. et Arn.).

A small tree, with stiff branches; leaves crowded near the ends of the branches, chartaceous to thick coriaceous, the upper side wrinkled with a close net-work, the lower side pubescent or glabrous when old, obovate to spathulate, or oblong, rounded at the apex or bluntly acuminate with revolute margins, 7 to 10 cm long, 2.5 to 3 cm wide on a petiole of 15 to 20 mm; inflorescence terminal, axillary or cauline, short tomentose, the thick peduncle about 2 to 10 mm long, the flowers subsessile; sepals ovate tomentose, 4 mm, corolla cream-colored, the tube short, 6 mm, its lobes half as long; stamens half the length of the tube; ovary tomentose, style of the same length as ovary, the two lobes of the stigma spreading; capsule quadrangular to oblong, tomentose, flattened, about 25 mm each way, with a longitudinal median groove; seeds rough, dull.

This species occurs on the island of Hawaii in the scrub forest at an elevation of 2000 feet and again in the scrub forests or open country at 7000 feet elevation. On Maui the writer collected specimens on the lava fields of Auahi, district of Kahikinui, southern slopes of Haleakala at an elevation of 1500 feet, which belong to this species. It differs from the Hawaii plants in the leaves only, which are of much thinner texture, being chartaceous and having rather indistinct veins, while in the plants from Kona and Kau, Hawaii, the veins are very strong and prominent. The specimen figured came from East Maui, southern slopes of Haleakala, where it grew on the rough *aa* flows along the government road. It is a small tree, 15 to 18 feet in height, with a small trunk about 5 inches in diameter.

Pittosporum cauliflorum Mann.

Hoawa.

PITTOSPORUM CAULIFLORUM Mann in Proc. Am. Acad. VII. (1867) 151, et Fl. Haw. Isl. (1867) 124;—Wawra in Flora (1873) 168;—Hbd. Fl. Haw. Isl. (1888) 24;—Del Cast. Ill. Fl. Ins. Mar. Pac. VI (1890) 110;—Pax in Engl. et Prantl. Pflzfam. III. 2. a. (1891) 111.

A loosely branching tree; leaves crowded at the ends of the stiff stout branches, coriaceous, closely areolate above, elongate-obovate or cuneate 15 to 20 cm long, 5 to 7.5 cm wide, rounded or shortly apiculate, gradually narrowing into a petiole of 12 mm, pale green, densely covered underneath with a soft fawn or pale lemon colored tomentum; flowers cauline on the bare branches below the leaves, peduncle 4 to 8 mm, bearing at the end 8 to 12 subsessile flowers; bracts 5 mm; sepals 3 mm, ovate obtuse, tomentose; corolla cream colored, with a tube of 8 to 10 mm; stamens half as long, with sagittate anthers; ovary tomentose, the stigma capitate, 2-lobed; capsule thick woody, the flattened valves with a median furrow and transverse waves 18 to 25 mm, with the endocarp pale orange; seeds flat angular, crenulate or tubercular at the back and edges.

A tree 30 feet in height, with a trunk of 8 to 10 inches in diameter. It was first collected by H. Mann on the Waianae range, on Mt. Kaala, and by Hillebrand in Makaleha Valley of the same range.

PLATE 58.

PITTOSPORUM HOSMERI var. **longifolia** Rock var. nov.
Flowering and fruiting branch much reduced.

The writer is not acquainted with this species. Hillebrand records three varieties of this species as follows: β. var. *fulvum*, Oahu, Ewa to Waialua; γ. var.
from Mt. Kaala, and finally δ var. *flocculosum*, also from Mt. Kaala.

It is exceedingly difficult properly to diagnose the Hawaiian species of Pittosporum and more so the varieties. *Pittosporum terminalioides* has all possible
intermediates finally approaching *P. confertiflorum*. It is perhaps one of the
many forms of the latter. The two species, together with *Pittosporum Hosmeri*,
have tuberculate seeds in common, while all the other species have the seeds
smooth and shining. *P. Gayanum* also belongs to this group as far as foliage is
concerned, but the seeds are smooth and not tuberculate.

The writer has abundant material, but even so, it is extremely difficult to separate them specifically, as all seem to run very much into each other.

P. glabrum is very close to *P. glomeratum* and differs from it only in the
sepals and pedicellate flowers, a characteristic which can not be very well relied
upon, as both forms occur often on one and the same plant. The capsules of *P.
confertiflorum* from the various localities have all possible shapes and forms, but
can not be separated successfully into varieties. It will have to remain a polymorphous species.

In conclusion the writer wishes to state that he has gathered much material
from localities from where Pittosporums had never been recorded. Some of
them undoubtedly are new, but owing to incomplete specimens, as the wanting
of flowers, or mature capsules, the writer thinks it advisable not to include them
in this already voluminous book, but rather to wait for additional material and
then make an exhaustive study of this very variable group of plants.

Pittosporum Hosmeri Rock.

Aawa hua kukui.

PITTOSPORUM HOSMERI Rock Bull. Torr. Bot. Club. 37 (1910) 297 pl. 1, et Rept. Board
Com. Agr. & For. (1911) 84, pl. 20.

Branches stout, young shoot pubescent, leaves crowded at the ends of the branches,
subcoriaceous, glabrous above, wrinkled with a close network, densely tomentose underneath with a light to dark brown wool, young leaves covered on both sides, entire with
revolute margins, 10 to 26 cm long, 3 to 6 cm wide, on petioles of 2 to 3 cm; inflorescence
axillary and cauline, a corymbose raceme, the tomentose peduncle 2 to 3 cm, bracteate,
the peduncle surrounded at the base with numerous linear subulate bracts, sepals tomentose, ovate acute 4 mm long; corolla cream-colored, the tube about 8 to 10 mm long, the
lobes 5 mm, ovate, with prominent veins; stamens as long as the tube, anthers oblong;
ovary tomentose, ovoid-oblong, the style nearly twice as long, slightly exserted; capsule
tomentose when young, glabrous and smooth when mature, valves woody, oblong to subquadrangular 55 to 75 mm long, 40 to 55 mm wide, and about 45 mm thick, opening into
two to four valves, with a longitudinal median groove, endocarp bright orange colored,
seeds arranged alternately in two rows on each placenta, black, rugose 6 to 7 mm in
diameter, differing from the other Pittosporums in that the capsules are not filled completely by the seeds, but are arranged only in two rows.

It is a medium-sized tree 18 to 25 feet or more in height with stiff more or
less ascending branches; it is most remarkable for the enormous capsules, which
are the largest in the genus. The type specimen was collected on the lava field

PLATE 59.

PITTOSPORUM HOSMERI var. **longifolia** Rock var. nov.
Trunk showing bark, and flowering and fruiting branch pinned to trunk. Growing on
the lava fields of South Kona, Kapua, Hawaii.

Pittosporaceae.

of Puuwaawaa, in North Kona, on the slopes of Mt. Hualalai, Hawaii, on June 17, 1909. Since that time the writer visited again this district and collected addi- tional material; most of the trees were then in flower. The writer made also extensive exploration of the forest surrounding Mauna Loa, especially the drier districts in South Kona, which resemble Puuwaawaa greatly as far as vegetation is concerned. In that latter locality the writer found this species very common, and it is certainly astounding that it has been kept from our knowledge for so long. The plants from this latter locality, however, differ somewhat from those from Puuwaawaa, in size of capsules, which are smaller, and in the size of leaves, which are much larger. The tree itself is much smaller and more nearly a shrub, while the trees at Puuwaawaa have often a diameter of a foot or so.

Near Kilauea Volcano at an elevation of 4000 feet is a small *Kipuka* or piece of land of great age which is surrounded by rough (*aa*) lava flows. The area of this *Kipuka* is 56 acres; on it are to be found not less than 42 species of trees. The vegetation is such that one would immediately look for Pittosporum, but in vain. The writer persisted, however, to locate a Pittosporum representative in the vicinity, and after a search of several days found a small triangular lot of about an acre in extent, which must have been once upon a time a part of the above *Kipuka;* it was surrounded by enormously thick *aa* flows, which were cov- ered with stunted *Ohia lehua* growth, whilst in that small pocket of land grew *Pittosporum Hosmeri* var. *longifolia*, together with Pelea and Xanthoxylum.

The trees from Kilauea are identical with those from Kapua, S. Kona, and also with specimens from the upper slopes of Hualalai, from the forests above Huehue at an elevation of 5000 feet, while the typical *Pittosporum Hosmeri* is peculiar to Puuwaawaa.

The variety is here described as follows:

Var. longifolia var. nov.
(Plates 58, 59, 60.)

Leaves lanceolate-oblong to obovate oblong, rounded or acuminate at the apex, 15 to 40 cm long, 5 to 9 cm wide, on petioles of 2 to 5 cm, glabrous above, densely covered under- neath with an ochraceous to rufous tomentum; flowers as in the species; capsules smaller subsessile, 10 on a common peduncle forming a cluster of often 12 cm in diameter, cap- sules globose, quadrangular to oblong, 2-3-4 valved, the valves woody, 4 to 5 cm long or 5 cm each way, glabrous, smooth, seeds as in the species. Capsule orange yellow when mature.

The tree is quite common at Kapua, S. Kona, Hawaii, on the lava flows, but does not reach such a height and size as at Puuwaawaa. The trees of the latter locality are loaded with fruit during June and July, while those of Kapua bear mature fruit during the month of February. However, the fruiting season of these, like nearly all the other Hawaiian trees, can not be relied upon. Occurs also at Kilauea, and Hualalai, Hawaii.

This species with its variety resembles somewhat *P. terminalioides* of the same regions, but has only the roughened seeds in common with it.

The fruits of *P. Hosmeri* and variety are a source of food for the native crow,

PLATE 60.

PITTOSPORUM HOSMERI var. longifolia Rock var. nov.
Growing on the lava flows of South Kona, Kapua, Hawaii; elevation 2000 feet.

PLATE 61.

PITTOSPORUM GAYANUM Rock.
Hoawa.
Fruiting branch; less than one-half natural size.

Pittosporaceae.

Corvus hawaiiensis or *Alala*, which pecks open the large woody capsules and feeds on the oily seeds within. The crow is peculiar to Kona, Hawaii. Nearly 80% of all the capsules of this species examined by the writer were eaten out by these birds, which are still very common.

Pittosporum Gayanum Rock sp. nov.
(Plate 61.)

A small tree 15 to 18 feet high with a round spreading crown, or when growing on the high central plateau near Waialeale in the dense rain forest, a tree with very few straight ascending branches; leaves crowded at the ends of the branches or scattered, obovate oblong, shortly acuminate, with revolute margins, glabrous above, veins very prominent impressed, dark green with dark brown or fulvous tomentum underneath, especially on the very prominent veins, the young leaves covered on both sides with a dark reddish-brown wool, 15 to 25 cm long, 4 to 10 cm wide, on somewhat margined petioles of about 2 cm; inflorescence axillary and cauline, peduncle short, 12 mm, with dark reddish brown tomentum, bracteate, bracts linear subulate, woolly as well as the ovate to linear lanceolate sepals; flowers on pedicels of 5 to 10 mm, sepals 3 mm, tube of the cream-colored corolla about 10 mm, the lobes 4 mm, stamens as long as the tube, anthers oblong, style exserted, three times the length of the tomentose ovary; capsule ovoid to cordate, pointed, densely tomentose with dark reddish brown wool, about 2 cm or more in diam. the valves rugose, wrinkled; seeds angular, shining black, smooth. about 5 mm long.

This very interesting tree is peculiar to the interior, high plateau of Kauai, especially the upper slopes of Waialeale. It grows in the swamps and swampy forests as well as along streambeds several miles inland from Kaholuamano, at an elevation of 4800 to 5000 feet. It is not uncommon in the more open flat swamps in company with the thousands of *Lobelia macrostachys* at this region, which is constantly wrapped in clouds. It is a rather curious plant, with a short trunk and perfectly straight branches, which are only few, three or four, and the large dark green and brown foliage. It is a constant species and grows all over the summit of Kauai. It was collected by the writer first in September, 1909, and again in October, 1909, in the Alakai swamp near the head of Wainiha, and on Waialeale October 20, 1911. The type is 8867 in the College of Hawaii Herbarium, Honolulu, T. H. The plant is named in honor of Mr. Francis Gay of Kauai, whose kind hospitality and help in exploring the Kauai forests the writer was fortunate to enjoy. At the very summit of Waialeale in the open bog the writer found a variety of this species perfectly glabrous; it was a shrub about 5 feet high, and may be described here as follows:

Var. Waialealae var. nov.

Leaves whorled at the ends of the branches, glabrous even the very young leaves, obovate oblong. acuminate dull green on both sides, 5 to 10 cm long, 2 to 3.5 cm wide, contracting into a petiole of 1 cm; capsules 2 cm each way, the valves deeply wrinkled glabrous, young capsules tomentose, seeds as in the species.

Type No. 8866 in the College of Hawaii Herbarium, collected by the writer October 10, 1911, at the summit bog of Waialeale, Kauai, elevation 5200 feet. It grew in company with *Pelea Waialealae. Labordea Waialealae, Lobelia Kauaiensis*, etc.

PLATE 62.

PITTOSPORUM INSIGNE Hbd.
Hoawa.
Fruiting branch, half natural size.

PLATE 63.

PITTOSPORUM HAWAIIENSE Hbd.
Hoawa.
Showing fruiting branch.

Pittosporaceae.

Pittosporum insigne Hbd.

Hoawa.

(Plate 62.)

PITTOSPORUM INSIGNE Hbd. Fl. Haw. Isl. (1888) 25;—Del Cast. Ill. Pl. Ins. Mar. Pac. VI (1890) 110;—Pax in Engl. et Prantl Pflzfam. III 2. a (1891) 111.

Leaves in distant whorls, thick, chartaceous, glabrous, obovate-oblong, acuminate 6 to 12 cm x 2.5 to 4 cm, contracting into a short petiole of 1 to 2 cm; flowers terminal in the uppermost leaf-whorls and axillary or all along the stem; inflorescence a corymbose raceme (or in East Maui specimens more or less glomerate) the flowers on pedicels of 1 to 2 mm, the rhachis tomentose, surrounded at the base with numerous linear bracts of 5 to 10 mm, bearing 15 to 25 flowers on pedicels of 4 to 8 mm (in specimens from the type locality); sepals ovate, acute, densely tomentose, tomentum light yellowish, corolla large, tube 10 to 12 mm, the lobes broad ovate about 8 mm; stamens half the length of the tube, style and ovary as long as the tube, the latter densely villous; capsule oblong about 25 mm long, deeply wrinkled, seeds smooth.

A very handsome tree with large cream-colored flowers; it reaches a height of about 25 feet and has stiff ascending branches. Hillebrand's description, which has been enlarged upon to suit the abundant material which is at the writer's disposal, agrees exactly with plants from the type locality. It is not uncommon on West Maui, above Kaanapali, at an elevation of about 3500 to 4000 feet, where it grows in the rain forest. It was also collected by the writer in Iao Valley, on the same island.

On East Maui, in the rain forest of Mt. Haleakala, at an elevation of 4000 feet, the writer met with a Pittosporum which he must refer to this species, though differing somewhat from the trees found on West Maui. This is, however, not surprising, since all Hawaiian Pittosporums are very variable. The East Maui plants differ from the West Maui ones in the inflorescence, which 's shorter peduncled and has almost sessile flowers: the latter agree, however, with those from the type locality. On the northern slope of Haleakala, at Nahiku, on the crater Hinai, at an elevation of about 3000 feet, the writer met with a large number of trees which will also have to be referred to this species; they differ from the type specimens in the young leaves, which are covered with light brown tomentum, and in some other minor points.

On the same mountain, at 2000 feet elevation, the writer collected Hillebrand's var. *β* of this species, which is easily distinguished by the long axillary peduncles, which measure often 5 cm. and more. The variety is a small tree, 15 to 18 feet in height.

Pittosporum Hawaiiense Hbd.

Hoawa.

(Plate 63.)

PITTOSPORUM HAWAIIENSE Hbd. Fl. Haw. Isl. (1888) 26;—Del Cast. Ill. Fl. Ins. Mar. Pac. VI. (1890) 110;—Pax in Engl. et Prantl. Pflzfam. III. 2. a (1891) 111.

Leaves scattering or in distant whorls, large obovate-oblong, acute strongly nerved, glabrous on both sides when old or pubescent underneath, young shoots covered with a dense fawn colored tomentum on both sides, thick chartaceous, 12 to 22 cm long, 5 to 7 cm wide, on petioles of 1.5 to 3 cm, flowers axillary or cauline, racemose rarely terminal on hirsute peduncles of about 15 mm, pedicels 3 to 7 mm; sepals ovate, triangular 3

169

PLATE 64.

PITTOSPORUM CONFERTIFLORUM Gray.
Fruiting branch pinned against trunk of tree, growing near Ukulele, Haleakala, Maui;
elevation about 6000 feet.

Pittosporaceae.

mm, bracts ovate lanceolate 5 to 8 mm; tube of corolla about 8 mm split up to the upper third, the lobes broadly ovate; stamens as long as the tube, anthers oblong-sagittate; ovary ovoid, densely tomentose style almost twice as long; capsule bluish-glaucous or colored, subquadrangular, about 3 cm or more in diameter, valves woody, deeply wrinkled; seeds black, smooth or minutely tuberculate.

This species is a small tree, 15 to 18 feet high, with straight ascending branches, bark white, smooth; flowers cream-colored. This particular species occurs on the island of Hawaii in the forests of Naalehu, Kau, at an elevation of from 2300 to 4000 feet or more, where it is quite plentiful. It was also collected by the writer on the great plateau of the Kohala mountains of the same island at an elevation of 4000 feet, but not at all common. Its distinctive characteristics are the capsules, which are bluish-glaucous and deeply wrinkled, as well as the very large foliage, which is, however, exceeded in size by *Pittosporum Hosmeri* var. *longifolia.*

Pittosporum Kauaiense Hbd.

Hoawa

PITTOSPORUM KAUAIENSE Hbd. Fl. Haw. Isl. (1888) 25;—Del Cast. Ill. Fl. Ins. Mar. Pac. VI. (1890) 111;—Heller Pl. Haw. Isl. (1897) 829.

Leaves chartaceous with strong prominent nerves, obovate oblong, 12 to 24 cm long, 4 to 8 cm wide, shortly acuminate, with a distinct petiole of 2 to 4 cm long, dark green, glabrous above, covered with a whitish or golden yellowish pubescence; inflorescence axillary or cauline, densely hirsute with brownish hair, peduncle short, about 8 mm, pedicels 4 mm, sepals scarcely 2 mm, acute, villous, corolla cream colored the lobes about 2 mm with a strong median nerve; stamens as long as the tube, style little longer; capsule subglobose 16 mm in diam., glabrous when mature, covered with brownish wool when young, with 4 deep longitudinal furrows; seeds smooth, shiny.

This is one of the tallest species of Pittosporum, reaching a height of 30 to 40 feet, with a trunk of about 10 inches in diameter, which is vested in a smooth whitish bark. It is peculiar to the island of Kauai, where it grows in the forest of Kopiwai, below Halemanu, 3600 feet, as well as at higher elevation. It is not common at Kaholuamano, but was again collected by the writer in Olokele canyon and in the woods of Makaweli, elevation 2000 feet. The trees from the lower locality differ from those of the type locality, Halemanu, in the capsules, which are wrinkled, but are otherwise the same. The pubescence of the underside of the leaves disappears with age.

Pittosporum confertiflorum Gray.

Hoawa.

(Plate 64.)

PITTOSPORUM CONFERTIFLORUM Gray Bot. U. S. E. E. (1854) 232, pl. 19;—H. Mann Proc. Am. Acad. VII. (1867) 150, et Fl. Haw. Isl. (1867) 123;—Hbd. Fl. Haw. Isl. (1888) 26;—Del Cast. Ill. Fl. Ins. Mar. Pacif. VI (1890) 110;—Pax in Engl. et Prantl. Pflzfam. III, 2. a (1891) 111.—**P. terminalioides** β. Gray l. c. p. 231.

Branches stout, leafy, woolly when young, leaves thick coriaceous, alternate or whorled obovate-oblong, shortly acuminate 12 to 20 cm long, 3 to 6 cm wide, contracting into a distinct petiole of 2.5 cm, pale fulvo-tomentose underneath, and occasionally above; inflorescence terminal, axillary and cauline, the numerous flowers densely packed in a corymbose raceme with an axis of about 25 mm; pedicels 6 to 12 mm; bracts linear oblong 16 mm; sepals orbicular ovate densely woolly, obtuse 6 mm; corolla cream-colored

Pittosporaceae.

or white, tube 10 to 12 mm or less, lobes about 6 mm, stamens nearly as long as the tube, anthers linear sagittate; pistil short, ovary sessile, oblong, tomentose; capsule globose-ovoid, somewhat flattened, the thick woody valves 2.5 mm, wrinkled or rough or sometimes smooth; seeds purple, compressed and angled, closely packed in two rows in each cell, testa dull, minutely tuberculate-rugose.

A tree 20 feet in height with stiff, stout, ascending branches. It is a somewhat variable species; the inflorescence is not always terminal, but also axillary and even cauline in specimens from Haleakala, Maui. The writer collected specimens of this species from the type locality southern slopes of Haleakala, Maui, where the tree is not at all common. It also grows near Kaupo at an elevation of about 5000 feet. The leaves in the writer's specimen are much larger than those figured by Asa Gray.

Hillebrand's var. β. from Kau and Kona agrees well with the writer's material from Lanai. The genus Pittosporum is exceedingly well represented on Lanai, the species *confertiflorum* evidently being very variable, as there are as many different forms as there are Pittosporum trees and one would be naming individual trees. It is indeed puzzling, the question of specific distinction in the Hawaiian Pittosporums, thanks to the insects on which the plants depend for pollination.

Hillebrand's typical var. β. occurs in nearly all the valleys of Lanai, as Kaiholena, Mahana, Koele, and also on the ridges. It differs from the species in its smaller leaves and lanceolate sepals, and is a small tree about 18 feet in height. In some of the Lanai specimens the capsules are deeply wrinkled, and quadrangular, with perfectly flat valves 3 cm. each way; one specimen, No. 8109, has a long bracteate peduncle of 4 cm., with large pedicellate flowers.

172

LEGUMINOSAE.

This, the second largest plant family—being only exceeded by the Composite family—consists of nearly 450 genera, with over 7000 species, and is of much greater economic importance than the latter.

The Leguminosae family is distributed all over the world, and is only absent from the very remote islands of the Antarctic, though only sparingly represented in New Zealand.

In regard to the sub-families, the Mimosoideae are entirely absent in Europe, while the Papilionatae are to be found in the Arctic as well as high Alpine regions of both hemispheres.

The family is represented in the Hawaiian Islands by 25 genera, only four of which, however, have arborescent species.

KEY TO THE GENERA.

SUB-FAM. MIMOSOIDEAE.

Leaves twice pinnate; flowers in heads or spikes:
Stamens indefinite; leaves mostly replaced by dilated petioles... 1. **Acacia**

SUB-FAM. CAESALPINIOIDEAE.

Leaves twice pinnate:
Pod-winged along the upper suture, calyx very oblique........ 2. **Mezoneurum**

SUB-FAM. PAPILIONATAE.

Leaves abruptly pinnate:
Pod four-winged... 3. **Sophora**
Leaves of three leaflets.. 4. **Erythrina**

ACACIA Willd.

Flowers hermaphrodite or polygamous; calyx campanulate, toothed or petals free or united; stamens numerous, free or united at the base; ovary sessile or raised, two to many ovuled. Legume oval, oblong or linear, straight or curved, flat or convex, membraneous, coriaceous, indehiscent. Unarmed or thorny trees or shrubs. Leaves bi-pinnate, or reduced to a phyllodium or dilated petiole. Flowers small, numerous, mostly yellow in globular heads or cylindrical spikes.

The genus consists of about 450 species, which are distributed over the tropical and subtropical regions of both worlds, being especially numerous in Africa and Australia. In these islands only three species are represented; one is doubtful (*Acacia Kauaiensis*, Hbd.).

KEY TO THE SPECIES.

Phyllodia instead of true leaves:
Pod flat, broad and straight.................................... **A. Koa**
Pod narrow and curved... **A. Koaia**

Acacia Koa Gray.
Koa or *Koa ka.*

(Plates 65, 66, 67, 68.)

ACACIA KOA Gray Bot. U. S. E. E. (1854) 480;—H. Mann Proc. Am. Acad. VII (1866) 165;—H. Mann Fl. Haw. Isl. (1867) 235;—Wawra in Flora (1873) 141;—Hbd. Fl. Haw. Isl. (1888) 112;—Del Cast. Ill. Fl. Ins. Mar. Pac. VI (1890) 160;—Engl. & Prantl Pflzfam. III. 3 (1894) 110;—Heller Pl. Haw. Isl. (1897) 830.—**Acacia heterophylla** Hook. et Arn. Voy. Bot. Beech. (1832) 81;—Benth. Mimos. in Hook. Lond. Journ. Bot. I. (1839) 368.

PLATE 65.

ACACIA KOA Gray.
Koa.
About one-third natural size. Showing true leaves and phyllodia, flowers and fruits.

Leguminosae.

Phyllodia falcate, coriaceous, 10 to 15 cm long, varying from 6 to 8 mm to 24 mm or more in breadth, narrowed at the base, acute or obtuse at the tapering apex; the smooth surface is striate with many nerves; on younger plants the phyllodia bear a bipinnate leaf; the leaflets 12 to 15 pairs, oblong, emarginate, crowded; peduncles solitary or fascicled in the axils, about 12 mm long, bearing a dense many flowered head of 8 mm in diameter, calyx teeth very short 5 in number, petals 5, oblong lanceolate, glabrous, more or less united, longer than the calyx, half the length of the stamens; legume broadly linear, straight or slightly falcate, 7.5 to 15 cm long, 16 to 18 mm broad, glabrous, flat, two-valved, about 12 seeded; seeds dark brown to black.

The *Koa* is one of our most stately forest trees and is next to the *Ohia lehua (Metrosideros polymorpha),* the most common. It is perhaps the most valuable tree which the islands possess, as it is adapted for construction as well as for cabinet work. The *Koa* reaches a height of more than 80 feet in certain localities, with a large trunk vested in a rough, scaly bark of nearly an inch in thickness. When growing in the open, it develops a beautiful, symmetrical crown, with usually short trunks of perhaps 15 to 20 feet in height and a diameter of more than 6 feet. The lower branches are then almost horizontal, far-spreading, while farther up the branches become peculiarly twisted and more or less ascending. When growing in the rain or fern forest, it develops a long, straight bole of considerable length and thickness, clothed in a rather smooth, gray bark; usually branching 40 feet or so above the ground. (See plate 68.) It is this sort of timber which is most valuable for construction work, while the *Koa* of the drier districts has a much more beautiful wood and is more suitable for cabinet work. The *Koa* has two kinds of leaves, true leaves and phyllodia. Young twigs or young trees always have first the true twice pinnate leaves, which gradually pass into phyllodia—that is, the petioles become dilated and take the place of the true leaf.

The adult trees bear phyllodia only, though an occasional twig near the base of the trunk will have true leaves. The *Koa* is found on all the islands of the group, and adapts itself to almost any condition. It descends to as low as 600 feet, and ascends to an elevation of 5000 feet, and sometimes higher. Beautiful trees can be observed on the slopes of Mauna Loa on the Island of Hawaii, not far from the volcano, as well as in South Kona on the same mountain. It is sad, however, to see these gigantic trees succumb to the ravages of cattle and insects.

Large tracts of *Koa* forest which twenty years or so ago were in their prime have now perished, and nothing is left but the dead trunks with their huge branches dangling on strings of bark, ready to drop from the dizzy heights, when stirred by the slightest gust of wind, crushing everything beneath them. Such is the condition of the *Koa* forest of today in certain tracts of land on Hawaii. Cattle are the great enemy of the *Koa*.

Above Kealakekua, in South Kona, of the once beautiful *Koa* forest 90 per cent of the trees are now dead, and the remaining 10 per cent in a dying condition. Their huge trunks and limbs cover the ground so thickly that it is difficult to ride through the forest, if such it can be called. It might be said, how-

PLATE 66.

ACACIA KOA Gray.
Koa.
Showing trunk, bark and flowering branch; near tree-molds, Kilauea, Hawaii; elevation
4000 feet.

Leguminosae.

ever, that there are still tracts of land where the *Koa* forest is in its natural condition. As already mentioned, the *Koa* adapts itself to almost any environment. Ancient *aa* (rough) lava flows have been covered by *Koa* trees to the exclusion of everything else. It is on these lava fields that the trees are still in good condition, as cattle usually avoid crossing these sharp, rugged fields of lava.

From the big trees found in Kona, Hawaii, the natives of by-gone days used to carve their great war canoes. Occasionally one can find an unfinished log which, owing to its enormous weight, was abandoned by the natives, who were unable to remove it to the lowlands and beach. Today the wood is used for furniture and is sold as Hawaiian mahogany, though, of course, it bears no relation to the tree of that name. The bark of the *Koa* was used by natives for tanning purposes.

At lower elevations, as on Oahu on the windward side, *Koa* is associated with the screw pine *(Pandanus odoratissimus)*, while at the middle forest zone, at 4000 feet, it is usually found in company with the *Naio (Myoporum sandwicense), Kolea (Suttonia), Metrosideros polymorpha*, and *Mamani (Sophora chrysophylla)*, while in the forks of its branches in accumulated humus flourish arborescent species of Lobelias of the genus *Clermontia*.

The *Koa* is peculiar to the Hawaiian Islands, but is closely related to a species *(Acacia heterophylla* Willd.), in Mauritius and Bourbon; while *Acacia laurifolia* is a seaside tree in Viti and Samoa; the vernacular name in Viti is *Tatakia*, and in Samoa *Tatakia* or *Tatagia*.

The *Koa* is attacked by several insects. A few lepidopterous insects feed on the *Koa* leaves, such as *Scotorythra caryopis* Meyr and *S. idolias* Meyr, which are often responsible for the defoliated *Koa* trees, as well as the *S. rara* (Bult.), the most common species of the genus. Of borers, several beetles live in the *Koa* trunks, such as *Aegosomus*, while the larvae of *Thyrocopa alboonubila* Walsm. are found in dead branches of *Koa*, as well as larvae of *T. abusa* Walsm. on the bark and dead twigs. Besides, other lepidopterous insects may be found in more or less decayed *Koa* trunks.

Acacia Koaia Hbd.
Koaia or *Koa oha.*

ACACIA KOAIA Hbd. Fl. Haw. Isl. (1888) 113;—Del Cast. Ill. Fl. Ins. Mar. Pacif. VI (1890) 160.
Leaves as in Koa; axillary racemes with not more than 3 heads, generally reduced to a single one; pod very narrow, not over 8 mm wide, and about 15.5 to 15 cm long; otherwise as in *Acacia Koa*.

The *Koaia*, unlike the *Koa*, is a rather small tree, reaching a height of only 20 to 25 feet. The trunk is not straight as in the *Koa*, but gnarled and twisted. The bark is rough and corrugated. It differs mainly from the *Koa* in its pods, which are very narrow, linear, while those of the *Koa* are broad. The leaves are the same as in the *Koa*.

177

12

PLATE 67.

ACACIA KOA Gray.
Koa.
Tree about 80 feet tall, with diameter of trunk about 4 feet; growing in the Kipuka
Puaulu, near Volcano Kilauea, Hawaii; elevation 4000 feet.

PLATE 68.

ACACIA KOA Gray.
Koa.
Showing straight growth of bole in wet or fern forest, near Volcano Kilauea, Hawaii;
elevation 4000 feet.

PLATE 69.

MEZONEURUM KAUAIENSE (Mann) Hbd.
Uhiuhi.
Flowering and fruiting specimen. About one-third natural size.

Leguminosae.

The *Koaia* inhabits the very dry districts on the leeward sides of the Islands of Molokai, Maui, and Hawaii. On Molokai, it grows at Kalae as well as on the edge of the dry canyon below Kamoku, in company with *Naio (Myoporum sandwicense), Walahee (Plectronia odorata), Aiea* (Nothocestrum), Dodonaea, etc. On Maui it can be found on the Kula slopes of Haleakala at an elevation of 2000 feet or more, together with the *Halapepe*, while on Hawaii it grows on the lava fields of North Kona, especially on the slopes of the ridge between Puuanahulu and Puuwaawaa, associated with Reynoldsia, Maba, Osteomeles *(Ulei),* etc., as well as on the lava fields of Kawaihae iuka, along the road together with the *Maua, Naio, Mamani,* and *Kului.*

Koaia wood, which is much harder than the *Koa* and closer grained, was used by the natives for spears and fancy paddles. It is endemic to the islands, and was first discovered by Dr. W. Hillebrand, and described by him in his valuable work on the Flora of the Hawaiian Islands.

He also describes a species of Acacia from Kauai, specimens of which were sent to him by Valdemar Knudsen of Kekaha, Kauai. He gave it the name *Acacia Kauaiensis*, but does not say whether it is a tree or shrub. As the writer did not meet with any trees that would answer the description given by Hillebrand, it is here omitted and simply mention made of it.

The *Koaia* flowers during the early part of the summer or late spring, but flowers and fruits usually can be observed on the same tree during July and August.

MEZONEURUM Desf.

Calyx short oblique, the lowest lobe larger than the four remaining; concave; petals 5 nearly all equal; stamens 10, free declinate, ovary sessile free, with 2 to many seeds; legume flat compressed, indehiscent, with a dorsal wing; seeds flat, compressed exalbuminous. Trees or climbing shrubs. Leaves bipinnate. Flowers red or yellow.

A genus of eleven species found in the tropics of the old world, distributed from India to Malay archipelago, Queensland, and New South Wales, with one species in tropical West Africa, and one in the Hawaiian Islands.

Mezoneurum Kauaiense (Mann) Hbd.
Uhiuhi; Kea on Maui.
(Plates 69, 70, 71.)

(The native name ''Kalamona'' is not applied to this plant, as stated by Hillebrand, but to an introduced species of Cassia.)

MEZONEURUM KAUAIENSE (Mann) Hbd. Fl. Haw. Isl. (1888) 110;—Del Cast. Ill. Fl. Ins. Mar. Pacif. VII. (1890) 157.—Caesalpinia Kavaiensis Mann Proc. Am. Acad. VII. (1866) 164, and Fl. Haw. Isl. (1867), 233;—Brigham Mem. B. P. B. Mus. III. (1911) 178.

Branches loose spreading, unarmed, the young shoots covered with a hoary pubescence; leaves abruptly pinnate with 1 to 5 pairs of pinnae, each pinnae with 4 to 8 pairs of leaflets, the common rhachis 7.5 to 12.5 cm, the pinnae 3.5 to 7.5 cm; leaflets oblong, 25 to 30 mm x 12.5 mm. obtuse at both ends membraneous, on petioles of 2 mm; stipules none or small wart-like; raceme terminal, hoary 25 to 75 mm long densely floriferous from the base; the pedicels 25 to 50 mm, jointed above the middle; bracts ciliate, caducous; calyx glabrous pinkish or red; petals pinkish purple or red, shorter than the calycine

181

PLATE 70.

MEZONEURUM KAUAIENSE (Mann) Hbd.
Uhiuhi.
Showing trunk with bark and flowering and fruiting branch pinned to it. (Trunk about
1 foot in diameter.) On the lava fields of Puuwaawaa, North Kona,
Hawaii; elevation 2000 feet.

PLATE 71.

MEZONEURUM KAUAIENSE (Mann) Hbd.
Uhiuhi.
Along the government road in North Kona, Hawaii; elevation 2000 feet.

PLATE 72.

SOPHORA CHRYSOPHYLLA Seem.
Mamani.
Flowering branch.

Leguminosae.

lobes; stamens exserted, the filaments hairy, broad and flat below; ovary glabrous, 3 to 5-ovuled; style incurved; stigma small; pod broad-oblong or obovate nearly 10 cm long by about 5 cm wide, with a dorsal wing of 6 to 2 mm in width running along its whole length and ending in an uncinate point, indehiscent, glaucous reddish when young; seeds 2 to 4, pale ovate, flat, 18 to 20 mm x 14 to 16 mm.

The *Uhiuhi* is a very beautiful tree with a trunk of sometimes more than one foot in diameter. The bark is rough-scaly and of a dark-gray to brown color. The leaves are pinnate, having 4 to 8 pairs of leaflets of about 1½ inches in length. The flowers are arranged in terminal racemes 1 to 4 inches long, and are of a beautiful dark-red color; legume is broad, oblong, 3 to 3½ by 2 inches, and is winged on one side; when young it is pinkish, glaucous, and very pretty.

The tree, which was first discovered on the Island of Kauai, inhabits the leeward side of the islands, especially the *aa* lava fields. It is not uncommon on the Island of Hawaii. At North Kona, between Huehue and Puuwaawaa, elevation 2000 feet, the writer observed the biggest trees. They are not, however, very tall, reaching a height of about 30 feet, with short trunks. On Kauai they are very scarce nowadays, only individual trees being found in a gulch below Puu ka Pele back of Waimea; on Hawaii they are only found in Kona, where quite a number of trees exist, the latter place being a new locality, as no *Uhiuhi* had been recorded previously from Hawaii.

The tree is known by the natives as *Uhiuhi* on Kauai and Hawaii, while on Maui, along Kaupo, the southern outlet of Haleakala crater, it is known as *Kea*. It blossoms in the early spring. On Hawaii it is associated with *Kokia Rockii* Lewton, the native red cotton or *Kokio*, *Erythrina monosperma* or *Wiliwili*, *Colubrina oppositifolia*, Dodonaea, Sideroxylon, *Maba sandwicensis*, Osteomeles, etc. It is also found on Oahu in the mountains of Waianae and on Wailupe. It has not been reported from Molokai or Lanai.

The wood of the *Uhiuhi* is extremely hard, close-grained, and very durable; it is of almost black color, with a light-colored sapwood. The natives made their spears from it, as well as the *laau melo-melo* or *laau makaalei*, a peculiar implement for fishing. The *laau melo-melo* had the shape of a club, to which a line was attached at the tapering end. When fishing, the natives used to drop the wood, which previously was besmeared with a sweet, sticky substance, into the water, through which it was slowly pulled in order to attract the fishes, which were then caught by a man with a net, who followed behind. The wood, being very heavy, will sink in the water even if a hundred years old, and was on that account selected by the natives for the above-described purpose.

The *Uhiuhi* is peculiar to these islands, outside of which it is not found. A species of Tortrix feeds on the flat seed-pods of the *Uhiuhi*; it is seldom that perfect pods are met with.

SOPHORA L.

Calyx with short teeth; vexilum broad, obovate or circular, often shorter, rarely longer than the carina; alae oblong; stamens free or rarely connected at the base in a ring, with dorsifixed anthers, ovary with many ovules; pod cylindrical often contracted between the

PLATE 73.

SOPHORA CHRYSOPHYLLA Seem.
Mamani.
Kipuka Puaulu, near Volcano Kilauea, Hawaii; elevation 4000 feet.

Leguminosae.

seeds, or slightly compressed, coriaceous, often four winged, fleshy or woody, usually indehiscent; seeds ovate or globose. Trees or shrubs, rarely perennial herbs with impari-pinnate leaves; leaflets usually small and numerous; flowers yellow or white, rarely purple, in simple terminal racemes or several forming a terminal panicle.

Only one species found in the Hawaiian Islands. The genus consists of more than twenty-five species, distributed over the warmer regions of both hemispheres. Trees or shrubs, distributed from Western Thibet to Ceylon, China and Japan, Siberia, Texas, California, South America, New Zealand, Bourbon, and one on our islands. *S. tomentosa* is a tropical cosmopolitan, and is found in all the islands of the South Seas, including New Guinea.

Sophora chrysophylla Seem.
Mamani.
(Plates 72, 73, 74.)

SOPHORA CHRYSOPHYLLA Seem. in Flora Vit. (1873) 66;—H. Mann Proc. Am. Acad. VII (1866) 164, et Fl. Haw. Isl. (1867) 192;—Hbd. Fl. Haw. Isl. (1888) 108;—Del Cast. Ill. Fl. Ins. Mar. Pacif. VI (1890) 157.—**Edwardsia chrysophylla** Salisb. in Trans. Linn. Soc. IX (1808) 302 t. 26, f. 1;—Ker. Bot. Reg. t. 738;—DC. Prodr. 2 (1825) 97;—Endl. Fl. Suds. (1836) no. 1610;—A. Gray U. S. E. E. (1854) 459;—Wawra in Flora (1873) 140.

Young shoots silky pubescent; leaves 15.5 to 15 cm long, with 6 to 10 pairs of leaflets; leaflets obovate oblong, 20 to 36 mm x 8 to 12 mm, obtuse, often retuse, with a cinereous silvery or tawny pubescence (when growing at high altitudes) or glabrous (at low eleva-tion); racemes terminal and lateral, 12 to 25 mm long, tomentose; calyx about 6 to 10 mm, cup-shaped lobes broad and obtuse; petals 25 mm long; yellow, the broad vexilum re-curved, the suberect alae and carina nearly as long; stamens as long as the carina; ovary tomentose; pod 10 to 15 cm long, 8 mm wide, often deeply constricted between the seeds, four-winged; indehiscent; seeds 4 to 8, oval somewhat compressed, yellow 8 mm long. The var. β mentioned in the Bot. of the U. S. Exploring Expedition is only a glabrous form of this species usually found in the lowlands where it is shrub, and never a tree.

The *Mamani* is a tree of 20 to 40 feet in height, with a trunk reaching some-times 2 feet in diameter. It is vested in a light-brown corrugated bark of a half inch in thickness. The leaves are 5 to 6 inches long, and have from 6 to 10 pairs of leaflets. The flowers are a bright yellow, and are arranged in droop-ing racemes, which are either terminal or lateral.

The *Mamani*, which may be found on all the islands with the exception of Oahu and Molokai, grows from almost sea level up to nearly 10,000 feet elevation. It inhabits the high mountains of Hawaii, Mauna Kea, Mauna Loa, and Hua-lalai up to 10,000 feet, where it forms the upper forest zone together with shrubby Composites, such as *Raillardia arborea* and *R. struthioloides* and other plants peculiar to these regions. On Kauai it never grows to a tree, while on the slopes of Mauna Loa, on Hawaii, near the volcano of Kilauea, it reaches its best development. Trees of 40 feet in height are not uncommon at an elevation of 4000 feet. In North Kona, on the slopes of Hualalai on the lava fields just below Huehue, it is about 2 to 4 feet high, branching from the base, and does not resemble the fine trees which may be found higher up at 7000 to 8000 feet

187

PLATE 74.

SOPHORA CHRYSOPHYLLA Seem.
Mamani.
Growing in Kipuka Puaulu, near Volcano Kilauea, Hawaii; elevation 4000 feet.
Tree 40 feet high.

Leguminosae.

on the same slopes. At low elevation the plant is entirely glabrous, while just below and above the snow-line it is covered with silvery-gray hair, which protects it from the severe cold which it experiences not only during the winter but also in the summer months. The writer experienced a temperature of 19° Fahr. during a night spent on Mauna Kea in the month of July. A few small trees were found on Lanai just above the homestead of the former manager of the Lanai Ranch Co., in a small gulch all by themselves. Whether they were planted there by human hand or by birds cannot be ascertained, but the former may be more reasonable, as they were not found elsewhere on Lanai.

The wood of the *Mamani* is exceedingly hard and very durable in the ground. It is therefore mainly used for fence posts by the cattle ranchers on the large estates on Hawaii. On Haleakala, Maui, the trees are of medium size, though reaching a similar development at Auahi as near the volcano at Puaulu. On the upper slopes of Haleakala they are shrubby. The wild cattle and horses, which are very numerous on the upper slopes of Mauna Kea, live almost exclusively on the young leaf shoots of the *Mamani* during the dry season, when there is no grass available. But, thanks to the hardiness of the trees, which are exceedingly deep-rooted, they are able to withstand these ravages of the descendants of Vancouver's cattle.

The *Mamani* is peculiar to the Hawaiian Islands, while *S. tomentosa* is found in the South Sea Islands, where it grows on the beach. In Viti or Fiji it is known by the name *Kau ni alewa*, or women's tree.

Two native beetles infest the *Mamani*. They belong to the peculiar genus Plagithmysus, and nearly every tree can be seen perforated with small holes, the work of the beetle. But to the credit of the beetle may it be said that they attack only trees already in a dying condition. The two species are *P. Blackburni* and *P. Darwinianus*.

ERYTHRINA L.

Calyx campanulate, truncate, or 5 toothed; vexilum large, conduplicate, alae short, often very small or wanting; carina longer or shorter than the alae, the two petals free or partially connate; vexillary stamens free, or connate with the others which are connate to the middle; ovary stipitate, with several ovules; style subulate, with a small terminal stigma; pod stipitate, linear, curved, compressed or cylindrical, tapering at both ends, contracted between the oval seeds; two valved, sometimes follicular or indehiscent. Trees or erect shrubs with stout, often prickly branches. Leaves pinnately three-foliolate, with glandular stipellae; flowers in terminal or axillary racemes, generally scarlet; bracts and bractlets small or wanting.

Only one species represented in the islands. The genus, which is distributed over the tropics and subtropics of both hemispheres, consists of thirty species. They range from the Himalayas to tropical West Africa, Brazil, Australia and tropical America, one species being cosmopolitan, with one species in the Hawaiian Islands, which is, however, found in the other islands of the Pacific.

189

PLATE 75.

ERYTHRINA MONOSPERMA Gaud.
Wiliwili.
Showing trunk, bark and fruiting branch. Lava fields near Puuwaawaa, Hawaii; elevation 2000 feet.

Leguminosae.

Erythrina monosperma Gaud.

Wiliwili.

(Plate 75.)

ERYTHRINA MONOSPERMA Gaud. Bot. Voy. Uranie (1826) 486, pl. 114;—Hook. et Arn. Bot. Beech. (1832) 81;—Endl. Fl. Suds. (1836) no. 1641;—A. Gray U. S. E. E. (1854) 444;—H. Mann l. c. p. 163, et Fl. Haw. Isl. (1867) 185;—Sinclair Indig. Fl. Haw. Isl. (1885) pl. 18;—Hbd. Fl. Haw. Isl. (1888) 99;—Del Cast. Ill. Fl. Ins. Mar. Pacif. VI (1890) 151, et Fl. Polyn. Franc. (1893) 47;—Heller Pl. Haw. Isl. (1897) 834.—**E. montana** Forst. in Pancher, Herb., et in Cuzent, Tahiti (1860) 240.—**E. tahitensis** Nadeaud Enum. (1873) n. 499.—**Corallodendron monosperum** O. Ktze. Rev. Gen. Pl. I. (1891) 173.

Leaflets ovate or deltoid, broader than long 5 to 6.5 cm x 6.5 to 9 cm, obtuse, entire, truncate or subcordate at the base, chartaceous, tomentose underneath; the petiole of the terminal leaflet 10 to 25 cm long, the petiolules of the lateral ones 5 mm; stipules gland-like; racemes in the axils of the ultimate leaves, fulvo-tomentose, stout, dense, nodose, with two or one flowers at a node, 15 to 20 cm long; bracts 2 mm or less; pedicels 4 to 8 mm; calyx thickly tomentose; minutely toothed; flowers pale yellow or brick red; vexilum 25 to 50 mm nearly as broad as long, about 3 times longer than the obtuse alae and carina; stamens about as long as the vexilum; anthers pointed, versatile; ovary tomentose, about 12 mm long, stipitate 3 to 5 ovuled, half the length of the style; pod 35 to 50 mm long, 1 to many seeded (the name monosperma is badly chosen); seeds about 12 mm, bright red.

The *Wiliwili* is a medium-sized tree of 20 to 30 feet, with stiff, gnarled branches and a spreading crown. The trunk is usually short, with few conical prickles on its otherwise smooth, thin, yellowish bark. It is usually of very large diameter, often 3 to 4 feet and more. The *Wiliwili* has the reputation of having the lightest wood of any of our island trees. It loses its leaves in the early fall or late summer and flowers from early spring to June or July, according to environment, before the new leaves appear, though sometimes flowers and leaves may be found together. The former are of a brick-red or white color, and not altogether unhandsome. The bright-red seeds are usually single, one in a pod, from which the tree derives its specific name monosperma (one-seeded). It is called tiger's-claw by the foreigners, on account of its flowers, which are claw-shaped.

The *Wiliwili* is the feature of lowland vegetation up to 1500 feet. It thrives best in the hottest and driest districts on the leeward sides of all the islands, especially on the scoria and among rocks. It grows usually in company with *Myoporum sandwicense (Naio), Reynoldsia sandwicensis, Nototrichium sandwicense, etc.* It is characteristic of the lava fields of North Kona, Hawaii, on the west end of Molokai, the gorges of Mauna Lei and Nahoku on Lanai, the lava fields on the southern slopes of Haleakala, Maui, in the dry canyons on Kauai, and even on the barren Island of Kahoolawe a few trees are still in existence. (See Plate XXVII.)

The very soft, white wood of the *Wiliwili* was and is still used by the natives for outriggers on their fishing canoes, but since it has become more and more scarce, the *Hau* is used as a substitute. The pretty red seeds are strung into leis and worn by the native women; those sold as *Wiliwili* leis in the curio shops are not of the native *Wiliwili*, but are the seeds of the so-called Red San-

191

Leguminosae.

dalwood or *Adenanthera pavonina*, a tree introduced into the islands from India. The wood of other species is manufactured into corks.

The *Wiliwili* is not peculiar to Hawaii, but is distributed from Hawaii to Tahiti and New Caledonia.

Erythrina indica Lam. is a cosmopolitan species of the South Seas, being found in Samoa, New Guinea, Solomon and Marshall Islands, and also has found its way even into North Australia. Its vernacular names are *Malatum* of the Tami Islands, *Gatae* in Samoa, where the natives have even a name for the flowers, which they call *alo'alo*. The bark is used as a remedy for colic, etc.

RUTACEAE.

The family Rutaceae belongs to the warmer regions of the globe, and wherever they appear form a distinct part, or contribute to the vegetative character of that particular region. This is especially true in the Hawaiian Islands, where the family is one of the most prominent features of the Hawaiian forest. The group of Xanthoxyleae-Evodiinae, to which our Hawaiian Rutaceae belong, finds its best development on the islands and on the western coast of the Pacific Ocean. The family is represented in the Hawaiian Islands by three genera, one of which, Platydesma, is endemic, while Pelea is found in New Caledonia and Madagascar. It has in these islands the largest number of species. The whole family consists of 111 genera with over 900 species. The group Aurantieae possesses the most useful members, namely, the fruit trees, such as oranges, citrons, etc.

KEY TO GENERA.

Leaves compound, alternate; flowers unisexual...................... 1 **Xanthoxylum**
Leaves simple, opposite or whorled.
    Stamens free; petals valvate.................................. 2 **Pelea**
    Stamens united; petals imbricate............................. 3 **Platydesma**

XANTHOXYLUM L.

Flowers polygamous or unisexual. Calyx lobes 1 to 5, small, more or less united. Petals 2 to 10, imbricate or valvate. Stamens 3 to 5, hypogynous, alternate with the petals, rudimentary or wanting in the pistillate flowers; filaments filiform or subulate; anthers elliptic to nearly orbicular or ovate. Pistils 1 to 5, raised on a fleshy gynophore, sometimes slightly united below, rudimentary in the staminate flowers. Ovaries 1-celled; styles short and slender, more or less united toward the summit; stigmas capitate; ovules 2 in each cavity, collateral, pendulous from the inner angle of the cell. Follicles 1 to 5; endocarp free. Seeds oblong, ovoid, or globose, suspended on a slender funiculus often hanging from the carpel at maturity; seed-coat black or reddish, shining. Embryo straight or curved. Cotyledons oval or obicular foliaceous.—Trees or shrubs, often prickly, but unarmed in the Hawaiian species, with acid aromatic bark, alternate equally or odd pinnate or three-foliolate leaves, rarely unifoliolate, dotted with pellucid oil glands. Infloresence terminal or axillary, cymose, paniculate, racemose or glomerate. Type species *Xanthoxylum Clava-Herculis* L.

The genus Xanthoxylum, or Zanthoxylum as it may also be written, consists of numerous species, which were all except nine placed in the genus Fagara by Engler in the Natürlichen Pflanzenfamilien. The writer, however, adheres rather to the old classification, as the distinctions on which Engler based his new

192

Rutaceae.

arrangement are not at all well brought out in the Hawaiian species. In most of the other works Engler's new combinations have been placed as synonyms.

The genus Xanthoxylum is distributed over North America, Eastern Asia and also most tropical countries. It is found in Polynesia, outside of the Hawaiian Islands, where seven species and numerous varieties have so far been discovered, only in Tahiti. All Hawaiian species are unarmed. The leaves are quite aromatic, most of them having a peculiar soapy odor, while one, *X. hawaiiense* Hbd. var. *citriodoro*, is strongly lemon-scented. The flowers of some species are also quite fragrant.

Most of our Xanthoxyla inhabit the dry regions on the leeward sides, especially old lava flows, where they reach their best development, as, for example, on the southern slopes of Mt. Haleakala, Puuwaawaa, North Kona, Hawaii, and on Mauna Kea in the open scrub-country. Several species occur only in the rain forests, as *X. oahuense* and *X. Bluettianum*. They are usually found at an elevation of 2500 to 4000 feet, but rarely higher. All Hawaiian Xanthoxyla are trees, except a new species found in the Kohala rain forests.

KEY TO SPECIES.

Petals 4, thin and slightly imbricate. Flowering panicles appear before the leaves in the axils of large scales.
    Leaflets pedately ternate, the lateral ones on long petiolules.
        All petiolules articulate at or below the middle.............. **X. Oahuense**
        Lateral petiolules without articulation...................... **X. hawaiiense**
            Leaflets ovate cuneate on petiolules of 16-20 mm......... **X. Bluettianum**
    Leaflets 7 to 3 foliolate the lateral leaflets sessile or on short petiolules.
        Leaflets 9-7 lanceolate with copious oil-dots................. **X. glandulosum**
        Leaflets 5-3 ovate or ovate oblong opaque................... **X. Kauaiense**
        Leaflets 3 or rarely 5, thick, tomentose truncate at the base... **X. Mauiense**
Petals 4 or 2, thick coriaceous and valvate. Small stipelliform leaflets at the base
    of the lowest leaflets... **X. dipetalum**

Xanthoxylum Oahuense Hbd.

Ae or *Heae.*

(Plate 76.)

XANTHOXYLUM OAHUENSE Hbd. Fl. Haw. Isl. (1888) 75;—Del Cast. Ill. Fl. Ins. Mar. Pac. VI. (1890) 130.—**Fagara Oahuensis** Engler in Engl. et Prantl Pflzfam. III. 4. (1895) 119.

A small tree, glabrous; leaves 3-foliolate, on long petioles of 8 to 10 cm, their leaflets on petioles of nearly even length, the terminal one 5 to 8 cm, the lateral ones 4 to 5 cm, all of which are articulate or thickened in the upper fourth, ovate or orbicular, 7 to 8 cm long, 5 to 7 cm or more wide, caudate-acuminate, the lateral ones unsymmetrical at the base, excised in the upper half, glabrous coriaceous, opaque, dark green, brownish-black when dry; panicles at the base of the branch 6 to 12 cm long, loosely and few-flowered; male flowers: sepals minute, petals greenish, ovoid-oblong blunt at the apex, imbricate in the bud, stamens slightly exserted 2.5 mm in length, with subglobose anthers; follicles 10 to 12 mm, rugose and pitted.

The Oahuan *A'e* or *Hea'e* is a small, rather handsome tree and is peculiar to the island after which it is named. It is one of the few Hawaiian Xanthoxyla which inhabits the wet middle, or rain forest zone, growing on the highest

PLATE 76.

XANTHOXYLUM OAHUENSE Hbd.
A'e or Hea'e.
Male flowering branch, and fruiting panicles in the upper corners; less than half
natural size.

Rutaceae.

ridges, as on Konahuanui, Niu Valley, and in the Koolau range, where the tree is not uncommon.

The bark, as of nearly all the other Hawaiian species of this genus, is thin and smoothish, with yellowish lenticels; in other species the bark is dark brown to black and has the appearance of having been burned; the granular mass will come off even when only touched, in others again the bark is covered with very narrow only slightly protruding confluent ridges. The wood of this, as of the other species, is yellow and bitter to the taste.

Xanthoxylum hawaiiense Hbd.
A'e or Hea'e.
(Plate 77.)

XANTHOXYLUM HAWAIIENSE Hbd. Fl. Haw. Isl. (188) 76;— Del Cast. Ill. Fl. Ins. Mar. Pacif. VI. (1890) 129.—Fagara hawaiiensis Engler in Engl. et Prantl Pflzfam. III. 4. (1895) 119.

A medium sized tree, glabrous; leaves pedately 3-foliolate, on petioles of 3.5 to 4.5 cm, the leaflets on petiolules of equal length, not articulate, but occasionally thickened near the blade, acuminate, ovate to deltoid, the lateral ones unsymmetrical or subcordate, 5 to 7 cm long, 4.5 to 5.5 cm wide; panicles in the axils of the leaves or at the end of the branches; follicles curved, almost smooth, but pitted, 1 cm in diameter.

Hillebrand records this tree from the central plateau on the Island of Hawaii at 5000 to 6000 feet elevation, evidently from between Mauna Kea, Mauna Loa and Mt. Hualalai. The writer did not meet with this tree on that great plain, but collected specimens of an evident variety of this species on the slopes of Mauna Kea near Keaumoku, among composites such as Raillardia and Lipochaeta, near the extinct crater of Nohonaohae at an elevation of perhaps 4000 feet.

On his last visit to North Kona, Puuwaawaa, he collected flowering specimens of a Xanthoxylum; in fact, the same species as found at Nohonaohae, referrable to X. hawaiiense. The specimens were collected on the lava fields beyond Puuanahulu joining the pahoehoe lava flow of 1859. The leaves of this tree as well as those from Nohonaohae are exceedingly strong lemon scented, exactly as those of Eucalyptus citriodora, which fact caused the manager of the Parker Ranch, on which land the trees are found, to believe that the tree was the lemon-scented gum.

It is peculiar that Hillebrand should not have noticed such a strong aromatic odor, which none of our other Xanthoxyla possess; he, however, fails to mention anything about it. The true species, answering Hillebrand's description in nearly every detail, was found by the writer on the southern slopes of Mt. Haleakala, Maui, where the tree is, however, not abundant. There the trees have not the slightest odor of lemon, but the ordinary, somewhat soapy smell, as have the rest of our Xanthoxyla. In the latter locality the trees were in fruit during November, 1910, where the writer collected his first material of this species (no. 8657 in the College of Hawaii Herbarium).

PLATE 77.

XANTHOXYLUM HAWAIIENSE Hbd.
A'e or Hea'e Tree.
Growing on the ancient lava fields of Auahi, district of Kahikinui, East Maui.
Tree about 20 feet in height.

Rutaceae.

The trees from Hawaii first mentioned differed somewhat from Hillebrand's description, and on this, as well as on the strength of its exceedingly aromatic odor, it is here described as a new variety.

Var. citriodora Rock var. nov.

Leaves 3-foliolate on a common pubescent petiole of 4 cm, leaflets deltoid 3.5 to 4 cm in diameter on not articulated petiolules, the median one 5 cm, the lateral one 3 cm, puberulous underneath, transparent, with a continuous row of pellucid oil glands along the entire margin, strongly lemon-scented when fresh, young leaves velvety tomentose. panicles pubescent at the end of the branchlets, sepals and petals pubescent, the latter 2.5 mm ovoid, stamens as long, anthers ovoid, the rudimentary ovary pubescent.

Hillebrand's variety β. the writer collected on Lanai. This variety has coriaceous leaves which are also larger, ovoid to orbicular and even deltoid; it is as a whole a much more robust tree and entirely glabrous. Collected without flower or fruit July 24, 1910, in Kaiholena Valley, Lanai, no. 8076 in College of Hawaii Herbarium. On Kauai the writer saw one tree and collected specimens of the same below Kaholuamano, growing on the edge of one of the canyons. It must be referred to Hillebrand's var. β., from which it, however, differs in the lateral petiolules, which are only 1.5 cm long. Collected Sept. 18, 1909, Kaholuamano, Kauai. (No. 5207 in College of Hawaii Herbarium.)

Var. velutinosum Rock var. nov.

Leaves 3-foliolate on a common petiole of 4 to 5 cm, leaflets on petiolules of nearly even length, ovate acuminate, not articulate, truncate to unevensided at the base, gray-velvety tomentose throughout on upper and lower surface, quite opaque, without marginal oil glands, and not lemon-scented, in fact without any odor, even when leaves are crushed; stipules below the leaf-whorls, spathulate, many nerved, pubescent.

This tree occurs on the lava fields of Puuwaawaa, North Kona, Hawaii, adjoining the lava fields of Puuanahulu, where the variety *citriodora* occurs. This variety differs from the latter in the shape of the leaves, which are inodoriferous and densely velvety tomentose and quite opaque and without marginal oil glands. Collected March, 1912; type no. 10205 in College of Hawaii Herbarium.

Xanthoxylum glandulosum Hbd.
A'e or *Hea'e.*

XANTHOXYLUM GLANDULOSUM Hbd. Fl. Haw. Isl. (1888) 74;—Del Cast. Ill. Fl. Ins. Mar. Pacif. VI. (1890) 129.—**Fagara glandulosa** Engl. in Engl. et Prantl Pflzfam. III. 4. (1895) 119.

Leaves 9 to 7 foliolate, 18 to 20 cm long, the leaflets lanceolate 7.5 to 9 cm x 2.5 to 3 cm, acute, contracting at the base, membraneous, glabrous, copiously punctate with large transparent oil-dots, the common petiole about 2.5 cm, that of the terminal leaflet about 18 mm, the lateral leaflets subsessile.

Hillebrand collected this species on West Maui, gulch of Lahainaluna. The writer found a small tree 10 feet high of this species in Waihou Gulch, near the spring at the head of the valley, back of Makawao on the northwestern slope of Mt. Haleakala on East Maui, elevation 3000 feet. The tree was neither in flower nor fruit; the 7-foliolate leaves were coriaceous and not membraneous. A va-

197

PLATE 78.

XANTHOXYLUM KAUAIENSE Gray.
A'e or Hea'e Tree.
The three-foliolate form growing on the aa lava fields on the southern slopes of
Mt. Haleakala, Auahi, Maui.

Rutaceae.

riety β. Hbd. with 7 to 5 leaflets, large, oblong, caudata-acuminaté, rounded at the base and dotted as before, occurs in the woods of Hilo, on the Island of Hawaii. The writer is not acquainted with this variety.

Xanthoxylum Kauaiense Gray.

A'e or *Hea'e*.

(Plates 78, 79.)

XANTHOXYLUM KAUAIENSE Gray Bot. U. S. E. E. (1854) 354;—H. Mann in Proc. Bost. Soc. Nat. Hist. X. (1866) 318; et Proc. Am. Acad. VII. (1867) 160, et Fl. Haw. Isl. Proc. Ess. Inst. (1869) 170;—Wawra in Flora (1873) 139;—Hbd. Fl. Haw. Isl. (1888) 73;— Del Cast. Ill. Fl. Ins. Mar. Pac. VI. (1890) 130.—**Fagara kauaiensis** Engler in Engl. et Prantl Pflzfam. III. 4. (1895) 119.

A small graceful tree, about 6 to 12 m high, with a straight trunk and a dense round crown; leaves 5 or 3-foliolate (in the trees of East Maui, southern slopes of Mt. Haie- akala) on petioles of 2.5 to 3.5 cm; the leaflets ovate or oblong, 4 to 6 cm long, 2 to 3 cm wide, subacuminate, coriaceous and quite opaque, or with a few transparent dots along the margin, glabrous, the petiolule of the terminal one occasionally but not always articu- late near the blade, 12 to 16 mm, those of the lateral ones 2 to 3 mm; panicles 1 to 4 near the base of the short branchlets 3.5 to 7 cm long, the compressed peduncle 12 to 20 mm, the pedicels 2 to 4 mm, the bractlets minute; flowers tetramerous, 0.5 mm, acute, petals 3 to 4 mm, stamens in the male flowers longer than the petals, (in sterile flowers according to Hillebrand 2 mm long) anthers ovoid, wanting in the fertile flowers; carpel single, with a globose subsessile stigma, rudimentary in the sterile flowers; follicle on a stipe of 4 mm, (teste Hillebr.) obovate, glabrous, faintly pitted and striate; seed solitary, 8 to 10 mm.

The Kauai *A'e* is a rather handsome tree with a beautiful round crown when growing in the open. It occurs most frequently at Kaholuamano, as well as at Halemanu, on the leeward side of Kauai, at an elevation of 3600 to 4000 feet, at the outskirts of the forest, which at this elevation is more of a dry nature and of a mixed type. It is quite common along stream beds in company with various species of Pelea, *Xanthoxylum dipetalum* var. γ, *Alphitonia excelsa*, *Cyanea lep- tostegia*, *Cryptocaria Mannii*, *Bobea Mannii*, and *Tetraplasandra Waimeae*.

The leaves of the Kauai trees of this species are all 5-foliolate, that is consisting of five leaflets, which are glabrous. The flowers of this species are fragrant; the wood is yellowish white.

The writer collected several forms, nos. 2103, 5677, in the type locality, flow- ering only.

On the Island of Maui on the eastern section, which is formed by the great mass of the largest extinct volcano, Mt. Haleakala, the writer found on its southern flank, on ancient, now wooded, *aa* lava flows, numerous trees belonging to this species. They differ, however, in some respects from the Kauai specimens in that the leaves are always three-foliolate and never five-foliolate, in being chartaceous instead of coriaceous, but otherwise exactly as in the specimens from Kauai. At Auahi, the name of the above-mentioned locality on Maui, the trees reach a handsome size and trunks of a foot and a half or even more in diameter are not uncommon, though growing never taller than 40 feet. The trees are quite numerous, especially on the southern border of Auahi, where the district of Kahikinui joins that of Kaupo; there the writer saw the finest specimens, which formed practically the sole tree-growth. On the northwestern slope of

199

PLATE 79.

XANTHOXYLUM KAUAIENSE Gray var. β Hbd.
A'e or Hea'e.
Branch pinned against trunk of tree. Growing on the aa lava flows of Puuwaawaa,
North Kona, Hawaii; elevation 3000 feet.

Haleakala the writer met with trees of this species in the forests above Makawao, but there the leaves were all five-foliolate, membraneous, and quite glabrous. This latter tree Hillebrand refers to his var. β. of the same species, though erroneously, in the writer's opinion. The Auahi specimens were collected in November, 1910 fruiting, no. 8658 in the College of Hawaii Herbarium. On his last visit to Auahi the writer photographed one of these trees, which is figured in this book. (See plate 78.)

Hillebrand's var. β. is five-foliolate and strongly pubescent underneath. The leaflets are, however, not smaller than in the species, at least in certain trees, for this variety seems to be quite a variable one. The true variety β. the writer collected at Puuwaawaa, lava fields of North Kona, fruiting (no. 3651), on June 17, 1909. On his last visit, March, 1912, he collected the variety again, but found numerous trees on the Puuwaawaa hill proper, which differed somewhat from those found on the plain below, in having much larger leaves and quite pubescent follicles; the leaflets are broadly ovate to ovate-acute, while those of the plain below are smaller of typical *X. kauaiense* shape, and have glabrous follicles. The leaf-branch and trunk figured is the true var. β. Hillebrand's material came from Kawaihaeiuka, a neighboring district. In that latter locality tree growth has disappeared to a certain extent, owing to cattle ranches; only the most hardy trees have survived.

Hillebrand's variety γ, with rather large leaflets, comes from Kauai from the forests above Waimea, meaning either Halemanu or Kaholuamano. The variety is represented in the College of Hawaii Herbarium by the number 5960 collected in the type locality, flowering Sept. 6, 1909.

In order to have this monograph on the genus Xanthoxylum complete, the writer wishes to describe a new species belonging to this genus. The same is, however, only a shrub three feet or even less high and occurs in the rain forests of the Kohala Mts. at an elevation of 4100 feet. It may be described as follows:

Xanthoxylum Bluettianum Rock sp. nov.

A sparingly branching shrub 1 m high, glabrous; leaves three-foliolate on petioles of 5 to 6.5 cm, leaflets ovate, acute, with a cuneate base, the lateral ones unevensided 5.5 to 8.5 cm x 3 to 5.5 cm, thick coriaceous opaque puberulous underneath, the petiolule of the terminal leaflet often articulate near the blade 2.5 to 3.5 cm, those of the lateral leaflets 16 to 20 mm; panicles at the base of the branchlets 8 to 12 cm long with a gray pubescent compressed peduncle of 5 cm. Flowers unknown. Follicles 1 cm, pitted striately rugose, curved; seeds 16 mm, the woody testa rugose under the black shining epidermis.

Hawaii: High mountains of Kohala at the edge of Honokanenui gulch at an elevation of 4100 feet, in company with *Schiedea diffusa* (fruiting June, 1910, Rock n. 8373, type in College of Hawaii Herbarium).

Named in honor of Mr. P. W. P. Bluett, Manager of Kohala Ditch, through whose kindly aid the exploration of Kohala was made possible.

PLATE 80.

XANTHOXYLUM MAUIENSE Mann var. **RIGIDUM** Rock var. nov.
Fruiting branch, about one-third of the natural size.

Rutaceae.

Xanthoxylum mauiense Mann.

Ae or Heae.

XANTHOXYLUM MAUIENSE Mann, Proc. Bost. Soc. Nat. Hist. X. (1866) 319, et Proc.
Am. Acad. VII. (1867) 160, et Fl. Haw. Isl. Proc. Ess. Inst. V. (1867) 170;—
Hbd. Fl. Haw. Isl. (1888) 74;—Del Cast. Ill. Fl. Ins. Mar. Pac. VI. (1890) 130.—
Fagara mauiensis Engler in Engl. et Prantl Pflzfam. III. 4. (1895) 119.

Leaflets 3 on a common petiole of 2.5 to 3 cm, ovate or ovate-oblong 6 to 8 cm long,
3.5 to 5 cm wide, acuminate or somewhat obtuse, pale coriaceous, quite opaque, puberulent above, gray-tomentose underneath as well as the petioles and petiolules in the writer's
specimens, the lateral ones subtruncate at the base, more or less cut in the upper half, on
petiolules of 2 to 4 mm, that of the median leaflet 16 to 18 mm, and often articulate near
the blade; panicles 3.5 to 10 cm long many flowered, the common peduncle 2.5 to 4.5 cm,
the pedicels about 4 mm, tomentose; follicles 8 to 10 mm, stipitate, lunulate-obovoid, the
apex almost lateral, after dehiscence recurved, rugose and pitted.

This species seems to be indeed a very variable one; the writer has collected
material of this species on Maui, Hawaii and Lanai, and even specimens of a
small tree were collected by him on Kauai, which seems to be intermediate between *X. mauiense* and *X. hawaiiense*; the petiolules of the lateral leaflets being
shorter than in *hawaiiense*, but longer than in *mauiense*. The specimens from
the above-mentioned islands vary considerably, especially those from Lanai, and
from Maui proper. Horace Mann's type came from West Maui, in which
latter locality the writer did not find any Xanthoxylum. The specimens on
which Mann based his species were collected by Remy n. 615. and Lydgate, but no
definite locality is given, other than West Maui. It is the writer's opinion
that the tree must be a dry district species, as all other varieties occur in the
mixed forests, rather than in mesophytic forests. The writer's specimen which
comes closest to the original description came from the lava fields of Puuwaawaa, North Kona, Hawaii, on the slopes of Mt. Hualalai (no. 3716), where the
genus Xanthoxylum has numerous representatives.

The leaves and inflorescence are quite pubescent, and the former opaque, and
as a whole answer well to Mann's description; there seems, however, to be a
transition type present which has the pubescent leaves, and besides being trifoliolate, has also five leaflets, which would remind one of *X. kauaiense*. The
species is dioecious, a fact of which Hillebrand was not certain.

Specimens gathered on the Island of Lanai, in Mahana Valley (no. 8112), undoubtedly will have to be referred to this species, though differing from it in
the less coriaceous and perfectly glabrous leaves, and may therefore be called
forma *glabrum* f. nov. Hillebrand describes a var. *β*. from Maunahui, Molokai,
which differs from the species in the very long petioles 5 to 10 cm, the leaves of
which are glabrous above and coarsely pubescent underneath, with pellucid dots
along the margin. The writer is unacquainted with this variety.

Another variety described by Hillebrand as var. *γ* the writer collected on Lanai.
This latter tree is indeed quite common on Lanai, occurring on the main ridges
Lanaihale and Haalelepakai; elevation 3000 feet. It may be described as follows:

PLATE 81.

XANTHOXYLUM DIPETALUM Mann var. **GEMINICARPUM** Rock var. nov.
Less than one-half natural size.

Rutaceae.

Leaflets thick coriaceous, opaque, obtuse or rounded, the lateral ones subsessile, truncate at the base, rhomboidal, the lower half much produced, almost auriculate, the rib puberulous or more often glabrate, the median leaflet rarely articulate; panicles simple or compound.

The writer's number 8071, collected in Mahana Valley, Lanai, is the typical var. γ, while number 8217 has the leaves not quite so coriaceous and has densely flowered panicles.

Var. **rigidum** Rock var. nov.
(Plate 80.)

A small tree 5 m high, with few very stiff stout branches, leaves three foliolate, on petioles of 5 to 6 cm, leaflets ovoid to ovoid-oblong, bluntly acute, truncate at the base, the lateral ones subsessile or on petiolules of 4 mm, the median leaflet on an articulate petiolule of 3 cm, 12 to 15 cm long, 8 to 12 cm wide, (having the largest leaves of any Hawaiian Xanthoxylum) thick coriaceous, opaque, with prominent stramineous midrib and veins; panicles densely flowered, 9 to 12 cm long. on flat, compressed peduncles of 3.5 to 4 cm, ultimate pedicels 6 mm, follicle as in the species.

Collected on the Island of Maui on the northwestern slopes of Haleakala in Waihou gulch, back of Makawao, elevation 3000 feet, March, 1912, in company with *Pseudomorus Brunoniana* and *Sideroxylon Ceresolii*. Type is number 10200 in the Herbarium of the College of Hawaii. It is a small tree 15 feet high and is peculiar to Mt. Haleakala, where it grows in the drier regions on the steep slopes of Waihou gulch.

From the Kaala Mt., Oahu, Hillebrand describes a variety δ with 3 to 5-foliolate leaves. The writer is not acquainted with this variety.

Var. **anceps** Rock. var. nov.

Leaves trifoliolate on petioles of 8 to 12 cm, pubescent with whitish hair, leaflets lanceolate to ovate-lanceolate, the lateral ones sessile, almost rhomboidal in outline, very unevensided, acuminate at the apex, the terminal leaflet on a petiole of 22 to 30 mm, which is not articulate, 10 to 15 cm long, 3.5 to 9 cm wide pubescent or glabrous above, pubescent underneath, especially along the prominent midrib; panicles large 15 to 20 cm, open, many flowered, pubescent throughout, with a common. broad and flat (compressed) peduncle of 6 to 9 cm, ultimate pedicels 5 mm; male flowers: sepals minute dentiform, pubescent, petals cream-colored, 5 mm long ovoid, acute. stamens slightly shorter, anthers orbicular, ovary pronounced, though rudimentary; follicle only 8 mm, minutely pitted.

A medium-sized tree 20 feet in height, pubescent throughout. It is peculiar to the Island of Hawaii, where it grows near the Volcano of Kilauea at an elevation of 4000 feet in the Kipuka Puaulu, which is so rich in species. A number of other species of Xanthoxylum are found in this small area (56 acres), which is surrounded by ancient aa lava flows which are in turn covered by a forest of *Acacia Koa*.

Specimens of this variety were collected flowering and fruiting by the writer in July, 1911. The type is number 10201 in the College of Hawaii Herbarium. The name *anceps* refers to the broad and compressed peduncle.

In the same locality another form was collected with 3 to 5 leaflets which are glabrous and coriaceous. In fruit only, the leaves resemble more var. *rigidum* (no. 10202).

205

PLATE 82.

XANTHOXYLUM DIPETALUM Mann var. **GEMINICARPUM** Rock var. nov.
Trunk 2½ feet in diameter, growing in Kipuka Puaulu Kilauea, Hawaii.

Rutaceae.

To the variety *anceps* must be referred another tree found in the same locality. The inflorescence is exactly as in the variety, but the leaves, which are also pubescent, have three but rarely five leaflets which are subcordate to truncate at the base; the lateral ones instead of being sessile are on petiolules of about 10 mm and are subcordate to unevensided; the leaflets remind one very much of those of *Pterotropia Kauaiensis*. The terminal leaflet is also articulate. Evidently the length of the petiolules of the lateral leaflets, on which Hillebrand laid so much stress, is not a good specific character. According to his key to the species, this latter form, which may be known now as forma *petiolulatum* f. n., would belong to *X. hawaiiense*, rather than to *X. mauiense*, but can not be separated from the latter, as it differs otherwise very materially from the former species, whose lateral leaflets are practically deltoid, with petiolules as long as the terminal one. These varieties and forms seem to be intermediates between *X. mauiense* and *X. hawaiiense*, though reminding one much more of the former than of the latter.

Xanthoxylum dipetalum Mann.

XANTHOXYLUM DIPETALUM Mann in Proc. Bost. Soc. Nat. Hist. X. (1867) 160, et Proc. Ess. Inst. V. (1868) 170;—Hbd. Fl. Haw. Isl. (1888) 76;—Del Cast. Ill. Fl. Ins. Mar. Pac. VI. (1890) 129.—Fagara dipetala Engl. in Engl. et Prantl Pflzfam. III. 4. (1895) 119.

Leaves 15 to 18 cm long including a petiole of 2.5 to 3.5 cm, pinnately 5 to 7 foliolate, the lowest pair of leaflets generally with a pair of stipelliform or auricular folioles close to its base; lateral petiolules 6 mm, the terminal one 12 to 18 mm, often articulate; leaflets oblong 7.5 to 8.75 cm long, 3.75 to 4.5 cm wide, obtuse, all contracting and nearly symmetrical at the base, coriaceous, with faint nerves and many pellucid dots, glossy; panicles terminal and oppositifolious, 7.5 to 10 cm long, with a peduncle of 2.5 to 3.75 cm and suberect branches, the ternate flowers on pedicels of 6 mm, the lateral pedicels minutely bracteate below the middle; male flowers: sepals 4, rounded, little more than 1 mm high; petals 2, lanceolate, thick coriaceous and valvate, 10 mm long, stamens 4, scarcely half the length of the petals, placed on the edge of the disc, with long apiculate anthers of 2 to 3 mm; ovary rudimentary.

This very interesting species, which is quite distinct from all the other Hawaiian Xanthoxyla, was first collected by Dr. Wm. Hillebrand and communicated by him to H. Mann, who described it. The writer is only acquainted with several forms or varieties of this species found on the other islands, but has never collected the species proper, found on Oahu by Hillebrand on the slopes of Waiolani, also called Lanihuli, in Nuuanu Valley. The dipetalous flowers occur in the species, and in the varieties the flowers are tetramerous. It is a tree about 30 feet high and quite glabrous. In regard to the dipetalous flowers Hillebrand quite correctly states: "The reduced number of the petals in the species is owing not to a suppression of a pair, but to coalescence of two contiguous petals; it is not so much therefore on the strength of these characters that the present species must claim a place distinct from the preceding ones within the genus, as for its mode of inflorescence and the presence of the supplementary pair of reduced leaflets in such an extraordinary position, where they appear like appendages of the lowest folioles."

PLATE 83.

XANTHOXYLUM DIPETALUM Mann var. **GEMINICARPUM** Rock var. nov.
Tree growing in the Kipuka Puaulu, near Volcano Kilauea, Hawaii; elevation 4000 feet.

Rutaceae.

H. Mann described Hbd.'s variety γ, doubtfully in the genus Connarus as *C.?* *Kauaiensis,* and remarks that the two lower lateral leaflets, which are very small and have strongly revolute margins, are perhaps a diseased state. This is, however, not the case, as in all forms examined from Kauai and Hawaii these stipelliform leaflets are present.

Hillebrand describes a variety β with generally 3-foliolate leaves and acute anthers which are longer than their filaments, from the Island of Hawaii, from the western, dry section of Kawaihaeiuka. The writer did not meet with this variety, though he found another form in the neighboring district of North Kona on the lava fields of Puuwaawaa, which proved to be new and is here described as follows:

Var. **tomentosum** Rock var. nov.

Leaves 5 to 7 foliolate, including the reduced pair of stipelliform leaflets, on petioles of 2.5 to 4 cm, densely tomentose throughout, as is the inflorescence; leaflets oblong to linear-oblong, or orbiculate, or obovate-oblong, rounded at the apex and base, or bluntly acute, or with even emarginate apex, 5.5 to 15 cm long, 3 to 8 cm wide, pubescent above, densely velvety tomentose underneath, the terminal petiolule 1 to 3 cm, articulate, the lateral ones 1 to 5 cm, densely tomentose, the stipelliform leaflets immediately below the last pair of normal leaflets, the margins revolute, or completely folded, opaque, without oil glands; veins and midrib prominent underneath; panicles 4 to 15 cm long including a peduncle of 5 mm to 7 cm; male flowers: sepals 4, rounded or acute, 2 mm high, hispid, petals 2, tomentose, broadly ovate, acute, stamens 4, oblong, 1.5 mm long. four times as long as filament; female flowers: stamens wanting, ovary ovoid, slightly raised on a disc, tomentose; stigma sessile, with two flat broad lobes; follicles woody, 2.5 cm long, 2 cm wide, tapering into a point of 3 to 5 mm, rugose and pitted; seed ovoid, black, 16 mm long, 12 mm wide, shining, raphe extending its entire length.

This very interesting tree occurs on the lava flows of Mt. Hualalai, at Puuwaawaa, North Kona, Hawaii, where it is, however, not common. It was first collected by the writer, fruiting and flowering, on June 17, 1909 (no. 3695), and again during March, 1912, when several forms of this variety were found, which have been here described collectively. Type is 10207 in College of Hawaii Herbarium.

Var. **geminicarpum** Rock var. nov.
(Plates 81, 82, 83.)

Leaves one to three foliolate with the ever present stipellifoim leaflets, on short petioles, leaflets entirely glabrous, thick coriaceous, with midrib and nerves prominent, united by a reticulate venation, ovate-oblong, or elliptical-oblong, acute or rounded at the apex, the terminal leaflet gradually tapering into a non-articulate petiolule of 1 to 3.5 cm, the lateral ones subsessile or on peduncles of often more than 5 cm; female flowers: sepals 4, ôvate, acute or rounded petals 2 to 4 reddish yellow, lanceolate, 10 mm, thick, acute, when 2; terete tapering styles distinct, united at the apex by the reddish, close grooved stigma; ovary 2, rarely 3-celled; follicles usually two,* with an ovoid, black smooth seed in each, occasionally with a single seed, the other rudimentary.

A large tree 40 feet high with a straight trunk, 2½ feet in diameter, bark gray, covered with lenticels. This interesting variety the writer discovered on the

---

* In the writer's material each fruit consists of two follicles, though the figure on plate 81 shows only a single one.

Rutaceae.

slopes of Mauna Loa at an elevation of 4000 feet, in the Kipuka Puaulu, near the Volcano Kilauea on Hawaii. Only two trees were observed; both were of the same size, about 40 feet in height, with stout, ungainly looking, ascending branches. Collected flowering and fruiting July 20, 1911. Type is no. 10208 in the College of Hawaii Herbarium.

Xanthoxylum dipetalum Mann. var. γ Hbd.
Kawau on Kauai.

XANTHOXYLUM DIPETALUM Mann. var. γ Hbd. Fl. Haw. Isl. l. c. p.;—Wawra in Flora (1873) 139.—**Connarus ? Kauaiensis** Mann Proc. Am. Acad. VII. (1867) 162.

Leaves on short petioles of 1 cm, 3 to 1 foliolate, with the supplementary pair of stipellifɔrm leaflets besides, obovate-oblong, thick coriaceous and quite opaque, with prominent veins and a distinct intramarginal nerve; panicles as in the species, few flowered; female flowers: sepals 4, 1 mm long, rounded, puberulous, as are the 4 lanceolate petals; stamens wanting, ovary glabrous, styles apparently two, but not distinct as in var. *geminicarpum*, appearing only to be grooved, united at the apex by a broad, flat, orbicular, grooved stigma; male flowers: petals 2, ovoid, smaller, only two-thirds the length of the female flower, anthers 4, less than half the length of the petals, 2.5 mm, including the 0.5 mm long filament, ovary rudimentary; follicle single, 3 cm long, including the 6 mm long acumen at the apex, slightly pitted, woody; seed ovoid, 2 cm, the hard woody testa covered with a black, shining, thin and brittle epidermis, the raphe extending its entire length; cotyledons thick fleshy, plano-convex, the radicle very short and enclosed.

This exceedingly interesting tree reaches a height of more than 30 feet with a trunk of often over a foot in diameter. It favors the outskirts of the forests on the leeward side of Kauai, especially at Kaholuamano and Halemanu above Waimea at an elevation of 3600 to 4000 feet. It is found in company with *Pelea anisata, Bobea Mannii, Pelea Kauaiensis, Elaeocarpus bifidus, Cyanea leptostegia, Tetraplasandra Waimeae, Sideroxylon sandwicense, Alphitonia excelsa, Pterotropia kauaiensis,* and others which make up this very interesting mixed forest.

On Kauai, to which island this tree is peculiar, its trunk was in great demand for *tapa* or *kapa* logs or anvils on which the strips of the *wauke* bark were beaten. The yellowish wood of this tree was especially in favor with the natives on account of the resonant tones it produced when struck with a *tapa* beater made of some of the hard woods, such as *Uhiuhi, Kauila,* and others. The sound of the *tapa* beating would be heard from valley to valley, and constituted a regular system of communication by means of a code.

This *Kawau* tree, or as it is also termed *Kawau kua kuku kapa,* is the subject of a *mele* or old Hawaiian song, which begins thus: "*Mehe Kawau laka ale i ka moana,* etc." As the *Kawau* so is the sound of the ocean. The old natives evidently had reference to the sounds produced by the pounding surf, which can be heard for a long distance, and compared it with the resonant sound produced when beating *tapa* on the *Kawau* log. According to Mr. Francis Gay of Kauai, the natives of that island preferred this tree to any other for the above described purpose.

Rutaceae.

PELEA Gray.

Flowers polygamous. Calyx lobes 4, rarely 5, imbricate. Lobes of corolla 4, rarely 5, valvate. Stamens 8, rarely 10, inserted at the base of a slightly 8 lobed discus, in the fertile flowers rudimentary, usually the height of the ovary, in the sterile flowers 4, often as long as the petals and occasionally longer and protruding; filaments flat; anthers short ovate or sagittate, introrse. Carpels 4, rarely 5, united, each with two collateral ovules, one ascending, the other pendulous. Capsule of 4 follicles either discreet and 4-coccous or more or less deeply 4-parted, in a few species cuboid; follicles 2-valved. Seeds crustaceous with black shining testa, on a short and broad funiculus. Embryo straight, in a fleshy albumen, with broad ovate cotyledons and short radicle.—Unarmed trees with opposite or whorled leaves, which are simple and entire, and have an intramarginal nerve. Flowers in axillary, simple or compound, mostly paniculate cymes.

The genus Pelea, which was dedicated by Asa Gray to the Hawaiian goddess of the Volcano, Pele, is not strictly Hawaiian, though the bulk of the species is found in these Islands. A few only occur outside the Hawaiian archipelago, as, for example, three in New Caledonia and one in Madagascar.

The Hawaiian Pelea are rather difficult for the systematist, as they are extremely variable and have numerous forms and varieties which link several species together. There are, strictly speaking, very few well defined species. The writer in this treatise on the arboreous species of this genus, has added five new species and five new varieties. The work of classifying all the variable species of Pelea was made extremely difficult and troublesome through the publication of supposed new species of Pelea by H. Léveillé based on material collected by Abbe U. Faurie, in the year 1910. It certainly is most regrettable that this material, which often is beyond recognition, was turned over to Mr. Léveillé, who was only too ambitious to swell the number of his new species. The descriptions are so incomplete that it was impossible to make use of them and consequently the work had to be ignored.

The writer still has numerous plants of Pelea which could not be placed, which are undoubtedly new, but the material is incomplete, either flowers or capsules being lacking, and it certainly would be of no help to describe these plants as new, without complete material, such as sterile and fertile flowers and fruits. Even Hillebrand's descriptions are not too complete, some of them are even dubious, and references to such will be found in their proper places. The writer could also have swelled the number of new species of Pelea as Mr. Léveillé did, to the sorrow of future workers on the Hawaiian Flora, but refrained from doing so on account of insufficient material. Of the new species of Pelea described in this book, the writer had abundant and complete material, having visited the various localities at different seasons in order to secure the plants in all stages of development. Léveillé describes, if so it can be called, five species of Pelea in Fedde Repertorium Vol. X. no. 10-14, 1911, and 10 species in Vol. X. no. 27-29, 1912, the names of all of which are as follows: *Pelea Leveillei* Faurie, *Pelea waianaiensis* Levl., *P. oahuensis* Levl., *P. penduliflora* Levl., *P. Feddei* Levl., *P. subpeltata* Levl., *P. nodosa* Levl., *P. singuliflora* Levl., *P. peduncularis* Levl., *P.*

211

Rutaceae.

grandipetala Levl., *P. Hillebrandii* Levl., *P. foetida* Levl., *P. sessilis* Levl., *Pelea?* *acutivalvata* Levl., *P. Fauriei* Levl.

The latter one the writer thinks to be only a mere variety of *P. clusiaefolia* Gray. It is a very small leaved form, but owing to the fact that it is found in the rather dry forests back of Kaluaha and Kamolo on the leeward side of Molokai, it can be easily the result of the location, a fact which has disproved many an apparently new species. Léveillé absolutely ignores fertile or sterile flowers and gives only a general description that may be applied to any species in the genus. An example may follow. *P. Hillebrandii, Rami fragiles, nodosi;—flores magni axillares cymosi pedicelli bibracteolati, caylce minuto, sepala obtusa, glabra, petala 4-5-plo longiora, glabra apice triangularia; stamina paulo breviora.*

This description, especially of the flower, is really a marvel, and anyone able to place *P. Hillebrandii* by it, must be a clairvoyant, and a clever one at that. Anyone acquainted with the extreme variability of the Hawaiian Pelea, their many intermediates, and who has at his disposal such a large material as is at the writer's disposal, cannot help but deplore such work, which is not to the advancement, but to the hindrance of botanical science.

The Hawaiian Pelea, for the sake of convenience, may be classed into four units, and embraced under a special name sp. (ecies) c. (ollectiva).

For example: *Pelea clusiaefolia* with all its varieties is closely related to *P. auriculaefolia, P. Cookeana, P. sapotaefolia, P. Waialealae, P. microcarpa, P. Fauriei* and perhaps *P. pallida.* All these species have a more or less variable, but always small capsule in common, and have all either quaternate or ternate leaves, and never opposite ones unless it be in very rare instances, or perhaps in a very dubious variety of some one of these species. The writer would propose for this group of species the name *Pelea sp. c. verticillifolia*; this expresses the conception of the group as a very closely related one, in a comprehensive and easy way.

The second and largest group has opposite leaves and is characterized by the large capsules, which are deeply parted but not discreet. The typical species of this group is *Pelea volcanica,* and is followed by *Pelea pseudoanisata, P. oblongifolia, P. rotundifolia, P. orbicularis, P. molokaiensis, P. Mannii, P. parvifolia, P. macropus, P. Kauaiensis,* and *P. sandwicensis.* *P. Balloui,* of which only young capsules (which are silky pubescent) are known, may also belong to this group for which the writer proposes the name *P. sp. c. megacarpa.* This in itself is a practical key which will facilitate the identification of species.

Another marked group, though small, has cuboid capsules and opposite leaves and is made up of the following members: *Pelea anisata, P. Wawraeana, P. Zahlbruckneri,* and may be termed *P. sp. c. cubicarpa.*

The fourth group is composed of the following, with *Pelea cinerea,* as the most variable one, in the lead; it is followed closely by *P. Knudsenii, P. multiflora, P.*

212

Rutaceae.

barbigera, and the *P. elliptica*. All these form a marked group which can be expressed by the name *Pelea sp. c. apocarpa.*

Drake Del Castillo, in his *"Illustrationes Florae Insularum Maris Pacifici,"* united the genera Melicope and Pelea with Evodia. The latter genus differs, however, from Pelea in the strictly tetramerous flowers, while the genus Pelea has never less than eight stamens. Melicope again differs from Pelea in the imbricate petals. The writer has here adhered to the original classification, upholding the genus Pelea, as has also been done by Engler in his treatise on the family Rutaceae.

KEY TO SPECIES.

I. **Verticillifoliae.**

Capsule syncarpous the carpels more or less united.

Flowers fasciculate on a short axis.

Leaves quaternate or ternate.

Capsule deeply parted, small.

Leaves obovate, shortly petiolate, capsule woody, small.
P. clusiaefolia

Leaves large obovate-oblong, attenuate at the base, subsessile, flowers small .... **P. Oookeana**

Leaves ovate, small, 2 to 5 cm, subsessile.... **P. Fauriei**

Leaves large, elongate oblong, spathulate, villous underneath
P. sapotaefolia

Leaves lanceolate-acute capsule thin........ **P. Waialealae**

Leaves sessile with an auriculate base....... **P. auriculaefolia**

Leaves ternate, obovate, petiolate, the midrib pubescent, capsule very small......................... **P. microcarpa**

II. **Megacarpae.**

Capsules large, deeply 4 parted.

Leaves opposite branches hirsute—tomentose.

Leaves oval, hirsute underneath........... **P. volcanica**

Leaves oval or oblong, strongly reticulated, glabrous underneath . . . . **P. sandwicensis**

Leaves orbicular, petiolate, mucronate...... **P. orbicularis**

Leaves opposite, branches glabrous.

Leaves coriaceous, velvety villous underneath on hirsute petioles . . . . **P. Kauaiensis**

Leaves orbicular, sessile, glabrous........... **P. rotundifolia**

Leaves obovate, retuse base, glabrous, chartaceous
P. Molokaiensis

Leaves elliptico-oblong, contracted, not emarginate
P. macropus

Leaves ovate to obovate oblong, shining on both sides, capsule very large, strongly anise-scented...... **P. pseudoanisata**

Leaves ovate, thick coriaceous, capsule silky tomentose, sepals and petals persistent............... **P. Balloui**

III. **Cubicarpae.**

Capsules cuboid, almost entire.

Leaves opposite, capsules small.

Leaves thin, glabrous, anise-scented......... **P. anista**

Leaves elliptico oblong, coriaceous, glabrous. **P. Wawraeana**

Leaves opposite, capsule large.

Leaves obovate-oblong, chartaceous......... **P. Zahlbruckneri**

PLATE 84.

PELEA CLUSIAEFOLIA A. Gray.
Alani.
Showing flowering and fruiting branch.

Rutaceae.

IV. Apocarpae.
Capsules apocarpous, carpels discreet.
　Leaves opposite, cobwebby, capsules glabrous.
　　Leaves oblong, cobwebby underneath, flowers up to 200
　　　　　　　　　　　　　　　　　　　　　　　　　P. multiflora
　　Leaves ovate to ovate-oblong, cordate, flowers up to 40
　　　　　　　　　　　　　　　　　　　　　　　　　P. Knudsenii
　　Leaves elliptico oblong, curved, concave, chartaceous, flowers
　　　3 to 5.................................. **P. barbigera**
　Leaves opposite, capsules pubescent.
　　Leaves thin chartaceous, obtuse, pale pubescent, capsule
　　　puberulous............................ **P. elliptica**
　　Leaves ovate oblong, subcoriaceous, tomentulose, capsule with
　　　fulvous tomentum....................... **P. cinerea**

Pelea clusiaefolia Gray.
Alani.
(Plate 84.)

PELEA CLUSIAEFOLIA Gray, Bot. U. S. E. E. (1854) 340, pl. 35;—Mann. Proc. Bost. Soc. Nat. Hist. X. (1866) 312, et Proc. Am. Acad. VII. (1867) 158, et Proc. Essex Inst. V. (1867) 165;—Wawra in Flora (1873) 107;— Hbd. Fl. Haw. Isl. (1888) 62;—Heller Plants Haw. Isl. (1897) 838.—**Clusia sessilis** Hook. et Arn. Bot. Beech. (1832) 80 (not Forster).—**Evodia clusiaefolia** Drake Del. Cast. Ill. Fl. Ins. Mar. Pacif. VI. (1890) 131.

A small glabrous tree; leaves in whorls of 4 or 3, occasionally 2, obovate or obovate-oblong, rounded or emarginate, with contracted base, thick coriaceous, with a prominent midrib and continuous intramarginal nerve which is close to the edge, shining above, dull underneath, 5 to 12 cm long, 3 to 6 cm wide, on either short petioles of 1 cm or even subsessile, or on petioles of 2.5 cm; flowers in axillary clusters, often cauline, the thick peduncle scarcely 2 mm in length, the pedicels 2 to 4 mm, minutely bracteate at the base; sterile flowers of the same size as the fertile, in the former some of the stamens are as long as the petals and even longer, protruding, the sepals and petals acute, the latter twice as long as the former, ovary glabrous, rudimentary, composed of 4 globose carpels, with apparently no style in the writer's specimens, but small sessile stigma; fertile flowers 4 to 6 mm, the petals more than twice the length of the sepals, stamens rudimentary, little longer than the rather depressed ovary, anthers sagittate on broad filaments, style 2 mm, with a 4 lobed stigma, the lobes rather thick and blunt; capsule 4 lobed, the carpels united to the middle, obtuse or obovate, prominently marked with concentric wrinkles, one to two seeded, 16 mm in diameter.

Wawra says of this species that the flowers are hermaphrodite; this is, however, not the case. All Hawaiian Peleae have fertile and sterile flowers with either one or the other organ rudimentary, making them appear to be hermaphrodite. The male flowers of this species were not known to Asa Gray.

Wawra in Flora records three forms: fm. α (*normalis*) from the Waianae Mts., fm. β (*macrocarpa*) and fm. γ *microcarpa*. Asa Gray enumerates two varieties—β and γ, so does Hillebrand.

The writer has large material of this species from many localities. It is one of the most common Pelea on Oahu, as well as on other islands, especially on Hawaii in the forests of Puna, near the Volcano Kilauea.

It is a medium-sized tree reaching a height of 25 to 30 feet in certain localities.

Specimens from Konahuanui, Oahu, have ovate acute leaves, but also varying tremendously, while others from the Waikane Mts., on the windward side of Oahu, have obovate subsessile leaves. From the same locality the writer collected specimens with linear oblong leaves 15 cm long, and 3 cm wide and petiolate.

A distinct variety recorded as β by Hillebrand the writer collected in the type locality, back of Wahiawa, in the north fork of Kaukonahua gulch; the leaves are narrow and on rather long petioles of 3 to 4.5 cm, flowering, fruiting May 15, 1909, no. 3053.

A more robust variety was collected on Hawaii in the Kohala mountains, with stout branches and petioles; flowering and fruiting June, 1910, no. 8366.

Hillebrand's var. γ was collected along the government road above Glenwood and near the Volcano of Kilauea on Hawaii, fruiting no. 8775, April, 1911; July, 1911; December, 1911.

Pelea Cookeana Rock sp. nov.

Branches densely foliate at the ends; leaves obovate-oblong, or obovate, or even ovate, quaternate, rounded at the apex or emarginate, attenuate at the base, rounded or subemarginate, slightly auriculate, subsessile, thick coriaceous, opaque, with a prominent midrib, leaves punctate underneath, intramarginal nerve almost straight, close to the edge of the leaf, 5.5 to 14 cm long, 2.5 to 6.5 cm wide; inflorescence as in *P. clusiaefolia* in fascicles; male flowers: sepals ovate acute, petals twice the length, acute, stamens 8, 4 as long as the petals, the remaining shorter and of unequal size, filaments broad, anthers very short, acute, deeply emarginate at the base, ovary glabrous, style 1 mm, with a bluntly 4-lobed stigma, lobes minute; female flowers smaller, petals slightly longer than the sepals, stamens minute, less than 1 mm, ovary flat, circular in outline, style filiform, 1 mm, with a 4-lobed stigma; capsule as in *P. clusiaefolia* but smaller.

This certainly very variable species, which is here named in honor of Mr. George P. Cooke of Molokai, occurs in the dense rain forests above Kamoku, on the leeward side of Molokai, at an elevation of 4000 feet. It is a small tree, though often inclined to be shrubby with rather stiff and stout branches. It occurs all over Molokai in various forms, but always in the dense rain forest. It is closely allied to *P. clusiaefolia*, and perhaps also to *P. auriculaefolia*. The leaves are, however, much larger, subsessile, of thick texture, the inflorescence smaller as well as the capsules; the tree has an entirely different aspect with its stout branches, which remind somewhat of *P. microcarpa* from Kauai.

The type material was collected on the Island of Molokai in the swampy forest above Kamoku camp, at an elevation of 4000 feet; flowering and fruiting no. 6262, March 23, 1910. Flowering April 10, 1910, no. 7075, from Wailau Pali, Molokai, elevation 4000 feet.

Pelea Fauriei Levl.

PELEA FAURIEI Levl. in Fedde Repert. X. 10-14 (1911) 153.

A clusiaefolia Gray affini distinguitur: cortice nigrescente, ramulis rugosis vel articulatis; foliis brevibus et minoribus 1 to 5 x 1 to 2 cm opacis, subsessilibus, profuse nigropunctatis et subtus conspicue tomentosis et validissime, reticulatis; capsula et cetera fere *P. clusiaefoliae.*

A *P. sessili* adhorret colore pallido foliorum; floribus breviter fasciculatis, et duplo majoribus.

Molokai: Kamolo, 1000 m, Pukoo, 600 m, maio-jun. 1910; Faurie no. 104, 203.

The plant in question was collected first by the writer in April, 1910, in the

Rutaceae.

woods of Kaluaha, Molokai, with flower buds; no. 7066. Owing to very incomplete material the writer is unable to enlarge upon Léveillé's description. In the writer's hand is a co-type of Faurie's no. 203, but without flower and fruit. The writer is very much inclined to reduce this plant to a variety of *P. clusiaefolia*, as it only differs from that species in the rather small subsessile leaves; but owing to insufficient material for study, it is left at present unmolested. It is a small tree, also shrubby.

Pelea sapotaefolia Mann.

PELEA SAPOTAEFOLIA Mann Proc. Bost. Soc. Nat. Hist. X. (1866) 312, et Proc. Am. Ac. VII. (1867) 158, et Fl. Haw. Isl. Proc. Ess. Inst. V. (1867) 165;—Wawra in Flora (1873) 109;—Hbd. Fl. Haw. Isl. (1888) 63;—Heller Pl. Haw. Isl. (1897) 840.—**Evodia sapotaefolia** Drake Del Cast. Ill. Fl. Ins. Mar. Pac. VI. (1890) 133.

A small tree much branched; the young naked leaf-buds hirsute, the branches and inflorescence glabrous; leaves verticillate, in fours, elongated-oblong or slightly spathulate-oblong, chartaceous, 10 to 22.5 cm long. 5 to 7.5 cm wide, somewhat attenuated at the base, or sometimes obtuse, on a petiole of 2.5 to 3.5 cm, with a strong, prominent midrib, the very numerous primary veins (30 to 50 pairs) running out nearly transversely towards the margin, where they unite with a distinct intra-marginal vein; the leaves are somewhat villous pubescent on the under surface, more especially on the midrib, but quite glabrous above; the texture and especially the venation of the leaves gives them somewhat the appearance of the larger forms of (*Sapota sandwicensis*) *Sideroxylon sandwicense*; flowers in axillary sessile clusters, the pedicels 4 to 6 mm long; calyx 4-parted, the lobes broadly ovate, imbricated in aestivation, about 2 to 3 mm long; petals 4, valvate, ovate, a third longer than the sepals, not thickened at the apex, stamens 8, much shorter than the petals—evidently from a fertile flower (Rock), filaments linear-lanceolate, glabrous; anthers deltoid-sagittate, adnate-introrse; hypogynous disk very short; ovary glabrous, depressed, globular, 4-lobed, 4-celled, the 4 carpels somewhat united; style a little longer than the ovary; 4-parted nearly to the base, the divisions clavate, stigmatic at and near the summit; the immature capsule is puberulent and deeply four-grooved.

The above is the original description of this species by Mann, as found in the Proceedings of the Boston Society of Natural History, Vol. 10, page 313. In Hillebrand's description of this species the fact that the immature capsule is deeply 4 grooved is omitted, and the writer thinks it altogether wrong to place this species in the key as having cuboid subentire capsules.

The writer collected specimens of a Pelea on Mt. Waialeale, the summit of Kauai, overlooking directly Kealia and Hanalei, on the windward side of Kauai, which he must refer as a variety to *Pelea sapotaefolia*. In trying to place the plant according to Hillebrand's key to the species, the writer was quite unsuccessful, as his key calls for cuboid capsules; however, in looking up the original description of Mann, which is very complete of this species, he came to the conclusion that the Waialeale plant is a variety of this species. The capsules are deeply 4-lobed when mature, and evidently likewise in the species found at Kealia, of which no one seems to have collected mature capsules. Owing to a plant collected by Knudsen at Waimea, Kauai, with cuboid capsules, Hillebrand, who seemed not to have collected the species, referred it to the latter, and merely took for granted that *P. sapotaefolia* had also cuboid fruits. The fact is strengthened by Heller's statement, who collected Hillebrand's variety β, which says:

217

Rutaceae.

"That this variety is specifically distinct from *P. sapotaefolia* is pretty evident."
He goes on saying: "One old capsule was found on the tree, but unfortunately
it dropped to the ground and could not be found in the dense tangle of ferns
and weeds which were growing at the foot of the tree. * * * From what I
recollect of it, it was entirely too deeply lobed to belong to the same section as
P. sapotaefolia."

Unfortunately the writer has not collected the species, having only little explored the forests of Kealia or Hanalei. However, there seems to be evident
proof that the true species *P. sapotaefolia* has not cuboid but deeply-grooved or
lobed capsules. The variety may be described as follows.

Var. dumosa Rock var. nov.

Shrubby, with rather stout branches, leaves smaller than in the species, whorled,
ovate oblong or slightly spathulate, attenuated at the base, rounded or emarginate at the
apex, glabrous above, villous underneath especially on the midrib, the petioles of the
young leaves hirsute; petioles shorter than in the species about 1.5 cm; flowers as in
the species, capsules 18 mm in diameter, deeply 4-parted to more than half the length of
the cocci, strongly marked with concentric wrinkles; endocarp glabrous.

This variety was collected by the writer on the summit of Mt. Waialeale, Kauai,
at an elevation of 5200 feet, flowering and fruiting September 24, 1909. The
type is numbered 4974 in the College of Hawaii Herbarium.

It is very unlikely that the variety γ *procumbens* Hillebrand, is in reality a
variety of *P. sapotaefolia*, and until better material is at hand nothing can be
done towards solving the question. The writer collected specimens of a pro-
cumbent Pelea on Waialeale (no. 8854) without fruits, which seems to answer
the description of Hillebrand's variety γ *procumbens*, but in the writer's mind
could not be associated with *P. sapotaefolia*.

Pelea Waialealae Wawra.
Anonia or *Alaniwai.*

PELEA WAIALEALAE Wawra in Flora (1873) 108;—Hbd. Fl. Haw. Isl. (1888) 63;—
Heller Pl. Haw. Isl. (1897) 841.—Evodia Waialealae Drake, Del Cast. Ill. Fl. Ins.
Mar. Pac. VI. (1890) 134.

A shrub or tree; leaves quaternate, lanceolate, 5 to 8 cm long, 1 to 3 cm wide, acute,
narrowing at the base into a margined petiole of 6 to 8 mm, coriaceous, glabrous, covered
underneath with minute dots, opaque, with prominent veins and midrib, marginal nerve
close to the edge; flowers fasciculate, shortly stalked, pedicels bibracteolate near the
base and puberulous; male flowers: sepals broader than high, 2 mm, rounded, petals 7 mm,
thin oblong acute, somewhat pubescent outside, stamens, 8, 4 as long or longer than the
petals, the remaining ones a little shorter, on very broad filaments. anthers oblong, ovary
rudimentary, with a 4-notched sessile stigma; female flowers: smaller than male flowers;
ovary glabrous, surrounded at the base with the rudimentary anthers which are scarcely
as high as the ovary; style filiform, 2 mm, stigma 4 lobed. each lobe 1 mm long; capsule
10 mm in diameter, glabrous, strongly veined, deeply parted, thin chartaceous, the cocci
globose, keeled along the sutures, endocarp glabrous, shining, seeds angular, black shining.

Wawra says in his description: "Male flowers much smaller than the female
flowers," a statement which the writer finds to be the reverse. In fact, nearly
all species of Pelea have the male flowers larger than the female flowers.

Rutaceae.

The *Anonia* or *Alaniwai* is one of the handsomest species of Pelea. It is recorded by Wawra and Heller as a shrub 3 feet high. The writer collected material of this species first September 24, 1909, and again October, 1911. It grows only on the Island of Kauai on the summit of Mt. Waialeale, a big flat swamp at an elevation of 5200 feet. It is a small tree with a straight trunk of 4 to 5 feet and reaches a height of 15 to 20 feet. The mountain is always enshrouded by clouds and it is extremely difficult to see farther than a few feet. On the day of the writer's last ascent the sky was perfectly cloudless and a thorough survey could be made of the vegetation, which resulted in the discovery of a number of new species, and also furnished additional data in regard to the plants already known. During the writer's first visit to this most interesting mountain, the cold was so intense, the wind blew with such great force, and rain came down in such torrents, that it was impossible to remain longer than a couple of hours. The second time, however, the writer was more fortunate. Collected flowering and fruiting September 24, 1909, no. 4975, and October, 1911, no. 8883 in the Herbarium of the College of Hawaii. Heller records the plant as a shrub 3 to 4 feet high from the bog of Wahiawa, Kauai; this latter locality is at a much lower elevation, about 3000 feet.

Pelea auriculaefolia Gray.

PELEA AURICULAEFOLIA Gray. Bot. U. S. E. E. (1854) 343, pl. 36;—Mann Proc. Bost. Soc. Nat. Hist. X. (1866) 313, et Proc. Am. Ac. VII. (1867) 158, et Proc. Ess. Inst. V. (1867) 166;—Heller Pl. Haw. Isl. (1897) 838.—**Platydesma auriculaefolia** Hbd. Fl. Haw. Isl. (1888) 72;—Del Cast. Ill. Fl. Ins. Mar. Pac. VI. (1890) 134.—**Platydesma auriculifolium** Engl. in Engl. et Prantl Pflzfam. III. 4 (1895) 128..

Following is a quotation of A. Gray's brief description of the above species:

"P. glabra; foliis ternis oblongo-spatulatis basi auriculatis sessilibus; flori'us fasciculatis ad axillas foliorum delapsorum secus caulem virgatum brevissime pedicellatis; capsula quadripartita."

He says: "The specimen, taken from an upright, nearly simple shrub, bears only a little fruit, and a few fertile ovaries, from which the perianth, stamens, etc., have fallen. The virgate stem is very leafy above; and the flowers have been produced lower down, in small fascicles from the axils of earlier leaves, now fallen. Plant glabrous throughout. Leaves verticillate in threes, coriaceous, pale, oblong-spathulate, obtuse, auriculate at the base, sessile, from 3 to 5 inches long, veined and dotted nearly as in the preceding species; the midrib salient underneath. Ovary more deeply lobed than in *P. clusiaefolia*, being united only at the base; style has mostly fallen. Capsule deeply four-parted; the cocci oval-oblong, otherwise similar, as apparently are the seeds to those of *Pelea clusiaefolia*.

"Forests of Hawaii, on the flank of Mauna Kea."

How Hillebrand could have taken this plant for a Platydesma is difficult to understand. Even Engler in the Natürlichen Pflanzenfamilien places it under the latter genus.

Rutaceae.

The writer did not meet with this plant in the forests of Mauna Kea, but on the slopes of Mauna Loa at about 5000 feet elevation the writer collected specimens of a Pelea which resembles very much the above species. The leaves are quaternate instead of ternate, are subsessile and very slightly auriculate; they are, however, decidedly punctate and so are the deeply-parted capsules which answer well Gray's description. It is an erect shrub or small tree with straight ascending branches; trunk about 3 inches in diameter; leaves quaternate subsessile; flowers arranged in fascicles as in *P. clusiaefolia;* female flowers: sepals acuminate, petals linear oblong, acute, little longer than the sepals; the 8 stamens short, rudimentary, little higher than the glabrous ovary; style filiform, 2 mm, with thickened clavate 4-lobed stigma.

It is still somewhat doubtful if this plant is actually *P. auriculaefolia,* as there is no description of either fertile or sterile flowers given by Gray, who had only a fruiting specimen. As the leaves are very variable in the Hawaiian Pelea, the plant collected on the slopes of Mauna Loa by the writer seems to be best at present referable to this species.

Collected flowering and fruiting in the forests above Naalehu, Kau, Hawaii, January 13, 1912; no. 10012.

On Molokai occur several Pelea with quaternate leaves, resembling this one in question, but are more affiliated with *P. clusiaefolia* than with *P. auriculaefolia.*

Pelea microcarpa Heller.
Kukaimoa.

PELEA MICROCARPA Heller Pl. Haw. Isl. Minnes. Bot. Stud. IX. (1897) 839, pl. 49.
A small tree with stout trunk and grayish bark; branches more or less curved upwards; leaves in threes or quaternate, near the ends of the branches, on flattened, somewhat hirsute petioles of 3 to 3.5 cm, obovate-oblong, or spathulate, rounded at the apex and retuse, quite glabrous above, pubescent below, especially along the midrib, 8 to 14 cm long, 4 to 6 cm wide, coriaceous, opaque, the secondary veins parallel, at almost right angles to the midrib, united by an intramarginal nerve which is very close to the edge; flowers all along the naked branches, in the axils of fallen leaves; peduncles exceedingly short, about 1 mm, 2 to 3 flowered, pedicels stoutish 2 mm; sepals ovate acute, 3 mm, about as broad as high, petals twice the length of sepals, acute, stamens 8, 4 protruding from the corolla, 4 smaller, half the length, or of unequal length, on broad filaments; style very short less than 1 mm, with a very indistinctly 4 notched stigma, capsule small, cuboid, 8 to 10 mm in diameter, merely notched or slightly lobed, glabrous.

This tree, 10 to 15 feet high, is called *Kukaimoa* by the natives. It is quite common in the forests of Kaholuamano, Kauai, at an elevation of 3600 to 4000 feet and inhabits the swampy forests together with *Pelea Kauaiensis.* It was first discovered by Heller. The writer found the tree quite numerous and collected flowering and fruiting specimens at different times (no. 5621, September 6, 1909, and no. 2010 flowering at Halemanu, Kauai).

Were it not for the small cuboid capsules the plant could be mistaken for *Pelea sapotaefolia,* of which Hillebrand omits the description of its fruits, while Mann says the immature capsule is puberulent and deeply four-grooved.

The native name of this species, which means "chicken droppings," originated

220

Rutaceae.

at first as an exclamation of disappointment, insofar as the capsules of this species resemble very much those of the *Mokihana*, but are without the fragrant odor of the latter. When the natives gathered the capsules for *leis* or wreaths, they quite often mistook the capsules of the species in question for *Mokihana* seeds and on finding them without odor, exclaimed "*Kukaimoa*," by which the tree is now known.

Pelea volcanica Gray.
Alani.

PELEA VOLCANICA Gray Bot. U. S. E. E. (1854) 346, pl. 38;—H. Mann in Proc. Bost. Soc. Nat. Hist. X. (1866) 315, et Proc. Am. Acad. VII. (1867) 159, et Fl. Haw. Isl. in Proc. Ess. Inst. (1867) 167;—Hbd. Fl. Haw. Isl. (1888) 67;—Engler in Engl. et Prantl Pflzfam. III. 4. (1895) 113 fig. 64. K-N.—**Evodia volcanica** Drake Del Cast. Ill. Fl. Ins. Mar. Pac. VI. (1890) 134.

Leaves opposite, oval, or ovate oblong, coriaceous, obtuse at both ends, occasionally retuse at the apex, glabrous above, glabrate underneath or slightly pubescent, especially on the prominent midrib, not shining, somewhat pellucid, the secondary veins nearly parallel, united by an arcuate intramarginal nerve, not distant from the edge of the leaf, 8 to 16 cm long, 5 to 9 cm wide, on petioles of 3 to 5 cm which are stout and apparently lignescent; inflorescence paniculate, axillary; female flowers: sepals ovate triangular, mucronulate, pubescent, 3 mm, petals ovate lanceolate, twice as long, glabrous, ovary pubescent; stamens short 1 mm, (as long as the petals in the male flowers) anthers sagittate (or oblong in the male flowers); style 4 mm long pubescent, especially in its lower half, stigma with 4 blunt lobes of 1 mm in length; capsule large 3.75 cm in diameter, but often with one, two, or three cocci abortive, cocci glabrous, somewhat lignescent, united in the axis, but recurved; the papery endocarp glabrous; seeds ovoid black shining.

According to Asa Gray, this tree reaches a height of 40 feet with a trunk of 1½ feet in diameter. It occurs on the slopes of Mauna Kea near the bullock plains in the forests bordering the latter. The writer's material (no. 3325) came from the northern slopes of Mauna Kea from the forests of Paauhau No. 2 at an elevation of 3000 feet; he also collected it in the Kohala mountains (no. 8399); flowering and fruiting June, 1910.

It is a striking species on account of its very large capsules, but is also very variable, as are nearly all Hawaiian Pelea. Complete material is needed to arrange satisfactorily and determine this rather difficult genus. The writer cannot help but deplore the awful chaos into which our Hawaiian Pelea have been thrown through the very inefficient and hasty work of H. Léveillé, which owing to the poor descriptions, which might fit any species in the genus, will have to be ignored.

In the dense rain forest of Hamakuapoko, Maui, the writer collected a specimen of a tree which is unquestionably *P. volcanica* Gray, fruiting September, 1910 (no. 8566).

Hillebrand in his flora enumerates two varieties. The first is var. *β grandifolia*, with very large leaves which are chartaceous, and a tomentose inflorescence; the capsules are 25 mm across and parted more than half way. It occurs in the woods near Hilo, Hawaii, but is not known to the writer.

The second variety, *γ ovalifolia*, is a tall tree with oblong or ovate oblong emar-

221

PLATE 85.

PELEA SANDWICENSIS Gray.
Alani.
Fruiting branch, about one-half natural size.

Rutaceae.

ginate, or subcordate leaves, with a 5 to 9 flowered panicle and capsules as in
the species. This variety was collected by Hillebrand on the Island of Maui in
the Valley of Waihee and on the southern slopes of Mt. Haleakala; the writer is
not acquainted with this plant.

Var. montana Rock var. nov.

A slender tree 20 to 30 feet tall, the branches hirsute, leaves obovate to elliptico-
oblong, bluntly acute at the apex, rounded at the base, very thick coriaceous, strongly
hirsute above when young but glabrate with age, densely pubescent underneath, the prominent midrib hirsute as are the 1.5 to 4 cm long petioles, margins revolute, the secondary
veins parallel at nearly right angles to the midrib and united by an intramarginal nerve
not distant from the edge of the leaf, 6 to 12 cm long, 4 to 6 cm wide; inflorescence
axillary paniculate, densely hirsute 1 to 5 flowered; female flowers: sepals ovate-
triangular acute 3 mm, pubescent, as are the ovate-lanceolate petals, the latter twice as
long as the sepals, stamens rudimentary the height of the yellowish hirsuite ovary, anthers
sagittate, acute, filaments broad, glabrous; style hirsute, not quite as long as the petals,
with a bluntly four-lobed stigma; capsule largest in the genus, 5 cm in diameter, puberulous, parted more than ¾, the cocci acute, at maturity the apex is deeply split, often one
or two abortive, always two seeded, the papery endocarp glabrous.

This variety the writer discovered on the upper slopes of Mt. Hualalai at an
elevation of 5000 to 6000 feet on the rim of a crater called Puuki. It is a slender
tree 25 to 30 feet in height, but has a rather small trunk of 3 to 5 inches diameter.
It has long and slender branches which are foliate only at the ends. The writer
met with it also lower down at 3500 to 4000 feet, but it was more numerous
around the rims and at the floors of extinct craters, scattered over the western
slope of Hualalai in close vicinity to the dismal cinder plain above Huehue.

The type is 3849 in the College of Hawaii Herbarium, flowering and fruiting
June, 1909. A very similar form with somewhat smaller capsules the writer
collected in the woods back of Waimea, Hawaii, fruiting June, 1910, no. 8426.

Here must also be referred a shrubby form with long rambling branches, often
a small tree, which may be known as:

Var. terminalis Rock var. nov.

Leaves smaller, more or less glabrous, on short petioles of 1 to 1.5 cm, linear-oblong,
acute, thick coriaceous, 3.5 to 12 cm long, 2 to 6 cm wide, on long slender rambling
branches; capsules smaller than in variety *montana*, about 4 cm in diameter, usually 4 to 6
on a common bracteate peduncle of 1 cm or more, usually terminal, the ends of the branchlets drooping under the weight of the mature capsules, occasionally also axillary; capsula
as in var. *montana*, smaller.

Collected at Auahi, southern slopes of Mt. Haleakala, Maui, on the lava fields
at an elevation of 2600 feet; type no. 8655, fruiting November, 1910, College of
Hawaii Herbarium.

On the Island of Lanai in the scrub vegetation of Mahana Valley occurs a
shrub with long rambling branches which becomes finally a vine entangling all
the neighboring trees and reaching way into their crowns. It is in all respects a
variety of *Pelea volcanica* and may be called:

Var. lianoides Rock var. nov.

Leaves as in the species, glabrate above, pubescent underneath, especially along the
salient midrib, on shorter petioles than in the species; inflorescence axillary, paniculate,
bearing from 3 to 10 flowers; female flowers large, pubescent, petals twice as long as the

223

Rutaceae.

sepals exactly as in the species; male flowers smaller, stamens of all sizes some as long as the petals; ovary pubescent stigma with 4-globular lobes, and sessile; capsule little smaller, endocarp glabrous.

This variety, which seems to be a typical liane, forming dense tangles, was collected flowering and fruiting by the writer in the valley of Mahana, Island of Lanai, on the dry open wooded forehills, on July 24, 1910. The type is no. 8057 in the College of Hawaii Herbarium.

Pelea sandwicensis Gray.
Alani.
(Plate 85.)

PELEA SANDWICENSIS Gray Bot. U. S. E. E. (1854) 345, t. 37;—H. Mann, Proc. Bost. Soc. Nat. Hist. X. (1866) 315, et Proc. Am. Acad. VII. (1867) 159, et Proc. Ess. Inst. V. (1867) 167;—Hbd. Fl. Haw. Isl. (1888) 66.—**Brunelia sandwicensis** Gaud. Bot. Voy. Uranie (1830) 39 sine descript;—Hook. et Arn. Beech. (1832) 80;— Endl. Fl. Suds. (1836) 184, no. 1589.—**Evodia sandwicensis** Drake Del Cast. Ill. Fl. Ins. Mar. Pacif. VI. (1890) 133.

New branchlets, inflorescence, etc., tomentose with a rather hirsute pubescence; leaves opposite, oval or oblong, thick coriaceous, glabrous above, more or less puberulent beneath, when young pubescent on the thick midrib, very veiny and reticulated, punctate, rounded at the apex or acute and mucronate, 7 to 15 cm long, 4 to 8 cm wide, on stout lignescent petioles of 20 to 35 mm; cymes axillary, short peduncled, 3 to 9 flowered; pedicels short, annulate by the broad scars of the ovate subulate bracts; sterile flowers: sepals ovate, acute, puberulous, 3 mm; petals 7 mm, oblong acute; stamens 8, 4 as long or longer than the petals, on broad filaments, 4 shorter of unequal length; anthers sagittate; ovary smaller than in the fertile flowers, pubescent, style pubescent 1.5 mm long with short bluntly notched stigma; fertile flowers smaller, ovary tomentose, style longer, with a bluntly, short-lobed stigma; stamens not quite the height of the ovary, anthers smaller; capsule finely tomentose, or glabrous when old, deeply four lobed, 20 to 24 mm in diameter, the cocci oval, endocarp finely pubescent.

A medium-sized tree, but perhaps one of the largest for the genus Pelea, reaching a height of 30 feet or little more, with a trunk 10 to 12 inches in diameter.

The *Alani* occurs in the wet forests of Oahu, especially of the main western range, where it is a common tree at an elevation of 2000 to 2500 feet. The writer met with it most plentifuly in the mountains of Punaluu, on the windward side of Oahu, as well as on Konahuanui, back of Honolulu. Several varieties of this species are known, perhaps doubtful. According to Dr. Wm. T. Brigham, the tough wood of this species was used for tapa beaters. (Flowering and fruiting November 14, 1908; no. 912, Mts. of Punaluu; fruiting Konahuanui, November, 1912, no. 10215 College of Hawaii Herbarium.)

Hillebrand's var. *β.* the writer collected at Wahiawa in the north fork of Kaukonahua gulch on Oahu, on May 15, 1909, fruiting no. 3046. The leaves are perfectly glabrous, and chartaceous, the capsules are larger and also glabrous, even when very young.

Pelea orbicularis Hbd.

PELEA ORBICULARIS Hbd. Fl. Haw. Isl. (1888) 67.—**Evodia orbicularis** Drake Del Cast. Ill. Fl. Ins. Mar. Pacif. VI. (1890) 133.

A rather small tree, stunted, the young shoots coarsely hirsute; leaves opposite, suborbicular, or orbicular, emarginate at both ends, mucronate at the apex, thick coriaceous,

Rutaceae.

dull, glabrous above, pubescent to hirsute underneath in the young leaves, pubescent along the prominent reddish midrib, the marginal nerve close to the edge and continuous 6 to 8 cm long, 5 to 7 cm wide, on petioles of 15 to 20 mm; panicles hirsute in the axils of the leaves, 6 to 15 flowered; male flowers: sepals ovate acute, 3 mm, petals little longer, stamens of unequal length some as long as the petals, anthers ovoid, ovary hirsute; female flowers: stamens rudimentary, half the height of the ovary, the latter 3 mm high, pubescent, deeply parted, style filiform, 1.5 mm, with a bluntly 4-lobed stigma, the lobes thick; capsule not known.

This small stunted tree is peculiar to the summits of Puu Kukui, West Maui, and to the summit of Mt. Waileale, Kauai, where it grows on the borders of the great swampy plateau and in little gulches of the summit swamp proper.

The writer collected specimens of this tree on West Maui, Puu Kukui elevation 5700 feet, flowering August 21, 1910, in company with Mr. G. Hammond, no. 8154; also on the edge of Honokawai Gulch at 4300 feet, flowering August 24, 1910, no. 8184.

On the summit of Kauai, Mt. Waialeale, the writer collected this species flowering on September 24, 1909, no. 4987, and again flowering October 20, 1911, no. 8880. The plants from this latter locality have the leaves from orbicular to ovate and even oblong on the same branch; however, they do not differ in other respects from those on West Maui, with the exception that they are shrubs on Waialeale, Kauai.

Pelea kauaiensis Mann.

Pilo ula.

PELEA KAUAIENSIS Mann in Proc. Bost. Soc. Nat. Hist. X. (1866) 313, et Proc. Am. Acad. VII. (1867) 158, et Fl. Haw. Isl. Proc. Ess. Inst. V. (1867) 166;—Hbd. Fl. Haw. Isl. (1888) 64.—**Pelea cruciata** Heller Pl. Haw. Isl. Minn. Bot. Stud. IX. (1897) 839, pl. 48.—**Evodia kavaiensis** Drake Del Cast. Ill. Fl. Ins. Mar. Pac. VI. (1890) 132.

Leaves opposite, ovate or elliptico-oblong, 10 to 22 cm long, 5 to 10 cm wide, thick coriaceous, (and not chartaceous) rounded or bluntly acute or emarginate at the apex, gradually tapering into a villous angular petiole of 2.5 to 3.5 cm, the marginal nerve remote from the edge, arched, uniting the secondary veins, which are parallel and almost at right angles to the midrib, pubescent above, especially along the impressed midrib, villous underneath, velvety, especially thick on the prominent midrib; finely reticulated on both sides; flowers single, 2 to 5 in a cluster, borne on slender pubescent pedicels of 2 mm; sepals ovate, rounded, broader than high, with subciliate margins; petals somewhat longer, oblong-ovate, the apices incurved, thin, glabrous, valvate, about 5 mm long, anthers rudimentary in the female flowers, of the height of the glabrous ovary; style filiform, nearly 2 mm, with an obtusely 4-lobed stigma; capsule glabrous, 15 to 30 mm in diameter deeply four parted, the cocci thick in the full grown fruits, one to two seeded, the cocci elongate, one or two often abortive.

The *Pilo ula* is a small tree, reaching a height of 15 feet, and has rather stout villous branches. Its trunk is short and only a few (6 to 8) inches in diameter. It inhabits the high central plateau of Kauai in the gray swampy, loamy soil near Kaholuamano, especially in the forests bordering the bog Lehua Makanoe. It grows in company with several species of Pelea, *Wikstroemia sandwicensis* var. *furcata, Platydesma campanulatum*, etc. It is not uncommon also at Halemanu above Makaweli. Heller in his "Plants of the Hawaiian Islands" described it as a new species *"Pelea cruciata"* and remarks as follows: "Mann's description

225

calls for a small capsule, while these are large.'' But had Heller seen the original description he would have noticed Mann's remark, ''Ripe fruit unknown,'' which accounts for his capsules being small, as they were not fully developed. The writer has abundant fruiting material in which the capsules are of various sizes from 12 mm to over 30 mm in diameter. Collected Halemanu flowering and fruiting February 14, 1909, no. 2292, and Kaholuamano, September, 1909, no. 5292, and fruiting October, 1911, no. 10214 in Herbarium, College of Hawaii. Faurie no. 226 with immature fruits March, 1910, in College of Hawaii Herbarium.

From within 5 minutes walk of the summit of Kauai, Mt. Waialeale, the writer collected a specimen of a Pelea which must be referred to this species; it is, however, a small stunted shrub, but answers otherwise the description of *P. Kauaiensis*. The capsules are much larger and all cocci are fully developed; the diameter of the mature capsule is 3.5 cm. Collected September 24, 1909, Waialeale, Kauai, 5000 feet elevation, no. 4990.

Hillebrand reports a variety *β. glabra* from the same locality with glabrous leaves which are on longer petioles; perhaps the writer's no. 1994 from Halemanu, without flowers or fruits.

Pelea rotundifolia Gray.

PELEA ROTUNDIFOLIA Gray. Bot. U. S. E. E. (1854) 344, pl. 37, fig. A;—H. Mann Proc. Bost. Soc. Nat. Hist. X. (1866) 315, et Proc. Am. Ac. VII. (1867) 159, et Proc. Ess. Inst. V. (1867) 167;—Wawra in Flora (1873) 137;—Hbd. Fl. Haw. Isl. (1888) 68;—Heller Pl. Haw. Isl. Minnes. Bot. Stud. (1897) 840.—**Evodia rotundifolia** Drake Del Cast. Ill. Fl. Ins. Mar. Pac. VI. (1890) 133.

A small tree or shrub, leaves sessile or subsessile, orbicular to ovate, rounded and emarginate or acute at the apex, cordate at the base, thick coriaceous, prominently nerved below, the intramarginal nerve arched, distant from the edge, with intervening meshes entirely glabrous 6 to 12 cm long, little less wide. flowers several in a short peduncled somewhat racemose cyme in the axils of the upper or occasionally lower leaves; bracts and bractlets opposite, minute, ovate, subulate: male flowers: sepals ovate, acute, puberulous, 4 mm high, petals more than twice the length, oblong, acute, glabrous; stamens 8, 4 longer than the petals, protruding, the remaining ones shorter and of unequal size, on broadened filaments; anthers sagittate, acute; rudimentary ovary pubescent, four lobed, pubescence encroaching on the lower part of the style, which is 2 mm in length and terminates into a bluntly 4 lobed stigma; female flowers shorter, about half the length of the male flowers. petals slightly longer than the sepals, the 8 stamens not longer than the ovary; ovules 2 in each cell; fruit nearly as in *Pelea volcanica*, but smaller, minutely pubescent, the carpels united at the base.

This peculiar species can be found not uncommon in the mountains back of Honolulu, and is easily recognized by its rather large sessile cordate leaves, and rambling or long drooping branches. Wawra quite correctly remarks that the otherwise excellent figure shows undeveloped flowers; the detailed drawings represent female flowers, so does Gray's description, as he had not seen the much larger male flowers. It is peculiar to Oahu and occurs throughout the main Koolau range at an elevation of 2000 to 2500 feet.

Flowering, Punaluu Mts., November 21, 1908, no. 577; flowering and fruiting,

Rutaceae.

Wahiawa, May 15, 1909, no. 3026; and Waikane Mts. flowering January 23, 1909, no. 1238. The inflorescence in the specimens from the last locality is more than 10-flowered.

Pelea molokaiensis Hbd.

PELEA MOLOKAIENSIS Hbd. Fl. Haw. Isl. (1888) 65.—**Evodia Molokaiensis** Drake Del Cast. Ill. Fl. Ins. Mar. Pac. VI. (1890) 132.

A small tree about 6 m high, the young shoots slightly puberulous, leaves 10 to 12.5 cm long, 6.5 to 8 cm or more wide, on petioles of 12 to 24 mm, or often subsessile, or on petioles of 8 mm (in Lanai specimens), quite glabrous, even on the reddish midrib, obovate, with retuse base and rounded or emarginate apex, the marginal nerve at some distance from the edge, with one or two sets of meshes intervening; flowers glabrous, or puberulous, 2 to 5 in a cyme or pseudo-raceme of 18 to 36 mm in length, the terete slender rhachis with 2 to 3 nodes, the pedicels 10 to 12 mm, nodose near the middle and thickened beyond; sepals triangular, 3 to 4 mm; petals reddish 5 to 6 mm; capsule as in *P. volcanica* 20 to 36 mm transversely.

According to Hillebrand this is the most prevailing form on Molokai and is also found on West Maui. The writer's material of this species is scanty and incomplete, several forms having been collected which may be referred to this species. A few plants have sessile leaves, others subsessile, others again on petioles as called for in the description, but the leaves are much smaller. On Lanai the writer collected specimens from a shrub with rambling branches which are undoubtedly *Pelea molokaiensis*, though differing somewhat from the original description. The leaves are prominently veined on both sides, while Hillebrand says: "nerves little prominent"; the species in question is evidently a very variable one, and as the writer's material of this species is without fruit in every case, the diagnosis is somewhat doubtful. However, no. 8023 from the main ridge of Lanai is here referred to *P. molokaiensis*, flowering July 25, 1910. At first glance it resembles somewhat *Pelea rotundifolia*. Hillebrand records a variety β (doubtfully) of this species from Oahu, Niu Valley; leaves as in *P. orbicularis*, all on long petioles.

Pelea macropus Hbd.

PELEA MACROPUS Hbd. Fl. Haw. Isl. (1888) 65.—**Evodia macropus** Del Cast. Ill. Fl. Ins. Mar. Pac. VI. (1890) 132.

A small tree about 5 m high, quite glabrous, leaves opposite obovately oblong, contracted and not emarginate at the base; flowers single, on a short peduncle of 2 to 4 mm, which bears 1 or 2 pairs of minute bractlets, the pedicels beyond them clavately thickened to the length of 24 to 30 mm; petals greenish; capsule nearly 3.75 cm transversely and 8 mm high, its carpels parted more than ½ their length.

This species was first collected by V. Knudsen of Kauai (no. 189), on which island it is found, probably in the forests of Halemanu, back of Waimea.

To the writer the species is not known, though a shrubby variety of it occurs on the high plateau of Kauai near Waialeale.

Pelea pseudoanisata Rock sp. nov.

A very variable small tree or shrub; branches ascending; every part of the plant emits an exceedingly strong odor of anise, leaves ovate, obovate oblong, or oblong, shining

Rutaceae.

on both sides, chartaceous to subcoriaceous, glabrous, densely punctate underneath slightly
pubescent along the salient midrib, prominently veined, the arcuate intramarginal nerve
somewhat distant from the edge of the leaf, rounded at both ends or retuse at the apex,
occasionally bluntly acute and mucronate, often submarginate at the base, 6 to 12 cm
long, 3 to 7 cm wide, on stout lignescent angular petioles of 1 to 2 cm; inflorescence a
cyme, axillary, usually in the axils of the lower leaves, single to 3 flowered, peduncle and
pedicels filiform, nodose, the former 6 to 10 mm long, the pedicels of variable length 2 to 3
cm, nodose, bibracteolate at each node, bracteoles linear-subulate pubescent; flowers large
in both sexes, female flowers greenish yellow to red, strongly anise-scented as is the whole
plant, sepals ovate, acute, 3 mm, almost deltoid, petals linear-oblong, acute, 1 cm long,
glabrous as are the sepals, stamens rudimentary, as high as the ovary, the latter 1.5 mm.
glabrous; style slender filiform, 6 mm, or more, often protruding beyond the petals,
glabrous, with a four lobed stigma, the lobes slender oblong, 1 to 1.5 mm in length,
puberulous; male flowers as large as the female flowers or smaller, petals broad, oblong,
acute, usually 12 mm long and 4.5 mm wide, glabrous, many nerved; stamens 8, 4 nearly
as long as the petals, the filaments broad, thin, and penninerved, the remaining 4, two-
thirds the length of the others, anthers oblong, deeply split at the base; ovary rudimentary; style slender 3 mm, with a very indistinctly four notched, almost capitate
stigma; capsule nearly 5 cm transversely, and 18 to 20 mm high, somewhat chartaceous,
glabrous, the 4 follicles united half their length, in shape much like that of *P. volcanica*,
recurved, 1 to 2 seeded, rarely one or two abortive; endocarp loose, chartaceous, glabrous;
seed large, 9 mm long, ovoid to sub-orbicular, black, shining.

This exceedingly interesting species, which has been called the *mokihana* of
Hawaii, is a small tree or shrub, and is peculiar to the summit ridges and
swamps of the Kohala mountains on Hawaii. It occurs only at an elevation of
4000 to 5000 feet, and is exceedingly common at the summit of the Kohala range
called Kaala. It inhabits the dense rainforest where moss covers the ground
over a foot deep and where most beautiful 5-feet-high violets abound. When
bruised it emits an exceedingly strong odor of anise, much more so than the true
mokihana of Kauai, *Pelea anisata*. If a branch is bruised accidentally by work-
ing one's way through the jungle, the odor emitted can be detected for a long
distance through the forest jungle. The species has the biggest capsule in the
genus and also the largest flowers.

The writer has excellent and most complete material of this species, which
seems to be related to *P. oblongifolia*, in all stages of growth. It was first collected by the writer on July 13, 1909, flowering and fruiting, in the forests of
Kohala, no. 4455; it was again collected in June, 1910, in the same locality and
on the summit of Kohala proper, where it is most abundant in the swampy jungle
bordering a big open bog. Certain forms resemble somewhat *Pelea parvifolia*
Hbd.

The type is no. 8306 in the College of Hawaii Herbarium and was collected at
the summit of Kohala, Hawaii. It also borders the edges of the great valleys of
Alakahi and Kawainui in the heart of the mountains at an elevation of 4200
feet, where they are enwrapped by clouds ten months or more of the year.

Pelea Balloui Rock sp. nov.

A small tree or shrub; leaves ovate or obovate rounded at both ends, occasionally
retuse at the apex, thick coriaceous, opaque, finely reticulated on both sides especially
underneath, the salient midrib reddish, pubescent, as is the under surface of the young
leaves, soon glabrate, the intramarginal nerve not distant from the edge of the leaf,
but with one set of meshes intervening 5 to 10 cm long, 3 to 7 cm wide, on petioles of

Rutaceae.

1 to 2.5 cm; inflorescence axillary, covered with a silky appressed yellowish green pubescence throughout, paniculate, branching from every node, bracteate throughout, bracts 1
mm, triangular, acute; peduncle 3 to 12 mm, the ultimate bibracteolate pedicels 5 mm;
sepals ovate, acute, not quite 3 mm, petals acuminate, 4 mm, both sepals and petals persistent with the capsule, (description drawn from persistent sepals and petals) flowers
unknown; capsule silky tomentose, parted more than half into 4 ovoid cocci which when
fresh are nearly as beaked as in *Platydesma rostrata*.

This rather interesting species, which is named here after Prof. Howard M.
Ballou, to whom the writer is indebted for corrections of the proof sheets of
this book, grows in the dense rain forest on the slopes of Mt. Haleakala, Maui,
along the trail leading from Ukulele to Waikamoi Gulch, at an elevation of 5000
feet. It was collected by the writer in the above locality, fruiting, October 25,
1910, in company with Mr. L. von Tempsky. The type is numbered 8609 in the
College of Hawaii Herbarium.

It is apparently related to the rather dubious *Pelea Mannii* Hbd., but differs
from the latter in the pedunculate inflorescence and the silky-haired rostrate
capsules; while the ovary in *Pelea Mannii* is glabrous.

Pelea anisata Mann.
Mokihana or *Mokehana.*

PELEA ANISATA Mann in Proc. Bost. Soc. Nat. Hist. X. (1866) 314, et Proc. Am.
Acad. (1867) 159, et Fl. Haw. Isl. Proc. Ess. Inst. V. (1867) 166;—Wawra in
Flora (1873) 109;—Hbd. Fl. Haw. Isl. (1888) 64;—Heller Pl. Haw. Isl. (1897)
837;—Brigham, Ka Hana Kapa, (1911) 163, fig. 97.—**Evodia anisata** Drake Del
Cast. Ill. Fl. Ins. Mar. Pac. VI. (1890) 130.

A slender tree; leaves opposite oblong, 5 to 12 cm long, 3.75 to 5.5 cm wide on
petioles of 2.5 cm, obtuse or rounded at both ends, or emarginate with an attenuate base,
chartaceous, the marginal nerve distant from the edge, with smaller secondary meshes
intervening; flowers small, 1 to 5 on a short peduncle of 4 mm, which is bracteate at the
apex, pedicels 2 mm, bracteolate at the middle; sepals obtuse, 2 mm, thin and transparent;
petals 4 to 7 mm long, oblong, acuminate, stamens 8, four longer than the petals, the
remaining 4 slightly shorter, or as long as the petals; ovary glabrous, style 1.5 mm, with
4 minute stigmatic branches; capsule coriaceous, small 12 mm in diameter, cuboid, subentire, the outer faces notched only by a shallow sulcus, the axis remaining entire after
dehiscence; all parts of this tree emit a very strong anise odor.

This very strongly scented tree, called *Mokihana* by the natives of Kauai, is
peculiar to the latter island. It is a slender tree reaching a height of over 20
feet, and a trunk of 10 inches or more in diameter, and is vested in a smooth
thin bark; all parts of the tree have a strong anise odor, which is retained even
for years in the dry wood as well as in the capsules. The latter are in great
favor with the natives and are threaded and worn by women and men alike as
leis or wreaths. It was one of their favorite perfumes and twigs as well as capsules were placed between their tapa cloth.

The tree is evenly distributed over the Island of Kauai, and is quite common
in the forest of Kaholuamano and Halemanu, above Waimea, as well as at Hanalei on the windward side; it, however, does not ascend higher than 4000 feet
and not lower than 3000 feet. This is not the only tree of this genus which
possesses an odor of anise. On the Island of Hawaii in the high swamp forest of

229

PLATE 86.

PELEA ZAHLBRUCKNERI Rock sp. nov.
Flowering and fruiting branch, less than one-half natural size.

Rutaceae.

the Kohala mountains grows a species with exceedingly strong anise odor, even more so than in the Kauai plant, but it does not retain its odor. The capsules are three times as large as those of the *Mokihana* and resemble very much the capsules of *P. volcanica*.

The *Mokihana* fruits abundantly during the early fall, especially during the month of September, when the trees are loaded with the mature capsules.

Pelea Wawreana Rock sp. nov.

Leaves elliptico-oblong or obovate-oblong, opposite, bright green, thick coriaceous, shining above, dull underneath, glabrous throughout, even on the reddish prominent midrib, rounded at the apex, often retuse, more or less pellucid, cuneate or often rounded at the base, veins prominent united by an arched intramarginal nerve which is close to the edge of the leaf at the base, and more or less distant toward the apex, the secondary veins about parallel in angles of about 85° to the midrib, 8 to 15 cm long, 4 to 7 cm wide, on stout petioles which are thickened near the blade, angular when young, 2 to 3 cm long; inflorescence axillary, 2 to 3 flowered, young bud pubescent; peduncle stiff. thick, about 5 mm or little longer, pubescent, bracteate, the pedicels half the length, bibracteolate at the middle; capsule cuboid, scarcely notched, 12 to 14 mm in diameter, about 10 mm high, the cocci one to two seeded, endocarp glabrous.

This species, named in memory of the author's compatriot, Dr. H. Wawra of the Austrian exploring expedition, is a small tree 10 to 15 feet high with a short trunk which is vested in a smooth brown bark; the branches are ascending, robust and very tough. It is probably related to *P. sapotaefolia*, from which it differs in the opposite glabrous leaves and much smaller cuboid capsules.

It is not uncommon on the slopes of Konahuanui, but especially along the Manoa cliff trail at an elevation of about 2000 feet, together with *Perrottetia sandwicensis*, Hibiscus, *Maba sandwicensis, Straussia Kaduana,* and others.

Collected November 30, 1912, and fruiting February 2, 1913, in company with Dr. E. A. Back. The type is no. 10220 in the Herbarium of the College of Hawaii.

A pubescent form of this species was collected at Wahiawa in the north fork of Kaukonahua Gulch of the Koolau range on May 15, 1909, flowering and fruiting (no. 3020).

The leaves are pubescent along the midrib; the inflorescence, which is 5 to 7 flowered, is covered with a yellowish tomentum, as are the sepals. The petals are glabrous; the female flowers are rather small, only 3 mm in length; stamens about 0.5 mm, ovary hirsute, style thick with a bluntly four-lobed stigma.

Pelea Zahlbruckneri Rock sp. nov.
(Plates 86, 87.)

Leaves opposite, large, elliptical oblong, obovate oblong, or oblong or suborbicular, thin chartaceous, rounded or retuse at the apex, almost cuneate at the base, midrib prominent, secondary veins more or less parallel, at not quite right angles to the midrib, united by an arched intramarginal nerve which is quite distant from the revolute margin of the leaf, glabrous above, puberulous or glabrate underneath, 8 to 24 cm long, 4.5 to 12.5 cm wide, on petioles of 2 to 6 cm, pale green, whitish when dry; cymes axillary, very slender, 2 to 4 flowered, peduncle somewhat compressed, 1 cm, bracteate, pedicels 4 mm, bibracteate at the base, bracts triangular to subulate; flowers very small, sepals triangular 1.5 mm, petals 3 mm, acute, stamens of unequal length, all shorter than the petals;

231

PLATE 87.

PELEA ZAHLBRUCKNERI Rock sp. nov.
Growing in the Kipuka Puaulu, near Kilauea Volcano, Hawaii; elevation 4000 feet.

the sagittate anthers on broad filaments; the glabrous ovary neither lobed nor notched, entire, crowned by a short style with a bluntly notched stigma; capsule large. 3 cm in diameter, chartaceous, entire, cuboid, scarcely even notched, glabrous, the ovary thin, transparent, glabrous endocarp entirely loose; the cocci appear to be somewhat divided after dehiscence of the capsule, each cocci 1 to 2 seeded; seeds large 8 mm, ovoid, black, shining.

This very interesting species, which seems to be related to Hillebrand's var. β of *Pelea sapotaefolia* as far as capsules are concerned, occurs in the park-like Kipuka Puaulu near the Volcano of Kilauea, on Hawaii, at an elevation of 4000 feet. It is a conspicuous tree on account of its peculiar branching habit, exceedingly large leaves, and very large cuboid capsules. It is quite plentiful in company with *Pelea volcanica, Pelea clusiaefolia*, Xanthoxylum, *Sapindus saponaria*, Suttonia and other trees. It was discovered by the writer in July, 1911, when he collected his type material, which is no. 10216 in the College of Hawaii Herbarium. Named in honor of Dr. A. Zahlbruckner, Director of the Botanical Museum in Vienna.

Pelea multiflora Rock.
(Plates 88, 89.)

PELEA MULTIFLORA Rock in Coll. Haw. Publ. Bot. Bull. I. (1911), pl. III.

Leaves opposite, oblong, rounded at the apex, subcordate at the base, dull green, glabrous above, densely covered underneath with an olivaceous tomentum, as well as the 2.5 to 4 cm long petiole, 10 to 20 cm long, 5 to 9 cm wide, thick coriaceous, quite opaque, marginal nerve wanting; young leaves golden yellow, densely hirsute; inflorescence 10 to 15 cm and more long, cymosely paniculate, densely tomentose, on a common peduncle of 4 to 6 cm, bracteate throughout, the bracts 1 to 1.5 cm, linear oblong, acuminate, ultimate pedicels 3 to 5 mm long; flowers 10 to 200 on a single inflorescence; floral bracts subulate, enclosing the persistent calyx which in turn encloses the four valvate petals of 5 mm in the fertile flowers; male flowers larger than the female flowers, calyx half the length of the corolla; stamens 8, four shorter than the petals, the remaining four as long as the corolla, and sometimes protruding, ovary rudimentary with 4 minute stigmatic branches; female flowers, calyx as long as the corolla, silky gray, the lobes acuminate, smaller than the male flowers; ovary large glabrous, four lobed, style 4 mm long with a white four lobed stigma, each lobe 2 mm long; follicles glabrous, 3 cm each way, carpels parted their entire length; endocarp yellow, shining, glabrous, more or less loose; each follicle 1 to 2 seeded, seeds ovoid, black, shining.

This exceedingly interesting species was discovered by the writer on the lava fields of Mt. Haleakala on the southern slopes, in the district of Kahikinui, on Maui. The particular locality where this tree occurs is called Auahi, and is situated at an elevation of 2600 to 3000 feet. It is the richest botanical section in the whole Territory, with the exception of Puuwaawaa on Hawaii.

The species in question is a good-sized tree 30 to 40 feet in height, with a trunk of over one foot in diameter, which is clothed in a gray smooth bark. The tree is badly attacked by a lichen, a species of *Usnea*, probably *australis*, which seems to check the growth of the trees; they are literally covered, trunk and branches, with this ungainly looking lichen.

The tree was discovered during November, 1910, when the first specimens were collected (no. 8646 flowering and fruiting). During the first part of March, 1912, the writer revisited that locality for the purpose of collecting additional material and also to secure photographs. Many trees were then in flower, and

PLATE 88.

PELEA MULTIFLORA Rock.
Male flowering branch, showing a (placed) mature capsule in the upper branch;
one-half natural size.

Rutaceae.

on the strength of the new material, the specific description is herewith enlarged. It is one of our most interesting species of Pelea in that it has the greatest number of flowers in its inflorescence, bearing often more than 200 flowers. It belongs to the same group as *Pelea cinerea* and *Pelea barbigera*, though it is specifically very distinct from both. At Auahi, to which place this tree is peculiar, it is associated with *Alectryon macrococcus, Pterotropia dipyrena, Bobea Hookeri, Alphitonia excelsa, Sideroxylon auahiense, Antidesma pulvinatum,* etc.

Pelea Knudsenii Hbd.

PELEA KNUDSENII Hbd. Fl. Haw. Isl. (1888) 70.—Evodia Knudseni Drake Del Cast. Ill. Fl. Ins. Mar. Pac. VI. (1890) 132.

A tree about 10 m high, the young shoots and inflorescence covered with a gray tomentum; leaves opposite, 12.5 to 15 cm long, 7.5 to 10 cm wide, on petioles of 5 to 6.5 cm, ovate or ovate-oblong, cordate at the base, or the basal lobes connate, with the petiole subpeltately inserted above the base, bluntish, glabrous above, pubescent underneath, the midrib and nerves densely villous with a soft grayish wool, thin chartaceous, with the marginal nerve in deep arches; flowers numerous 20 to 40, in a large pyramidal panicle of 5-6.5 cm in length, with 3 to 4 pairs of divaricate branches, the stiff angular peduncle about 24 mm, the ultimate pedicels very short, with the last bractlets close to the calyx; bracts 8 to 6 mm; calyx and corolla villous externally, the sepals 6 mm; the oblong petals scarcely longer; disk 8 lobed hairy; ovary sparsely pubescent.

The plant was collected by Valdemar Knudsen of Kauai, for whom it was named by Hillebrand. It is recorded as growing at an elevation of 1500 feet back of Waimea, Kauai, and is, of course, a dry district plant. It is not known to the writer, who collected extensively in the above referred to locality, but never met with this species. It is evidently closely related to the writer's *Pelea multiflora*, which differs, however, from the foregoing in the exceedingly large inflorescence, which is 15 cm long, in the 6 cm long peduncle, and in the number of flowers, which is up to 200; the ovary in this species is glabrous.

The capsule of *P. Knudsenii* is not known, but is unquestionably apocarpous, under which latter heading it is placed in Hillebrand's key to the species.

Pelea barbigera (Gray) Hbd.
Uahe a Pele.

PELEA BARBIGERA (Gray) Hbd. Fl. Haw. Isl. (1888) 70.—Melicope barbigera Gray Bot. U. S. E. E. (1854) 351, t. 39, fig. B;—H. Mann Proc. Bost. Soc. Nat. Hist. X. (1866) 316, et Proc. Am. Acad. VII. (1867) 159, et Fl. Haw. Isl. Proc. Ess. Inst. V. (1867) 168.—Melicope cinerea fm. barbigera Wawra in Flora (1873) 139.—Evodia barbigera Drake Del Cast. Ill. Fl. Ins. Mar. Pac. VI. (1890) 130.

Leaves elliptical, oblong, 10 to 16 cm long, 5 to 6.5 cm wide, on petioles of 2.5 to 5 cm, contracting but obtuse at both ends, pale green, dull, not shining above, beneath densely clothed, especially along the midrib, with a cobwebby wool, which disappears with age, chartaceous with faint nerves, the leaves all curved, the upper surface convex, the lower concave; flowers 3 to 5 on a stiff angular gray tomentose peduncle of 20 to 24 mm, the pedicels 2 to 6 mm long, and bracteolate at the middle, the bracts and bractlets usually large for the genus, 8 to 6 mm; sepals and petals gray-tomentose, the former ovate-acute, 3 to 4 mm, the latter 5 to 6 mm; ovary sparingly pubescent, with distinct style and 4 short stigmatic branches; follicles discreet, one or another abortive, obovoid, 25 mm in diameter, glabrous, rather thin, concentrically striate, endocarp glabrous; one to two seeded.

235

PLATE 89.

PELEA MULTIFLORA Rock.
Flowering branch pinned against trunk of tree: growing on the lava fields of
Auahi, Mt. Haleakala, Maui.

Rutaceae.

This rather interesting species, called *Uahe a Pele* by the natives, meaning smoke of Pele, owing to the peculiar smoky gray color of the leaves, is only found on the Island of Kauai, where it inhabits the drier districts especially near Kaholuamano and Halemanu, above Waimea, at an elevation of 3600 to 4000 feet. It is a rather small tree or often only a shrub. It is quite different from *Pelea cinerea* in general aspect as well as in the leaves, which are thinner and curved, and mainly in its fruits, which are glabrous, and have also a glabrous endocarp. It comes, however, nearest to that species, though specifically distinct from it and not a mere form, as Wawra tried to make out.

Pelea elliptica Hbd.

PELEA ELLIPTICA Hbd. Fl. Haw. Isl. (1888) 69.—**Melicope ? elliptica** Gray Bot. U. S. E. E. (1854) 353;—Mann. Proc. Bost. Soc. Nat. Hist. X. (1866) 317, et Proc. Am. Ac. VII. (1867) 159, et Fl. Haw. Isl. Proc. Ess. Inst. V. (1867) 168.—**Pelea Kaalae** Wawra in Flora (1873) 110.—**Evodia elliptica** Drake Del Cast. Ill. Fl. Ins. Mar. Pac. VI. (1890) 131.

A small tree; leaves thin chartaceous, with pellucid dots, elliptico-oblong 7.5 to 12.5 cm long, 2.5 to 3.5 cm wide, on petioles of 8 to 16 mm, broadly obtuse or rounded, even emarginate at both ends, faintly nerved, with the sinuous marginal nerve rather distant from the edge, sparsely dotted underneath with a pale pubescence, but soon glabrous and pale; flowers 1 to 3 on a short angular peduncle of 2 to 6 mm, the pedicels 6 mm, bracteolate below the middle with dentiform bractlets; sometimes several cymes in one axilla; sepals and petals coriaceous, persistent below the capsule, both canescent in the bud, but sub-glabrate in a later period; sepals 2 mm, obtuse, petals valvate in the bud, oblong 3 to 5 mm; style obscurely 4-lobed, almost capitate in the sterile flowers; follicles discreet to the base, gray, puberulous, 8 to 10 mm, thin papery, dehiscent in both sutures, one or more abortive.

The plant was first collected by the U. S. Exploring Expedition on Kaala of the Waianae range, Island of Oahu. The writer is not familiar with this species, as he has never collected it. Hillebrand describes five varieties of this species, two from Maui, one from Niu Valley, Oahu, and the last var. ε. from Kalae and Mauna Loa, Molokai.

Pelea cinerea (Gray) Hbd.
Manena on Maui.
(Plate 90.)

PELEA CINEREA (Gray) Hbd. Flora Haw. Isl. (1888) 68.—**Melicope cinerea** Gray, Bot. U. S. E. E. (1854) 350, t. 39, fig. A;—H. Mann in Proc. Bost. Soc. Nat. Hist. X. (1866) 316, et Proc. Am. Ac. VII. (1867) 159, et Fl. Haw. Isl. Proc. Ess. Inst. V. (1867) 168:—Wawra in Flora (1873) 139.—**Evodia cinerea** Drake Del Cast. Ill. Fl. Ins. Mar. Pac. VI. (1890) 131.

Young shoots covered with a grayish or ochraceous tomentum; leaves opposite, ovate oblong 7.5 to 10 cm long, 3.75 to 5 cm wide, on petioles of 16 to 24 mm, shortly acuminate, subcoriaceous, with faint nerves, the marginal nerve distant and arcuate, tomentulose to pubescent underneath, glabrate when old; flowers 3 to 5 in a short cyme or raceme, the angular peduncle 6 to 12 mm, the pedicels 4 to 8 mm, bibracteolate at the middle; petals 4 mm, valvate in the bud, but some edges forced out before expansion, gray puberulous; ovary tomentose; capsule 20 to 24 mm transversely, the follicles cohering slightly at the base only, soon glabrate, thick coriaceous, opening only along the ventral suture, generally all maturing; the thick endocarp pubescent; seeds 1 or 2 in each follicle, 4 to 6 mm in diameter; cotyledons plano-convex, extending the whole length and breadth of the albumen.

PLATE 90.

ṖELEA CINEREA (Gray) Hbd. var. γ Hbd.
Manena Tree.
Growing in the Kipuka Puaulu, near Volcano Kilauea, Hawaii; elevation 4000 feet.

Rutaceae.

Specimens of this species were first collected by the U. S. Exploring Expedition on the Island of Oahu, on the Waianae range, in a ravine of Mt. Kaala. This species is a typical dry district Pelea and is found on nearly all the islands of the group in various forms, which do not differ much from the species. In certain localities they are small trees or shrubs, while again in others they are handsome trees with trunks of often a foot or more in diameter. The writer has not collected the species on this island (Oahu), but has abundant material from the other islands.

Hillebrand's var. β. with an olivaceous tomentum, and coriaceous leaves, the writer collected on Maui in the dry gulches back of Makawao, on the northwestern slope of Mt. Haleakala; no. 8550, flowering and fruiting September, 1910. The leaves in this variety are quite pale, with revolute margins and more or less glabrous on both sides; the peduncles are 3-flowered, the flowers are smaller than in the species; the capsules are of a sulphur-yellow and are densely tomentose; the tree is conspicuous on account of its leaves, which are whitish pale underneath. Another variety, enumerated as γ in Hillebrand's Flora, and described as *Pelea Hawaiiensis* by Wawra in Flora (1873) 110, occurs in Hawaii in the Kohala range, evidently in the dry districts near Mahukona, as this particular species has never been found in the rain forest, but always on ancient lava flows or in *kipukas*.

To this variety evidently will have to be referred the various specimens collected by the writer on the Island of Hawaii. At Puuwaawaa, North Kona, Hawaii, on the ancient lava fields, it occurs quite plentifully (no. 10211). The young shoots as well as the leaves are tomentose, but become glabrate when old; the capsules are 2 cm in diameter, light ochra-yellow and densely tomentose; the leaves are thick coriaceous, with prominent veins. In the Kipuka Puaulu, on the slopes of Mauna Loa, near Kilauea Volcano, the writer met with the finest trees of this variety, one of which is here figured. The capsules are of a darker yellow and larger. The trunk of this tree is vested in a smooth pinkish, light brown bark, which is about half an inch thick and of a dirty brownish yellow color inside. (No. 10210, fruiting July, 1911.) Another form of this variety was collected (no. 8774) in the same locality, with acute glabrous leaves and 5-15 or more flowered panicles; petals elongate acute tomentose outside, four stamens protruding, four half as long, filaments puberulous, as long as the petals (3.5 mm), anthers oblong, 1 mm, ovary hirsute.

Hillebrand's var. δ the writer collected on the lava fields of Puuwaawaa at an elevation of 2000 feet. It is quite distinct from the variety found a thousand feet higher. It differs mainly in the thinner perfectly glabrous acute leaves; the peduncles in the writer's specimens are about 8 mm, each bearing a single fruit; follicles larger, 3 cm in diameter, covered with a reddish yellow velvety tomentum. Collected June 6, 1909, fruiting (no. 3561). It is a shrub with

PLATE 91.

PLATYDESMA CAMPANULATUM Mann.
Pilokea.

Rutaceae.

rather rambling branches. Hillebrand's material came from Kau and South Kona.

Var. racemiflora Rock var. nov.

Leaves ovate, cordate at the base, bluntly, acute, glabrous above, puberulous underneath, on compressed hirsute petioles; panicles racemose, terminal and in the axils of the leaves, often more than 6 cm long, with yellowish pubescence; flowers small, numerous, stamens wanting in the fertile flowers, ovary tomentose.

This new variety is a small tree with broad flat crown, and reaches a height of 10 to 15 feet. The branches are stout and woody to the last ramification. It occurs on the rough *aa* lava flows on the southern slope of Mt. Haleakala, Maui, between the huge blocks of lava, at an elevation of 1500 feet, where it is in company with *Reynoldsia sandwicensis* and *Alphitonia excelsa*, the most predominant trees in the district. It was collected by the writer in flower, November, 1910. The type is no. 8676 in the College of Hawaii Herbarium. The native name of the tree is *Manena*.

PLATYDESMA Mann.

Flowers hermaphrodite. Sepals 4, roundish, broadly imbricate. Petals 3, large, imbricate or convolute. Discus flat, slightly 4 to 8 lobed. Stamens 8 inserted at the margin of the discus; the filaments flat, ovate or ovate-lanceolate, united into a wide tube, with elongate sagittate anthers, with linear anther cells converging at the apex. Carpels 4, united, each with 5 to 8 ovules suspended from a broad funiculus, hemitropous. Ovary deeply lobed. Style terminal, undivided, with thick stigma. Fruit a dry 4-lobed indehiscent or loculicidal capsule, with thin endocarp, with 2 or more seeds in each cell. Seeds subglobose, with black shining crustaceous testa, and with albumen. Embryo in the middle of the albumen, with thin, broad, roundish cotyledons and short radicle.—Small trees or shrubs with strong pepsin odor, and opposite or whorled, single entire leaves. Flowers large in axillary cymes.

The genus Platydesma is peculiar to the Hawaiian Islands and consists of three endemic species, only one of which is arborescent. *Pl. rostratum,* a shrub branching from the base, with rostrate or beaked capsules, is peculiar to Kauai, while *Pl. cornutum* is found on Oahu. *Pl. campanulatum* occurs principally on Oahu, but is represented on the other islands in various forms. *Pelea auriculaefolia* Gray has erroneously been referred to Platydesma by both Hillebrand and Engler. Léveillé described two species collected by Abbé Faurie, both from the Punaluu Mts., Oahu. One, *Platydesma Fauriei,* is undoubtedly *Pl. campanulatum*; the other, *Pl. oahuensis,* is probably referable to *Pl. cornutum,* which the writer collected in the Punaluu Mts. Léveillé in his description of his second new species says: *petalis luteis?* None of the Hawaiian Platydesma have yellow petals, but are of a waxy white or cream color.

Platydesma campanulatum Mann.
Pilo kea.
(Plate 91.)

PLATYDESMA CAMPANULATUM Mann Proc. Bost. Soc. Nat. Hist. X. (1866) 317, et Proc. Am. Ac. VII. (1867) 160, et Fl. Haw. Isl. Proc. Ess. Ins. V. (1867) 169, et Mem. Bost. Soc. Nat. Hist. I. 4. (1869) 530, pl. 22;—Wawra in Flora (1873)

241

Rutaceae.

139;—Hillbr. Fl. Haw. Isl. (1888) 71;—Del Cast. Ill. Fl. Ins. Mar. Pac. VI. (1890) 134;—Engler in Engl. et Prantl Pflzfam. III. 4 (1895) 127, fig. 69, A-F;—Heller Pl. Haw. Isl. in Minnes. Bot. Stud. IX. (1897) 841.—**Platydesma Fauriei** Levl. in Fedde Repert. X. no. 10-14. (1911) 153.—**Melicope spathulata** Gray, Bot. U. S. Expl. E. (1854) 352; (doubtful).

A variable species; leaves opposite, obovate oblong, bluntly acuminate at both ends, or rounded at the apex, narrowing at the base, chartaceous, often rather thick when fresh, with transparent dots, the nerves not prominent, with the exception of the midrib which is salient, punctate on the underside, glabrous above, occasionally sparingly pubescent along the veins and midrib, leaves varying in size on different parts of the tree, from 7.5 to 35 cm long, by 2.5 to 10 and 15.5 cm wide, the petioles from 1 to 5 cm in length; peduncles of about the same length as the petioles, bearing ovate subulate bracts; cyme 3 to 5 flowered, occasionally single flowered; pedicels 4 to 6 mm long, bracteolate; flowers hermaphrodite, 18 to 20 mm long, 12 to 14 mm in diameter, campanulate; sepals round, 8 to 10 mm long, decussatingly imbricate, clothed with a sericeous pubescence extending also to the pedicels; petals 4, cream colored, alternate with the sepals, strongly imbricate, 16 to 18 mm long, obovate, thick, waxy, minutely sericeous, bearded on the margins; stamens 8, nearly as long as the petals, inserted on the margin of the thin hypogynous disc; the dilated filaments monadelphous to the middle; anthers sagittate, introrsely dehiscent, 4 mm long; ovary globular, the four rounded carpels joined only by the central columnar style, which is four times their length; stigma terminal, entire, slightly four-grooved; ovules 5 in each cell, collateral; capsule of 4 distinct erect cocci, 16 to 22 mm long and 10 to 12 mm in diameter, whole capsules 30 mm transversely; endocarp smooth, crustaceous, and half enclosed by the persistent cup-shaped calyx; seeds resembling very much those of Pelea. The capsule often rots away but the seed remain attached to the placenta for some time. Two seeds usually ripen.

This exceedingly interesting tree, which must have been much more common than it is now, can still be found in the mountains behind Honolulu on the slopes of Konahuanui, and also in the whole Koolau range, especially in the mountains of Punaluu, on the windward side of Oahu. The tree is, however, not confined to the Island of Oahu, but is found also on the other islands of the Hawaiian group, with the exception of Molokai and Lanai. The writer observed it only as a shrub outside of Oahu, while on the latter island it reaches a height of 15 to 20 feet or perhaps a little more; the trunk is, however, not more than 5 inches or so in diameter. The whole plant, when bruised, emits an exceedingly strong odor of pepsin, which is not unpleasant. This species is the type of the genus and has the largest capsules, while the other two species have much smaller and quite different capsules. It is certainly very variable. It was collected by the writer first at Punaluu, no. 65, flowering August, 1908, and again November 13, 1908, flowering and fruiting no. 630; flowering and fruiting November 30, 1912, Manoa Valley, Mt. Olympus, no. 10225.

Hillebrand describes two varieties. β. var. *pallida* from Kaala, Oahu; and East Maui, Hamakua. It differs from the species in the densely pubescent or tomentose leaves. The second, γ var. *macrophylla*, he records from Kauai.

The writer collected this variety on Kauai in the mountains of Halemanu and Kaholuamano back of Waimea at an elevation of 3600 feet. The leaves are quite large, some of them 36 cm long, on petioles of 4 cm, and are densely tomentose underneath, especially along the midrib; the flowers are arranged in cymes on a peduncle of less than one millimeter, at the nodes of the naked branches; flowers as in the species; a very robust form which evidently belongs

Rutaceae.

here was collected along the Honomanu trail on the northern slopes of Mt. Haleakala, Maui, elevation 2500 feet, with enormous leaves 20 cm wide; another form at 4000 feet elevation on the same island in the forests near Olinda, with smaller leaves, flowering, September, 1910; no. 8534.

Hillebrand's var. γ. *macrophylla* with large glabrous leaves is from Kauai.

On the Island of Hawaii, in the Kohala Mts. proper, west of Honokanenui gorge, the writer collected specimens of a tree 15 to 20 feet high, with very robust branches; the leaves are glabrous, thick coriaceous, and probably belong to Hillebrand's var. γ. The leaves are on petioles of 5 to 5.5 cm and differ therefore from the latter variety, which has the leaves on short petioles of 6 to 8 mm; it may be known as forma *coriaceum* f. nov.

Collected June, 1910, fruiting, no. 8367, in College of Hawaii Herbarium.

Var. sessilifolia Rock var. nov.

A shrubby plant, with erect stems foliose at the apex; leaves large, opposite, perfectly sessile with a broad base, oblong or obovate oblong, gradually tapering toward the base, very thin chartaceous, transparent, midrib and veins prominent, rounded at the apex, glabrous above, pubescent underneath, 26 to 38 cm long, 9 to 14 cm wide, flowers as in the species, the petals acute; capsule exceedingly large, the erect cocci separated by a very broad sinus of 4 mm.

Collected in the dense forests of the summit mountain of the Kohala range, Hawaii, fruiting July 12, 1909, type no. 4222 in the College of Hawaii Herbarium.

EUPHORBIACEAE.

This is an exceedingly large family, consisting of more than 208 genera with many species, distributed over all parts of the world, with the exception of the Arctic and Alpine regions.

The genus Euphorbia is the most widely distributed of the family, reaching as far as the polar borders of the northern and southern hemispheres.

In the Hawaiian Islands the family is represented by five genera, four of which have arborescent species.

KEY TO THE GENERA.

Plants not milky:
I. **PHYLLANTHEAE.** Flowers monoecious or dioecious; ovary cells two-ovulate:
   Leaves alternate entire, fruit a berry, three celled, seeds arillate.... **Neowawraea**
   Leaves alternate, entire; fruits flat, one-seeded.................. **Antidesma**
II. **CROTONEAE.** Flowers monoecious or dioecious; ovary cells one-ovulate:
   Leaves alternate, crenate or serrate; fruits capsular, two-three celled
   .... **Claoxylon**
   Leaves alternate, lobed; stone fruit one-seeded, splitting into two-four cocci
   .... **Aleurites**
Plants milky:
III. **EUPHORBIEAE.** Flowers mostly monoecious, rarely dioecious; ovary three celled, one-ovulate:
   Leaves opposite, linear; fruit a three celled capsule............. **Euphorbia**

NEOWAWRAEA Rock gen. nov.

Flowers dioecious. Male flowers: sepals 5, of unequal shape and size. Petals none. Stamens 3 to 4, rarely 5, inserted between the sinuses of the hypogynous disc, consisting

243

PLATE 92.

NEOWAWRAEA PHYLLANTHOIDES Rock gen. et sp. nov.
Showing male flowering branch, and female branch in fruit; about one-half natural size.

Euphorbiaceae.

usually of 4 glands. Female flowers unknown. Fruit a globose berry, reddish-black, with persistent calyx. Endocarp of 3 thin membraneous cocci each with two seeds, rarely 4, which are enclosed in an arillus. Embryo filling the whole cavity of the seed, cotyledons flat, subrotundous, radicle exserted, albumen scanty.—An unarmed tree with alternate, ovate, glabrous, entire leaves. Flowers in fascicles all along the stipulate branchlets.

This proposed new genus, which is here dedicated to the memory of the author's compatriot, Dr. H. Wawra, Ritter von Fernsee, of the Austrian Exploring Expedition, consists of a single remarkable species, of which only three male and one female trees are in existence. It is evidently related to Phyllanthus. Owing to the fruit being a berry it would come closer to Bischofia, from which it, however, differs in the presence of a discus and the fasciculate inflorescence.

Neowawraea phyllanthoides Rock sp. nov.

A tree 10 to 12 m high, with a straight trunk of about 4 dm or more in diameter; bark light brown, rough and scaly; branches semi-erect, with many small branchlets which are covered with light gray, oblong lenticels; leaves ovate, rounded or truncate at the base, bluntly acute at the apex, light green above, glaucous underneath, penninerved, the lateral veins nearly parallel, at angles of about 60° to the midrib, thin, chartaceous, glossy above, dull underneath, glabrous, 8 to 14 cm long, 4 to 9 cm wide, on petioles of 15 to 20 mm; stipules triangular, subcaudate, membraneous, caducous; inflorescence axillary, fasciculate, all along the branchlets; male flowers in dense fascicles or close clusters, very small 1.5 mm in diameter, on short pedicels of 2 mm, which are surrounded at the base by several roundish bracts, in the shape of a cup, out of whose center the pedicels arise. The 5 sepals are minute, unequal, petals wanting, stamens 3 to 4, rarely 5, inserted between the sinuses of an hypogynous disc, usually consisting of 4 glands, female flowers not known; fruit an indehiscent globose berry, 6 mm in diameter, with the calyx persistent, reddish-black, juicy, staining purplish, endocarp thin membraneous, divided into three cocci, each with two arillate seeds, rarely 4; seeds pale yellow, about 2 mm long, convex outside, acute angled inside, hilum suborbicular to ovate situated in the upper third of the seed; embryo 2.3 mm long, cotyledons flat, filling the whole cavity of the seed, 1 mm long, 1.3 mm wide, radicle 1 mm, protruding; albumen scanty.

This very interesting and remarkable tree, for which an old native Hawaiian gave the name *Mehamehame,* is exceedingly rare, only three males and one female tree being in existence. In regard to the native name, the writer is not inclined to accept it. The outward appearance of the tree resembles somewhat our Hawaiian Antidesma, which are also called *Hame* or *Mehame* or *Mehamehame.* The old native might have easily taken it for such. It is very doubtful if the natives ever had a name for the tree, as it is peculiar to such a small area, located in a most inhospitable place on the southern flanks of the great volcano Mauna Loa on rough *aa* lava flows, made accessible only very recently.

It was discovered by the writer in the above locality at an elevation of 2000 feet, called Kapua, during the month of February, 1912; but was at that time neither in flower nor in fruit. A careful search of the ground beneath the trees, revealed no sign of seeds of a previous season. This, however, was explained on a later visit in the month of July (15), 1912, in company with Mr. W. M. Giffard, when it was found that the trees first examined were all male and in flower. Only one other tree was seen, which fortunately turned out to be a female tree bearing fruit. It is a striking tree of medium height, and is quite

245

PLATE 93.

NEOWAWRAEA PHYLLANTHOIDES Rock gen. et sp. nov.
Branches pinned against trunk of tree. Growing on the lava fields of Kapua,
South Kona, Hawaii.

Euphorbiaceae.

conspicuous in that small area on account of its pale glaucous foliage. The wood is exceedingly heavy, close grained and very hard. The sap wood is red, while the heartwood is black, making a beautiful contrast. The type is no. 10030 in the College of Hawaii Herbarium.

It is associated with *Antidesma pulvinatum, A. platyphyllum, Pittosporum Hosmeri* var. *longifolia, Maba sandwicensis, Alphitonia excelsa, Colubrina oppositifolia, Santalum Freycinetianum, Osmanthus sandwicensis, Tetraplasandra Hawaiiensis*, and many other interesting tree species.

ANTIDESMA Linn.

Flowers dioecious. Calyx 3 to 5 lobed. Discus teeth free, rarely united. Male flowers: Stamens 2 to 5, opposite the sepals; anthers bent inward in the bud, later erect. The rudimentary ovary small. Female flowers: Ovary 1—very rarely also 2-celled. Style 3, very short, 2 lobed. Stone fruit small often oblique. Seeds without caruncle.

A genus of trees and shrubs, with more than 70 species in the warmer regions of the old world. It is distributed from tropical Africa to Australia, Japan and the islands of the Pacific.

Two species or probably three are to be found in these islands, with one in the Viti (Fiji) Islands, one in Samoa, and two in New Guinea. The only representative of the genus in tropical Polynesia, a doubtful one, is recorded by Hemsley from Admiralty Island. None have so far been discovered in America.

KEY TO THE SPECIES.

Leaves ovate or obovate, glabrous.................................... **A. platyphyllum**
Leaves cordate with a patch of hairs in the angles of rib and veins...... **A. pulvinatum**

Antidesma platyphyllum Mann.
Hame or *Haa.*
(Plate 94.)

ANTIDESMA PLATYPHYLLUM Mann Proc. Am. Acad. VII. (1867) 202;—Hbd. Fl. Haw. Isl. (1888) 402;—Del Cast. Ill. Fl. Ins. Mar. Pacif. VII. (1892) 289;—Heller Pl. Haw. Isl. (1897) 842.

Leaves ovate to obovate or orbicular 8 to 12 cm long, 4 to 10 cm wide, on petioles of about 5 mm, shortly acuminate, glabrous, shining above but punctato papillose, chartaceous to coriaceous, panicles puberulous; male flowers: subsessile along the simple branches of a paniculate rhachis of about 8 cm; bracts conchoid, as long as the calyx or longer; calyx less than 2 mm, puberulous, with 5 to 4 roundish lobes; petals rudimentary, disc glabrous, lobed, stamens 5 or 4, long exserted; ovary rudimentary, with peltate stigmas. Female flowers: pedicellate along the branches of a solitary, axile, paniculate rhachis of 5 to 14 cm; bracts linear; calyx less than 2 mm, 5 to 8 cleft; disc small, annular; ovary glabrous; style terminal; drupe reddish or dark purplish, fleshy, compressed, suboblique the osseous putamen irregularly ridged. Cotyledons suborbicular, as broad as the scanty albumen, 2 or 3 times as long as the radicle.

The *Hame* or *Haa* is a very handsome tree, reaching a height of 20 to 30 feet, with a trunk of a foot or more in diameter; the bark is fibrous, deeply corrugated, and whitish. It has no round crown, as the few branches are rather ascending and have only a few branches. It is conspicuous by its large leaves, which are bright green and glossy, and is on that account often mistaken for the *Maua* tree (*Xylosma Hillebrandii* or *X. Hawaiiense*), which it resembles

247

PLATE 94.

ANTIDESMA PLATYPHYLLUM Mann.
Hame or Haa.
Fruiting branch, less than one-half natural size.

greatly. During the months of June, July, and August, and on Kauai as late as October, the trees are loaded with the very dark-red, fleshy, compressed berries, which are of the size of a large pea; they are arranged all along the branches on a paniculate rachis. On the lava fields of Kona, especially at Kapua, it fruits in December and January.

The *Hame* inhabits the dry as well as the wet forests on all the islands, especially at an elevation of 1500 to 3000 feet. It is not uncommon above Makawao, Maui, where it grows in company with Sideroxylon, Labordia, Pelea, Pittosporum, Ochrosia, Xanthoxylum, Straussia, etc. On Molokai it inhabits the dry sections and is also found in the wettest district along the stream in Wailau valley proper, which has an enormous rainfall. On Hawaii it is plentiful in North and South Kona, on the slopes of Hualalai, and the slopes of Mauna Loa, also Waipio valley and the mountains of Kohala. It can also be found along the Keanae ditch trail on the windward side of Maui, but not growing to any size. On Kauai a variety grows just below Kaholuamano, 3000 feet elevation, associated with *Cyanea leptostegia*, Xanthoxylum, Charpentiera, Osmanthus, etc.

The wood of the *Hame* or *Haa* is close-grained, rather hard, and of a reddish-brown color. It was used by the natives for *Olona* anvils. The *Olona* formed one of their principal fiber plants, which was beaten to thin strips on *Hame* logs. The wood, which takes a fine polish, is excellent for cabinet work, but, unfortunately, it is not found in sufficient quantities to be of any commercial value. The red coloring matter of the fleshy berries was used in conjunction with the *Kamani* oil, into which such tapa was placed as was intended to be worn as bathing malos by the chiefs; this infusion gave it a bright color.

From Kauai, Hillebrand describes a variety β with broad obtuse leaves which are shining on both faces.

$\times$ **Antidesma Kapuae** Rock nov. hybr.

(Antidesma platyphyllum Mann $\times$ *A. pulvinatum* Hbd.)

Leaves as in *A. platyphyllum*, but quite acuminate, while the fruits are almost exactly like in *A. pulvinatum* Hbd.

Both *A. platyphyllum* and *A. pulvinatum* are extremely common in Kapua on the lava fields of South Kona, Hawaii, at an elevation of 2000 feet. Here the writer met with trees whose leaves are identical with those of *A. platyphyllum*, while the fruits are those of *A. pulvinatum*. It could not be placed either to the one or the other, and is here mentioned as a probable hybrid.

Antidesma pulvinatum Hbd.

Haa, or *Mehama.*

(Plates 95, 96 and 97.)

ANTIDESMA PULVINATUM Hbd. Fl. Haw. Isl. (1888) 403;—Del Cast. Ill. Fl. Ins. Mar. Pac. VII. (1892) 289.

Young branches and inflorescence ochraceous, tomentose; leaves ovate, cordate, shortly acuminate, thin chartaceous, dark green above, lighter and tomentose underneath, with

PLATE 95.

ANTIDESMA PULVINATUM Hbd.
Haa or Mehame.
Fruiting branch, less than one-half natural size.

PLATE 96.

ANTIDESMA PULVINATUM Hbd.
Haa or Mehame.
Fruiting branch pinned against trunk of tree; showing deep longitudinal corrugation of
bark. Growing on the lava fields of Kapua, South Kona, Hawaii.

PLATE 97.

ANTIDESMA PULVINATUM Hbd.
Haa or **Mehane** tree.
Growing on the *aa* lava fields of Kapua, South Kona, Hawaii.

prominent veins, and always with a villous patch in the angles of rib and veins; panicles short, branching only near the base; ovary tomentose; drupe much smaller than in *A. platyphyllum*, 4 to 6 mm, black; female calyx tomentose, 5 to 6 cleft; style branches very short, subentire.

This species, unlike the previous, is confined to the dry districts, especially to the *aa* (rough) lava fields. It does not reach the height of *A. platyphyllum*, but has a beautiful round, symmetrical crown. The trunk is short and about 10 inches to over one foot in diameter. The bark is deeply corrugated, longitudinally furrowed, fibrous, and whitish. The leaves are ovate, generally heart-shaped at the base, not glossy, of a dull-green, and have villous patches on the underside in the angles of rib and veins, giving them a brownish color. The berries are much smaller than in the *Hame* or *Haa*, and are blackish.

It inhabits the dry region of the lower elevations and may be found on the southern slope of Haleakala on the *aa* lava fields of Auahi in company with Reynoldsia, *Maba sandwicensis*, *Xylosma Hillebrandii*, etc. On Oahu it is found in the Waianae range, but it is most plentiful on the lava fields of South Kona, Hawaii, especially at Kapua (2000 feet), where it forms about 60 per cent of the tree growth.

CLAOXYLON Juss.

Dioecious, rarely monoecious. Discus of various formation. Male flowers: calyx subglobose, 3 to 4 cleft; filaments free, anthers extrorse; without rudimentary ovary. Female flowers: calyx less divided, 2 to 4 lobed. Discus entire or lobed. Ovary 3 to 2 celled. Styles short, free or united at the base. Seeds without caruncle, globose. Albumen fleshy. Cotyledons flat.—Glabrous or tomentose trees or shrubs. Leaves alternate, petioled, often large, subcoriaceous, entire or serrate; inflorescence axillary single or fasciculate, shorter than the leaves. Flowers small, the male flowers usually fascicled, the female flowers single under each bract.

The genus Claoxylon consists of over 40 species, and is distributed in the tropics of the old world, from Africa to the islands of the Pacific. Two species occur in these islands, two in New Guinea *(C. longifolium* (Bl.) Mull.-Arg., and *C. bicarpellatum* Laut. & Sch.*)*. One species is recorded from New Caledonia, one from Tahiti, and two from Viti or Fiji Islands. Of the Hawaiian species only one is arborescent.

Claoxylon sandwicense Mull.-Arg.
Poola.
(Plate 98.)

CLAOXYLON SANDWICENSE Mull.-Arg. in Linnaea XXXIV. (1865) 165; et in DC. Prodr. XV. 2. (1866) 780;—H. Mann Proc. Am. Acad. VII. (1867) 203;—Seem. Flora Vit. (1867) 224;—Wawra in Flora (1875) 148;—Hbd. Fl. Haw. Isl. (1888) 398;—Del Cast. Ill. Fl. Ins. Mar. Pac. VII. (1890) 291;—Pax in Engl. et Prantl Pflzfam. III. 5 (1896) 48.

A small soft wooded tree, with pale spreading branches, the youngest shoots tomentose; leaves obovate-oblong or lanceolate, 10 to 20 cm long, 5 to 7 cm wide, on petioles of 2.5 to 5 cm, shortly acuminate or obtuse, crenate-serrate with callous teeth; membraneous, lurid green, scabro papillose, but glabrate; flowers clustered in distant fascicles of 2 to 4 and minutely bracteate along a simple rachis of from 7 to 12 cm in length. Male flowers: calyx 6 mm, parted to the base into 3 (rarely 2 or 4) triangular lobes; no disc or glands,

PLATE 98.

CLAOXYLON SANDWICENSE Mull.-Arg.
Poola.
Flowering and fruiting branch, from the forest about Glenwood above Hilo, Hawaii.
About one-half natural size.

Euphorbiaceae.

stamens about 200; female flowers: calyx 2 to 3 mm, sepals ovate, glands 3, oblong, nearly the size of the sepals; ovary tomentose or silky; styles short, spreading; capsule dividing into 3 cocci, 5 mm high and 6 mm broad, deeply furrowed; seeds globose, rugose; embryo axile, cotyledons orbicular, twice as long as the radicle.

The *Poola* is a very small, soft-wooded tree, reaching a height of not more than 15 to 18 feet, rarely 20. The trunk is usually branching 6 to 8 feet above the ground with pale, spreading branches, forming rather an unsymmetrical crown.

On East Maui, on the southern slopes of Haleakala, on the lava fields of Auahi, it grows to a small tree at an elevation of 2000 to 2500 feet, in company with Alectryon, Xanthoxylum, Xylosma, Pelea, Tetraplasandra, etc. On Hawaii it is not uncommon on the lava fields of Puuwaawaa, where it is a small tree. The plants from the latter locality differ somewhat from those of other localities, in that their leaves turn to a steel-blue color on drying, and in some other minor points. On Lanai, the *Poola* is most plentiful in the valleys of Kaiholena and Mahana. It is endemic to the Hawaiian Islands. No record remains as to the usefulness of this tree.

The second Hawaiian species, *C. tomentosum* (Hbd.) Heller, is a shrub, and occurs on Kauai only.

ALEURITES Forst.

Monoecious to almost dioecious. Male flowers: calyx irregularly 2 to 3 cleft. Petals longer than the calyx. Stamens inserted on a conical receptacle, in 1 to 4 whorls, the 5 outer ones epipetalous. Alternipetalous disc-glands 5, without rudimentary ovary. Female flowers: corolla the same as in the male flower. Disc much reduced. Ovary 2 to 5-celled. Style divided into two thick, linear branches; stone fruit indehiscent, exocarp thin, endocarp crusty, 2 to 5 celled. Testa thick, woody. Albumen thick, hard, very oily.—Trees with stellate pubescence. Leaves alternate, long petioled, large, 5 to 7 nerved at the base, entire or 3 to 5 to 7-lobed; peduncle at the apex with two glands. Flowers in loose, widely branched cymose corymbs.

A small genus of 3 to 5 species, of which *A. moluccana* (L.) Willd. is the most common and widely distributed species; it occurs in the tropics and sub-tropics of the old world, in the West Indies and Brazil, Pacific islands, etc.

Aleurites moluccana (L.) Willd.
Kukui.
(Plate 99.)

ALEURITES MOLUCCANA (L.) Willd. Sp. Pl. IV. (1805) 590;—Mull. Arg. in DC. Prodr. XV. 2. (1866) 723;—H. Mann Proc. Am. Acad. VII. (1867) 203;—Seem. Fl. Vit. (1867) 223;—Nadeaud Enum. Tahit. Plants (1873) No. 462;—Hbd. Fl. Haw. Isl. (1888) 400;—Del Cast. Ill. Fl. Ins. Mar. Pac. VII. (1892) 289, et Fl. Polyn. Franc. (1893) 183;—Pax in Engl. et Prantl Pflzfam. III. 5. (1896) 73, fig. 44;—Heller Pl. Haw. Isl. (1897) 842.—Brigham Ka Hana Kapa (1911) 138, fig. 84.—Jatropha moluccana Linn. Spec Pl. ed. 1. (1753) 1006.—Aleurites triloba Forst. Char. Gen. (1776) 112. t. 56., et Prodr. (1786) no. 360, et Incon. (ined. cf. Seem.) t. 262;—Hook. et Arn. Bot. Beech. (1832) 69, et 95;—Endl Fl. Suds. (1836) no. 1554;—Guill. Zeph. Tait. (1836-37) no. 180;—Jardin Iles Marqu. (1858) 25.—Telopia perspicua Soland. Prin. Fl. Ins. Pac. (1858) 332, et in Park. Draw. Tah. Pl. 105, et. 106 (ined. cf. Seem.).—Camirium moluccanum O. Ktze. Rev. Gen. Pl. II. (1891) 595.

Leaves of variable shape, ovate or rhombeo-lanceolate, undivided or 3, 5 to 7 lobed, with triangular acuminate lobes, pale, with the rib and nerves tomentose; corymb 10 to

PLATE 99.

ALEURITES MOLUCCANA (L.) Willd.
Kukui.
Flowering and fruiting branch, reduced.

Euphorbiaceae.

15 cm long. Male flowers: calyx ovoid in the bud petals white to cream colored, oblanceolate; stamens about 18, anthers erect, introrse. Female flowers: calyx 6 mm; ovary hairy, 2-celled; fruit fleshy, coriaceous, globose, about 5 cm or more in diameter, with 4 shallow furrows; seeds 1 or 2, rugose-gibbous.

The *Kukui* is one of the most common of Hawaiian forest trees, growing at elevations of from about sea level to about 2200 feet. It reaches a height of sometimes 80 feet and more, especially in narrow, rocky gorges, such as Mauna Lei on Lanai, and other narrow valleys. The trunks reach large dimensions, and it is not uncommon to find them several feet in diameter. Of all Hawaiian trees the *Kukui* has the lightest colored foliage, it being covered with a silvery-gray powder which makes it very conspicuous in the forest, and can be recognized from far off. The trunks are not always erect, but sometimes are twisted and running on the ground, as are also the huge branches. It is mainly in narrow gorges that the tree has a perfectly straight trunk, branching 40 feet or so above the ground.

It inhabits the lower slopes of the mountains in the dry region as well as on the windward side, where the rainfall is usually heavy. It is common on all the islands from almost sea level up to 2200 feet, but not higher.

The nuts especially were a necessity to the natives, who made their torches from the seeds, strung on coconut or palm-leaf midribs. An oil was expressed from the nuts, which they burnt in stone lamps. Of the acrid juice of the fleshy covering of the nuts they prepared a black dye, used in tattooing. From the bark of the root a similar dye was used in coloring canoes black. The trunk itself was sometimes made into canoes. while the soot of the burning nuts was used as canoe paint. The trunk, when bruised, exudes a gum or resin called *pilali* by the natives, who employed it for various purposes. The gummy substance is said to be chewed by the Tahitians, especially that exuding from the fruits. The nuts contain 50 per cent of oil, which is known as *Kekuna* in India and Ceylon, and *Kukui* in Hawaii. In former times the yearly production of the *Kukui* nut oil in the Hawaiian Islands amounted to 10,000 gallons, and was exported to Europe. The cake, after expression of the oil, is a good food for cattle, and also useful for manuring. Medicinally, the oil is used as a purgative, and also makes an ideal dressing for ulcers.

The nuts are also roasted by the Hawaiians and, when chopped, are mixed with seaweed and served at *luaus* or native feasts as a relish. In Samoa the nuts are strung similarly to the old Hawaiian method and used as house lamps, 50 to 60 nuts being necessary for one night. They are boiled before being strung on the midribs of palm leaves. It is called *lama* and *tuitui* in Samoa, *nibbol* by the Tami Islanders in New Guinea, and *raguar* in the Caroline Islands; it is the *lauci, sikeci* and *tuitui* in the various dialects of Fiji.

The wood of the *Kukui* is of a light color, soft and absolutely not durable. It decays very easily when cut full of sap. Many insects bore into the wood, but especial mention may be made of the big beetle Aegosoma, belonging to the Longicorn family, which is also a great enemy of the *Koa* and other trees.

257

PLATE 100.

EUPHORBIA LORIFOLIA (Gray) Hbd. var. **GRACILIS** Rock var. nov.
Koko or Akoko.
Fruiting branch pinned against trunk of tree; bark is incised, note flow of latex. Growing on the lava fields of Puuwaawaa, North Kona, Hawaii; elevation 3000 feet.

Euphorbiaceae.

EUPHORBIA L.

Cyathium campanulate, 4 to 5 lobed, the lobes entire or slit, often hidden by glands. Glands between the lobes, rarely less, entire or two horned or digitate. Male flowers: numerous without calyx, very rarely with a small scale on the articulation of the stamens. Female flowers: single from the middle of the cyathium, finally stipitate and exserted from the cyathium, naked or with a calyx formed by three small scales. Styles 3, free or united, entire or bifid. Capsule separating into 3 two-valved cocci.—Herbs, shrubs or trees, abounding in milky juice. Leaves entire, opposite, or alternate. Cyathia in terminal cymes or in the axis of two dichotomous branches, or in the axils of the leaves; stem often thick fleshy, cactus-like or even leafless.

The genus consists of more than 600 species, and is distributed especially over the warmer regions; it is absent in the Arctic regions, and only very sparingly represented in the colder parts of the temperate zone.

In the Hawaiian Islands ten species are endemic, of which only three become small trees.

All Hawaiian Euphorbiae are called *Akoko* or *Atoto* by the natives. The name *Atoto* appears also in Tahiti for *Euphorbia atoto*, which is called *Totolu* and *Totoyava* by the Fijians. *Euphorbia atoto* is credited to the Hawaiian Islands by Seeman, who mistook for it the closely allied *Euphorbia cordata* of our seashores.

KEY TO THE SPECIES.

Leaves linear oblong; flowerheads terminal or axillary, single; capsule small. **E. lorifolia**
Leaves obovate oblong; flowerheads in open axillary cymes; capsules large. **E. Rockii**

Euphorbia lorifolia (Gray) Hbd.
Koko or *Akoko.*
(Plate 100.)

EUPHORBIA LORIFOLIA (Gray) Hbd. Flora Haw. Isl. (1888) 395;—Del Cast. Ill. Fl. Ins. Mar. Pacif. VII. (1892) 285.—**E. multiformis** var. **lorifolia** Gray in H. Mann, Proc. Am. Acad. VII. (1867) 202.—**E. multiformis** var. **angustifolia** Boiss. in DC. Prodr. XV. 2 (1866) 11 (ex parte).

A small tree, with stiff branches which are nodose with short internodes and puberulous; leaves opposite, linear or oblong, somewhat spathulate, 2.5 to 5 cm long, 4 to 10 mm wide, on petioles of 1 mm or almost sessile, obtuse or truncate, often retuse at the apex, entire, slightly contracted and subtruncate or uneven sided at the base, chartaceous or somewhat fleshy; stipules very low, triangular with a broad base; flowerheads terminal and axillary, generally single or (in the Maui specimens) 2 to 3 in the leaf-axils, subsessile, supported by several short bracts; involucre less than 3 mm, pubescent outside, glabrous within, with 4 suborbicular glands; the lobes obovate or quadrate, with ragged margins; bracteoles 3 to 4 fid; styles free to the base, shortly bifid with clavate branches; capsule erect on a short stalk, 3 mm in diameter, puberulous, obtuse at the angles, the cocci broader at the base; seeds rugose, scrobiculate.

Var. gracilis Rock. var. nov.

Branches not erect and stiff, but very slender and drooping; leaves linear oblong, acute at both ends, chartaceous, opposite, on petioles of 2 to 3 mm, midrib and veins very prominent, pubescent underneath, pellucid, capsules smaller, the cocci of equal width. Type no. 3593 in College of Hawaii Herbarium.

This variety is peculiar to Puuwaawaa, North Kona, Hawaii, where it grows on the *aa* lava fields. It reaches a height of 20 to 25 feet and a diameter of

PLATE 101.

EUPHORBIA ROCKII Forbes.
Koko.
Showing fruiting branch and flowers, reduced.

Euphorbiaceae.

often more than 10 inches. The trunk is vested in a pinkish, rather thin bark which is smooth when young, but often forms thick knobs which are deeply wrinkled in very old trees. It has a tremendous flow of latex, which does no⁺ coagulate on the tree, but becomes yellow, especially in old trees.

The species occurs in the gulches back of Makawao, Maui, and also on the slopes of Mauna Kea, Hawaii, near the crater Nau, on the boundary of the Parker and Horner ranches. The writer met with it also on the Island of Lanai in the dry gulches of Mahana.

The new variety, however, occurs only on the slopes of Hualalai between Hue-hue and Puuwaawaa, Hawaii, at an elevation of 3000 feet, on the rough *aa* lava fields and also in the more humid forest of Waihou. The area with which this tree is practically covered amounts to about 5000 acres. During a recent visit in North Kona, engaged in botanizing in this most interesting locality, the writer was struck by the tremendous flow of latex and the large amount which could be procured from a single tree. Thinking it worth while to take some latex samples for examination, the writer sent a large bottleful to the U. S. Agricultural Experiment Station in Honolulu for analysis.

This Station has since published the results of the analysis in the form of a Press Bulletin No. 37, entitled "*Euphorbia lorifolia,* a Possible Source of Rubber and Chicle," by Wm. McGeorge, Assistant Chemist, and W. A. Anderson, Superintendent Rubber Substation

Euphorbia Rockii Forbes.
Koko.
(Plate 101.)

EUPHORBIA ROCKII Forbes Occas. Pap. Bernice P. Bishop Mus. Vol. IV. 3. (1909) 38, pl. 1.

Leaves opposite, obovate-oblong, obtuse, uneven-sided with a clasping base, nearly sessile, 8 to 12 cm long, 2.5 to 3 cm wide; flowers in open axillary cymes 3 to 3.5 cm long; involucre campanulate, minutely hairy or glabrous on the outside, pubescent on the inside, lobes ovate, minute, glands transversely oblong, not appendiculate; style branches short, nearly free; capsules large 18 to 24 mm. glabrous, pink or dark crimson, on nodding peduncles.

This tree, which was discovered by the writer in August, 1908, when in full fruit is exceedingly handsome. It reaches a height of about 15 to 20 feet, with a trunk of about eight inches in diameter. The bark is smooth and whitish. Like all Euphorbiae, it exudes a sticky, milky sap when bruised. The branches are flat and spreading, giving the trees a broad, flat crown. The flowers are small and inconspicuous and are borne on dichotomous cymes. The three-cornered capsules are bright pink or deep scarlet when mature, of an inch or more in length clothing the whole crown in scarlet, which is beautifully contrasted with the dark-green, glossy, sessile foliage.

The *Euphorbia Rockii* is peculiar to the Island of Oahu, and is only found on the windward side, in the mountains of Punaluu above Kaliuwaa valley, at an elevation of 2000 feet or more. On the summit ridge it grows to a shrub.

261

while in the shaded ravines it becomes a tree 15 to 18 feet in height. It associates with *Pittosporum glomeratum, Straussia* sp., *Psychortia hexandra, Pterotropia gymnocarpa,* Cyrtandra, many Lobelias and other plants peculiar to the rain forest, of which this tree is also typical.

ANACARDIACEAE.

This family, which consists of 58 genera with over 420 species, reaches its best development in the tropical regions of the old and new world, but mainly in the Malayan Archipelago. Only a few genera occur in the extra tropical regions of the northern and southern hemispheres, as in the Mediterranean, and Manchurian-Japanese regions, in the forests of North America, and in the Andes region of South America.

Among the most useful members of this family are the Mango (*Mangifera indica*), *Wi (Spondias dulcis), Cacheu-nut (Anacardium occidentale)* and many others.

RHUS L.

Flowers polygamous, calyx 5-lobed. Petals longer than the calyx, both imbricate. Stamens inserted below a broad discus, with subulate filaments, and ovate anthers, in the female flowers often small. Ovary ovate or subglobose, with a single ovule suspended from an erect funis; styles terminal 3, free or somewhat united, with truncate or capitate stigmas. Drupe globose or compressed, with thin glabrous or tomentose exocarp. Seeds ovate or reniform with thin testa.—Shrubs or trees with alternate, simple, trifoliate or pinnate leaves, and usually small flowers arranged in compound panicles.

The genus Rhus has the largest number of species of any genus of the above family. It consists of over 120 species and subspecies, and is distributed over the tropics, subtropics and temperate zones, but chiefly in South Africa. Several species are found in the Viti (Fiji) and Society Islands.

The Hawaiian variety of *R. semialata* differs from the species in having the rhachis of the leaf not winged.

R. semialata extends from the Himalaya Mts. through China to Japan.

The Japanese Sumach (*R. vernix*) has been introduced into the islands here.

Some species of Rhus are poisonous to the touch, others are employed for tanning and dyeing purposes.

The Tahitian name of *R. Taitensis,* peculiar to the South Sea Islands (Samoa, Viti, and Tongan Islands) is *"Waiwai,"* in Samoa *"Tavai."*

Rhus semialata Murr. var. sandwicensis Engl.

Neneleau or *Neleau.*

RHUS SEMIALATA Murr. var. SANDWICENSIS Engl. in DC. Monogr. IV. (1883) 380;— Hbd. Fl. Haw. Isl. (1888) 89;—Del Cast. Ill. Fl. Ins. Mar. Pac. VI. (1890) 145;— Engler in Engl. et Prantl Pflzfam. III. 5 (1896) 168.—R. semialata Murr., Mann Proc. Am. Acad. VII. (1867) 162, et Fl. Haw. Isl. (1867) 177.—Rhus sandwicensis Gray Bot. U. S. E. E. (1854) 369.—Toxicodendron semialatum (Murr.) O. Ktze Rev. Gen. Pl. I. (1891) 154.

Branches feruginous at the ends; leaves impari-pinnate, with 2 to 6 pairs of leaflets, the rachis 10 to 30 cm long, terete, not margined, petiolate in the lower third or fourth; leaflets oval or oblong, more or less acute or acuminate, 5 to 15 cm long and 2.5 to 8 cm wide, almost sessile, feather veined, downy underneath, subglabrous above; panicle terminal, very large and compound, very dense, 30 cm long, many flowered, flowers small yellowish, calyx 1 mm, deeply 5-cleft, tomentose; petals 5, 2 mm, obovate, glabrous or ciliate; anthers 5, ovoid, obtuse, on very short filaments, styles 2 to 3, short, with capitate stigmas; fruit 3 to 4 mm, ovoid, somewhat flattened, tomentose.

The *Neneleau*, or Hawaiian Sumach, is a small tree of 15 to 25 feet in height. It sometimes sends up numerous shoots from the roots and thus forms dense clumps of great extent. The trunk is seldom a foot in diameter and is vested in a smooth bark; the leaves are pinnate, of a bright green with red veins and petioles, and when it is in flower is quite an attractive looking tree. The flowering panicle is terminal rusty tomentose, and very dense. The flowers are very small and pale yellow. The *Neneleau* is strictly of the lowland and lower forest zone between 600 to 2000 feet elevation, and may be found in more or less isolated clusters. On Kauai it grows above Makaweli together with the *Kukui* (*Aleurites moluccana*), *Sapindus oahuensis*, Pisonia, etc., while on Hawaii it is most common all along the road back of Hilo. It is also found in Kona and back of the Waimea village. On Maui it grows on the windward (Kailua) and leeward slopes of Haleakala (at Auahi), together with the *Puhala* (*Pandanus odoratissimus*), and it is not uncommon in Nuuanu Valley, on Oahu.

The wood of the *Neneleau* is soft and very light, of a yellowish gray color, and has a rather coarse grain with darker streaks. It, however, is tough and is largely used for ox plows by the ranchers.

In North Kona above Kailua, Hawaii, there is a large grove of *Neneleau*, though now almost dead, due to a fungus pest which has also made its appearance in Hilo.

The species of which this Hawaiian tree is a variety is a small tree whose habitat is in the outer Himalaya Mts., from the Indus to Assam, growing at an elevation of 6000 feet, and on the Khasia Mts. at altitudes between 3000 and 5000 feet. The fruit is used by the hill tribes of the Himalaya as a remedy for colic. From the pulp which surrounds the drupes, the *omlu*, a vegetable wax, is prepared by the Nepalese, which is similar to the Japanese wax of commerce. The *Neneleau*, however, is peculiar to Hawaii.

AQUIFOLIACEAE.

Of the family Aquifoliaceae only about 176 species are known, of which more than 170 belong to the genus Ilex. The remaining species belong to 3 genera. The center of distribution of Ilex is in the central and southern part of America, with nearly half as many species in Asia and a few in the Pacific Isles. One genus (Nemopanthes) is North American, while the genus Phelline and others belong to the Australian floral region.

PLATE 102.

ILEX SANDWICENSIS (Endl.) Loes.
Kawau or Aiea on Kauai.
Fruiting branch about one-half natural size. Typical Oahu specimen.

Aquifoliaceae.

ILEX L.

Flowers through abortion dioecious. 4 to many lobed, usually isomerous, calyx rarely oligomerous, and ovary pleiomerous.

Subgenus **BYRONIA** (Endl.) Loes.

Inflorescence single or in the leaf axils or single lateral at the base of young shoots, usually long peduncled, one or several times dichotomous or trichotomous, cymose or irregularly forked, rarely umbellately contracted. Flowers isomerous, or oftener at least the female flowers heteromerous. Petals occasionally shorter than the ovary. Staminodia of the female flower often without anthers, resembling entirely the petals. Ovary 5, or more often 6, to many celled, occasionally 22 celled. Ovules single in each cell. Trees with chartaceous or mostly thick coriaceous, entire, or rarely serrulate leaves.

The genus Byronia, established by Endlicher, was reduced by Loesener to a subgenus under the genus Ilex, which was again divided into two classes, A. *Eubyronia*, into which falls the Hawaiian representative, now *Ilex sandwicensis* (Endl.) Loes., and B. *Micrococca* Loes. with a single species found in Japan.

Ilex sandwicensis (Endl.) Loes.
Kawau, or *Aiea* on Kauai.
(Plate 102.)

ILEX SANDWICENSIS (Endl.) Loes. in Engler et Prantl Pflzfam. Nachtr. I. γ 218.— Ilex ? anomala Hook et Arn. Bot. Beech. (1832) 111 t. 25.—**Byronia sandwicensis** Endl. in Ann. Wien. Mus. I. (1836) 184,—et Fl. Suds. (1836) no. 1577;—A. Gray Bot. U. S. E. E. (1854) 296. pl. 26;—H. Mann Proc. Am. Acad. VII. (1867) 161, et Fl. Haw. Isl. Essex Inst. V. (1867) 171;—Wawra in Flora (1873) 170;— Hbd. Fl. Haw. Isl. (1888) 78;—Del Cast. Ill. Fl. Ins. Mar. Pac. VI. (1890) 138;— Brigham Ka Hana Kapa (1911) 178, fig 105.—**Byronia anomala** Heller Pl. Haw. Isl. (1897) 847, et **B. sandwicensis** Endl. Heller l. c. p. 848.

Leaves elliptico-oblong or obovate to ovate, 5 to 12 cm long, 2 to 6 cm wide, on petioles of 5 to 25 mm, obtuse, narrowing toward the base, entire or rarely serrulate, coriaceous, dark green above, lighter underneath, glossy above, with impressed nerves; flowers numerous in cymose panicles of 5 to 10 cm in length, the naked compressed two-edged peduncle 2.5 to 5 cm, pedicels 6 mm, bibracteolate below the middle, the bractlets 2 to 3 mm; calyx 4-lobed, the lobes rounded, corolla rotate white, deeply 6 to 10 cleft, female flowers with staminodia often without anthers, as many as the lobes of the corolla and alternate with them; ovary closely sessile in the calyx, globular, 12 to 18 celled; in sterile flowers smaller and imperfect; stigma sessile, broad, radiate with 12 to 18 lines, persistent, ovules single in each cell, stamens half the length of the corolla, filaments flattened, anthers didymous, drupe spherical, smooth, 12 to 18 grooved when mature or dry, black, dull, with purplish fruit flesh, containing 2 to 18 separable pyrenae.

The writer has abundant material of this species from various localities all over the group, and after comparing the many specimens he comes to the conclusion that, as so many of our Hawaiian trees are polymorphous or variable, the *Kawau* or *Aiea* proves to be no exception. Hillebrand in his Flora of the Hawaiian Islands fails to mention that the flowers are often sterile and that the anthers are often wanting in fertile flowers.

It is a handsome tree reaching a height of 20 to 40 feet, with a trunk of often one foot in diameter. It is, however, occasionally a shrub with stiff ascending branches and leaves crowded at the ends of the latter. Such shrubs can be found near Kilauea Volcano on Hawaii, elevation 4000 feet, among the sub-xerophytic vegetation, or in open swampy country. It is one of the most common forest trees on all the islands and is more or less confined to the rain forests, though occa-

PLATE 103.

PERROTTETIA SANDWICENSIS A. Gray.
Olomea or Waimea on Maui.
Fruiting branch, about one-half natural size.

sionally met with in the drier districts. It can be found usually in company with *Perrottetia sandwicensis (Olomea), Cheirodendron Gaudichaudii (Olapa)*, Straussia, Bobea, *Elaeocarpus bifidus (Kalia)*, and others peculiar to that zone. The tree is seldom tarnished by insects or blight, and the dark glossy leaves make the tree a conspicuous object in the forest, and more so when it is in full bloom, exhibiting its cymes of white flowers in the upper axils, and abundant small black fruits below the leaves, along the stem.

The leaves vary tremendously in size, shape and texture, and so does the inflorescence, which is sometimes very shortly peduncled and appears to be terminal. A form with very small leaves is not uncommon on Kauai, while the biggest fruited specimens the writer collected on the slopes of Mt. Hualalai, in North Kona, Hawaii.

The wood of the tree is whitish and rather soft. It has been employed for saddle-trees by the Hawaiians of today.

CELASTRACEAE.

With the exception of the Arctic Zone, the Celastraceae are to be found in all floral regions, but especially in southern and tropical Africa, including Madagascar; also in tropical and subtropical Asia, in China, and Japan.

The genus Perrottetia, which occurs in the Indo-Malayan region, is also to be found in tropical America, with one species in the Hawaiian Islands. The family consists of 38 genera with numerous species.

PERROTTETIA H. B. K.

Flowers hermaphrodite or unisexual; calyx broad, flat cupshaped to obconical; lobes triangular 5, short, erect, open or imbricate in the bud. Petals 5, erect, similar to the sepals, occasionally ciliate, valvate in the bud. Disc flat, cup or ring-shaped, entire, or minutely wavy, or undulate. Stamens 5, inserted in the margin of the disc; in the male flowers longer than the petals, in the female flowers very short, sterile, filaments filiform or subulate, anthers broad round or oval, versatile; ovary ovate, or lageniform, free from the disc, mostly 2 celled or oftener apparently 4-celled at the base. Ovules 2 in each cell. Style short, stigma 2 or 3 to 4 parted, 1 to 2 erect ovules in each cell. Fruit a thick fleshy globose berry with persistent calyx, corolla, disc and stamens, 2 to 4 celled, cells 1 to 2 seeded. Seeds round with thin fleshy albumen.—Unarmed trees or shrubs with alternate, thin coriaceous serrate leaves; stipules triangular, small and deciduous. Inflorescence single in the leaf-axils, paniculate or cymosely branched. Flowers small.

Perrottetia sandwicensis A. Gray.
Olomea, or *Waimea* on Maui.
(Plate 103.)

PERROTTETIA SANDWICENSIS A. Gray Bot. U. S. E. E. (1854) 291, pl. 24;—Mann, Proc. Am. Ac. VII (1867) 161, et Fl. Haw. Isl. (1867) 172;—Wawra in Flora (1873) 141;—Hbd. Fl. Haw. Isl. (1888) 79;—Del Cast Ill. Fl. Ins. Mar. Pac. VI. (1890) 139;—Loes. in Engl. et Prantl Pflzfam. III. 5. (1896) 220, et Nachtr. I. (1897) 224,—Heller Pl. Haw. Isl. (1897) 848.

Leaves alternate, ovate oblong, somewhat acuminate, either obtuse or acute at the base, serrate, rather chartaceous, pinnately veined, shining above, pale underneath, veins and nerves as well as petioles red, the latter 12 to 25 mm in length; stipules minute,

PLATE 104

SAPINDUS SAPONARIA Linn.
Ae and Manele.
Showing a fruiting branch and seeds at the base.

caducous; flowers small, polygamo-dioecious, greenish, pedicellate, numerous in compound panicles from the axils of the leaves, peduncle puberulent or tomentose, branching divaricately; sepals 5, ovate lanceolate; petals 5, triangular ovate, acute; stamens 5, alternate with the petals; anthers 2-celled; ovary ovoid, in the male flowers abortive and sterile; ovules 2 in each cell; fruit bright red, globose, slightly depressed, about 6 mm when mature; seeds marked with minute transverse wavy lines.

A tall shrub or tree 10 to 18 feet or more in height, nearly glabrous. The branches are short and stiff, but when growing at higher elevation become long and more or less drooping.

During the month of October and November, when the tree is in full fruit, it is not unattractive. The bright red berries gracefully droop on densely clustered panicles from every branch. The *Olomea* inhabits both the dry and the wet forests on all the islands, ranging from 1000 feet to 6000 feet elevation.

It is most common on Maui, in Koolau, the northern gap or outlet of Haleakala crater, where the tree forms a forest to the exclusion of nearly everything else at an elevation of 6000 feet. The undergrowth in this *Olomea* jungle consists of the native Begonia, *Akaakaawa*, which stands 10 feet high. It is not uncommon near Kilauea Volcano, Hawaii, in the dry forest 4000 feet above sea level, while it is a common feature especially in the rain forests on all the islands.

The wood of the *Olomea* is of medium strength, of a golden brown color with reddish tint, and was used by the natives for producing fire by friction. Two sticks called *Aunaki* were used, the upper of *Olomea* wood and the lower of the much softer *Hau*. In the Hawaiian mythology their origin is explained thus: During the first appearance of the sun which caused the separation of the heavens, Lailai (goddess) is taken up to him ornamented with the dress of the dawn, while he encloses the fire on earth in the rubbing sticks called *Aunaki*.

SAPINDACEAE.

The family Sapindaceae, which is almost purely tropical, consists of not less than 118 genera with over one thousand species, nearly one-third of which (belonging to five genera of the tribe Paullinieae) are climbing or twining plants peculiar to America. The only exception is Cardiospermum, which is found in all tropical countries, besides one other climbing species, *Paullinia pinnata,* occurring in Africa. The remaining genera, consisting either of shrubs or trees, are distributed over Asia, Africa, Australia, and Oceanea.

In the Hawaiian Islands only four genera are represented, three of which have arborescent species.

KEY TO THE GENERA.

Petals present:
Sepals and petals 5; fruit 1-3 cocci, leaves simple or abruptly pinnate.... **Sapindus**
Petals wanting:
Sepals 5; fruit of one or two cocci................................... **Alectryon**
Sepals 2-5; fruit a winged capsule.................................. **Dodonaea**

PLATE 105.

SAPINDUS SAPONARIA L.
A'e or **Manele**.
Buttressed trunk of a very large A'e tree. Growing at the Kipuka Puaulu, near the
Volcano Kilauea, Hawaii; elevation 4000 feet.

Sapindaceae.

SAPINDUS L.

Sepals 5, round or ovate, concave, either small, glabrous and petaloid, or larger, and densely villous outside, the two outer smaller. Petals usually 5 densely tomentose outside, each with a scale at the base. Disc annular, rarely incomplete; stamens 8 (10) free, generally hairy. Fruit of 3 to 1 cocci, indehiscent, with coriaceous exocarp, mesocarp fleshy containing saponine, putamen chartaceous. Seeds globose or elliptical, with a hard bony testa. Embryo oily. Large or medium sized trees with numerous leaflets and occasionally winged rhachis, one Hawaiian species only with simple leaves. Flowers in terminal and axillary panicles.

A genus of eleven species, mainly medium-sized or large trees, occuring in tropical and sub-tropical countries, with the exception of Africa and New Holland. All species of Sapindus have leaves consisting of many leaflets, with the exception of one species occurring in these islands, which has simple and entire leaves.

Sapindus Saponaria, described by Linnaeus, is found in America in many forms, which have been mistaken for different species.

The genus is represented in these islands by two species, while one other occurs in the Viti (Fiji) Islands. The species of Sapindus found in Tahiti, the Marquesas, and Easter Island, is identified by some botanists with the already mentioned *S. Saponaria* L.

KEY TO THE SPECIES.

Leaves abruptly pinnate... **S. Saponaria**
Leaves simple, entire... **S. Oahuensis**

Sapindus saponaria L.

A'e and *Manele*.

(Plates 104, 105, 106.)

SAPINDUS SAPONARIA L. Spec. pl. ed. 1 (1753) 367;—Forst. Prodr. (1786) 178;—DC. Prodr. I. (1824) 607;—Endl. Fl. Suds. (1836) No. 1534;—Seem. Fl. Vit. (1866) 47;—Del Cast. Ill. Fl. Ins. Mar. Pacif. VI. (1890) 143, et Fl. Polyn. Franc. (1893) 35;—Radlk. in Engl. et Prantl Pflzfam. III. 5. (1896) 315, fig. 164.—**S. microcarpa** Jardin Hist. Nat. Iles Marquises (1858) 25.—**S. Thurstonii** Rock Bull. Hawaii Board Agric. and For. I. (1911) 6, fig. 2, pl. 3.

A deciduous tree; leaves alternate; leaflets opposite or slightly alternate, the rhachis slightly marginate or winged in young leaves; leaflets subsessile in 4 to 6 pairs, chartaceous, elliptical-oblong, slightly falcate, 6 to 12 cm long, 2 to 3.5 cm wide, acuminate, rounded at the base, glabrous above, tomentose underneath; the pubescent panicles terminal, about 12 cm long; flower-buds green, strongly pubescent; fruits consisting of 1 to 2 globose cocci, 17 to 20 mm in diam. which are connate, or when single bear the rudiments of two abortive ones; pericarp coriaceous, endocarp pergameneous, pale, seeds globose, dark reddish brown or black, 10 to 12 mm in diam. with a long testa bearing no tufts of hair at the base (in the Hawaiian specimens).

The *A'e* or *Manele* is a very beautiful tree, attaining a height of about 80 feet, when growing in the middle forest zone at an elevation of 4000 feet.

The bark on young trees is of a light-brown color and smooth, and falls off in large scales from mature trees, exposing the smooth inner layers.

The leaves are abruptly pinnate, light-green, and have a winged rhachis when young. The small flowers are on terminal panicles and of a yellowish color. The berries are round, and two or three may be found attached to each

271

PLATE 106.

SAPINDUS SAPONARIA L.
A'e or Manele.
Tree growing in the Kipuka Puaulu, Hawaii; elevation 4000 feet.

Sapindaceae.

other with a parchment-like covering, but are usually single with two abortive ones at the base; the seed is round, brownish-black, and hard. The tree loses its leaves in the winter months; but as the young leaves come out before all the old ones drop, it is hardly bare for any length of time. Owing to the ravages of a caterpillar which feeds on the flowers, making the whole inflorescence wilt before expansion, very few trees, indeed, bear fruits.

S. Saponaria L. is the second species of the genus Sapindus found in these islands. It is called *A'e* on Mauna Loa, while on Hualalai it is known as *Manele*. The wood is whitish and is of medium strength.

After reexamination of extensive material of this plant, the writer came to the mature conclusion that the Hawaiian *A'e* or *Manele* is identical with the American *Sapindus saponaria* L. The tree was first found by the writer on the Island of Hawaii on the lava fields of Puuwaawaa, in North Kona, in the year 1909. Mr. L. A. Thurston called the writer's attention to some very large trees near the Kilauea Volcano, in the Kipuka Puaulu, and on visiting this most interesting district the writer found the trees identical with those from Puuwaawaa, the only difference being in the size of trunk (5 to 6 feet) and height of tree (80 feet), while in the latter locality the tree is rather small. After examining the material and comparing it with specimens of the introduced *Sapindus saponaria* L., growing about town, the writer came to the conclusion that the Hawaii plant was new to science. It certainly differed materially from the trees growing at Honolulu.

The writer after careful examination (unfortunately after the publication of the name *Sapindus Thurstonii*) came to the conclusion that these differences were not specific and that the tree is identical with the American *Sapindus saponaria* L., and as such it is here published. The tree had, however, never been recorded growing in its native state on Hawaii, save by J. Remy (No. 566 bis), who collected on these islands in the early days, and is only cited in the publication by Drake del Castillo.

It is desired to state that the trees of *Sapindus saponaria* L. from Hawaii forests reach a larger size than was ever recorded of that species in other parts of the world. The diameter of some of the trees measures six feet and is also buttressed, as can be seen in the accompanying illustration. The bark of old trees comes off in huge thick scales, exposing the smooth inner layers. The Hawaiian trees are also deciduous.

Sapindus Oahuensis Hbd.

Aulu and *Kaulu* on Oahu, *Lonomea* on Kauai.

SAPINDUS OAHUENSIS Hbd. in Radlkofer, Berichte d. K. Bayer. Acad. (1878) 401,—et Fl. Haw. Isl. (1888) 85;—Radlk. in Engl. et Prantl Pflzfam. III. 5. (1896) 316.— **Celastrina?** Wawra in Flora (1873) 141.

A glabrous tree, with whitish bark covered with lenticels, the wood pale; leaves ovate, 10 to 20 cm long, 5 to 12 cm wide, on petioles of 2.5 to 7 cm, acuminate, rounded or truncate at the base, but slightly decurrent, quite entire, thick chartaceous. pale glabrous;

273

PLATE 107.

ALECTRYON MACROCOCCUS Radlk.
Mahoe.
Showing fruiting branch, with young and mature fruits; less than one-half natural size.

Sapindaceae.

panicles tomentose with a fulvous pubescence, either several in the axils of the uppermost leaves and then 5 to 10 cm long, or single, terminal and 10 to 12 cm long, with the lowest bracts foliaceous, the branches alternate and patent, the pedicels 2 mm, minutely bracteolate about the middle; sepals unequal, orbicular, 3 mm; tomentose, slightly connate at the base; petals 5, little longer, equal, pubescent and ciliate; stamens 8, inserted on the thick margin of a pentagonal glabrous disc 2 mm; ovary glabrous, 3 to 2 lobed; stigma subsessile, lobes broad, rounded; cocci either 2, connate, or oftener a single one with the rudiments of 1 or 2 abortive ones at the base; the single coccus obovoid, 30 to 20 mm; pericarp leathery, shining; endocarp pergameneous, pale, villous in the immature state; seed obovoid, 20 to 12 mm; testa black, osseous, rugose, with a broad truncate, rather carunculate base; embryo curved, cotyledons accumbent to the short tapering radicle. Hillebrand's var. β differs from the species in its leaves, which are narrowing at the base, and are shorter petioled; the flowering panicle is also denser and not open as in the species.

This tree, which reaches a height of 20 to 30 feet, is endemic to the Hawaiian Islands, and is found on Oahu and Kauai. It develops a rather short trunk of about eight inches in diameter, and is vested in a whitish bark which is covered with lenticels. While all other known species of Sapindus have pinnate leaves, the *Aulu* or *Lonomea* is a remarkable exception, in having single, oblong, entire leaves, which never show any indication of division.

The small, yellow flowers are arranged in long, terminal panicles, which are covered with a rusty-brown down.

It is distinctly a tree of the lower forest zone, and inhabits the leeward sides of the Islands of Oahu and Kauai. On the former island it is found in the valleys of Makaha and Makaleha of the Kaala range, while a variety of it grows in the valley of Niu. On the latter island it is scattered on the lower levels at an elevation of 1000 feet back of Makaweli and Waimea, together with the *Aleurites moluccana (Kukui), Ochrosia sandwicensis*, Straussia, etc.

The wood of the *Aulu* is whitish and of no value. On Kauai the seeds were used as a cathartic by the natives. A dose consisted of 7 to 8 seeds.

The variety occurs in Nui Valley, on Oahu, but all the trees found in Nui by the writer were attacked very badly by a moth (Rhyiocoppha sp.?), which gave the trees an ungainly appearance; in fact, most of them were devoid of leaves.

ALECTRYON Gartn.

(*Mahoe* Hillebr.)

Flowers regular, calyx short, cup-shaped, 4 to 5 toothed, valvate or somewhat imbricate. Petals 4 to 5, with 2 scales, or wanting. Discus complete. Stamens 8 to 10. Ovary 2 to 3 celled, and usually of 2 to 3 cocci, style with a short 2 to 3 lobed stigma, rarely undivided; cell one ovuled. Fruit of 2 or 3 or, through abortion, of one coccus. Cocci large globose or ovate, often of the size of a pea, occasionally keeled, coriaceous or cortico-crustaceous, opening in an irregular fissure. Seeds nearly globose or compressed, with shining brown, smooth testa, arilate. Trees with abruptly pinnate leaves consisting of 1 to 5 pairs of leaflets, entire, or serrate, papillose on the underside in a few species. Flowers small, in thyrses or less branched panicles.

The genus Alectryon consists of 16 species, which are all arborescent and are distributed over the Malayan, Papuan and Pacific islands, represented by the species of Nephelium in the two latter groups.

The type of the genus is the Titaki of New Zealand, *A. excelsus*, which, like our Hawaiian species, the *Mahoe* tree, has edible fruits.

275

PLATE 108.

ALECTRYON MACROCOCCUS Radlk.
Mahoe tree.
Growing on the lava fields of Auahi land of Kahikinui, southern slopes of Mt. Haleakala, Maui; elevation 2600 feet.

Sapindaceae.

Alectryon macrococcus Radlk.
Mahoe.
(Plates 107 and 108.)

ALECTRYON MACROCOCCUS Radlk. in Sitzber. k. Bayer. Acad. XX (1890) 255, et in Engl. et Prantl Pflzfam. III. 5. (1895) 333, et in Bull. Hawaii Bd. Agric. and Forest. I. (1911) 1;—Rock Rep. Hawaii Board Agric. and For. (1910) 81, pl. 19. et Bull. Bd. Agric. and For. I (1911) 2, pl. 1. in part.—**Mahoe** gen. nov.† Hbd. Fl. Haw. Isl. (1888) 86.—**Dodonaea** sp. Del Castill. Ill. Fl. Ins. Mar. Pac. VI. (1890) 144 in obs. ad. Dod. visc.—Vulgo **Mahoe** in Molokai et Maui (quo nomine in Nuov-Zealandia Melicytus ramiflorus Forst. salutatur t. Kirk. in Forest Fl. N.-Zeal. 1889. 3.).

Medium sized tree; branches terete, glabrous, young branches striate, with new leaves covered with an appressed yellowish silky tomentum; leaves with 2 to 5 pair of leaflets; the latter large, opposite, elliptical or subovate, obtuse at both ends, or with an acuminate apex, petioled, entire undulate, coriaceous to chartaceous, 10 to 18 cm long, 4 to 10 cm wide, the lateral nerves oblique; shining above, densely tomentose underneath with a yellowish brown tomentum; panicles axillary; female flowers small, on pedicels of 2 mm, calyx 5-lobed, the lobes 2 mm, subacute, persistent with the young fruits; petals none, rudimentary; stamens 6-8, in sinuses within the pubescent discus-margin, filaments very short, hirsute; anthers red, 1 mm long, subdidymous at the base; ovary compressed, densely hirsute, 1 to 2 celled; style short, almost arched, with a bifid stigma; male flowers unknown; fruits of 1 to 2 cocci; young fruits covered densely with yellowish-golden setulose hair, crowned by the remnants of the style, mature fruits glabrous, dark brown corticose-coriaceous, globose 3 to 6 cm in diameter; or of one coccus with 1 to 2 abortive ones, largest for the genus; arillus scarlet, seeds with a crustaceous testa, brown, shining, (In the Herbarium of the College of Hawaii No. 8642).

The *Mahoe*, which is the single representative of the genus Alectryon in the Hawaiian Islands, is a medium-sized tree 20 to 25 feet tall, with a trunk of perhaps 6 to 8 inches in diameter. The bark is brown, somewhat rough; the wood is hard, dark yellowish-brown, and very tough.

It is an ungainly tree. The branchlets and inflorescence, as well as young fruits, are covered with a dense coat of silky-brown hair; the leaves are large, having from 2 to 4 leaflets, which are glabrous above and tomentose underneath.

The fruits of the *Mahoe*, which are of very large size, have the color of a potato and are perfectly smooth. They hang in clusters from the branches and become ruptured when mature, the fissure being irregular, exposing a bright scarlet aril and the glossy surface of the chestnut-brown orbicular seed, giving a not altogether unpleasing contrast. Flowering and fruiting trees were observed by the writer during the month of November, who would judge, however, that the flowering period would fall during the late summer months, as most of the trees bore young fruits and old ones from the previous year.

The *Mahoe* inhabits the dry regions on the leeward side of the islands. It is very scarce on Oahu, where it grows in Makaha valley of the Kaala range, and practically extinct on Molokai; on Kauai it was found by Mr. Francis Gay back of Makaweli, while the writer discovered a new locality from which it had not been reported previously. About seven miles from Ulupalakua, on the Island of Maui, is a small area of forest on the lava fields of Auahi. Unpromising as it looks from the road, this forest is botanically, nevertheless, one of the richest in the Territory. It is there that the *Mahoe* is not uncommon, and still

277

Sapindaceae.

thrives in company with many other rare trees peculiar to that small area, such as Pelea, Xanthoxylum, Bobea, Pittosporum, Pterotropia, Tetraplasandra, etc. Owing to its scarcity, it is unknown to most of the old natives, who have heard of it only in rare instances from their ancestors.

The wood, which is very hard and tough, has not been made use of by the natives, as far as can be ascertained. The bright scarlet fruit flesh is eaten by the natives, as well as the kernel of the seed, and are not altogether unpleasant to the taste.

The *Mahoe* is endemic to the Hawaiian Islands, and is remarkable for its fruits, which are the largest in the genus.

The name *Mahoe*, meaning "twins," undoubtedly refers to the double fruits, which are not uncommon in our Alectryon.

DODONAEA.

Flowers dioecious, regular (often appearing as if hermaphrodite). Sepals 3 to 7 imbricate or valvate; petals none. Disc developed or in the fem. flowers forming a short carpophore. Stamens 8 or less, rarely more, with short filaments and elongate anthers. Ovary usually orbicular or obcordate, mostly 3- also 2- or 4, rarely 5-6 ridged with as many cells as ridges and with 2 ovules in each cell, the upper ascending and apotropous, the lower pendulous and epitropous, styles short, with 3 to 6 short stigmating lobes. Capsule papery or coriaceous, 3-2-6 celled, winged, rarely without wings. Seeds single or 2 in each cell, globose or lentiform. Embryo spirally twisted, containing aleuron as well as saponine.—Trees or shrubs often only bushes with a viscous surface; leaves simple, or pinnate (not in the Hawaiian species), often covered with resinal glands. Flowers pediceled, axillary or terminal, single, or in racemes or panicles.

The genus Dodonaea consists of 46 species, 44 of which are endemic in Australia, including the cosmopolitan *D. viscosa* L., which can be found in all tropical countries.

In Hawaii three species occur; the above-mentioned *D. viscosa* L., besides *D. eriocarpa* Smith, and *D. stenoptera* Hbd., the latter a shrub 2 to 4 feet high and peculiar to Molokai. Outside of the Australian and Hawaiian species, there is only one other species, *D. madagascariensis* Rdlk., which is peculiar to Madagascar. They are trees or shrubs, or also bushes.

The leaves in the Hawaiian Dodonaea or *Aalii*, as they are called by the natives, are simple, usually covered with glands which secrete a resin.

KEY TO THE SPECIES.

Capsule broadly winged, with wings projecting above:
    Capsule glabrous, flat, 2-winged.................................... **D. viscosa**
    Capsule pubescent, 3-4 winged.................................... **D. eriocarpa**

Dodonaea viscosa L.
Aalii or *Aalii kumakua*.

DODONAEA VISCOSA L., Mant. II. (1771) 238;—Forst. Prodr. (1786) no. 164;—DC. Prodr. I. (1824) 616;—Hook. et Arn. Bot. Beech. (1832) 61;—Endl. Fl. Suds. (1836) no. 1539;—Guill. Zeph. Tait. (1836-1837) no. 335;—A. Gray Bot. U. S. E. E. (1854) 260;—Pancher in Cuz. (1860) l. c.;—Seem. Fl. Vit. (1866) 49;— Mann. Proc. Am. Acad. VII. (1867) 175;—Nadeaud Enum. Tahit. Pl. (1873)

Sapindaceae.

447;—Sinclair Indig. Fl. Haw. Isl. (1885) pl. 39;—Hbd. Fl. Haw. Isl. (1888) 87;—Del Cast. Ill. Fl. Ins. Mar. Pac. VI. (1890) 144, et Fl. Polyn. Franc. (1893) 36;—Radlk. in Engl. et Prantl Pflzfam. III. 5. (1895) 357;—Heller Pl. Haw. Isl. (1897) 849.

Branches angular, stiff, glabrous, glutinous at the ends; leaves lanceolate, oblanceolate or obovate, acuminate, or obtuse, entire, chartaceous panicles terminal and axillary 2.5 to 5 cm long; male flowers: sepals 4, glabrous, 2 mm; stamens 7 to 9; ovary rudimentary; female flowers: sepals 4, stamens wanting; ovary shortly stipitate, viscid, glabrous, 2 to 3 celled, each cell with 2 ovules; style several times as long as the ovary with two linear lobes glued together; capsule bright yellow, red or brown, membraneous, flat, orbicular, faintly ridged along the middle, 2 to 3 winged the latter 4 to 6 mm broad; seeds 4 mm, ovate, flattened.

The *Aalii* or *Aalii Kumakua* is a small tree, reaching a height of 15 to 25 feet or more; the branches are angular, stiff, and glutinous at the ends. It develops a rather short trunk of only a few feet in height with a diameter of 5 to 10 inches. The bark is thick, longitudinally and very closely wrinkled or corrugated, and of a reddish-brown color. Plants may be found only a foot high and bearing profusely, while sometimes trees can be observed up to 30 feet in height. The male and female flowers are borne on different trees, but female trees are met with much oftener than male trees. The *Aalii* varies tremendously in habit and stature. The two-winged, papery capsules are of a bright red, or pale yellow, and very conspicuous on that account. It has been said that owing to the viscousness of the very light capsules, they easily adhere to the plumage of birds, to which agents the plant owes its world-wide distribution; the capsules of the Hawaiian Dodonaea are only viscous when young, and are perfectly glabrous and papery when mature.

The wood of the *Aalii* is of a golden-brown color, with black heartwood, and is extremely hard. Its density and heaviness would make it a very desirable wood for cabinet work and many other purposes. In New Zealand it has been employed as a substitute for brass for machine bearings, with good results.

The *Aalii* is common on all the islands of the Hawaiian archipelago, and is gregarious at elevations of 1000 to 4000 feet. On Oahu it can be found on the main range, as well as on the Waianae mountains, but is especially common in Palolo valley at an elevation of 1000 feet. As already mentioned, it is a cosmopolitan, and occurs in all tropical countries from Australia to New Zealand, Chatham Islands, Tahiti, Viti, and Samoan Islands, to Africa, America, and Asia. In Hawaii it has a variety named by Hillebrand β. var. spathulata. J' is a stunted shrub and occurs on the higher elevations, especially on Hawaii. It forms almost 50 per cent of the vegetation at the summit slope of Mt. Hualalai (8270 feet).

Undoubtedly the wood was employed by the natives for various purposes, but no information can be obtained from this generation. The leaves were used as medicine.

It is known to the Samoans as *Togovao*, who employ its leaves for baths as a remedy for rheumatism and other inflammations. In the Viti Islands it is

279

PLATE 109.

DODONAEA ERIOCARPA Smith.
Aalii Kumakani.
Typical specimen from the upper slopes of Mt. Haleakala.   Male flowering branch.
Mature capsules at the left.

the *Wase*, and in Tahiti, *Apiri*. It is the *Ake* of Rarotonga and New Zealand; in the latter place often called *Akeake*.

Dodonaea eriocarpa Smith.

Aalii kumakani.

(Plate 109.)

DODONAEA ERIOCARPA Smith in Rees. Cycl. XII. No. 6;—DC. Prodr. I. (1824) 617;— Endl. Fl. Suds. (1836) No. 1540;—Gray Bot. U. S. E. E. (1854) 260;—Mann Proc. Am. Acad. l. c. et Flora Haw. Isl. l. c. p. 176;—Hbd Fl. Haw. Isl. (1888) 88;— Del Cast. l. c.;—Heller. Pl. Haw. Isl. (1897) 839.

Flowers polygamous, with male, female and hermaphrodite flowers on the same plant; leaves narrow, lanceolate or oblanceolate, acute, puberulous when young; panicle terminal, pubescent; sepals 5, ovate, pubescent, stamens 10, round a ciliate torus in the male flowers; ovary pubescent, shortly stipitate; style short, stigmas indicated by 4 dots, or 3 to 6 mm long in the female flowers; capsule turgid; 8 to 16 mm high, 3 to 4 winged, pubescent along the margins of the wings; seed ovoid.

The *Aalii kumakani* is a small shrub, or tall, much-branched shrub or medium-sized tree of 20 feet or so in height. It differs very little from the *Aalii kumakua*, and that mainly in the pubescent capsules, which are three or four-winged, instead of having two wings. It is a shrub on the leeward side of Kauai, above Waimea on the open, barren slopes at an elevation of 2000 feet, and is a small tree on the upper slopes of Mt. Haleakala at elevations of 6000 to 8000 feet, where it grows in gulches and along dry stream beds in company with a species of Suttonia, with the Silversword, *Argyroxiphium sandwicense* var. *macrocephalum, A. virescens*, the green sword plant, and numerous other Compositae, as Raillardia, and Artemisia. It is a handsome tree with dark-green, viscous, shining leaves, forming a beautiful, symmetrical, round crown. It also occurs on Hawaii in the dry regions of Kau, and on the central plateau on the slopes of Mauna Loa.

On Molokai above Kamalo grows another species (*Dodonaea stenoptera* Hbd.) peculiar to the above locality. It is, however, never a tree and therefore here omitted.

RHAMNACEAE.

The family Rhamnaceae occurs in all regions whose climate permits lignaceous growth. The genus Rhamnus is the widest distributed; its center of development is Europe and extra tropical Asia. Here in the Hawaiian Islands the family, with its 45 genera, has only two representatives, the genera Alphitonia and Colubrina, with only one endemic species belonging to the latter genus.

KEY TO THE GENERA.

Fruit three-grooved at the apex, the calycine cup not extending beyond the base.

Colubrina

Fruit not grooved, globose, the calycine cup extending to the middle...... Alphitonia

COLUBRINA Brongn.

Sepals, petals and stamens 5. Calycine cup hemispherical, not extending beyond the ovary. Disc broad annular, more or less flat. Style trifid. Ovary immersed in the cup of the calyx, three-celled. Fruit dry or with somewhat fleshy exocarp, enclosed at the

PLATE 110.

COLUBRINA OPPOSITIFOLIA Brongn.
Kauila.
Flowering and fruiting branch pinned against trunk of tree. Growing on the ancient lava flows of Puuwaawaa, Mt. Hualalai, Hawaii; elevation 2000 feet.

Rhamnaceae.

base by the calycine cup. Endocarp divided into three cocci, opening elastically. Seeds with thick smooth testa, occasionally with small arillus. Albumen present.—Unarmed shrubs or trees with glabrous or more or less tomentose leaves which are usually alternate, or opposite in one of the Hawaiian species, cordate to elongate, three to penninerved. Flowers usually in axillary, short peduncled cymules or single.

The genus Colubrina consists of about 15 species distributed mainly in tropical America and the warmer regions of North America. One is endemic in the Hawaiian Islands, and one is widely distributed in the tropics of the old world.

Colubrina oppositifolia Brongn.
Kauila.
(Plates 110 and 111.)

COLUBRINA OPPOSITIFOLIA Brongn. (In Herb. Gray) H. Mann Proc. Am. Acad. VII (1867) 161, et Fl. Haw. Isl. Essex Inst. V. (1867) 173;—Wawra in Flora (1873) 170;—Hbd. Fl. Haw. Isl. (1888) 80;—Del Cast. Ill. Fl. Ins. Mar. Pac. VI. (1890) 140;—Weberb. in Engl. et Prantl III. 5. (1896) 415.

A medium sized tree (and not a shrub) 10 to 12 m high with a trunk of often 3 dm and more in diameter; leaves opposite, ovate or oblong 7 to 15 cm long, 3 to 6 cm wide, on petioles of 3 to 5 cm, thin chartaceous, bright green on both sides, entire; penninerved, with a gland at the base of each nerve on the lower face; flowers 5 to 10 in an umbellate cyme on a common peduncle of about 1 cm or more, the pedicels 6 to 12 mm, with minute ovate bractlets at the base; calyx cup-shaped 3 mm, parted to the middle; petals not exceeding the calyx and enclosing the short stamens; anthers ovoid; style very short, three-lobed; fruit subglobose, 3-grooved at the apex, about 10 to 12 mm in diameter, the calycine cup not exceeding the lower third; exocarp woody, not separating from the endocarp, cocci 3; seeds reddish-brown, angular convex; cotyledons rather thick and fleshy, nearly as long and broad as the thin albumen; radicle short.

This is the *Kauila* of South and North Kona, Hawaii. It is in the latter locality that the tree is quite common, while in South Kona on the lava fields of Kapua the tree is quite scarce. Between Puuwaawaa and Huehue, on the slopes of Hualalai in North Kona, the tree reaches its best development. Trees 35 feet or more in height are not uncommon, with a trunk of often a foot or more in diameter. The bark is of a light brown color and scales off in large round flakes. It is associated with *Kokia Rockii* (*Kokio*), *Mezoneurum Kauaiense* (*Uhiuhi*), *Myoporum sandwicense* (*Naio*), and many others.

The wood of this *Kauila* is harder than the *Kauila* (*Alphitonia excelsa*) of Kauai, Hawaii and Maui; it is exceedingly hard, close grained and of a dark red color, without black streaks such as occur in *Alphitonia excelsa*.

The wood of this tree was used by the natives for spears on account of its hardness and durability. It is peculiar to the Hawaiian Islands, as it is not known from other parts of the world. A second species occurs in the islands, which is a small rambling shrub (*Colubrina asiatica*) and is at once distinguishable by its alternate leaves. Its native name is *Anapanapa* or *Kukuku*. It is extremely poisonous and was often used for stupefying fish. It grows only near the sea. It is a cosmopolitan and is widely distributed over the tropics of the old world.

PLATE 111.

COLUBRINA OPPOSITIFOLIA Brongn.
Kauila tree.
Growing along the North Kona road between Huehue and Puuwaawaa, Hawaii;
elevation 2000 feet.

Rhamnaceae.

ALPHITONIA Reissek.

Flowers polygamous; sepals, petals and stamens 5; disc flat annular. Style 2 to 3 fid. Ovary 2 to 3 celled. Fruit below and at the middle invested by the cup-shaped calyx-tube and coalesced with the same; exocarp strongly developed, brittle, but not so much in the Hawaiian plants. Endocarp divided into 2 or 3 cocci with woody or crustaceous partitions opening inward by a longitudinal slit. Seeds with aril, often enclosing the seed completely. After the falling away of the pericarp, the seeds remain on the receptacle; in the Hawaiian plant the pericarp never falls away but it is often not even cracked owing to the calyx tube investing the drupe up to the middle and even beyond. (A fact which Hillebrand pointed out and correctly). A tree with leaves, petioles, and inflorescence tomentose. Leaves alternate, coriaceous, penninerved, broadly ovate to lanceolate, glabrous above, with a whitish to reddish brown tomentum underneath. Flowers in terminal or lateral loose cymes.

The genus Alphitonia consists of a single extremely variable species, which is distributed from Australia to Polynesia and Borneo.

In Hawaii the tree is known as *Kauila.* Hillebrand in his Flora of the Hawaiian Islands described it as a new species, *"Alphitonia ponderosa."* It is true it is a quite different plant from those in the writer's possession from Australia. In the Australian plants the fruits are barely 6 mm. in diameter and are cracked to the base, while the Hawaiian plants have the fruits 14 mm. in diameter; they also are hardly even split; only on rare occasions the writer found cracked fruits on a tree.

He, however, refers this tree to *A. excelsa,* as he has not seen the intermediates of the Australian and South Polynesian plants.

Alphitonia excelsa Reiss.
Kauila, Kauwila or *O'a* on Maui.
(Plate 112.)

ALPHITONIA EXCELSA Reiss. ex Endl. Gen. (1840) 1098;—Seem. Fl. Vit. (1866) 43;— H. Mann, Proc. Am. Acad. VII. (1867) 161, et Fl. Haw. Isl. (1867) 174;—Wawra in Flora (1873) 170;—Del Cast. Ill. Fl. Ins. Mar. Pacif. VI. (1890) 140 (ex parte) et Fl. Polyn. Franc. (1893) 33;—Weberb. in Engl. et Prantl III. 5. (1896) 419;— Brigham Ka Hana Kapa (1911) 174, fig. 103.—Colubrina excelsa Fenzl. in Hugl. Enum. (1837) 20.—Rhamnus zizyphoides Soland. in Forst. Prodr. (1786) no. 510 absqu. char.);—Sprgl. Syst. I. (1825) 768;—DC. Prodr. II. (1825) 27;—Pancher, in Tahiti, (1860) 230.—Pomaderris zizyphoides Hook. et Arn. Bot. Beech. (1832) 61;— Endl. Fl. Suds. (1836) no. 1570;—Guill. Zephyr. Tait. (1836-1837) no. 330;—A. zizphoides Gray Bot. U. S. E. E. (1854) 278 t. 22;—Nadeaud Ennm. (1873) no. 451.— A. franguloides Gray l. c. 280 t. 22.—Zizphoides argentea Soland. Prim. Fl. Pac. 378, et in Parkins Draw. Tahit. Pl. (ined. cf. Seem, l. c.)—A. ponderosa Hbd. Fl Haw. Isl. (1888) 81;—Del Cast, l. c. 140;—Heller Pl. Haw, Isl. (1897) 849.

Leaves ovate, ovate-oblong, lanceolate, generally acute, entire, dark green above, with a rust colored tomentum underneath; flowers in the axils of the youngest leaves, in short tomentose dichotomous cymes; calyx 6 mm, lobes expanded; petals half as long as calyx lobes, spathulate, enclosing the short stamens; anthers ovoid, style very short 2 to 3 fid; fruit globose 14 to 18 mm in diam. ringed at the middle by the border of the adnate calyx in the Hawaiian plants, almost indehiscent; arillus a dark red separable film enveloping the whole seed. Cotyledons broad, oblong.

The *Kauila* is a stately tree and attains its greatest height, 80 feet, on the Island of Kauai, especially in the forest of Kopiwai. It has a straight trunk of 1½ to 2 feet in diameter with a whitish deeply corrugated bark in the dry districts.

PLATE 112.

ALPHITONIA EXCELSA Reiss.
Kauila or **O'a.**
Fruiting branch pinned against trunk of tree. Growing on the *aa* (rough) lava fields of
Auahi, Kahikinui, southern slopes of Haleakala, Maui; elevation 2600 feet.

It inhabits the dry regions on the leeward slopes of all the islands, but is nowhere common except on Kauai and at Auahi, district of Kahikinui, on Maui, where it is gregarious on the *aa* lava fields. It is in this latter place that the writer met with trees whose trunks were more than 2 feet in diameter.

On the islands of Molokai and Lanai it is very scarce indeed and found only on exposed ridges as straggling shrubs. On Maui, on the southern slopes of Haleakala at an elevation of 2600 to 3000 feet, it is a beautiful tree with a straight trunk. The name *Kauila* is unknown on the Island of Maui, for this species; it is always referred to as the *O'a*, while the name *Kauila* is applied to *Colubrina oppositifolia*, from Hawaii.

On Oahu it can be found on Mt. Kaala on dry exposed ridges, while on Hawaii it is not uncommon in Kau and North and South Kona; but never in company with *Colubrina oppositifolia*, which inhabits the more ancient lava flows.

The wood, which is of a beautiful reddish color with black streaks, is very durable, close and hard grained and exceedingly heavy. It was employed by the natives for their spears as well as for tapa beaters or mallets and other tools.

The *Kauila* or *O'a* is indigenous to Hawaii, but not endemic, as it is also found in most of the Polynesian islands of the South Seas, Australia and Borneo.

It is known as *Doi* in Fiji and as *Toi* in Tahiti, while the Samoan name of the species is also *Toi*.

The Samoans use the leaves for medicinal purposes. They are also often ground between stones, and are used in washing out the lime from the hair.

In Australia the tree is known as Mountain Ash, Red Ash, Leather Jacket, and Cooper's Wood. The aboriginals of Australia have also several names for it; among them are *Mee-a-mee, Culgeraculgera,* and *Murrrung* in the Ilaawara district of New South Wales.

ELAEOCARPACEAE.

The family Elaeocarpaceae is rather small, consisting of only seven genera, with somewhat more than 120 species. It is distributed over the tropics of the old and new world, and reaches its most northern point in Japan, where two species, belonging to the genus Elaeocarpus, are to be found.

The genus Elaeocarpus, represented in these islands by one species, is the largest in the family, with more than 60 species. The distribution of the family ranges from the West Indies to the latitude of the Island of Chiloe, and from Japan to New Zealand.

ELAEOCARPUS L.

Flowers usually hermaphrodite. Sepals 5. Petals 5, usually bifid at the apex, at the base flat, free, valvate in the bud. Androgynophor mostly 5 lobed. Stamens numerous, anthers linear, often ciliate, with two adnate cells opening at the apex into transverse valves. Ovary 2 to 5 celled with several ovules in each cell. Stone fruit with hard, 3 to 5 celled, 1 to 5 seeded stone, usually very hard and rugose. Trees with usually alternate leaves, which are either entire or serrate. Flowers in simple axillary, often many flowered racemes.

PLATE 113.

ELAEOCARPUS BIFIDUS Hook. et Arn.
Kalia.
Flowering and fruiting branch about one-half natural size.

Elaeocarpaceae

A genus of more than 60 species of trees. It is distributed from India through the Malayan Archipelago to Australia, New Caledonia, and New Zealand; also over the Philippines to Japan, with a single species in Hawaii.

Elaeocarpus bifidus Hook. et Arn.

Kalia.

(Plate 113.)

ELAEOCARPUS BIFIDUS Hook et Arn. Bot. Beech. (1832) 110, t. 24;—Endl. Fl. Suds. (1836) no. 14;—A. Gray, Bot. U. S. E. E. (1854) 205;—H. Mann, Proc. Am. Acad. VII (1867) 158, et Fl. Haw. Isl. (1867) 143;—Wawra in Flora (1873) 171;— Hbd. Fl. Haw. Isl. (1888) 53;—Del Cast. Ill. Fl. Ins. Mar. Pac. VI. (1890) 126;— Heller Pl. Haw. Isl. (1897) 850.—**Beythea bifida** End. Gen. Pl. Walp. Rep. I. (1840) 365 et V. 121.

Leaves ovate to ovate-oblong 10 to 18 cm long, 5 to 9 cm wide, on petioles of 5 cm, acuminate, crenate or bluntly serrate, often nearly entire, chartaceous; stipules lanceolate, 2 mm long, caducous; racemes 25 to 50 mm long with 5 to 8 flowers on pedicels of 12 mm; sepals narrow lanceolate, petals as long as sepals, about 8 mm, greenish, linear oblong, shortly bifid or scarcely emarginate, pubescent on both faces; stamens 13 to 16, 1/3 the length of the sepals, with short filaments; anthers obtuse or emarginate, ovary ovoid, 2 to 3 celled, tapering into the simple 2 to 3 grooved style; ovules 3 to 6 in each cell, stone fruit olive-shaped, 25 to 30 mm long, the putamen thick woody; seeds generally solitary, rarely two, with a thin testa.

The *Kalia* is a perfectly glabrous tree, reaching a height of 30 to 40 feet, with a trunk of several inches to sometimes a foot in diameter. The bark is dark-gray, one-fourth of an inch thick, and roughened. Its branches are drooping and sending out many branchlets, which are gummy at their ends. The flowers of the *Kalia* are attacked by an insect, which accounts for the monstrous deformation of the flowers, which can be seen on nearly every tree. The insect is a species of Acari. The layman would certainly mistake it for the flowers, as its bright-red color is not altogether unattractive. The writer on all of his rambles found very few trees, indeed, which had normal flowers. The real flowers, however, are small and greenish and rather inconspicuous. The drupe is olive-shaped and over an inch long, with usually one seed, rarely two.

The *Kalia* is most common on Kauai, where it inhabits the leeward side at an elevation of 3500 to 4000 feet. It is distinctly a tree of the rain forest, and is never found in the dry region or on lava fields.

It loves boggy forests and gray loam. It associates with Straussia, Bobea, *Cheirodendron platyphyllum, Cryptocarya Mannii, Pelea* sp., etc. On Oahu it is not uncommon and can be found on all the ranges, windward and leeward. It is, however, not as common as on Kauai, where it forms 30 per cent of the leeward forest. On all the explorations undertaken by the writer he was unable to find a single tree on any of the other islands, making the tree peculiar to Kauai and Oahu. This may be explained on account of the large seed, which is impossible to be carried either by birds or winds, and as the tree inhabits the middle forests zones, the ocean currents can have nothing to do with its dispersal, especially as the seeds are not buoyant.

PLATE 114.

HIBISCUS ARNOTTIANUS Gray.
Kokio Keokeo.
Native white Hibiscus from Oahu. Flowering branch, reduced one-half.

The bast of the *Kalia* was made into cordage, while its slender branches were employed for *"ahoa"* or thatching rods for house building, the larger branches being selected for rafters.

MALVACEAE.

The family Malvaceae is distributed all over the world with exception of the frigid zones. The most northern species is *Malva rotundifolia* L., which can be found in Sweden and Russia. The farther we advance towards the tropics the richer in species becomes this very useful family. The members of this family inhabit usually the lower regions, but in the South American Andes they can be found at considerable elevation. A few genera have a very restricted distribution, as, for example, Hibiscadelphus, which is peculiar to Hawaii, while the genus Hoberia is only found in New Zealand. On the other hand, we find genera as Hibiscus, Abutilon, Sida and others distributed over both hemispheres. In the Hawaiian Islands we have several genera, of which two are endemic (Kokia and Hibiscadelphus), and also Hibiscus and Thespesia, all of which have arborescent species.

KEY TO THE GENERA.

Style branches long as many as divisions in the ovary.
    Calyx persistent with fruit..................................... **Hibiscus**
    Calyx deciduous before maturity of fruit........................ **Hibiscadelphus**
Style branches simple, club-shaped or divided into short erect clavate branches.
    Bracteoles small or narrow..................................... **Thespesia**
    Bracteoles large ovate, sinuate or slightly lobed.................. **Kokia**

HIBISCUS L.

Involucre none or consisting of 3 to many bracts. Staminal column antheriferous below the truncate or 5 toothed apex. Ovary 5-celled, with several ascending ovules in each cell. Style-branches short, 5, somewhat thickened towards the apex. Capsule loculicidal; endocarp always smooth and glabrous, rarely detached.—Trees, shrubs, or herbs, the trees usually clothed with a stellate pubescence. Leaves lobed or entire. Flowers usually large, and of a conspicuous color, mostly single, axillary. The calyx remains with the fruit.

The genus Hibiscus is exceedingly large, consisting of not less than 180 species, which occur nearly all in the tropics with the exception of two found in Europe.

KEY TO THE SPECIES.

Flowers yellow.
    Leaves cordate, acuminate..................................... **H. tiliaceus**
Flowers white.
    Leaves entire, ovate, bluntly acuminate......................... **H. Arnottianus**
    Leaves crenate, suborbicular, tomentose......................... **H. Waimeae**
Flowers red.
    Leaves crenate, acuminate, style branches horizontal............. **H. Kokio**

PLATE 115.

HIBISCUS WAIMEAE Heller.
Kokio Keokeo.
Kauai white Hibiscus, one-half natural size.

Malvaceae.

Hibiscus tiliaceus L.

Hau.

HIBISCUS TILIACEUS Linn. Spec. plant. ed. I. (1753) 694;—Forst. Prodr. (1786) no. 261;—DC. Prodr. I. (1824) 454;— Endl. Fl. Suds. (1836) 182, no. 1504;—Seem. Fl. Vit. (1865) 18;—Mann in Proc. Am. Acad. VII. (1867) 157, et Fl. Haw. Isl. Proc. Ess. Inst. V. (1867) 140;—Wawra in Flora (1873) 173;—Mrs. Sincl. Indig. Flow. Haw. Isl. (1885) pl. 1;—Del Cast. Ill. Fl. Ins. Mar. Pac. VI. (1890) 121;— Brigham Ka Hana Kapa, Mem. B. P. B. Mus. III. (1911) 132, fig. 82.—**Paritium tiliaceum** A. St.-Hil. Flora Bras, mer. I. (1827) 256;—Gray Bot. U. S. E. E. (1854) 178;—Nadeaud Enum. Tahit. Pl. (1873) no. 429;—Hbd. Fl. Haw. Isl. (1888) 49.

Leaves on long petioles, orbicular-cordate, shortly acuminate, entire, palmately 7 to 9 nerved; stipules large ovate, caducous; involucre campanulate, half the length of the calyx with 10 to 12 acute lobes; lobes of the calyx lanceolate; petals large yellow, usually with a dark center or pure yellow; capsule about 2.5 cm in diameter, opening into 5 valves; 3 naked seeds to each cell.

The *Hau* is one of the most common trees found on the lowlands and on the beaches on all the islands; it is a cosmopolitan and occurs in all tropical coun-tries, but is especially plentiful in the South Sea Islands. It is a very useful tree and is much desired on account of its shade, and is therefore trained into *lanais* or arbors. The wood serves for outriggers of canoes, while the bark fur-nishes a tough and pliable bast for ropes. In Fiji the bark is chiefly used for the women's *"liku,"* a dress consisting of a number of fringes attached to a waist-band. The bark is stripped off, steeped in water to render it soft and to allow the fibers to separate. According to Dr. Hillebrand, a decoction is made of the flowers by the natives as a useful emollient in bronchial and intestinal catarrhs. The Vitian and Tahitian name is *Fau, Pago* at Guam, *Varo* or *Baro* in Madagascar, and *Au* in Rarotonga.

Hibiscus Arnottianus Gray.

Kokia keokeo.

(Plate 114.)

HIBISCUS ARNOTTIANUS Gray Bot. U. S. E. E. (1854) 176;—Mann in Proc. Am. Acad. VII. (1867) 157,—et Fl. Haw. Isl. Proc. Ess. Inst. V. (1867) 139;—Wawra in Flora (1873) 173;—Hbd. Fl. Haw. Isl. (1878) 48;—Del Cast. Ill. Fl. Ins. Mar. Pac. VI. (1890) 121;—Heller in Minnes Bot. Stud. Bull. IX. (1897) 851.— **H. Boryanus** H. et A. Bot. Beech. (1832) 79. (n. DC.);—Endl. Flora Suds. (1836) 182, no. 1495.—**Hibiscus Fauriei** Leveil. Fedde Repert. X. 6/9. (1911) 120.

Leaves large of variable size, ovate, bluntly acuminate, entire, 3-nerved, chartaceous, dark green; stipules subulate, caducous; flowers solitary in the axils, white with pinkish veins, or pure white even the pistil, (Molokai, Wailau), pedicels articulate near the end; involucral bracts 5 to 7, triangular to lanceolate, 4 to 6 mm long, calyx 16 to 24 mm, tubular, 5-toothed splitting laterally when with fruit; petals white, obovate-oblong, or lanceolate and free, (very variable), 7.5 to 10 cm or more long; staminal column long ex-serted, 10 to 15 cm long, red or white, sending off filaments of 12 to 16 mm, from its upper half or third; style branches 6 to 8 mm, erect; capsule elongate, as long as the calyx, chartaceous; seeds 5 mm, reniform.

In regard to the nomenclature of this species there seems to have been some doubt. Heller and others thought that the white native Hibiscus was without a name, as Gray in his description of *H. Arnottianus* says: flowers red * * *.

293

PLATE 116.

HIBISCUS KOKIO Hbd.
Kokio or Pualoalo.
Red native Hibiscus, somewhat reduced.

Malvaceae.

This also accounts for the publication of a *Hibiscus Fauriei* by Léveillé, coming from the mountains behind Honolulu, where the tree is quite common. In order to straighten matters out the writer sent specimens to the Gray Herbarium to be compared with Asa Gray's type. Dr. B. L. Robinson kindly replied as follows: "There can be no question that the white flowered species (no. 8831) from Oahu is precisely the real *H. Arnottianus* Gray.

"The red flowered species (a photograph was sent) as far as can be made out from the photograph corresponds very well with authentic material of *H. Kokio* Hbd.; the chief difference being the larger petioles." This, however, may be due to the fact that the plant was grown in cultivation; it came from the garden of Mr. Gerrit P. Wilder. This now settles the controversy in regard to one of the most beautiful native flowering trees which the Islands possess. Along streambeds in the mountains of Koolau, Oahu, it is usually a tree 30 feet tall and when in flower makes a beautiful display. It is also cultivated by residents of Honolulu. On the other islands it is not uncommon, but varies to some extent. A pure white flowered one occurs on the beach of Wailau Valley, on Molokai.

Hibiscus Waimeae Heller.
Kokia keokeo.
(Plate 115.)

HIBISCUS WAIMEAE Heller in Minnes. Bot. Stud. Bull. IX. (1897) 851, pl. 53.—**Hibiscus Arnottianus** Gray forma Mrs. Sinclair Indig. Flow. Haw. Isl. (1885) pl. 8.

Leaves suborbicular about 5 cm or more in diameter, pale green, crenate, pubescent on both sides, velvety to the touch; petioles half the length of the leaves; stipules small; flowers axillary near the ends of the branches, large white or tinged with pink, on pubescent pedicels; calyx broadly tubular, pubescent outside, woolly within, petals 10 to 15 cm long, 18 to 25 mm wide, prominently veined, pubescent on the outside; staminal column rather stout, long exserted, red, otherwise as in *H. Arnottianus* Gray.

This rather distinct plant occurs as a tree 20 to 30 feet in height on the leeward side of Kauai below the forests of Kaholuamano at the bottom of vertical cliffs, in dry situations, and in gulches on open grass lands below Halemanu, Kauai, at an elevation of 2500 feet up to 3000 feet, in company with *Dracaena aurea, Osmanthus sandwicensis* and others. It is also cultivated now in Honolulu.

Hibiscus Kokio Hbd.
Kokia ula or *Pualoalo.*
(Plate 116.)

HIBISCUS KOKIO Hbd. mss. in Flora (1873) 174;—Hbd. Flora Haw. Isl. (1888) 48;— Del Cast. Ill. Fl. Ins. Mar. Pac. VI. (1890) 121.—**H. Arnottianus** A. Gray forma Mrs. Sinclair Ind. Fl. Haw. Isl. (1885) pl. 9.

Leaves ovate or elliptical-oblong, rather acuminate, sinuately crenate, scarcely palmate-nerved, chartaceous, glabrous, on petioles of 6 to 18 mm or more; flowers axillary, solitary; pedicels 18 to 30 mm, pubescent, articulate in the upper third; involucral bracts 6 to 7, linear, 8 to 12 mm long; calyx tubular or subcampanulate, 8 to 30 mm, cleft to the middle into 5 acute lobes, glabrate; petals 5 to 6.5 cm, entire, red; staminal column

295

PLATE 117.

HIBISCADELPHUS GIFFARDIANUS Rock.
Hau Kuahiwi.
Showing flowering branch and mature fruits in lower left hand corner, reduced.
Showing flowering and fruiting branch; one-half natural size.

shorter, red, the short filaments crowded near the five-toothed apex; style branches 8 to 10 mm, spreading horizontally, ciliate; capsule glabrous, 18 mm; seeds 5 mm, reniform covered with a coarse brownish pubescence.

This species is somewhat rare, at least not so common as the white native Hibiscus. The writer met with two varieties on Molokai— one at Mapulehu, where it is a shrub at about 1000 feet elevation; the other at the bottom of Wailau Valley, only a few hundred feet above sea level. On Kauai only, it is apparently a tree. Mr. Lydgate informed the writer that he saw a tree about 40 feet in height back of Lihue, along the pole-line. As the writer did not see specimens, it is doubtful whether it is *H. Kokio* or Forbes' *H. Kahilii*, a tree 27 feet high, which, however, seems not to differ very much from the former, according to Forbes, only in the pubescent calyx and in other minor points, one of which, according to his figure, seems to be the bluntly acute or somewhat obtuse apices of the leaves. His specimen came from near the Wahiawa swamp, Kauai. *H. Kahilii* Forbes Occ. Pap. B. P. B. Mus. V. (1912) 4, with plate.

HIBISCADELPHUS Rock.

Bracteoles 5 to 7, very narrow linear or dentate, free. Calyx deeply and unevenly 2 to 3 cleft. Staminal column antheriferous below the 5-dentate apex. Ovary 5-celled, with 1 to 3 ovules in each cell; style branches 5, suberect with capitate flesh-colored stigmas. Capsule woody or coriaceous, 5 valved; endocarp chartaceous, detached. Seeds reniform, covered with a dirty white tomentum.—Medium sized trees with a stellate tomentum. Leaves cordate, unevenly 3 to 5 pointed or rounded and entire. Flowers single or several in the axils of the leaves at the ends of the branches; color of petals magenta, yellowish and green. Calyx deciduous before maturation of the fruit.

The genus Hibiscadelphus established by the writer consists of 3 species which are peculiar to the dry sections of Hawaii and Maui. Of two of the species only an individual tree is in existence, while of the third several can still be found on the slopes of Mt. Hualalai, in the forest of Waihau, in North Kona, Hawaii.

The genus, of which *Hibiscadelphus Giffardianus* is the type, is closely related to Hibiscus, from which it differs mainly in the deciduous calyx, and quite different flowers.

KEY TO THE SPECIES.

Flowers 5 to 6 cm long.
 Involucral bracts 2 cm, filiform, free........................... **H. Giffardianus**
 Involucral bracts linear-spathulate, one nerved................... **H. Wilderianus**
Flowers 2.5 to 3 cm long.
 Involucral bracts dentiform, 1 mm............................ **H. Hualalaiensis**

Hibiscadelphus Giffardianus Rock.

Hau kuahiwi.

(Plate 117.)

HIBISCADELPHUS GIFFARDIANUS Rock in Bull. Hawaii Bd. of Agric. and Forestry I. (1911) 10. pl. 4.

A medium sized tree; bark smooth, fibrous, whitish; branches terete, glabrous, covered with leaf scars; leaves on long petioles orbicular in outline cordate, bluntly acute at the apex, 12-15 cm each way, unevenly lobed or pointed, chartaceous, covered on both sides

PLATE 118.

HIBISCADELPHUS HUALALAIENSIS Rock.
Hau Kuahiwi.
Showing flowering and fruiting branch; less than one-half natural size.

Malvaceae.

with a stellate tomentum, palmately 7-nerved, with hispid glands in the angles of ribs and veins on both sides; stipules small triangular caducous; flowers solitary or several in the axils of the leaves on the ends of the branches; bracteoles 5 to 7 very narrow, 2 cm long, free, filiform; calyx saccate, deeply and unevenly 2 to 3 cleft, lobes acuminate, many-nerved, yellowish green outside, with stellate hairs, glabrous inside; corolla convolute, curved, only the very apex slightly opening, on account of the almost completely contorted aestivation; on pedicels of 2 to 3 cm, petals 5 to 6 cm long acute at the apex, oblong very uneven-sided, deep magenta inside, grayish-green outside with a stellate hispid tomentum on the exposed parts, especially on the prominent nerves; staminal column 1/3 longer than the petals, with numerous long filaments on nearly half its length, hispid at its base; style branches sub-erect 5 mm, hispid; stigmas flesh-colored; capsule coriaceous to woody oblong tapering toward the apex 4 to 5 cm x 2 to 2.5 cm, broadest at the base, rugose, yellowish-green, covered with stellate hairs; the calyx and bracteoles deciduous before maturation of fruit; endocarp chartaceous shining glabrous, loose; seeds large 7 to 10 mm, reniform, covered with dirty whitish-gray wool.

The *Hau Kuahiwi* is a remarkable tree. At first appearance one would think it to be the common *Hau* (*Hibiscus tiliaceus*), but at closer inspection one cannot but wonder at the most peculiar shape of the flowers, which are of a deep magenta, and the large yellowish tuberculate capsules. It is a rather low tree, with not erect but rather inclining trunk of a foot in diameter, with a many-branching round crown. The genus "Hibiscadelphus," meaning "brother of Hibiscus," was described by the author and the species named in honor of Mr. W. M. Giffard of Honolulu, in whose company the writer collected his first specimens.

It differs from the genus Hibiscus in its very peculiar flowers and mainly in the calyx, which is not persistent with the capsules, but drops together with the bracts as soon as the capsules are formed.

Unfortunately the tree, of which a specimen is figured in this book, is the only one in existence. It is unique among all Hawaiian plants, and the author is sorry to relate that nothing has been done to protect it. Like many other Hawaiian trees, it will succumb to the ravages of cattle, which inhabit a great many of our native forests.

This single tree is found on a small Kipuka of 56 acres called Puaulu, on the land of Keauhou, near Kilauea Volcano, at an elevation of 4200 feet, on the Island of Hawaii. It is surrounded by a great many rare trees, which will share its fate sooner or later. Among them are beautiful trees of *Sapindus saponaria*, Pelea, Xanthoxylum, Urera, Straussia, Ochrosia, etc.

The genus consists of three species—the above described one on Hawaii, one on Maui with only a single tree left, and the third on Hualalai, Hawaii. The wood is white, not so soft as in the *Hau*, while the bark is whitish and fibrous.

Hibiscadelphus Wilderianus Rock.

Hau kuahiwi.

HIBISCADELPHUS WILDERIANUS Rock in Bull. Haw Bd. of Agric. & For. I. (1911) 12. pl. 5.

A tree 5 m, trunk erect; leaves orbicular in outline trilobed wavy, cordate with a broad sinus at the base, with subacute or blunt apex, on petioles of 7 to 10 cm, palmately 5 to 7 nerved, puberulous above, with minute stellate hair underneath; nerves prominent,

PLATE 119.

HIBISCADELPHUS HUALALAIENSIS Rock.
Hau Kuahiwi tree.
Growing in Waihou forest slope of Mt. Hualalai, North Kona, Hawaii; elevation 3000 feet.

Malvaceae.

hispid; the subulate stipules small and puberulous; flowers solitary on pedicels of 1.5 to 4 cm, bracteoles linear, spathulate, free, 2 cm long one-nerved; calyx saccate unevenly tri-lobed, the lobes triangular acute; hirsute outside, puberulous inside, 2.5 cm long, flowers nearly the same size as in *H. Giffardianus*, petals greenish yellow outside, yellowish inside, many and strongly ribbed, the nerves branching at the apex, densely hirsute especially on the very prominent nerves, 4 to 5 cm long, contorted, with blunt or acute apex; staminal column long exserted, antheriferous to the five lobed apex, the lobes acuminate, less than 2 mm; stamens numerous, filaments 6 mm long, anthers dark red; style branches erect, 3 mm; capsule ovoid 3.5 cm x 4 cm greenish-black, woody, tuberculate, stellate hispid, seeds same as in the previous species.

Of this interesting tree only one is in existence and when last visited (1912) by Mr. Gerrit P. Wilder, who also collected the first open flowers from which the description is drawn, the tree was found to be in a dying condition; the branches were completely covered with a species of *Usnea,* probably *australis.* The tree occurs on the ancient lava fields of Auahi, on the land of Kahikinui, southern slope of Mt. Haleakala, on the lee side, where rain is very infrequent. Mr. Wilder visited the tree twice, and only on the last trip was enabled to find one open flower and a few more or less developed buds. Seeds of this species were planted by Mr. Wilder, who succeeded in raising one single plant. As the tree is situated on a cattle ranch, it will be only a very short time until it will have disappeared from its natural habitat. It was first discovered by the writer in November, 1910. The type is 8663 in the Herbarium of the Board of Agriture and Forestry, now in the safe-keeping of the College of Hawaii Herbarium.

Hibiscadelphus Hualalaiensis Rock.

Hau kuahiwi.

(Plates 118, 119.)

HIBISCADELPHUS HUALALAIENSIS Rock in Bull. Hawaii Bd. Agric. & For. I. (1911) 14. pl. 6.

Tree 5 to 7 m high, with an erect trunk 0.3 m in diameter, bark white, branches terete, with young leaves densely hirsute, leaves somewhat reniform, or bluntly and shallow trilobed, on long petioles (10 to 16 cm) with scattered stellate hair above, to-mentose underneath, the main nerves branching several times; flowers usually single on tomentose pedicels of 1.5 to 2 cm; bracteoles minute dentiform about 1 mm, calyx irregularly 3 to 6 lobed, the lobes acuminate of unequal size, some only 2 mm, others 15 mm, flowers half the size as in the two other species, 2.5 to 3 cm curved, petals green, somewhat reddish inside, contorted, many ribbed hirsute near the bluntly acuminate lobes and on the nerves, silky at the base, the margins even ciliate; corolla only slightly opening, apex of the petals recurved; staminal column exserted one-third its length, bearing numerous filaments, with semicircularly curved anthers; style branches erect, ciliate, with clavate hirsute stigmas; ovary conical densely silky tomentose five celled, with 3 ovate ovules in each cell of which the upper is ascending the lower horizontal; capsule small ovate, 2 cm long, 1.5 cm wide covered with yellowish stellate hair; seeds reniform, covered with a yellowish white wool.

This exceedingly interesting and distinct species was found by the writer in the year 1909 on the lava fields of Mt. Hualalai, in North Kona, Hawaii, and in the forest of Waihou of the same district, where about a dozen trees are still in existence. The writer revisited the above locality in March, 1912, and found the trees in flower, while on his previous visit. June 18, 1909, only a few worm-eaten capsules could be found. The trees are badly attacked by several species of moths which feed on the leaves and also mature capsules. Mr. Gerrit Wilder, however, succeeded in growing a few plants from healthy seeds collected by the writer.

THESPESIA Corr.

Involucral bracts 3 to 5, small. Calyx not punctate, usually cup-shaped and truncate. Staminal column antheriferous below the toothed apex. Ovary 5-celled, with few ascending ovules in each cell; style club-shaped. 5-grooved. Capsule woody or coriaceous, almost baccate, dehiscent or almost indehiscent. Seeds woolly; cotyledons black-punctate.—Trees with entire leaves. Flowers large, single in the axils of the leaves.

This genus possesses only a few species in tropical Asia and Polynesia. *T. populnea* (L.) Corr., the Hawaiian *Milo*, is a cosmopolitan beach-tree, occurring in tropical Africa, Asia and Polynesia; in Hawaii it is not as common now as in the early days.

Thespesia populnea (L). Corr.

Milo.

THESPESIA POPULNEA (L.) Corr. in Ann. Mus. Par. IX. (1807) 290, t. 8. fig. 2;—DC. Prodr. I. (1824) 457;—H. et A. Bot. Beech. (1832) 60;—Endl. Fl. Suds (1836) 182. no. 1506;—Gray Bot. U. S. E. E. (1854) 179;—Seem. Fl. Vit. (1865) 18;—Mann in Proc. Ess. Inst. V. (1867) 140;—Mrs. Sincl. Indig. Flow. Haw. Isl. (1885) pl. 10;—Hbd. Fl. Haw. Isl. (1888) 49;—Del Cast. Ill. Fl. Ins. Mar. Pac. VI. (1890) 119;—Brigham Ka Hana Kapa, Mem. B. P. B. Mus.. III. (1911) 135.—**Hibiscus populneus** Linn. Spec. pl. ed. I. (1753) 694.—**H. bacciferus** Forst. Prodr. (1786) no. 260.

Leaves roundish, cordate, acuminate entire, 10 to 12.5 cm in diameter, glabrous; peduncles as long as the petioles; involucral bracts lanceolate equalling the calyx, soon deciduous; calyx truncate 12 mm; petals obovate-oblong 5 cm, yellow; capsule globose, 24 to 30 mm in diameter, almost woody, very tardily dehiscent; seed 8 mm, villous at the base and angles.

The *Milo*, like the *Hau*, is a tree not uncommonly found along the sandy beaches on all the islands. Its habit of growth is, however, different, as it develops a straight trunk of often 2 feet or more in diameter, with a thick corrugated bark.

It is a favorite shade tree, reaching a height of over 40 feet, and is often planted. The name *Milo* occurs also in Tonga, Samoa, and Tahiti for the same tree, while it is called *Miro* in Rarotonga and *Mulo* in Viti.

Hillebrand in his Flora p. 50 remarks that the tree was regarded sacred in Tahiti and used to be planted in Morais or temples and its leaves were employed in religious ceremonies. That the tree was held in high esteem by the Hawaiians is shown by the fact that several of them surrounded the house of King Kamehameha I. at Waikiki.

The wood of the *Milo* is very beautiful, being of a rich brown color and capable of taking a fine polish. It is made into *poi* calabashes by the natives, and is highly prized, though not so much as those of the less common *Kou* (*Cordia subcordata*).

Malvaceae.

KOKIA Lewton.

Tree 4 to 8 m high, woody throughout. Flowers single in the axils of the upper-most leaves; peduncle bearing below the middle a broadly sessile, obliquely clasping cadu-cous, ovate bract. Bracteoles 3, persistent, accrescent, ovate, entire, sinuate or slightly lobed, narrowed at the base, not in the least auriculate, coriaceous, glabrous, strongly reticulated, 7 to 13 nerved. Calyx urceolate, thin scarious, punctate with black warts; lobes 5, shallow, rounded, the scarious almost hyaline margins overlapping and completely enclosing the bud. Calyx tube often with median transverse vein, the upper half of the calyx usually soon breaking off at this point, giving the appearance of being truncate. At the base of the calyx at the point of insertion of the petals there is a ring of stiff brownish hairs. Floral nectary naked, extra floral nectaries not evident. Corolla two to three times the length of the bracteoles, red. Ovary 5-celled, with one ascending ovum in each cell. Capsule ovoid, ligneous, opening tardily. Seeds ovoid, sharply angled on the ventral side, rounded on the dorsal, covered with short brick-red tomentum. Cotyledons punctate with black dots. Bark containing a reddish brown sap.

This genus established by Lewton consists of two species and one variety. The type is *Kokia Rockii* Lewton, no. 691082 in the U. S. National Herbarium. The co-type is in the Herbarium, College of Hawaii, no. 3549.

The writer sent specimens of this plant to Mr. Fairchild, agricultural explorer in charge of the U. S. Department of Agriculture, Washington, D. C., at his request, as there were no specimens of this plant in the U. S. Nat. Herbarium, Mr. Fairchild's attention having been called to this interesting plant in the writer's report to the Board of Commissioners of Agriculture and Forestry, 1910. The plants were sent under the name *Gossypium drynarioides* Seem., with the remark that it is at least a new variety of the plant by the above name, which is found on Molokai, while the writer's material came from a new locality: slopes of Mt. Hualalai, lava fields of Puuwaawaa, Kona, Hawaii. The specimens, with additional notes on the living trees, were furnished Mr. Lewton, who then proceeded to describe the plant under a new genus. Specimens of the original *Gossypium drynarioides* Seem. from Molokai were also sent. Hille-brand found one tree on Oahu, with lanceolate bracts, which he called variety β. Mr. Lewton named this variety *Kokia lanceolata* on the strength of a few scraps of lanceolate bracts in the Gray Herbarium. The writer does not think it justifiable to create a new species on such incomplete material and more or less on the strength that it grew on another island. The writer knows the Ha-waiian flora thoroughly, and is well acquainted with tremendous variations found in all Hawaiian plants, and therefore prefers to retain the varietal rank rather than specific. The plant in question has, however, become extinct. The fact that Lewton's third species grows on another island is not sufficient to make it a species. Besides, Makapuu Point, on Oahu, where IIbd's var. β grew, is exactly opposite the point on Molokai where *Kokia drynarioides* grows, and is only about 25 miles distant.

KEY TO THE SPECIES

Bracts broadly obovate, 6.5 cm x 8 cm............................ **K. Rockii**
Bracts broadly ovate, entire, 2.5 to 3 cm x 2.5 cm.............. **K. drynarioides**

PLATE 120.

KOKIA ROCKII Lewton.
Kokio.
Flowering branch, flowers bright red of silky texture.   About one-third natural size.

Malvaceae.

Kokia Rockii Lewton.

Kokio.

(Plates 120, 121.)

KOKIA ROCKII Lewt. in Smithson. Misc. Coll. LX. 5. (1912) 3, pl. 1, 2, 3, 4;—Rock in Report. Haw. Bd. Agric. & For. (1912) pl. 19-20;—**Gossypium drynarioides** Rock in Rep. Haw. Bd. Agr. & For. (1910) 71. pl. 13.

Bracts broadly obovate 6.5 cm long 6.5 to 8 cm broad, with three to five blunt and shallow lobes, very strongly reticulated and veined below. Leaves glabrous below except for a dense patch of rusty hairs 2 to 2.5 cm in diameter at point of attachment of the petiole, the pulvinus of which is also hairy; staminal tube 9 to 10 cm long curved; seeds 2 cm long by 1 cm wide; lint 3 mm long.

The *Kokio* or native red cotton (not to be mistaken for the *Kokio ula* or *Pualoalo*, red native Hibiscus) is an exceedingly rare tree of 12 to 13 feet in height, with a trunk up to one foot in diameter and vested in a thin grayish-brown bark, which is covered with lenticels. The trunks of the Hawaii plants are straight and not gnarled. It is sparingly branching and woody in its last ramification. The leaves resemble those of a young *Kukui* tree, though they have the color of a maple leaf with the autumn tints from reddish-yellow to green.

The tree is of striking beauty when in flower and is worthy of cultivation.

The writer observed a young tree in Kona, Hawaii, which was literally loaded with the bright red blossoms which excel in beauty many a Hibiscus flower. On the Island of Hawaii the writer discovered several trees of this species, some of which were in excellent condition. It inhabits the dry region of North Kona and is scattered all along the Government Road between Huehue and Puuwaawaa, elevation 2000 feet. There it is associated with the *Lama* (*Maba sandwicensis*), *Kauila* (*Colubrina oppositifolia*), *Halapepe* (*Dracaena aurea*), etc.

The bark, which contains a rich reddish-brown juice, is used by the natives, who dye their fish nets with it. They strip the tree for several feet of its bark, which is macerated, and the juice thus obtained is used as a dye. The wood is soft and of a reddish-brown color.

This particular *Kokio* is endemic and peculiar to the Island of Hawaii, where it is still in its prime and, if properly protected from cattle and man, should not become extinct.

The writer is glad to relate that the owners as well as the lessee of the land on which these few trees are growing, have already fenced these trees, so as to protect them from the ravages of cattle. A regulation has also been posted to prevent the natives from stripping the trees of their bark, and thus the writer hopes that this interesting species may live many more years. Abundant seed has been collected and forwarded to the U. S. Department of Agriculture in Washington, D. C. A quantity of seed has also been distributed here in Honolulu, and people interested in showy flowers have been urged to plant them Quite a number are now growing in Honolulu.

305

PLATE 121.

KOKIA ROCKII Lewton.
Kokio tree.
Growing on the lava flows of Puuanahulu, Kona, Hawaii; elevation 2500 feet.

Malvaceae-Theaceae.

Kokia drynarioides (Seem.) Lewt.

Kokio.

KOKIA DRYNARIOIDES (Seem.) Lewt. in Smithson. Misc. Coll. LX. 5. (1912) 3. pl. 5.—
Gossypium drynarioides Seem. Fl. Vit. (1865) 22;—H. Mann in Proc. Am. Acad. VII.
(1867) 157; et Fl. Haw. Isl. Proc. Ess. Inst. V. (1867) 141;—Hbd. Fl. Haw. Isl.
(1888) 51;—Del Cast. Ill. Fl. Ins. Mar. Pac. VI. (1890) 120.—**Hibiscus drynarioides**
Kuntze Rev. Gen. Pl. I. (1891) 68.

Leaves on long petioles, membraneous, glabrous, but with a few brownish hairs at
the base of the veins, cordate 7 to 5 lobed, the deltoid lobes about 3.5 cm deep, the basal
sinus quite open; flowers single in the axils of the uppermost leaves, on stout peduncles
of 2.5 to 5 cm, which bear at the middle a broadly sessile and obliquely clasping caducous
bract of 8 to 10 mm in length; involucral bracts broadly ovate to sub-cordate, obtuse,
entire, 7 to 13-nerved, 2.5 to 3 cm long, and 2.5 cm or more broad, glabrous, coriaceous;
calyx urceolate, truncate, thin scarious; petals red, obovate-oblong, entire, 7.5 to 10 cm
long, silky outside; staminal column of same length, truncate or obsoletely 2 to 3-toothed
at the apex, antheriferous in the upper third with short filaments; style shortly exserted,
clavate, 5-grooved; ovary 5-celled, each cell with one ascending ovule; capsule ovoid
2.5 cm, thick woody, opening tardily near the apex; seeds obovoid, covered with a short
reddish-brown tomentum.

Of this exceedingly interesting species there has been only one tree in existence
up to a few months ago. This same tree which was declared dead, showed still
some signs of life and produced a few capsules with mature seeds; but this is
evidently the last, only a small branchlet having produced a few leaves. Seeds
of this tree have been planted by the manager of the Molokai Ranch Co. and by
Mr. G. P. Wilder, who secured the last ones to be had. A few have been sent
to Washington to the Bureau of Plant Introduction. Thus it is hoped still to
perpetuate this most interesting plant. Several trees occurred on the west end
of Moloaki, at Mahana, all having now died, owing to ravages of cattle, sheep
and goats, which eat off the bark and leaves. On Oahu, at the eastern end, on
the hills of Makapuu and Koko Head, grew a variety of this species with lanceolate involucral bracts, which has long been extinct. It was described by Lewton
as a new species, though really only of varietal rank.

It should be called *Kokia drynarioides* var. *lanceolata.* The reasons for this
change are explained in the generic discussion.

THEACEAE.

The family Theaceae, with its 16 genera and about 174 species, is rather confined to the tropical and subtropical regions of the world. A few appear in the
temperate regions of the northern hemisphere in America and Asia. The genus
Eurya is the only representative of this family in the Hawaiian Islands, where it
has one endemic species. To this family belongs *Thea sinensis* L., the Tea of
commerce, which is found wild in the interior of the south Chinese island Hai-
nan, and Upper Assam in Bengal, from whence it was introduced as an agricultural plant into China and Japan about 810 A. D.

Theaceae.

EURYA Thunb.

Trees or shrubs with coriaceous leaves. Flowers single or exceptionally in very short racemes, which are axillary.

Subgenus TERNSTROEMIOPSIS Urb.

Flowers dioecious, corolla fleshy. Male flowers, with 10 to 15 stamens in one row, the anthers twice as long as the filaments, linear lanceolate, split down to the base. Ovary 3-celled, in each cell 15 ovules, of which the most are pendulous while the upper are nearly horizontal. Styles 3, with ovate lanceolate stigmas. Fruit a berry with 12 seeds in each cell. Cotyledons shorter than the radicle of the embryo.—Leaves spiral. To this subgenus belongs the Hawaiian species (*Eurya sandicicensis* Gray) only.

The genus to which the Hawaiian species belongs consists of about 36 species and several subspecies which are distributed over Mexico, South America and the East and West Indies.

Eurya sandwicensis A. Gray.

Anini or *Wanini.*

EURYA SANDWICENSIS A. Gray. Bot. U. S. E. E. (1854) 209;—H. Mann. Proc. Am. Acad. VII (1867) 156, et Fl. Haw. Isl. (1867) 134;—Wawra in Flora (1873) 168;—Hbd. Fl. Haw. Isl. (1888) 41;—Del Cast. Ill. Fl. Ins. Mar. Pac. VI. (1890) 117;—Szyszyl. in Engl. et Prantl Pflzfam. III. 6. (1895) 189, et Engl. in Nachtr. (1897) 247;—Heller Pl. Haw. Isl. (1897) 856.—**Ternstroemiopsis sandwicensis** Urban in Ber. Deutsch. Bot. Ges. XIV. (1896) 49.

A small tree 5 to 6 m in height, or at higher altitudes a shrub 2 to 3 m, the ultimate branchlets pubescent; leaves obovate oblong, obovate or oval, obtuse, or bluntly acuminate at the apex, cordate at the base, closely serrate, thick coriaceous, or subchartaceous, somewhat shining above, 5 to 7.5 cm long, 25 to 30 mm wide, on short petioles of 2 to 3 mm; flowers solitary in the axils, subsessile or on pedicels of 6 mm; sepals dark purplish, coriaceous, suborbicular, persistent; petals deciduous in the fertile flowers, somewhat fleshy, ovate or obovate, about 8 mm, yellowish; stamens free, very short; anthers mucronate; styles 2 to 3, distinct; berry dryish, globose, black, about 10 mm in diameter, tuberculate, crowned by the styles; seeds 12 in each cell, globular-reniform, with a thin testa; albumen scanty; cotyledons thick and broad; radicle somewhat longer.

Hillebrand in his Flora of the Hawaiian Islands describes a variety β, with larger leaves, rounded or acute at the base, from Kealia, Kauai.

Wawra in Flora (1873), page 168, describes this particular form as *Eurya sandwicensis* Gray, fm. *grandifolia* Wawra, *arbuscula foliis tenerioribus, sparsis, 4 poll. longis, 1½ poll. latis, basi rotundatis vel acutis, minutissime serrulatis; pedunculis 4 lin. longis.* Kauai um Kealia, etc. 2025.

The variety is not known to the writer. The species occurs on all the islands of the group, especially in the middle forest zone up to 5000 feet and even higher. It is a small, rather glabrous tree, but more often a shrub. It is known to the old natives as *Wanini*, or *Anini.* On the summit of Waialeale, Kauai, the writer met with this species as a stiff shrub, with very large fruits, as compared with those of the middle forest zone, where the berries do not become larger than 6 mm.

The *Wanini* is peculiar to the Hawaiian Islands, outside of which it has not been found.

GUTTIFERAE:

The family Guttiferae reaches its highest development between the tropics of Cancer and Capricorn, and only the genus Hypericum is found also outside the tropics. To this family belong the Mammei apple, the Mangosteen, and other edible fruits. The genus Calophyllum is here represented by only one cosmopolitan species.

CALOPHYLLUM L.

Flowers polygamous; sepals and petals not always distinguishable from each other, together 4 to 12, in 2 to 3 rows, imbricate; stamens many, free or hardly united at the base, filiform, with ovate or elongate anthers, long style and peltate stigma. Fruit a drupe with thin sarcocarp, with crustaceous stone and globose or ovoid seed. Trees with shiny coriaceous leaves, with numerous parallel nerves, and medium sized or rather small flowers, arranged in racemes or panicles.

The genus Calophyllum with its 55 species occurs in the old world, with the exception of 4 species which are found in tropical America. Only one species, *C. Inophyllum*, the true Hawaiian *Kamani*, is represented in these islands. It is the most noteworthy species of those occurring in the old world. It produces the real *Balsamum Mariae*, and a resin called *Tacamahak*.

Calophyllum inophyllum Linn.
Kamani.
(Plate 122.)

CALOPHYLLUM INOPHYLLUM Linn. Spec. Plant. I. (1753) 513;—Forst. Prodr. (1786) no. 225;—DC. Prodr. I. (1824) 562;—Guillem. Zeph. Tait. (1836-1837)—no. 337;—Endl. Fl. Suds. (1836) no. 1397;—A. Gray, Bot. U. S. E. E. (1854) 218;—Pancher in Cuzent, Tahiti (1860) 223;—Seem. Fl. Vit. (1865) 12;—Parkins Draw. Tah. Pl. (ined. cf. Seem.) t. 55;—H. Mann, Proc. Am. Acad. VII. (1867) 156, et Fl. Haw. Isl. in Proc. Essex Inst. V. (1867) 133;—Nadeaud Enum. Tahit. Pl. (1873) no 440.—Wawra in Flora (1874);—Hbd. Fl. Haw. Isl. (1888) 40;—Del Cast. Ill. Ins. Mar. Pac. VI. (1890) 116, et Fl. Polyn. Franc. (1893) 10;—Engler in Engl. et Prantl Pflzfam. III. 6. (1895) 222. Fig. 105;—Wilder Fr. Haw. Isl. (1911) 152. pl. 74.—Brigham Ka Hana Kapa (1911) 171, fig. 102.

Leaves coriaceous, shining, broadly oblong or obovate, 20 cm x 10 cm rounded or emarginate, on petioles of about 2.5 cm; racemes axillary, 5 to 17 cm long, the pedicles 2.5 to 3.5 cm with short, soon deciduous bracts at the base; sepals 4, rounded 8 to 10 mm long; petals 4, rarely 6 to 8, white, oblong 14 to 16 mm; stamens numerous, style 4 to 6 mm; fruit globose 2.5 to 4 cm thick; the flowers are fragrant.

This beautiful cosmopolitan tree, which grows always near or at the sea-shore, reaches a height of 50 to 60 feet or even more; it forms large groves in certain districts of the islands. One is especially remarkable on the Island of Molokai, at the entrance of the valley of Halawa, which has been referred to by the earliest navigators. Trees of this species, which was found here by the first white men and is therefore counted as indigenous, occur on all the islands of the group on the sea-shores. It is also known through all tropical Asia and Polynesia. Its Tahitian name is *Tamanu*, while it is known in Samoa as *Tefau*. The Samoans employ the oil of the nuts as a remedy for eye catarrh, while in

PLATE 122.

CALOPHYLLUM INOPHYLLUM Linn.
Kamani.
Trunk of tree with fruiting and flowering branch pinned to it.   Leaves badly infested with scale.

Guttiferae-Flacourtiaceae.

Nauru (Micronesia) it is employed for skin diseases. In Fiji the tree is known as *Diol.* Seeman in his Flora of Fiji writes: ''The most valuable oil produced in Fiji is that extracted from the seeds of this tree. The natives use it for greasing their bodies and polishing their arms.''

The Hawaiians used the wood for calabashes or poi bowls. In India the tree is known as Alexandrian Laurel and its wood is used for cabinet work, machinery, railway sleepers and mast spars. The wood is moderately hard, close grained and of a reddish brown color. The resin exuding from the bark is useful in indolent ulcers.

FLACOURTIACEAE

This family, consisting of 70 genera and more than 500 species, is exclusively tropical. Not a single species is found either in Europe or North America. They are distributed from India to Australia, Africa and the Pacific islands. Nearly all Flacourtiaceae inhabit the lowlands or lower forest zone.

The family is represented in the Hawaiian Islands by two species belonging to the genus Xylosma.

XYLOSMA Forst.

Flowers dioecious, rarely polygamous. Calyx lobes 4 to 5, somewhat united at the base, imbricate, usually ciliate. Petals none. Stamens numerous, surrounded by an annular discus, the latter often consisting of several glands; filaments free, filiform, long; anthers round or elliptical, 2-celled, extrorse, versatile. Ovary wanting in the male flowers, surrounded by a discus or rarely by staminodia, 1-celled, free, with 2 to 3 placentas, each with 2 or (4 to 6) ascending, epitropous ovules. Style short, occasionally entirely missing. Stigma peltately lobed. Fruit a 2 to 8 seeded berry with little fruit flesh. Seeds obovoid with rich albumen, embryo large, with broad cotyledons.—Small trees or shrubs, often with axillary thorns, but unarmed in the Hawaiian species. Leaves alternate, shortly petioled, entire ,or dentate-crenate, coriaceous without stipules. Flowers small, in short axillary racemes with small bracts.

A genus of 45 species, distributed over all tropical countries, with the exception of Africa. Thirty-two species alone are found in America, while only four are known from Polynesia, including the two Hawaiian species.

KEY TO THE SPECIES.

Leaves entire; stigma sessile, generally 3............................ **X. Hawaiiense**
Leaves crenate or sinuate; stigmas raised on a style, generally 2....... **X. Hillebrandii**

Xylosma Hawaiiense Seem.
Maua.

XYLOSMA HAWAIIENSE Seem. Flora Vit. (1865) 7;—Mann Proc. Am. Acad. VII. (1867) 150, et Fl. Haw. Isl. Proc. Ess. Inst. V. (1867) 122;—Wawra in Flora (1873) 171; Hbd. Fl. Haw. Isl. (1868) 20;—Del Cast. Ill. Fl. Ins. Mar. Pac. VI. (1890) 109.—**Myroxylon Hawaiiense** (Seem.) O. Ktze. Rev. Gen. Pl. (1891) 44;—Warburg in Engl. et Prantl III. 6a. (1893) 41;—Heller Pl. Haw. Isl. Minnes. Bot. Stud. Bull. IX. (1897) 856.

Leaves distichous on petioles of 12 mm, ovate or rounded 7.5 to 10 cm long, 6 to 7.5 cm wide, shortly acuminate, entire, thick, coriaceous, glabrous; flowers small greenish or

PLATE 123.

XYLOSMA HILLEBRANDII Wawra.
Maua.
Fruiting branch, one-half natural size.

reddish, about 8 in racemes of 10 to 15 mm in length, often several racemes from one gemma, the pedicels of about the same length, bracteolate below the middle; male flowers: sepals 4, connected at the base, ovate, obtuse 3 mm, margins ciliate; stamens 2 or 3 times as long, on a raised torus and surrounded by a crenulate disc; female flowers: sepals 5, quincunial; ovary surrounded by a crenulate disc and a few rudimentary stamens; stigma sessile, peltately 2 to 3 (or 4) lobed, the lobes reflexed; placentas 3 (-4) with 3 pendulous ovules to each; berry reddish somewhat dry 8 to 12 mm long, ovoid; seeds 5 mm; embryo straight in copious albumen, but shorter, the radicle shorter than the broad foliaceous cotyledons.

The *Maua* is a very handsome tree, conspicuous in the forest by its reddish young leaves. It thrives best in the drier districts on the Islands of Oahu and Kauai only. The *Maua* of Molokai, Hawaii, and Maui is botanically referred to another species.

In the forest of Kopiwai, a semi-dry district on the leeward side of Kauai. it grows to a height of 30 feet, developing a more or less straight trunk of sometimes more than a foot in diameter, with a smooth bark. It is conspicuous on account of its large ovate or rounded leaves, which are of a dark-green color with reddish hue and shining. It is not uncommon at an altitude of 2000 feet, and sometimes as high as 3000 feet, where it can usually be found in company with the *Hame* or *Haa, Kopiko. Ahakea*, and others.

It is confined, like the *Kalia*, to the Islands of Oahu and Kauai. In the former island it grows in nearly all the valleys of the leeward side, but has also been observed in Punaluu, on the windward side of Oahu; at lower elevation it usually is not taller than 20 feet, or sometimes even less.

On Kauai it is found in the lower forest zone above Waimea, in the woods of Kopiwai, where it is associated with the *Alphitonia excelsa (Kauila), Dracaena aurea*, the *Halapepa, Santalum pryrularium*, Sandalwood, and others; also at Kaholuamano and probably in the woods above Koloa. It is not found outside of the Hawaiian group, but has a relative in the Marquesas, Tonga and Viti islands.

There seem to be intermediate leaves between this species and the following; on Lanai occurs a tree with entire leaves, while others have a faint suggestion of crenate leaves; evidently the two species are very little distinct specifically. The following may only be a good variety of the former.

Xylosma Hillebrandii Wawra.
Maua.
(Plate 123.)

XYLOSMA HILLEBRANDII Wawra in Flora (1873) 171;—Hbd. Fl. Haw. Isl. (1888) 20;— Del Cast. Ill. Fl. Ins.. Mar. Pac. VI. (1890) 109.—Myroxylon Hillebrandii (Wawra) O. Ktze. Rev. Gen. Pl. I. (1891) 44;—Warburg in Engl. et Prantl Pflzfam. III. 6 a. (1893) 41.

Leaves on petioles of 12 mm, ovate-oblong, 6 to 10 cm long, 3 to 7 cm wide, somewhat obtuse, or acute, contracted at the base or rounded, repandly crenate, even sinuate, the teeth tipped with a callous gland, membraneous. chartaceous or in very dry districts coriaceous, glabrous and shining, racemes puberulous. 12 to 25 mm long, with 10 to 12 flowers on pedicels of 2 to 6 mm, which are bracteolate above the base and articulate; male flowers: sepals 4, broadly ovate or triangular. with a white pubescence on both faces,

313

PLATE 124.

WIKSTROEMIA OAHUENSIS (Gray) Rock.
Akia.
Flowering branch, two-thirds natural size.

ciliate, disc 4-lobed; female flowers: sepals 4, occasionally 5, stigma 2-lobed, on a short style; placentas (2, rarely 3), each with 3 pendulous ovules; fruit subglobose to obovoid, beaked with the permanent style..

This tree, which is also called *Maua* by the natives, is to be found on all the islands of the group, with the exception of Oahu and Kauai. It differs mainly from its cogener in its leaves, which are not entire, but crenate. It is a much smaller tree in certain localities, only reaching a height of 10 to 15 feet, prefering the very dry lands on the leeward sides of Lanai, Molokai, Hawaii, and Maui. On the latter island on the southern slopes of Haleakala, and on Hawaii in the rain forest of Kau, it reaches its best development: there have been observed trees 40 feet in height with a trunk of over one foot in diameter. This *Maua* presents a very poor appearance on the west end of Molokai, where individual trees are still to be found on the slopes of Mahana valley. Windswept and stunted, it stands as a relic of by-gone days, the remnant of what was once a beautiful forest. Its associates, *Gardenia Brighami (Nau), Reynoldsia sandwicensis (Ohe), Kokia drynarioides (Kokio)*, and others, of which only a few are left, have experienced a similar fate, and in time not far hence will be things of the past. On Hawaii, it grows on the *aa* (rough) lava fields of Puuwaawaa and Huehue, North Kona, and Kawaihaeiuka (2000 feet), and at an elevation of 4000 feet on the slopes of Mauna Loa on the land of Keauhou near Kilauea volcano. Here the tree is larger and of similar size to the *Maua* of Kauai and Oahu. On Lanai it may be found on the dry ridges as well as on the flat land of Kaa, where a peculiar forest of an area of perhaps 30 acres has withstood the ravages of cattle and sheep, but, as on Molokai, is rapidly succumbing.

On Maui it grows above Makawao and on the southern slopes of the crater of Haleakala on the lava field of Auahi. district of Kahikinui, at a height of 2600 feet above sea level. Both *Mauas* blossom usually in midsummer, but no particular month can be stated, as the flowering period varies greatly according to locality and environment.

This species is closely related to the Tahitian *Xylosma suaveolens* Forst., while the other *Maua* approaches very closely *Xylosma orbiculatum* from the Viti, Marquesas, and Tongan islands.

This species is quite variable. Specimens from the west of Molokai are quite distinct from those of East Maui, above Makawao; from the latter place the racemes are the longest in any specimen of this species, being 25 to 30 mm long on the naked branch below the leaves, while in those from Molokai the racemes are very short and axillary only. In regard to the leaves, the crenation differs very much also, some having almost entire leaves.

THYMELAEACEAE.

The family Thymelaeaceae is a rather small one, consisting of 37 genera with about 455 species. With the exception of the Polar zones, the family is distributed over the whole globe, and ranges from Terra del Fuego to Canada,

315

in America, and in the old world from New Zealand to Norway. It is poorly represented in the tropical and temperate regions, but is very rich in species in the sub-tropical regions of Africa and Australia, and in the steppes of Asia. In the Hawaiian Islands the family is represented by the genus Wikstroemia, which has about eight species in this archipelago, all of which, with the exception perhaps of one, are endemic. Three species become trees. The others are small shrubs.

WIKSTROEMIA Endl.

Flowers hermaphrodite, tetramerous. Receptacle long cylindrical. Calyx lobes spreading, petals none. Stamens in two alternate rows, inserted in the upper portion of the receptacular tube, the upper near the top of the tube opposite the lobes. Hypogynous scales 4 to 2. Ovary sessile, glabrous or tomentose. Style very short, the large globose stigma therefore almost sessile. Fruit a drupe, or dry, and then enclosed by the receptacular base. Albumen scanty or none. Embryo with fleshy cotyledons.—Shrubs or trees with opposite or rarely alternate leaves. Flowers terminal in short racemes or spikes. Bracts none.

This genus, whose Hawaiian species are known to the natives by the name *Akia*, is composed of about 20 species, found in the Indo-Malayan region, China, Australia and the Hawaiian Islands; in the latter locality about eight species are endemic. All have a very tough bark and furnished one of the strongest Hawaiian fibers. The Hawaiian *Akia* or *Akea* contain an acrid narcotic and were used for stupefying fish.

KEY TO THE SPECIES.

Leaves ovate, small, 3.5 cm, glabrous.
  Spikes short, glabrous...   **W. oahuensis**
Leaves large. ovate-oblong. occasionally pubescent.
  Spikes tomentose, thick.
    Branches often drooping, spikes often 3 cm long..............   **W. sandwicensis**
    Branches stiff, erect, spikes 4 to 7.5 cm, many forked.........   **W. furcata**

Wikstroemia oahuensis (Gray) Rock.

Akia.

(Plate 124.)

WIKSTROEMIA OAHUENSIS (Gray) Rock.—**Wikstroemia foetida** var. **Oahuensis** Gray in Seem. Journ. Bot. III. (1865) 302;—Seem. Flora Vit. (1866) 207;—H. Mann in Proc. Am. Acad. VII. (1867) 199;—Wawra in Flora (1875) 175;—Hbd. Fl. Haw. Isl. (1888) 385.—**Wikstroemia indica** Del Cast. Ill. Fl. Ins. Mar. Pac. VII (1892) 280.—**Diplomorpha Oahuensis** Heller in Minnes. Bot. Stud. Bull. IX. (1897) 860.

Leaves ovate or ovate-lanceolate 2.5 to 5 cm long, 12 to 25 mm wide, on petioles of 2 to 4 mm, acute at the apex, rounded or slightly contracted at the base, glabrous, pale underneath, thin chartaceous; flowers 6 to 12 on pedicels of 1 mm, clustered at the head of a short terminal peduncle, the cluster at most elongating into a spikelet of 4 mm in length; perianth pale or greenish yellow, tubular, puberulous, about 7 mm long, including the spreading lobes, which are somewhat obtuse, and perhaps half, often less, the length of the tube; lower stamens at the middle of the tube or somewhat higher; hypogynous scales 4 to 5, linear, connate at the base, as long as the ovary, which is glabrous except the apex which is often, but not always, strigose-pubescent, style very short, with capitate stigma; drupe ovoid, 6 to 8 mm, reddish yellow.

This species of *Akia* is usually a shrub 2 to 4 feet high, but on the upper slopes of Mt. Konahuanui it is a small tree 12 to 15 feet in height, where it

Thymelaeaceae.

grows in company with *Cheirodendron platyphyllum, Lobelia macrostachys, Pittosporum spathulatum*, several species of Pelea, *Scaevola glabra* and others. On the low lands on the outskirts of the forest on open glades, as in Niu Valley, it is only 2 feet or so in height. The trunk and branches are clothed in a black, very tough, fibrous bark, which, owing to its strength, was employed by the natives for ropes and other purposes where strong fiber was needed; it almost equals the *Olona* in strength. The plant is poisonous and was employed by the natives, similarly to the *Auhola* or *Auhulu* (*Tephrosia piscatoria*) for fishing. The plant was pounded to pulp and thrown into the water, which stupefied the fishes in the immediate neighborhood, which floated to the surface of the water. This mode of fishing has been forbidden of late.

Wikstroemia sandwicensis Meisn.

Akia.

WIKSTROEMIA SANDWICENSIS Meisner in DC. Prodr. XIV. (1856) 545;— Gray in Seem. Jour. Bot. III. (1865) 303;—Seem. Fl. Vit. (1866) 206;—Mann Proc. Am. Acad. VII. (1867) 199;—Hbd. Fl. Haw. Isl. (1888) 386;—Del Cast. Ill. Fl. Ins. Mar. Pac. VII. (1892) 280;—Gilg. in Engl. et Prantl Pflzfam. III. 6a. (1894) 235.— W. foetida var. glauca Wawra in Flora (1875) 176—Diplomorpha sandwicensis Heller in Minnes. Bot. Stud. Bull. IX. (1897) 861.

Leaves dark green, glabrous, or slightly pubescent underneath, especially along the midrib and veins, chartaceous and faintly nerved, ovate or ovate oblong to lanceolate, 5-10 cm long, 2.5-4 cm wide, on petioles of 6-8 mm which are often pubescent, acute at both ends or often rounded at the base; adult spikes 4-30 mm long on peduncles of 2-6 mm, suberect or drooping, usually terminal, densely flowered near the apex, the rachys thick squarrose and tomentose, sometimes dichotomously forking; perianth on a short pedicel of 1 mm, silky tomentose 5-6 mm long, the lobes somewhat obtuse; scales 4 linear, free, as long as the ovary, drupe ovoid 8-10 mm, usually only two maturing at the apex of the spike.

To this species will have to be referred Léveillé's *Wikstroemia Fauriei*, which is based mainly on the pubescent leaves.

The writer has large material of this species (*W. sandwicensis*) with perfectly glabrous leaves, and again specimens with leaves which are pubescent underneath. Pubescence in Hawaiian plants is not at all a characteristic to be relied upon, which anyone who has collected in these islands can readily verify. If one should make new species of a plant based on such characteristics there would be no end and the number of Hawaiian plants would reach several thousand.

This species occurs mainly on Hawaii on the lava fields and on the great central plain on the outskirts of the forest and in the *Koa* forest at an elevation of 5000 feet, where it is a small tree 15 feet high. At this elevation it is much branching and the branches are drooping and sparingly foliose. Like all other Hawaiian *Akia*, the bark is very tough and blackish. It fruits prolifically during the winter months. Hillebrand records it from Hilo, where Faurie's specimens were collected also.

PLATE 125.

JAMBOSA MALACCENSIS (Linn.) P. DC.
Ohia Ai or **Ohia,** Mountain Apple.
Flowering branch, about one-half natural size.

Thymelaeaceae-Myrtaceae.

Wikstroemia furcata (Hbd.) Rock.

Akia.

WIKSTROEMIA FURCATA (Hbd.) Rock.—**Wikstroemia sandwicensis** Meisn. var. **furcata** Hbd. Flora Haw. Isl. (1888) 386;—Del Cast. Ill. Fl. Ins. Mar. Pac. VII. (1892) 280.

Leaves 6 to 14 cm long, 2 to 5 cm wide, dark green above, pale underneath, glabrous on both sides, shortly contracted at the base, acute or rounded or subcordate, acute or obtuse at the apex, on petioles of 4 to 8 mm, chartaceous; spikes 5 to 7.5 cm long repeatedly forking 3 to 5 times, yellowish pubescent, many flowered, the perianth silky tomentose on a pedicel of 2 mm, tube of perianth yellowish, about 4 mm, the spreading lobes acute, about one third the length of the tube, apex of ovary silky pubescent, as well as the short style and thick stigma; drupes much larger than in *W. sandwicensis*, 15 mm long, ovoid, bright red; seed ovoid to acute, testa thin, black, and shining.

Found on Kauai, especially in the swampy jungles back of Kaholuamano and Halemanu at an elevation of 4000 feet. It certainly is a very striking plant, especially during the month of October, when the small trees are loaded with the rather large, bright red fruits. The branches are erect and not drooping, and rather stout.

It differs from *W. sandwicensis* in the long and many-forked spike, the large leaves, and the large bright red drupes. The native name, like that of all other species, is *Akia.*

MYRTACEAE.

The family Myrtaceae consists of 72 genera with about 2750 species, which belong to two main evolutional centers, one in tropical America, the other on the Australian continent. It is less numerous in species in Polynesia, tropical Asia, Africa and subtropical America. In the Mediterranean region only one species occurs, the ordinary Myrtle. The family cannot adapt itself to cold climates; only a few species of Eucalypti occur in such regions in Tasmania as are covered with snow for several months in the year.

In the Hawaiian Islands four genera are represented, three of which possess one species each, while the genus Metrosideros has several species, of which one occurs from sea-level to 9000 feet elevation in the most varied forms.

Of early introduction are the various Guayava species (Guava) and of late the genus Eucalyptus, with about 60 to 70 species.

KEY TO THE GENERA.

Fruit a berry.
    Petals falling off single; staminal discus distinct.................... **Jambosa**
    Petals cohering, falling off together; staminal discus not distinct....... **Syzygium**
Fruit a capsule.. **Metrosideros**

JAMBOSA DC.

Receptacle obconical, funnel-shaped, cup-shaped or cylindrical, gradually tapering into the peduncle, and prolonged over the ovary; dilated discus-like at the insertion of the stamens. Calyx lobes comparatively large, usually semicircular. Flowers single or in terminal or lateral cymes or corymbs.

319

PLATE 126.

SYZYGIUM SANDWICENSE (Gray) Ndz.
Ohia Ha or Paihi.
Flowering and fruiting branch, about one-half natural size.

Myrtaceae.

The genus Jambosa consists of about 120 species, which are distributed over the Indo-Malayan, but especially Malagassic, regions; also over north-eastern Australia and Polynesia.

In the Hawaiian Islands the genus is represented by one cosmopolitan species.

Jambosa malaccensis (Linn.) P.DC.
Ohia ai, Mountain Apple.
(Plate 125.)

JAMBOSA MALACCENSIS (Linn.) P. DC. Prodr. III. (1828) 286;—Hook. et Arn. Bot. Beech. (1832) 83;—Endl. Flora Suds. in Ann. Wien. Mus. (1836) 181, n. 1466;—Guillem. Zeph. Tait. (1836-1837) no. 298;—Pancher in Cuz. Tahiti, (1860) 232;—Jardin Hist. Nat. Iles Marqu. (1858) 24;—Nadeaud Enum. Tah. Pl. (1873) 488;—Niedenzu in Engl. et Prantl Pflzfam. III. 7. (1893) 84;—Wilder Fruits Haw. Isl. (1911) 20. pl. 8.—**Eugenia malaccensis** Linn. Spec. Pl. ed. I. (1753) 470;—Forst. Prodr. (1786) no. 220;—Gray Bot. U. S. E. E. (1854) 510;—Seem. Fl. Vit. (1866) 77;—Mann Proc. Am. Acad. VII. (1867) 166, et Fl. Haw. Isl. Proc. Ess. Inst. V. (1867) 245;—Mrs. Sinclair Ind. Flow. Haw. Isl. (1885) pl. 41;—Hbd. Fl. Haw. Isl. (1888) 128;—Del Cast. Ill. Fl. Ins. Mar. Pac. VI. (1890) 169, et Fl. Polyn. Franc. (1893) 67;—Heller in Minnes. Bot. Stud. Bull. IX. (1897) 862;—Brigham Ka Hana Kapa Mem. B. P. Bish. Mus. III. (1911) 156, fig. 93.—**Jambosa domestica** Rumph. Herb. Amb. I. (1741) 127. t. 37;—Blume Mus. Bot. (1849) 91.—**J. pur- purascens** DC. l. c.

Leaves opposite, elliptical or obovate-oblong, 15 to 20 cm long, 5 to 7.5 cm wide, on petioles of 12 mm, suddenly acuminate, dark green and shining, not dotted, the sinuate marginal nerve distant from the edge; cymes axillary, usually cauline, short, about 5 cm long, their lowest branches 8 to 12 mm long and 3 flowered, the middle and terminal branch racemose; pedicels short, gradually enlarging into the calyx; calyx turbinate, produced beyond the ovary, with 4 rounded lobes; petals obovate, red, reddish-purple or white, 6 mm; the red or white stamens 18 mm long; fruit obovate, about 7.5 cm in diameter, umbilicate at the top and crowned by the truncate scar of the calyx-lobes, deep crimson, pale pinkish, or white; seed generally one.

Occasionally a tree of 60 feet in height. It is the mountain apple of the white man and the *Ohia ai* or edible *Ohia* of the native Hawaiian. So much has been written about this cosmopolitan species that only a brief account of it will be given in the following lines.

The *Ohia ai* was undoubtedly brought to Hawaii by the natives long before the arrival of the first white man, and was the only Hawaiian fruit before the coming of the latter. It is widely distributed over the islands of the Pacific, where it is known by various names. It favors the windward sides of the islands in the valleys and gorges, where it forms almost pure stands, along streambeds. It is restricted to the lowlands and never ascends into the mountains.

It flowers and fruits at various times of the year according to locality. In one district the trees can be seen in flower while in another the trees are loaded with the bright red watery apples.

The *Ohia ai* played an important role in the legends of Hawaii and Polynesia as a whole, and was regarded as sacred, and from its wood many idols were carved.

The white variety is known in Hawaii as *Ohia ai hua keokeo*, and in Fiji as

PLATE 127.

METROSIDEROS POLYMORPHA Gaud.
Ohia Lehua.
High mountain form from Mt. Haleakala, Maui; belongs to section II. var. η reduced.

Myrtaceae.

Kavika vulavula, while the red is called *Kavika damudamu* by the Fijians. In Samoa the tree is called *nonufi afi'a* or *nomula* for the red variety, while the white variety is known as *nonuui.* The bark of the trees is used as an astringent, while the flowers and leaves are used for lung troubles.

The trunks of the trees were hewn into posts and rafters for houses, also used in making the enclosures about temples. From it were also made the sticks to couple together the double canoes.

SYZYGIUM Gaertn.

Staminal discus wanting. Sepals usually short and broad or entirely missing. Petals usually united and falling off together at the opening of the flowers.—Otherwise as in Jambosa.

The genus Syzygium consists of more than 140 species, of which only two or three are found in tropical Africa. The majority of the species of this genus occur in the East Indian-Malayan archipelago or region, while four are found in Australia, of which two are endemic. The Hawaiian Islands possess a single endemic species which is known by the natives as *Ohia ha* or *Paihi.*

Syzygium sandwicense (Gray) Ndz.
Ohia ha or *Paihi* on Maui.
(Plate 126.)

SYZYGIUM SANDWICENSE (Gray) Ndz. in Engl. et Prantl Pflzfam. III. 7. (1893) 85.—
Eugenia sandwicensis Gray Bot. U. S. E. E. (1854) 519;—Mann Proc. Am. Acad.
VII. (1867) 166, et Fl. Haw. Isl. (1867) 246;—Wawra in Flora (1873) 171;—
Hbd. Fl. Haw. Isl. (1888) 129.—Del Cast. Ill. Fl. Ins. Mar. Pac. VI. (1890) 170;—
Heller in Minnes. Bot. Stud. Bull. IX. (1897) 862.

Sometimes a tree of 20 m; branches angular, sharply margined; leaves obovate or obovate-oblong, rounded and usually emarginate at the apex, glabrous, dark green or yellowish brown with red veins, subcoriaceous, 4-10 cm long, 3-5 cm wide, on petioles of about 12 mm, the marginal nerve continuous; cymes single or compound in the axils of the upper leaves, the common peduncle angular and elongate, 2.5-3.5 cm, the pedicels only about 3 mm, articulate and bibracteolate below the calyx; bractlets small triangular; calyx turbinate, 3-4 mm long, 4-lobed, imbricate, early deciduous; petals obovate, often emarginate, pinkish, about 2 mm, generally discreet, but sometimes united and falling off together; stamens 20-30, shorter than the petals; style short; ovary 2-celled, with 10 or more ovules in each cell; berry turbinate or globose, flat at the top, 8-10 mm in diameter, red; seeds 1 or 2, with a pale thin testa, the thick cotyledons not consolidated.

The *Ohia ha,* or *Paihi* as it is called on Maui, occurs on all the islands of the group and becomes often a tree 60 feet or more in height, with a diameter of trunk of one to one and a half feet.

The bark is reddish brown and smooth and it can therefore be distinguished easily from the *Ohia lehua* (Metrosideros), which has rough scaly bark. The wood of the *Ohia ha* is hard and durable and is of a reddish color. It inhabits the forests of lower elevations, but can often be found also up to 4000 feet, as, for example, on Kauai in the forests of Kaholuamano and Halemanu. It reaches its best development in the dense rain forest, while on open, exposed ridges it becomes stunted and is inclined to be shrubby. During the late summer

323

PLATE 128.

METROSIDEROS POLYMORPHA Gaud.
Ohia Lehua.
From near Kilauea Volcano, Hawaii; belongs to section III. var. ι; reduced.

Myrtaceae.

months the trees are often loaded with the bright red berries, which are edible, though somewhat insipid. The inflorescence is often monstrously deformed, similarly to that of the *Kalia* tree (*Elaeocarpus bifidus*), the work of a species of Acari.

The wood was used as fuel and also in house-making, while the bark was employed in staining tapa a black color.

METROSIDEROS Banks.

Flowers perigynous. Receptaculum funnel-shaped or campanulate. Calyx-lobes deltoid or obtuse, 5. Petals 5, rounded. Stamens numerous, usually in a row; filaments free, long; anthers elongate, dorsifixed, versatile. Ovary united at the base with the receptaculum, 3-celled. Style very long; stigma simple. Seeds many, covering the whole placenta, only partially fertile; testa thin; embryo straight; cotyledons flat or folded, longer than the radicle.—Trees or shrubs, rarely climbers (in New Zealand). Leaves opposite. Flowers in terminal or axillary cymes.

The genus Metrosideros consists of over 20 species, of which only one occurs in the Cape Colony, one in the Sunda Islands, and the remainder are distributed over Australia and Polynesia. The Hawaiian Islands possess five species, of which one is cosmopolitan (*M. polymorpha*) and occurs here in numerous varieties, while the others are peculiar to the Hawaiian Islands.

This genus furnishes the bulk of the Hawaiian forests; next in number is the *Acacia Koa*.

For the numerous varieties of the *Ohia lehua* the natives of the olden days had many names, as, for example, *Lehua mamo*, an orange yellow flowering *Metrosideros polymorpha*; *Lehua kumakua*, with sessile cordate leaves; *Lehua laulii*, with very small leaves; *Lehua puakea*, with white flowers, and others.

KEY TO THE SPECIES.

Leaves on short petioles.
    Leaves suborbicular, cordate ovate or oblong; capsule almost free.... **M. polymorpha**
    Leaves linear or elliptical, acute at both ends.................. **M. tremuloides**
    Leaves rugose and impressed above; capsule adnate to near the apex **M. rugosa**
Leaves on long petioles of 2 to 5 cm.
    Leaves ovate to ovate-oblong; capsule hidden in the calyx tube..... **M. macropus**
    Leaves acuminate-caudate, capsule projecting beyond the calyx-tube **M. tremuloides** var. **Waialealae**

Metrosideros polymorpha Gaud.

Ohia lehua or *Lehua.*

(Plates 127, 128, 129, 130, 131, 132.)

METROSIDEROS POLYMORPHA Gaud. Bot. Voy. Uranie (1826-1830) 482. pl. 108 et 109;—DC. Prodr. III. (1828) 225;—H. et A. Bot. Beech. Voy. (1832) 82;—Endl. Fl. Suds. (1836) 181. no. 1452;—A. Gray Bot. U. S. E. E. (1854) 562;—Seem. Fl. Vit. (1866) 80;—Mann in Proc. Am. Acad. VII. (1867) 166, et Fl. Haw. Isl. Proc. Ess. Inst. V. (1867) 243;—Wawra in Flora (1873) 171;—Mrs. Sinclair Indig. Flow. Haw. Isl. (1885) pl. 2;—Hbd. Fl. Haw. Isl. (1888) 125.—Metrosideros collina Gray Bot. U. S. E. E. (1854) 558. pl. 68;—Nadeaud Enum. Tahit. Pl. (1873) no. 484;—Del Cast. Ill. Fl. Ins. Mar. Pac. VI. (1890) 167, et Fl. Polyn. Franc. (1893) 64;—Ndz. in Engl. et Prantl III. 7. (1893) 87.— M. lutea Gray Bot. U. S. E. E. (1854) 560 pl. 69. B.—M. villosa Smith in Trans.

PLATE 129.

TRUNK OF METROSIDEROS POLYMORPHA Gaud., showing scaly bark and young branches growing from the base of the trunk. In the forests of Kaholuamano, Kauai; elevation 4000 feet.

Myrtaceae.

Linn. Soc. III. (1797) 268.—**M. spectabilis** Gaertn. Fruct. I. (1788) 172, pl. 34. fig. 9;—Sol. Prim. Fl. Ins. Pacif. 263 (ined.) et in Parkins. Draw. Tah. Pl. t. 54.— **M. diffusa** Hook. et Arn. Bot. Beech. (1832) 63, (non Smith).—**M. obovata** Hook. et Arn. Bot. Beech. (1832) 63. pl. 12.—**Melaleuca villosa** Linn. fig. m-p.—**Nania collina** O. K. Rev. Gen. Pl. I. (1891) 242.—**Nania pumila** Heller in Minn. Bot. Stud. Bull. IX. (1897)864.—**Nania glabrifolia** Heller l. c. 866.— **Nania lutea** Heller l. c. 867.—× **Nania Fauriei** Levl. in Fedde Repert. X. 10/14 (1911) 150.—× **Nania Feddei** Levl. l. c. 150.—**N. polymorpha** var. **nummularifolia** Levl. Repert. X. 10/14 (1911) 149.

Branches angular or terete, tomentose or glabrate; bracts of leafbuds short, scarlet, early deciduous; leaves opposite on short or long petioles, lanceolate, oblong, ovate. obovate or orbicular, at the base acute, rounded or cordate, glabrous or tomentose underneath, with faint nerves; flowers in terminal cymose corymbs, pedicellate or subsessile, 3 on a branchlet or peduncle, red, salmon, pink, or yellow, bractlets 3 mm caducous; calyx turbinate, 3 to 5 mm, glabrose or tomentose, with deltoid or rounded lobes; petals 3 to 6 mm, oblong or obovate; capsule semi-adnate, at last almost free, 3-lobed, 3-valved, glabrous or tomentose; seeds linear fusiform.

The numerous varieties of *Metrosideros polymorpha* may be arranged into three sections as follows:

Sect. I. Glabrae.
Leaves glabrous on both sides, calyx also glabrous.
Sect. II. Hemilanatae.
Leaves glabrous on both sides, calyx silvery or whitish tomentose or woolly.
Sect. III. Tomentosae.
Leaves whitish or grayish tomentose, calyx tomentose or woolly.

Sect. I. Glabrae.

α Small plants usually only found at the summit swamps as on Mt. Puukukui, and Mauna Eke on Maui, (no. 8145).

Leaves small cordate, suborbicular, glabrous on both faces, strongly but finely reticulated; calyx glabrous or here and there with a small patch of minute silky pubescence; petals and stamens red, the former slightly ciliate at the margins.

β Trees on the main range of Oahu, at an elevation of 1000-2000 feet. Niu Valley, (no. 4829), Pauoa Valley (no. 1010), Manoa Valley.

Leaves small ovate-elliptical, acute or rounded at the apex, tapering at the base into a somewhat margined petiole; calyx perfectly glabrous, the lobes triangular acute, branchlets red; resembles *M. tremuloides*. Inflorescence occasionally but sparingly sprinkled with a silky pubescence.

γ Large trees, probably the typical *M. polymorpha* on the main range, Koolau Mts. (no. 1279), Oahu; also from Kauai.

Leaves elliptical to ovate-oblong, larger, glabrous on both faces bluntly acute, dark green, with a straight marginal nerve, shortly petioled; calyx and corolla glabrous or very finely pubescent, of a silky white.

Sect. II. Hemilanatae.

δ Trees or shrubs. Kamoku forest, Molokai, (no. 6181).

Leaves ovate to ovate-oblong, obtuse at both ends, rather large, long petiolate, glabrous on both faces with indistinct marginal nerve; calyx and pedicels densely white tomentose, the rounded sepals green and glabrous, petals red and margins not ciliate.

ε Creepers in swampy open places, or bogs, on Molokai, Kawela, (no. 5087 and 6097), resembles var. *α* sect. I. glabrae.

327

PLATE 130.

METROSIDEROS POLYMORPHA Gaud.
Ohia Lehua Tree.
Showing large bunch of aerial roots common to this species. Growing on lava
fields, Hawaii.

PLATE 131.

STILT-ROOTS OF METROSIDEROS POLYMORPHA Gaud. **Ohia Lehua.** Note the remnants of tree-fern trunk in the upper portion of tree trunk. For explanation see text. Forests near Glenwood, Hawaii; elevation 3500 feet. The tree to the left is **Straussia** sp.

PLATE 132.

GROVE OF METROSIDEROS POLYMORPHA Gaud., **Ohia Lehua;** near the Volcano of Kilauea, Hawaii, elevation 4000 feet. Some of the trees are nearly 100 feet high.

Leaves small, suborbicular, cordate, subsessile, pale green or yellowish, glabrous on both faces; inflorescence and calyx densely tomentose or white woolly, the lobes green, pubescent, with ciliate margins, red-punctate on the outer face, petals glabrous; leaves often slightly pubescent when young.

ζ   Large trees found on Kauai, above Waimea, (no. 2044).

Leaves large, ovate oblong, shortly petiolate, the petioles and part of leaf-midrib pubescent, thick coriaceous, subcordate at the base; young branches and inflorescence covered with a white pubescence; calyx, sepals and petals white tomentose or woolly, the latter showing the red through the white pubescence, the margins white ciliate.

η   Trees, at high elevation 6000-7000 feet. Mt. Haleakala, Maui, (no. 8593).

Branches stout, stiff and gnarled, scaly; leaves small, thick coriaceous, suborbicular, cordate, sessile, or auriculate at the base; inflorescence densely and thickly white woolly, as are the pedicels and calyx lobes, petals red, glabrous, the margins only white ciliate.

θ   Trees, main ridge of Mahana, Lanai, (no. 8055).

Leaves ovate, or suborbicular, cordate at the base, thin, subcoriaceous, entirely glabrous on both faces, very shortly petiolate; calyx slightly or thinly pubescent, of a dark silvery or dirty gray color, sepals green and puberulous or glabrous; petals and stamens yellowish, or salmon pink, the former glabrous with slightly ciliate margins; here also belongs a form with longer petiolate leaves, which are suborbicular and cordate, pale green; calyx and sepals densely white woolly, petals large, yellow, glabrous, with ciliate margins; the petioles pubescent.

Sect. III. Tomentosae.

ι   Trees at 4000-9000 feet elevation Kilauea, Hawaii, also Oahu, Pauoa Valley (no. 722); Hualalai, Hawaii (no. 3626).

Leaves large orbicular, cordate at the base, coriaceous, glabrous above, or finely pubescent, tomentose underneath of a dirty gray color, petioles short, tomentose, inflorescence and calyx pubescent; often yellow flowered.

κ   Creepers from the summit swamp of Kohala, Hawaii, (no. 8414).

Leaves small, orbicular, emarginate at the apex, cordate at the base, sessile, glabrous above, densely covered underneath with a yellow strigose pubescence; inflorescence, calyx and sepals with yellowish strigose hairs, petals red, slightly pubescent, margins ciliate.

The *Ohia lehua* is the most prevalent tree in the forests of the islands of the Hawaiian archipelago.   It can be found from sea-level to an elevation of 9000 feet.   It certainly deserves its specific name *polymorpha* as it is the most variable tree which the Islands possess.   On the summits of Kohala, Hawaii, Mt. Waialeale on Kauai, and Puukukui, West Maui, which have an elevation ranging from 5000-5600 feet, it is a creeper, only a few inches in length, though flowering.   It grows in company with native violets, geraniums and sundews (*Drosera longifolia*) while in the middle forest zone it becomes a giant of often 100 feet in height, with a trunk of several feet in diameter.   At the seashore, as for example at Napoopoo, Hawaii, it is a stunted gnarled tree 10-15 feet in height growing on ancient *pahoehoe* lava in company with *Reynoldsia sandwicensis*, the *Ohe kukuluaeo* of the natives, and other trees.   On the windward side of Hawaii, not far from Hilo, it covers the vertical cliffs down to the water's edge, but does not attain any size.   Its best development and the largest forests composed of this tree are found on the volcanic slopes of Mauna Loa and Mauna

PLATE 133.

METROSIDEROS TREMULOIDES (Heller) Rock.
Lehua Ahihi.
Flowering branch, one-half natural size.

Kea, on the island of Hawaii, and it is there that the trees reach their biggest size.

On Hawaii the *Ohia lehua* is usually associated with the tree ferns, the *Hapu* and *Hapu Iii* (which see). In such forests, the seeds of the *Ohia* trees fall on the moist woolly trunks of the tree ferns; there they germinate. At first the young tree finds enough nourishment in the humus, dead leaves, etc., which collect in the axils of dead fern leaves all along the tall fern trunks, but finally it sends its roots down along the fern trunks into the ground. As the tree grows larger and taller, the fern becomes enclosed between the stilt-like roots of the *Ohia* tree, until finally the fern dies and decays, leaving the stilt roots standing some 15-20 feet above the ground, after which the real trunk of the tree commences. Such stilt-like *Ohia* trees are very common in the Hawaiian forest, but mainly on Hawaii. The accompanying illustration shows an *Ohia* tree with stilt-roots between which remnants of a decayed tree-fern trunk are still visible.

The wood of the *Ohia lehua* is of a dark reddish color, durable, hard and equal in strength to the Oak. It was employed by the natives for the carving of their idols, spears, mallets, etc., but is used now for paving-blocks, flooring, and interior house finishings. Mills have been erected on Hawaii at Pahoa where lumber is turned out at a profit. Several railroads, especially the Santa Fé railroad of the mainland, have ordered large shipments of *Ohia* ties.

The flowers of the *Ohia lehua* are of a bright red, pale yellow to orange yellow and pink-salmon, while some are even white. They are the source of food for some of the native birds, as the *Iiwi* and *Olokele*, both of which possess a bright red plumage, matching the scarlet *Lehua* blossom while flitting from flower to flower for their honey.

The name *Lehua* is an interesting one. *Lehua* in everyday language means "hair." It was undoubtedly applied to the tree in question on account of the numerous long red stamens resembling fine hair, which makes the *Ohia lehua* flower attractive.

The tree in its various forms is not peculiar to Hawaii, but is well distributed over Polynesia and New Zealand, where the tree is known as *Rata* and *Pohutukawa*. It has the most numerous varieties, however, in the Hawaiian Islands. A number of species have been described from other islands of the Pacific, which later turned out to be identical with the *Ohia lehua*.

Metrosideros tremuloides (Heller) Rock.

Lehua ahihi.

(Plate 133.)

METROSIDEROS TREMULOIDES (Heller) Rock comb. nov.—**Nania tremuloides** Heller in Minnes. Bot. Stud. Bull. IX. (1897) 866.—**Metrosideros polymorpha** Gaud. var. η Hbd. Flora Haw. Isl. (1888) 127.

A small tree, with slender trunk and smooth grayish bark, glabrous throughout, even the inflorescence; branches slender, loosely spreading; leaves narrowly lanceolate, acute or acuminate at both ends, bright green, shining above, paler underneath, coriaceous, on

333

PLATE 134.

METROSIDEROS RUGOSA A. Gray.
Lehua papa.
Two-thirds natural size.

Myrtaceae.

flat slightly winged petioles of about 6 mm in length, not prominently veined, but midrib conspicuous; cyme branches divaricate, peduncles slender of varying length though hardly longer than 10 mm; pedicels half the length; calyx campanulate, the lobes rounded and equaling the tube in length, margins scarious; petals, bright red, almost orbicular twice the length of the calyx lobes, stamens bright red, barely 2 cm in length, capsule half free.

The *Lehua ahihi* is one of the handsomest species of the genus Metrosideros. The fine bright green graceful foliage stands quite distinct from all the other species and varieties and certainly deserves specific rank. It can be found on Oahu at the lower elevation around Tantalus back of Honolulu, and in nearly all the neighboring valleys on their upper slopes at about 1000-2000 feet elevation. When in full flower the slender branches are drooping and almost continually in motion, whence its specific name.

Var. **Waialealae** Rock. var. nov.

Leaves larger, bright green above pale underneath, with bright red midrib and leaf-margin, 5 to 7 cm long, 2 to 2.5 cm wide, coriaceous, acute at the base, acuminate-caudate at the apex, the apex curved, the bright red petiole 15 to 20 mm long, flat and somewhat margined; flowers as in the species; fruits very large, the same size as in **M. macropus,** the calyx-lobes persistent but the capsule projecting almost its whole height beyond the calyx, almost free; seeds linear, lunulate, pointed at each end.

This variety is peculiar to the summit ridge of Mt. Waialeale on Kauai, where it was observed and collected by the writer. It certainly is the most beautiful Metrosideros or *Ohia lehua* known to him. It only grows at a certain ridge at the summit of the mountain of Kauai where it forms pure stands with hardly any other tree around it. It is a small tree 25 feet high. Collected flowering and fruiting Sept. 24, 1909, Mt. Waialeale, Kauai, elev. 5200 feet, type no. 5083, in College of Hawaii Herbarium.

Metrosideros rugosa Gray.
Lehua papa.
(Plate 134.)

METROSIDEROS RUGOSA Gray Bot. U. S. E. E. (1853) 561. t. 69 B.;—Mann in Proc. Am. Acad. VII. (1867) 166, et Haw. Isl. (1867) 244:—Wawra in Flora (1873) 173;—Hbd. Fl. Haw. Isl. (1888) 127;—Niedz. in Engl. et Prantl Pflzfam. III. 7. (1893) 87.—**Metrosideros polymorpha** Del Cast. Ill. Fl. Ins. Mar. Pac. VI. (1890) 167 (ex parte).—**Nania rugosa** Kuntze Rev. Gen. Pl. (1891) 242;—Heller in Minnes. Bot. Stud. Bull. IX. (1897) 864.

A small tree or shrub, with quadrangular branchlets, only the ultimate ones tomentose; leaves orbicular, about 2.5 cm in diameter, thick and coriaceous, strikingly rugose above and deeply impressed along the veins, which are remarkably strong and ridged underneath, the under-surface thickly tomentose with a ferruginous wool as are the leaf-buds on both faces, the petiole scarcely 2 mm; cymes small, solitary or in pairs at the summit of the branches, the peduncles and their divisions short and stout, thick tomentose, the whole subtended by rather conspicuous and coriaceous bud-scales; bractlets as long as the calyx, oval tomentose, soon deciduous; flowers subsessile, about as large as in the common species; calyx tomentose; petals and stamens red, the former pubescent; ovary deeply immersed in the tube of the calyx, its summit only free.

This species, which is called *Lehua papa* by the natives, is peculiar to the Island of Oahu, where it can be found at the summits of the ridges of the main range, and on the vertical cliffs or *pali* on the windward side of the island. It certainly is quite distinct from the ordinary *Ohia lehua* and can be distinguished from it at a glance by the deeply rugose small leaves. It is never a large tree, but only of about 10-15 feet in height or more often a shrub. Flowering, Koolau Mts. Punaluu, Nov. 14-21, 1908. no. 294, College of Hawaii Herbarium.

Metrosideros macropus Hook. et Arn.

Ohia lehua.

METROSIDEROS MACROPUS Hook. et Arn. Bot. Beech. (1832) 83;—Endl. Fl. Suds. in Ann. Wien. Mus. (1836) 181, no. 1453;—Gray Bot. U S. E. E. (1854) 564. t. 70;—Mann in Proc. Am. Acad. VII. (1867) 166, et Fl. Haw. Isl. (1867) 244;—Wawra in Flora (1873) 172;—Hbd. Fl. Haw. Isl. (1888) 127;—Del Cast. Ill. Fl. Ins. Mar. Pac. VI. (1890) 168;—Ndz. in Engl. et Prantl Pflzfam. III 7. (1893) 87.—Nania macropus O. Kuntze Rev. Gen. Pl. (1891) 242;—Heller in Minnes. Bot. Stud. Bull. IX. (1897) 865.

A well proportioned tree glabrous throughout; the branchlets angled; leaves ovate or ovate-oblong, coriaceous rather dull, acute at the base, copiously feather-veined; petioles 2.5 to 5 cm long usually margined, and standing nearly at right angles to the stem; cymes terminal usually geminate, subsessile, many-flowered, crowded, evolved from a large scaly bud, the scales of which remain persistent for some time as ovate or oblong pointed bracts, 12 mm in length; pedicels about 4 mm long, subtended by similar smaller ovate lanceolate bractlets which are deciduous; flowers larger than in the largest flowered forms of *M. polymorpha*; petals and stamens red or yellow, ovary three-celled, free nearly to the middle; capsule nearly included in the turbinate tube of the calyx, of which the lobes are persistent, free to the middle, three-valved, many seeded; seeds fusiform, subulate, not much pointed.

This species is peculiar to the Hawaiian Islands and differs from the cosmopolitan *M. polymorpha* in the long petioled leaves, large floral scales, and much larger flowers. It is a tree of considerable size and can be found in the mountains of Oahu on the main Koolau range, as well as on Molokai and on Kauai.

Hybrids of this and the cosmopolitan species can be met with wherever they occur together.

ARALIACEAE.

The family Araliaceae, which is chiefly tropical, consists of 51 genera and numerous species. In Polynesia it is represented by the genera Plerandra, Reynoldsia, Meryta, and others; while in Hawaii, the most northern islands of Polynesia, it has two endemic genera, Pterotropia and Cheirodendron, besides several species of Tetraplasandra, which now includes also Triplasandra, which genus has been merged into the former by Harms. The genus Tetraplasandra is not peculiar to the islands, as it has two species which occur outside of Hawaii, one in New Guinea and the other in Celebes. Reynoldsia, which is represented in Hawaii by one species, has also one species in the Society Islands and one in Samoa.

Araliaceae.

KEY TO THE GENERA.

Leaves pinnate, alternate.
  Leaflets entire:
    Leaflets 13-21, flowers racemose umbellate, arranged in a long drooping
      panicle . . .. **Pterotropia**
    Leaflets 5-13, inflor. racemose-umbellate or umbellate and panicu-
      late . . .. **Tetraplasandra**
  Leaflets sinuate crenate... **Reynoldsia**
Leaves digitate, opposite... **Cheirodendron**

TETRAPLASANDRA A. Gray.
(Triplasandra Seem.)

Calyx border undulate or denticulate, petals 5 to 8, valvate in the bud. Stamens as many as petals or 2 to 3 times or even 6 times as many, arranged in 1 or 4 series, with rather thick filaments and ovate or lanceolate anthers. Ovary quite inferior, ovate, 13-7-5-2 celled. The stigmas on a short stylopod or subsessile; drupes globose to ovate-elongate or cylindrical, with a somewhat fleshy covering. Pyrenae chartaceous, crustaceous or coriaceous, compressed. Seeds often ribbed or furrowed. Unarmed glabrous or tomentose trees or shrubs with a glutinous sap. Leaves large, alternate impari-pinnate, with 5 to 13 entire leaflets; petiolule of the terminal leaflet usually articulate. Stipules wanting or rudimentary. Inflorescence a racemose umbellate panicle or a simple or compound umbel; bracts caducous, small or larger; peduncles not articulate, often very thick.

The genus Tetraplasandra derives its name from the Greek τετραπλασιος (tetraplasios), fourfold, and ανδρα (andra), stamens, having four times as many stamens as petals. It consists of possibly 12 species, two of which are not found in the Hawaiian Islands; *T. paucidens* Miq. occurs in New Guinea, while *T. Koerdersii* Harms is found in Celebes. Of Hawaiian species, only two were described originally, *T. hawaiiensis* A. Gray and *T. Waimeae* Wawra. All the species of Triplasandra (established by Seeman) have been merged into Tetraplasandra by H. Harms. The writer has since added two new species: *T. Lanaiensis* and *T. Waialealae*.

KEY TO THE SPECIES.

I. **EUTETRAPLASANDRA.** Stamens 2-6-8 times as many as petals.
  Leaves tomentose underneath.
    Inflorescence paniculate.
      Stamens 4 times as many as petals.............. **T. Hawaiiensis**
  Leaves glabrous underneath.
    Inflorescence umbellate.
      Stamens numerous, 6-8 times as many as petals... **T. Waimeae**
    Inflorescence compound umbellate.
      Stamens 4 times as many as petals; ovary 6 celled.. **T. Waialealae**
      Stamens twice as many as petals; ovary 3 celled... **T. Lanaiensis**
      Stamens 2-3 times as many as petals.
        Drupe ovoid with conical vertex............. **T. Lydgatei**
        Drupe cylindrical truncate.
          Stamens 10-15; ovary 5-6 celled......... **T. Oahuensis**
          Stamens 12-18; ovary 4-3 celled......... **T. Kaalae**

II. **NOTHOTETRAPLASANDRA.** Stamens as many as petals, 5-8; ovary, 5-2 celled.
  Inflorescence umbellate or compound umbellate.......... **T. meiandra** and varieties

337

22

PLATE 135.

TETRAPLASANDRA HAWAIIENSIS A. Gray.
Ohe.
Showing fruiting branch and flower buds pinned against trunk of tree, bark in the dry
districts rough and scaly. South Kona, lava fields of Kapua; elevation 1200 feet.

Araliaceae.

Tetraplasandra hawaiiensis A. Gray.
Ohe.
(Plate 135.)

TETRAPLASANDRA HAWAIIENSIS A. Gray Bot. U. S. E. E. (1854) 728, t. 94;—
H. Mann. Proc. Am. Acad. VII. (1867) 169;— Hbd. Fl. Haw. Isl. (1888) 154;—
Del. Cast. Ill. Fl. Ins. Mar. Pacif. VI. (1890) 183;—Harms in Engler et Prantl
Pflzfam. III, 8 (1898) 30, Fig. 2, g-h.

Branchlets with the leaf-stalks, inflorescence and the exterior of the flowers canescent
with a soft tomentum; leaves alternate, exstipulate, 3 to 4.5 cm long, pinnately 5 to 7 foliolate; leaflets oblong or elliptical 10 to 17 cm long and 5 cm or more in width, obtuse at both
ends, entire, coriaceous, glabrous above, densely canescent-tomentose underneath, the ribs
hirsute; peduncle terminal stout, bearing an ample and open panicle of compound or de-
compound umbels; peduncles and pedicels articulate, densely tomentose; calyx tube cup-
shaped, the truncate limb very short, entire; petals 5 to 8 tomentose as is the calyx,
cohering at the apex, 6 to 8 mm long; stamens 4 times as many as petals or less in one
circle, recurved; ovary 7 to 13 celled; the apex crowned with a short and conical stylopod
which bears an obscurely 7 to 13 rayed stigma; ovules solitary; fruit a globose baccate
drupe 1 cm in diameter, many ribbed when dry, containing 7 to 13 flat chartaceous compressed pyrenae.

The *ohe*, not to be mistaken for the *ohe* of the lowlands, is a beautiful tree
with a broad, flat crown reaching a height of 40 to 80 feet, with a trunk of 1 to 2
feet or more in diameter. The writer met with huge trees in Kona, Hawaii, in
the semi-wet forest, overtowering the tallest *Ohia* trees. The bark is whitish and
more or less smooth.

It can be distinguished from afar on account of its large pinnate leaves,
which are 1 to 1½ feet long, having from 5 to 9 oblong leaflets, which are light-
green above and pale-ocher colored underneath, due to a dense tomentum. The
flowering panicles are often more than one foot long, bearing umbellate racemes
along umbellate and racemose tertiary and secondary branches. The globose
fruits become many-ribbed when dry.

The *ohe* inhabits the drier as well as very wet regions and is not uncommon
in the valley of Wailau, Molokai, where it grows on the steep pali or cliff covered
with tropical verdure. On Lanai, from which island it had not been been recorded previously, it can be found near the summit ridges of Haalelepakai and
Lanaihale, at an elevation of 3000 feet, and also on Mahana ridge.

On Maui it growes above Kaanapali, and on Hawaii it is found in the rain
forests of Puna and semi-wet forests of South Kona, together with Xylosma,
Pelea, etc.

Its associates are usually species of Straussia, Bobea, Metrosideros, Cheirodendron, and such as are peculiar to the rain forests.

Tetraplasandra Waimeae Wawra.
Ohe Kikoola.
(Plate 136.)

TETRAPLASANDRA WAIMEAE Wawra in Flora (1873) 158;—Hbd. Fl. Haw. Isl. (1888)
155;—Del Cast. Ill. Fl. Ins. Mar. Pacif. VI. (1890) 184;— Heller Pl. Haw. Isl.
(1897) 871;—Harms in Engl. et Prantl Pflzfam. III, 8 (1898) 30.

Leaves 30 to 45 cm long, leaflets 5 to 13, oblong or ovate-oblong, 10 to 15 cm long, 3.5
to 5 cm wide, on petioles of 12 to 18 mm, obtuse with rounded, the laterals ones with unsymmetrical, bases, chartaceous to coriaceous, glabrous; inflorescence a terminal umbel of

PLATE 136.

TETRAPLASANDRA WAIMEAE Wawra.
Ohe kikoola.
Growing in the mountains of Kauai in the forest of Kaholuamano; elevation 3600 feet.

Araliaceae.

10 to 12 rays, with or without a short common rhachis, each 10 to 15 cm long and bearing at its apex an umbel of 15 to 30 flowers on thick and long pedicels of 2.5 to 5 cm; calyx 8 to 12 mm long broad tubular, slightly constricted below the wavy denticulate border; petals 7 to 8, triangular lanceolate, 12 mm long, pink or reddish, coriaceous, glabrous, at last expanded, the open corolla measuring sometimes 3.5 cm in diameter, the largest in the genus; stamens 6, 7 or 8 times as many as petals, 8 to 10 mm long, in two rows; ovary 6 to 8 celled, the stigma on a short stylopod of 1 mm; drupe globose, about 3 cm or often more in diameter, somewhat fleshy, strongly ribbed when dry; pyrenae compressed, thick coriaceous, deeply notched at the upper inner angle, and with two prominent ridges on each side.

The *Ohe kikoola* is a medium-sized tree with an erect trunk of 30 to 40 feet in height and a diameter of a foot or more. The erect bole is vested in a grayish-white smooth bark. It divides very sparingly near the top into rather short ascending branches, which bear large leaf whorls at the apex. The leaves are over a foot long and consist of 5 to 13 leaflets. The inflorescence is a terminal umbel of several rays, bearing at its apex peculiar rose-colored flowers, which are the largest in the genus, measuring an inch or more in diameter. The drupe is globose, an inch or more across, somewhat fleshy, and becomes ribbed on drying.

The tree is peculiar to the Island of Kauai, where it grows on the leeward side above Waimea at an altitude of 3600 feet, in the drier forest or outskirts of the woods around Kaholuamano. It is associated with *Cyanea leptostegia*, *Cryptocaria Mannii, Bobea Mannii, Sidero ylon sandwicense, Elaeocarpus bifidus*, etc. It also is not uncommon at Halemanu, where it was first collected by Dr. Wawra of the Austrian Exploring Expedition ship "Donau," and named by him after the district of Waimea.

The wood is whitish, of a silky, wavy green, and of medium strength.

Tetraplasandra Waialealae Rock.

TETRAPLASANDRA WAIALEALAE Rock Coll. Haw. Publ. Bull. 1, (1911) 10, pl. I.
Leaves 30 to 45 cm long; leaflets oblong acuminate thick coriaceous, unevensided at the base, otherwise rounded; inflorescence a terminal compound umbel of usually 4 peduncles, each about from 7 to 10 cm long, bearing 6 rays about 6 cm long, each bearing an umbel of 2-5 pedicels about 2 cm long; calyx tubular purplish-black with an undulate border; petals 5 to 7, triangular, thick, with a prominent median nerve, glabrous; stamens in two circles, four times as many as petals; ovary 6 celled; stigma on a conical stylopod of 5 mm.

This remarkable tree, which as far as is known has no native name, is of rather small size, 15 to 25 feet high, with sub-erect long branches, bearing, crowded at their ends, irregularly pinnate leaves. The leaflets are dark-green and glossy; the trunk is rather short, is vested in a white bark, and is about 6 to 8 inches in diameter.

The inflorescence is compound umbellate, not as large as that of the *Ohe kikoola*, but is also terminal.

This interesting tree, which the writer discovered on the summit of Mt. Waialeale, on Kauai, 5200 feet elevation, was named by him after that wonderful mountain. Unlike the *Ohe kikoola*, which grows in the dryer forest on Kauai back of Waimea, it inhabits the high summit swamp, where the rainfall is immense. This swamp is enshrouded by clouds nearly all the year round, and is swept by the strong trade winds for over nine months of the year.

PLATE 137.

TETRAPLASANDRA MEIANDRA (Hbd.) Harms. var. γ.
Flowering and fruiting branch pinned against trunk of tree. Growing at Puuwaawaa,
North Kona, Hawaii, elevation 2800 feet. Trunk about a foot in diameter.

Araliaceae.

Tetraplasandra Waialealae is really the only tree of any size at the summit, where the rest of the vegetation is stunted. It is associated with *Pelea Waialealae*, the *Anonia* of the natives, *Lagenophora mauiensis, Sanicula sandwicensis* var., *Lobelia kauaiensis, Lobelia macrostachys* var., *Drosera longifolia, Dubautia Waialealae, Geranium humile* var. *Kauaiense,* etc.

It is the second species of Tetraplasandra which has been so far recorded from Kauai, and is peculiar to Waialeale, though it may be found along the Kaluiti and Kailiili streams a little below the summit. The wood is soft and white.

Tetraplasandra Lanaiensis Rock.

TETRAPLASANDRA LANAIENSIS Rock. Coll. Haw. Publ. Bull. 1. (1911) 12, pl. 2.
Leaves 30 to 38 cm long, leaflets 5 to 7, oblong obtuse or bluntly acuminate, uneven-sided at the base, midrib prominent. 8 to 10 cm long, 4 to 5 cm wide, dark green above, light underneath, the terminal leaflet on a petiolule of 4 cm which is articulate near the blade, the lateral ones on petiolules of 1 to 1.5 cm, subcoriaceous; inflorescence thrice umbellate, not erect, but drooping, the 3 to 5 peduncles on a common rhachis of about 2.5 cm, about 20 cm long, bearing umbels of 17 to 21 slender droopings rays of 8 to 10 cm length, these again umbellate with 7 to 13 pedicels; calyx tubular 6 mm with a denticulate border, petals 5 to 6, lanceolate, greenish-yellow, 7 mm long, stamens twice as many as petals, ovary 3-celled, stigmas sessile.

This tree was discovered by the writer on the Island of Lanai and described by him under the above name. It is rather small, only about 20 feet high, with a trunk of a few inches in diameter. It branches irregularly, and as it was crowded in with other trees it was impossible to form an idea of its general aspect.

It is remarkable in the genus Tetraplasandra for its large inflorescence, which, instead of being erect, is drooping, and for its very small flowers. The leaves are dull and of a light-green color, making the tree quite conspicuous among the dark-leaved Maba, Suttonia, and Sideroxylon, with which it is associated. The tree is peculiar to the Island of Lanai and was seen only in Kaiholena Valley, crowded by other trees at an elevation of 2000 feet. Kaiholena Valley, belonging to the drier regions of Lanai, is extremely interesting and harbors a very multiformous tree flora.

Tetraplasandra Lydgatei (Hbd.) Harms.

TETRAPLASANDRA LYDGATEI (Hbd.) Harms in Engl. et. Prantl Pflzfam. III. 8 (1898) 20.—**Triplasandra Lydgatei** Hbd. Fl. Haw. Isl. (1888) 153;—Del Cast. Ill. Fl. Ins. Mar. Pacif. VI (1890) 184.

Leaves 20 to 30 cm long; leaflets 5 to 9 on petioles of 8 to 16 mm, oblong 7.5 to 9 cm long, 2.5 to 4 cm, obtuse and slightly emarginate, contracting at the base, thin chartaceous; inflorescence compound-umbellate from a short common rhachis of about 12 mm, the 4 or 5 slender peduncles bearing umbels of about 12 slender pedicels of 16 to 18 mm; calyx broad obconical, 5 mm, with an undulating border; petals 5, cohering at their apices, 6 mm; stamens 12, about 1/3 shorter, with straight or recurved anthers; ovary 4 celled, inferior, the disk slightly raised, with sessile stigmas; drupe ovoid-globose, 8 to 10 mm in diameter, obtusely 4 angled, the short conical apex finally elongated into a short stylopod.

343

PLATE 138.

TETRAPLASANDRA MEIANDRA (Hbd.) Harms. var. δ
Flowering branch pinned against trunk of tree. Growing on the lava fields of Auahi,
East Maui, southern slopes of Haleakala, elevation 3000 feet. Diameter of trunk 2 ft.

Araliaceae.

This species, which like the two following has no native name, is a small tree originally found by John Lydgate in the valley of Wailupe on Oahu, and resembles somewhat *Pterotropia gymnocarpa* from the same mountain range.

It has not been collected by the writer, and as there are no specimens of this plant in herbaria in the Territory of Hawaii, the above short description will have to suffice.

Tetraplasandra oahuensis (A. Gray) Harms.
Ohe mauka.

TETRAPLASANDRA OAHUENSIS (A. Gray) Harms in Engl. et Prantl Pflzfam. III, 8 (1898) 30.—Gastonia? oahuensis A. Gray U. S. E. E. (1854) 726.—H. Mann Proc. Am. Acad. VII (1867) 169.—Triplasandra Oahuensis Seem. in Journ. Bot. VI (1868) 139;—Hbd. Fl. Haw. Isl. (1888) 153;—Del Cast. Ill. Fl. Ins. Mar. Pacif. VI (1890) 184.

Leaves about 3 cm long; leaflets 7 to 13, ovate or broad oblong, 5.5 to 8.5 cm long, 2.5 to 5 cm wide, on petiolules of 3 to 6 mm, obtuse, coriaceous glabrous; inflorescence compound umbellate, 3 to 5 peduncles, 5 to 7.5 cm long, either free or united on a short rhachis of about 12 mm, each bearing an umbel of 16 to 20 pedicels of 12 mm in length; calyx cylindrical 4 to 6 mm; petals 5 to 6, about 6 mm long; stamens 10 to 15, half as long as the petals, with recurved anthers; ovary 5 to 6 celled; drupe ovoid or short cylindrical, 6 to 8 mm, inferior 5 to 6 ribbed or angled, truncate, the stigmas on a short stylopod.

This species and a variety *β.* occur on the Island of Oahu on the slopes of Waiolani and Konahuanui back of Honolulu. It differs from the foregoing species mainly in the drupe, which is cylindrical and truncate, while the former has ovoid drupes with conical vertices.

It is a small tree about 20 feet in height and is peculiar to Oahu. The writer observed several trees at the head of Pauoa Valley and on the slopes of Konahuanui. It is sparingly branching about 6 feet above the ground; the trunk is vested in a gray, smooth bark, and is about 6 to 8 inches in diameter. According to Horace Mann, its native name is *Ohe mauka* or the mountain *Ohe*, while *Reynoldsia sandwicensis* is *Ohe makai;* the latter, however, is also known as *Ohe kukuluaeo.*

Tetraplasandra Kaalae (Hbd.) Harms.

TETRAPLASANDRA KAALAE (Hbd.) Harms in Engl. et Prantl Pflzfam. III, 8 (1898) 30.—Triplasandra Kaalae Hbd. Fl. Haw. Isl. (1888) 154;—Del Cast. Ill. Fl. Ins. Mar. Pacif. VI (1890) 184.

Leaves about 3 dm long, with widely clasping base, leaflets 7 to 11, ovate or ovate-oblong. 7.5 to 10 cm long, 5 to 7.5 cm wide, on petiolules of 12 to 24 mm, obtusely acuminate, rounded and unsymmetrical at the base, thick coriaceous, glabrous underneath, dark green; inflorescence thrice umbellate, 3 to 5 peduncles rising from a short common rhachis, each 4 to 6.5 cm long, with an umbel of about 12 rays of 2.5 to 3.5 cm or more long, these again umbellate with 10 to 12 pedicels of 8 to 12 mm; calyx obconical, glabrous, 2 mm; petals 6 at last expanded. 6 to 8 mm; stamens three times as many as petals or less, 18 to 12; ovary 4- rarely 3-celled; stigmas sessile on a conical apex.

This tree was first collected by Hillebrand on the summit of Mt. Kaala of the Waianae range on Oahu at an elevation of 4000 feet. It is, like the two foregoing species, a small tree 12 to 16 feet in height and of no economic value.

PLATE 139.

TETRAPLASANDRA MEIANDRA (Hbd.) Harms, var. ζ.
Fruiting specimen, much reduced.

Araliaceae.

Tetraplasandra meiandra (Hbd.) Harms.

(Plates 137, 138, 139.)

TETRAPLASANDRA MEIANDRA (Hbd.) Harms in Eng. et Prantl Pflzfam. III, 8 (1898) 30.—**Triplasandra meiandra** Hbd. Fl. Haw. Isl. (1888) 152;—Del Cast. Ill. Fl. Ins. Mar. Pacif. VI (1890) 184.—**Triplasandra Waimeae** (Wawra) Heller Pl. Haw. Isl. (1897) 871.—**Heptapleurum (?) Waimeae** Wawra in Flora (1873) 158. (Wawra's specific name Waimeae should hold good on account of priority, but as there is already a species with that name in Tetraplasandra, Hillebrand's meiandra is here adhered to.)

Leaves 3 to 4.5 cm long, the petiole dilated at the base and clasping; leaflets 7 to 13; inflorescence umbellate but variable: either the pedicels at the end of 3 to 5 terminal peduncles (simply umbellate, but then shrubs), or at the ends of rays which proceed from the ends of 3 to 5 peduncles, the latter rarely united by a common rhachis (compoundly umbellate); bracts broadly ovate, 4 to 8 mm long, caducous long before the flowers expand; calyx cylindrical, ovate or obovate, with a short denticulate or undulate border; petals 5 to 8, triangular or linear lanceolate; stamens as many, shorter, or as long as the petals (in one variety only). Ovary 2 to 6 celled; stigmas 2 to 6, sessile on the conical vertex, or, when 4 to 6, raised on a short stylopod, drupe cylindrical, ovate, oblong, or obovate, or subglobose.

Hillebrand, in his Flora of the Hawaiian Islands, says in a foot note on page 152:

"Under this collective species I have united the following forms, which are exceedingly rare, each corresponding to a single or a few individuals, found in closely-circumscribed localities."

He then describes six varieties, as follows:—

Stigmas 2, rarely 3.
 a. 7 to 12 leaflets.
 β. 7 to 9 leaflets.
 γ. 11 leaflets.
Stigmas 3 (4).
 δ. 7 to 9 leaflets.
Stigmas 3-4-5.
 ε. 9 to 13 leaflets.
Stigmas 4-5-6.
 ζ. Leaflets as in δ, drupe ovoid.

The above key to the varieties of this species can not be relied upon, as one may find plants with only 2 stigmas and 13 leaflets, and plants with 4 stigmas, 6 stamens and 9 leaflets. The specimens from Oahu are more or less shrubs, and have rather long rays or peduncles, while the plants from the other islands are always trees, and have rather short rays. It is unfortunate that Hillebrand did not define them more clearly. However, complete material is not always possible to obtain, and therefore an exact diagnosis not always possible, as the stamens play an important part in the identification of this very variable species.

Only such variations are here cited as are trees, and the writer is sorry to state that, owing to incomplete material from other varieties occuring in the Kohala Mountains, Hawaii, and West Maui mountains, certain trees are herewith omitted. They are, however, all referable to *Tetraplasandra meiandra.* It is the writer's intention later to monograph this interesting family.

On Hawaii on the lava fields of Puuwaawaa, North Kona, grow a few speci-

PLATE 140.

REYNOLDSIA SANDWICENSIS A. Gray.
Fruiting branch.

Araliaceae.

mens of a tree which may be referred to Hillebrand's var γ. It is a medium-sized tree 35 feet or so in height, with bright-green imparipinnate foliage. The inflorescence, which is compound umbellate, arises usually in the axil of the two uppermost branchlets.

On Maui, on the lava fields of Auahi, situated on the southern slopes of Hale-akala, grows a beautiful tree which has to be referred to variety ∂, though differing from the plants on Lanai; the drupes of var. δ resemble very much var. ζ which see. It is a handsome tree of 50 feet or so in height, with a trunk of almost two feet in diameter. The trunk is perfectly straight and vested in a smooth gray bark. The branches are thick and ascending, bearing at their ends large leaf-whorls, underneath which are umbels with small greenish flowers.

The writer found many varieties from new localities, such as Haleakala, West Maui, Kau forests, Kohala Mountains, etc., which all come under *Tetraplasandra meiandra;* while Hillebrand's varieties came mostly from Oahu. They are, however, not quite so rare as Hillebrand thought them to be; the forests have merely been opened up nowadays by ditch trails, while in Hillebrand's time the rain forests were almost inaccessible.

Varieties of the above species occur both in extremely wet forests and in exceedingly dry or mixed forests. It is in the latter regions that they reach their best development. They are there associated with Pterotropia, Alectryon, Pelea, Xanthoxylum, Hibiscadelphus, etc.

Variety ζ, which is here illustrated, grows in the forests of Kau above Naalehu on Hawaii. Hillebrand's plant came from the woods of Hilo, where it was collected by Mr. J. Lydgate. In Kau it is a medium-sized tree, 35 feet in height, with a rather short trunk and large, stout, ascending branches; the leaves are over a foot long and consist of 7 to 13 leaflets; the inflorescence is a compound umbel with usually five rays, each ray bearing an umbel of 5 to 16 peduncles, each peduncle having again from 5 to 12 pedicels half an inch long, petals 7, stamens as many; the ovarian portion is ovoid and has a conical vertex with four stigmas raised on a minute stylopod.

As far as known the natives made no use of this tree. Its wood is white and soft and of no value, as is the case with all the rest of the species belonging to this genus and those closely allied to it.

Varieties of this species grow also above Awini in the rain forests of Kohala, Hawaii; in the mountains of West Maui, on the ridges of Honokawai; on the summit ridge of Lanai, Haalelepakai; in the Punaluu Mountains, and Konahuanui on Oahu, as well as in Niu and Wailupe Valley of the same island. On Molokai, it grows in the forests of Kamoku; in the swamp forest on the windward side of Haleakala a new variety is not uncommon. The species and its forms grow at altitudes of from 1000 to 4000 feet, and are either small shrubs or medium-sized trees in the wet forests. and larger trees in the dry regions (on lava fields).

349

PLATE 141.

REYNOLDSIA SANDWICENSIS A. Gray.
Fruiting branch pinned against trunk of tree; diameter of the latter 2 feet; growing on the land of Kapua, South Kona, Hawaii; elevation 1800 feet.

Araliaceae.

REYNOLDSIA A. Gray.

Calyx border short, undulate. Petals 8 to 10, linear-lanceolate, valvate in the bud. Stamens as many as petals and somewhat shorter. Ovary 8 to 10 or 15 to 22 celled. Stigmas arranged in a circle around the very short, thick style. Drupe globose, somewhat fleshy. Pyrenae laterally compressed, chartaceous or crustaceous. Embryo small at the apex of an even fleshy albumen.—Unarmed, glabrous trees. Leaves large, imparipinnate, with 3 to 9 oval or cordate sinuate-crenate or (in the species not from Hawaii) entire leaflets; exstipulate. Flowers racemose-umbellate on the alternate branches of a terminal panicle. Bracts minute linear.

A genus of three species, one inhabiting Tahiti (*R. verrucosa* Seem.), one Samoa (Savaii) *(R. pleiosperma* A. Gray), and the third our islands.

Reynoldsia sandwicensis A. Gray.
Ohe, or *Ohe makai.*
(Plates 140, 141, 142.)

REYNOLDSIA SANDWICENSIS A. Gray U. S. E. E. (1854) 724, pl. 92;—H. Mann Proc. Am. Acad. VII (1867) 169;—Wawra in Flora (1873) 142;—Hbd. Fl. Haw. Isl. (1888) 156;—Harms in Engl. et Prantl Pflzfam. III, 8 (1898) 30.—**Eschweileria Sandwicensis** Durand Ind. Gen. 167;—Del Cast. Ill. Fl. Ins. Mar. Pac. VI. (1890) 182.

Leaves about 3 dm long, glabrous, the slender petioles shortly toothed at the dilating base (according to Hillebr. but not in the writer's specimens); leaflets 7 to 11, ovate to cordate, 7 to 10 cm x 5 to 8.5 cm on petiolules of 2 cm in the upper pair of leaflets and 4 cm in the lower pair, obtuse or bluntly acuminate, repando, or sinuate crenate, stiff membraneous, light green, glossy; inflorescence of 3 terminal peduncles, rising from a short common rhachis, each about 12 to 20 cm long and branching from the base upward, the branches horizontal, 4 to 5 cm when with flower, 7 to 9 cm when in fruit, and racemose umbellate in their upper halves, with pedicels of 10 to 12 mm; calyx obconical truncate, 2 to 3 mm; petals 8 to 10, about 6 mm long, cohering; ovary 8 to 10 celled, wholly inferior; drupe globose 6 to 8 mm in diameter ribbed when dry; pyrenae crustaceous, with smooth sides.

The *Ohe* is a very peculiar Hawaiian tree, which sheds its leaves in the winter months and flowers before the reappearance of the leaves in the early summer. When bare, it resembles somewhat the *Wiliwili,* which also sheds its leaves during the rainy season.

It reaches a height of from 15 to 60 feet and develops thick and often short trunks with bluish-gray, smooth bark, and a spreading crown with straight ascending branches. The leaves, which are about a foot long, consist of 7 to 11 leaflets, heart-shaped at the base. The flowers are arranged on stiff, erect terminal peduncles, rising from a short common rhachis, branching from the base upward, and racemose-umbellate in the upper half.

It is peculiar to the very dry districts of the lowland zone and especially on *aa* lava fields, where the heat is intense and rain is very infrequent. The trunk exudes a very thick resin or gum which is of a clear yellowish-golden color.

On Maui it is not uncommon on the lava fields near Ulupalakua on the southern slopes of Haleakala, as well as on Molokai, where it can be found at the western end at Mahana in gulches, and on the heights above Kamolo, associated with *Dracaena aurea (Halapepe).* On Hawaii, on the lava fields of North and South Kona, it reaches its best development, trunks with a diameter of 1½ to 2 feet being not uncommon. It also grows on Lanai on the slopes above Manele

PLATE 142.

REYNOLDSIA SANDWICENSIS A. Gray.
Growing on the lava fields of Kahikinui, southern slopes of Mt. Haleakala, Island of Maui. Elevation 1500 feet.

Araliaceae.

and Kalama in company with a variety of *Santalum Freycinetianum* (Sandal-wood). Owing to the softness of the whitish wood, it is of no commercial value. The gum or resin which the tree is capable of producing was used by the natives for various purposes.

The wood was used for making the *kukuluaeo,* or stilts, employed by the old Hawaiians in a game by that name, and it is spoken of as the *"He ohe kahi laau hana ia i mea kukuluaeo."*

In Tahiti the name *"Ofe"* is applied to a tree of the same family to which our Reynoldsia belongs.

PTEROTROPIA Hbd.
(*Dipanax* Seem.)

Calyx border slightly prominent and repandly dentate. Petals 5 to 9, valvate in the bud, thick, cohering or finally spreading. Stamens as many as petals, shorter than the latter; anthers ovate to oblong. Ovary 2 to 5 celled; stigmas sessile on the top of the conical vertex or raised on a conspicuous style. Drupe somewhat succulent, ovoid or sub-globose, with conical apex, round not angular, ringed above, below or at the middle, or at the base by the calycine border and naked above. Pyrenae with a thin endocarp, ovoid or slightly compressed, with a broad back and a prominent ridge on either side.— Trees with glutinous sap. Leaves alternate, large, impari-pinnate, with 13 to 21 ovoid or oblong entire leaflets, with a scattering scaly or stellate pubescence, but occasionally glabrous. Inflorescence terminal and lateral; flowers umbellate-racemose on the umbellate racemose branches of a panicle with a short rhachis. Pedicels not articulate; bracts minute, deciduous. (The name Dipanax is not as old as Mann's section name Pterotropia and the latter is therefore retained.)

A Hawaiian genus of three species. Tall or medium-sized trees with straight trunks and smooth bark. Easily distinguished from all other Hawaiian Araliaceae by their leaves, which reach a size of over three feet and have from 9 to 21 leaflets, and their large inflorescence, which is racemose-umbellate and drooping below the leaf-whorls, often two feet and more long; in *P. gymnocarpa* apparently above the leaf-whorls.

The native name for all three species is *Ohe ohe.* They are peculiar to the dry districts, with the exception of *P. gymnocarpa,* which occurs in the rain forest.

The only distinguishing character between *P. Kavaiensis* (Mann) Hbd. and *P. dipyrena* (Mann) Hbd. is the number of stigmas. In Hillebrand's key to the species he also mentions the definite number of leaflets, which, since, more material is at hand, can no longer be relied upon.

Specimens of *P. dipyrena* collected by the writer in Kau have 21 leaflets, which are truncate, and flowers with 2 to 3 stigmas. The same number of leaflets and stigmas occurs in plants from East Maui on the southern slopes of Haleakala on the lava fields of Auahi, and also on plants back of Ulupalakua.

As the number of stigmas varies in that species and differs mainly from the Kauai species in the fact that they are sessile, the writer is almost persuaded to unite them both under *P. dipyrena.*

The character of the fruit as given in Hillebrand's Flora regarding the two

PLATE 143.

PTEROTROPIA GYMNOCARPA Hbd.
One-half natural size.   Fruiting specimen.

Araliaceae.

species in question is also uncertain, since drupes ringed above and below the middle can be observed in *P. Kavaiensis;* the drupes of *P. dipyrena* are ringed above the middle only.

KEY TO THE SPECIES.

Drupe ringed at the base.
    Stigmas 2 to 3, sessile...................................... **P. gymnocarpa**
Drupe ringed either above or below or at the middle.
    Stigmas 2, 3 to 4, sessile.................................... **P. dipyrena**
    Stigmas 4 to 5 on a conspicuous style....................... **P. Kavaiensis**

Pterotropia gymnocarpa Hbd.
(Plate 143.)

PTEROTROPIA GYMNOCARPA Hbd. Fl. Haw. Isl. (1888) 151;—Harms in Engl. et Prantl Pflzfam. III, 8 (1898) 31.—**Heptapleurum gymnocarpum** Del Cast. Ill. Fl. Ins. Mar. Pac. VI (1890) 183.—**Dipanax gymnocarpa** Heller Pl. Haw. Isl. (1897) 870.

Leaves 3 to 4 dm long, leaflets 9 to 11 (according to Hillebrand 15 to 17), 8 to 18 cm long, 4.5 to 8 cm wide, ovate oblong, the lower pair diminishing in size on petioles of 2 to 18 mm, obtuse or obliquely acuminate, with rounded base or unevensided, chartaceous to coriaceous, glabrous underneath, shining above; rhachis of panicle rather short, with 3 to 5 umbellately radiating primary branches of 10 to 20 cm, the flowers about 12 in an umbel at the ends of racemose and umbellate secondary branches of 5 to 9 cm, on pedicels of 8 to 20 mm; calyx very short; petals 6, rarely 7, cohering at the apex, about 8 mm in length; ovary 2 to 3 celled (in one of the writer's specimens all ovaries are two celled, one of which is abortive); stigmas sessile; drupe globose (according to Hillebr.) or oblong-turbinate in the writer's specimens, 12 to 15 mm long, and about 7 mm in diameter, nearly entirely free and naked, the adherent calyx forming a low disk at its base; pyrenae thin papery, ovoid, beaked above and faintly notched below the beak.

This is a small or medium-sized tree reaching a height of 15 to 30 feet. It differs from the other two species in its smaller leaves and leaflets, which become quite glabrous when old, while only the very young branchlets are mealy.

The branching habit is similar to Oahuan species of Tetraplasandra, rather than Pterotropia, and it is often mistaken for such at first glance. It inhabits the main range of Oahu, to which island it is peculiar. It is, however, easily distinguished from Tetraplasandra by its rather dark foliage.

Fine trees may be found in the forest on the windward side of Punaluu and above Kaliuwaa valley at an elevation of 2000 feet or more, usually along streambeds and in gulches. It is associated with *Pelea sandwicensis, Euphorbia Rockii, Hibiscus Arnottianus, Syzygium sandwicense, Elaeocarpus bifidus,* Pittosporum, etc.

On Mt. Olympus at the head of Palolo Valley near the summit ridge fine trees may be observed; also on Mt. Konahuanui of the same range. The biggest trees occur in the Punaluu Mountains of the Koolau range. Hillebrand's specimens came from Niu Valley. This tree is in every respect a Pterotropia but in habit, as it does not reach the height of the other two species, which is sometimes 60 to 80 feet.

The trees from Mt. Olympus have a two-celled ovary, while those from other localities are three-celled. The inflorescence is not drooping, but almost erect above the leaves.

PLATE 144.

PTEROTROPIA DIPYRENA (Mann) Hbd.
Showing fruiting specimen. Much reduced.

Araliaceae.

Pterotropia kavaiensis (Mann) Hbd.
Ohe ohe.

PTEROTROPIA KAVAIENSIS (Mann) Hbd. Fl. Haw. Isl. (1888) 150;—Harms in Engl. et Prantl Pflzfam. III, 8 (1898) 31.—Heptapleurum (Pterotropia) kavaiense Mann Proc. Am. Acad. VII (1867) 168;—Del Cast. Ill. Fl. Ins. Mar. Pac. VI. (1890) 183.—Agalma kavaiense Seem. Revis. Hederac. (1868) 103.—Dipanax kavaiensis Heller Pl. Haw. Isl. (1897) 871.

Leaves impari-pinnate, 6 to 9 dm long; leaflets 11 to 21, ovate oblong, 7 to 19 cm long, 4 to 8 cm wide, on petioles of 2 to 15 mm (the last upper pair of leaflets almost sessile in some specimens, the lowest pair of leaflets much smaller than the others, but on the longest petiolules), acuminate or rounded at the apex, rounded or truncate at the base, coriaceous, sprinkled above, but densely tomentose underneath; panicle large and ample, its 5 primary branches 1 to 3 dm long mostly alternate on a common rhachis of 5 to 7 cm, the secondary branches 4 to 7 cm, mostly alternate; petals 6 to 7, rarely 9, densely tomentose especially in the bud; ovary generally 4-celled, or 3 to 5 celled, stigmas on a distinct stylopod of 1 mm; drupe ovoid about 12 mm, ringed below, at, or above the middle, the pyrenae chartaceous.

This species differs very little from *P. dipyrena,* and is only distinguishable from the latter in the raised stigmas, the number of which is usually four in *P. kavaiensis* and two to three to four in *P. dipyrena.* The characters of the leaves can not at all be relied upon, the leaflets of *P. dipyrena* varying from linear oblong to ovoid, and are either cordate, truncate or rounded at the base, on petiolules of about 1 mm to 30 mm; the stigmas are more or less sessile in *P. dipyrena.*

Pterotropia kavaiensis, in the writer's mind, should be united with *P. dipyrena,* but as only one good flowering specimen from one locality is at present in his possession, he defers such action until the future, when more complete material shall be at hand.

The *Ohe ohe* of Kauai is a very beautiful and symmetrical tree reaching a height of 50 feet and occasionally more, with a trunk of over one foot in diameter. It divides near the top into a few ascending stout branches, at the end of which are large leaf-whorls. The crown is flat and is about one-fifth the height of the tree. When growing, crowded by other trees, it branches 10 or 15 feet above the ground and is not as symmetrical as trees growing apart. It is a tree which inhabits the mountains on the leeward side of Kauai, above Waimea, in the dry regions at an elevation of 2800 to 4000 feet.

Its associates are *Bobea Mannii, Cryptocaria Mannii, Cyanea leptostegia, Tetraplasandra Waimeae,* Metrosideros, etc. It can be recognized from afar, as it usually towers above the trees surrounding it, giving the landscape a peculiar aspect.

The wood of the *Ohe ohe* is white and rather soft.

Pterotropia dipyrena (Mann) Hbd.
Ohe ohe.
(Plates 144, 145.)

PTEROTROPIA DIPYRENA (Mann) Hbd. Fl. Haw. Isl. (1888) 150; Harms in Engl. et Prantl Pflzfam. III, 8 (1898) 31.—Heptapleurum (Pterotropia) dipyrenum Mann Proc. Amer. Acad. VII (1867) 160.—Dipanax Mannii Seem. Journ. Bot. VI (1868) 41;—Del Cast. Ill. Fl. Ins. Mar. Pac. VI (1890) 182;—Heller Pl. Haw. Isl. (1897) 870.

PLATE 145.

PTEROTROPIA DIPYRENA (Mann) Hbd.
Ohe Ohe.
Growing at an elevation of 4500 feet above Ulupalakua on the southeastern slopes of
Mt. Haleakala, Maui.

Araliaceae.

Leaves 36 to 100 cm long, composed of 15 to 21 leaflets varying greatly in size and shape, usually ovate oblong 8 to 21 cm long, 4 to 11 cm wide, cordate, truncate or un-evensided at the base, acuminate at the apex, the longest pair of leaflets at about the middle of the leaf, the lowest pair the broadest but shorter, on short petioles in the smaller leaf-forms, and on petioles of often 25 mm in the large leaf forms, glabrous above, fur-furaceous below; panicle very large almost one meter long (in the Kau, Hawaii, speci-mens, but about 36 cm in some of the Maui specimens) rising from a common rhachis of sometimes 15 cm, with 8 drooping rays, each ray often 7.5 dm long, covered with a brown tomentum, the secondary branches 4 to 10 cm long, alternate, the flowers racemose and subumbellate on pedicels of about 1 cm, bracts short triangular; calyx small with an undulate border; petals 6 to 8, 12 mm long, lanceolate, cohering, but finally free; stamens 6 to 8, anthers white; drupe ovoid to subglobose, ringed with the calyx border above the middle, stigmas 2 or 3 or 4, slightly raised or sessile on a conical disk; pyrenae coriace-ous inseparable.

The *Ohe ohe* of Maui and Hawaii is like that of Kauai, a stately tree 50 to 60 feet and sometimes even 80 feet in height. It has a straight bole for 30 feet or more, with few stout ascending branches. The trunk, which is clothed in a whit-ish-gray smooth bark, is often a foot or more in diameter. The tree was first described by H. Mann, who collected it on the Island of Lanai, recording it as a small tree 12 to 20 feet in height. It has since been found on Maui and Ha-waii. It is, however, still most numerous on the southeastern and strictly south-ern slopes of Mt. Haleakala, Island of Maui. In the former locality above Ulu-palakua it is the only species alive, as can be seen in the picture, all the rest of the vegetation having been killed by cattle, goats and sheep.

On the lava fields of Auahi, district of Kahikinui, the writer found some very big trees in company with *Pelea multiflora, Bobea Hookeri, Alectryon macro-coccus, Xanthoxylum* sp., *Tetraplasandra meiandra*, and many others. It is more or less peculiar to the dry districts, but is also not uncommon in the rain forest on the northeastern slope of Haleakala along the Kula pipe line trail, especially on the crater of Puukakai at an elevation of about 4500 feet.

On Hawaii it has been found by Hillebrand in the dry district of Kawaihae-iuka, but could not be located during a visit made by the writer in that locality, though the writer was fortunate, however, to find it in the forests of Hilea in Kau, the most southern point on the Island of Hawaii, at an elevation of 2000 feet. In this latter locality occur the biggest trees of this species, while in the Kaiholena Mountains, elevation 4000 feet, of the same district, the trees are smaller and resemble the description (outward appearance) given by Mann of the trees which he found on Lanai.

The wood of the *Ohe ohe* is rather soft and of no particular value. It is a hardy tree and can stand the ravages of cattle and other enemies better than any other Hawaiian tree.

CHEIRODENDRON Nutt.

Calyx border with 5 short teeth. Petals 5, valvate in the bud, triangular. Stamens 5 shorter than the petals, anthers ovoid. Ovary 5 to 2 celled, stigmas sessile on a conical elevation of the disk, or apical on a thick and short style. Fruit globose, ribbed when dry, with somewhat fleshy exocarp; pyrenae laterally compressed, coriaceous. Albumen even, not wrinkled, fleshy to horny.—Glabrous unarmed trees. Leaves opposite,

PLATE 146.

CHEIRODENDRON GAUDICHAUDII (DC.) Seem.

Fruiting branch pinned against trunk of tree, diameter of the latter nearly 2 feet. Growing in Kipuka Puaulu, near Volcano Kilauea, Hawaii; elevation 4000 feet.

Araliaceae.

digitate with 3 to 5 leaflets, long petiolate, entire or toothed. Flowers umbellate on the ultimate division of a terminal or lateral panicle, with opposite horizontal branches, which are articulate at all nodes and below the calyx. Bracts small opposite.

A genus of two species peculiar to the Hawaiian Islands, but related to Nothopanax, a genus occurring in New Zealand, Samoa and Tasmania. *Nothopanax samoense* Gray is called *Tane-tane* by the Samoans.

KEY TO THE SPECIES.

Leaflets 3 to 5, longer than broad................................. Ch. Gaudichaudii
Leaflets 3, broader than long....................................... Ch. platyphyllum

Cheirodendron Gaudichaudii (DC.) Seem.
Olapa, or *Kauila Mahu* on Kauai.
(Plates 146, 147.)

CHEIRODENDRON GAUDICHAUDII (DC.) Seem. Journ. Bot. V. (1867) 236;— Hbd. Fl. Haw. Isl. (1888) 148;—Harms in Engl. et Prantl Pflzfam. III, 8 (1898) 48.— **Panax?** Gaudichandi DC. Prodr. IV (1830) 253;—Hook. et Arn. Bot. Beechey (1832) 84;—Endl. Fl. Suds. (1836) no. 1340;—Del Cast. Ill. Fl. Ins. Mar. Pacif. VI (1890) 181.—**Aralia trigyna** Gaud. Bot. Voy. Uranie (1826) (but appeared in reality 1830) 474, pl. 98.—**Hedera Gaudichaudii** A. Gray. Bot. U. S. E. E. (1854) 719, t. 90;—H. Mann Proc. Am. Acad. VII (1867) 168;— Wawra in Flora (1873) 142.—**Cheirodendron trigynum** (Gaud.) Heller Pl. Haw. Isl. (1897) 870.

Had Gaudichaud's Botany of the Voyage Uranie appeared really in 1826, as indicated on the title page, Heller's combination would hold good; Gaudichaud's description, however, appeared in 1830 after the publication of the species by DeCandolle in his Prodromus (1830).

Leaflets 3 to 5, the outer ones smaller, petioled, ovate, oblong or obovate, the margin generally thickened and toothed or serrulate, with a gland in the notch of each serrature, or entire (in specimens from the Punaluu mountains, Oahu) with no signs of any dentation, chartaceous to coriaceous, glabrous, shining above; panicle subpyramidal, shorter than the leaves, compact, with 4 to 5 nodes to the rhachis; flowers 4 mm greenish; pedicels 2 mm; petals thick ovate 2 to 3 mm, soon caducous; stamens nearly as long; ovary generally 3 celled, or 2 or 4 celled, rarely 5 celled; stigmas short and thick, recurved, sessile or subsessile on a short stylopod; drupe ovoid 6 mm long, 2 to 5 angled when dry.

Hooker et Arnott's *Panax? ovatum* is *Cheirodendron Gaudichaudii* (DC.) Seem. var. δ. Hbd. l.c.

The *Olapa,* as the tree is usually called on all the islands, reaches a height of 40 to 50 feet and sometimes more. It derives its name "Cheirodendron" from the Greek (Keiros—hand and Dendron—tree) on account of its leaves, which consist usually of five leaflets, giving it the shape of a hand. It is one of our most common forest trees, and is always conspicuous in the woods by its foliage, which is constantly in motion, even if there is hardly any breeze. Its trunk is sometimes two feet and even more in diameter, and is vested in a smooth, yellowish bark when growing in wet forest, and rough, scaly bark in dry districts. All parts of this tree, as well as of the *Lapalapa,* emit a very strong carroty odor when bruised, not unlike turpentine, and the wood of both species is said to burn when green. Several varieties are recognized which are peculiar to certain sections of the various islands, and are as follows:—

PLATE 147.

CHEIRODENDRON GAUDICHAUDII (DC.) Seem.
Tree growing on the old lava fields of Auahi, southern slope of Mt. Haleakala, Maui;
elevation 2800 feet.

Araliaceae.

var. *a.*—Leaflets 5 to 3, ovate oblong, deeply crenate or serrate; panicles short, styles 3, rarely 2 to 4. (E. Maui and Hawaii.)

var. *β.*—Leaflets generally 3, rarely 5, ovate to suborbicular, remotely dentate, on a long common petiole, panicle large; stigmas 3 or 2. (W. Maui, Molokai, Hawaii.)

var. *γ.*—Leaflets 3, entire, the common petiole rather long; panicle large, open, panicle drawn out, stigmas 3 to 2. (Koolau Range, Oahu.)

var. *δ.*—Leaflets 3, rarely 5, remotely and faintly dentate, on rather short petioles, styles 3, 4 or 5. (Oahu, Koolau range; Mt. Kaala, and Niihau.)

var. *ε.*—Leaflets subentire, small, membraneous, styles 2 to 5. (Woods of Kauai.)

The *Olapa* is most common on East Maui, in the middle forest zone on the slopes of Haleakala at an elevation of 4000 feet, and it is here that it attains its best development. As mentioned before, it is common on all the islands of the group at elevations from 2000 to 4000 feet.

The performers of the native *hula*, or dance, were divided into two groups, the *Olapa* and the *Hoopaa*. The former, who undoubtedly derive their name from the *Olapa* tree, were those whose part in the dance was the agile one, who could best illustrate, by the graceful bending of their bodies, the motion of the leaves of the *Olapa* trees. From the leaves and bark the natives extracted a bluish dye, which they employed in dyeing their *tapa*, or paper cloth.

Cheirodendron platyphyllum (Hook. et Arn.) Seem.
Lapalapa.
(Plate 148.)

CHEIRODENDRON PLATYPHYLLUM (Hook. et Arn.) Seem. Journ. Bot. V. (1867) 236;—Hbd. Fl. Haw. Isl. (1888) 149;—Heller Pl. Haw. Isl. (1897) 869;—Harms in Engl. et Prantl Pflzfam. III, 8 (1898) 48.—Panax? platyphyllum Hook. et Arn. Bot. Beechey (1832) 84;—Endl. Fl. Suds. (1836) no. 1342;—Del Cast. Ill. Fl. Ins. Mar. Pacif. VI (1890) 182.—Hedera platyphylla A. Gray Bot. U. S. E. E. (1854) 720, t. 91;—Mann Proc. Am. Acad. VII (1867) 168;—Wawra in Flora (1873) 157.

Leaflets 3, ovate, broader than long, 4 to 8 cm x 5 to 7.5 cm, mucronate or suddenly and shortly acuminate, truncate at the base, or sometimes cuneate, entire or shortly dentate or almost sinuate-dentate (Waialeale, Kauai, plants), with thickened margin, coriaceous and shining, on long spreading petioles about 4 cm, the common petioles 6 to 8 cm long; panicles single, or three together, very open, 10 to 15 cm long, pedunculate; umbellets 4 to 7 flowered, the pedicles 2 to 6 mm; flowers 6 mm; stigmas 5, rarely 4, incurved or truncate, triangular on a very short and thick stylopod; drupe subglobose, 6 to 7 mm in diameter, 5 to 4 angled when dry.

The *Lapalapa*, somewhat smaller than the *Olapa*, is a very handsome tree, though by far not as common as the latter, as it is only found on the high plateau of Kauai up to the summit of Waialeale, and on the Koolau mountain range of Oahu. It is easily distinguished from the *Olapa* by its leaves, which are much broader than long and are on long, spreading petioles with only three leaflets. What has been said of the *Olapa* in regard to the constant motion of its leaves applies also to the *Lapalapa*.

It is confined to the Islands of Kauai and Oahu and inhabits the very wet or rain forests at an elevation of 4000 feet up to 5000 feet; it hardly descends lower than 3000 feet. It thrives best in swampy ground, and is a common fea-

PLATE 148.

CHEIBODENDRON PLATYPHYLLUM (Hook. et Arn.) Seem.
Flowering branch, reduced.

ture of the vegetation on the high plateau of Kauai, bordering the extensive open bogs of Kauluwehi, Alakai, and Lehua makanoe. At the summit of Waialeale it is a small tree or rather shrub, with almost sinuate leaves. At lower elevations the leaves are entire. It is associated with Pelea, Dubautia (the high mountain forms), Labordea, *Lobelia Gaudichaudii, Scaevola glabra*, etc. On Oahu it is confined to the summit ridges of the Koolau range, especially Konahuanui, and has also been found on Kaala of the Waianae range.

The wood of the *Lapalapa* is whitish, with a yellow tinge, and is said to burn when green.

EPACRIDACEAE.

The family Epacridaceae has only a limited distribution. The bulk of its species is to be found in Australia and Tasmania, with quite a number of genera in New Zealand. The family possesses 21 genera of which 273 species occur in Australia. Of all the 21 genera only one genus with one subgenus is not to be found in Australia or Tasmania. A few endemic species occur in New Caledonia and the most southern part of South America, besides a few species of large genera in India and the Malayan-Archipelago. Here in the Hawaiian Islands we have two species represented, of the subgenus Cyathodes, formerly recognized as a genus, but now a subgenus of Styphelia by Drude.

STYPHELIA Sol.

Corolla campanulate, funnel-shaped or tubular. Stamens enclosed in the tubes of the corolla; anthers hardly visible, or exserted on long filaments. Style longer than the stamens, stigma simple small. Disc a ring or composed of 5 lobes or scales. Ovary usually 5-celled, rarely through abortion 3- or 2-celled. Fruit a berry or drupe.—Shrubs or low trees with usually broad or narrow lanceolate, spathulate-elliptical leaves, the flowers single, axillary, or in racemes, with 2 to several bracts.

This is the richest genus in the family Epacridaceae of which the largest number of species belongs to Australia. The Hawaiian species *St. Tameiameia* and *St. Grayana* come under the fourth subgenus Cyathodes which may be described as follows:

Subgen. Cyathodes Lab.

Calyx surrounded by many bracts; corolla funnel-shaped, its tube hardly protruding from the calyx, inside and at the throat without glands and beardless; stamens enclosed; ovary 5-10 celled.

The subgenus Cyathodes occurs in Tasmania, New Zealand, and in the Hawaiian Islands with two species.

Styphelia tameiameia F. Muell.

Pukeawe or Puakeawe.

STYPHELIA TAMEIAMEIA F. Muell. Fragm. VI. (1867) 55;—Drude in Engl. et Prantl Pflzfam. IV. 1. 78.—Cyathodes tameiameia Cham. in Linnaea I. (1826) 539;—Endl. Fl. Suds. (1836) 170. No. 1070;—DC. Prodr. VII (1839) 741;—

Epacridaceae.

Th. Nuttal in Transact. Am. Phil. Soc. VIII. (1843) 270;—A. Gray Proc. Am. Acad. V. (1862) 325;—Mann Proc. Am. Ac. VII. (1867) 188;— Wawra in Flora (1873) 59;—Hbd. Fl. Haw. Isl. (1888) 272;—Del Cast. Ill. Fl. Ins. Mar. Pac. VII. (1892) 224;—Heller Pl. Haw. Isl. in Minnes. Bot. Stud. Bull. IX. (1897) 872.

Leaves stiff coriaceous, linear or oblong 8-12 mm long, 2-4 mm broad, on broadish petioles of less than 1 mm, acute or somewhat obtuse, shortly mucronate, cuneate or somewhat obtuse at the base, naked, smooth above, waxy-white or glaucous underneath and striate with 9-13 longitudinal nerves, which fork or branch more or less, particularly in the obovate leaves; peduncle with flower shorter than the leaf; bracts (5-9) and sepals obtuse coriaceous; corolla whitish, 3 mm long, the tube included in the calyx, the acute lobes ½ the length of the tube, with 5 lines of hairlets running down the tube; anthers oblong, obtuse, subexserted, about as long as their filaments; disc small; ovary 5-8 celled; style as long as the ovary, thick tapering; drupe globose 4-6 mm in diameter, red, white or pink, rather dry; seeds ovoid, with thin testa; embryo axile two-third the length of the mealy albumen, the radicle scarcely distinguishable from the cotyledons.

The *Pukeawe*, or as it is also called *Maiele*, *Puakeawe* and *Kawau* on Lanai, is a shrub in the lower elevations, but becomes a small tree 10-15 feet in height in the upper regions at 6000-7000 feet elevation. The trunk is rather twisted and vested in a finely corrugated brown bark; the tallest specimens were observed by the writer on the upper slopes of Mt. Hualalai on Hawaii at an elevation of 6000 feet. The species occurs on all the islands of the group and can be found at all elevations. The species besides being found in Hawaii exists also in Tahiti and Eimeo of the Society group.

Interesting legends are connected with this plant in Hawaii; it was a favorite of the Kahuna or native priest. David Malo, the Hawaiian historian, tells us that it was used in incremating the body of any one who had made himself an outlaw beyond the protection of the tabu. Dr. N. Emerson gives an interesting explanation of this procedure of incremation. He also says: "When a kapu-chief found it convenient to lay aside his dread exclusiveness for a time, that he might perhaps mingle with people on equal terms without injury to them or to himself, it was the custom for him and according to one authority those with whom he intended to mingle joined with him in the ceremony—to shut himself into a little house and smudge himself with the smoke from a fire of the *Pukeawe* shrub. At the conclusion of this fumigation a priest recited a *Pule Huikala*— prayer for a dispensation.

The *Pukeawa* is familiar to all who have been at all in the Hawaiian forests, especially around the Volcano of Kilauea on Hawaii where the plant is very common in company with the *Olelo* berries. It is very striking on account of its heath-like appearance, and the white or red dry berries. On the high mountains at from 10,000 feet elevation up to the limit of plant growth occurs another species, which is a shrub. Its scientific name, which was *Cyathodes imbricata* Stschegleew, will have to be changed, as there is already a *St. imbricata* in that genus as a synonym, and therefore will be known from now on as *Styphelia Grayana* (Stschegleew) Rock.

MYRSINACEAE.

The family Myrsinaceae consists of 32 genera and about 770 species. The family is a distinctly tropical one and is distributed over the whole world. In the eastern hemisphere it ranges from the island of Tsu Sima, Korea straits, to Victoria in Australia, and in the western hemisphere from Florida to Argentine.

In the Hawaiian Islands only two genera are represented, Suttonia and Embelia, the former occurs outside of Hawaii only in New Zealand and has arborescent forms, while the genus Embelia has two species in these Islands, which are climbers, but consists of more than 92 species which have a wide distribution (Africa, India, Hawaii, Australia).

SUTTONIA Hook.

Flowers hermaphrodite, 4 or 5-merous. Sepals shortly, or very shortly united, or free at the base, imbricate or open, with ciliolate margins. Petals free, valvate or very obscurely imbricate, broadly or rarely narrow-elliptical, or very rarely obovate, rounded or subacute at the apex, with papillulose or ciliate margins, often punctate or lineate. Anthers usually sessile and little shorter than the petals, introrse, somewhat acute at the apex or subobtuse, and papillose. Ovary ovoid, style wanting or very short; stigma capitate and often fimbriate. Placenta 2-4 ovulate. Fruits globose or ovoid, 1-seeded, crowned by the stigma; endocarp crustaceous to chartaceous. Seeds globose with the rudiments of the placenta, albumen horny, embryo cylindrical. Trees or shrubs with entire, very variable leaves. Inflorescence lateral, fasciculate in the axils of fallen leaves, few-flowered. Flowers small, pedicellate.

The Hawaiian species of the genus Suttonia form a section by themselves "Subgenus *Rapaneopsis* Mez;" with pentamerous flowers.

The Hawaiian *Kolea* were originally placed in the genus Myrsine by A. DeCandolle, and later transferred to the genus Suttonia by Mez. The whole genus consists of 17 species, 11 of which are endemic in the Hawaiian Islands; of the remaining 6, 5 are found in New Zealand and one in Norfolk Island. Originally only four Hawaiian species were known and are described in Hillebrand's Flora of the Hawaiian Islands. Since then 4 were added by Mez, and 3 distinct new species and 3 new varieties by the writer. H. Léveillé described 10 new species of which 6 are now synonyms; one of his species, *Suttonia molokaiensis*, is a small leaved form of *Sideroxylon sandwicense*. As the description of the remaining ones is so vague, and material of them not in the writer's possession, they are very dubious and are here ignored.

KEY TO THE SPECIES.

Leaves tomentose underneath.
    Branches glabrous, leaves 65 mm.............................. S. Kauaiensis
    Branches covered with ferruginous tomentum, leaves 100 mm or more S. Wawraea
Leaves glabrous.
    Leaves thin, without marginal nerve, petals markedly punctate..... S. Lanaiensis
    Leaves large 210 mm, elongate elliptical, petiolate, chartaceous.... S. Fernseei
    Leaves succulent, spathulate, 75 mm, petiole margined............ S. spathulata

Myrsinaceae.

Leaveš ðark, chartaceous, pale veined, not punctate; drupe very
small 3 mm, spheroidal.. **S. volcanica**
Leaves ovate to suborbicular, glaucous, margins revolute, style
distinct.. **S. Knudsenii**
Leaves thick coriaceous, 100 mm long or more, reticulate, cuneate
at the base.. **S. Lessertiana**
Leaves coriaceous, small, 24 mm, emarginate at the apex.......... **S. Sandwicensis**
Leaves elliptical-oblong, petiolate, 50 mm long, strongly reticulate. **S. Hillebrandii**
Leaves sessile, very narrow, lanceolate, apex caudate, acuminate.. **S. lanceolata**

Suttonia kauaiensis (Hbd.) Mez.

SUTTONIA KAUAIENSIS (Hbd.) Mez Das Pflzenreich 9. IV. 236. (1902) 335;—Pax in
Engl. et Prantl Pflzfam. IV. 1. (1908) 278.—**Myrsine kauaiensis** Hbd. Fl. Haw. Isl.
(1888) 280;—Del Cast. Ill. Fl. Ins. Mar. Pac. VII. (1892) 227.—Heller in Minnes.
Bot. Stud. IX. (1897) 873.

A small tree 12 m in height; branches slender, glabrous; leaves pilose when young,
glabrate when old, on petioles of 4-15 mm, oblong or oblong-lanceolate, shortly and obscurely
acuminate at the apex or somewhat obtuse, reticulate on both sides, the adult leaves densely
set with blackish minute dots; inflorescence of 1-5-7 flowers, bracts linear, 2-2.5 mm, the
slender pedicels 5.7 mm, glabrous or pilose; flowers 3 mm long; sepals connate one-third
their length, often covered with long hair at the dorsal side, ovate; petals elliptical,
subrotundate at the apex, with elongate, brownish, or shortly linear dots; stamens with
large, ovate-elliptical, somewhat acuminate anthers, slightly papillose; ovary glabrous, ovoid,
style short and thick, stigma obtuse, very obscurely 5-angular; drupe globose, 4 mm.

This species was first collected by V. Knudsen (no. 191) of Kauai. It grows
in the outskirts of the forests of Halemanu and Kaholuamano on Kauai. Specimens which evidently belong to this species were collected by the writer in the
type locality (Halemanu) flowering (no. 1567) Febr. 14, 1909; and in Milolii
gorge (no. 2355) Febr. 26, 1909. In this latter form the young leaves are
membraneous and puberulous; without flower or fruit.

The typical *Suttonia kauaiensis* was collected in the forests of Kaholuamano,
at an elevation of 3800 feet, flowering March, 1909, (no. 2359). The pedicels
are glabrous, as well as the flowers, with the exception of the ciliate margin of
sepals and petals; the leaves are subemarginate at the base.

Suttonia Wawraea Mez.

SUTTONIA WAWRAEA Mez Das Pflzreich 9. IV. 236. (1902) 335.—**Myrsine Gaudichaudii**
var. **hirsuta** Wawra in Flora (1874) 524.—**Myrsine Kauaiensis** var. β **hirsuta** Hbd.
in Fl. Haw. Isl. (1888) 281; Del Cast. Ill. Fl. Ins. Mar. Pac. VII. (1892) 227.

A small tree or shrub; young branches densely and shortly covered with a turbid
brown-ferruginous tomentum; leaves on petioles of 4 mm, elliptical or obovate-elliptical,
somewhat obtuse at the apex, 8-16 cm long, 40-60 mm wide, the medium nerve covered
with an appressed reddish tomentum, the under side of the young leaves with a scattered
pubescence of the same color, prominently reticulate on both sides, the upper side glabrous,
punctulate, with transparent dots; flowers 6-10, 14 mm long, pedicels densely tomentose 5-7
mm long; flowers densely tomentose, sepals connate at the base one-fourth their length,
ovate, somewhat acute, with the margins very densely villous-ciliate; petals linear, anthers
barbellate at the apex; stigma in the female flowers echinate-capitulate; drupe dark
bluish, glaucous, globose 8 mm in diameter, crowned by the persistent stigma; seeds globose,
many-ribbed, 6 mm in diameter, endocarp thin, papery.

Myrsinaceae.

This exceedingly interesting and handsome species, which is undoubtedly very closely related to *S. Kauaiensis*, occurs only in the very dense forest of the interior of Kauai, often bordering the extensive bogs. It is quite conspicuous on account of its dark green leaves which are dark reddish pubescent underneath, and also for its fruits, which are blackish blue with glaucous hue. It rarely attains a height of more than 12 feet and is often shrubby; the writer collected it on the borders of the bog Kauluwehi, elevation 4300 feet, in the heart of the Kauai forests, fruiting October, 1911, (no. 10229); and flowering, Kaholuamano forests (no. 2362), March 3-10, 1909; (no. 5956) fruiting from the tabular summit of Kauai Sept. 4, 1909. Abbe Faurie flowering March, 1910, (no. 424).

Suttonia lanaiensis (Hbd.) Mez.

SUTTONIA LANAIENSIS (Hbd.) Mez Das Pflzenreich 9. IV. 326. (1902) 336.—**Myrsine Lanaiensis** Hbd. Fl. Haw. Isl. (1888) 281.—Del Cast. Fl. Ins. Mar. Pac. VII. (1892) 227.

A small tree, glabrous throughout, the bark of the rather stiff branches covered with lenticels; leaves on petioles of 4-18 mm, elliptical, or obovate-oblong, shortly acute at the base, moderately acuminate at the apex, pale, dull, membraneous to chartaceous, minutely dotted above, very obscurely so underneath, 85 mm or more long, 40-60 mm wide, flowers rameal and in the axils of leaves, flowers usually 5-8 or even more, pedicels 5-6 mm, slender, glabrous; flowers 3 mm long; sepals almost free, ovate to suborbicular, with the margins papillose-fimbriate; petals elliptico-lanceolate, subacute, dotted with black roundish dots or lines; anthers ovate, subacute, the apex papillulose; ovary ovoid, narrowed toward the apex, glabrous, style none, stigma large, pulvinate; drupe globose, depressed 5-6 mm in diam. reddish, with chartaceous putamen, 1-seeded, with the rudiments of 2 or three ovules; embryo arcuately curved in horny albumen.

This handsome species, which has hitherto been thought to be peculiar to the Island of Lanai, has also been collected on the eastern part of Maui in open dry gulches back of Makawao at an elevation of 2500 feet, where it reaches a height of 30 feet.

It is exceedingly common on the Island of Lanai in the open dry gulches, such as Kaiholena, Mahana and Koele, where it is a small tree, and quite conspicuous on account of its pale, graceful foliage, which has always a pinkish tint. It is associated with *Rauwolfia sandwicensis, Xanthoxylum hawaiiense* var. *β.*, *Pisonia sandwicensis*, and many others.

It is collected by the writer on Lanai, flowering July 27, 1910, (no. 8027); and flowering and fruiting Sept., 1910, (no. 8533) in a gulch above Makawao, Island of Maui.

Var. coriacea Rock var. nov.

A tree with stout and robust branches; leaves thick coriaceous, ovate-oblong, somewhat shining above, copper colored on both sides, dull underneath, prominently veined, very minutely punctate above, subacute or slightly emarginate at the apex, somewhat acute at the base, slightly contracted on puberulous stout petioles of 10-12 mm; flowers 8, on stout pedicels of 6 mm, glabrous, otherwise as in the species; fruit not seen.

Of this variety only one tree was observed in the xerophylous forest on the western end of Lanai, called Kaa, where a remnant of what must have been

Myrsinaceae.

once an interesting forest is still to be found. The tree was at once conspicuous by its thick leathery bronze colored leaves; it was just beginning to flower. It is associated with *Osmanthus sandwicensis, Xylosma Hillebrandii,* and *Maba sandwicensis.* From a distance the tree looked almost exactly like a Sideroxylon or Chrysophyllum. Collected flowering July 27, 1910, (no. 8078), type in the Herbarium of the College of Hawaii.

Suttonia Fernseei Mez.

SUTTONIA FERNSEEI Mez. in Das Pflzenreich 9. IV. 236. (1902) 336.—Myrsine Gaudichaudii var. grandifolia Wawra in Flora (1874) 524.

Branches very thick, at the very apex beset with minute ferruginous scales; leaves on petioles of 7 mm or more, elongate and narrowly elliptical, acute at the base, shortly contracted, 210 mm or more long, 65 mm broad, membranaceous to chartaceous, somewhat shining, reticulate; flowers 5-8, 12 mm or more long, pedicels slender, glabrous, 8 mm; flowers 3 mm long, glabrous; sepals connate one-third their length, the lobes triangular, with the margins densely ciliate, petals acute, very obscurely marked with lines; anthers of the female flowers little reduced, acute; ovary glabrous, with a sessile capitate stigma.

This species named by Mez in honor of Wawra, Ritter von Fernsee, was collected by the latter on the Island of Kauai (no. 2019). It is not known to the writer. It may, however, be identical with an exceedingly large Suttonia tree with a trunk of 2 feet in diameter, and very large leaves, found at Opaiwela near Kaholuamano, Kauai. Owing to the size of the tree it was impossible to secure specimens. The writer did not meet with any other tree of this sort, and was assured by Mr. Francis Gay of Kauai, who is more familiar with the Kauai forests than any other man, that the one in question is the only one known to him in the surrounding forests.

On the Koolau range on the Island of Oahu, in the mountains of Punaluu, the writer collected specimens of a Suttonia (no. 473) but without flower or fruit, whose leaves answer well Mez's description of *S. Fernseei,* and it is here doubtfully referred to that species. Among the numerous duplicates of the various Suttonia, the writer found a sheet numbered 2364 collected at Kaholuamano, Kauai, March, 1909, but without flower or fruit; it must however be referred to *S. Fernseei,* as the leaves answer the description.

Suttonia spathulata Rock sp. nov.
Kolea.

A small tree 6-8 m high, glabrous throughout; branches stiff, more or less ascending; leaves decidedly spathulate, bluntly acute at the apex or rounded, thick fleshy, rather succulent, on short margined petioles of 5-8 mm, or often subsessile, dark green above, light underneath, petioles reddish, veins quite inconspicuous, sparingly punctate with minute black dots, 5-7.5 cm long, 2-3 cm wide; branchlets densely flowered their whole length, (flowers unknown); fruits usually 4-6 in a cluster on pedicels of 10 mm, bracts broad, triangular; pedicels and the persistent ovate sepals glabrous, the latter with slightly fimbriate margins; fruit globose, black, 6 mm in diameter, crowned by the stigma.

This rather striking species is a small tree of 15-20 feet or little more, and is peculiar to Mt. Haleakala, Maui, where it grows on the northwest slope at an elevation of 6500 feet in the gulches back of the extinct crater of Puunianiau,

Myrsinaceae.

associated with *Dodonaea eriocarpa, Argyroxiphium virescens, Raillardia platyphylla, Santalum Haleakalae, Geranium arboreum,* and others.

It was collected by the writer fruiting on Oct. 11, 1910. The type is number 8591 in the Herbarium of the College of Hawaii.

It is at once distinguished from other Suttonia by its small spathulate, very thick leaves, and branchlets, which are densely covered with the rather large fruits. In the dry specimens the leaves turn pale and the fruits yellowish.

Suttonia volcanica Rock sp. nov.

Kolea.

A small tree 4-5 m high, with slender branches, glabrous throughout; leaves dark green, very prominently and pale veined, midrib red, pale underneath, not dotted, thin chartaceous, shining above, dull underneath, ovate-oblong, bluntly acuminate or acute, or slightly obtuse, rounded at the base, 5-10 cm long, 2-4.5 cm wide, on somewhat margined petioles of 6-8 mm; the slender branchlets densely covered with mature fruits; (flowers unknown); fruits 2-8 in a cluster on very slender glabrous pedicels of 6-8 mm; bracts reddish-brown, dentiform to linear, the persistent calyx parted two-third its length into 5-7 triangular lobes of 1 mm, with slightly ciliate margins; fruit subglobose or rather spheroidal, black when mature, very small for a Suttonia, 3-4 mm in diameter, glabrous, crowned by the stigma.

This species is remarkable for its very small fruits, which are densely clustered around the slender branchlets, and for its leaves, which are chartaceous, thin, and prominently veined, but not punctate. It was found by the writer on the great central plain between Mauna Loa and Mt. Hualalai on Hawaii on the cinder slopes of a crater called Puuokeanue, at an elevation of 5300 feet in company with *Solanum incompletum, Santalum Freycinetianum,* and *Raillardia* sp. It was collected fruiting Feb. 13, 1912. The type is no. 10230 in the Herbarium of the College of Hawaii.

Var. lavarum Rock var. nov.

Leaves elliptical-oblong, to oblong-lanceolate, of the same texture and venation as the species, obscurely acute, or obtuse, slightly contracted at the base, dark green above, dull and lighter underneath, not punctate, 6-12 cm long, 2-3.5 cm wide, on black petioles 10-15 mm, inflorescence in fascicles, mainly in leaf-axils and also along the branches but not very numerous; inflorescence of 8 flowers, on slender pedicels 4-7 mm, bracts as in the species; calyx parted one-half its length into 5-7 ovate rounded lobes with ciliate margins; petals pubescent with ciliate-fimbriate margins, densely punctate with rather large black dots; anthers sagittate, with pubescent apex; ovary globose, with sessile capitate stigma; fruits as in the species, little larger.

The variety *lavarum* occurs on the southern slopes of Mt. Haleakala, Maui, on the *aa* lava fields of Auahi, on the land of Kahikinui, an exceedingly dry locality at an elevation of 2000 feet. It was collected by the writer flowering and fruiting November, 1910. The type is number 8678 in the College of Hawaii Herbarium.

It is a small tree and quite distinct from *Suttonia Lessertiana* and its numerous variations, which occur at little higher elevation in the same locality. In texture and venation of leaf, shape and size of fruit, as well as general aspect, it is almost identical with *Suttonia volcanica* from Mauna Loa, Hawaii, of which it is here made a variety.

PLATE 149.

SUTTONIA LESSERTIANA (A. DC.) Mez.
Kolea.
Flowering branch, from a tall tree found in the rain forests of Naalehu, Kau, Hawaii;
one-half natural size.

Myrsinaceae.

Suttonia Knudsenii Rock sp. nov.

A small tree or shrub, branches tortuose, glabrous; leaves ovate to obovate, or suborbicular, glabrous on both sides, venation prominent, reticulated, the margins revolute, quite opaque, sparingly punctate underneath, dark green, with glaucous hue, shining above, dull beneath, quite chartaceous, 4.5-7 cm long, 3-4.5 cm wide, on petioles of 2-4 mm; inflorescence fasciculated at intervals of 15 mm along the slender branchlets and in the axils of the leaves, of 3-12 flowers, puberulous, pedicels of 2-2.5 mm, the bracts 1 mm, triangular, with ciliate margins; calyx 2 mm, parted more than half its length into acute lobes, densely punctate, with fimbriate margins, corolla twice as long as the calyx, ornamented with dark dots, anthers oblong, puberulous at the apex, ovary ovoid, with distinct style; fruit unknown.

This exceedingly handsome species is peculiar to the Island of Kauai and is only found in the forests of Halemanu, in the interior swampy woods; it is distinguished from the other Suttonias by its thin leaves which are ovate to suborbicular and are of a glaucous color, and in the very shortly pedicellate red flowers. It is a striking species and is here named for Mr. Augustus Knudsen, of Waiawa, Kauai, to whom the writer is greatly indebted for extended hospitality and facilities for collecting in the mountains of Kauai. The type is number 2337 in the College of Hawaii Herbarium. Collected February 14-26, 1909, Halemanu, Kauai, flowering.

A form with somewhat smaller leaves, which are acute at the apex instead of rounded, and more elliptical in outline, must be referred here as forma *elliptica* fm. nov. (no. 1661), flowering, February, 1909, Halemanu, Kauai.

Suttonia Hillebrandii Mez.
Kolea.

SUTTONIA HILLEBRANDII Mez Das Pflzenreich 9. IV. 236. (1908) 337.

Branches entirely glabrous, leaves on petioles of about 3 mm, acute at the base, shortly contracted, quite acuminate at the apex, rarely somewhat obtuse, about 50 mm long, 20 mm broad, not punctate; inflorescence 5 or more flowered, 10 mm long, pedicels slender, glabrous, 7 mm long sepals 1/3 connate, the lobes ovate somewhat acute, the margins remotely dentate and ciliate, lineate; ovary globose, stigma thick capituliform.

This species, which is not known to the writer, was collected by Wawra on the Island of Kauai, evidently at Halemanu. There are several forms found on the Island of Oahu which are certainly referable to this species; some of them are varieties.

On the Island of Oahu in the Koolau range, Mountains of Waikane, the writer collected specimens of a tree which is a good variety and may be described as follows:

Var. emarginata Rock var. nov.

A small tree; leaves lanceolate oblong, glabrous throughout, chartaceous, 3.5 to 8 cm long, 12 to 15 mm wide, contracting at the base into a slightly margined petiole of 2 to 3 mm, veins prominent; intramarginal nerve continuous and very close to the edge, rounded at the apex and always emarginate; dark green above, lighter beneath; inflorescence in the axils of the leaves and along the branchlets, 3 to 8 flowered, pedicels slender, puberulous, as are the petals, which are sparingly punctulate with reddish dots or even lined; stamens oblong, little shorter than the petals; ovary ovoid, style distinct; fruits large, black, 8 to 9 mm in diameter.

373

PLATE 150.

SUTTONIA LESSERTIANA (A. DC.) Mez.
Kolea.
Fruiting branch from a stunted tree found on open exposed ridges on Mt. Konahuanui,
Oahu; about one-half natural size.

Myrsinaceae.

In Niu Valley, Oahu, occurs a small tree which belongs to this variety. In specimens from the latter locality the fruits are densely clustered along the branchlets, especially on defoliate ones, making them appear like axillary racemes.

Collected flowering (no. 1217)) January 23, 1909, Waikane Mts., Oahu, and Niu Valley, fruiting Aug. 22, 1909 (no. 4807), and Feb. 8, 1913, fruiting (no. 10232), same locality.

Suttonia Lessertiana (A. DC.) Mez.
Kolea.
(Plates 149, 150, 151.)

SUTTONIA LESSERTIANA (A.DC.) Mez Das Pflzenreich 9. IV. 236. (1902) 336;—Pax in Engl. et Prantl Pflzfam. Nachtr. IV. 1. (1908) 278.—Brigham Ka Hana Kapa in Mem. B. P. Bish. Mus. (1911) 148. fig. 89.—**Myrsine Lessertiana** A. DC. in Ann. Sc. Nat. 2. Ser. XVI. (1841) 85 et in DC. Prodr. VIII. (1844) 96;—Gray in Proc. Am. Acad. V. (1862) 331;—Seem. Fl. Vit. (1866) 149;—Mann in Proc. Am. Acad. VII. (1866) 188;—Hbd. Fl. Haw. Isl. (1888) 279;—Del Cast. Ill. Ins. Mar. Pac. VII. (1892) 227;—Heller in Minnes. Bot. Stud. IX. (1897) 874.— **Myrsine Gaudichaudii** Wawra (non DC.) in Flora (1874) 523;—Gray l. c. 331; Seem. l. c.;—Mann l. c. 188;—Hbd. l. c. 280;—Heller l. c. 873.—**Myrsine Fauriei** Lévl. in Fedde Repert. X. 10-14. (1911) 154.—**Suttonia Fauriei** Lévl. in Fedde Repert. X. 24-26. (1912) 373.—**Suttonia cuneata** Lévl. et Faurie in Fedde Repert. X. 27-29. (1912) 443;—**Suttonia pukooensis** Lévl. l. c. 444.

Branches thick or very thick, quite glabrous, old ones verrucous; leaves very shortly petioled or often broadly sessile, broad or narrow elliptical, or elliptical-lanceolate or obovate, somewhat obtuse at both ends or rounded at the apex, often acute at the base, of variable length and width, coriaceous, the adult leaves densely and minutely punctulate above with black dots, the veins little prominent and connected by a straight marginal nerve; flowers in the axils of the oldest leaves and all along the branchlets and on projecting spurs of the bare branches, in fascicles of 3 to 7 or more, pedicels slender, glabrous, 5 to 6 mm with flowers, and longer with fruits; flowers 3 to 3.5 mm long, glabrous, sepals shortly (1/5) united at the base, lobes 5 to 7 ovate somewhat acute, the margins very shortly fimbriate; petals broadly elliptical twice the length of the calyx, yellowish with reddish dots, apex obtuse, the margin papillose; stamens little shorter than the petals, anthers ovate, apex papillulose, emarginate at the base; ovary ovoid-conical, stigma sessile or on a short style, capitate, fimbriate or 5-laciniate on the fruit; drupe globose, reddish or black, 4 to 6 mm with chartaceous pyrena.

This species is one of the most variable ones in the genus, and that to such an extent that hardly two trees are alike. The leaves are the most variable part of the plant; also shape and branching habit vary greatly. It certainly is a graceful tree in the rain forests of Oahu and Hawaii, as well as on the other islands of the Hawaiian group. Should one undertake to describe all the various forms as new species, as H. Léveillé did, one would certainly be naming individuals, and swell the synonyms of *Suttonia Lessertiana,* into which most of H. Léveillé species have wandered to remain there forever; the remaining ones are synonyms of *S. sandwicensis.*

As already stated the species occurs on all the islands of the group in many forms which are too numerous to cite, but have been incorporated in the description to some extent. The trees reach often a height of 60 feet or so, with a trunk of one to two feet in diameter, and clothed in a gray bark which

PLATE 151.

SUTTONIA LESSERTIANA (A. DC.) Mez.
Kolea Tree.
Growing in the Kipuka Puaulu, near the Volcano of Kilauea, Hawaii. elevation 4000 feet.

Myrsinaceae.

is either smooth or covered with lenticels; when cut into, a red sap exudes very freely, which was employed by the natives of by-gone days for dyeing the tapa or paper cloth. The wood is quite handsome, of a pink color and mottled throughout. It is not very hard, but was used by the natives for house posts and beams; it takes a fine polish and could be employed for cabinet work as it can be easily worked. The biggest trees the writer observed on the Island of Hawaii on the slopes of Mauna Kea and Mauna Loa, as well as in Waihou forest on the flanks of Mt. Hualalai. It favors an elevation of from 3000-4000 feet, but descends lower on Oahu, though higher on Hawaii. It grows in the rain forests, though its best development is attained in the more open park-like forests situated on the above mentioned mountains.

On the Island of Lanai occurs a tree which must be referred to *S. Lessertiana*, but from which it differs in the decidedly ovate fruits, or even elongate-ovate, and is here named forma *ovicarpa* fm. nov. Collected in Mahana Valley, Lanai, fruiting Aug. 1st, 1910; no. 8102.

Suttonia sandwicensis (A. DC.) Mez.
Kolea laulii.
(Plate 152.)

SUTTONIA SANDWICENSIS (A. DC.) Mez Das Pflanzenreich 9. IV. 236. (1902) 336.—
Myrsine sandwicensis A. DC. in Ann. Sc. Nat. 2. Ser. XVI. (1841) 85 et in DC.
Prodr. VIII. (1844) 96;—Gray Proc. Am. Ac. V. (1862) 331;—Seem. Fl. Vit.
(1866) 149;—Mann Proc. Am. Ac. VII. (1867) 188;—Wawra in Flora (1874)
523†;—Hbd. Fl. Haw. Isl. (1888) 281;—Pax in Engl. et Prantl Pflzfam. IV. 1.
(1889) 92;—Del Cast. Ill. Fl. Ins. Mar. Pac. VII. (1892) 227;—Heller in Minnes.
Bot. Stud. Bull. IX. (1897) 874 (not Myrsine lanceolate).—Myrsine Vanioti Lévl.
in Fedde Repert. X. 10./14. (1911) 157.—Myrsine sandwicensis var. mauiensis
Lévl. l. c. 157.—M. sandwicensis var. punctata Lévl. l. c. 157.—Suttonia mauiensis
(Lévl.) Lévl. in Fedde Repert. X. 27/29 444.—S. punctata (Lévl.) Lévl. l. c.
144, identical with Myrsine sandwicensis DC. var. β denticulata Hbd. l. c.

A small tree or shrub of myrtillaceous habit, with the young branches somewhat tomentulose, or in Kauai specimens covered with a rufous tomentum. leaves on petioles of up to 3 mm, obovate or lanceolate-obovate, acute at the base, emarginate at the apex, 14 to 24 mm long, 6 to 10 mm broad, coriaceous, with hidden veins, quite opaque, rugose underneath, glabrous, the young leaves often densely punctulate with reddish dots; inflorescence of 3 to 7 flowers, on not protruding gemmae, the pedicels 4 to 6 mm; flowers 2 to 2.5 mm long; sepals little connate, ovate, the margins papillulose-ciliate; petals elliptical-lanceolate, acute, scarcely twice as long as the sepals, yellowish or reddish, with reddish-brown streaks; stamens only half as long as the corolla, anthers shortly acuminate at the apex; ovary ovoid, gabrous, stigma subsessile, large, capitate-pulvinate; drupe black or bluish and glaucous, globose or ovoid, 3 to 5 mm in diameter.

This very handsome species is usually found as a shrub, but also as a tree, especially in the forest of the southern slopes of Mauna Loa at an elevation of 5500 feet, where it attains a height of 25 feet. It is quite conspicuous in the woods on account of its small foliage which is less than an inch long, dark green above and pale underneath. It occurs on all the islands of the group and is more or less uniform, with the exception of on Kauai, where it is quite

PLATE 152.

SUTTONIA SANDWICENSIS (A. DC.) Mez.
Kolea Laulii.
Flowering branch, about one-half natural size.

Myrsinaceae.

variable. It is plentiful in different forms in the forests of Halemanu, above Waimea, Kauai, where it is a small tree or shrub.

It is not found at low elevations where *S. Lessertiana* abounds, but is more or less restricted to the higher levels, that is between 3000-5500 feet, or occasionally even higher. To this species are referred Léveillé's numerous new species, which are not even forms of *S. sandwicensis*. His *S. punctata* is identical with Hillebrand's var. *β. denticulata* a low shrub, which occurs on the high plateau of Kauai in open bogs, or often also in the swampy forests. The writer had at his disposal co-types of Léveillé's plants, which were kindly loaned to him by the Brothers of the Catholic school of Hilo, to whom Abbé Faurie sent one set of his duplicates. With the help of these plants the writer was enabled to straighten out Léveillé's species, which could not have been done satisfactorily with Léveillé's short description only.

Var. apodocarpa (Lévl.) Rock.

Suttonia apodocarpa Lévl. et Faurie in Fedde Repertor. X. 27/29 (1912) 44.

Leaves linear, indistinctly multipunctate, 1 to 2 cm long, 2 to 5 mm wide, acuminate glabrous, rugulose, with revolute margin, fruits usually single or 2 to 4 in a cluster, on very short pedicels, (according to Léveillé sessile, but his specimen at my disposal bears neither flower nor fruit) globose, 3 to 4 mm, crowned by the capitate stigma. Abbé Faurie's number is 446, coll. Waimea, Kauai, Febr., 1910.

The writer's own material of this plant, which is not specifically distinct from *S. sandwicensis*, but is a variety, was collected on the central plateau of Kauai in September, 1909, fruiting no. 5605. Hillebrand's var. *β.denticulata* occurs also in that locality, flowering and fruiting no. 4967, Sept., 1909, and Oct., 1911.

Suttonia lanceolata (Wawra) Rock.
Kolea.

Myrsine sandwicensis var. **lanceolata** Wawra in Flora (1874) 526.—**Myrsine lanceolata** Heller in Minnes. Bot. Bull. IX. (1897) 873, not **M. angustifolia,** Heller —**Suttonia angustifolia** Mez Das Pflzenreich 9. IV. 236. (1902) 337.

Branches slender, glabrous, nodose, dark reddish brown, foliate only at the apex; leaves, linear-lanceolate, dark green above, pale underneath, caudate-acuminate at the apex, acute at the base, sessile or subsessile, minutely reticulate underneath, minutely punctulate above, with black dots, 40 to 65 mm long, 5 to 8 mm wide; flowers single or two in the axils of the leaves on short pedicels of 2 mm; flowers 3 mm, glabrous, sepals ovate, subacute, sparingly punctate, half the length of the corolla; petals oblong, subacute, sparingly punctate, with a reddish thickened margin, stamens the height of the ovary, which is less than half the length of the petals, anthers acute, glabrous, ovary conical with a sessile capitate stigma; drupes usually on the naked branchlets, bluish-black, glaucous, 8 mm in diameter.

This very distinct species is peculiar to the high mountains of Kauai, and is not uncommon at the summit of Kauai, Mt. Waialeale, elevation 5200 feet, where it grows as a small tree 15 feet or more in height in the open boggy country, in company with *Labordea Waialealae, Pelea Waialealae, Dubautia paleata, Tetraplasandra Waialealae, Lobelia Kauaiensis*, and others. It is an exceedingly handsome species on account of its beautiful delicate foliage. Lower down, in the great bogs of Lehua makanoe and Kauluwehi (4500 feet) it is a shrub 8 feet in height.

Collected by the writer on September 24, 1909, fruiting (no. 4958), on the summit of Waialeale, Kauai, and flowering and fruiting October 20, 1911, (no. 8887), Mt. Waialeale, Kauai.

SAPOTACEAE.

The family Sapotaceae, which consists of about 445 species distributed in more than 31 genera, occurs in the tropics of the whole world, but is absent in Europe and extra-tropical Asia. In the Hawaiian Islands two genera are represented: Chrysophyllum with a single species, and Sideroxylon with four distinct species and several varieties, all of which are peculiar to these Islands. The Sapotaceae are characterized mainly by their milky sap, and regular cyclic construction of their flowers. All Sapotaceae are woody plants with entire leaves, save in a single exception.

KEY TO THE GENERA.

Corolla 8 to 10 lobed, without staminodia, fruit small, black, olive shaped.
.... **Chrysophyllum**
Corolla 5 lobed, with staminodia, fruit large, globose or ovate.......... **Sideroxylon**

CHRYSOPHYLLUM L.

Calyx with 5, rarely 6 to 7 imbricate lobes. Corolla with campanulate or short cylindrical tube of 5, rarely 6 to 7, occasionally, as in the Hawaiian species, 8 to 10 imbricate segments. Stamens as many as segments in the corolla, filaments filiform; anthers short. ovoid, opening outside or laterally, occasionally abortive. Ovary 5 to 10 celled, pubescent. Style short, with small capitate stigma. Berry rarely more than one-celled, and with several compressed seeds; usually with one ovate or olive shaped seed, testa opaque, shining. Cotyledons thin, foliaceous.—Milky trees with alternate ovate or lanceolate leaves, without stipules. Flowers usually small, whitish or yellowish, shortly stipitate in axillary fascicles.

The genus Chrysophyllum, with its 70 species, is mainly tropical and is most numerous in species in tropical America.

In Hawaii the genus is represented by a single species, *Ch. Polynesicum* Hbd., which is peculiar to these Islands, and inhabits the dry regions on the leeward sides, but is by no means common.

Chrysophyllum Polynesicum Hbd.

Keahi.

CHRYSOPHYLLUM POLYNESICUM Hbd. Fl. Haw. Isl. (1888) 277;—Engler in Engl. et Prantl Pflzfam. IV. 1. (1890) 149.—**Isonandra polynesica** Benth. et Hook. Gen. Pl. II. (1876) 658;—Del. Cast. Ill. Fl. Ins. Mar. Pacif. VII. (1892) 229.

Branches stiff, cinereous; young leaves and inflorescence rusty-tomentose, leaves scattering, oblong or obovate 5 to 10 cm long, 5.5 to 5 cm wide, on petioles of 12 to 25 mm, rounded or emarginate at the apex, thick coriaceous, glabrate with age; flowers axillary on prominent nodes, 3 to 6 in a cluster, on pedicels of 4 to 6 mm, which are bracteate at the

Sapotaceae.

base; calyx persistent, coriaceous, deeply 4 to 5 parted; corolla little longer 4 to 5 mm, urceolate, divided into twice as many lobes as the calyx; staminodia none; stamens inserted at the base of the corolla, as many as lobes; ovary hairy 4 to 5 celled; style angular; fruit a somewhat fleshy black shining olive-shaped berry with a thin fibrous endocarp, about 16 mm long, 1- rarely 2-seeded, the single seed ovoid, with thick, bony, shining, pale brown testa; hilum obliquely basal, leaving a broad roundish deep scar; embryo axillary, cotyledons oblong, obtuse, radicle very short, inferior.

The *Keahi* is a medium-sized milky tree with a roundish crown, and rough drooping branches. The leaves resemble somewhat those of the Sapota pear, or more so the *Alaa* (*Sideroxylon sandwicense*), and is hardly distinguishable from it when without fruit or flower.

The flowers are borne all along the branchlets and very densely. It is a very prolifically bearing tree and can be found loaded with the black, olive-shaped shining fruits during the months of May to August. It inhabits the very dry regions on the leeward sides of most of the islands, and is very common on Lanai, where it grows in company with *Sideroxylon sandwicense*, *S. spathulatum*, the leaves of which look all very much alike and when not in fruit are exceedingly difficult to distinguish. On Molokai it is also common, as well as on the Island of Maui on the slopes of Haleakala, district of Kahikinui, while it has so far not been found on Hawaii. Together with Sideroxylon, Nothocestrum, Suttonia, Osmanthus, Reynoldsia, Gardenia, Antidesma, *Bobea Hookeri*, and Rauwolfia, it forms the typical dry forest at the lower elevation on Mt. Haleakala, on the lava fields of Auahi.

The *Keahi* is peculiar to the Hawaiian Islands. As far as can be ascertained, the natives made no use of this tree, though the wood is quite hard and durable, while the fruits are not edible.

SIDEROXYLON L.

Flowers occasionally polygamous; calyx lobes 5 to 6, imbricate; corolla broad-campanulate, with short or longer tube and 5 to 6 obtuse or acute segments. Staminodia 5 to 6, petaloid, or only scale-like to filiform. Stamens 5 to 6, with short or long filaments and ovate to lanceolate anthers. Ovary glabrous or pubescent, 5 to 2 celled. Style short or long, with small stigma. Berry ovoid to globose, usually small or often large, with thin pericarp, with 5 to 2 seeds, more often one-seeded. Seeds with shining hard testa and elongate linear hilum; albuminous. Cotyledons broad, flat.—Trees with usually coriaceous leaves, with and without stipules, and small sessile or peduncled flowers.

A genus of over 100 species, occurring in the tropical and subtropical regions of the old and new world. In the Hawaiian Islands the genus is represented by several species usually growing in the dry districts on the lee sides on the various islands. Originally only two species were known from Hawaii, to which the writer had added two new ones.

What has been said of the polymorphism of the genus Pittosporum in Hawaii, holds also good for the genus Sideroxylon.

The tremendous variations which we find in the species growing in Hawaii make it indeed difficult to separate all these forms satisfactorily. The fruits of the Hawaiian Sideroxyla are of various shapes and colors, the largest fruits

381

PLATE 153.

SIDEROXYLON SANDWICENSE (Gray) Benth. and Hook.
Alaa.
Showing fruiting branch, about two-third natural size.

Sapotaceae.

occurring in *S. rhynchospermum* Rock. They are ovoid and of a deep purplish black color. The fruits of *S. sandwicense* (Gray) B. & H. are pear-shaped to ovoid and also black and long peduncled, while those of *S. auahiense* Rock and its varieties on Hawaii are bright citron yellow, globose to top-shaped and sessile. The writer has collected large material of this genus from numerous localities. That *S. auahiense* is a good species is brought out by the fact that the latter grows in company with *S. sandwicense* with black ovoid fruits on the lava fields of Auahi, Maui, and nothing is more in contrast than to see these two species growing side by side, especially when loaded with respectively the bright yellow and the black fruits. On the slopes of Haleakala, back of Makawao, the writer collected specimens of a tree with large cone shaped, whitish-gray fruits, whose seeds differ decidedly from all the other Hawaiian species, while in the same locality only 50 yards off grew the typical *S. sandwicense*.

On Molokai occurs a very small-leaved species, which was unfortunately not in fruit, perhaps a form of *S. spathulatum* Hillebr. from Lanai. On the latter island the writer collected the largest leaved Sideroxylon with long pear-shaped black fruits. Another form was in flower only, the latter being of exceedingly large size compared with the other Hawaiian Sideroxyla. All the specimens collected by the writer on Kauai are one seeded, while those from the other islands are all five seeded, save a few exceptions.

The Hawaiian species of Sideroxylon may be arranged as follows:

KEY TO THE SPECIES.

Flowers 2 to 4, in clusters, pedicellate.
 Fruits globose ovoid to obovate, purplish black.
  Seeds thick, rounded at both ends........................ **S. sandwicense**
  Seeds thin flat, beaked at both ends..................... **S. rhynchospermum**
Flowers single and sessile.
 Fruits globose citron or orange yellow.
  Seeds as in **S. sandwicense** but smaller.................. **S. auahiense**
Flowers 2 to 3, pedicellate.
 Fruits conical, brownish yellow.
  Seeds small, linear-elongate, dull........................ **S. spathulatum**
Flowers single, pedicellate.
 Fruits large conical, grayish-white.
  Seeds elliptical elongate, dull; radicle long, protruding...... **S. Ceresolii**

Sideroxylon sandwicense (Gray) Benth. & Hook.
Alaa or *Aulu, Kaulu* according to Hillebrand.
(Plate 153.)

SIDEROXYLON SANDWICENSE (Gray) Benth. & Hook. Gen. Pl. II. (1876) 655;— Hbd. Fl. Haw. Isl. (1888)) 276;—Engl. in Engl. et Prantl Pflzfam. IV. I. (1890) 144. fig. 77, L (Sect. VIII., in Nachtr. Sect. IX.);—Del Cast. Ill. Fl. Ins. Mar. Pac. VII. (1892) 288.—**Sapota Sandwicensis** A. Gray in Proc. Am. Ac. V. (1862) 328;—H. Mann Proc. Am. Ac. VII. (1867) 188;—Wawra in Flora (1875) Addenda 252.

Leaves coriaceous, obovate-oblong, on petioles of 2.5 to 3.5 cm, equally rounded at both ends, or contracted at the base, quite entire, old leaves glabrous on both faces, often clothed with a brownish pubescence underneath, shining above, veins prominent straight

PLATE 154.

SIDEROXYLON RHYNCHOSPERMUM Rock.
Alaa.
Showing fruiting branch and seeds; about one-half natural size.

and close, connected by an intra-marginal nerve; flowers in clusters of 2 to 4 on tomentose pedicels of about 20 mm; calyx 5 lobed, (3 int. 2 ext.) broadly ovate, covered with a rusty brown tomentum, the two inner only pubescent on the exposed parts; corolla glabrous, slightly longer than the calyx, parted to little beyond the middle into 5 obtuse broad lobes, 6 mm, includ. the corolla tube; staminodia linear in front of the sinus; stamens inserted at the base of each lobe, perfectly glabrous, anthers sagittate, opening laterally, included; ovary conical densely hirsute with long stiff hair, 5-celled with one ascending ovule in each cell; style short, grooved at the apex; berry globose, or pear-shaped, to obovate, black, 3 cm in diameter, or 3 to 4.5 cm when obovate or ovate, rather dry, 5 to 1 seeded, each seed enclosed in a thin chartaceous pyrena, 20 mm long, 8 mm thick when single, more or less compressed when many, the crustaceous testa yellowish brown and shining, the elongate scar of the raphe occupying nearly the whole central angle; cotyledons nearly as long and broad as the albumen, the minute radicle inferior.

The *Alaa* is a fine tree of often 50 feet in height and is conspicuous in the forest by its leaves, which are of bronze to reddish brown color underneath, due to a hairiness of that color. It is usually found in the dry districts of nearly all the islands, and is especially common on Lanai in the valleys of Kaiholena and Mahana. On Maui big trees can be found above Makawao, in the gulches of the north-western slopes of Mt. Haleakala, as well as at Auahi, on the south side of the said mountain. On Hawaii this species is wanting, but the genus is represented by another species, *S. auahiense* var. *aurantium* Rock, with globose orange colored sessile fruits. The natives employed the milky sap as a bird glue. Hillebrand remarks in his Flora that the fruit of this tree is rarely met with perhaps on account of dimorphism in the flower. This the writer cannot verify, as all the trees found by him bore fruit in abundance, with the exception of on Kauai, where none of the trees bore perfect fruits, but were all abortive and consequently of very small size. The fruits are not always globose, but are quite often ovate, obovate and even long pear-shaped and of a black color. It inhabits mainly the dry districts, but can also be found along the Manoa Valley trail and Tantalus on Oahu, as well as at Kahuku, Waialua, and the Waianae range.

Hillebrand records a variety β. *auratum* with leaves and calyx, as well as corolla, densely ferruginous. The flowers are also generally single. Collected by Hillebrand on the dry forehills of Molokai and Lanai. From the latter islands the writer collected material which he must refer to this variety, though the flowers are not always single but often two in each leaf axil. Rock, Lanai, Kaiholena Valley, July, 1910. No. 8064.

Sideroxylon Ceresolii Rock spec. nov.

Leaves perfectly glabrous when old, chartaceous, (not thick leathery) obovate-oblong, bluntly acuminate, gradually tapering into a margined petiole of 2.5 to 3 cm; fruits single in the axils of the leaves, on peduncles of 5 mm, berry ovoid, acuminate at the apex, grayish-white in color, very soft and fleshy, 4 cm long, 2.5 cm wide, yellowish inside, 5-seeded, seeds elliptical-elongate, acute at both ends but not beaked, or somewhat obtuse, thin flat, dull brown, mottled, 24 mm long, 10 mm wide at the middle, testa rather thin, the raphe not quite as long as the ventral angle; cotyledons as broad as the albumen but only 2/3 its length, the inferior radicle 8 mm long, protruding half its length.

Collected on the Island of Maui in Waihou gulch on the northwestern slope of Mt. Haleakala, elevation 3000 feet, in company with my friend, Dr. P. Cere-

385

PLATE 155.

SIDEROXYLON RHYNCHOSPERMUM Rock.
Alaa.
Showing fruits and seeds about natural size.

Sapotaceae.

sole, after whom the tree is named. Rock & Ceresole, March, 1912; type in College of Hawaii Herbarium, No. 10150.

A medium-sized tree 20 to 30 feet in height with straight ascending branches. The fruit and seeds of this species differ very materially from all other known Hawaiian Sideroxyla.

Sideroxylon rhynchospermum Rock.
Alaa.
(Plates 154, 155.)

SIDEROXYLON RHYNCHOSPERMUM Rock in Torrey Bot. Cl. Bull. Vol, 37, 6. (1910) 295, fig. 2 & 3 a. b. et Report Hawn. Bd. Com. Agr. & For. (1911) 84, pl. 21.

A tree 10 to 20 m high, dividing freely into ascending branches; bark brownish, with shallow, narrow longitudinal corrugations about 3 mm thick, trunk up to 45 cm in diam. four feet from the ground; leaves coriaceous, obovate oblong 14 to 18 cm x 4.5 to 8 cm, on petioles 2.5 to 3 cm, alternate, exstipulate, quite glabrous with age, some pubescence remaining on the sides and angles of midrib and veins, especially on the lower surface, shining above, dull beneath, midrib prominent, with lateral veins leaving midrib at wide angles, parallel and connected with a continuous intra-marginal nerve; young leaves densely covered with appressed brown hair on both surfaces; flowers in cluster 2 or 3 on tomentose pedicels 12 to 20 mm long; calyx 5 parted to near the base, lobes acute, 3 to 5 mm; corolla light yellow, longer than the calyx, 4 to 5 parted to the base, lobes acute; staminodia half as long linear; stamens 5, inserted at the base of the corolla, glabrous, anthers ovate, the cells confluent at the apex, opening laterally; ovary hirsute, 5-celled, style short; fruit a purplish black plum-like berry 4.5 to 5.5 cm long, 3.5 cm wide, rather fleshy, 3 to 5 seeded; seeds enclosed in a papery pyrena 25 to 30 mm x 12 to 14 mm, perfectly flat, about 3 mm thick, beaked at both ends of the ventral angle, which is occupied by the scar of the raphe, the crustaceous testa thin, of a light brown color.

This rather handsome tree was first collected by Dr. H. L. Lyon in the woods of Nahiku, on the north-eastern slopes of Mt. Haleakala, Maui, at an elevation of 1300 feet. The species differs from the other Hawaiian Sideroxyla in the large black ovoid fruits and mainly in the very flat thin-beaked seeds. It grows in the rain forest of Nahiku, where precipitation is exceedingly heavy; while most of the other Hawaiian Sideroxyla are peculiar to the dry regions. When the writer visited the forests of Nahiku in the year 1911, the trees were neither in flower nor in fruit. The trees are not very abundant, but only individual trees could be seen scattered through the forest.

Sideroxylon auahiense Rock.
Alaa.

SIDEROXYLON AUAHIENSE Rock Coll. Haw. Publ. Bot. Bull. 1. (1911) 18. pl. 5.

Leaves coriaceous, pale green, glabrous on both sides when old, shining above, covered with a gray silvery tomentum when young, elliptical oblong, bluntly acuminate or rounded, 8 to 12 cm long, 4 to 6 cm wide, on petioles of 3 to 4 cm, veins parallel leaving midrib at wide angles of about 80°; flowers single, rarely two in the axils of the alternate leaves, calyx hirsute, 5 parted to near the base, the lobes rounded, corolla lobes 5, obtuse, staminodia shorter than the lobes, 5, triangular; stamens wanting in the female flowers; ovary hirsute with a dense circle of long reddish hair at its base, 5-celled; style short conical; berry sessile or subsessile, pale citron yellow, with a grayish hue, rather globose with the apex drawn out into a short acumen; 3.5 to 4.5 cm in diam., bright yellow inside, quite fleshy; seeds 20 mm long, 10 mm wide, enclosed in a thin papery pyrena, the thick hard testa pale yellow, with reddish spots, shining; the scar of the raphe shorter than the ventral angle; cotyledons broad, the minute radicle inferior.

387

PLATE 156.

SIDEROXYLON AUAHIENSE var. **AURANTIUM** Rock var. nov.
Alaa.
Showing fruiting branch with mature fruits; specimen from Kapua, South Kona.
Less than one-half natural size.

PLATE 157.

SIDEROXYLON AUAHIENSE var. **AURANTIUM** Rock var. nov.
Alaa.
Fruiting branch pinned against trunk of tree, showing thick scaly bark. Growing on the lava fields of Puuwaawaa, North Kona, Hawaii.

PLATE 158.

SIDEROXYLON AUAHIENSE var. **AURANTIUM** Rock var. nov.
Alaa Tree.
Growing at Puuwaawaa, on the lava fields of Mt. Hualalai, North Kona, Hawaii.

Sapotaceae.

This species, which is a tree 25 to 30 feet high, has a rather broad round crown, and pale glaucous, terete, glabrous branches. The tree differs from *S. sandwicense* mainly in its pale yellow sessile fruits, in its single unisexual flowers, and very pale glabrous foliage. It was discovered by the writer during the month of November, 1910, on the Island of Maui, southern slopes of Mt. Haleakala, on the lava fields of Auahi, district of Kahikinui, elevation 3000 feet. It grows in company with *Alectryon macrococcus, Pelea multiflora, Pterotropia dipyrena* and *Sideroxylon sandwicense*, as well as with another Sideroxylon with perfectly globose, orange-colored fruits which are smaller than in the species in question, and may be described as follows:

Var. **aurantium** Rock var. nov.
(Plates 156, 157, 158.)

Leaves elliptical-ovate to linear-oblong, acuminate or rounded at the apex, covered with a bronze-colored tomentum underneath, pale green and dull above; flowers single; fruits perfectly sessile deep orange-colored, globose, 2 to 2.5 cm in diam., one to five seeded, seeds smaller than in the species, enclosed in a thick pergameneous pyrena.

This variety is a medium-sized tree, of different habit than the species, with straight ascending branches. The biggest tree the writer observed on the lava fields of Puuwaawaa, North Kona, Hawaii, with trunks of nearly two feet in diameter, and clothed in a thick gray very rough bark, while the younger trees have a smooth grayish-white bark. The variety occurs on the Island of Hawaii in North and South Kona, as well as at Auahi, Maui, and can be distinguished at a glance from the species, even at a distance.

SIDEROXYLON SPATHULATUM Hbd. Fl. Haw. Isl. (1888) 277;—Engl. in Engl. et Prantl Pflzfam. IV. i. (1890) 144;—Del Cast. Ill. Fl. Ins. Mar. Pac. VII. (1892) 228;—Rock Coll. Haw. Publ. Bot. Bull. 1. (1911) 20.—**Sapota sandwicensis** var. β Gray Proc. Am. Acad. V. (1862) 328.

A small stiff-branched tree or shrub 4 to 5 m in height; leaves spathulate or ellipticooblong, bluntly acuminate, contracting into a margined petiole of 12 to 18 mm, rusty-tomentose underneath, thick coriaceous, with the veins little prominent; flowers single or in clusters of 2 to 3, on short pedicels of 2 to 4 mm; calyx and corolla rusty-tomentose 4 mm high, their lobes somewhat acute; stamens inserted at the middle of the corolla, at the base of the lobes, the short filaments slightly reflected, not hairy below, the anthers apiculate; staminodia broad, half the width of the lobes; ovary hairy, with short style; berry dark orange colored and glabrous when mature, covered with a rufous tomentum when young, 3.5 cm long, by little over 2 cm wide, conical in outline, with an acuminate apex, 5-seeded, each seed enclosed in a membraneous yellow pyrena, 20 mm long, 7 mm wide. rounded at both ends, grayish-brown, rather dull, linear elongate, cotyledons nearly as long and broad as the albumen, radicle about 3 mm long and superior, fruit flesh light yellow.

This species is quite common on the Island of Lanai in the valleys of Kai-holena and Mahana, as well as on the windward side toward Halepalaua, and in the Kaa forest. It grows in company with *Chrysophyllum polynesicum, Bobea Hookeri, Osmanthus sandwicensis*, etc. The writer met with this same species on the southern slopes of Mt. Haleakala, on the lava fields of Auahi, at an elevation of 2000, near the government road, in company with *Reynoldsia sandwicensis, Antidesma pulvinatum*, etc.

391

Sapotaceae.

Var. β **densiflorum** Hbd.

Leaves large 7.5 cm long, generally glabrous when old; flowers in clusters of 4 to 6 in the axils of the upper closely set leaves, on pedicels of 4 mm, completely covering the end of the branch.

Hillebrand records this variety from the leeward slopes of Mt. Kaala of the Waianae range on Oahu. The plant is not known to the author, but he collected specimens of another variety, coming rather close to this one, on Molokai, near Kapulo'u below Kamoku camp in the rather dry district, in company with *Myoporum sandwicense, Ochrosia sandwicensis,* and *Nothocestrum latifolium.* It may be described as follows:

Var. **molokaiense** (Lévl.) Rock comb. nov.

Myrsine molokaiensis Levl. in Fedde Rep. Spec. nov, regn. veg. X. 10-14 (1911) 154 et **Suttonia molokaiensis** Levl. nov. nom. in Fedde, l. c. X. 24-26 (1912) 373.

Leaves elliptical oblong, dark green, glabrous above, with a fine silvery pubescence underneath, young leaves yellowish pubescent; flowers either single or 4 to 6 in the axils of the upper leaves, often very densely flowered, on pedicels of 10 to 12 mm, whole inflorescence of a golden yellow, the glabrous petals longer than the calyx, staminodia petaloid, ovary densely hirsute with distinct style; fruit subglobose, beaked, resembling the fruit of *S. spathulatum.*

In Abbé Faurie's collection, which I have at hand, is a plant numbered 435 and labelled "*Myrsine molokaiensis* Levl. sp. nov. Molokai, Kamolo 1000 m. leg. Faurie Junio 1910." The plant is at a first glance recognizable as a Sideroxylon and is identical with my number 6154 *Sideroxylon spathulatum* var. *molokaiense* Rock.

At first the writer could not believe that such a gross error could be committed, but after reading the most incomplete description by Léveillé, which says: "Affinis *M. sandwicensis* DC. a quo secernitur foliis supra atro-viridibus, subtus incanis vel incano-tomentosis," it can be no other plant than Faurie's specimen marked 435. Faurie's specimen is in fruit, but quite immature.

The material collected by the writer came from almost the identical locality where Faurie collected his plants, but a little more toward the west. However, one cannot depend very well on Faurie's exactness in citing localities, as can be seen in Léveillé's publication, who places Hilo on the Island of Maui and Mt. Haleakala on a different island than Maui. Some plants are simply marked: Sandwich. It is indeed very regrettable that the material of Abbé Faurie (which is often beyond recognition) fell in the hands of H. Léveillé, whose ambition seems to be to bring the number of his new species up to 1000. A goodly number of his new species are European weeds which have been imported by the cattle estates with grass seeds, and have become scattered over the mountains in the pasture lands which he calls *in herbidis;* may it be said that in these vast meadows not even a native grass can be found, still less herbaceous native plants, which have been crowded out by imported grasses and such weeds which Léveillé describes now as new species, and thus would change the whole endemic aspect of our most interesting flora.

EBENACEAE.

The family Ebenaceae is almost exclusively tropical and subtropical, inhabiting especially the eastern hemisphere. They have reached their best development in the East Indies and the Malayan Archipelago. In the Hawaiian Islands the family is represented by the genus Maba only. The family is closely related to the Symplocaceae, from which it however differs in the superior ovary and the unisexual flowers.

MABA J. R. et G. Forster.

Flowers usually 3- rarely 3-6-fid. Calyx enlarged with fruit. Male flowers: Stamens 3 to several, usually 9; filaments free or united to 2 to 3; anthers elongate, opening laterally. Ovary 3- or 6-celled, with 6 ovules. Style 3-fid or 3 single styles. Fruit usually an ovate or globose, glabrous or pubescent 1 to 6 seeded berry.—Trees or shrubs with alternate, simple and entire leaves. Flowers solitary or in short axillary cymes.

The genus Maba consists of about 63 species and is distributed over the same regions as the family with the exception of South Africa. In the Hawaiian Islands only two species and one variety are to be found. One of the two species, *Maba Hillebrandii* Seem., is endemic, while *Maba sandwicensis* occurs also in Fiji.

KEY TO THE SPECIES.

Leaves pale green, smooth on both faces, calycine lobes obtuse........ **M. sandwicensis**
Leaves dark green, wrinkled on the upper face, calycine lobes acute... **M. Hillebrandii**

Maba sandwicensis A. DC.
Lama.
(Plates 159, 160.)

MABA SANDWICENSIS A. DC. Prodr. VIII. (1844) 242;—A. Gray Proc. Am. Acad. V. (1862) 327;—Mann Proc. Am. Acad. VII. (1867) 188;—Wawra in Flora (1873) 59;—Hbd. Fl. Haw. Isl. (188) 274.—Gurke in Engl. et Prantl Pflzfam. IV. 1. (1891) 160;—Del Cast. Ill. Fl. Ins. Mar. Pacif. VII. (1892) 230.—Ebenus sandwicensis O. Ktze. Rev. Gen. Pl. II. (1891) 408.

Leaves distichous, coriaceous, with hidden veins, pale green, elliptical, or, ovate-oblong 3.5 to 5 cm long. 1.5 to 2.5 cm wide, on petioles of 4 to 6 mm, shortly acuminate, entire glabrous, but silky haired when young; flowers single, rarely the male in clusters of 2 to 5, the very short peduncle covered with about 6 small, ovate-obtuse, deciduous bracts; calyx coriaceous, silky with oppressed hair, 4 to 5 mm, shortly 3 to 4 fid with obtuse lobes, corolla coriaceous, 5 to 6 mm, densely hairy in the upper half, 3 toothed, the lobules blunt, and sinistrorsely convolute in the bud; male flowers, stamens free, 12 to 18, around the hirsute rudiments of an ovary, 1/3 the length of the corolla, glabrous, anthers short, oblong, as long as the filaments; female flowers without stamens, the ovary hairy; style very short 3-rayed; fruit dry or somewhat fleshy; 18 mm high, pubescent when young, 3-celled, with 1 seed in each cell, but generally one-seeded when mature; seeds oblong with thin testa and smooth albumen; cotyledons half the length of the radicle, complanate, oblong, obtuse.

The *Lama* is a beautiful medium sized tree reaching a height of 20 to 40 feet. The leaves are thick, leathery, dull green and are arranged alternately in opposite rows, making the little branchlets resemble pinnate leaves.

393

PLATE 159.

MABA SANDWICENSIS DC.
Lama.
Fruiting branch, typical Oahu specimen; one-half natural size.

Ebenaceae.

The *Lama* inhabits the wet as well as the dry regions on all the islands of the group. The small leaved form occurs on the Koolau range of Oahu, as in Manoa Valley and Niu as well as all along toward Kahuku. Back of Hilo on Hawaii it is a very common tree, reaching a height of 40 feet; in this latter locality it is quite common in company with Straussia, Metrosideros, etc., following immediately the Pandanus forest. The trunk of the *Lama* is vested in a black rather smooth bark, but in old trees the bark becomes rough and scaly, forming irregular squares of a dark gray color. The tree is common on all the islands of the group, but especially so in the dry districts, where it forms often pure stands, as in the low lands of Kapua in South Kona where the writer met with the finest trees with perfectly straight trunks of a foot in diameter. It grows in company with *Aleurites Moluccana, Pittosporum Hosmeri* var. *longifolia,* and *Antidesma pulvinatum.* The berries, which are of a reddish yellow color when mature, are quite palatable and are eaten by the natives and birds. The trees fruit prolifically during the late winter months, especially in the month of February, when the trees are loaded with the bright colored fruits.

The wood is very hard, close grained, and of a rich reddish brown color when old; it was employed in building houses for the gods. A block of *Lama* wood was always placed upon the *Kuahu,* altar, in the temple of the goddess of the sacred Hula dance, Laka, which latter personality it represented. This uncarved block was wrapped in choice yellow tapa, scented with turmeric and was set conspicuously upon the altar.* The wood was also used in making sacred inclosures for other tabu purposes.

A variety β Hbd. with ovate or ovate oblong, larger leaves, which are broadly rounded at the base, and pubescent underneath, occurs on the lava flows and on the leeward sides of the islands in general, but always in dry situations. On Kauai the variety has the largest leaves 10 to 12.5 cm x 5 to 5.5 cm.

Maba Hillebrandii Seem.

MABA HILLEBRANDII Seem. in Flora Vitiensis (1866) 151;—H. Mann l. c.;—Hillebr. Fl. Hw. Isl. (1888) 275;—Gurke in Engl. et Prantl Natürl. Pflzfam. l. c.;—Del Cast l. c.—**Ebenus Hillebrandii** O. Ktze. Rev. Gen. Pl. II. (1891) 408.

Leaves oblong, 8 to 12 cm long, 3.5 to 6 cm wide, on petioles of 4 mm, obtuse or bluntly acute, contracted, rounded or truncate or even emarginate at the base, glabrous, dark green, coriaceous, smooth on the lower face, but deeply rugose on the upper by a close and fine areolar network; bracts and calyx glabrous, coriaceous, the latter 3-fid almost to the middle with broad triangular acute lobes; corolla 7 mm, hairy, shortly 3-toothed; stamens 9, short, glabrous, with pointed anthers; fruit obovoid, about 2 cm long and 15 to 18 mm in diameter, pubescent at the apex only.

This species, which is quite different from the *lama,* is endemic in the Hawaiian Islands and is peculiar to Oahu, where it can be found in the hills of

---

* Emerson, Unwritten Literature of Hawaii.

PLATE 160.

MABA SANDWICENSIS DC. var. *β*. Hbd.
Lama.
Fruiting branch pinned to trunk of tree. Growing on the lava fields of
Kapua, S. Kona, Hawaii; elevation 1500 feet.

Ebenaceae-Oleaceae.

Kahuku and Waialua; the writer met with it in Niu Valley where it is quite plentiful at an elevation of 2000 feet. Hillebrand records it also from Wailupe Valley.

OLEACEAE.

The family Oleaceae, which consists of about 370 to 390 species, inhabits the temperate, subtropical and tropical regions of the earth, especially in East India, where some of the genera like Jasminum and others are rich in species. Only about 12 species belonging to this family occur in Europe; in Polynesia and Australia about 26; in America and Africa each about 46 species. In the Hawaiian Islands the family is represented by the genus Osmanthus with a single species.

OSMANTHUS Lour.

Flowers hermaphrodite, polygamous or dioecious, calyx short, 4 toothed or 4 lobed. Tube of corolla short. Stamens 2, rarely 4, with short filaments inserted on the tube of the corolla and enclosed by the same. Anthers laterally dehiscing. Style short. Stigma small, entire or 2-lobed.—Shrubs or trees with evergreen leaves. The small flowers are arranged on axillary simple or compound racemes.

The genus Osmanthus with its 10 species is distributed in South Asia, East Asia, Polynesia and North America, with one species—*Osmanthus sandwicensis* (A. Gray) Knobl.—in the Hawaiian Islands.

Osmanthus sandwicensis (A. Gray) Knobl.
Pua or *Olopua*.
(Plates 161, 162, 163.)

OSMANTHUS SANDWICENSIS (A. Gray) Knobl. in Bot. Centralbl. LXI (1895) 82, et in Engl. et Prantl Pflzfam. IV. 2. (1895) 9.—Olea sandwicensis A. Gray Proc. Am. Acad. V. (1862) 331;—H. Mann Proc. Am. Acad. VII (1867) 197;—Wawra in Flora (1874) 548;—Hbd. Fl. Haw. Isl. (1888) 301;—inclus. var. β Hbd. from Kauai;—Del Cast. Ill. Fl. Ins. Mar. Pac. VII (1892) 231;—Heller Pl. Haw. Isl. (1897) 876.

A large tree often 20 m high, quite glabrous; leaves pale underneath, darker above, coriaceous elliptico-oblong or lanceolate acute, or acuminate or obtuse, 7 to 15 cm long, 2.5 to 7 cm wide, on petioles of about 12 mm; racemes axillary tomentose, short; flowers hermaphrodite; calyx obtusely 4-toothed; corolla about 4 mm, pale yellow, rotate, deeply 4 parted; anthers always 4, alternate with the lobes of the corolla and as long as the latter (in the writer's specimens) sessile on the short tube, oblong obtuse; ovary conical, elongate, stigma subsessile, 2-lobed; drupe ovoid, peaked or obtuse, 12 to 22 mm long, bluish-black, when mature rather dry, but the exocarp somewhat fleshy and staining, with an osseous putamen and a single seed; embryo straight in the axis of horny albumen, the obtuse cotyledons as long as the superior radicle.

The *Pua* or *Olopua* is one of the most common Hawaiian trees, but rarely inhabiting the rain forests or even their outskirts. It is more confined to the lower forest zone, especially on the leeward sides of all the islands, and is usually the predominating tree on the lava fields of Hawaii. The *Pua*, like all Hawaiian trees, is very variable and only a trained eye can at first glance decide if it is the *Pua* or not. The leaves are often very large and again very small, as in the Molokai specimens, which have elliptical lanceolate leaves, while those of

397

PLATE 161.

OSMANTHUS SANDWICENSIS (Gray) Knobl.
Pua or **Olopua**.
Fruiting branch, less than one-third natural size.

PLATE 162.

OSMANTHUS SANDWICENSIS (Gray) Knobl.
Pua or **Olopua.**
Trunk of tree showing roughness of bark; about 3 feet in diameter. Growing in Kipuka
Puaulu near Kilauea Volcano, Hawaii; elevation 4000 feet.

PLATE 163.

OSMANTHUS SANDWICENSIS (Gray) Knobl.
Pua or **Olopua.**
One of the biggest pua trees in the islands, growing in the Kipuka Puaulu near Kilauea
Volcano, Hawaii; height of tree about 60 feet.

Oleaceae-Loganiaceae.

Kauai are exceedingly large and oblong acuminate. It flowers usually in March in certain localities, but the writer found the trees in South Kona on the lava fields of Kapua loaded with the ripe bluish fruits during the month of January. It is a graceful tree and reaches often a height of 60 feet, with a trunk of 3 feet in diameter; the bark is thick and very corrugated, often divided into oblong scales. It occurs on all the islands of the group, especially on the dry leesides from 600 to 4000 feet elevation. On Kauai it grows in the great Waimea Canyon and at Halemanu, as well as Milolii and in Kopiwai forest, where the writer met with handsome specimens. The biggest tree the writer saw in the Kipuka Puaulu on the edge of an old *aa* lava flow near the Volcano Kilauea, on the slopes of Mauna Loa, elevation 4000 feet.

The wood of the *Pua* is extremely hard, close grained and very durable; it is of a dark brownish color with blackish streaks, exceedingly heavy and takes a most excellent polish. The wood was often used by the natives for various purposes such as adze-handles. In helping to shape the fish hooks, the *Pua* wood was used, as well as the rough *pahoehoe* lava rock, as rasps.

LOGANIACEAE.

The family Loganiaceae, with its 31 genera and more than 370 species, is decidedly tropical; only few representatives are found outside the tropics, and only two genera are found distributed in the tropics of the whole world, while the remaining ones are restricted to certain regions. In the Hawaiian Islands only one genus (Labordia) of this family occurs, which is endemic.

LABORDIA Gaud.

Flowers hermaphrodite or unisexual, pentamerous. Calycine lobes large, lanceolate or foliaceous, occasionally unequal. Corolla distinctly tubular, with narrow, lanceolate contorted lobes. Stamens with short filaments and enclosed linear anthers. Ovary 2 to 3 celled, with cylindrical style and elongate clavate stigma; ovules many. Fruit a capsule. Seeds ovoid or ellipsoidal imbedded in an orange colored or greenish pulp; with fleshy albumen. Embryo straight with short cotyledons and longer radicle.—Small trees or shrubs; stipules sheathing. Inflorescence a terminal cyme, corymbiform or paniculate, sometimes reduced to a single flower.

The genus Labordia consists of numerous species, and is endemic to the Hawaiian Islands. Only a few become trees, while the majority of them are shrubs inhabiting the middle forest zone along stream beds or in swampy grounds in dense shades up to an elevation of over 5000 feet. Only one or two occur on the forehills of the dry districts at the outskirts of the forests, as for example in Mahana Valley on Lanai. The native name of nearly all the species is *Kamakahala*. The majority of the species have green flowers, while some have orange colored thick fleshy corollas.

H. Baillon in his treatise on the tribe of Labordia remarks that in his opinion the Genus Labordia cannot be sustained. He goes on to say that owing to the imbricate and more often twisted corolla the genus should rather be classified under the family Apocynaceae than Loganiaceae. "The existence of stipules

401

26

PLATE 164.

LABORDIA MEMBRANACEA Mann.
Fruiting specimen; from the mountains back of Honolulu. One-half natural size.

Loganiaceae.

between the leaves would be the only characteristic which might separate them from the former family, had it not been demonstrated that too much value altogether has been attached to the presence or absence of these organs, etc.'' Owing to limited space it is here impossible fully to discuss this interesting question. A definite settlement in regard to the nomenclature of our Hawaiian Labordia will have to be deferred until the future. The writer possesses numerous new species of Labordiae and complete material of those already known, which will be worked up after the writer's return from Europe, where he will have opportunity to compare his specimens with the types in the various Herbaria of Europe. Only after then can a satisfactory treatise on this difficult group be published.

KEY TO THE SPECIES.

Corolla yellow.
    Flowers single, enclosed within the foliaceous calyx lobes.
        Capsule small crested...................................... **L. molokaiana**
    Flowers several in a sessile cyme.
        Capsule 40 mm long, not crested.......................... **L. membranacea**
        Capsule 5 mm high, three valved, minutely pedunculate....... **L. sessilis**
Corolla greenish.
    Flowers in a paniculate cyme................................. **L. tinifolia**

There are undoubtedly several more Labordia which become trees, but owing to the general chaos in which this genus is at present, it was decided by the writer to limit the number of arborescent species to be described to four, as the diagnosis of the latter is fairly certain.

Labordia Molokaiana H. Baillon.
Kamakahala.

LABORDIA MOLOKAIANA H. Baillon in Bull. Soc. Linn. Paris, I. (1880) n. 30. 240;—Del Cast. Ill. Fl. Ins. Mar. Pac. VII. (1892) 237.—Labordia lophocarpa Hbd. Fl. Haw. Isl. (1888) 289;—Solereder in Engl. et Prantl Pflzfam. IV. 2. (1892) 32.

A tree 10 m high, glabrous, the younger branches fleshy, slender, and sharply ridged or angular; stipular sheath large, emarginate laterally; leaves elliptical or obovate-oblong, 4 to 10.5 cm long, 2.5 to 3 cm wide, shortly acuminate, suddenly narrowing into a petiole of 4 to 12 mm, thin chartaceous, dark underneath when dry, pale even whitish when fresh, and somewhat fleshy in texture, glabrous or distantly hispidulous; inflorescence a single terminal flower on a puberulous pedicel of 4 to 10 mm; bractlets lanceolate or spathulate, 12 mm; calyx as long as the corolla, the lobes 14 to 20 mm, divided into 4 to 5 broad foliaceous sepals, shortly acuminate, 9 to 11 nerved; corolla deep yellow, enclosed in the calyx, glabrous outside, puberulous inside, the broad tube 10 to 12 mm long; style 4 mm, shorter than the broad clavate stigma; capsule 12 to 14 mm high, 2 to 3 valved, the valves broadly winged at the back, above, with the wings rounded and generally not confluent at the apex.

In regard to the nomenclature of this species there seems to be some doubt whether it is Hillebrand's *Labordia lophocarpa* or Gaudichaud's *L. fagraeoidea*, but to the writer's mind it must be identical with the former. However, the question cannot be decided definitely until material has been examined on which Baillon based his description. Baillon states in regard to *L. Molokaiana* as follows:* ''The *L. Molokaiana* gathered on Molokai by Mr. J. Remy (no. 363)

_____

* Translated from the original.

PLATE 165.

LABORDIA TINIFOLIA Gray.
Kamakahala.
Fruiting branch, photographed from an herbarium specimen; two-thirds natural size.

Loganiaceae.

which has much narrower, lanceolate and longer petioled leaves, with less closer internodes, is perhaps but another variety of *L. fagraeoidea.* Their inflorescences are contracted and pauciflorous, and the divisions of their corollas are linear.''

In the writer's opinion the plant is quite distinct from Gaudichaud's *L. fagraeoidea.*

The species Labordia are certainly very badly confused, earlier authors, as Mann, giving only three or four line descriptions which may be applied to several variable species, have later been enlarged upon by other authors simply taking for granted that their specimens are referable to either the one or the other, increased the confusion rather than clearing matters up. Until type-material of all the previous authors has been examined and compared, a satisfactory treatise on this difficult genus cannot be undertaken.

L. Molokaiana occurs on Molokai principally, where it was collected by the writer at the pali of Wailua in the dense rain forest, at an elevation of 3000 feet. The specimens agree exactly with Hillebrand's description of *L. lophocarpa*, which is a synonym of the former (flowering and fruiting no. 7044, April 15, 1910). Hillebrand enumerates two varieties, *pluriflora* and *phyllocalyx* which may be distinct species.

Labordia membranacea Mann.
Kamakahala.
(Plate 164.)

LABORDIA MEMBRANACEA Mann in Proc. Am. Acad. VII. (1867) 197.—Wawra in
Flora (1872) 516;—Hbd. Fl. Haw. Isl. (1888) 291;—Solereder in Engl. et Prantl
Pflzfam. IV. 2 (1892) 32;—Del Cast. Ill. Fl. Ins. Mar. Pacif. VII. (1892) 237.

Branches thick, fleshy, pubescent with short dark brown hair, terete, or slightly angled; leaves broadly ovate, shortly acuminate, (not membraneous when fresh) rather fleshy, succulent, pale underneath, dark green and shining or somewhat dull above, petioles thick fleshy, midrib thick, prominent, veins transparent; interpetiolar stipules very short, rounded or truncate; inflorescence terminal, a three-flowered cyme, subsessile or sessile in the axis of the uppermost leaflets, with two linear bracts at the base; peduncles terete fleshy, alternately bracteolate, bracteole, linear subulate; calyx divided nearly to the base into five linear acute segments 1.5 cm long, hirsute with blackish hairlets as is the whole inflorescence; corolla pale yellow, the long slender tube urceolate, about 2 cm long, the lobes (5) reflexed, about 2/3 the length of the tube, acuminate; anthers sessile at the throat of the tube, between the sinuses of the corolla-lobes, slightly exserted; ovary two-celled, oblong-conical, about 1 cm high, style short about 2 mm, stigma large, clavate 5 mm long, 2.5 mm thick, slightly notched or grooved at the apex. Capsule two-valved, very large 40 mm long, 18 mm broad, conical-oblong, the valves not ridged at the back.

Mann describes a small tree from the mountains behind Honolulu under *Labordia membranacea*, though very briefly. The writer found numerous trees which will have to be referred to Mann's species. Like all Labordiae it is somewhat variable. It is however easily distinguished, by the large oblong leaves and exceedingly large capsules. The writer has enlarged upon Mann's description. The flowers of this species are hermaphrodite. It occurs in the dense rain forests of the main range of Oahu, especially between Manoa and Mt. Olympus trail, where it is a small tree 10 to 18 feet in height.

Loganiaceae.

Labordia sessilis Gray.

LABORDIA SESSILIS Gray in Proc. Am. Acad. IV. (1860) 323;—H. Baillon Bull. Mens. Soc. Linn. Paris. I. (1880)240.—**L. fagraeoidea** Hbd. Fl. Haw. Isl. (1888) in part.

Leaves subsessile, thick leathery, oblong, or lanceolate oblong, acute at the apex, cuneate at the base, 7.5 cm to 12.5 cm long, pale underneath, veins transparent, stipules united, tubular, long; sepals oblong-lanceolate, capsules 5 mm high, minutely pedunculate or sessile in the axis of the last leaves within the stipules, three-valved.

This species which is certainly distinct from *L. fagraeoidea*, is a tree often 35 to 40 feet in height, but occasionally a shrub, and occurs only in the rain forests of Oahu, on the main range. It is especially common in Manoa Valley at an elevation of 2500 feet. It can easily be recognized by its oblong-lanceolate pale green foliage and transparent venation. The capsules are exceedingly small and hidden in the stipules.

Labordia tinifolia Gray.
(Plate 165.)

LABORDIA TINIFOLIA Gray in Proc. Am. Acad. IV. (1860) 322;—Mann in Proc. Am. Acad. VII. (1867) 197.—Wawra in Flora (1872) 515;—Baill. in Bull. Mens. Soc. Linn. Paris. (1880) 238-240;—Hbd. Fl. Haw. Isl. (1888) 292;—Solereder in Engl. et Prantl IV. 2. (1892) 32;—Del Cast. Ill. Fl. Ins. Mar. Pac. VII. (1892) 237;— Heller Pl. Haw. Isl. (1897) 877.

A small tree 6 to 8 m high, with slender and pale terete branches; leaves elliptical or obovate or ovate-oblong, 5 to 10 cm long, 18 to 37 mm wide, on petioles of 4 to 12 mm, acute or acuminate at both ends, or obtuse at the apex, chartaceous glabrous; flowers many in a paniculate cyme 3.5 to 10 cm in length, with a peduncle of 12 to 30 mm in length, the ultimate pedicels 6 to 18 mm, subequal; bractlets subulate; calyx 3 mm, divided beyond the middle into 5 triangular acute lobes; corolla greenish, very slender, salver-shaped, the tube 6 to 8 mm, glabrous, but pubescent within, the lobes about one-third as long; capsules globose, short, ovoid, or obovoid somewhat obtuse or acute, 8 to 12 mm long, slightly sulcate, 2 valved or very rarely 3-valved, the valves rounded at the back.

This species is a small tree of 15 to 20 feet or more in height and occurs on Kauai, Maui, Lanai, Molokai, and according to Hillebrand also on Oahu; as it is found on these various islands at different altitudes it is somewhat variable. The trunks of the trees are straight, especially in the specimens from the forests above Makawao (no. 8616). The bark resembles very much that of the *Aalii, Dodonaea viscosa*, or that of *Styphelia tameiameia*. It is of a dark brown color, and is closely and deeply corrugated, the furrows are not straight, but seem to encircle the trunk, somewhat cork-screw fashion. The peduncle varies considerably in length, as do also the leaves in size. On Lanai the tree was observed on the dry forehills of Mahana and Kaiholena Valleys, (no. 8000 and no. 8099). On West Maui it grows above Kaanapali at 2000 feet elevation (no. 8169). It is typical of the drier regions and hardly ever ascends into the rain forest. It comes very close to *L. triflora* Hbd. and seems to differ from the latter in not having cordate and subsessile leaves. On Kauai, along the trail to Opaiwela stream near Kaholumano it grows as a shrub; the leaves are larger and the capsules ovoid, acute.

APOCYNACEAE.

The family Apocynaceae consists of about 1000 species, the larger number of which belong to the tropics. Of its 133 genera only five are represented in the Hawaiian Islands, three of which have arborescent species. One genus (Pteralyxia K. Sch.) is endemic, with a single species. The largest number of Apocynaceae are climbing shrubs, while erect shrubs or trees are not as numerous. In these Islands we have only one climbing plant of this family, the well-known *Maile* of the natives, *Alyxia olivaeformis* Gaud., while the remaining ones are trees, with the exception of the cultivated *Vinca rosea*, which has also become naturalized, having escaped from cultivation. Annuals are not known in this family. Of interest and usefulness is the milky sap which nearly all members of this family possess, as it contains caoutchouc. Not a few of the species of Apocynaceae are extremely poisonous, and undoubtedly these strong poisonous substances are to be found in the milky sap.

KEY TO THE GENERA.

Discus wanting.
    Endocarp winged, drupe always 1-celled, large, bright red........... **1. Pteralyxia**
    Endocarp compressed, deeply furrowed underneath, drupe 2-celled, large, yellow.
    .... **3. Ochrosia**
Discus present.
    Leaves whorled, drupe smooth, small, black, obcordate............. **2. Rauwolfia**

PTERALYXIA K. Sch.

Calyx deeply 2-parted, with almost free, imbricate lobes, glandless. Corolla tubular, without scales at the constricted throat, and short obtuse sinistrorse lobes. Stamens inserted below the throat, ovate-lanceolate, acute. Discus absent. Ovary superior, with 2 pendulous ovules in each cell. Style filiform, with subglobose, thickened stigma, which is shortly 2-lobed. Drupe dry, obovate, bright red. Putamen with 2 large winged lateral angles and 2 sharp middle-crests. Seeds large (3 to 3.5 cm long, and 1 to 1.5 cm in diam.), with ruminate albumen.

A Hawaiian genus with a single arborescent species, peculiar to the Island of Oahu. The species was first described by Hillebrand in the genus Vallesia as *V. macrocarpa* Hbd. According to K. Schumann the plant is nearest related to the genus Alyxia.

Pteralyxia macrocarpa (Hbd.) K. Sch.

Kaulu.

PTERALYXIA MACROCARPA (Hbd.) K. Schum. in Engl. et Prantl Pflzfam. IV. 2. (1895) 151.—**Vallesia macrocarpa** Hbd. Fl. Haw. Isl. (1888) 297;— Del Cast. Ill. Fl. Ins. Mar. Pacif. VII. (1892) 232.

A small tree with short and thick diverging branches and very tenacious milky sap; leaves obovate or obovate-oblong, on petioles of about 5 cm; rounded at the apex, coriaceous, pale, glabrous, veins prominent, strictly parallel; cymes contracted, 6 to 12 flowered, terminal, sessile on short leafy spurs or branches, pedicels very short, with squamaceous bractlets; calyx 2 mm, lobes obtuse short; corolla pale yellow, tube 6 to 8 mm, lobes 2 to 3 mm; stamens with very short filaments, anthers acute; style nearly the length of the tube; drupes dry, 5 cm long, 2.5 cm or more wide, bright red; seed elliptical, 36 mm long, 16 mm broad and 12 mm deep, pointed at both ends; albumen deeply wrinkled by transverse sinuous folds; embryo axile, straight, nearly as long as the albumen, the linear oblong fleshy cotyledons about as long as the inferior radicle and scarcely broader.

407

PLATE 166.

RAUWOLFIA SANDWICENSIS A. DC.
Hao.
Fruiting branch photographed from an herbarium specimen. About one-half natural size.

Apocynaceae.

This most interesting species is a small tree 15 to 25 feet in height and resembles somewhat the *Alaa* or *Sideroxylon sandwicense*. The native name of this rather rare tree is *Kaulu*, according to Hillebrand. The locality for the tree is Oahu, Nuuanu Valley, and Makaleha Valley of the Waianae range. In the latter place the tree was observed by C. N. Forbes and also by a student of the College of Hawaii, but has not been collected by the writer. The tree seems to be conspicuous on account of its bright red double fruits.

RAUWOLFIA Linn.

Calyx small, deeply 5-cleft, with obtuse or acute, imbricate lobes, glandless. Corolla salver-shaped, cylindrical, constricted at the scaleless throat, tube dilated at the place of insertion of the stamens, lobes sinistrorse. Stamens small, with obtuse or acute anthers, inserted at the middle of the tube or higher. Discus cup-shaped, truncate or lobed. Ovaries 2, superior, entirely free, or connate, at the base; ovules paired in each cell, pendulous; style filiform, with a short cylindrical stigma with a membraneous ring at the base. Drupes distinct, frequently connate at the base, obcordate, with crustaceous putamen. Seeds with uniform albumen.—Glabrous rarely tomentose trees or shrubs with usually opposite or whorled leaves. Flowers small in compound often umbellate cymes, at first terminal.

The genus Rauwolfia consists of about 45 species, which occur in the tropics of the old and new world. In the Hawaiian Islands only one species is represented. The Hawaiian species has often been confused with *Ochrosia parviflora* (Forst.) DC. and has even been described twice by De Candolle, once as *Ochrosia sandwicensis*, which now stands as a synonym.

Rauwolfia sandwicensis A. DC.

Hao.

(Plate 166.)

RAUWOLFIA SANDWICENSIS A. DC. Prodr. VIII. (1844) 339;—H. Mann Proc. Am. Acad. VII. (1867) 197;—Wawra in Flora (1874) 367;—Hbd. Fl. Haw. Isl. (1888) 295;—Del Cast. Ill. Fl. Ins. Mar. Pac. VII. (1892) 232;—K. Schum. in Engl. et Prantl Pflzfam. IV. 2. (1895) 153;—Heller Plants Haw. Isl. (1897) 878.— Cerbera parviflora Hook. et Arn. (not Forst.) Bot. Beech. (1832) 90.—Ochrosia sandwicensis A. DC. Prodr. VIII. (1844) 357 (not Gray).

Leaves 5 in a whorl, elliptico oblong, acuminate at both ends, pale chartaceous, on petioles of 1.5 to 3 cm (in all of the writer's material and not 2 to 3 mm as given in Hillebrand), with 5 to 12 stipitate glands in each axilla; flowers crowded into 4 umbellately compound cymes of the same length or longer than the petioles, at first terminal then axillary; the common peduncle 1 to 3.5 cm, pedicels about 2 mm; calyx 5 mm, parted to near the base into 5 oblong obtuse lobes; tube of the yellowish-green corolla 8 mm, scantily hairy inside, dilated below the constricted throat, the lobes 3 mm; anthers subsessile, sagittate, shortly exserted; discus small, annular or 5 lobed; ovules 4 in each carpel; drupe compressed. obcordate, deeply emarginate at the top, 8 to 12 mm in height and more in width, fleshy, black when mature; albumen scanty, radicle terete, superior.

The *Hao* is a medium-sized tree with milky sap. When growing in localities with rich soil and occasional rainfall it develops a straight trunk 6 to 12 inches in diameter and a total height of sometimes over 20 feet. When growing on the rough *aa* lava flows on the leeward sides of the Islands, as on Auahi, Maui, on the southern slopes of Mt. Haleakala, it is a more or less stunted shrub.

It resembles the *Holei* very much and when not in flower or fruit is not often easily distinguished from it. The leaves are of a lighter green than the *Holei* and not quite as thick in texture; it differs mainly from it in its small black fruits which are obcordate.

409

PLATE 167.

OCHROSIA SANDWICENSIS A. Gray.
Holei.
Showing fruiting branch about one-half natural size.

PLATE 168.

OCHROSIA SANDWICENSIS A. Gray.
Holei.
Growing in the Kipuka Puaulu, near the Volcano Kilauea, Hawaii; elevation 4000 feet.

PLATE 169.

OCHROSIA SANDWICENSIS A. Gray.
Holei Tree.
In the Kipuka Puaulu, Kilauea Volcano, Hawaii.

Apocynaceae.

It inhabits the dry regions on the leeward sides of all the islands at an elevation of about 2000 feet. On Lanai, in the valleys of Kaiholena and Mahana, it develops a straight trunk; the branches are somewhat stiff and densely studded with leaf-scars. It associates with *Reynoldsia sandwicensis*, Pittosporum, Antidesma, and other trees peculiar to the dry regions. On Oahu it is more or less shrubby, sepecially so in Niu Valley and on Tantalus, while on Kauai big trees may be found above Makaweli.

The wood of the *Hao* is of medium strength, fairly close grained, and dark yellowish in color. It is never used for firewood, as the natives claim that the smoke is poisonous. As it burns to ashes and leaves no charcoal, it was never employed by the natives for the production of the latter. It is called the Hawaiian Ironwood on account of its durability.

OCHROSIA Juss.

Calyx small, deeply 5-cleft, with imbricate obtuse lobes, glandless. Corolla salvershaped, with cylindrical tube which is dilated at the point of the insertion of the stamens, and is constricted at the glabrous throat, lobes dextrorse. Stamens oblong lanceolate, with acute anthers. Discus wanting, or very indistinct, short, annular. Ovary superior with few ovules in each cell arranged in two rows. Carpels frequently connate at the base. Drupes in pairs or through abortion single, diverging, rather dry, united at the base or free, with thin exocarp and woody endocarp which is dorsally compressed and deeply furrowed on the ventral side. Seeds few, three for the most in a double drupe. Trees with whorled coriaceous leaves, which are narrowly parallel-veined; flowers of medium size and often very fragrant, arranged in cymes from the axils of the uppermost leaves.

The genus Ochrosia supposedly consists of 13 to 15 species, and extends from the Mascarene Islands, through Malaysia and tropical Australia into Polynesia. Only one species, *Ochrosia parviflora* (Forst.) Hemsl., is widely distributed over the Pacific Islands. *Ochrosia sandwicensis*, one of the Hawaiian species, together with the New Caledonian *Ochrosia elliptica*, comes very near to *Ochrosia oppositifolia* (*O. borbonica*) and may only be a variety of the latter.

Ochrosia sandwicensis Gray.

Holei.

(Plates 167, 168, 169.)

OCHROSIA SANDWICENSIS Gray (not DC.) Proc. Am. Acad. V. (1862) 333;—H. Mann Proc. Am. Acad. VII. (1867) 197;—Wawra in Flora (1874) 366;—Hbd. Fl. Haw. Isl. (1888) 296;—Del Cast. Ill. Fl. Ins. Mar. Pac. VII. (1892) 234;—K. Schum. in Engl. et Prantl Pflzfam. IV. 2. (1895) 156;—Brigham in Ka Hana Kapa (1911) 154, fig. 2, (the plant figured in Dr. Brigham's work is not *Ochrosia sandwicensis*, but *Xylosma Hillebrandii* Wawra).

Leaves 3 to 4 in a whorl, elongate oblong, on petioles of about 15 to 25 mm, shortly acuminate, chartaceous, shining above, the close and faint nerves parallel and at almost right angles to the midrib, and united by a distinct intramarginal nerve; cymes compound, 10 to 16 cm long, divaricately branching, the angular peduncle about 3 cm, the lateral pedicels about 3 to 4 mm, the medium flower subsessile; bracteoles short, ovate to dentiform; calyx 2 to 7 mm with acute lanceolate teeth or lobes, corolla yellowish to cream colored, quite fragrant, hairy inside, dilated below the throat, lobes linear oblong, equal, stamens inserted above the middle, with short hairy filaments and elongate included

413

anthers; stigma included, clavate; drupes dry, yellow when mature, ellipsoid or ovoid-elongate; seeds 1 on each side of the placenta and peltately attached to it; testa thin, chartaceous; albumen hard and fleshy; embryo axillary; radicle superior, as long as the cotyledons.

The *Holei* is a small milky tree, or sometimes shrub reaching a height of 10 to 25 feet, having long drooping branches. The trunk usually divides a few feet above the ground or has a single bole of eight inches in diameter vested in a brownish smooth bark. It is conspicuous in the forest by its oblong dark green leaves, which are arranged in whorls, and by its large light yellow to orange colored double fruits, which are suspended on long terminal or axillary peduncles. The flowers are yellowish and very fragrant.

The *Holei*, which has become rather scarce, inhabits the dry districts on the leeward side of the islands, and is only abundant on the Island of Maui, at an elevation of 2500 feet, back of Makawao, slopes of Haleakala, and on the lava fields of Auahi. On Hawaii several trees can be found in Puaulu, on the land of Keauhou, three miles from the Volcano of Kilauea, at an elevation of 4000 feet, as well as on the lava fields of Puuwaawaa, slopes of Hualalai.

The *Holei* is endemic to the Hawaiian Islands. The natives knew how to extract a yellow dye from the bark and roots, wherewith to stain their tapa or paper clothing. The wood of the *Holei* is hard, fine grained and of a dark yellowish brown color.

Hillebrand's var. *β.*, which he describes as:

"Leaves opposite 7-9 in. x 2½-3 in., on petioles of 1-1½ in., coriaceous, with prominent nerves. Cymes densely flowered," has been raised to specific rank by K. Schumann under the name:

Ochrosia compta K. Schum.
Holei.

OCHROSIA COMPTA K. Schum. in Engl. et Prantl Pflzfam. IV. 2. (1895) 156.—O. sandwicensis var. *β.* Hbd. Fl. Haw. Isl. (1888) 297.

Leaves coriaceous, flowers in contracted dense inflorescences.

This is all the description given by Schumann in Engler & Prantl Natürliche Pflanzenfamilien. The writer has never met with this plant, but desires to express the opinion that it is a rather doubtful species and perhaps only a form of *Ochrosia sandwicensis*. Especially when Schumann himself thinks *O. sandwicensis* to be only a form of *O. oppositifolia*, a species occurring in Madagascar, Mauritius, Java and Singapore.

BORRAGINACEAE.

The family Borraginaceae is distributed over the temperate and tropical regions of both worlds. The main center of distribution lies in the Mediterranean region. Pacific North America, especially California, is the second main center

Borraginaceae.

with numerous endemic species. Of most of the species of Cordia, Brazil as well as the rest of tropical South America possesses by far the majority.

In Hawaii 3 genera are represented, of which only the genus Cordia has a single cosmopolitan species which attains the size of a tree.

CORDIA Linn.

Calyx tubular or campanulate, 3 to 5 toothed, or split at the apex; after flowering often enlarged. Corolla funnel or salver shaped, with 4 to many, but usually 5, rarely imbricate lobes. Stamens as many as corolla lobes, inserted in the tube. Style usually prolonged, twice bifid, with a capitate or clavate stigma. Ovules erect. Drupe surrounded or more or less enclosed by the persistent calyx, 4-celled of which usually only one contains a developed seed. Seed with very scanty albumen and irregularly folded, thick or more often very broad thin and fan-shaped folded cotyledons, and short superior radicle.—Trees or shrubs with alternate, often almost opposite, petiolate, entire or serrate leaves. Flowers usually white or dark orange yellow, arranged in expanded or contracted cymes.

The genus Cordia consists of about 230 species distributed in the warmer regions of both hemispheres, especially in tropical America. In the Hawaiian Islands only the cosmopolitan *Cordia subcordata* Lam. (*Kou*) is represented.

Cordia subcordata Lam.
Kou.

CORDIA SUBCORDATA Lam. Ill. I. (1791) no. 1899;—Cham. in Linnaea IV (1829) 474;—Endl. Fl. Suds. (1836) no. 1212;—DC. Prodr. IX. (1845) 477;—Pancher in Cuzent Tahiti (1860) 235;—Seem. Fl. Viti (1866) 168, t. 34;—H. Mann Proc. Am. Acad. VII. (1867) 194;—Nadeaud Enum. Pl. Tahit. (1873) no. 375;—Wawra in Flora (1874);—Sinclair Indig. Flowers Haw. Isl. (1885) pl. 7;—Hbd. Fl. Haw. Isl. (1888) 321;—Del Cast. Ill. Fl. Ins. Mar. Pac. VII. (1892) 240, et Fl. Polyn. Franc. (1893) 128.—C. Sebestana Forst. Prodr. (1786) 108 (non Linn.);—Soland. Prim. Fl. Ins. Pacif. (ined.) 235, et in Parkins Draw. of Tahit. Pl. t. 29 (ined.) cf. Seem.) Endl. l. c. no. 1208;—C. orientalis Roem. et Schult. Syst. IV (1819) 449;—Guill. Zephyr. Tait. (1836-1837) n. 239.

Leaves ovate or subcordate 12.5 to 15 cm long, 8 to 10 cm wide, on petioles of 2.5 to 3 cm or more, acuminate, entire or wavy, glabrous excepting slight tomentose patches or streaks in the axils of the principal veins; flowers in short terminal or lateral subracemose panicles; calyx coriaceous, broadly and irregularly 3 to 5 toothed; corolla orange colored, its tube little longer than the calyx, with rotund, broadly expanded limb, 5 to 7 lobed; drupe ovate, submucronate, enclosed within the calyx.

The *Kou*, which is indigenous in the Hawaiian Islands, though presumably brought here by the Hawaiians centuries ago, can only be found along the seashore here and there. Nowadays it is exceedingly scarce, but in times gone by it was rather plentiful, and much planted by the Hawaiians near their dwellings or grass huts. The wood of the *Kou* was much sought for, on account of its beautiful grain, for calabashes or poi bowls, spittoons, etc. It is a tree 30 to 50 feet in height and had trunks of sometimes three feet in diameter.

Today trees are never larger than 15 to 20 feet, with trunks only a few inches in diameter. The writer observed it growing wild on the Island of Lanai, along the beach near Manele, and also on Maui near the lava fields beyond Makena, together with the Algaroba (*Prosopis juliflora*), which has taken possession of the country there, being on the leeside of Mt. Haleakala.

PLATE 170.

NOTHOCESTRUM BREVIFLORUM Gray.
Aiea.
Flowering branch, reduced one-half.

The *Kou*, whose Tahitian name is *Tou*, and is known in Samoa and Fiji as *Tou* or *Hauanave* and *Nawanawa* respectively, ranges all the way from the Hawaiian Islands to Madagascar, the Moluccas, and tropical New Holland.

The wood is used by the Samoans for rafts, and the fruits for paste for their tapa clothing. The wood, which is much prized by the natives, is rather soft but durable.

SOLANACEAE.

The family Solanaceae is distributed over the tropical and temperate regions of the old and new world. The center of distribution is in Central and South America. In the Hawaiian Islands the family has one endemic genus which is closely related to a genus occurring in Brazil, but is not known from any other part of the world. Of the genus Solanum six species are also peculiar to these islands, but only one is a tree.

KEY TO THE GENERA.

Corolla salver-shaped, 4 lobed, anthers sessile......................... **Nothocestrum**
Corolla rotate, 5-lobed, anthers connivent............................ **Solanum**

NOTHOCESTRUM Gray.

Calyx campanulate, 4-dentate or the teeth almost bilabiate. Corolla silky, salver-shaped, 4-lobed, the lobes ovate, valvate and folded in the bud. Anthers 4, sessile below the throat, linear, acute, the cells opening inward and lengthwise. Ovary globose to ovoid, 2-celled; ovules many. Style very short with a 2-lobed stigma. Fruit a berry. Seeds reniform, suspended from a funicle, the testa chartaceous and pitted. Embryo peripherical, curved around a fleshy albumen; the thick clavate radicle longer than the cylindrical cotyledons.—Soft wooded trees or shrubs with single or fasciculate, greenish-yellow, inconspicuous flowers.

The genus Nothocestrum consists of 4 species and is peculiar to the Hawaiian Islands, where all of its species are known by the name *Aiea*. The genus Nothocestrum is closest related to the genus Athenaea Sendtn. which possesses about 14 species peculiar to Brazil. The Hawaiian genus differs from the latter mainly in the tetramerous flowers which are salver-shaped, and besides in the calyx, which does not become enlarged at the maturity of the fruit, as is the case in Athenaea.

KEY TO THE SPECIES.

Flowers single, rarely 2 or 3; berry longate........................... **N. longifolium**
Flowers several on short axillary spurs; berry globose.
    Tube of corolla enclosed in the calyx.
        Leaves elliptical-oblong; fruit enclosed in the calyx........... **N. breviflorum**
    Tube of corolla longer than the calyx.
        Leaves ovate or ovate-oblong, often sinuate; calyx remains open with
           fruit . . . . **N. latifolium**
        Leaves ovate-cordate; fruit not closed over by calyx........... **N. subcordatum**

PLATE 171.

NOTHOCESTRUM BREVIFLORUM Gray.
Aiea Tree.
Injured trunk of Aiea tree, growing on the lava fields of Puuwaawaa, North Kona, Hawaii; elevation 2400 feet.

Solanaceae.

Nothocestrum longifolium Gray.
Aiea.

NOTHOCESTRUM LONGIFOLIUM Gray. in Proc. Am. Acad. VI. (1862) 48;—Seem. Flora Vit. (1866) 173;—Mann in Proc. Am. Acad. VII. (1867) 191;—Wawra in Flora (1873) 62:—Hbd. Fl. Haw. Isl. (1888) 308;—Del Cast. Ill. Fl. Ins. Mar. Pacif. VII. (1892) 249.

A small tree or shrub with slender ascending branches, quite glabrous; leaves thin membraneous, lanceolate or elliptical-oblong, acuminate at both ends or occasionally only acute or somewhat obtuse, 10 to 20 cm long, 3.5 to 8.5 cm wide, on petioles of 8 to 20 mm; flowers axillary, usually single, but not uncommonly 2 or 3, on pedicels of 8 to 30 mm; calyx tubular, 8 to 12 mm with flowers, 14 to 16 mm with fruit, glabrous, sharply or obtusely, always unevenly, 4-toothed; corolla pale yellow, the tube not longer than the calyx, the lobes of variable size, narrowly margined, glabrous when open, silky pubescent when in the bud, but with a remnant of pubescence on the back of the petals when open; anthers partly exserted; stigma clavate, included in the tube; berry elongate or fusiform, 12 to 20 mm long, orange-colored, rather fleshy, included in the calyx or exserted beyond.

This rather slender species is more often a shrub than a tree, and is peculiar to the rain forests on all the islands of the group. It usually sends out thin slender stems which do not branch, reaching a height of 7-10 feet, bearing leaf whorls at the ends, or it is a regular shrub with long and slender branches. Occasionally it is a tree 15-20 feet high. As such it was observed and collected by the writer in the Kipuku Puaulu, near the Volcano Kilauea on Hawaii at an elevation of over 4000 feet. This is the only record where it was not found in the rain forest proper. It is not uncommon on Oahu, on the Koolau range, and can be collected in the mountains back of Honolulu.

A variety β *brevifolium* Hbd. occurs in the mountains of Kauai, where it was collected by the writer along Opaiwela stream in the forests of Kaholuamano.

Nothocestrum breviflorum Gray.
Aiea.
(Plates 170, 171.)

NOTHOCESTRUM BREVIFLORUM Gray in Proc. Am. Acad. VI. (1866) 49;—Seem. Flora Vit. (1866) 173;—Mann Proc. Am. Acad. VII. (1867) 191;—Hbd. Fl. Haw. Isl. (1888) 308;—Del Cast. Ill. Fl. Ins. Mar. Pac. VII. (1892) 248.

A stout tree about 10 to 12 m high; branches stiff, ascending; leaves oblong or elliptical-oblong, 5 to 12 cm long, 3 to 6 cm wide, on petioles of 3 to 5 cm, acute or obtuse on both ends, thin chartaceous, tomentose underneath, flowers many, clustered on short axillary spurs, the pedicels 4 to 10 mm, calyx campanulate with flowers, globose with fruit and closed over it, dentate, almost bilabiate; corolla greenish yellow, tube enclosed in the calyx, lobes with yellowish, coarse pubescence outside, with the exception of the margins which are glabrous, glabrous inside; anthers not protruding, linear, acute, glabrous; ovary ovoid, style short; berry globose or oblong, orange-red, 6 to 8 mm, or more long.

The *Aiea* of Hawaii is a medium sized tree, 30-35 feet high, with a trunk of often 1½ feet in diameter; the bark is perfectly smooth and of a chocolate brown or grayish color; the wood is soft and whitish-green, and full of sap. It is peculiar to the Island of Hawaii, where it occurs in the dry districts especially on the *aa* lava flows of North Kona, at Puuwaawaa on the slopes of Mt. Hualalai, where it is exceedingly common. In that locality the writer met with the biggest trees. The trunks, owing to their softness are easily damaged and often

PLATE 172.

NOTHOCESTRUM LATIFOLIUM Gray.
Aiea Tree.
Fruiting branch pinned against trunk of tree. Growing on the lava fields of
Auahi, East Maui.

Solanaceae.

eaten out by thirsty cattle, and are often covered with peculiar looking scars, and covered with knobs, increasing the ungainly appearance of the tree. It may be said here that none of the species of Nothocestrum (*Aiea* trees) deserves any claim to beauty; in fact they are the most ugly trees which the Hawaiian Islands possess. In the forests of Naalehu, southern slopes of Mauna Loa, Hawaii, the writer met with a form of this species, which owing to the fact that it grew in a wetter forest had a somewhat different aspect. The fruits were more or less oblong instead of globose, but agreed otherwise well with *N. breviflorum*. Collected fruiting June, 1909, North Kona, Hawaii, (no. 3552); and flowering and fruiting Jan. 15, 1912, in Hilea forests, Kau, Hawaii, (no. 10016).

The tree is usually found at an elevation of between 2000-2500 feet.

Nothocestrum latifolium Gray.

Aiea.

(Plates 172, 173.)

NOTHOCESTRUM LATIFOLIUM Gray in Proc. Am. Acad. VI. (1862) 48;—Seem. Flora Vit. (1866) 173;—Mann Proc. Am. Acad. VII. (1867) 191;—Wawra in Flora (1873) 62;—Hbd. Fl. Haw. Isl. (1888) 308;—Del Cast. Ill. Fl. Ins. Mar. Pacif. VII. (1892) 249;—Heller in Minnes. Bot. Stud. Bull. IX. (1897) 885.

A small tree; branches rigid, ascending; leaves broad ovate, or obovate-oblong, or suborbicular (Lanai spec.) entire or with very shallow sinuses, acute or obtuse and often rounded at the apex, covered with an ochraceous tomentum when young, puberulous at a later age, of somewhat thick texture when fresh, thin chartaceous in dried specimens, pellucid, 4 to 12 cm long, 3 to 7 cm wide, on petioles of 10 to 50 mm; flowers clustered on short spurs, the pedicels 4 to 18 mm, calyx urceolate, about 6 mm, truncate, at length globose, tomentose or glabrate, open with fruit; corolla greenish-yellow, silky, the tube twice as long as the calyx, the lobes less than half its length; anthers protruding, somewhat shorter than in the foregoing species; ovary globose, style as long as tube, berry globose 4 to 6 mm, whitish.

This species of *Aiea* occurs on all the islands of the group with the exception of Hawaii. Like the former it prefers the dry forehills on the leeward sides as well as *aa* lava fields. It is one of the most common and ungainly looking trees on the Island of Lanai, where it can be found in the Kaa desert, the most western point of Lanai. It is taller than any other tree in that locality and can be recognized from a distance by its long stiff ascending branches, which are only slightly foliate; on Molokai it is common at Mapulo'u in the dry canyons and rocky situation 2000 feet above Kaunakakai, where it associates with Sideroxylon, *Acacia Koaia*, *Myoporum sandwicense*, and other trees; collected March 22, 1910, Mapulo'u, Molokai, no. 6155 fruiting; flowering at Mauna Lei, Lanai, July 26, 1910, (no. 8082).

On the Island of Maui, on the southern slopes of Haleakala on the lava fields of Auahi, land of Kahikinui, occurs a variety enumerated as β by Hillebrand in his Flora. During the winter months, especially in the month of November, the trees are adorned with large dark green foliage hiding the ugly gnarled stiff branches, while in the month of March they are either bare or with only very scanty foliage.

PLATE 173.

NOTHOCESTRUM LATIFOLIUM Gray.
Aiea Tree.
Growing on the aa lava fields of Auahi, Haleakala, East Maui; elevation 2600 feet.

Solanaceae.

The leaves are large with sinuate margins, subcordate at the base, densely tomentose, dark green with pale venation; inflorescence also covered with a dirty yellowish pubescence; otherwise as in the species. At the same locality occurs, however, also the species with entire leaves or just a slight indication of a wavy margin.

The tree illustrated was photographed when the foliage was scanty.

The wood of this, as well as of the other species, is soft and of a green color; it was used by the natives in the olden days for finishing off canoes. The reddish yellow berries are sometimes eaten.

Nothocestrum subcordatum Mann.
Aiea.

NOTHOCESTRUM SUBCORDATUM Mann Proc. Am. Acad. VII. (1867) 191;—Wawra in Flora (1873) 62;—Hbd. Fl. Haw. Isl. (1888) 309;—Del Cast. Ill. Fl. Ins. Mar. Pac. VII. (1892) 249.

A medium sized tree about 10 m high; leaves ovate or cordate, 7.5 to 12.5 cm long, 5 to 10 cm wide, on petioles of 3 to 4.5 cm, bluntly acuminate, thick coriaceous, glabrous; flowers clustered, but often only a single one developed, on pedicels of 4 to 5 mm; calyx 4 to 8 mm, glabrous, campanulate with flowers, globose with fruit but not closed over it; corolla exserted, silky yellow, its tube 8 to 10 mm, the limb half as long and 4 to 5 lobed; berry globose.

This species, which is undoubtedly closely related to *N. latifolium*, if at all distinct from it, occurs in the ravines of Mt. Kaala of the Waianae range, and in the Valley of Wailupe, at the eastern end of Oahu. It is not known to the writer. Wawra collected it at Halemanu on Kauai, (no. 2140).

SOLANUM L.

Calyx 5 to 10 toothed or lobed, only rarely enlarged with fruit. Corolla rotate or broad campanulate, 5-lobed. Filaments very short, inserted at the base of the corolla; anthers oblong or linear, erect and connivent in a cone round the style, opening at the apex by 1 to 2 pores. Berry globose or elongate.—Herbs, shrubs or trees, prostrate, erect, or climbing, with entire or lobed leaves. Flowers in umbellate cymes or racemes, or often a corymbose panicle, rarely single. Corolla white, yellow, purple, blue or red.

This genus, which numbers more than 900 species, is distributed over the tropical and temperate parts of the whole globe; the largest number of species occurs however in South America. The Hawaiian Islands possess 6 endemic species of which only the one here described is a tree, the remaining five being shrubs. Besides the six endemic species quite a number of species are cultivated for ornamental purposes, and a few are weeds along the roadside, as the nightshade (*Popolo*) etc. To this genus also belongs the Potato, *Solanum tuberosum* L., and the Egg plant, *S. Melongena*.

Solanum Carterianum Rock sp. nov.
Puananahonua.

A medium sized or small tree 5 to 7 m high, with very few stiff branches, straight trunk of 15 to 20 cm in diameter, vested in a grayish smooth bark; branches covered

PLATE 174.

MYOPORUM SANDWICENSIS (A.DC.) Gray.
Naio or **Bastard Sandalwood.**
Flowering and fruiting branch, less than one-half natural size.

Solanaceae-Myoporaceae.

throughout with a pale yellow to cinereous, long, stellate pubescence; leaves pale green and velvety tomentose above, densely covered beneath, especially on the veins and mid-rib, with a stellate pale tomentum, as well as the petioles, which are 20 to 30 mm long, elliptical-oblong, long acuminate at the apex, shortly contracted at the base, acute, chartaceous, entire, 12 to 25 cm long, 3.5 to 7 cm wide; inflorescence a terminal corymb, when fully developed 15 cm long, standing erect on a common stiff peduncle of 8 cm, densely covered with a long stellate woolly tomentum, calyx densely tomentose, divided to the middle into ovate acute lobes of 4 mm length, corolla parted two thirds its length into ovate-oblong acute lobes, which are of a blue color, and glabrous inside, but densely tomentose outside, with a prominent median nerve; stamens on short filaments, anthers pale, short, oblong, not attenuate, broader at the apex than at the base, 2.5 mm long, with two ovoid apical pores; ovary villous, style long protruding, 6 mm, hairy; berry globose, black covered with a short stellate pubescence when young, 10 to 12 mm in diameter on pedicels of 6 mm; the peduncle and pedicels woody and thick, when with fruit.

This most remarkable species was discovered by the writer on the Island of Oahu in the lower forests near Waiahole, at the entrance of Waianu Valley, on January 22, 1909; only a single tree was seen, for which an old native gave the name as *Puananahonua*. He remarked that he knew of the tree when he was a boy, and that his parents used the fruits for medicinal purposes.

This is the only species of Hawaiian Solanum which becomes a tree, all the rest of them being shrubs. It is remarkable for its large entire leaves, but mainly for its terminal woody corymbose inflorescence which reaches a length over 15 cm; also for the bright blue corolla, and long filiform style.

It is named in honor of Ex-Governor George R. Carter, who made the publication of this volume possible.

Collected at Waianu, Oahu, flowering and fruiting, January 22, 1909, (no. 1191), type in the College of Hawaii Herbarium.

MYOPORACEAE.

The main regions of the distribution of this family are situated in Australia and in the neighboring islands. Only a few out of the 102 species are found outside of Australia, one each in China and Japan, one in Mauritius, one in South and West Africa, and another species in the West Indies. Here in the Hawaiian Islands we have also only one species represented. The family consists only of 4 genera, nearly all Australian.

MYOPORUM Banks et Sol.

Calyx 5-lobed, unchanged at maturity of the fruit. Corolla with short tube sub campanulate, or with longer tube and funnel shaped, actinomorphous. Stamens 4, two large, rarely 5. Ovary 2 to 10 celled; and as many seeded. Trees or shrubs or bushes with erect and prostrate stems. Flowers single or fasciculate in the leaf-axils.

The genus numbers about 25 species, which are divided into 5 sections. It is distributed over Australia, China, Japan, Mauritius and the Hawaiian Islands with a single species which comes under section II. Polycoelium.

The only useful species of Myoporum are *M. platycarpum* R. Br., the sandal or sugar tree or dog wood of the Australians, which exudes a sort of manna, and

425

PLATE 175.

MYOPORUM SANDWICENSE (A.DC.) Gray.
Naio.
Trunk of large tree showing peculiar scaly bark, more than two feet in diameter; growing in forest above Makawao, Maui; elevation 2500 feet.

Myoporaceae.

also a resin which is used as sealing wax. and the Hawaiian species, *M. sandwicense* (DC.) A. Gray, or *Naio* or Bastard Sandalwood, used as a substitute for the true sandalwood after the exhaustion of the latter.

Myoporum Sandwicense (DC.) A. Gray.
Naio or Bastard Sandalwood.
(Plates 174, 175, 176.)

MYOPORUM SANDWICENSIS (DC.) A. Gray in Proc. Am. Acad. VI. (1866) 53;—
H. Mann. in Proc. Am. Acad. VII (1867) 194;—Wawra in Flora (1874);—
Hbd. Fl. Haw. Isl. (1888) 339;—Del Cast. Ill. Fl. Ins. Mar. Pacif. VII. (1892)
258;—v. Wettstein in Engl. et Prantl Pflzfam. IV. 3. 1. (1895) 360;—Heller Pl.
Haw. Isl. (1897) 892.—**Polycoelium sandwicense** A. DC. Prodr. XI. (1847) 706.—
Myoporum tenuifolium Hook. et Arn. in Bot. Beech. (1832) 93.

Leaves crowded towards the ends of the branches, alternate, elliptico lanceolate or oblong lanceolate, very acute, or acuminate, chartaceous, or fleshy when growing at the sea-shore or even at low elevations (300 feet) 6 to 15 cm long, 1 to 5 cm wide on petioles of about 1 cm or less, acute at both ends, entire, or serrate in the specimens from Mt. Hualalai, North Kona, Hawaii, the young leaves very viscous in all specimens; flowers in clusters of 5 to 8, white or deep pink colored, on pedicels of 8 mm; calyx 1 to 3 mm. parted to the base into ovate-lanceolate acute lobes; corolla campanulate 5 to 8 mm, cleft to the middle into 5 to 6 or rarely 7 obovate lobes; stamens as many as lobes, shorter than the latter, all alike, or two little exceeding the others; style short, flattened, incurved near the apex; stigma truncate. Drupe dry or somewhat fleshy and white globose or ovate, about 2 mm in diameter, crowned by the style, ribbed when dry; embryo cylindrical cotyledons as long as the radicle.

On the Island of Molokai is a very narrow leaved form, with linear lanceolate very acuminate leaves, which are viscous; and with small pink flowers. It grows on all the islands of the group, from high elevations down to near or at the sea-shore, where it forms globose tussocks with salty fleshy leaves.

The *Naio* or Bastard Sandalwood is a very handsome tree which reaches a considerable size. Its thick bark is of a dark gray color and deeply irregularly corrugated. It inhabits all the islands of the group and according to Hillebrand is supposed to reach its best development on the high mountains of Hawaii, Mauna Kea and Mauna Loa, up to 10,000 feet elevation, which, however, is not the case. Next to *Ohia* and *Koa*, it is one of our most common forest trees, growing at all elevations from sea level, where it is a small shrub 2 feet high, up to 10,000 feet. On the Island of Maui, in the dry forest back of Makawao (elevation 2500 feet), as well as at Auahi, southern slopes of Haleakala, it attains its greatest height and diameter of trunk; trees of 50 to 60 feet with trunks of more than 3 feet in diameter are not uncommon. It prefers the leeward sides of the islands, especially the *aa* lava fields, regions with very little rainfall, as well as the high mountains of Mauna Kea, Mauna Loa, Hualalai and Haleakala, where it forms the upper forest zone together with the *Mamani* (*Sophora chrysophylla*), Raillardia, Coprosma, and Styphelia, reaching a height of about 20 feet, and withstanding heavy frosts. At the lower levels it is associated with the *Maua, Holei, Aalii, Kauila, Uhiuhi*, etc. Hillebrand in his flora says that it is wanting on Molokai. The writer, however, found it very abundant above Kaunakakai, on the open dry ridges at Mapulou, where it grew together with *Koaia* and *Alaa*. The tree is glabrous throughout, has from narrow lance-

427

PLATE 176.

MYOPORUM SANDWICENSE (A.DC.) Gray.
Naio, Bastard Sandalwood.
A large Naio tree, growing on the lava fields of Auahi, southern slopes of Haleakala,
Maui; elevation 2600 feet.

olate to obovate pointed glossy leaves which are crowded at the ends of the branches. The flowers, which are of a white or pink color, are borne all along the slender branches and are quite fragrant.

The dark yellowish green wood becomes very fragrant on drying and resembles the odor of true Sandalwood. After the supply of the latter became exhausted in the islands, it was shipped to China as a substitute. The *Naio* is peculiar to this archipelago, though undoubtedly it must have originated either from Australia or New Zealand, the home of most of the Myoporums.

Dead trees or old trunks are called *Aaka* by the natives.

RUBIACEAE.

The family Rubiaceae with its 4500 or more species and about 350 genera is a decidedly tropical one. The distribution of its species over Africa, Asia and America is rather even. Polynesia possesses also a large number of species. In the Hawaiian Islands this family is represented by 13 genera of which 4, (Straussia, Bobea, Gouldia and Kadua) are endemic. Eight of the 13 genera have arborescent species while the remaining 5 have shrubby or also herbaceous species only, and are therefore here omitted. A large contingent of the Hawaiian Flora is made up of this family which is the largest next to (Lobelioideae) Campanulaceae and Rutaceae. The family is easily distinguished by its opposite leaves and interpetiolar stipules.

Ovules many in each cell.
  Ovary 2- rarely 3-4 celled.
    Fruit a bluish-black, indehiscent fleshy berry.................... **Gouldia**
  Ovary 1-celled.
    Fruit larger globose or pyriform, succulent or dry, crowned with the calycine
      limb . . .. **Gardenia**
Ovules one in each cell.
  Flowers hermaphrodite or polygamous.
    Ovary 2 to 10-celled.
      Flowers greenish, the corolla-lobes imbricate in the bud........ **Bobea**
    Ovary 2-celled.
      Flowers white fragrant, the corolla lobes valvate............ **Plectronia**
      Flowers white small, rotate................................ **Straussia**
      Flowers larger, white funnel-shaped, drupe crowned by the long calycine
        limb... **Psychotria**
    Ovary 4-celled.
      Flowers in globose heads; drupes united into a fleshy compound
        fruit... **Morinda**
  Flowers dioecious, stigma bifid to the base, anthers 4 to 11............ **Coprosma**

GOULDIA Gray.

Calyx short, cup-shaped, 4-toothed. Corolla salver-shaped, coriaceous, with 4 thick, fleshy lobes and glabrous throat. Stamens 4. inserted in the tube or throat. Ovary 2-celled; style with 2 filiform branches. Fruit a berry with 2 drupaceous divisions, bisulcate.—Shrubs or small trees with coriaceous leaves and short interpetiolar, caducous stipules.

PLATE 177.

GOULDIA AXILLARIS Wawra.
Manono.
Fruiting branch; reduced.

Rubiaceae.

The genus Gouldia is strictly Hawaiian, and consists of a goodly number of ill-defined species, most of which are shrubs, only very few becoming trees. As they are at present in a mixup, and difficult to determine without type material, it is thought wise to mention only these few.

KEY TO THE SPECIES.

Panicles axillary and short, leaves pubescent underneath................... **G. axillaris**
Panicles terminal, large, loose.. **G. elongata**

Gouldia axillaris Wawra.
Manono.
(Plate 177.)

GOULDIA AXILLARIS Wawra in Flora (1874) 297;—Hbd. Fl. Haw. Isl. (1888) 170;—
Del Cast. Ill. Fl. Ins. Mar. Pacif. VI. (1890) 189.—**G. sandwicensis** var. **hirtella**
Gray Proc. Am. Ac. IV. (1860) 310, in part.

Branches angular, solid, densely and evenly foliose throughout, coarsely pubescent; leaves on petioles of 4 to 12 mm, elliptical, obovate-oblong or lanceolate, 5 to 15 cm long, 1.5 to 5 cm wide, more or less acuminate, contracted or rounded at the base, bluish-green when fresh, membraneous to chartaceous, with not very distinct nerves, coarsely but sparingly pubescent underneath; stipules 6 mm; panicles numerous, pubescent, short, 2.5 to 5 cm long, in the axils of mostly older leaves or on the naked branches, with slender peduncles of 4 to 12 mm; the lowest bracts 6 to 12 mm or foliaceous; corolla puberulous, small; anthers subexserted; berry pale blue or blackish, 3 to 4 mm in diameter; seeds 20 to 22 on each placenta.

This species is a small tree about 20 to 25 feet high, and is very variable. It occurs practically on all the islands of the group in the rain or middle forest zone at an elevation of about 3000 feet. Specimens from South Kona, in the forests back of the lava fields of Kapua, Hawaii, have exceedingly large fruits, and larger panicles all along the branches, as well as terminal; collected fruiting February, 1912, (no. 10030). Other numbers in the Herbarium of the College of Hawaii are 3706 from Hualalai, Hawaii; 7016 from Maunahui, Molokai; 8535 from Mt. Haleakala, Maui.

Gouldia elongata Heller.
Manono.

GOULDIA ELONGATA Heller in Minnes. Bot. Stud. Bull. IX. (1897) 897.—**G. terminalis**
Hbd. Fl. Haw. Isl. (1888) 169 in part.

Branches subherbaceous near the ends, drooping, slender, four-angled, glabrous throughout; or the young leaves finely puberulous underneath; bark gray, smooth; leaves elliptical-lanceolate, slightly more contracted at the apex than at the base; 5 to 7.5 cm long, 3 cm or more wide, entire, midrib prominent, impressed above, on short petioles about 2 cm; panicles terminal or occasionally axillary, pyramidal, very large and loose; pedicels slender; berries small, 2 mm in diameter, bluish.

This *Manono* is usually a shrub, but it was also observed as a tree in the forests of Kaholuamano, Kauai. Plants occur on Maui (no. 8531) which would be referable to this species, but differ to some extent, as in the contracted panicle, which comes closer to *G. sambucina*. The latter is also a small tree described by Heller. It occurs in the forests of Kaholuamano, Kauai. The leaves of this latter species are very wide and thick coriaceous.

PLATE 178.

GARDENIA REMYI Mann.
Nanu or Nau.
Flowering and fruiting branch; reduced.

Rubiaceae.

GARDENIA Ellis.

Calyx usually tubular and truncate, toothed or lobed, persistent.   Corolla salver-shaped, campanulate, or funnel-shaped with cylindrical tube; lobes occasionally more than 5.   Stamens 5 to 11, inserted in the throat, enclosed or shortly protruding.   Ovary 1-celled, with 2-several parietal placentas; style often with clavate stigma protruding.   Fruit coriaceous or succulent, often irregularly opening, smooth or ribbed, globose or pyriform.—Shrubs or trees with chartaceous or coriaceous leaves, and interpetiolar, often connate and sheathing stipules.   Flowers occasionally very large, terminal or axillary, white, yellow or purple.

The genus consists of about 70 species which are distributed over tropical Africa, Asia and Australia.   About 10 species have been described from the Pacific isles, two of which are peculiar to Hawaii, while the remaining ones occur in Tahiti (1), Fiji (6) and in Samoa (1).

KEY TO THE SPECIES.

Branches not glutinous, fruit globose.................................... **G. Brighami**
Branches glutinous, fruit quadrangular, pyriform........................ **G. Remyi**

Gardenia Brighami Mann.

Nau.

GARDENIA BRIGHAMI Mann in Proc. Am. Acad. VII. (1867) 171;—Hbd. Fl. Haw. Isl. (1888) 171;—Del Cast. Ill. Fl. Ins. Mar. Pac. VI. (1890) 191;—Brigham Ka Hana Kapa in Mem. B. P. B. Mus. III. (1911) 146.

Branches dichotomous, densely foliose, scarcely glutinous at the ends; leaves on short petioles of 4 mm, ovate, shortly acuminate, chartaceous, with prominent straight nerves, shining above, papillose and puberulous when young; stipules triangular or truncate; flowers single, terminal, subsessile; calyx tube shortly produced above the ovary, 10 mm long, 4 lobed; anthers subsessile, linear, their apices exserted; style as long as the tube (14 to 18 mm), the two clavate branches nearly half its length; fruit globose, with 4 faint lines, about 2.5 cm in diameter, coriaceous, indehiscent, tipped with the contracted limb of the calyx, 1-celled, with 4 (or 3 or 5) parietal placentas projecting about 4 mm from the pergameneous endocarp; seeds many in a yellowish pulp, horizontal, flattened, obtusely 3 or more angled.

The *Nau* is a small tree, reaching a height of 15 to 18 feet, or is even smaller when it is a shrub.   It has a trunk 6 to 8 inches in diameter and is vested in a smooth or slightly roughened bark.   The flowers are of a beautiful white and very fragrant and would be worthy of cultivation on that account.   During the month of March the trees are usually loaded with the globose fruits, which turn black when mature.   Hillebrand remarks that the fruits do not open on the tree, though the writer saw them split into several divisions on most of the trees on Molokai.

The *Nau* is peculiar to the very dry districts on the leeward sides of the islands, and is especially common on Molokai, where it forms the remnants of the dry forest on the slopes of Mauna Loa which forms the west end of that Island.   The trees on Molokai are taller than on the other islands.   It associates with the *Keahi, Chrysophyllum polynesicum, Kokia drynarioides, Reynoldsia sandwicensis, Xylosma Hillebrandii, Nototrichium sandwicense,* etc.   On Lanai it is also very common in the Valleys of Mahana and Kaiholena, as well as on the slopes of the Kaa desert, where it can be found with some of the above mentioned trees and also with *Bobea sandwicensis, Nothocestrum* sp., *Osmanthus*

433

PLATE 179.

PLECTRONIA ODORATA (Forst.) F. v. M.
Walahee or Alahee Trees.
Growing on the extreme western end of Molokai.

Rubiaceae.

sandwicensis, various Sideroxylons and others. On Hawaii the writer found a small tree on the lava fields of Puuwaawaa, elevation 2000 feet, North Kona, while on Oahu it is recorded from Nuuanu and the dry forehills of Makaleha. The wood of the *Nau* is whitish yellow. The yellow pulp of the fruit was employed in dyeing *tapa*, or *kapa*, yellow.

Gardenia Remyi Mann.
Nanu or *Nau.*
(Plate 178.)

GARDENIA REMYI Mann in Proc. Am. Acad. VII. (1867) 171;—Hbd. Fl. Haw. Isl. (1888) 172;—Del Cast. Ill. Fl. Ins. Mar. Pac. VI. (1890) 191;—Brigham Ka Hana Kapa Mem. B. P. B. Mus. III. (1911) 146. fig. 88.

Leaves obovate oblong, 10 to 22.5 cm long, 5 to 10 cm wide on petioles of 4 to 8 mm, shortly acuminate, contracted at the base, chartaceous, papillose underneath, prominently nerved; stipules truncate and sheathing, flowers terminal, single, sessile; calyx-tube angular, 18 mm long with 4 to 5 lobes which are falciform, and dilated toward the obtuse apex, net-veined, spreading with the plane vertical about 3 to 5 cm long, equalling or exceeding the corolla; corolla white, the tube 2.5 cm, the 7 to 8 obovate-oblong suberect lobes about 20 mm long, narrowed at the base and separated by broad sinuses; anthers enclosed; fruit 4 to 5-angled, pyriform, 3.5 to 5 cm, the permanent calyx-lobes surrounding a disc 6 to 8 mm in diameter.

The *Nanu* or *Nau*, unlike the afore described, is a tall tree reaching a height of 20 to 40 feet with a rather large broad crown. The branches are more or less horizontal in large trees; the trunk is short. The leaves which are larger than in the foregoing species are light green and covered as with a layer of varnish due to a glutinous substance which exudes from the young shoots. The large sweet-scented flowers are terminal and single and have no flower stalk. The fruit, which is quadrangular, is crowned by four wings, which are the persistent lobes of the calyx, a characteristic which is absent in the other Hawaiian *Nau*.

The *Nanu* or *Nau* may be found on the slopes of Tantalus and especially in Palolo Valley on Oahu, where it is a smaller tree, while on Molokai back of Kaluaha large trees can be found in company with *Acacia Koa (Koa), Bobea elatior, Straussia Kaduana*, etc. It grows on the leeward sides of some of the islands and also in the rain forests on the windward sides, as for example on Maui, where it is scattered between the valleys of Waikamoi and Honomanu on the northern slope of Haleakala, where the rainfall is exceedingly large, as well as on Kauai in the forests of Hanalei. Like the former it is endemic to the Hawaiian Islands; both species were discovered by Horace Mann and also described by him in his "Enumeration of Hawaiian Plants"; the former he named in honor of his companion, Prof. Wm. T. Brigham, the latter for the French Botanist Jules Remy.

The glutinous leaf buds were used by the natives as a cement, and the yellow fruit-pulp for dyeing purposes.

435

PLATE 180.

BOBEA ELATIOR Gaud.
Ahakea.
Fruiting branch; reduced.

Rubiaceae.

PLECTRONIA Linn.

Calyx short, cup-shaped, truncate or 4 to 5 toothed. Tube of corolla short or prolonged, corolla funnel shaped or campanulate, with obtuse or acute lobes. Stamens 4 to 5, inserted near the throat. Ovary 2-celled; style with thickened, obtuse, capitate stigma. Drupe 2-seeded, one cell often abortive.—Shrubs or trees, occasionally climbers, armed or unarmed, with coriaceous leaves and interpetiolar stipules. Flowers small in fascicles or corymbose cymes.

A genus of more than 80 species distributed over the warmer or hottest regions of the old world, with the exception of Europe. In the Hawaiian Islands we have only one species, the *Walahee* or *Alahee*, distributed however over the South Pacific Islands.

Plectronia odorata (Forst.) F. v. M.
Walahee or *Alahee*.
(Plate 178.)

PLECTRONIA ODORATA Forst. F. v. Muell. ....? Hbd. Fl. Haw. Isl. (1888) 175;—Del Cast. Ill. Fl. Ins. Mar. Pac. VI. (1890) 194;—K. Schum. in Engl. et Prantl Pflzfam. IV. 4. (1891) 92;—Heller Pl. Haw. Isl. (1897) 902.—**Coffea odorata** Forst. Prodr. (1786) no. 94.—**Ixora odorata** Sprengl. Syst. veg. I. (1825) 409.—**Canthium lucidum** H. et A. Bot. Beech. (1832) 65;—Mann Proc. Am. Acad. VII. (1867) 169;—Wawra in Flora (1874) 298.—**Myonima umbellatum** Hook. et Arn. Bot. Beech. (1832) 86.—**Pavetta dubia** Endl. Fl. Suds. (1836) 176. no. 1296.—**Canthium odoratum** Seem. Fl. Vit. (1866) 132.

Leaves elliptical-oblong, acuminate or somewhat obtuse, dark green, glossy above, paler beneath; stipules mucronate; flowers white, fragrant in cymose corymbs 2.5 to 3.5 cm long; calyx 2 mm, dentate; corolla 6 mm long, 4 to 5 fid, pilose at the insertion of the stamens, the latter exserted; style little longer, glabrous, stigma short ovoid or rather the 2 thick lobes co-adnate; drupe obovoid, compressed, black and juicy when mature, emarginate, grooved on each side, 8x10 mm, 2-celled. Seed incurved.

The *Walahee* or *Alahee* is a shrub or small tree reaching a maximum height of 20 feet. It has a round crown, bright green, very glossy leaves; the white fragrant flowers add to the beauty of the little tree during the summer months.

It inhabits the dry regions of the low land or lower forest zone up to 2000 feet, and is rather a common tree on all the islands. On the west end of Molokai, *Walahee* trees form the sole arborescent growth in the little gulches (see plate 178).

The wood of the *Alahee* is very handsome, exceedingly hard, and durable. It was used by the natives for their implements with which they tilled the soil. The leaves were used in coloring articles black.

BOBEA Gaud.

Flowers polygamous-dioecious. Calyx cup-shaped, truncate, 4-toothed or 4-lobed. Corolla salver-shaped, lobes imbricate in the bud. Stamens inserted in the throat, their apices protruding. Ovary 2 to 11-celled; style in the male flowers with 2-, in the female flowers with 2 to 11 filiform branches. Drupe globose, somewhat dry or fleshy, furrowed when dry, with 2 to 11 osseous, uniseriate pyrenae. Seeds straight.—Trees with subcoriaceous to chartaceous, pale green leaves, and interpetiolar easily caducous stipules. Flowers usually 3, or single, in axillary symes.

PLATE 181.

BOBEA HOOKERI Hbd.
Ahakea.
Flowering and fruiting branch; reduced.

Rubiaceae.

The genus Bobea, named by Gaudichaud in honor of M. Bobe-Moreau, a physician and pharmacist in the French Marine, consists of 4 or perhaps 5 species, which are all peculiar to the Hawaiian Islands. They form two groups, one composed of *Bobea elatior* and *B. Mannii* which are perhaps a single species, and *B. timonioides*, *B. sandwicensis* and *B. Hookeri*, only differing from each other mainly in the number of pyrenae.

KEY TO THE SPECIES.

Limb of calyx cup-shaped, truncate, drupe with 2 to 11 pyrenae.
    Leaves glabrous; peduncle erect.................................... **B. elatior**
    Leaves hairy underneath, peduncle drooping........................ **B. Mannii**
Limb of calyx cup-shaped, 4 toothed.................................. **B. timonoides**
Limb of calyx broadly 4 lobed.
    Flowers in cymes; drupe with 2 pyrenae........................... **B. sandwicensis**
    Flowers single; drupes with 4 to 6 pyrenae....................... **B. Hookeri**

Bobea elatior Gaud.
Ahakea.
(Plate 180.)

BOBEA ELATIOR Gaud. Bot. Voy. Uranie (1826-30) 473. pl. 93;—A. Gray Proc. Am. Acad. IV. (1860) 36;—Mann Proc. Am. Acad. VII. (1867) 170;—Hbd. Fl. Haw. Isl. (1888) 173;—K. Schum. in Engl. et Prantl IV. 4. (1891) 96;—Del Cast. Ill. Fl. Ins. Mar. Pac. VI. (1890) 192;—Heller in Minnes. Bot. Stud Bull. IX. (1897) 893.—**Burneya Gaudichaudii** Cham. et Schlecht. in Linn. IV. (1829) 190.—**Timonius Gaudichaudii** DC. Prodr. IV. (1830) 461;—Endl. Fl. Suds. (1836) 176, no. 1288.

Leaves pale, obovate oblong, 5 to 10 cm long, 2.5 to 5 cm wide, on petioles of 6 to 24 mm, acuminate, chartaceous, glabrous; stipules oblong-lanceolate, 8 to 12 mm, rather convolute in the bud; flowers 3 (accord. Hillbd. 3 to 7) in a cyme, with a common peduncle of 5 to 7.5 cm, the middle flower sessile, the lateral ones on pedicels of 12 to 18 mm; bracts and bractlets cup-shaped, low; calyx 4 to 5 cm, the cup-shaped truncate limb as long as the adnate portion; corolla greenish, glabrous, the lobes in the bud silky near the apex, the tube 4 to 8 mm, plicate at the throat, the obovate or rounded lobes 3 to 5 mm; anthers sessile at the middle of the tube; style 3 to 11 cleft; drupe rather fleshy, purplish ovoid 6 to 10 mm in diameter, or spheroidal crowned by the calycine limb which surrounds a glabrous disk of 2 mm in diam.; pyrenae 3 to 11, thick walled, complanate.

This *Ahakea* is a tree 30 feet or so tall with often a large trunk of 1½ feet in diameter. It occurs in the rain forests of the Islands of Oahu, Kauai, and Hawaii, and can be recognized by its rather pale green foliage, which is often reddish-veined.

It is not uncommon back of Honolulu in the Valleys of Pauoa and Palolo as well as in the whole Koolau range. The biggest trees were observed in the mountains of Punaluu on the windward side of Oahu. The wood of the *Ahakea* is yellow and was employed by the natives for poi boards and the top-rims of outrigger canoes, which in modern ones are painted yellow, to take the place of the yellow *Ahakea* wood.

Few are the natives now-a-days who are familiar with the *Ahakeas* of the Hawaiian forests.

At a lower elevation, about 1000 feet, there occurs an apparent variety of the

439

PLATE 182.

BOBEA HOOKERI Hbd.
Ahakea.
Flowering and fruiting branch pinned against trunk of tree. Growing on the lava fields
Auahi, southern slopes of Mt. Haleakala, Maui.

Rubiaceae.

true *B. elatior*, with smaller leaves, and fruits with only two pyrenae. The whole aspect of the tree is different from the true *B. elatior* occurring 1000 feet higher.

Hillebrand enumerates a variety *β. brevipes*, and gives the length of the peduncles at 3 lines or 6 mm; in a foot note, however, he states: "the single flowers are on a peduncle of 12 to 20 lines or 24 to 40 mm.

On the Island of Molokai in various districts, as in Wailau Valley, Mapuleho, and Kaluaha occurs a species of Bobea which at first glance would appear to be *B. elatior*. However, the flowers are single and usually with 1 pyrenae. The tree is entirely glabrous in all parts. It may be Gray's *B. brevipes*, but his description: "*pedunculis brevibus unifloris?*" would speak against it, and therefore the writer would suggest the name: *Bobea elatior* Gaud. var. *Molokaiensis* Rock var. nov. The type is 7028 in the College of Hawaii Herbarium. Collected flowering and fruiting Wailau Valley, Molokai, April, 1910. It is a small tree about 20 to 25 feet in height with a slender straight trunk.

On the Island of Kauai the writer observed several trees of Bobea, one occurring in the mountains of Halemanu in the dense forest, a rather large tree with a broad round crown. It is known to the natives as *Akupa*. Its leaves are ovate, bluntly acute, or obtuse or rounded at both ends and are on petioles of 4 mm, or even subsessile, the branchlets, petioles and leaves are hirtulose with whitish hair. As the tree was neither in flower nor in fruit its diagnosis is uncertain; it will probably prove to be a new species of Bobea when complete material is at hand.

On the lower mountain slopes back of Makaweli, Kauai, occur a few small trees which may be referred to Hillebrand's *Bobea Mannii*, though all peduncles, which are rather short, drooping and hirsute, are single flowered and would therefore come under Gray's *B. brevipes*. There is however some doubt in the writer's mind in regard to the specific value of *Bobea Mannii* which, with the exception of the three flowered inflorescence, agrees well with Gray's *B. brevipes*. Until the type material can be examined, these questions cannot be definitely settled.

Bobea Hookeri Hbd.
Ahakea.
(Plates 181, 182, 183.)

BOBEA HOOKERI Hbd. Flora Haw. Isl. (1888) 175;—K. Schum. in Engl. et Prantl Pflzfam. IV. 4. (1891) 96.—**Rhytidotus sandwicensis** Hook. f. Icon. Plant. (1870) tab. 1071;—Del Cast. Ifl. Fl. Ins. Mar. Pac. VI. (1890) 192.

Branches and branchlets terete, the latter nodose, stipules triangular puberulous, 4 mm; leaves ovate, slightly and irregularly crenulate, or with a transparent wavy margin, acuminate, 6 to 9 cm long, 3 to 5 cm wide, chartaceous, with pellucid veins, dark green above, lighter underneath, with reddish midrib and petioles, the latter 6 to 12 mm, pubescent, as are the young leaves; flowers single, usually axillary or in the axils of fallen leaves, on peduncles of 1 mm to 2.5 cm and even slightly longer; calyx-tube 3 mm, pubescent, with 4 many-nerved ovate-oblong lobes of 4 to 5 mm, reticulately veined; corolla tube

441

PLATE 183.

BOBEA HOOKERI Hbd.
Ahakea Tree.
Growing on the *aa* lava fields of Auahi, southern slopes of Mt. Haleakala, Maui; elevation 3000 feet.

Rubiaceae.

cylindrical, silky pubescent, 5 mm, the lobes one-third as long, with a patch of yellowish hair underneath each lobe; anthers linear, slightly exserted, sessile; style densely tomentose, protruding, divided into 4 to 6 filiform stigmatic branches, which are erect and not spreading; fruits globose, 8 to 12 mm, purplish, with a gray pubescence, pyrenae 4 to 6, crowned by the calyx lobes.

This species differs very little from *Bobea sandwicensis* Hbd. Its outward appearance, color of leaves, and branching habit, are exactly the same in both species. When neither in flower nor fruit it would be absolutely impossible to separate the two species. The only difference is that in the species in question the flowers are single and the fruits have from 4 to 6 pyrenae, while in *Bobea sandwicensis* the inflorescence is cymose but usually of only 3 flowers, and with fruits of 2 pyrenae; otherwise the trees could not be distinguished.

Bobea Hookeri Hbd. was collected by the writer on Molokai in the open dry gulches below Mr. G. P. Cooke's residence, Kauluwai, at an elevation of 2000 feet, only a single tree was observed, (no. 6177 flowering and fruiting March 26, 1910). It also grows on the lava fields of Auahi, district of Kahikinui, southern slopes of Mt. Haleakala, Maui; there the writer met with a single tree with a large trunk vested in a gray large-scaly bark, (see plates 182 and 183); it had three main trunks each of a foot or more in diameter. It is associated with *Alectryon macrococcus, Tetraplasandra meiandra* var., Pittosporum, *Dracaena aurea*, and others. It is one of the rarest trees in the territory. Hillebrand records it from Oahu, from the valleys of Wailupe and Makaleha, but it was never met with by the writer on Oahu.

Bobea sandwicensis Hbd.
Ahakea.

BOBEA SANDWICENSIS Hbd. Fl. Haw. Isl. (1888) 174;—Del Cast. Ill. Fl. Ins. Mar. Pac. VI. (1890) 193.—**Chomelia ?** sandwicensis Gray in Proc. Am. Acad. IV. (1860) 38.—**Guettardella** sandwicensis H. Mann Proc. Am. Acad. VII. (1867) 170.
Branchlets pubescent, leaves as in *Bobea Hookeri* but pubescent underneath and puberulous above; inflorescence cymose, 3 flowered in the writer's material, 3 to 7 flowered according to Hillebrand, peduncle tomentose about 10 mm, the lateral flowers sessile, calyx and corolla silky tomentose, yellowish-green; bracteoles 1 mm; calyx as in *Bobea Hookeri*, the lobes larger; tube of corolla cylindrical, 8 mm, anthers exserted, style in all the writer's specimens only 1.5 mm long and slightly bifid, exserted or quite short according to Hillebrand; drupe globose 5 mm in diameter, blackish, with a gray pubescence, with two bony pyrenae.

The writer collected this species on the Island of Lanai on the dry open slopes below Koele, and near the edge of the Mauna Lei canyon. It is quite numerous and grows in company with *Siderorylon spathulatum, Gardenia Brighami, Chrysophyllum polynesicum*, and others.

It is a medium sized tree about 20 to 25 feet in height, has a short trunk (about 4 feet), but a large round and spreading crown, and is very freely branching. (Flowering and fruiting July 26, 1910. Rock and Hammond, no. 8038.)

PLATE 184.

STRAUSSIA KADUANA Gray.
Kopiko kea.
Flowering branches; reduced; typical Oahu specimen.

Rubiaceae

Hillebrand records it from West Maui, Molokai and Lanai; it is known to the writer only from the latter island. The size of calyx and corolla varies considerably in this species; the larger flowers being an indication of dimorphism.

Bobea timonioides Hbd.
Ahakea.

BOBEA TIMONIOIDES Hbd. Fl. Haw. Isl. (1888) 174;—K. Schum, in Engl. et Prantl Pflzfam. IV. 4. (1891) 96.—**Obbea timonioides** Hook. f. Icon. plant. (1870) tab. 1070 et Gen. Plant. II. (1873) 102;—Del Cast. Ill. Fl. Ins. Mar. Pac. VI. (1890) 193.—**Chomelia?** sp. Wawra in Flora (1874) 330.

A small tree with the ultimate branches slender and straggling, pubescent and ciliate on the deep cicatrices of the fallen stipules; leaves pale, ovate to ovate-lanceolate, sometimes falcate, on petioles of 8 to 12 mm, acuminate, chartaceous, glabrous or slightly puberulous on the nerves underneath; stipules triangular, acute pubescent; cymes many, tomentose, 3 to 7-flowered, the common peduncle 8 to 12 mm, the lateral flowers on pedicels of 2 to 4 mm; bractlets minute; calyx and corolla densely tomentose, the former turbinate, with the free limb cup-shaped, and 4-toothed; tube of corolla 6 to 8 mm, the obovate lobes 1/3 shorter; anthers sessile, above the middle of the tube, elongate, included or the tips exserted; disc conical, hairy; style thick, pubescent, about ½ the length of the corolla, deeply bifid into 2 pointed branches; ovary 2-celled, the single seed suspended from a short and broad funis.

Hillebrand records this tree from South Kona, Hawaii, and Kawaihaeiuka of the same island. This tree is not known to the writer, but is undoubtedly very close to *B. sandwicensis* from which it seems only to differ in the toothed calyx and one seeded fruits. These last three species may form in reality only a very variable species.

STRAUSSIA A. Gray.

Flowers hermaphrodite. Calyx cup-shaped, persistent, 4 to 5 toothed or truncate. Corolla short funnel-shaped with glabrous tube, sparingly pubescent at the throat. Stamens inserted at the throat, half exserted; anthers basifixed, with thickened connective. Ovary 2-celled; style short with two branches. Fruit convex.—Trees with coriaceous, obovate, obtuse, or acute leaves, and interpetiolar broad rather obtuse stipules. Flowers small, white, in pedunclued, terminal cormybose cymes.

The genus Straussia consists of 7 species, all of which are peculiar to the Hawaiian Islands. Heller's two new species, *St. psychotrioides* and *St. pubiflora*, described in the Minnesota Botanical Studies Bull. IX. (1897) 904 & 905, are not very distinct species and will undoubtedly be referred to *St. Kaduana.*

The genus is not found at higher elevation than 4500 feet, but descends somewhat lower than 1000 feet. To the five species originally known the writer has added two new ones; a third new one was described by H. Léveillé.

KEY TO THE SPECIES.

Leaves on short petioles of 2 to 12 mm.
    Leaves obovate-oblong, obtuse, panicle long drooping.............. **St. Kaduana**
    Leaves cuneate, subsessile, prominently nerved, panicles 25 cm long. **St. longissima**
    Leaves obovate-suborbicular pubescent, panicle short pubescent..... **St. oncocarpa**
    Leaves ovate acute or suborbicular glabrous, small, subsessile....... **St. Fauriei**

PLATE 185.

STRAUSSIA LONGISSIMA Rock sp. nov.
Flowering and fruiting branch, less than one-half natural size.

Rubiaceae.

Leaves on petioles of 12 to 45 mm.
    Leaves obovate-elliptical oblong, acuminate, pubescent underneath... **St. leptocarpa**
    Leaves acute at both ends, obovate-oblong, panicle erect............ **St. Mariniana**
    Leaves large, oblong, rounded at both ends, pubescent underneath... **St. Hillebrandii**
    Leaves large, obovate with cuneate base, glabrous.................. **St. hawaiiensis**

Straussia kaduana (Cham. et Schlecht.) Gray.
Kopiko kea.
(Plate 184.)

STRAUSSIA KADUANA (Cham. et Schlecht.) Gray in Proc. Am. Acad. IV. (1860) 43;—H. Mann in Proc. Am. Acad. VII. (1867) 170;—Wawra in Flora (1874) 321;—Hbd. Fl. Haw. Isl. (1888) 179;—Del Cast. Ill. Fl. Ins. Mar. Pac. VI. (1890) 197;—K. Schum. in Engl. et Prantl Pflzfam. IV. 4. (1891) 112;—Heller in Minnes. Bot. Stud. IX. (1897) 903.—**Coffea kaduana** Cham. in Linnaea IV. (1829) 33;—DC. Prodr. IV. (1830) 502;—Hook. et Arn. Bot. Beech. (1832) 86;—Endl. Fl. Suds. (1836) 176 no. 1297.—**Apionaema obovatum et penduliflorum** Nutt. in Herb. Kew. (Hbd.).

Leaves obovate or obovate oblong, 5 to 10 cm long, 3 to 5 cm wide, on short petioles of 4 to 12 mm or even sessile, rounded or shortly acuminate, cuneate toward the base, chartaceous to coriaceous, with nerves prominent or little prominent, glabrate or puberulous underneath, turning black when dry; stipules short 4 to 6 mm, broadly triangular; panicle 4 to 12.5 cm long, erect or nodding, puberulous or glabrate, with only 1 or 2 approximate whorls of rays toward the end of a long peduncle; calyx 1 mm, the limb denticulate; corolla about 4 mm, naked at the throat, its 4 to 6 lobes generally longer than the tube, often 2 to 3 times as long; drupe obovoid or top-shaped, almost quadrangular, with a broad, flat disc, 10 to 14 mm long, and about 8 mm broad near the top.

This is a very variable species and occurs mainly in the mountains of the Island of Oahu, where it is quite common. The flowers, which are very small and white, are arranged on rather long drooping panicles; the drupes are yellow and resemble a coffee-drupe. It is a medium sized or small tree of 15 to 20 feet in height, and is often quite stunted and shrubby when growing on the crests of mountain ridges. It occurs on Lanai on the Mahana ridge (no. 8044) in company with *Pittosporum confertiflorum*, Xanthoxylum, Gouldia, *Tetraplasandra meiandra*, and others.

The wood being whitish, it is called *Kopiko kea* by the natives. Hillebrand records is also from Molokai; he enumerates two varieties which are here included in the species. A very interesting new species was found by the writer when in company with Mr. G. P. Wilder, in Nuuanu Valley, Oahu, and is described as follows.

Straussia longissima Rock sp. nov.
(Plate 185.)

Leaves obovate-oblong, acute at the apex or rounded, strictly cuneate at the base, sessile or on petioles of 2 m, 2 to 15 cm long, 4 to 8 cm wide, light green above and glabrous, with prominent strong nerves and midrib, which, like the whole underside of the leaves, are covered with a rufous pubescence; stipules broadly triangular to oblong, acute; panicles exceedingly long up to 25 cm, pendulous, the common peduncle up to 18 cm long, the shortest 10 cm, with three whorls, each of four rays, the whole inflorescence including peduncle rufous pubescent; calyx limb truncate to dentate, pubescent, corolla small 2.5 mm, white, naked at the throat, the 4 lobes as long as the tube, glabrous; drupe obovoid to oblong 12 to 14 mm long, 6 mm wide, with a small conical disc, not ribbed.

Rubiaceae.

This exceedingly interesting Straussia, with decidedly specific characters, is a tree 12 to 20 feet high with ascending branches and is remarkable for the very long pendulous panicles, the longest in the genus. It is restricted as far as known to Nuuanu Valley in one of the small side gulches of Konahuanui, along a small streambed at a thousand feet elevation. It is associated with *Charpentiera obovata, Hibiscus Arnottianus, Perrottettia sandwicensis*, Cyrtandra and others.

It was collected when in company with Mr. Gerrit P. Wilder, flowering and fruiting May, 1912. The type is No. 10200 in the College of Hawaii Herbarium.

Straussia oncocarpa Hbd.
Kopiko.

STRAUSSIA ONCOCARPA Hbd. Flora Haw. Isl. (1888) 180;—Del Cast. Ill. Fl. Ins. Mar. Pac. VI. (1890) 197.

Leaves obovate or suborbicular 5 to 7.5 cm long, 3.75 cm wide, on petioles of 4 to 12 mm, rounded at both ends, subcoriaceous, pubescent underneath, the costal glands hidden under the hairs; stipules triangular, obtuse 3 to 4 mm; panicle short, 2.5 to 5 cm long, bearing one whorl of short rays, rusty-pubescent, as are also the calyx and corolla; calyx distinctly dentate; corolla naked at the throat, its tube 4 mm; the lobes as long; drupe obovoid, 4-ribbed, tumid at the base, 12 mm long, 8 mm wide, with a small disc.

Hillebrand records this species from Ulupalakua, Maui, only. The writer collected the typical *St. oncocarpa* on the Island of Lanai, (nos. 8024 and 8025) at the head of Waiakiola gulch, at an elevation of 2800 feet. It is a tall tree 40 to 50 feet in height. The leaves are on slender petioles of little over 2.5 cm, about twice as long as in Hillebrand's specimens. On East Maui specimens were collected of this species which answer the original description in every detail with the exception that some of the leaves are subcordate at the base and strongly nerved (no. 8540); this latter tree occurs in the open drier gulches back of Makawao and is only about 25 feet tall. In the same locality occurs a tree which must be referred to the same species, the leaves are larger, pale green the panicle is 1 to 2 whorled, otherwise as in the species.

Hillebrand's var. β. the writer collected on Kauai at Kaholuamano, probably the type locality (no. 1935) fruiting, March 3-10, 1909. The panicles are shorter, less than 2.5 cm and contracted; the leaves are obovate-oblong and rounded, though cuneate at the base.

Var. subcordata Rock var. nov.

Leaves as in the species, but thin chartaceous, glabrous on both sides and subcordate at the base, on very short petioles; panicles of 3 whorls, pubescent, slender, 12 cm long including the peduncle, which measures often more than 7 cm; calyx-limb dentate; corolla lobes half the length of the tube.

This variety occurs at the Wailau pali on the Island of Molokai, at an elevation of 4000 feet. It is a small tree 25 feet in height. Collected April, 1910, flowering, no. 7072 in the College of Hawaii Herbarium.

Rubiaceae.

Var. **scoriacea** Rock var. nov.

Branches light gray, terete and striate. Leaves suborbicular, shining, coriaceous, pubescent along the prominent nerves and midrib, on petioles of 2 to 2.5 cm; the flat glands triangular and very conspicuous in the axils of the nerves; panicles of 1 to 2 whorls, rather short, 2.5 to 3 cm, densely tomentose, with a dirty yellowish-gray tomentum; calyx and corolla pubescent, the former truncate; drupes angled, obovate, rather small, 7 mm, pubescent.

As the name implies, this variety occurs on the scoria or *aa* lava fields of Manuka in Kau on the southern slopes of Mauna Loa, Hawaii. It is a small tree 15 feet in height and grows in company with *Nototrichium sandwicense, Santalum Freycinetianum, Osteomeles anthyllidifolia,* and others. Collected July, 1911, flowering and fruiting. The type is no. 10201 in the College of Hawaii Herbarium.

Straussia Fauriei Lévl.
Kopiko.

STRAUSSIA FAURIEI Lévl. in Fedde Repert. X. 10/14 (1911) 155.
Branches stout; leaves obovate or suborbicular, 3 to 7.5 cm long, 2 to 6 cm wide, rounded or acute at the apex, somewhat contracted at the base, slightly subcordate, sub-sessile or on petioles of 1 mm, reddish to bronze-colored when dry, glabrate, with strong prominent nerves; panicles erect, short, rusty tomentose, peduncle 15 to 25 mm; calyx limb truncate or wavy, corolla lobes twice the length of the tube, puberulous, slightly bearded at the throat; the drupe is obovate, crowned by the calycine limb and a small conical disc which is not protruding.

This marked species is a small tree 10 feet or little more in height and occurs on Oahu as well as on Lanai on the crests of the mountain ridges exposed to the wind and cold and therefore appears stunted. The species was first discovered by the writer in the Punaluu Mts., Oahu, on Aug. 23rd, 1908 (no. 25), was again collected on December 3, 1908 (no. 634); and also on the Island of Lanai (no. 8047) on the top of the ridges leading to the summit Lanaihale. In the Lanai specimens the leaves are 3x2 cm, while the Oahu specimens have larger leaves. The panicles are usually one-whorled. Collected also by Abbé Faurie (no. 400) at Nuuanu pali, December, 1909.

Straussia leptocarpa Hbd.
Kopiko.

STRAUSSIA LEPTOCARPA Hbd. Fl. Haw. Isl. (1888) 180;—Del Cast. Ill. Fl. Ins. Mar. Pac. VI. (1890) 197;—K. Schum. in Engl. et Prantl Pflzfam. IV. 4. (1891) 112.
Leaves obovate or elliptical oblong, 10 to 12.5 cm long, acuminate, contracted below triangular, obtuse, 3 mm; panicle furfuraceous-pubescent, erect, short, with 2 to 3 whorls, the peduncle about 2.5 cm; calyx and corolla puberulous in the bud, the latter four to six-lobed, with faint hairs at the throat, the lobes scarcely longer than the tube; stamens 4 to 6; ovary semi-superior; drupe slender, ellipsoidal or fusiform, 12 mm long and 4 mm broad at the middle, the conical apex or disc projecting beyond the calycine limb.

Hillebrand records this species as a shrub from East Maui, woods of Pumelei. The writer collected specimens from apparently this species from West Maui, and also East Maui, in open gulches above Makawao, where it is a small tree

449

PLATE 186.

STRAUSSIA HAWAIIENSIS Gray.
Kopiko.
Flowering and fruiting branch, less than one-half natural size.

Rubiaceae.

15 to 20 feet in height. Hillebrand's description, which is cited above, answers very well to the writer's specimens. It may be remarked that *St. leptocarpa* and *St. oncocarpa* come very close to each other, as the number of whorls in the panicle and dentate calyx limb cannot always be relied upon as constant characters. The writer has observed subtruncate and decidedly dentate calyx limbs on a single panicle. In the writer's specimens (no. 8541) from Makawao, Maui, the peduncles are from 4.5 to 5 cm long, and glabrate, while the leaves are on petioles of 12 to 20 mm. Specimens from West Maui, above Kaanapali, (no. 8167) come much closer to *St. leptocarpa* than no. 8541, though the leaves are much smaller (4 to 5 cm) than the description calls for; the panicles are smaller, and pubescent, the peduncle is exactly 2.5 cm or 1 inch. The species is peculiar to the open dry forehills of West and East Maui.

Straussia Mariniana (Cham. et Schlecht.) Gray.
Kopiko.

STRAUSSIA MARINIANA (Cham. et Schlecht.) Gray in Proc. Am. Acad. IV. (1860) 43;— Mann in Proc. Am. Acad. VII. (1867) 170;—Hbd. Fl. Haw. Isl. (1888) 179;— Del Cast. Ill. Fl. Ins. Mar. Pac. VI. (1890) 197;—Heller in Minnes. Bot. Stud. Bull. IX. (1897) 904.—**Coffea Mariniana** Cham. in Linnaea IV. (1829) 35;—DC. Prodr. IV. (1830) 86;—Endl. Fl. Suds. (1836) 176. no. 1298.—**Apionema sulcatum** Nuttal in Herb. Kew, teste Hillebrand.

Leaves obovate-oblong, or elliptical-lanceolate, acute at both ends or the apex bluntly acuminate, 10 to 15 cm long, 5 to 6.5 cm wide, on petioles of 12 to 15 mm, chartaceous to coriaceous, glabrate underneath, and dark green, with rather prominent reddish rib and nerves; stipules obovate from a broad base, somewhat obtuse, 6 to 12 mm long; panicles glabrous, erect, 5 to 8 cm (impossible to be 4 lines=8 mm, according to Hillebrand) in the writer's specimens, including a peduncle of about 3 to 3.5 cm; calyx truncate; corolla with a pilose patch at the base of each lobe; the lobes scarcely longer than the tube; drupe as in *Straussia kaduana*.

This species, which is distinguished from *Straussia kaduana* mainly in the bearded corolla, and the more or less elliptical-lanceolate leaves, which are acute at both ends and twice as long petioled as in the latter species, occurs on Oahu, Maui, and Kauai. On the latter island the writer collected it in the forests above Makaweli at an elevation of 3000 feet (no. 5833) and also in the woods of Kaholuamano, though from this locality the leaves have pubescent glands in the axils of the nerves, (no. 5352). An apparent variety with oblong leaves was collected at Kaholuamano, Kauai, in Sept., 1909, (no. 5346); the panicles in this variety are slightly pubescent, but the throat of the corolla appears to be naked. As it is a very variable species no exact limits of either *Straussia kaduana* or *St. Mariniana* can be set. It would perhaps be best to unite both into one species.

Straussia hawaiiensis Gray.
Kopiko ula.
(Plate 186.)

STRAUSSIA HAWAIIENSIS Gray in Proc. Am. Acad. IV. (1860) 43;—H. Mann Proc. Am. Acad. VII. (1867) 170;—Hbd. Fl. Haw. Isl. (1888) 180;—Del Cast. Ill. Fl. Ins Mar. Pacif. VI. (1890) 196.

PLATE 187.

STRAUSSIA HILLEBRANDII Rock sp. nov.
Kopiko.
Fruiting branch, about one-third natural size.

Rubiaceae.

Leaves thick, chartaceous, with stout nerves, obovate 10 to 18 cm long, 5.5 to 8.5 cm wide, petioles of 1.5 to 3 cm, somewhat rounded at the apex or bluntly acute, obovate oblong, contracting or cuneate toward the base, glabrous, except on the flat glands in the axils of the nerves, which are usually large and pubescent; midrib impressed above, reddish underneath, stipules triangular, obtuse, 6 mm; peduncles from 16 mm to 8 cm long, whole length of panicle 16 cm or even more, panicle wide and spreading, often 12 cm in diameter, of 3 to 4 whorls, of usually 3 rays, whole inflorescence covered with a rufous pubescence, calyx truncate; corolla 3 to 4 mm, the 4.5 lobes as long as the tube or little longer each with a patch of hairlets at the base; drupe obovoid, small, 6 mm or less, crowned by the truncate limb of the calyx.

This species, which is a tree 20 to 35 feet tall, occurs in the forests of South Kona, Hawaii, on the slopes of Mauna Loa, especially in the more uniform forests above the lava fields of Kapua at an elevation of 3000 feet; the trunk is about one foot in diameter and vested in a smooth black bark. It is associated with *Metrosideros polymorpha, Myoporum sandwicense, Xylosma Hillebrandii, Clermontia coerulea*, and others. Hillebrand's description of the tree is not quite correct: he says: ''panicles as in No. 2,'' *(Straussia Mariniana)*. This latter species however has panicles only 4 lines long according to his description, while *St. hawaiiensis* has exceedingly large panicles. Gray's description of this species is too vague to permit a certain diagnosis. However the plant figured (plate 186) is none other than *St. hawaiiensis* and was collected in the type locality. The leaves are over 18 cm long, and the panicles 16 cm long, including the peduncle, while on the same tree some panicles are only 3 cm long, but none are 8 mm as stated by Hillebrand. Collected flowering and fruiting Feb., 1912, (no. 10028). The flat circular glands in the axils of veins, are well brought out in the accompanying plate (plate 186).

Straussia Hillebrandii Rock sp. nov.
Kopiko.
(Plates 187 and 188.)

Leaves obovate oblong, rounded at both ends, or cuneate at the base, chartaceous to coriaceous, glabrous and dark green above, but with a scattered rufus pubescence underneath, especially on the very prominent reddish midrib and nerves, whose axils are entirely destitute of glands, so conspicuous in *St. hawaiiensis*, 10 to 15 cm long, 6 to 9 cm wide, on petioles of 10 to 45 mm; stipules ovate-oblong, acute, 12 mm long; panicles stout, rusty pubescent, large and open, 12 to 16 cm long, 7 to 10 cm wide, erect or drooping, with 3 whorls, each with 4 to 6 rays which in turn branch dichotomously, the free peduncles 6 to 10 cm long; calyx dentate to subtruncate, subglabrous; corolla 3 mm, the 4 lobes longer than the tube, puberulous inside, anthers partly exserted, style exserted, with two long clavate stigmatic branches; drupe small, obovoid, 6 mm, crowned by the minute dentate calyx-limb.

This new species of *Kopiko*, named in memory of Dr. W. Hillebrand, occurs on the Island of Hawaii, on the slopes of Mauna Loa, only 3 miles from the volcano of Kilauea in the famous Kipuka Puaulu, which has already furnished a number of new species and even a new genus.

The species comes close to *Straussia hawaiiensis* in one way and in the other to *St. oncocarpa*. Hillebrand, in a foot note under *St. Hawaiiensis* says: ''A specimen, probably from the Kohala range, has the leaves rounded at the base

PLATE 188.

STRAUSSIA HILLEBRANDII Rock.
A new **Kopiko** tree.
Growing in the Kipuka Puaulu, Kilauea, Hawaii.

Rubiaceae.

and pubescent underneath along the nerves, which are almost destitute of glands; the panicle is also pubescent and inclined.''

This seems to apply very much to the species in question, but it is really quite distinct from *St. Hawaiiensis*, in the leaves, fruits and dentate calyx-lobes, besides in the whole aspect of the tree, which is much smaller (see plate 188). Collected flowering and fruiting in the above mentioned locality, April, 1911, and July, 1911, type no. 8779 in the College of Hawaii Herbarium.

The species also occurs on the Parker ranch, Hawaii, and in the forests of Paauhau, Hamakua, Hawaii.

Var. **Molokaiensis** Rock var. nov.

Leaves as in the species, chartaceous, quite large; panicles slender, drooping, pubescent, about 10 cm long, including the 6 cm long peduncle; calyx-limb dentate; corolla as in the species; drupe oblong, larger than in the species.

The panicles of this variety are not so open and wide, but rather close and of only 1 to 2 whorls. It occurs in the rain forests of Molokai, especially at Kaluaha on the leeward side. It was collected flowering and fruiting April, 1910, the type is no. 7085 in the College of Hawaii Herbarium.

PSYCHOTRIA Linn.

Flowers hermaphrodite. Calyx short, 5 to 6 toothed. Corolla funnel-shaped, tubular or campanulate. Stamens inserted in the throat, partly exserted. Ovary 2- (rarely 3-5) celled. Fruit 2 to 5 seeded.—Shrubs or trees, rarely herbs. Leaves whorled or opposite, stipules interpetiolar. Flowers in terminal cymose corymbs, rarely axillary, white in the Hawaiian species.

The genus Psychotria consists of about 350 species or more. It is distributed over tropical Africa, the Malayan archipelago, East India. Brazil; it also occurs in China, but is not known from Japan. In the Hawaiian Islands three species are found of which two, *P. grandiflora* and *P. hirta,* are peculiar to Kauai, while the third, *P. hexandra,* occurs on Oahu and Kauai but on none of the other islands of the group. The genus occurs also in Fiji and other Pacific Islands.

KEY TO THE SPECIES.

Flowers in a trichotomous corymbose cyme.
    Leaves acute at both ends, glabrous.............................. **P. hexandra**
    Leaves obovate, cuneate, pubescent underneath...................... **P. hirta**
Flowers large in a panicle with verticillate rays........................ **P. grandiflora**

Psychotria hexandra Mann.

PSYCHOTRIA HEXANDRA Mann in Proc. Am. Ac. VII. (1867) 170;—Wawra in Flora (1874) 328;—Hbd. Fl. Haw. Isl. (1888) 181;—Del Cast. Ill. Fl. Ins. Mar. Pac. VI. (1890) 198;—Heller Pl. Haw. Isl. (1897) 902.

Branches quadrangular, compressed; leaves obovate or obovate-oblong, 7.5 to 15 cm long, 2.5 to 3.5 cm wide, on petioles of 6 to 25 mm, shortly and abruptly acuminate, cuneate at the base, membraneous, pale and glabrous underneath; stipules one on each side, broad, oblong, 8 to 12 mm long, caducous, leaving a fringe of hairlets in the axils; flowers in a terminal semi-erect, corymbose, glabrous cyme of not more than 5 to 6 cm, the peduncle 12 to 25 m; bracteoles below the calyx ovate, acute 4 to 2 mm; calyx 6 mm, with 6 toothlets;

455

PLATE 189.

PSYCHOTRIA HEXANDRA Mann.
Fruiting branch, little more than one-half natural size.   From the mountains behind
Honolulu, Oahu.

Rubiaceae.

corolla waxy white, funnel shaped, villous at the throat, 6-lobed; anthers subsessile at the throat, acute, little exserted; style slightly exserted, the short lobes dilated; drupe 12 mm crowned with the calycine limb; pyrenae with 3 ridges at the back.

This species, for which there is no native name as far as can be ascertained, was originally discovered on Kauai. It was however found by the writer on the Island of Oahu, in the forests of the Koolau range. It is a small tree 15 to 20 feet in height and occurs along the Manoa cliff trail back of Honolulu, as well as in the forest of Punaluu, on the windward side of Oahu. The flowers of this species are white and much larger than those of Straussia *(Kopiko)*.

On Kauai in the mountains of Kaholuamano and Halemanu occur two other species, one of them a small tree, first described by Wawra as a variety *hirta* of the above species, but raised since to specific rank by Heller and now known as *Psychotria hirta* (Wawra) Heller. It differs from *P. hexandra* in the leaves, which are obovate cuneate at the base and pubescent underneath; the calyx teeth are also shorter. The third species, *Psychotria grandiflora* Mann, is a shrub and was collected by the writer in the swampy forests of Halemanu near Alakai swamp. It is the handsomest species, as it has the largest flowers, which are pure white to cream colored on long drooping panicles. Hillebrand records it as a tree, but it was observed by the writer only as a shrub.

COPROSMA Forst.

Flowers unisexual, dioecious in all Hawaiian species. Calyx cup-shaped, truncate or more or less toothed or lobed, larger in the female flowers than in the male. Corolla funnel-shaped or campanulate 4 to 9 lobed, lobes in the female flowers often reflexed. Stamens 4 to 9 inserted at the base of the corolla-tube, exserted. Ovary 2, very rarely 4-celled; style divided to the base, pubescent. Drupe ovate or globose, fleshy.—Prostrate or erect shrubs or trees with opposite or rarely verticillate leaves, entire or dentate stipules. Flowers white or greenish, quite inconspicuous, single or in few flowered cymes, terminal or axillary.

The genus Coprosma, which consists of about 45 to 50 species, of which the majority are found in New Zealand, has quite a number of species in the Hawaiian Islands. So far 15 species have been found in these islands, of which 4 were described lately,—two by the present writer in this volume and two by H. Léveillé in Fedde repertorium *(C. Fauriei* and *C. parvifolia)*. The latter was first collected by the writer on West Maui, while Faurie's specimen came from Molokai. *C. Fauriei* is not a good species and is referable to *C. Kauaiensis* (Gray) Heller. A few species occur in the Fiji and Norfolk Islands, 8 in Australia, 1 in the Malay Peninsula, and 1 or 2 in Chile.

None of the Hawaiian species has a foetid odor, as the generic name would imply.

KEY TO THE SPECIES.

Leaves opposite.
    Flowers sessile on short axillary spurs............................ **C. montana**
    Flowers raised on distinct peduncles..............................
        Drupes beaked with the long tubular limb of the calyx.
            Flowers 3-5-6, subsessile at the end of a short peduncle. **C. rhynchocarpa**
            Flowers single or in racemes, pedicellate.................. **C. Vontempskyi**

457

PLATE 190.

COPROSMA RHYNCHOCARPA Gray.
Pilo.
Fruiting branch, less than one-half natural size.

Rubiaceae.

Drupes crowned by the calycine teeth.
    Flowers 2-3, sessile at the end of a short peduncle........... **C. Grayana**
    Flowers 2 on axillary peduncles of 5 mm, drupes largest of all Hawaiian
        species . . . . **C. Waimeae**
Drupes naked at the apex.
    Flowers numerous, crowded on short peduncles............. **C. pubens**
    Flowers 3, sessile on a peduncle of 2 cm................... **C. Kauaiensis**
Leaves ternate.
    Flowers many, crowded at the ends of long peduncles.............. **C. longifolia**

Coprosma montana Hbd.
Pilo.

COPROSMA MONTANA Hbd. Fl. Haw. Isl. (1888) 185;—Del Cast. Ill. Fl. Ins. Mar. Pac. VI. (1890) 201;—K. Schum. in Engl. et Prantl Pflzfam. IV. 4. (1891) 132.— **C. Menziesii** var. γ Gray in Proc. Am. Acad. IV. (1860) 49;—Wawra in Flora (1874) 326.

A small tree 5 to 6 m in height, with stiff, stout ascending branches, densely foliose, covered with stipules below and more or less pubescent; leaves obovate or spathulate, 18 to 25 mm long, 10 to 12 mm wide, penninerved, bluntly acuminate or rounded, the base contracting into a margined petiole, thick coriaceous, shining; stipules broad triangular, ciliate at the upper border; flowers axillary, sessile on very short and thick spurs; female flowers: calyx 2 mm, urceolate, the limb denticulate; corolla 4 mm, deeply 5 to 6 parted, with reflexed lobes; styles 6 mm; drupe yellow or reddish, ovoid, 6 to 8 mm, tipped with the short calycine limb.

This species, which is occasionally a shrub of 3 to 4 feet and often even prostrate as recorded by Hillebrand, is also a small tree 15 to 18 feet in height, especially on Mauna Kea, Hawaii, at an elevation of 10000 feet, above the crater of Kaluamakani and on Papalekoki as well as Moano and Nau, where it grows in company with arborescent compositae such as *Raillardia struthioloides, R. arborea,* as well as with the leguminous tree, *Sophora chrysophylla,* the *Mamani* of the natives. It is decidedly a high mountain species, as it grows to a small tree on Mt. Haleakala on Maui, on the crater of Puunianiau in company with *Mamani* and *Santalum Haleakalae,* a species of sandalwood peculiar to that mountain. On Mt. Hualalai, Hawaii, 8000 feet, it is a shrub 4 feet high and grows with *Dodonaea viscosa.* The leaves are thick glabrous but almost succulent in all locations.

Two varieties β and γ occur in the high mountain swamps of Puukukui, West Maui, and Waialeale, Kauai, respectively. The varieties are prostrate, but occasionally shrubby.

Coprosma rhynchocarpa Gray.
Pilo.
(Plate 190.)

COPROSMA RHYNCHOCARPA Gray in Proc. Am. Acad. IV. (1860) 48;—Mann Proc. Am. Acad. VII. (1867) 169;—Wawra in Flora (1874) 325;—Hbd. Fl. Haw. Isl. (1888) 187;—Del Cast. Ill. Fl. Ins. Mar. Pac. VI. (1890) 201.

Leaves elliptical or obovately oblong, 4 to 7 cm long, 15 to 25 mm wide, on petioles of 6 to 18 mm, acuminate at both ends, chartaceous, papillose to pubescent or sparsely hispid underneath; stipules 5 to 7 mm, a loose funnel-shaped sheath, the free portions triangular,

459

PLATE 191.

COPROSMA VONTEMPSKYI Rock sp. nov.
Pilo tree.
Growing in the forests about Olinda, slopes of Mt. Haleakala, Maui; elevation 4000 feet.

Rubiaceae.

the upper border ciliate with pale fawn-colored hair as is the base, and thus resembling *C. stephanocarpa*; flowers 3-5-6, subsessile at the end of a short peduncle of 4 to 6 mm; the bracts 2 to 3 mm; male flowers sometimes racemose; calyx minute; corolla 4 mm long, 6 to 8 lobed; female flowers: calyx 6 mm, the limb twice as long as the adnate portion and equalling the corolla, constricted below, tubular or funnel-shaped, with 5 to 6 small teeth; styles 6 mm; drupe yellowish red, globose or ovoid, 6 to 8 mm, crowned with the long, beak-like limb of the calyx.

The species occurs as a tree of 15 to 20 feet or so in height with a trunk of a foot in diameter on the upper slopes of Mt. Hualalai, at Hinakapauula, elevation 6000 feet. It however descends as low as 4000 feet. Nearly every trunk of these trees, which are very numerous at the above locality, is rotten, though the outward appearance of the tree is healthy; the trunks are without bark and full of holes, and are entirely hollow being inhabited by thousands of sow-bugs, *(Philoscia angusticauda)*. It is also common at Paauhau, 3000 feet elevation on Parker ranch, Hawaii, and was also collected by the writer on the slopes of Mauna Loa in the upper part of the rain forest of Kau above Naalehu and Waiohinu, 5000 feet elevation. Specimens from this latter locality differ somewhat from those of Hualalai in that the calycine limb is only half the length of that occurring on Hualalai and Paauhau.

Coprosma Vontempskyi Rock sp. nov.
Pilo.
(Plate 191.)

A small tree with rather slender branches, which are terete; leaves membraneous, ovate or linear oblong, acuminate at both ends, pubescent above and underneath especially along the midrib, 3.5 to 5.5 cm long, 14 to 20 mm wide, on a somewhat margined pubescent petiole of about 10 mm; stipules thin, 2 mm, sheathing, acute, pubescent, with slightly ciliolate margins, flowers unknown; drupes single or in racemes of 2.5 cm length on pedicels of 3 mm, when single the peduncle measures 5 mm, with foliaceous bracts of 6 mm length; drupe ovoid, 6 mm long, 4 mm wide, crowned by the calycine, dentate limb of 3 to 4 mm.

This interesting species seems to be an intermediate between *C. cymosa* and *C. rhynchocarpa*. It has the typical, though somewhat shorter, calycine limb of the latter species, and the inflorescence of the former. In general habit it is however quite different, as well as in many other respects. It occurs in the rain forest above and below Olinda on Maui, on the slopes of Mt. Haleakala, where it was collected by the writer in September, 1910. It is named after the writer's friend, Mr. L. v. Tempsky, the manager of Haleakala ranch, to whom he is greatly indebted for often extended hospitality and without whose aid the exploration of Mt. Haleakala could not have been accomplished in such a satisfactory way.

The type is 8529 in the College of Hawaii Herbarium.

Coprosma Grayana Rock sp. nov.
(Plate 192.)

Branches pale terete, glabrous, leaves opposite, elliptical-oblong, acute or bluntly acuminate at both ends, midrib and veins prominent, dark green, dull, lighter underneath,

461

PLATE 192.

COPROSMA GRAYANA Rock sp. nov.
Pilo.
Fruiting branch, one-half natural size.

Rubiaceae.

chartaceous, glabrous on both sides, 8 to 12 cm long, 3 to 4 cm wide; on petioles of 3 to 4 cm; stipules broad sheathing, thin, 8 mm high, slightly broad, ciliate at the upper border; flowers 2 to 3, sessile at the end of a short axillary peduncle of 2 to 5 mm; bracts 2.5 mm; (flower buds only known) calyx urceolate, very short dentate; corolla about 4 mm; drupes oblong-ellipsoidal bright red, usually single, 12 mm long, crowned by the calycine teeth; seeds whitish, rounded at the apex, acute at the base, oblong.

This new species, which is a tree 20 feet or more high, with a trunk of several inches in diameter was discovered by the writer in the forests of Naalehu, Kau, Hawaii, in the tropical rain forest situated on the southern slopes of Mauna Loa at an elevation of 3000 feet. The bark of this tree is fawn-colored and corky, the sap-wood yellow like that of the *Noni (Morinda citrifolia)*, the heartwood is blackish; when cut into an exceedingly large amount of sap squirts out in all directions, having a very peculiar oily odor. The wood is quite close grained and comparatively hard. It was collected in flower buds and fruit on January 9, 1912. The type is no. 10005 in the College of Hawaii Herbarium.

Coprosma pubens Gray.
Pilo.

COPROSMA PUBENS Gray in Proc. Am. Acad. IV. (1860) 49;—Mann Proc. Am. Acad. VII. (1867) 169;—Wawra in Flora (1874) 324;—Hbd. Fl. Haw. Isl. (1888) 188;—Del Cast. Ill. Fl. Ins. Mar. Pac. VI. (1890) 201.

Leaves lanceolate or obovate-oblong, 5 to 12.5 cm long, 2.5 to 3.5 cm wide, on petioles of 10 to 20 mm, acuminate, narrowing at the base, chartaceous glabrous, or pubescent at higher elevations, dark when dry; stipules 4 to 8 mm, loosely sheathing on half their length, the free portions triangular, strigose-pubescent; flowers numerous, glomerate at the apex of short peduncles; male flowers: calyx 2 mm, corolla 6 to 8 mm long, 6 to 7 lobed; female flowers: calyx 2 to 4 mm, cylindrical, the very short limb dentate; corolla 4 mm; styles 18 to 16 mm; drupes reddish, ovoid or ellipsoidal, 8 to 12 mm long, naked at the top, the pointed apex projecting beyond the calycine scar.

This species, often a shrub, was however observed only as a small tree 15 to 18 feet in height. It occurs only in the rain forests and is quite common in the mountains of Kohala, Hawaii, where the writer collected it, as well as in the valleys of Waipio, Puakalehua, Waimanu, etc. According to Hillebrand it occurs on all the islands of the group, but the typical *C. pubens* was collected only on Hawaii by the writer. It is distinguished from the other species of Coprosma in the numerous flowers, which are glomerate at the end of a short peduncle, and the narrow ellipsoidal fruit.

Coprosma kauaiensis (Gray) Heller.
Koi.

COPROSMA KAUAIENSIS (Gray) Heller Pl. Haw. Isl. (1897) 894.—**Coprosma pubens** var. **Kauaiensis** Gray in Proc. Am. Acad. IV. (1860) 49;—Wawra in Flora (1874) 323.—**C. stephanocarpa** β. var. **Kauaiensis** Hbd. Fl. Haw. Isl. (1888) 187;—Del Cast. Ill. Fl. Ins. Mar. Pac. VI. (1890) 201.

Leaves obovate-oblong, or ovate, bluntly acute at both ends, 6.5 cm to 3 cm, dull green, pubescent underneath, on petioles of 4 to 8 mm; peduncle naked about 2 cm long with 3 sessile flowers at the apex, supported by spathular bracts of 3 mm; calyx of female flower urceolate 3 to 4 mm with 5 to 6 lanceolate lobules; drupe small obovate, very obtuse

463

PLATE 193.

COPROSMA LONGIFOLIA Gray.
Pilo.
Fruiting branch, about one-half natural size.

Rubiaceae.

The *Koi* is a tree 15 to 20 feet in height with a trunk of a few inches in diameter. It is like the *Olena* peculiar to the Island of Kauai, where it occurs in the forests of Kaholuamano. The name *Pilo*, by which all other Hawaiian Coprosmas are known on the other islands, is applied on Kauai to a species of Pelea and to one of Platydesma.

Coprosma Waimeae Wawra.
Olena.

COPROSMA WAIMEAE Wawra in Flora (1874) 327;—Heller Pl. Haw. Isl. (1897) 895.—
   C. foliosa Hbd. Fl. Haw. Isl. (1888) 186, in part

Leaves elliptical-oblong, acuminate at both ends or shortly acute, on petioles of 5 mm, glabrous; stipules broadly triangular or ovate and long or caudately acuminate; drupes orange colored, largest of all Hawaiian species, ovate, 12x8 mm, crowned by the calycine teeth.

This species, which Hillebrand incorrectly referred to *C. foliosa*, is certainly distinct from all the other Hawaiian species, and as Wawra remarked in a footnote, has the largest fruits of all Hawaiian Coprosmas. It is a small tree and occurs in the forests of Halemanu and Kaholuamano, Kauai, above Kekaha and Waimea at an elevation of 3600-4000 feet.

The native name, *Olena*, meaning yellow, is derived from the yellow color of the wood.

Coprosma longifolia Gray.
Pilo.
(Plate 193.)

COPROSMA LONGIFOLIA Gray in Proc. Am. Acad. IV. (1860) 48;—Mann Proc. Am. Acad. VII. (1867) 169;—Wawra in Flora (1874) 324;—Hbd. Fl. Haw. Isl. (1888) 188;—Del Cast. Ill. Fl. Ins. Mar. Pac. VI (1890) 200;—Heller Pl. Haw. Isl. (1897) 895.

Leaves ternate, elliptico-oblong or lanceolate of even breadth in their greatest length, 6.5 to 10 cm long, 1.5 to 2.5 cm wide, on petioles of 12 to 18 mm. acute at both ends, chartaceous, stipules thin 6 to 12 mm, connate; flowers 6 to 15, glomerate at the end of axillary peduncles of 6 to 10 mm; bracts 6 mm, sometimes foliaceous; male flowers: calyx 2 mm, 5 to 8 toothed, corolla 6 to 8 mm, with 5 to 8 lobes; stamens long exserted 12 to 16 mm; female flowers: calyx urceolate, 4 mm, corolla 4 mm, with revolute lobes; styles 8 to 12 mm; drupes ellipsoidal 6 to 8 mm long, reddish, tipped with the short calycine teeth.

On the lower slopes of Mt. Konahuanui, Oahu, at an elevation of 2500 feet or higher, this very distinct species occurs as a tree 15 feet or more high with a short trunk of several inches in diameter. It is quite striking in its appearance, especially during the early winter months when the tree is loaded with the bright reddish drupes or fruits, contrasted with the graceful foliage. According to Hillebrand the species occurs on Kauai, besides Oahu, but was only seen on the latter island by the writer, where it is plentiful on the whole Koolau mountain range.

PLATE 194.

MORINDA CITRIFOLIA Linn.
Noni.
Flowering and fruiting branch, one-half natural size.

Rubiaceae.

MORINDA Linn.

Calyx cup-shaped truncate or toothed. Corolla salver-shaped to campanulate. Stamens inserted in throat of the tube, included or exserted. Ovary 4-celled; style with two branches. Drupes or berries united into one fleshy fruit. Seeds obovoid or reniform.—Trees or shrubs (occasionally climbing and epiphytic but not in Hawaii) with opposite leaves, and interpetiolar stipules, connate with the petioles. Flowers in globose heads, on axillary, terminal single or clustered peduncles.

The genus consists of about 46 species distributed over both hemispheres, but especially in the old world and the Pacific islands. Only two species occur in Hawaii, one of which is endemic.

KEY TO THE SPECIES.

Leaves oblong, fruit 2.5 cm in diameter.................................... **M. trimera**
Leaves ovate, fruit 5 to 10 cm in diameter................................ **M. citrifolia**

Morinda citrifolia Linn.
(Plate 194.)

MORINDA CITRIFOLIA Linn. Spec. Pl. ed. 1. (1753) 176;—DC. Prodr. IV. (1830) 446;—Hook. et Arn. Bot. Beech. (1832) 65;—Endl. Fl. Suds. (1836) 176;—Seem. Flora Vit. (1866) 129;—Mann Proc. Am. Ac. VII. (1867) 170;—Wawra in Flora (1874) p. ?;—Mrs. Sincl. Indig. Fl. Haw. Isl. (1885) t. 40;—Hbd. Fl. Haw. Isl. (1888) 177;—Del Cast. Ill. Fl. Ins. Mar. Pac. VI. (1890) 195;—K. Schum. in Eng. et Prantl Pflzfam. IV. 4. (1891) 138;—Heller Pl. Haw. Isl. (1897) 901;—Brigham Kn Hana Kapa Mem. B. P. B. Mus. III. (1911) 144. fig. 87.

Leaves broadly ovate 15 to 20 cm long, 10 to 15 cm wide, on short petioles,. somewhat obtuse, thick; stipules broad and rounded, connate into a sheath enclosing the peduncle; flowerheads on short bractless peduncles placed opposite the leaves; calycine limb short, truncate; corolla white, tubular to funnel-shaped, 5-cleft, pilose at the insertion of the sessile anthers below the middle of the corolla; syncarpium 5 to 10 cm, fleshy.

This well known cosmopolitan species, which Hillebrand believes to be of aboriginal introduction, occurs only on the lowlands in the vicinity of native dwellings, or now growing apparently wild but more correctly on overgrown forsaken native dwelling-sites. The species has an exceedingly wide distribution and is cultivated by the Polynesians as a dye-plant. It is also used medicinally by the Hawaiians and from the mature fruits they extract an oil of very unpleasant odor, used for the hair; ripe fruits are also used as a poultice. The wood is intensely yellow when fresh cut. The root yields a yellow dye while the bark furnishes a red dye. It is a small tree 15 feet in height with a trunk of usually a few inches in diameter; the leaves are large and shining and have impressed veins. The fruit when mature is foetid and of a yellow color. In Fiji the fruit is eaten either raw or cooked. The leaves are also used medicinally against diarrhoea and disturbances in menstruation, as well as for fever.

Morinda trimera Hbd.
Noni-kuahiwi.

(Plate 195.)

MORINDA TRIMERA Hbd. Fl. Haw. Isl. (1888) 177;—K. Schum. In Engl. et Prantl Pflzfam. IV. 4. (1891) 148.—**M. trinerva** Del Cast. Ill. Fl. Ins. Mar. Pac. VI. (1890) 196, should be trimera, evidently a misprint.

Branches pale terete, covered with numerous warts and lenticels; leaves elliptical or obovate-oblong, 10 to 18 cm long, 3.5 to 6 cm wide, on petioles of 2.5 to 3.5 cm, acuminate

PLATE 195.

MORINDA TRIMERA Hbd.
Noni-kuahiwi.
Fruiting branch, from the type locality.

at both ends, chartaceous to membraneous, pubescent underneath; stipules 6 mm, acuminate; peduncles in the axils of old leaves and cauline 3.5 to 4 cm long, pluribracteate at the base; flowers 8 to 12 in a glomerule, connate with their bases; calyx 2 to 3 mm, free from the ovary, truncate, with 3-toothlets; corolla 8 mm, puberulous, tubular, 3-toothed; anthers 3, subsessile on the lower third of the corolla, included; ovary small, globose depressed, immersed in an annular disc at the bottom of the calvx; style of the length of the calyx, bifid; drupe or berry of 4 distinct woody pyrena, fleshy, adherent with and enclosed within the globose calyx, each pyrena with 1 erect seed, and the calyxes connate into a syncarpium which measures about 2.5 cm in diameter.

This exceedingly rare species was first collected by J. Lydgate in the forests of Hamakua and Waikapu, Maui. The writer's attention was called to a tree growing in the forest above Makawao, Maui, by Mr. L. v. Tempsky, who having become interested in native trees, happened to find it though practically hidden by *Kopiko* trees and *Ie-ie* vines. It turned out to be this rare species.

A large tree of this species was found by the writer along the ditch trail on the windward side of Mt. Haleakala, near Honomanu gorge. The tree is freely branching and has a trunk of over one foot in diameter. The wood is yellow.

According to Hillebrand a variety occurs on Mt. Puakea of the Waianae range, Oahu. Its leaves are thicker and obtuse; the corolla is four-toothed and possesses 4 stamens instead of three. First collected by Dr. H. Wawra.

CAMPANULACEAE.

Tribe Lobelioideae.

While the family Campanulaceae numbers 59 genera, only the tribe Lobelioideae, with 22 genera, is of importance as far as Hawaii is concerned. Of this tribe, the Hawaiian Islands possesses six genera, five of which are endemic, the remaining one being the cosmopolitan genus Lobelia. Nowhere, with the exception of South America, does this tribe reach such a wonderful development as in the Hawaiian Islands. It has the largest number of species of any plant family represented here in these islands; next to it ranks the Compositae.

Many of our Lobelioideae are arborescent, some of them reaching a height of 40 feet, and are a typical feature in the forests of Hawaii. The tribe in general is mainly tropical, and reaches to the southern temperate zone. Quite a number inhabit North America, and two the Mediterranean regions. The Hawaiian Islands, with its numerous arborescent forms, ranks next to South America, which has the largest number of species, as Centropogon Presl., with 80 to 90 species, and Siphocampylus Pohl, with 100 species, especially numerous in the Andes and Brazil. But if we compare South America in size with the Hawaiian Islands, which has up to 100 species of the tribe Lobelioideae, we find that really nowhere in the world does this tribe reach such a wonderful development in such a comparatively small area. The other islands of the Pacific are void of Lobelioideae, and only Tahiti and the Society Islands, with Raiatea, have in all four species belonging to three different genera.

The Hawaiian species present sometimes really grotesque and specialized

469

PLATE 196.

CLERMONTIA DREPANOMORPHA, Rock.
About two-thirds natural size; showing flowers and fruits.

forms, while others again (new forms) run into each other to such an extent that it is difficult to recognize specific distinction. While most of them are shrubs or small trees, only those are included here which reach a height of about 18 to 40 feet. *Delissea undulata,* which attains a height of over 30 feet on Mauna Loa, Hawaii (see plate XVI), is here omitted, as its stem is rarely thicker than two inches.

The genus Lobelia, which is represented by five very handsome species, some reaching a height of 18 feet *(L. macrostachys* in Kau, Hawaii), possesses about 200 species, which are distributed over Africa and South America, while very few are to be found in Central America. They usually inhabit high mountains, like Abyssinia, Ruwenzori, Kenia, etc., in company with arborescent Compositae.

In the Hawaiian Islands the genus Lobelia is confined to the middle forest zone, but does occasionally ascend into the upper forest zone to an elevation of 6500 feet. (*L. hypoleuca,* Puunianiau crater, Haleakala.)

KEY TO THE GENERA.

Milky shrubs or trees with axillary inflorescences.
    Berry large yellow, an inch or more in diameter:
        Corolla deeply slit to the base; flowers 2-6 in simple cymes...... **Clermontia**
    Berry small, occasionally large, but then purple:
        Corolla slit beyond the middle, flowers in racemes............... **Cyanea**

CLERMONTIA Gaud.

Calycine lobes either as long as the corolla and then bilabiate and deciduous or shorter than the corolla, bluntly lobed or acute, free and persistent; corolla nearly unilabiate, staminal column free from the corolla; the two lower anthers penicillate, the upper ones naked; fruit a globose or pear-shaped berry with a broad epigynous disc; seeds brown shining. Shrubs or trees (with thick latex) branching candelabra like. Inflorescence a two to many flowered cyme.

The genus Clermontia, which is peculiar to Hawaii, consists of 17 species, 13 of which can be included in the term tree.

The most common of the shrubby ones is *C. macrocarpa* Gaud., which grows at an elevation of from 1000 to 2500 feet, and even higher, is replaced in the middle forest zone by *C. persicaefolia, C. oblongifolia* on Oahu, and *C. drepanomorpha,* etc., on Hawaii. Their branching habit is always candelabra-like, and not more than 6 or 8 feet above the ground.

KEY TO THE SPECIES.

I. **CLERMONTIA GENUINAE.**
    Calyx lobes connate, as long as the corolla; at maturity the entire tube falls with the corolla.
    Peduncle two flowered.
        Peduncle long filiform pendulous......................... **C. grandiflora**
        Peduncle arched, drooping, 1-10 cm long; fleshy, corolla dark purple
                C. drepanomorpha
    Peduncle short, erect.
        Corolla and calyx not or little curved when open, slender, whitish
                C. persicaefolia
        Corolla and calyx strongly arched, green.............. **C. oblongifolia**

PLATE 197.

CLERMONTIA PERSICAEFOLIA Gaud.
Less than half natural size.

Peduncle 20-25 mm, drooping.
    Corolla long, slender, dark, purplish-black.............. **C. Kohalae**
Peduncle two to four flowered.
    Corolla smaller, dark, purplish; calyx green; branches slender; leaves with a
        purplish black tinge............................... **C. leptoclada**
    Corolla large, green, purplish or white, ovarian portion strongly ribbed
                                        C. Hawaiiensis

II. CLERMONTIOIDEAE.

Calyx lobes free, shorter than the corolla, persistent.
Peduncle short 15 mm or less.
    Calyx five toothed; corolla puberulous..................... **C. Gaudichaudii**
    Calyx with minute acute teeth; corolla dark purplish-red... **C. Peleana**
    Calyx five lobed; corolla glabrous, thick, fleshy........... **C. arborescens**
    Calyx with five short obtuse lobes; corolla and calyx covered with tubercles
                                         C. tuberculata

Peduncle 2 cm or more in length; two to three flowered.
    Corolla bluish-white or purplish-green..................... **C. coerulea**
Peduncle two-six flowered; flowers whitish-green.............. **C. Haleakalensis**

Clermontia grandiflora Gaud.

CLERMONTIA GRANDIFLORA Gaud. Bot. Voy. Uranie (1826) 459; pl. 73; Presl Monogr. Lobel. (1836) 48.—DC. Prodr. VII (1839) 342;—A. Gray Proc. Am. Acad. V. (1862) 150;—H. Mann Proc. Am. Acad. VII (1866) 184;—Hbd. Fl. Haw. Isl. (1888) 240;—Del Cast. Ill. Fl. Ins. Mar. Pacif. VII. (1892) 221.—**Delissea filigera** Wawra in Flora (1873) 31;—Not Kauai, but Maui:—Wälder ober Waihee.

Leaves obovate to oblong 7 to 10 cm x 2.5 to 3 cm on petioles of 1 to 4 cm, shortly acuminate, bluntly serrulate or dentate, chartaceous glabrous dull; peduncle filiform, pendulous 2 to 8 cm long bracteate at the middle, two flowered, pedicels slender bracteolate about the middle, sometimes cymosely 4 to 5 flowered by dichotomy of pedicels; calyx glabrous greenish or purplish, thin, the lobes tubular, strongly curved before expansion 5 to 6 cm long; corolla purplish somewhat longer than the calyx, berry pear-shaped about 2 cm orange yellow.

This quite distinct species occurs on the Islands of Molokai, Lanai, and Maui, where it inhabits the rain forest from an elevation of 2000 to 5000 feet, or a little higher. It is very common on West Maui, but especially at the summit of Puu Kukui (5788 feet), at the edge of Iao valley, in company with *Lobelia Gaudichaudii*, Labordea, *Wilkesia Grayana*, etc. On Molokai it can be found in the forest above Mapulehu and along a stream back of Kamoku. It is quite conspicuous by its green, purplish-streaked corolla, which is pendulous on long filiform peduncles, which characterizes it from all the other species. It is most plentiful at 4000 feet elevation on the windward slope of Haleakala, East Maui, in the dense mossy rain forest along Waikamoi, Puohaokamoa and Honomanu gulch. On Lanai it grows in the more open dry districts at the ridge of Kaiholena valley, where it is a shrub, while in the other more shaded localities it becomes a small tree 15 to 18 feet in height.

The specific name grandiflora is rather misleading, as it is by no means the largest flowering Clermontia, being exceeded by *C. drepanomorpha* and *C. arborescens.*

Clermontia drepanomorpha Rock sp. nov.

(Plate 196.)

Leaves oblong or obovate, lanceolate 10 to 18 cm x 1.5 to 4 cm glabrous above or sparsely hispid underneath along the prominent reddish midrib, dark green above, lighter

PLATE 198.

CLERMONTIA OBLONGIFOLIA Gaud.
Less than one-half natural size; showing flowers and flower buds.

underneath, on petioles of 3 to 5 cm, denticulate in the upper two-thirds with callous teeth, entire in the lower; peduncle glabrous 6 to 8 cm long with flower, 10 cm long with fruit, pedicels 2 cm, two flowered; bracts and bractlets triangular; calyx dark purplish, the ovarian portion 1.5 to 2 cm triangular to globose, the lobes as long as the corolla, the peduncles drooping, but the flowers erect; corolla purple, curved 4 to 6 cm long by 1.5 to 2 cm wide, fleshy; staminal column glabrous purplish; anthers bluish-lilac, hirsute along the sutures, the lower anthers penicillate; berry large globose yellow 3 cm in diameter; seeds yellowish-brown, smooth.

This remarkable species was discovered by the writer on the open swamp lands in the mountains of Kohala, Hawaii; also along Alakahi and Kawainui gorges at an elevation of 4000 to 5000 feet. It is a small tree 12 to 20 feet in height, and is peculiar to the boggy regions of West Hawaii, where the rainfall is enormous. It was collected flowering and fruiting in July, 1909, and again the following year during the same month on the high plateau, summit of Kohala; the type is No. 4745 in the Herbarium of the College of Hawaii.

It grows in company with several species of Pelea, Cheirodendron, Tetraplasandra, and a number of other species of Clermontia. It is remarkable for its handsome flowers, which are even larger than those of *C. arborescens*.

The birds are very fond of its very large, bright-yellow fruits, which they hollow out until only the skin remains on the stalks. This, however, is the case with most of our Lobelioideae. The trunks of this species are thickly covered with moss up to the ultimate branchlets. The wood is soft and whitish.

Clermontia persicaefolia Gaud.

(Plate 197.)

CLERMONTIA PERSICAEFOLIA Gaud. Bot. Voy. Uranie (1826) pl. 72;—DC. Prodr. VII (1839) 342;—Hbd. Fl. Haw. Isl. (1888) 241;—Del. Cast. Ill. Fl. Ins. Mar. Pacif. VII (1892) 222;—Heller Pl. Haw. Isl. (1897) 907.—Clermontia persicifolia Presl Monogr. Lob. (1836) 48.—Clermontia grandiflora var. β oblongifolia Gray. in part, Proc. Am. Acad. V. (1862) 150;—H. Mann l. c. p. 184 in part.—Lobelia persicifolia Endl. Fl. Suds. (1836) no. 1061.—Clermontia parviflora Wawra Flora (1873) 47.

Leaves lanceolate or oblong 8 to 10 cm x 1 to 2 cm acuminate or obtuse, coarsely crenate or serrulate, the base gradually contracting into a long petiole of 4 to 6 cm subcoriaceous, glossy above, glabrous and glaucous underneath; peduncles 10 to 14 mm, two flowered, with a pair of bracts below the middle; pedicels 12 to 15 mm long bibracteolate at or near the base; calyx and corolla slender almost white, with purplish tinge, greenish when young, smaller than *C. macrocarpa*; the ovarian portion is turbinate.

A handsome shrub or small tree 15 to 18 feet in height, sometimes growing on other trees. It is peculiar to the Island of Oahu, where it can be found in the rain forests of the main range, and not uncommon on the mountain Waiolani, and also near the crater in Palolo valley at an elevation of from 1300 to 2000 feet. It is much branching and has a beautiful, round, symmetrical crown; flowers in spring. It also occurs on Mt. Kaala of the Waianae range.

Wawra's *Clermontia parviflora* No. 2206 in the Herb. Museum Caes. Palat Vindob., which the writer had occasion to examine, is really Gaudichaud's *Cl. persicaefolia*.

Campanulaceae.

Clermontia oblongifolia Gaud.
(Plate 198.)

CLERMONTIA OBLONGIFOLIA Gaud. Bot. Voy. Bonite (1838) 459 pl. 71;—Presl Monogr. Lob. (1836) 48;—DC. Prodr. VII (1839) 342;—Wawra in Flora (1873) 47;—Hbd. Fl. Haw. Isl. (1888) 241;—Del Cast. VII (1892) 222;—Heller Pl. Haw. Isl. (1897) 908.—**Lobelia oblongifolia** Endl. Fl. Suds. (1836) no. 1061.— **Clermontia grandiflora** var. **oblongifolia** Gray Proc. Am. Acad. V. (1862) 150 pro parte;—. Mann l. c. p. 184 pro parte.

Leaves oblong 8 to 12 cm x 3 cm obtuse or rounded, crenate or bluntly serrulate toward the apex, contracting into a long petiole of 4 to 8 cm, chartaceous pale, whitish underneath; peduncle 10 to 16 mm long, two rarely three flowered, with one or two pairs of dentiform bracts; pedicels of the same length as peduncle, with two bractlets near the base; calyx pale greenish, the lobes as long as the corolla, strongly arcuate, circa 6 cm long by 12 mm wide; berry globose not furrowed, seeds dark brown.

It is a small and handsome tree, reaching a height of about 15 to 25 feet, but is often found as a shrub in the more open country or swampy flat lands, as at the head of Pauoa valley on Oahu, to which island it was thought to be peculiar. It has since been found by the writer on Maui in Honomanu gulch, and on Molokai at Maunahui, as on the ridges of Manoa, Palolo, Niu and Waipio valleys, Oahu. Its large, very arched, green flowers are not particularly handsome.

All Clermontiae are known to the natives as *Ohawai* or *Haha*. The milky, viscous sap was employed as bird lime in the olden days by the native bird-hunter.

Var. Mauiensis Rock var. nov.

Leaves acuminate 15 to 19 cm long, 3.5 to 4.5 cm wide, glabrous, pale green, on shorter petioles (4 cm); peduncle 1.5 cm long 2-3 flowered, pedicels somewhat longer, bracts 4 mm, bracteoles 2 mm; calyx green; corolla purplish; staminal column and anthers dark purple, the former glabrous, the latter hirsute along the sutures.

A small tree 15 to 18 feet high, resembling very much the species on Oahu. This tree is not at all common, but can be found on the Island of Maui on the windward slopes of Mt. Haleakala along the Kailua ditch trail in the valley of Honomanu at an elevation of 2800 to 3000 feet in the rain forest. The type specimen is No. 8804 in the College of Hawaii Herbarium. Collected flowering April, 1911. The tree grows in company with *Cl. macrocarpa*, which is the most common species in that locality, and *Cl. arborescens*.

Clermontia Kohalae Rock sp. nov.

Leaves linear oblong bluntly acuminate or obtuse 7 to 16 cm long, 2 to 3 cm wide, gradually narrowing into a petiole of 2 to 4 cm, glabrous, dull, pale underneath, with impressed veins chartaceous denticulate or serrate in the upper two-thirds, entire at the base; peduncle 15 to 35 mm, two flowered, hispid or even scabrous, with two triangular bracts above the middle; pedicels as long as the peduncles bibracteolate; the ovarian portion of the calyx turbinate, green, the lobes as long as the corolla, dark blackish purple, slender, not fleshy, suberect or slightly arcuate, glabrous; corolla of the same color as the calycine lobes, glabrous; staminal column glabrous; anthers pale. hirsute along the sutures, the two lower anthers only penicillate; berry subglobose circa 2 cm in diameter; seeds pale brown smooth shining.

This species, new to science, is a small tree 15 to 18 feet in height with a trunk of a few inches in diameter, branching candelabra-like a few feet above

Campanulaceae.

the ground. It was discovered by the writer in July, 1910, in the lower forests of Kohala, Hawaii, and in the gulches on the windward side, along the streams at an elevation of 1500 to 2500 feet, where it is not uncommon. It is exceedingly handsome when in flower; the numerous dark-purple corollae in the axils of the leaves give it a pleasing appearance. It flowers during the summer months. The type is No. 8810 in the Herbarium of the College of Hawaii.

This very interesting and handsome Lobelia is peculiar to Kohala, Hawaii, after which district it is named. It was also observed along the lower Kohala ditch trial when in company with Mr. Bluett.

Clermontia leptoclada Rock sp. nov.

Branches slender loosely foliose; leaves oblong acuminate at both ends 12 to 18 cm long by 2.5 to 4 cm wide, denticulate with callous teeth, dark green above, with a dark purple-bluish tinge at the margins and apex, glabrous above, coriaceous, with impressed veins, pale underneath and sparingly hispid along the veins and midrib, on petioles of 4 to 6 cm; flowers all along the slender stem on cymosely branching hirsute peduncles of 2.5 to 4 cm, which are bracteate in the upper third; pedicels two usually three to four 1.5 to 3.5 cm long, bibracteolate at the middle, the bractlets linear subulate 5 mm long; calyx, ovarian portion subglobose, the tube as long as the corolla, purplish with prominent hispid nerves; corolla slightly arcuate 4.5 cm long, lobes linear lanceolate, dark purple, hispid with white hair; staminal column purplish puberulous, the anthers hirsute along the sutures, bluish purple, the lower ones penicillate; fruit globose 2.5 cm in diameter; seeds brown smooth shining.

This species, which becomes a tree of 18 to 20 feet in height, was discovered by the writer near the summit of the Kohala mountains on Hawaii, along the Alakahi and Kawainui ditch trail at an elevation of 4200 feet, during the month of July, 1909, at which time it was found in flower and fruit. It is one of the many remarkable Lobelioideae which inhabits our high swampy plateaus. The type is No. 4760 in the Herbarium of the College of Hawaii.

Clermontia Hawaiiensis (Hbd.) Rock.
(Plate 199.)

CLERMONTIA HAWAIIENSIS (Hbd.) Rock.—Clermontia macrocarpa var. Hawaiiensis Hbd. Fl. Haw. Isl. (1888) 241.

Leaves ovate-obovate, oblong, undulate dark green, glossy above, glabrous, lighter underneath, pubescent along the veins and midrib; the veins impressed; 15 to 22 cm long, 3 to 6 cm wide on petioles of 2.5 to 3 cm reddish; peduncles 2 to 4 flowered, 3 to 6 cm long, pedicels 2 to 4 cm long; peduncle bibracteate in the upper fourth, bracts foliaceous 2 to 3.5 cm long, linear oblong denticulate, pedicels bibracteolate at the middle and at their common base, puberulous, calyx subglobose, the ovarian portion pronouncedly 10 ridged, the dorsal one almost wing-like, the tube green or purplish 0 to 6.5 cm long, as long or even longer than the corolla; the dorsal slit extending to the base, the lateral slits beyond the middle, each lobe strongly nerved, each nerve being a continuation of a ridge of the ovarian portion of the calyx; corolla slightly arched thickened toward the apex in the bud; staminal column glabrous, green or purple, anthers pale purple or dark hirsute along the sutures or glabrous, the two lower only penicillate, berry large 3 cm in diameter, 10 ridged, orange yellow.

This shrub or small tree reaches a height of 20 or more feet. It is a very variable species; the leaves are sometimes oblong or ovate, the peduncle either very long and then twice as long as the pedicels and two-flowered, or as long as the pedicels or little longer and then four-flowered; the two inner pedicels

PLATE 199.

CLERMONTIA HAWAIIENSIS (Hbd.) Rock.
Ohawai.
Flowering and fruiting specimen from near the Volcano of Kilauea, Hawaii; elevation
4000 feet.   One-half natural size.

Campanulaceae.

shorter and thicker(almost four-cornered) than the two outer pedicels. In the four-flowered specimens the corolla is purple, while in the long peduncled, two-flowered specimens the corolla is either whitish or green.

This species occurs in the semi-wet forest on the land of Keauhou about three miles from the Volcano House. It becomes exceedingly plentiful as one penetrates into the interior. It usually grows on the trunks of Cibotium tree ferns or is also occasionally terrestrial. It is associated with *Acacia Koa, Metrosideros polymorpha, Perrottetia sandwicensis, Straussia* sp., *Myoporum sandwicense*, etc.

The specimens found lower down along the government road come nearer to *Cl. macrocarpa;* while the plants found back of Hilo are *Clermontia macrocarpa.* The plants found below the Volcano House and those beyond Shipman's paddock on Keauhou, cannot be very well separated, and therefore the writer found it advisable to make it a species, as the plants from the type locality can certainly not be called a variety of *Cl. macrocarpa.*

Collected April, 1911, July, 1911, and July 9, 1912, in company with Mr. W. M. Giffard. The type is No. 8803 in the College of Hawaii Herbarium.

Clermontia Gaudichaudii (Gaud.) Hbd.

Haha or *Hahaaiakamanu.*

CLERMONTIA GAUDICHAUDII (Gaud.) Hbd. Fl. Haw. Isl. (1888) 243;—Del. Cast. Ill. Fl. Ins. Mar. Pacif. VII (1892) 211.—Delissea clermontioides Gaud. Voy. Bon (1838) pl. 47, (1866) p. 64;—Gray Proc. Am. Acad. V (1862) 147;—H. Mann. l. c. p. 178;—Wawra in Flora (1873) 8.—Clermontia clermontioides Heller Pl. Haw. Isl. (1897) 906. Clermontia Clermontioides (Gaud.) Heller, would really be correct but owing to the silliness of the combination, Hillebrand's name is here retained.

Leaves elliptico oblong to lanceolate 8 to 12 cm x 1.5 to 4 cm on petioles of 2 to 3 cm, acute at both ends, crenulate, glabrous, pale and dull, chartaceous; peduncle short about 1 cm; pedicels 12 to 15 mm, bracts 1 mm; calyx broad campanulate about 15 mm high with 5 short acute teeth; corolla arched as much as in *C. oblongifolia*, about 4 cm long and 1 cm wide, greenish purple; anthers pale, glabrous; berry globose, furrowed, 22 to 25 mm in diameter.

This species, which is peculiar to the middle forest region of the Island of Kauai, is either a shrub or small tree, with many candelabra-like branches forming a beautiful round or flatish crown. It grows mainly along stream beds, and is plentiful along Waialae gulch (4000 feet). It also grows in the swampy high plateau in gray, muddy soil, or can often be found on other trees between their main branches in accumulated humus.

It ascends even as high as to the foot of Mt. Waialeale (4600 feet), where it grows in company with the curious *Gunnera petaloidea*, or *Apeape*, along Kaluiti and Kailiili streams.

The natives, as well as the birds, are very fond of the large, sweet, yellow berries, from which the tree receives its name, *Haha* or *Oha* being the native generic name for all Clermontiae. while *ai a ka manu* is the specific one, meaning "eaten by the birds."

479

PLATE 200.

CLERMONTIA PELEANA Rock sp. nov.
Flowering specimen from near Kilauea, Hawaii.   More than one-half natural size.

PLATE 201.

ÇLERMONTIA ARBORESCENS (Mann) Hbd.
Ohawai.
Less than half natural size; showing flowering branch and fruit.

PLATE 202.

ÇLERMONTIA TUBERCULATA Forbes
Natural size, showing flowerbuds.   Note tubercles on the inflorescence.

Campanulaceae.

Clermontia Peleana Rock sp. nov.
(Plate 200.)

Leaves oblong acuminate 18 to 20 cm long by 3.5 to 4.5 cm wide, dark green above, glossy somewhat lighter underneath, with dark purple veins and midrib, irregularly crenate to nearly the base of the leaf, which is on a petiole of 4 to 6 cm; flowers axillary usually two on a short peduncle of 1.5 cm with two small linear bracts at the middle; pedicles 3 to 4 cm with two bracteoles at their common base; calyx dark green, the ovarian portion turbinate 1.5 to 2 cm in diameter, with minute teeth; corolla strongly arched when open, 4 to 5 cm, dark blackish purple, thin not fleshy, silky, the apex almost returning to the level of the base; staminal column glabrous dark purple, as are the anthers of which the two lower are penicillate; style glabrous with a bluntly two-lobed stigma; fruit unknown.

This species, which is a small, glabrous tree 20 feet in height, has long, more or less rambling branches. It was discovered by the writer on the Island of Hawaii, in the middle rain forest zone, at an elevation of 3800 feet, four or five miles below Kilauea volcano, along the government road. Only three plants were observed, one of which had never flowered. It is a very handsome species, and is associated with *Clermontia Hawaiiensis, Cheirodendron Gaudichaudii, Cyrtandra,* Cibotium tree ferns, Ilex, etc.

It is named after the Hawaiian goddess Pele, whose abode is in the fires of Kilauea, in the vicinity of which this tree grows.

The type is in the Herbarium of the College of Hawaii, No. 8800, collected flowering in July, 1911, and July 10, 1912.

Clermontia arborescens (Mann) Hbd.
Oha wai.
(Plate 201.)

CLERMONTIA ARBORESCENS (Mann) Hbd. Fl. Haw. Isl. (1888) 242;—Del. Cast. Ill. Fl. Ins. Mar. Pacif. VII (1892) 221.—Cyanea arborescens Mann. Proc. Am. Acad. VII (1866) 183.—Delissea Waihiae Wawra in Flora (1873) 8.

Leaves obovate oblong 12 to 16 cm x 4 to 5 cm, on petioles of 3 to 6 cm, shortly acuminate or rounded, narrowing at the base, crenate or serrulate, coriaceous, dark green, glossy above, paler underneath; peduncle very short fleshy, two flowered only, the pedicels about 25 mm or also 35 cm, bracts small, bractlets at the base of the pedicels; calyx green with a campanulate tube of about 20 mm and thick obtuse or deltoid lobes of very variable length, separated by sinuses when small and partly connate when large; corolla exceedingly thick and fleshy, strongly arched about 6 cm long of an even width, greenish white or sometimes cream colored with a tinge of reddish purple; anthers glabrous; berry yellow very deeply furrowed and crowned by the calycine lobes; seeds pale yellow shining.

It is one of the most common Clermontia, next to the Oahuan *C. macrocarpa,* but unlike the latter inhabits the middle forest zone between 2000 and 4000 feet. It occurs on the three central islands, but is absent on Oahu, Kauai, and Hawaii. It is peculiar to the wet forests, where it is a small tree 15 to 25 feet in height. The yellow berries, which reach the size of a little lime, are eaten by birds and the natives. It is conspicuous by its monstrous fleshy inflorescence, which is, next to that of *C. drepanomorpha,* the largest in the genus. The *Oha wai* can be found along the Kula pipe line trail, East Maui, where it is extremely common. Also on West Maui (Kaanapali), Molokai (Pelekunu), Lanai (Haalelepakai), usually in company with species of Cyanea and *Clermontia grandiflora.*

PLATE 203.

CLERMONTIA COERULEA Hbd.
One-third natural size; showing flowers and fruits.

Campanulaceae.

Clermontia tuberculata Forbes.

(Plate 202.)

CLERMONTIA TUBERCULATA Forbes Occas. Papers B. P. Bish. Mus. V. (1912) 8, pl. 3.

Leaves obovate to oblong, serrulate, glabrous, coriaceous, the veins on the under-side minutely tuberculate 19.5 cm to 4 cm, with petioles 2 to 3 cm long; peduncle two-flowered 5 mm long pedicels 3 cm, both covered with small tubercles; calyx tube campanulate with short obtuse lobes, which together with the thick fleshy corolla is covered with pronounced tubercles; anthers dark red, glabrous; berry globose, strongly tuberculate on the outside 1.3 cm in diameter; seeds smooth, yellow, shiny, ovoid.

This small tree, which reaches a height of about 12 to 15 feet, was discovered by Mr. C. N. Forbes of the Bishop Museum, who collected it on the Island of Maui on the slopes of Haleakala, in the wet forests near Ukulele (5000 feet).

The writer collected specimens of this species a year later from the identical tree from which Mr. Forbes derived his material. One other tree was seen along a stream bed, its branches touching the rushing waters, between Puukakai hill and the Kula pipe line trail, when in company with Dr. P. Ceresole.

It comes nearest to *Clermontia arborescens* Hbd., but does not grow to such a size. It is a very distinct species, differing from all other Clermontiae in its tuberculate inflorescence, a character which, however, occurs in certain species of Cyanea new to science.

Clermontia coerulea Hbd.

(Plate 203.)

CLERMONTIA COERULEA Hbd. Fl. Haw. Isl. (1888) 243;—Del. Cast. Ill. Fl. Ins. Mar Pacif. VII (1892) 211.

Leaves oblong 12 to 15 cm long 2 to 4 cm wide on petioles of 3 to 5 cm shortly acuminate, contracting at the base, minutely denticulate, glabrous above, membraneous, with a scattered pubescence along the midrib underneath; peduncle slender 2.5 to 4 cm long, with a pair of short bracts considerably above the middle, pedicels of the same length or longer (in Hillebrand's specimen the pedicels are shorter) than the peduncle, bracteolate below the middle; (Hillebrand's statement that the bracteoles are at the middle is incorrect; his specimen of *C. coerulea* which I examined has the bracteoles also below the middle) calyx colored, the tube about 15 mm, turbinate, the lobes either large 15 to 17 cm or minutely denticulate; corolla moderately curved about 4 cm long greenish in Kau specimens, purplish in Kona specimens, of a thin texture; berry globose yellow about 2 cm in diameter somewhat furrowed.

What *Clermontia macrocarpa* is to Oahu, *Clermontia coerulea* is to Hawaii, especially on the southern end. It is the most common Clermontia on the slopes of Mauna Loa in Kau, from where it ranges way over to North Kona. It can be found at an elevation of 2000 feet above Naalehu, Kau, in wet rain forests up to an elevation of 4000 feet. It also occurs in the wet forest back of Kapua, where it extends up into the Koa belt. It is not uncommon in the forests above Kealakekua and on the slopes of Hualalai back of Huehue. In Kau it is a tree 15 to 20 feet in height with a trunk of about 4 to 5 inches in diameter, and is freely branching. In the specimens from Kau, the calycine lobes are minutely denticulate, while in the Kona specimens the lobes are broad deltoid. In the latter locality it is a shrub.

PLATE 204.

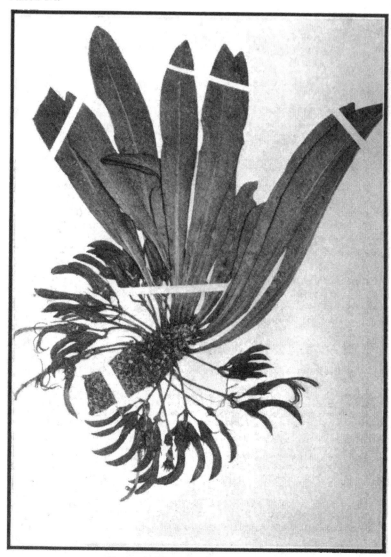

CLERMONTIA HALEAKALENSIS Rock.
Less than half natural size.

PLATE 205.

CLERMONTIA HALEAKALENSIS Rock.
Growing on the inner crater wall of Puunianiau, slopes of Mt. Haleakala; elevation 7000 feet. Island of Maui.

PLATE 206.

CYANEA ARBOREA (Gray) Hbd.
Portion of crown of leaves with inflorescence; less than one-third natural size.

Campanulaceae.

Clermontia Haleakalensis Rock, sp. nov.

(Plates 204, 205.)

Leaves 20 to 30 cm long including the short margined petiole, fleshy, 1.5 to 4 cm wide, obtuse, oblong lanceolate, dark green above, pale underneath, midrib thick prominent, veins impressed, pellucid, the upper half crenate, lower half entire, glabrous, gradually tapering into a short margined petiole; cymes in the axils of the leaves, peduncle 2 to 5 cm long, bearing usually 6 flowers on pedicels of 1 to 1.5 cm, the bracts linear subulate about 7 mm, the pedicels bibracteolate below the middle; calyx tube oblong turbinate 1.5 cm slightly pubescent, the lobes linear subulate 5 mm long, corolla whitish green 3.5 to 4 cm long, curved, the dorsal slit not always extending to the base, sometimes only to the middle, lobes linear lanceolate glabrous; staminal column white pubescent at the base, as is the disc, glabrous in the upper part, the two lower anthers penicillate; style slightly pubescent, inner side of the staminal column hispid with white hair in the lower half, berry oblong, seeds smooth whitish.

A small tree 10 to 20 feet tall, with few very robust branches, having at first glance the aspect of a Dracaena. It is soft-wooded, and glabrous. This very curious tree, which has almost an antediluvian appearance, comes nearly between Clermontia and Cyanea. Its decidedly cymose inflorescence places it with the former genus, while the dorsal slit of the corolla does not always extend to the base, but the middle. It also has a characteristic of the genus Delissea, and that is the thickened portion or knob in the flower bud about the middle, indicating the termination of the dorsal slit; though the seeds, which in Delissea are deeply wrinkled, are smooth and shining in the species in question.

This remarkable tree is undoubtedly one of the oldest forms of our Hawaiian Lobelioideae, as it is so strikingly different from all the rest of the Lobelioideae inhabiting these islands.

This particular species was discovered by the writer October 11, 1910, on the Island of Maui, on the western slopes of Mt. Haleakala, on the crater of Puunianiau, at an elevation of 7000 feet, in a locality where no one would expect to find a member of this wonderful tribe. It grows in open, dry scrub in company with plants belonging to the upper forest zone, such as *Raillardia platyphylla, Argyroxiphium virescens, Sophora chrysophylla, Santalum Haleakalae,* etc. Unfortunately, only three trees are in existence, and as they are peculiar to the above locality, it will not be long before they will have shared the fate of so many of our native trees, becoming extinct, as cattle have free access and browse on the lower branches within their reach. The writer appealed to the manager of Haleakala ranch to protect these trees from the ravages of cattle, which he kindly promised to do.

The type specimen is No. 8595 in the Herbarium of the College of Hawaii.

CYANEA Gaud.

(*Kittelia* Reichb., *Marcrochilus* Presl.)

Calycine lobes of variable length, from dentate to foliaceous; the dorsal slit of the corolla extending to the middle. The two lower small anthers or all penicillate; seeds crustaceous shining smooth. Shrubs or small trees with erect simple stem or branches, occasionally covered with thorns. Leaves entire, lobed, or pinnate. Flowers bluish or purple or white in axillary racemes.

PLATE 207.

CYANEA ARBOREA (Gray) Hbd.
Side view.   At Ulupalakua, Maui.   Note the dense inflorescence.

PLATE 208.

CYANEA ARBOREA (Gray) Hbd.
Front view.   Growing in a small gulch at Ulupalakua, Maui; elevation 5500 feet.

PLATE 209.

ÇYANEA LEPTOSTEGIA A. Gray.
Hahalua.
Plant reaches a height of forty feet.   Growing in the forest of Kaholuamano on Kauai.

Campanulaceae.

The genus Cyanea is endemic in the Hawaiian Islands and possesses more species than either Clermontia or Delissea. All the species are shrubby, with three exceptions. One species, *C. leptostegia*, reaches 40 feet in height, and is the tallest of any of our Lobelioideae. The genus consists of many species, 31 having been so far described, while many more have been discovered by the writer which will be published in a monograph on this tribe, bringing the number of species of Cyanea probably up to 45, or even more.

The genus Cyanea consists of milky shrubs or trees with a single erect or branching stem, which includes a medullary cavity. Flowers are arranged in racemes.

KEY TO THE SPECIES.

Calycine lobes shorter than the tube.
    Flowers grayish white or cream colored........................... **C. arborea**
Calycine lobes longer than the tube.
    Flowers dark purple.. **C. leptostegia**

Cyanea arborea (Gray) Hbd.
(Plates 206, 207, 208.)

CYANEA ARBOREA (Gray) Hbd. Fl. Haw Isl. (1888) 261;—Del Cast. Ill. Fl. Ins. Mar. Pacif. VII (1892) 219.—**Delissea coriacea** var. *β* A. Gray l. c. p. 148;—H. Mann l. c. p. 178.—**Delissea arborea** H. Mann l. c. p. 180.—**Cyanea longifolia** Heller l. c. p. 909.

Leaves sessile oblanceolate 40-65 cm x 7-12.5 cm, shortly acuminate or rounded and apiculate, gradually narrowing toward the base, faintly dentate, but almost entire and wavy towards the base, glabrous or pubescent along the rib, glossy, chartaceous to coriaceous; peduncle slender but stiff 15-30 cm long, almost naked above, closely many flowered in the last fourth, pedicels short 3.8 mm; bracts 2-4 mm; bractlets 1 mm; calyx subglobose, glabrous, shortly toothed, the tube 6 mm; corolla slender moderately curved, suberect 5 cm long, 5 mm wide, glabrous grayish white, rather thin, with a deep dorsal slit and connivent lobes; staminal column glabrous; berry globose, faintly ribbed, 10-12 mm in diameter.

A tree 12 to 24 feet tall of palm-like habit with a crown of leaves at the apex of the stem, the latter measuring about 4 inches in diameter or more.

This is one of the most handsome Lobelias which the islands possess. Unfortunately it is exceedingly scarce, and the writer fears that it has become extinct.

Where there was once a forest at Ulupalakula there is now only grassland with planted Eucalypti. The writer met with only one single plant in a small gulch which was inaccessible to cattle. For three days the writer searched for this beautiful Lobelia, and he had nearly abandoned all hope when he saw this handsome plant hidden in a small and very narrow gulch. It evidently is the last of its race. In the whole district of Ulupalakua there is now no forest at all, only here and there stands a tree of the araliaceous species *Pterotropia dipyrena*.

Cyanea comata, another beautiful lobeliaceous plant once common in this district, has vanished forever.

The plant is peculiar to Haleakala, Ulupalakua, Maui, and was once plentiful at an elevation of 4000 to 5000 feet. It flowers in the early spring.

493

Campanulaceae-Goodeniaceae.

Cyanea leptostegia A. Gray.
Hahalua.
(Plate 209.)

CYANEA LEPTOSTEGIA A. Gray Proc. Am. Acad. V. (1862) 149;—Mann. Proc. Am. Acad. VII (1866) 184;— Wawra in Flora (1873) 47;—Hbd. Fl. Haw. Isl. (1888) 261;—Del. Cast, Ill. Fl. Ins. Mar. Pacif. VII (1892) 219;—Heller Pl. Haw. Isl. (1897) 908.

Leaves sessile narrow lanceolate, 40 to 48 cm x 4 to 5 cm denticulate or subentire, glabrous shining chartaceous, the midrib of the leaves hollow, leaves of young plants lobed, the lobes extending sometimes to the midrib; peduncle (with flower) 2 to 3 cm slender, naked below, many-flowered at the apex, 10 to 20 flowers in a crowded cluster on pedicels of about 8 mm, bracts linear, twice as long as the bractlets; calyx glabrous, the tube cylindrical, lobes linear or filiform, sometimes 4 cm long; corolla dark purplish red, glabrous, semierect and slender about 4 cm long and 4 mm broad, anthers glabrous; berry ovoid, yellow, crowned by the filiform calycine lobes.

The *Hahalua,* which reaches a height of sometimes 40 feet, or about 13 m, has a pronounced palm-like habit, possessing a single erect trunk which is densely covered in its upper portion with rhomboid leaf-scars, bearing at the end a crown of sessile leaves.

The *Hahalua* is peculiar to the Island of Kauai, where it inhabits the middle forest zone on the leeward side in the drier and more open districts. It is associated with *Antidesma platyphyllum* var. β., *Xylosma Hawaiiense, Maba sandwicensis* var., *Pisonia sandwicensis, Cyanea spathulata,* and *Cyanea hirtella.* It flowers in the summer months.

Numerous species of caterpillars feed on the fruits and withered flowers

The leaves of the young plants are always lobed, a characteristic found quite often in young plants of Cyaneae, especially in those of Section III Palmae-formes. The milky juice of this species is yellow.

GOODENIACEAE.

The family Goodeniaceae consists of 13 genera, of which 10 are only found in Australia. The species number 291, of which 27 are not found in Australia. In the Hawaiian Islands only the genus Scaevola is represented of this family, with a few species.

SCAEVOLA L.

Flowers hermaphrodite, zygomorphous, pentamerous. Calyx tube adnate to the ovary, the limb very short, annular, truncate or 5-parted. Tube of corolla dorsally slit to the base, all lobes nearly of equal length or the two superior ones shorter. Filaments linear, anthers free. Ovary inferior, rarely very shortly superior, bi-locular, ovules solitary in each locule, erect, anatropous. Style entire, the margin of the indusium ciliate, very rarely glabrous; stigma truncate or subbilobate. Fruit indehiscent, exocarp fleshy succulent, or suberose, endocarp hard, ligneous, or bony, rarely crustaceous. Seeds solitary. Embryo as long as the albumen, with terete or foliaceous cotyledons.—Herbs, shrubs or small trees with alternate, rarely opposite leaves, which are toothed, serrate, or entire. Flowers rarely solitary, usually in cymes, bracteate and bracteolate, sessile or pedicellate. Corolla white, purple or yellow.

The genus consists of 83 species, distributed over Australia, but mainly West

Goodeniaceae.

Australia, India, a few in New Caledonia and 6 endemic species in the Hawaiian Islands, with one other *S. frutescens* (Mill.) Krause, of wide distribution.

KEY TO THE SPECIES.

Leaves obovate oblong, toothed or serrate.
    Cymes short, crowded, leaves pubescent......................... **S. procera**
    Cymes long, many flowered; leaves glabrous................... **S. Chamissoniana**

Scaevola Chamissoniana Gaud.
Naupaka or *Naupaka kuahiwi.*

(Plate 210.)

SCAEVOLA CHAMISSONIANA Gaud. Bot. Voy. Uranie (1826) 461. t.82;—Hook. et Arn. Bot. Beech. Voy. (1832) 89;—Endl. Fl. Suds. Ann. Wien. Mus. I. (1836) 170 no. 1043;—DC. Prodr. VII. (1839) 506;—A. Gray in Proc. Am. Acad. VII. (1867) 187;—Hbd. Fl. Haw. Isl. (1888) 267;—Del Cast. Ill. Fl. Ins. Mar. Pac. VI. (1890) 216;—Heller in Minnes. Bot. Stud. Bull. IX. (1897) 913;—Krause Das Pflzenr. LIV. 4. 277. (1912) 123.—**S. Chamissoniana** Gaud. var. γ Hbd. Fl. Haw. Isl. (1888) 267.—**S. ciliata** G. Don Gen. Syst. III. (1834) 728.—**S. ligustrifolia** Nutt. in Trans. Am. Phil. Soc. N. S. VIII. (1843) 253.—**Temninckia Chamissoniana** de Vriese Gooden. (1854) 8;—Walp. Ann. II. (1852) 1057.—**Lobelia Chamissoniana** O. Ktze. Rev. Gen. Pl. II. (1891) 378.

A shrub or small tree 5 to 6 m high; branches terete glabrous or in the axils of leaves sparsely white-villose; leaves chartaceous, obovate or obovate lanceolate, acuminate at the apex, cuneate at the base, narrowing into a petiole of 6 to 12 mm, margins serrate-dentate, glabrous on both sides, 4 to 10 cm long, 2 to 4.5 cm wide; flowers in subdivaricate cymes, 7 to 15 flowered, as long as the leaves or longer; bracts small linear, acute 2 to 5 cm long, ovary obovoid, glabrous, 3 to 4 mm long; calyx 1 to 2 mm long, shortly 5-lobed, sparsely ciliolate; corolla white with purple streaks or pure white, the erect tube narrow cylindrical, 1.5 to 2 cm long, glabrous outside, sparsely pubescent inside, lobes about half the length of the tube or shorter, winged; stamens almost the length of the tube, the filiform filaments somewhat dilated at the base, anthers small, oblong, truncate; style slightly protruding from the corolla, pubescent below, glabrous above; indusium glabrous, the superior margin sparsely and shortly ciliate. fruit ellipsoidal, glabrous, 6 to 10 mm long, 4 to 5 mm thick.

This species is one of the most common shrubs or often small trees which one is likely to meet everywhere in the lower or middle forest zone. It is in flower nearly all the year round and is quite a conspicuous object in the forest on account of its white flower, which appears to be only a half a flower, though complete. It occurs on all the islands of the group from 800 feet elevation up to 4000 feet and even higher; several varieties have been described. Krause in his monograph on the Goodeniaceae of the world distinguishes three varieties of this species: (1) var. *pubescens* (Nutt.) Krause, from Kohala, Oahu, (2) var. *bracteosa* Hbd. from Maui, Hawaii, and Molokai, and (3) var. *cylindrocarpa* (Hbd.) Krause, from Lanai.

There are many more varieties of this species in the writer's possession, which belong all to shrubs and therefore do not come within the scope of this book. Plate 210 shows a branch from the typical *S. Chamissoniana*, as it occurs in the forests of Oahu.

Here may be recorded another species, the *Ohenaupaka* of the natives or *Scaevola glabra* H. et A. This latter plant often reaches a height of fifteen

PLATE 210.

SCAEVOLA CHAMISSONIANA Gaud.
Naupaka.
Flowering and fruiting branch, reduced.

feet, but is seldom a tree; it grows usually in out-of-the-way places, as on the summit ridges of the mountains of Oahu, and in the swampy forest and borders of great bogs on Kauai, usually at an elevation of from 3000-5000 feet. The flowers are the largest of the Hawaiian *Naupaka* and are bright yellow.

Scaevola procera Hbd.

Naupaka or *Naupaka kuahiwi.*

SCAEVOLA PROCERA Hbd. Fl. Haw. Isl. (1888) 268;—Del Cast. Ill. Fl. Ins. Mar. Pac. VII. (1892) 217;—Heller in Minnes. Bot. Stud. Bull. IX. (1897) 914;—Krause Das Pflzenreich LIV. 4. 277. (1912) 123.—**Lobelia procera** O. Ktze. Rev. Gen. Pl. II. (1891) 378.

Branches terete, densely and shortly cinereous tomentose, adult ones somewhat glabrous, and barbellate in the leaf-axils; leaves chartaceous obovate-oblong or lanceolate-oblong, acuminate at the apex, contracting into a petiole of 1 to 1.6 cm rarely longer, margin acutely serrate-dentate, or the base entire, 6 to 15 cm long, 2.5 to 4.5 cm broad, sparsely hispidulous above, pubescent beneath, with distinct and prominent nerves; flowers large in axillary divaricate trichotomous cymes which are cinereous tomentulose, and shorter than the leaves; bracts linear lanceolate, acute, 2 to 4 mm long, ovary obovoid-oblong, puberulous or subglabrous, about 4 mm; calyx lobes very short, obsoletely deltoid-ovate, subacute, with ciliolate margins; corolla white with purple streaks, 1.8 to 2.5 cm long, outside sparcely but inside densely puberulous, the subpatent lobes shorter than the tube, with somewhat broad wings; stamens at the base little dilated, the filiform filaments 7 to 8 mm long, anthers elliptical-oblong, truncate, much shorter than the filaments; style somewhat complanate, sparsely puberulous, quite glabrous at the apex, little shorter than the corolla; indusium with the upper margin shortly ciliate; fruit ovoid, glabrous, 6 mm long, 3 to 4 mm thick, indistinctly and longitudinally costate.

This rather handsome species occurs as a shrub and small tree 15 feet or so high on several islands of the Hawaiian group, but is most common on Molokai. It resembles somewhat *S. mollis.* It was first found by Hillebrand on Molokai at the Pali of Pelekunu Valley. It was collected by the writer March. 1910, flowering and fruiting back of Kamoku, near Kawela swamp (no. 6159), and again at Wailau pali (no. 7031 and 7036), Molokai. On Kauai he collected it back of Lihue on the Haupu range with almost entire leaves, flowering March 19, 1909. (College of Hawaii Herbarium.)

COMPOSITAE.

The Composite, or Sunflower, family, is the largest family of plants, comprising over 800 genera, with more than 10,000 species. The Composite family is considered one of the youngest of the plant families, as some of its tribes are still in full evolution.

It is distributed over the whole Globe, and is represented in these islands by about 60 species, only a few of which become trees. Of striking character is the well-known Hawaiian Silversword, *Argyroxiphium sandwicense (Hinahina),* with its variety *macrocephalum* from Haleakala crater. Some of the arborescent species of Hawaiian Compositae inhabit the high mountains of the group, up to an elevation of over 10,000 feet.

PLATE 211.

DUBAUTIA PLANTAGINEA Gaud.
Naenae.
Flowering branch, about one-half natural size.

Compositae.

KEY TO THE GENERA.

Flowerheads small, yellowish:
  Style of fertil flowers bifid:
    Bracts of involucre in one row free........................... **Dubautia**
    Bracts of involucre connate................................. **Raillardia**
Flower heads large, two inches or more, brownish yellow:
    Style of all florets entire or shortly bidentate..................... **Hesperomannia**

DUBAUTIA Gaud.

Flowerheads homogamous, discoid, all florets hermaphrodite and fertile. Involucre turbinate, with 5 to 10 equal bracts in one row; receptacle naked or paleaceous, the paleae corresponding in number to the inner florets; corolla tubular with a 5-fid limb; anthers purple, shortly appendiculate; style-branches revolute; achenes hispid, 4 to 5 ribbed, with several shortly ciliate rays in a single row.—Shrubs or small trees with opposite or ternate leaves which are either sessile or subsessile, the leaves are parallel nerved, with a slightly branching middle nerve, and remind one of the leaves of species of Plantago or Bupleurum. Inflorescence terminal, paniculate or corymbose.

The genus Dubautia is strictly Hawaiian and is closely allied to the genus Raillardia, which is also peculiar to the Hawaiian Islands. It consists of seven species, only two of which attain the height which entitle them to be called trees; the remaining five are shrubs. The Dubautiae or *Naenae*, as the Hawaiians term these plants, are peculiar to the wet regions of the middle forest zone, and reach their best development on the Island of Kauai, where five species are found.

Dubautia plantaginea Gaud.
Naenae.
(Plate 211.)

DUBAUTIA PLANTAGINEA Gaud. Bot. Voy. Uranie (1826) 469. pl. 84;—Less in Linnaea VI. (1831) 162;—Endl. Fl. Suds. (1836) n. 998;—A. Gray Proc. Am. Ac. V. (1862) 134;—Wawra in Flora (1873) 76;—Hbd. Fl. Haw. Isl. (1888) 222;—Hoffmann in Engl. et Prantl Pflzfam. IV. 5. (1889) 248. fig. 120. G.;—Del Cast. Ill. Fl. Ins. Mar. Pac. VI. (1890) 212;—Heller in Minnes. Bot. Stud. Bull. IX. (1897) 918.

Leaves opposite, lanceolate 10 to 20 cm x 8 to 20 mm, acute gradually contracting at both ends, clasping with the narrow base, entire or remotely denticulate in the upper half, strongly 7 to 13 nerved; panicle pubescent, pyramidal, 15 to 25 cm long, projecting beyond the leaves, with horizontal branches, the lowest 5 to 7.5 cm long, the ultimate pedicels 2 to 3 mm, racemosely arranged; heads cylindrical, florets 7 to 10, involucral bracts 7 to 8; receptacle mostly naked; corolla orange colored, exserted; style branches revolute; pappus-rays linear-subulate, with upright ciliae.

The *Naenae* is a small tree of 10 to 16 feet in height with a short trunk of a few inches in diameter. The branches are very slender, spreading, and bear at their ends long, lanceolate, bright-green opposite leaves, which are strongly 7 to 13 nerved. It is a strikingly handsome tree when in full flower, which is from about July to August, varying, of course, according to locality. The small yellow flowers are borne on a large pyramidal panicle which projects beyond the leaves, about ten inches or more in length, drooping or standing erect. The corolla is orange-colored with a slender tube which dilates into a bell-shaped (campanulate) limb with reflexed lobes. The flowers have the odor of bee's-wax, and are often purplish instead of yellow.

499

PLATE 212.

RAILLARDIA ARBOREA Gray.
Naenae.
Photographed from an herbarium specimen, about one-half natural size.

Compositae.

The *Naenae* is more or less common on all the islands, but particularly on Oahu, where it can be found at an elevation of 2000 feet at the head of Pauoa valley, at the foot of Konahuanui. On Maui it is very common at the west end at a lower elevation along Honakawai gulch, back of Kaanapali, as well as at Honokahau. On Haleakala it is plentiful along the gulches near Kula, at 3000 feet, and is scattered in the rain forest near Waikamoi and Puukakai above Olinda at an elevation of 4000 feet. Occasional plants can be found in the crater of Haleakala in Kaupo Gap at an elevation of 5000 to 6000 feet, together with *Raillardia* sp., *Argyroxiphium virescens, Lobelia hypoleuca, Geranium multiflorum*, etc. On Hawaii it is found in the mountains of Kohala, as well as on the slopes of Hualalai at about 6000 feet, in company with Dodonaea, Styphelia, Coprosma, etc., on black cinder. On Kauai it is gregarious along Waialae stream together with *Dubautia laevigata* and other plants.

It is peculiar to the rain forest, where it reaches its best development, but can occasionally be found in the drier districts. On Oahu it is also plentiful in the mountains of Punaluu at an elevation of 2000 feet.

Another species, *Dubautia laxa* Hook. et Arn. occurs on Oahu, though a shrub. The writer discovered a variety of this latter species on Kauai at the central plateau in the swampy forests and on the borders of the great open bogs at an elevation of 4500-5000 feet. It is a small tree 15 to 18 feet in height with few spreading branches, which, together with the leaves are hirsute with whitish-gray hair. The inflorescence is a large hirsute corymb, bearing dark orange-yellow heads of 6 mm in diameter on pedicels of 12 mm. It differs from the species in the large, orange colored flower-heads which are on long pedicels, while in the species they are nearly subsessile. It may be known as *Dubautia laxa* H. et A. var. *pedicellata* Rock var. nov.

RAILLARDIA Gaud.

The genus Raillardia differs from Dubautia in its plumose pappus-rays and usually naked receptacle; flower-heads as in Dubautia.—Shrubs or trees with ternate, alternate, or opposite leaves, with various venations; flowers in terminal racemes, panicles or corymbs, yellow.

The genus Raillardia is peculiar to the Hawaiian Islands, though it is of American affinity, as it is closely related to the California genus, Raillardella, established by Gray, with four species peculiar to the high mountains of the Sierra Nevada and Yosemite district at elevations from 8000 to 11,000 feet. Most of the Hawaiian Raillardiae inhabit our high mountains to an altitude of 11,000 feet, but a few species (shrubby) occur as low as 2500 feet, or even lower. The arborescent species are found at high elevations only. The California Raillardella are acaulescent herbs with stout, creeping rootstocks.

The species of Raillardia are not at all clearly defined in Hillebrand's Flora, and need a revision. A few species run into each other so that it is sometimes

501

PLATE 213.

RAILLARDIA MENZIESII Gray.
Fruiting branch pinned against trunk of tree; growing in the upper forest of Mt.
Haleakala; elevation 6000 feet.

Compositae.

very difficult to distinguish them. Some species will have to be united, and perhaps one or two new species described, as they do not fit in Hillebrand's key to the species.

KEY TO THE SPECIES.

Leaves with a viscous pubescence; inflorescence paniculate........... **R. arborea**
Leaves silky pubescent, lanceolate acute........................... **R. struthioloides**
Leaves glossy, stiff ciliate; flower heads in a foliose raceme.......... **R. Menziesii**

Raillardia arborea Gray.

Naenae.

(Plate 212.)

RAILLARDIA ARBOREA Gray in Proc. Am. Acad. V. (1862) 134;—H. Mann Proc. Am. Acad. VII. (1867) 176;—Hbd. Fl. Haw. Isl. (1888) 228;—Hoffm. in Eng. et Prantl IV. 5. (1889) 248;—Del Cast. Ill. Fl. Ins. Mar. Pac. VI (1890) 213.

Young branches and inflorescence hirsute with glandular hairs; leaves ternate, close, sessile with a broad base, but not clasping, 3 to 5 nerved, hispid and viscid as is the inflorescence; the foliose panicle 8 to 10 cm long, involucre of 9 to 14 bracts with 22 to 45 florets; corollae glandular; achenes glabrous.

This species, which inhabits the dry upland slopes of Mauna Kea, is by no means common. It is usually a shrub or, when growing in black cinder at an elevation of 10,000 to 11,000 feet, a tree of about 20 feet in height with a trunk a foot in diameter. The writer saw only a few trees; the best developed specimen grew at a little over 10,000 feet on the slopes of Mauna Kea above Kemole; above Waikii at 9000 feet elevation it was a shrub, as well as back of Nau crater on the windward slope at 8000 feet. These arborescent Raillardia have a peculiar odor, and their presence can be detected long before the plants are reached, when once familiar with the odor. This applies also more or less to the shrubby species of the lower forests. *Raillardia arborea* is associated with *Styphelia Grayana, Geranium cuneatum* var. γ., *Raillardia struthioloides, Sophora chrysophylla, Rubus Hawaiiensis, Coprosma montana, Rumex giganteus*, etc. It can stand severe frost, and is sometimes covered with snow during part of the year.

Raillardia struthioloides Gray.

Naenae.

RAILLARDIA STRUTHIOLOIDES Gray in Proc. Am. Acad. V. (1862) 134;—H. Mann Proc. Am. Acad. VII. (1867) 176;—Hbd. Fl. Haw. Isl. (1888) 228;—Del Cast. Ill. Fl. Ins. Mar. Pacif. VI. (1890) 214.

A small tree 6 to 7 m high, with a trunk of about 22 cm in diameter, the branches canescent with a silky not glandular pubescence; leaves closely crowded, erect, imbricate, or at length spreading, lanceolate, 5 cm long, 8 to 14 mm wide, acute, broadly sessile, entire, coriaceous, rather concave when young, with 3 to 5 indistinct nerves, dull opaque, canescent with soft appressed hairs, scabrous on the margin, but not ciliate; inflorescence a raceme or panicle 10 to 15 cm long, with recurved pedicels; heads 12 mm; involucre 8 mm, pubescent, of 7 to 11 bracts; florets 12 to 22, the corolla almost tubular, not exserted.

This species, which is usually a shrub, but often a tree of 20 feet or so in height, ascends the highest of any of our Raillardia, as it can be found at an elevation of 11,500 feet on Mauna Kea. The trunk is not thicker than about nine inches. It differs from *R. arborea* in not being viscous, but covered with

503

PLATE 214.

RAILLARDIA MENZIESII Gray.
Naenae tree.
Growing on the slopes of Mt. Haleakala, Maui, near Puunianiau crater; elevation 6000 feet.

Compositae.

a silky canescent pubescence which is not glandular. The leaves are lanceolate aꞏute, leathery in texture, and concave when young. The flowers are yellow. It is found lower down in company with *Argyroxiphium sandwicense*, or Silver-sword, Silene, etc.

Raillardia Menziesii Gray
Naenae.
(Plates 213, 214.)

RAILLARDIA MENZIESII Gray Proc. Am. Acad. V. (1862) 133;—Mann Proc. Am. Acad. VII. (1867) 176;—Wawra in Flora (1873) 79;—Hbd. Fl. Haw. Isl. (1888) 228;—Hoffm. in Engl. et Prantl Pflzfam. IV. 5. (1889) 248;—Del Cast. Ill. Fl. Ins. Mar. Pac. VI. (1890) 214.

A shrub or small tree, branches stiff and stout, or at lower elevation profusely branching, densely foliose, cinereous or with a rufous hispid not glandular pubescence; leaves ternate or opposite, sessile, elliptical-oblong, or lanceolate, acuminate, entire, or faintly and remotely denticulate, coriaceous, 3 to 5 nerved, glabrate when full grown, but retaining a fringe of stiff scabrous ciliae among the margins; heads 10 mm or less, few in a foliose raceme or panicle of 5 cm or more, on pedicels of 2 to 8 mm; involucre obconical, or oblong, florets 2 to 25, but usually only 2 to 10, corollae funnel-shaped, not exserted; achenes glabrous or slightly hispid, ribbed.

The typical *Raillardia Menziesii* Gray, (no. 8621 and 8546, in the Herbarium of the College of Hawaii) is a shrub with stiff stout branches and thick, fleshy leathery, ternate leaves, and occurs on and near the summit of Mt. Haleakala at an elevation of from 7000-10000 feet. At 6000 feet elevation, and in gulches at 7000 feet, above Ukulele, on the same mountain, there are quite a number of trees some of them 20 feet high and pictured on plate 214; the leaves are thinner, opposite, and approach more *Raillardia linearis* Gaud. In order to ascertain the identity of the tree, the writer sent several specimens of the species in question to the Gray Herbarium for comparison. In the absence of Prof. M. L. Fernald, Mr. E. W. Sinnott kindly compared the material, of which he writes as follows: "Of *R. Menziesii* we have but two sheets, one of them the type. Your specimens no. 8621 and 8546 (the latter from the summit of Mt. Haleakala with ternate leaves) are obviously typical *R. Menziesii* upon comparison. The other two, no. 8573 and 8590, (the latter a specimen from the tree figured on plate no. 214) are probably referable to the same species, but seem to approach *R. linearis* Gaud. These two species are placed next each other by Dr. Gray, in his review of the genus in 1862."

The writer collected the typical *R. linearis* on the lava fields of Auahi, Kahikinui, southern slopes of Mt. Haleakala where it is a shrub 3 feet high at 2000 feet elevation. At present it will be advisable to retain the tree in question under *R. Menziesii* rather than create a new species, until the vast Hawaiian composite material is thoroughly worked up and monographed.

HESPEROMANNIA A. Gray.

Heads homogamous, all florets hermaphrodite and equal. Involucre turbinate-campanulate, the bracts imbricate, in many rows, dry, thin, chartaceous to coriaceous, the

505

PLATE 215.

HESPEROMANNIA ARBORESCENS A. Gray.
Flowering and fruiting specimen; one-half natural size.

Compositae.

inner bracts longest, linear lanceolate, the outer ones short, ovate. Receptacle flat naked. Corollae regular, slender, deeply 5-cleft into linear acute straight lobes. Stamens affixed to the base of the corolla, the anthers long linear, united until fertilization, exserted. Style filiform, long exserted, shortly bi-dentate or entire. Achenes linear-oblong, 5-angular, with several faces ribbed. Pappus of many pluri-seriate stiff and scabrous capillary bristles which are twice the length of the achene.—Trees or shrubs with very hard grained wood. Leaves alternate, penni-nerved, entire. Heads large and few in terminal clusters, or in the forks of the branches. Corolla brownish-yellow.

This most interesting Hawaiian genus consists of three species two of which become arborescent. The genus belongs to the tribe *Mutisieae* which is chiefly American, but especially occurring in the South American Andes. It has been called the Hawaiian Thistle tree.

Hesperomannia arborescens Gray.

(Plate 215.)

HESPEROMANNIA ARBORESCENS Gray in Proc. Am. Acad. VI. (1866) 554;—H. Mann in Proc. Am. Acad. VII. (1867) 176;—Brigham in Mem. Bost. Soc. Nat. Hist. I. 4. (1868) 527. p. 20;—Wawra in Flora (1873) 76;—Hbd. Fl. Haw. Isl. (1888) 232;—Del Cast. Ill. Fl. Ins. Mar. Pacif. VI. (1890) 215.

Leaves glabrous, dark on both faces, thin chartaceous, or often somewhat fleshy in texture when fresh, and minutely pubescent with grayish hairlets when young, especially along the veins and midrib, obovate-oblong 12 to 34 cm long, 4 to 20 cm wide, with reddish midrib and petiole, the latter 2 to 4 cm; bluntly acuminate, crenate-dentate, often sub-entire; heads about 5 cm high, 5 to 7 in a terminal cluster or cymose umbel on thick pedicels of about 10 to 14 mm; involucre 2.5 cm high, quite glabrous, its bracts in 4 to 7 rows, corolla 24 to 30 mm, divided to the middle, anthers 8 to 10 mm, achenes glabrous, 12 to 14 mm, linear-oblong, the tawny pappus twice that length.

The first tree of this species was discovered by H. Mann, on the Island of Lanai on the highest ridge; Hillebrand writes that he saw about eight, four years later. Dr. R. C. L. Perkins who thoroughly explored the islands for insects, and consequently became familiar with the Hawaiian Flora to some extent, informed the writer that he saw 2 trees of this species on Lanai about 10 years ago. When exploring the Island of Lanai in the year 1910, from June to August, the writer failed to find even a sign of this tree anywhere on the island. However, large trees of apparently this species were found by C. N. Forbes in the Koolau Mts. on Oahu, and the writer found a tree about 20 feet in height on the lower slopes of Mt. Konahuanui, back of Honolulu, practically at the head of Pauoa Valley. Its leaves were exceedingly large, though the last terminal ones answered the description by Gray. It was in flower and fruit and is figured on plate 214.

Mr. C. N. Forbes described a very interesting species from Kauai in the Wahiawa Mts. where it was collected by J. M. Lydgate. It has the habit of growth of a lobelia. The large flower-heads are on slender filiform pedicels. The leaves are entire. It was named by him *H. Lydgatei* Forbes.

507

ADDENDA.

Descriptions of New Species other than Trees.

Lobelioideae.

Cyanea pilosa Gray.

Var. densiflora Rock var. nov.

Leaves oblong-obovate, same as in the species; somewhat fleshy, white or silvery underneath, dark green above; the hirsute 10-16 flowered peduncle very short, pedicels hirsute; flowers white or with purplish tinge; staminal column white glabrous; anthers white, hirsute, the lower ones penicillate only; berry dark orange colored, 10-ribbed, crowned by the small linear calycine lobes, sparingly hispid.

Hawaii:—Southern slopes of Mauna Loa in the forest back of Naalehu, Kau, in swampy jungle, terrestrial. elevation 4000 feet; flowering and fruiting January 9, 1912; Rock no. 10001 in the Herbarium of the College of Hawaii.

Var. glabrifolia Rock var. nov.

Herbaceous, terrestrial, about 9-10 dm high, the stem strigosely hispid; leaves elliptical oblong, acuminate at both ends, thin chartaceous, pale green above, paler underneath, 18-28 cm x 5-8 cm, on hirsute petioles of 2½-3 cm, young leaves densely hispid underneath, old ones glabrous above, hispid along the midrib and veins; flowers several on a hirsute peduncle of about 7 cm, bracteate above the middle; pedicels 6-10 mm long, filiform, sparingly hispid and bibracteolate at the base; bracteoles linear lanceolate, about 4 mm long; calyx greenish, the ovarian portion 5 mm, the lobes of nearly the same length (4 mm); corolla greenish white, sparingly hispid, 2 cm long; staminal column glabrous, whitish, the anthers densely hirsute; berry glabrous, oblong, dark orange, crowned by the calycine teeth; seeds light yellow.

Hawaii:—In dense swampy forest near Kilauea, elev. 3700 ft., but especially numerous in Mr. W. M. Giffard's mountain lot, Kalanilehua; outside the fenced portion in the forest it is scarce owing to cattle which are allowed to graze in portions of the forest. The plant is usually small and can easily be overlooked, as it grows in dense shaded places, hidden under the numerous ferns and other foliage. Rock no. 8805, flowering and fruiting July, 1911; Type in College of Hawaii Herbarium.

Var. Bondiana Rock var. nov.

Plant about 8 dm high, terrestrial, stem hirsute; leaves short petiolate, coriaceous, ovate oblong, glabrous above, covered with a soft light brown tomentum underneath, acuminate at both ends, 10-14 cm x 3.5-5.5 cm; peduncles very short 3 mm, few flowered. hirsute, as are the pedicels and calyx, the lobes of the latter of the same length as the ovarian portion, linear; (flower buds only) corolla purple, sparingly hispid; berry glabrous yellow, globose.

Hawaii:—Mountains of Kohala, about 7 miles above Awini, near summit in exceedingly dense swampy forest, altitude about 5000 feet; flowerbuds and fruiting June, 1910. Rock, no. 8727 in the herbarium College of Hawaii, T. H.

Named in honor of Dr. B. D. Bond of Kohala for many courtesies received from him by the author.

Var. **megacarpa** Rock var. nov.

Plant erect, terrestrial, stem hirsute, leaves large, obovate oblong, blunt at the apex, narrowing suddenly into a fleshy petiole of 5 cm, with few scattered single hairs above, sparingly hispid underneath, 20-22 cm x 9.5-10.5 cm; berries large, 22 mm in diameter, globose, crowned by the broadly triangular 8 mm long calyx lobes (flowers unknown).

Hawaii:—Mts. of Kohala in swampy forest back of Waimea, along the Alakahi gorge, elev. 4200 ft. Only one plant observed; fruiting June. 1910, Rock no. 8728, in the herbarium, College of Hawaii, T. II.

Cyanea Bishopii Rock sp. n.

Cyanea Kunthiana? Hillebr. Fl. Haw. Isl. (1888) 264;—Drake Del Cast. Ill. Fl. Ins. Mar. Pac. VII. (1892) 219.

Plant subherbaceous, woody only at the base 10-14 dm high, rarely branching, leaves crowded at the top, obovate oblong, bluntly acuminate at the apex, gradually tapering into a margined petiole of ca 3 cm; leaves 20-30 cm long, 4-7 cm wide (measured at their widest portion) sparingly hispid with scattered whitish hairlets above, pubescent underneath especially along the veins and midrib; inflorescence densely clustered along the stem, immediately under the leaves, extending down for about 12-15 cm; flowers numerous on a short hirsute many bracteate peduncle, ca 8 mm in length; pedicels 5-6 mm when with flowers, 12 mm when with fruit, bibracteolate above the middle, bracteoles linear subulate ca 3 mm; calyx hirsute the subglobose ovarian portion 6 mm, calycine lobes as long as the tube or longer; corolla slender, somewhat curved, 3 cm long, 4 mm wide, hirsute, pale purple or lilac with whitish streaks. lobes very short, 3-4 mm, retrorsely dentate above, the dorsal slit extending one-third the length of the tube; staminal column sparingly hispid, anthers densely covered with strigose pale purplish hair, the lower ones only penicillate; berry subglobose, deep orange ca 8 mm in diam., crowned by the calycine lobes.

Maui:—Back of Lahaina, West Maui, 4000 ft. on the ridge overlooking Wailuku, coll. by E. F. Bishop, Jan., 1871. Slopes of Haleakala, wet forest between Waikamoi and Honomanu gulch, along Kula pipe line trail in dense swampy jungle, elev. 4200 ft., west of Olinda, East Maui; fruiting October, 1910; Rock no. 8572; flowering May, 1911; Rock no. 8806, Herbarium, College of Hawaii.

Cyanea stictophylla Rock sp. nov.

Plant 2 m high, erect, not branching; leaves 20-30 cm long, 4-4.5 cm wide, linear lanceolate, bluntly acuminate at both ends, narrowing into a petiole of 2.5-3 cm, glabrous above and evenly punctate with glandular points, hirsute underneath especially along the midrib and veins, with an undulate or irregularly notched margin, peduncles axillary 1-2.5 cm long, hirtellous, bracteate at the apex, pedicels hirtellous 7-15 mm long, bibracteolate below the middle; calyx green puberulous, ovarian portion ovoid, calycine lobes triangular about 2 mm (flowers unknown).

Hawaii:—Mts. of Kaiholeua, in rain forest southern slopes of Mauna Loa, Kau, elevation 6000 ft., Jan., 1912; Rock no. 10055, shortly after flowering with immature fruits. Type in Herbarium, College of Hawaii. The plant belongs to the group to which *Cyanea pilosa* belongs, to which it is related.

Cyanea aculeatiflora Rock sp. nov.

Plant 3-7 m tall single stemmed or occasionally branching not far above the ground, covered with leaf-scars especially in the upper half; leaves at the ends of erect stems, large 40-60 cm x 10-20 cm, thick and stiff, dark green above, lighter underneath, the midrib as well as the 15 cm long fleshy petiole muricate; the upper side muricate at the angles of the veins, densely hispid underneath; inflorescence muricate throughout with aculeate tubercules; arranged in cymes in the axils of the leaves, on a common peduncle of about 8 cm with large foliaceous bracts of 3-4 cm, the ultimate pedicels 1 to 1.5 cm; calyx oblong, 2 cm long the oblong liner muricate lobes 2.5 cm x 0.5 cm; corolla dark purple, curved, muricate with yellow spines, the lobes bluish white, spreading, muricate on the outside; staminal column glabrous, purple, longer than the 5 cm long tube, of the corolla, anthers dark purple, glabrous, the two lower penicillate; style thickening towards the shortly two-lobed hirsute stigma; fruit unknown.

Maui:—Northwestern slopes of Haleakala in dense rain forest along streams or swampy ground, terrestrial, from Waikamoi to Honomanu gorge, elev. 4000 ft.; flowering Sept., 1910, Rock. no. 7513, type Herb., Board of Agriculture & Forestry, T. H. It grows in company with *Clermontia arborescens, Cyanea hamatiflora*, Tetraplasandra, etc.. The young plants are covered with spines throughout while the trunk of old ones is prickly only at the base.

Cyanea hamatiflora Rock sp. n.

Plant 3-4 m high, unarmed, glabrous, erect not branching; leaves broadly lanceolate, somewhat acute, broadly sessile at the base 60-70 cm long, 10-14 cm wide, puberulous above, pubescent underneath, midrib thick fleshy red, irregularly serrate with callous teeth; flowers on short peduncles in the axils of the leaves under which they are hidden; bracts lanceolate acuminate with a prominent median nerve, pedicels 5-6 mm with linear lanceolate bracteoles at their base; calyx ovate, green, 1.5 cm x 6-7 mm, lobes of irregular length, the lower two usually much shorter than the remaining three, lanceolate, obtuse the lower 12-14 mm, the upper 15-18 mm x 4 mm; corolla purplish red, unilabiate, the dorsal slit extending more than one-third of its length, lobes sharply curved at the apex only, thick in texture and somewhat hirsute, staminal column glabrous, anthers sparingly hispid along the sutures, the two lower ones long penicillate. The whole inflorescence exudes a very viscid resinous substance especially when with young flowerbuds, which adhere to the paper in the Herbarium.
Fruit obovate-oblong dark purplish-red 10-12 ribbed, crowned by the long calycine lobes, 4 cm long, 2.5 cm wide, purple inside, seeds dark brown, shining.

Maui:—Slopes of Mt. Haleakala, elev. 4000 ft. in dense rain forest, between Waikamoi and Honomanu. The plant is conspicuous by its broad sessile light green leaves, which stand out horizontally. It grows in company with *Cyanea aculeatiflora, Clermontia arborescens, Cyrtandra* sp., Phyllostegia, Stenogyne, etc.

Rock n. 8514 flowering Sept., 1910; type in Herbarium, Board of Agriculture & Forestry, T. H.

Cyanea Gayana Rock sp. nov.

Trunk 1.5-3 m high, hardly woody, erect, stem smooth, not branching, (only when broken) foliose at the apex. leaves thick fleshy, lanceolate oblong, bluntly acuminate, denticulate, gradually narrowing into a margined petiole of 1 cm, making it appear subsessile, the lower portion entire, dark green above glabrous or puberulous, veins and midrib bright red thick fleshy, lighter underneath, and covered with grayish pubescence; peduncles thick fleshy, multi-bracteate from the base, hispid strigose, bearing flowers from half its length to the apex; pedicels densely hirsute 1-1.5 cm long, bracteate at the base; calyx dark, hirsute as is the corolla, tube ovate-obconical, 6-8 mm, the lobes triangular dentiform, 4 mm; corolla, suberect magenta-red with darker streaks, 3-4 cm long by 4 mm wide, the dorsal slit extending to the base; staminal column glabrous as well as the anthers, of the latter the two lower only penicillate; fruit ovoid of a glaucous color about 2-1.5 (?) cm long, crowned by the calycine teeth.

Kauai:—Mountains back of Waimea, woods of Kaholuamano, elev. 4000 ft., along streams only, near Waialae and Waiakealoha on the high plateau in company with numerous other Lobelioideae, Kadua, Cyrtandra, Hillebrandia, *Clermontia Gaudichaudii*, etc. Rock n. 2463, flowering March 10, 1909, and n. Sept., 1909, fruiting, (but fruits were lost, description of fruit from notes),

Rock, 1905, flowerbuds Oct. 20, 1911. Named in honor of Mr. Francis Gay of Kauai to whom the writer is greatly indebted for extended hospitality on Kauai, and without whose aid the writer would have been unable to make such a thorough botanical survey of that part of Kauai.

Type in Herbarium, Board of Agriculture and Forestry, T. II.

Cyanea rivularis Rock sp. n.

A shrub 4-5 cm high, stem simple or branching at the base, leaf whorls at the end of the tomentose branches; leaves linear oblong bluntly acuminate at both ends, crenate or serrate with callous teeth; 20-30 cm long, by 3-8 cm wide; pubescent above, densely velvety tomentose underneath, and pale; on tomentose petioles of 4-8 inches; whole inflorescence tomentose including the blue corolla; peduncle 4-8 cm long, naked two-thirds of its length, many flowered, the pedicels 1-1.5 cm, bracts linear subulate; calyx dark purplish green, its teeth sharply triangular, corolla 3 cm long, light pale to whitish with dark ultramarine blue streaks, velvety tomentose with short white hairlets, the dorsal slit extending one-third its length, curved with a knob in the bud showing the termination of the dorsal slit, lobes short; staminal column glabrous, white, anthers bright blue, slightly pubescent at the base, only the two lower ones penicillate, stigmatic lobes pubescent outside; berry dark bluish-black, globose 1-1.5 cm in diameter, crowned by the calycine teeth, seeds whitish large, and somewhat minutely wrinkled.

Kauai:—Mts. above Waimea along streambeds at the high plateau only, elev. 4200 ft. or more. The banks near the head of Waialae stream are covered with this species their palm-like stems gracefully waving in the wind. Also near Waiakealoha waterfalls (Rock no. 5365, Waiakealoha, Sept., 1909, flowering, and Waialea stream; Rock no. 9010 flowering and fruiting Oct 15, 1911). Abundant in company with *Lobelia hypoleuca, Cyanea Gayana*, etc.

Cyanea atra Hbd. var. lobata Rock v. nov.

Erect single stemmed with subentire and lobed leaves, petiole muricate, 6-7 cm, leaves coriaceous, when not lobed the margin is almost fringed; or lobed iregularly deeply but not to the rhachis; tuberculate above, covered with an olivaceous tomentum underneath; peduncle longer than in the species, 3-4 cm, many flowered bracts and bractlets as in species; pedicels 15-18 mm; calyx and corolla as in the species, the staminal column and anthers glabrous.

Maui:—Upper ditch trail leading from Ukulele, elevation 5000 ft. to Waikamoi gulch in dense rain forest. Only few plants observed, when in company with Mr. L. v. Tempsky of Makawao, (Rock no. 8337, flowering October, 1910).

Clermontia multiflora var. micrantha Hbd.
forma montana Rock f. n.

A shrub 2-3 m high, many branched; leaves smaller than in the variety, thick coriaceous. veins and denticulate margins pink as is the petiole; flowers somewhat larger, pinkish-purple, calyx lobes glabrous, corolla slightly hirtellous, peduncle usually 2-flowered. berry 1.5 cm or more long, not subglobose, but ovoid oblong.

Maui:—On the highest ridge leading to Puukukui, West Maui Mountains, in swampy forest at an elevation of 4600 ft. Rock and Hammond, flowering and fruiting, August, 1910, no. 8179, in Herbarium, College of Hawaii. Differs from var. *micrantha* in the two-flowered peduncle and in the larger ovoid-oblong fruits.

511

Clermontia parviflora Gaud. var. calycina Rock v. nov.

A shrub; leaves as in the species on somewhat longer petioles; flowers usually three on a peduncle, calyx lobes subulate 5 mm long, corolla larger than in the species, bluish gray, pubescent.

Hawaii:—High plateau of Kohala Mts., back of Waimea along Alakahi ditch trail, elevation 4000 ft. (Rock no. 4793, flowering July 12, 1909).

The plant has decidedly the aspect of *C. parviflora*, but differs from it in its larger flowers and short calycine lobes.

Clermontia Gaudichaudii Hbd.
Var. γ singuliflora Rock v. nov.

A shrub 1.5-2 m high, glabrous throughout, leaves coriaceous, coarser dentate, veins dark prominent, flowers somewhat larger single on long pedicels; calyx-lobes dentate, anthers glabrous, the lower ones penicillate.

Hawaii:—Not uncommon on the northern slope of Mauna Kea, Hamakua, on trees, usually Cheirodendron or Cibotium, upper forest of Paauhau No. 1, (Rock no. 3252, flowering June 1909).

Differs from the species in its single flowers and long pedicels.

All adopted genera, with their species, are preceded by an asterisk, while generic synonyms are without such. All plants described by the author in this book as new, are in bold type.

*Acacia Willd. 173
  Koa Gray 173
  Koaia Hbd. 177
Agalma Miq. 357
*Alectryon Gaertn. 275
  macrococcus Radlk. 277
*Aleurites Forst. 255
  moluccana (L.) Willd. 255
*Alphitonia Reissek. 285
  excelsa Reiss. 285
AMARANTACEAE 135
ANACARDIACEAE 262
*Antidesma L. 247
  × Kapuae Rock 249
  platyphyllum Mann 247
  pulvinatum Hbd. 249
Apionaema Nutt. 447, 451
APOCYNACEAE 407
AQUIFOLIACEAE 263
Aralia L. 361
ARALIACEAE 336
*Artocarpus Forst. 115
  incisa Forst. 115
Beythea Endl. 289
*Bobea Gaud. 437
  elatior Gaud. 439
  var. Molokaiensis Rock 441
  Hookeri Hbd. 441
  sandwicensis Hbd. 443
  timonoides Hbd. 445
Boehmeria Jacq. 123
BORRAGINACEAE 414
*Broussaisia Gaud. 151
  arguta Gaud. 151
  pellucida Gaud. 152
Brunelia Pers. 224
Burneya Cham. et Schl. 439
Byronia Endl. 265
Caesalpinia L. 181
CAESALPINIOIDEAE 173
*Calophyllum L. 309
  inophyllum L. 309
Camirium O. Ktze. 255
CAMPANULACEAE 469
Canthium Lam. 437
CELASTRACEAE 267
Celastrina ? Wawra 273
Celtis L. 113
Ceodes Forst. 145

Cerbera L. 409
*Charpentiera Gaud. 135
  obovata Gaud. 135
*Cheirodendron Nutt. 359
  Gaudichaudii (DC.) Seem. 361
  platyphyllum (H. & A.) Seem. 363
Chomelia ? sp. Wawra 445
Chomelia ? Gray 443
*Chrysophyllum L. 380
  Polynesicum Hbd. 380
*Cibotium Kaulf. 89
  Chamissoi Kaulf. 93
  Menziesii Hook. 91
*Claoxylon Juss. 253
  sandwicense Mull.-Arg. 253
*Clermontia Gaud. 471
  arborescens (Mann) Hbd. 483
  coerulea Hbd. 485
  drepanomorpha Rock 473
  Gaudichaudii (Gaud.) Hbd. 479
  Gaudichaudii Hbd. var. γ singuliflora Rock 512
  grandiflora Gaud. 473
  Haleakalensis Rock 489
  Hawaiiensis (Hbd.) Rock 477
  Kohalae Rock 476
  leptoclada Rock 477
  mutliflora Hbd. var. micrantha Hbd. forma montana Rock 511
  oblongifolia Gaud. 476
  var. Mauiensis Rock 476
  parviflora Gaud var. calycina Rock 511
  Peleana Rock 483
  persicaefolia Gaud. 475
  tuberculata Forbes 485
Clermontia genuinae 471
Clermontioideae 473
Clusia L. 215
Coffea L. 437, 447, 451
*Colubrina Brongn. 281
  oppositifolia Brongn. 283
Colubrina Fenzl. 285
COMPOSITAE 497

Connarus ? Mann 210
*Coprosma Forst. 457
  Grayana Rock 461
  Kauaiensis (Gray) Heller 463
  longifolia Gray 465
  montana Hbd. 459
  pubens Gray 463
  rhynchocarpa Gray 459
  Vontempskyi Rock 461
  Waimeae Wawra 465
Coralladendron O. Ktze. 191
*Cordia L. 415
  subcordata Lam. 415
*Cryptocarya R. Br. 149
  Mannii Hbd. 149
Crotoneae 243
CRYPTOGAMIA 89
*Cyanea Gaud. 489
  aculeatiflora Rock 509
  arborea (Gray) Hbd. 493
  atra Hbd. var. lobata Rock 511
  Bishopii Rock 70, 509
  Gayana Rock 510
  hamatiflora Rock 510
  leptostegia Gray 494
  pilosa Gray
    var. Bondiana Rock 508
    var. densiflora Rock 508
    var. glabrifolia Rock 508
    var. megacarpa Rock 509
  rivularis Rock 511
  stictophylla Rock 509
Cyanea Gaud. 483
CYATHEACEAE 89
Cyathodes Lab. 365
Delissea Gaud. 473, 479, 483, 493
Dicksoniae sp. autt. Hk., Bk. 89
DICOTYLEDONEAE 113
Dipanax Seem. 353, 355, 357
Diplomorpha Meissn. 316-317
*Dodonaea L. 278
  eriocarpa Smith 281

513

viscosa L. 278
Dodonaea sp. Del Cast 277
*Dracaena Vandelli 109
aurea Mann 109
Draco O. Ktze. 109
*Dubautia Gaud. 499
laxa H. et A. var. **pedi-cellata** Rock 501
plantaginea Gaud. 499
EBENACEAE 393
Ebenus Hiern. 393, 395
Edwardsia Salisb. 187
ELAEOCARPACEAE 287
*Elaeocarpus L. 287
bifidus H. & A. 289
EMBRYOPHYTA ASI-PHONOGAMA 89
EMBRYOPHYTA SIPHO-NOGAMA 96
EPACRIDACEAE 365
*Erythrina L. 189
monospeima Gaud. 191
Eschweileria Zipp. 351
Eugenia L. 321, 323
*Euphorbia L. 259
lorifolia (Gray) Hbd. 259
var. **gracilis** Rock 259
Rockii Forbes 261
EUPHORBIACEAE 243
Euphorbieae 243
Eupritchardia O. Ktze. 101, 103, 104
*Eurya Thunb. 308
sandwicensis Gray 308
Eutetraplassandra 337
Evodia Forst. 215-237
Fagara L. 193-207
FLACOURTIACEAE 311
*Gardenia Ellis 433
Brighami Mann 433
Remyi Mann 435
Gastonia ? Gray 345
GOODENIACEAE 494
Gossypium L. 305, 307
*Gouldia Gray 429
axillaris Wawra 431
elongata Heller 431
Guettardella Champ. 443
GUTTIFERAE 309
Hedera L. 361, 363
Heptapleurum ? Wawra 347
Heptapleurum Mann 355, 357
*Hesperomannia Gray 505
arborescens Gray 507
*Hibiscadelphus Rock 297
Giffardianus Rock 297
Hualalaiensis Rock 301
Wilderianus Rock 299
*Hibiscus L. 291
Arnottianus Gray 293
Kokio Hbd. 295
tiliaceus L. 293
Waimeae Heller 295

Hibiscus L. 302, 307
*Ilex L. 265
sandwicensis (Endl.) Loes. 265
Isonandra auct 380
Ixora L. 437
*Jambosa DC. 319
malaccensis (L.) P. DC. 321
Jatropha L. 255
Kittelia Reichb. 489
*Kokia Lewt. 303
drynarioides (Seem.) Lewt. 307
var. lanceolata(Lewt.) Rock 307
Rockii Lewt. 305
*Labordia Gaud. 401
membranacea Mann 405
molokaiana Baillon 403
sessilis Gray 406
tinifolia Gray 406
LAURACEAE 149
LEGUMINOSAE 173
LILIACEAE 109
Livistona ? 100, 101
*Lobelia L.
Gaudichaudii DC. var. **longibracteata** Rock 78
Lobelia Endl. 475, 476
Lobelia Adans. 493, 497
Lobelioideae 469
LOGANIACEAE 401
*Maba J. R. & G. Forst 393
Hillebrandii Seem. 395
sandwicensis A. DC. 393
Macrochilus Presl. 489
Mahoe Hbd. 277
MALVACEAE 291
Melaleuca L. 327
Melicope Forst. 235, 237, 242
*Metrosideros Banks 325
macropus H. & A. 336
polymorpha Gaud. 325
rugosa Gray 335
tremuloides (Heller) Rock 333
var. **Waialealae** Rock 335
*Mezoneurum Desf. 181
Kauaiense (Mann) Hbd. 181
Mimosoideae 173
MONOCOTYLEDONEAE 96
MORACEAE 114
*Morinda L. 467
citrifolia L. 467
trimera Hbd. 467
Morus L. 114
Myonima Comm. 437
MYOPORACEAE 425
*Myoporum Banks et Sol. 425

Sandwicense (DC.) Gray 427
Myroxylon Forst. 311-313
MYRSINACEAE 367
Myrsine L. 368, 369, 370, 375, 377, 379
Myrsine Levl. 392
MYRTACEAE 319
Nania Miq. 327-336
*Neowawraea Rock 243
phyllanthoides Rock 245
*Nothocestrum Gray 417
breviflorum Gray 419
latifolium Gray 421
longifolium Gray 419
subcordatum Mann 423
Nothocnide Blume 123
Nothotetraplassandra 337
*Nototrichium Hbd. 139
sandwicense Hbd. 141
NYCTAGINACEAE 143
Obbea Hook. 445
*Ochrosia Juss. 413
compta K. Sch. 414
sandwicensis Gray 413
Ochrosia DC. 409
Olea L. 397
OLEACEAE 397
Oreodaphne? Mann 149
*Osmanthus Lour. 397
sandwicensis (Gray) Knobl. 397
PALMAE 99
Panax? DC. 361, 363
PANDANACEAE 96
*Pandanus L. 96
odoratissimus L. 97
Papilionatae 173
Paritium A. St.-Hil. 293
Pavetta L. 437
*Pelea Gray 211
anisata Mann 229
auriculaefolia Gray 219
Balloui Rock 228
barbigera (Gray) Hbd. 235
clusiaefolia Gray 215
cinerea (Gray) Hbd. 237
var. **racemiflora** Rock 241
Cookeana Rock 216
elliptica Hbd 237
Fauriei Lévl. 216
kauaiensis Mann 225
Knudsenii Hbd. 235
macropus Hbd. 227
microcarpa Heller 220
molokaiensis Hbd. 227
multiflora Rock 233
orbicularis Hbd. 224
pseudoanisata Rock 227
rotundifolia Gray 226
sandwicensis Gray 224
sapotaefolia Mann 217
var. **dumosa** Rock 218
volcanica Gray 221

var. **lianoides.** Rock 223
var. **montana** Rock 223
var. **terminalis** Rock 223
Waialealae Wawra 218
Wawraeana Rock 231
Zahlbruckneri Rock 231
Perlarius O. Ktze. 123
*Perrottetia H. B. K. 267
sandwicensis Gray 267
Phyllantheae 243
Pinonia Gaud. 89
*Pipturus Wedd. 123
albidus Gray 123
*Pisonia Plum. 143
inermis Forst. 147
sandwicensis Hbd. 145
umbellifera (Forst.) Seem. 145
PITTOSPORACEAE 153
*Pittosporum Banks. 153
acuminatum Mann 155
cauliflorum Mann 159
confertiflorum Gray 171
Gayanum Rock 166
var. **Waialealae** Rock 166
glabrum H. et A. 155
glomeratum Hbd. 157
Hawaiiense Hbd. 169
Hosmeri Rock 161
var. **longifolium** Rock 163
insigne Hbd. 169
Kauaiense Hbd. 171
spathulatum Mann 157
terminalioides Planch. 159
*Plantago L.
pachyphylla var. **glabrifolia** Rock 77
*Platydesma Mann 241
campanulatum Mann 241
var. γ macrophyllum Hbd. forma **coriaceum** Rock 243
var. **sessilifolia** Rock 243
Platydesma Hbd. 219
*Plectronia L. 437
odorata (Forst.) F. v M. 437
Polycoelium A. DC. 427
Pomaderris Labill. 285
*Pritchardia Seem. et H. Wendl. 99
arecina Becc. 107
eriophora Becc. 105
eriostachia Becc. 107
Gaudichaudii H. Wendl. 100
Hillebrandi Becc. 103
lanigera Becc. 103
Martii H. Wendl. 101

minor Becc. 104
remota Becc. 104
Rockiana Becc. 105
*Pseudomorus Bureau 114
Brunoniana (Endl.) Bureau 114
Psilotrichium Blume. 141
*Psychotria L. 455
grandiflora Mann 457
hexandra Mann 455
hirta (Wawra) Heller 457
*Pteralyxia K. Sch. 407
macrocarpa (Hbd.) K. Sch. 407
*Pterotropia Hbd. 353
dipyrena (Mann) Hbd. 357
gymnocarpa Hbd. 355
Kavaiensis (Mann) Hbd. 357
Ptilotus R. Br. 141
Rademachia Steudl. 115
*Raillardia Gaud. 501
arborea Gray 503
Menziesii Gray 505
struthioloides Gray 503
*Rauwolfia L. 409
sandwicensis A. DC. 409
*Reynoldsia Gray 351
sandwicensis Gray 351
RHAMNACEAE 281
Rhamnus L. 285
*Rhus L. 262
semialata Murr. var. sandwicensis Engl. 262
Rhytidotus Hook f. 441
RUBIACEAE 429
RUTACEAE 192
SANTALACEAE 126
*Santalum L. 126
ellipticum Gaud. 131
Freycinetianum Gaud. 127
var. **Lanaiense** Rock 129
Haleakalae Hbd. 133
pyrularium Gray 133
SAPINDACEAE 269
*Sapindus L. 271
Oahuensis Hbd. 273
saponaria L. 271
Sapota Gaertn. 383, 390
SAPOTACEAE 380
SAXIFRAGACEAE 151
Sideroxylon L. 381
auahiense Rock 387
var. **aurantium** Rock 391
Ceresolii Rock 385
rhynchospermum Rock 387
sandwicense (Gray) B. et H. 383
spathulatum Hbd. 391

var. β densiflorum Hbd. 392
var. **molokaiense** (Lévl.) Rock 392
*Scaevola L. 494
Chamissoniana Gaud. 495
glabra H. et A. 495
procera Hbd. 497
SOLANACEAE 417
*Solanum L. 423
Carterianum Rock 423
*Sophora L. 185
chrysophylla Seem. 187
Sponia Comm. 113
*Straussia Gray 445
Fauriei Lévl. 449
hawaiiensis Gray 451
Hillebrandii Rock 453
var. **Molokaiensis** Rock 455
kaduana (Ch. et Sch.) Gray 447
leptocarpa Hbd. 449
longissima Rock 447
Mariniana (Ch. et Sch.) Gray 451
oncocarpa Hbd. 448
var. **scoriacea** Rock 449
var. **subcordata** Rock 448
*Styphelia Sol. 365
Grayana (Stschegl.) Rock 366
tameiameia F. Muel. 365
*Suttonia 367
Fernseei Mez. 370
Hillebrandii Mez. 373
var. **emarginata** Rock 373
Kauaiensis (Hbd.) Mez. 368
Knudsenii Rock 373
Lanaiensis (Hbd.) Mez. 369
var. **coriacea** Rock 369
lanceolata (Wawra) Rock 379
Lessertiana (A. DC.) Mez. 375
Sandwicensis (A. DC.) Mez. 377
var. **apodocarpa** (Lévl.) Rock 379
spathulata Rock 370
volcanica Rock 371
var. **lavarum** Rock 371
Wawraea Mez. 368
Suttonia Lévl. 392
*Syzygium Gaertn. 323
sandwicense (Gray) Ndz. 323
Telopia Sol. 255
Tenninckia 495
Ternstroemiopsis Urb. 308
*Tetraplasandra Gray 337

515

Hawaiiensis Gray 339
Kaalae (Hbd.) Harms
  345
Lanaiensis Rock 343
Lydgatei (Hbd.) Harms
  343
meiandra (Hbd.) Harms
  347
Oahuensis (Gray) Harms
  345
Waialealae Rock 341
Waimeae Wawra 339
THEACEAE 307
*Thespesia Corr. 302
  populnea (L.) Corr. 302
THYMELAEACEAE 315
Timonius DC. 439
Toxicodendron L. 262
*Trema Lour. 113
  amboinensis Blume 113
Triplasandra Seem. 337

ULMACEAE 113
*Urera Gaud. 119
  Kaalae Wawra 123
  Sandvicensis Wedd. 119
    var. Kauaiensis Rock
    123
URTICACEAE 117
Vallesia Ruiz et Pav. 407
Villebrunea Gaud. 119
Washingtonia H. Wendl.
  101, 103, 104
*Wikstroemia Endl. 316
  furcata (Hbd.) Rock 319
  oahuensis (Gray) Rock
  316
  sandwicensis Meisn. 317
*Xanthoxylum L. 192
  Bluettianum Rock 201
  dipetalum Mann 207
    var. geminicarpum
    Rock 209

    var. tomentosum Rock
    209
    var. γ Hbd. 210
  glandulosum Hbd. 197
  hawaiiense Hbd. 195
    var. citriodora Rock
    197
    var. velutinosum Rock
    197
  Kauaiense Gray 199
  Mauiense Mann 203
    forma glabrum Rock
    203
    var. anceps Rock 205
    forma petiolulatum
    Rock 207
    var. rigidum Rock 205
  Oahuense Hbd. 193
*Xylosma Forst. 311
  Hawaiiense Seem. 311
  Hillebrandii Wawra 313

INDEX TO THE HAWAIIAN AND ENGLISH NAMES OF TREES.

Aalii 278
Aalii Kumakua....... 278
'' kumakani 281
Aawa hua kukui...... 161
Ae...193, 195, 197, 199, 203
A'e 271
Ahakea...438, 441, 443, 445
Aiai 114
Aiea.....265, 419, 421, 423
Akia........316, 317, 319
Akoko 259
Alaa 383, 387
Alahee 437
Alani........215, 221, 224
Alaniwai 218
Anini 308
Anonia 218
Aulu 145, 273, 383

Bastard Sandalwood.... 427
Breadfruit 115

Haa 247, 249
Haha 479
Hahaaiakamanu 479
Hahalua 494
Hala 97
Halapepe 109
Hame 247
Hao 409
Hapu 93
Hapu Iii 91
Hau 293
Hau kuahiwi...297, 299, 301
Heae ....
...193, 195, 197, 199, 203
Heii 91
Hoawa ....
...155, 157, 159, 169, 171
Holei 413
Holio 149
Hona' 123

Iliahi 127, 131, 133

Kalia 289
Kamakahala 403, 405
Kamani 309
Kanawau 151
Kauila 283, 285
Kauila mahu 361

Kaulu 273, 383, 407
Kawau 210, 265, 366
Kea 181
Keahi 380
Koa 173
Koa ka 173
Koa oha 177
Koaia 177
Koi 463
Kokio 307
Kokio ula 295
Kokio keokeo 293, 295
Koko ....>......259, 261
Kolea ....
...370, 371, 373, 375, 379
Kolea laulii......... 377
Kopiko...448, 449, 451, 453
Kopiko kea 447
Kopiko ula 451
Kou 415
Kukaimoa 220
Kukui 255
Kului 141

Lama 393
Lapalapa 363
Lauhala 97
Lehua 325
Lehua ahihi 333
Lehua papa 335
Lonomea 273
Loulu...100, 101, 103,
104, 105, 107
Mahoe 277
Maiele 366
Mamake 123
Mamaki 123
Mamani 187
Mancle 271
Manena 237
Manono 431
Maua 311, 313
Mehame 249
Milo 302
Mokihana 229
Mountain Apple 321

Naenae 499, 503, 505
Naio 427
Nanu 434

Nau 433, 434
Naupaka 495
Naupaka kuahiwi...495, 497
Neleau 262
Neneleau 262
Noni 467
Noni kuahiwi 467

O'a 285
Ohawai 476, 483
Ohe 339, 351
Ohe kikoola 339
Ohe kukuluaeo 351
Ohe makai 351
Ohe mauka 345
Ohe Ohe 357
Ohia 321
Ohia ai 321
Ohia ha 325
Ohia lehua 325, 335
Olapa 361
Olena 465
Olomea 267
Olopua 397
Opuhe 119

Paihi 323
Papahekili 155
Papala 135
Papala kepau 145, 147
Pilo 459, 461, 463, 465
Pilo kea 241
Pilo ula 225
Poola 253
Pua 397
Puahanui 151, 152
Puakeawe 365
Puananahonua 423
Puhala 97
Pukeawe 365

Sandalwood 127
Screw-pine 97

Uahea pele 235
Uhiuhi 181
Ulu 115

Waimea 267
Wanini 308
Walahee 437
Wiliwili 191

517

ERRATA.

Page 76, line 28, and page 79, line 15, for *Styphelia imbricata* read *Styphelia Grayana*.

Page 97, line 3 from bottom, for *Gynopogon oliviformis* read *Alyxia olivaeformis*.

Pages 160, 162, 163, for **longifolia** read **longifolium**.

Page 191, line 10, for **monosperum** read **monospermum**.

Page 225, line 10, for **Waileale** read **Waialeale**.

Page 231, line 7, for **Wawreana** read **Wawraeana**.

Page 242, line 7 from bottom, and page 243, line 5, should read *macrophyllum*.

Page 242, line 9 from bottom, should read *pallidum*.

Page 243, line 13, for *sessilifolia* read *sessilifolium*.

Page 252, for **Mehane** read **Mehame**.

Page 285, lines 36 and 38, for **Zizphoides** read **Zizyphoides**.

Page 295, lines 19 and 35, for *Kokia* read *Kokio*.

Page 347, line 35, for δ read ε.

Page 366, line 7 from bottom, for *Olelo* read *Ohelo*.

1

PRESS OF THE
HAWAIIAN GAZETTE CO., LTD.
HONOLULU. T. H.

CPSIA information can be obtained
at www.ICGtesting.com
Printed in the USA
BVHW040836060719
552539BV00027B/165/P

9 781375 486576